D0141860

CHILDREN AND THEIR WORLD

CHILDREN AND THEIR WORLD

Strategies for Teaching
Social Studies

THIRD EDITION

DAVID A. WELTON
Texas Tech University

JOHN T. MALLAN
Syracuse University

HOUGHTON MIFFLIN COMPANY   BOSTON

Dallas   Geneva, Illinois   Palo Alto   Princeton, New Jersey

Cover photograph by Ken O'Donoghue.

Part One Opener: © Susan Lapides 1987.
Part Two Opener: © Susan Lapides 1987.
Part Three Opener: © Jean-Claude Lejeune 1987.

Excerpt on pp. 27–30 from "Essentials of the Social Studies," *Social Education,* 45 (March 1981), pp. 162–164. Used by permission of the National Council for the Social Studies.

Excerpt on p. 56 reprinted with permission of Macmillan Publishing Company from IN-TERNATIONAL ENCYCLOPEDIA OF THE SOCIAL SCIENCES, David L. Sills, Editor. Volume 1, p. xxii. Copyright © 1968 by Crowell Collier and Macmillan, Inc.

Excerpt on p. 81 from LANGUAGE IN THOUGHT AND ACTION, Second Edition, by S. I, Hayakawa, copyright © 1964 by Harcourt, Brace, Jovanovich, Inc. Reprinted by permission of the publisher.

Excerpt on pp. 113–114 from PREPARING INSTRUCTIONAL OBJECTIVES by Robert F. Mager, Copyright © 1984 by David S. Lake Publishers, Belmont, CA 94002.

Excerpt on p. 160 from *Revision of the NCSS Social Studies Curriculum Guidelines,* 1979. Used by permission of the National Council for the Social Studies.

Table on p. 176 from "In Search of a Scope and Sequence for Social Studies," *Social Education,* 48 (April 1984), pp. 249–262. Used by permission of the National Council for the Social Studies.

Excerpts on pp. 197, 202, and 206 from "What Should Be Taught Where?" *Social Education,* 47 (February 1983), pp. 94–101. Used by permission of the National Council for the Social Studies.

Excerpt on pp. 247–248 reprinted from TREASURY OF JEWISH FOLKLORE, Edited by Nathan Ausubel. Copyright © 1948, 1979 by Crown Publishers, Inc. Used by permission of Crown Publishers, Inc.

Excerpts on pp. 376–377 from *Education and the Human Quest* by Herbert A. Thelen, New York: Harper & Row, 1960. Reprinted by permission of the author.

Procedure on p. 403 from Fannie R. Shaftel/George Shaftel, ROLE PLAYING IN THE CUR-RICULUM, 2nd ed., © 1982, pp. 109–110. Adapted by permission of Prentice-Hall, Inc., Englewood Cliffs, New Jersey.

Excerpt on pp. 457–458 reproduced by permission of the publisher from Berger and Winters, SOCIAL STUDIES IN THE OPEN CLASSROOM: A PRACTICAL GUIDE (New York: Teachers College Press © 1973 by Teachers College—Columbia University. All rights reserved.) pp. 14–15.

Copyright © 1988 by Houghton Mifflin Company. All rights reserved.

No part of this work may be reproduced or transmitted in any form or by any means, electronic or mechanical, including photocopying and recording, or by any information storage or retrieval system without the prior written permission of Houghton Mifflin Company unless such copying is expressly permitted by federal copyright law. Address inquiries to College Permissions, Houghton Mifflin Company, One Beacon Street, Boston, MA 02108.
Printed in the U.S.A.
Library of Congress Catalog Card Number: 87-80876
ISBN: 0-395-44732-1

CDEFGHIJ-RM-9543210-89

To . . .
David Jr., Stephen, Christopher,
Lynda, and Shawn

. . . as they encounter their world.

CONTENTS

Chapter 5 Social Studies Programs: Who Teaches What, When?

PREFACE

We have written this book out of the conviction that elementary social studies can be approached as something students do and use, not simply something they are expected to know. By no means are we suggesting that social studies content is unimportant, however. Events over the last decade—particularly the emergence of state-mandated curriculum requirements—have made us increasingly aware of the need for a balanced approach to social studies. In such an approach, legitimate "know about" dimensions coexist well with an emphasis on the development of skills. Helping prospective teachers develop and manage this approach is at the heart of this book.

AUDIENCE AND PURPOSE

Children and Their World: Strategies for Teaching Social Studies, Third Edition, is intended for undergraduate students taking a first course in teaching elementary and middle school social studies. Inservice teachers and graduate students should continue to find this edition as useful as previous editions.

This book has been designed to help students understand the complex nature of elementary and middle school social studies. We take serious exception to the contention that "anyone can teach social studies," because it ignores the significant differences between demands that a subject like social studies imposes on a teacher as compared to those imposed by a subject such as mathematics. Any unwillingness to consider the nature of those differences risks misunderstanding the nature of both "beasts." We have tried to address those differences, along with elements that are unique to social studies, in a manner that is clear and direct and that appeals to undergraduate students.

This book is also based on the premise that learning is an *active* process. That premise, though hardly new or earthshaking, applies equally to students in elementary or middle school classrooms and to the students who read this book. A major purpose of this book is to present instructional models that provoke learner involvement. For prospective teachers especially, our purpose is to suggest that successful social studies teaching depends on one's ability to relate the three elements that form the triumvirate of teaching: (1) social studies content; (2) teaching methods; and (3) the ability to *apply* content and method in the classroom. The key to effective instruction lies, we believe, in *application;* content and teaching methods are certainly essential but they are not sufficient in and of themselves. Because we view teaching as an applied skill, we make every effort to relate subject-matter content to teaching methods, and teaching theory to actual practice.

REVISIONS IN THIS EDITION

This text has been extensively revised and updated throughout to incorporate the most recent research in social studies education and to reflect emerging changes and emphases in the field. A new chapter on instructional themes, which includes global education, multicultural education, law-related education, and sex-equity education, has been added. Several other chapters—including those on the nature of social studies, the nature of social ideas, social studies programs, access skills, and evaluation strategies—have been substantially reorganized and rewritten. In addition, the chapter on concept-based instruction—while retaining its emphasis on concepts as the building blocks of social studies instruction—has been greatly simplified, retitled "The Nature of Social Ideas," and moved to a more pivotal, upfront position in the text.

The treatment of several topics from earlier editions has been significantly expanded and updated in this revision. These topics include a reconceptualization of the field of social studies; developmental considerations that have an impact on social studies programs; the role and use of textbooks; social studies for young children; and the nature of skills-based teaching. New topics have also been added throughout the book. For example, state-mandated curricula; skills as "skill rules"; schema theory in relation to concept-oriented teaching; findings from the effective teaching research; and using computer-based instruction each now receives full discussion.

A significant aspect of this revision is the inclusion of new model student activities dealing with global education; examples and nonexamples of concepts; presenting information in table form; conducting surveys; role playing for young children; and gathering and interpreting data. Model student activities retained from previous editions have been updated throughout.

Finally, the book has been tightened throughout. Its overall part and chapter organization, its internal heading structure, and its writing style have been extensively overhauled to give it a very clear, direct quality.

COVERAGE AND FEATURES

This edition of *Children and Their World* is organized into three sections. Part One, "Foundations," contains three chapters that examine the nature of social studies as a teaching field, the social science disciplines, and the nature of social ideas. Part Two, "An Instructional Framework," examines the diverse elements that are essential to social studies teaching. Chapter 4 illustrates the planning process and the nature of content utilization; Chapter 5 focuses on social studies programs; Chapter 6 identifies instructional themes; Chapter 7 considers the issues and techniques associated with values education; and Chapter 8 treats teaching and questioning strategies. Chapters 9 through 11 deal with skills-based teaching. Chapter 9 identifies strategies related to reading, listening, and observing skills that enable students to gain access to information. Chapter 10 focuses on information-processing skills, while Chapter 11 explores strategies related to maps and globes, tables and graphs, and other media forms.

Part Three, "Management and Organization," contains five chapters that consider the various management dimensions associated with teaching social studies.

Chapters 12 and 13 focus on managing group dynamics and group-based instruction. Chapter 14 treats strategies related to individualized instruction including special considerations for exceptional students. Chapter 15 examines the variety of instructional resources available to social studies teachers. Chapter 16 explains the different evaluation strategies that teachers might employ. The book ends with an Epilogue in which we identify our perceived priorities for social studies in the 1990s and beyond.

In order to make this text easy to study and more appealing to use, we have included the following features:

Key Questions and *Key Ideas* at the beginning of each chapter that serve as advance organizers for the content to be covered.

Introductions that treat one or more issues within the chapter and that provide an overview of what is to come.

Model Student Activities that are appropriate for use with elementary students in the form in which they are presented, and that also illustrate lesson formats that can be adapted to other social studies topics or content.

Commentaries that are set off from the text and in which we extend ideas introduced previously or offer our point of view on various problems and issues.

Summaries that highlight the major concepts presented within each chapter.

Suggested Activities that are designed to stimulate further thought or provide opportunities for students to apply the concepts treated within the chapter.

Suggested Readings that list, with annotations, additional sources for students to locate detailed information on topics considered within the chapter.

ACKNOWLEDGMENTS

We are keenly aware of our indebtedness to many people who helped to make this book possible. Countless elementary and middle school students—including even Keith whom we describe on page 431—helped us to learn what it means to teach a subject like social studies, and who, collectively, played a significant though immeasurable role in shaping this book. Equally important are the college students and inservice teachers with whom we have been privileged to work, and whose questions (and responses to our answers) have indicated directions in which we needed to go and areas where we needed to be clearer than we were. We are also grateful to our colleagues, at both Texas Tech and Syracuse University, who have influenced and inspired us in so many ways.

We gratefully acknowledge the contributions of the following reviewers for the thoughtful advice and criticism they offered at various stages in the development of this book:

Dr. Thomas E. Bibler
University of Tennessee at Chattanooga

Dr. Robert A. Blume
University of Florida

Dr. Maurice Bozman
Salisbury State College, Maryland

Dr. Karen S. Buchanan
North Carolina Central University

Dr. Gloria Contreras
University of Texas at Austin

Dr. Gillian E. Cook
University of Texas at San Antonio

Dr. Boots Dilley
Marshall University, West Virginia

Dr. Dale D. Downs
Eastern Illinois University

Dr. Max Ferguson
Southern Utah State College

Dr. Rosalind Hammond
Bowling Green State University

Dr. James G. Hauwiller
Montana State University

Dr. Thomas M. McGowan
Indiana State University

Dr. Jerry R. Moore
University of Virginia

Dr. Elmo Moretz
Eastern Kentucky University

Dr. Rae K. O'Neill
University of Rhode Island

Dr. Robert Otto
Western Kentucky University

Dr. Muriel Radebaugh
Eastern Washington University

Dr. Charles SaLoutos
University of Wisconsin—Platteville

Dr. Hal Skinner
Sonoma State University, California

Dr. Josiah S. Tlou
Virginia Polytechnic Institute

Of these reviewers, we wish to extend our special thanks to Dr. Thomas McGowan for his rigorous examination of the manuscript, and for his perceptive reactions and creative suggestions that went far beyond what was expected. We also extend special thanks to the editorial staff at Houghton Mifflin who were clearly our partners in this endeavor.

Finally, we owe special acknowledgment to our families who know only too well the trials and joys associated with producing a book such as this, and with whom we intend to become reacquainted.

David A. Welton

John T. Mallan

CHILDREN AND THEIR WORLD

PART ONE

Social Studies: Foundations

PROLOGUE

"The dogmas of the quiet past are inadequate to the stormy present. Let us disenthrall ourselves." Abraham Lincoln

Remember when you

☐ couldn't understand why Australia was a continent but Greenland wasn't?

☐ thought Paris, Boston, and Chicago were states?

☐ had current events every Friday?

☐ memorized the Preamble to the Constitution, the Gettysburg Address, or the presidents of the United States, in order?

☐ were taught that "mail carriers deliver the mail" when you already knew it?

☐ couldn't remember the capital of Afghanistan or Belgium's major export?

☐ laboriously recopied from at least two encyclopedias your report on mythology, "the South," or Andrew Jackson?

INTRODUCTION: Reflecting on What's Ahead

Many things are done in the name of teaching social studies, some of which you may remember fondly and others that you have long since forgotten. Frankly, some of the things you studied might not have been taught at all were it not for the "Joan of Arc" syndrome.

The "Joan of Arc" syndrome, which is a fairly common occurrence in schools generally and in social studies in particular, is illustrated in the following conversation. Note that it doesn't really matter who the speakers in the conversation are; they could be two teachers, a parent and a teacher, or even two students. The only qualification is that one of them has spent time studying the topic under consideration.

"I heard that they're taking Joan of Arc [or any other topic] out of the social studies curriculum. Children won't be studying about her any more."

"What! What are they doing that for?"

"I guess it's because they can't figure out why they should keep her in."

"Why they should keep her in!!! Isn't it obvious? I learned about Joan of Arc in school—you did too. I mean, well . . . look at what it's done for us!

Look at where *we* are today! Joan of Arc is something that *everyone* needs to know."

"You're saying that because we learned it when we were in school, students today should learn it too."

"Exactly! I learned it, they should learn it too!"

Of the multitude of things that children could study in school, why do you suppose that fifth graders typically study American history and geography, and sixth graders study various nations and cultures around the world? We consider which topics are studied at what grade in detail in Chapter 5, but part of the answer lies in the "Joan of Arc" syndrome; these are topics that fifth and sixth graders have studied for almost as long as there has been something called "social studies" (or "fifth or sixth grade").

During the early decades of this century, many students left school at the end of the sixth grade or shortly thereafter. At that time, it was essential to "cover the earth" by the sixth grade lest students leave school with significant gaps in their knowledge of history and geography. But for students today, sixth grade is typically the midpoint, not the end of their public school careers. In other words, the amount of time available for instruction has almost doubled, yet what is taught as elementary and middle school social studies is sometimes little more than an updated version of what students studied in earlier eras. Social studies is not the only subject area affected by the "Joan of Arc" syndrome; in one form or other its effects extend to every subject area.

Tradition, which is what the "Joan of Arc" syndrome really refers to, is a remarkably powerful force for preserving existing policies or practices. It doesn't matter whether the practice is purely personal, such as the routine you follow when you get up in the morning, or academic, such as determining the content of a third-grade curriculum. Our tendency is to maintain the status quo, to continue doing what we've always done because—well, because that's the way we've always done it.

Occasionally we make adjustments in our personal and professional practices. Oversleeping, for example, can cause radical departures from one's daily routine. Instructional practices can also change. For example, what were once taught as facts may now be presented as the myths they really are; Columbus's "discovery" of America, and George Washington's involvement with that infamous cherry tree are two of the better examples of this. But even this kind of instructional tinkering can encounter resistance. For example, despite considerable evidence about the Viking presence in North America, countless teachers still teach about Columbus's discovery of the new world. It's not that those teachers don't know better—in fact, most textbooks present fairly extensive treatments of the Vikings (and somewhat less comprehensive treatments of the Native Americans who preceded them). Rather, we suspect that after devoting considerable time to studying about Columbus's expeditions, most adults are familiar with his activities and thus feel comfortable sharing that knowledge with children. In view of our tendency to cling to the familiar and the known (and to avoid the unfamiliar and the unknown), you can imagine the kind of reception that proposals to overhaul an entire curriculum might receive.

Our point here is that the "Joan of Arc" syndrome is an interfering mechanism that tends to keep us from examining what we do and what we have done, both personally and in the name of teaching social studies. Because something is an interfering mechanism does not mean it is necessarily bad however. Indeed, much of what has traditionally been taught as social studies should continue to be taught in the future. At the same time, we should consider elements that could be included in social studies programs but usually are not. For example, there are questions and concerns that sometimes bother students—things children think are important—but that are typically not part of most school's programs. Such questions may be similar to those listed below:

Is it okay to lie sometimes? When?

How do other people feel about me? Can I be sure?

If cooperation is so important, why don't you get graded on it in school?

Why are some of the best movies rated "R"?

Must I like everybody? What happens if I don't?

Is anyone really free?

Why can't everyone have all the money they need?

These questions reflect legitimate human and social concerns that students may think about and, in some cases, worry about. Our question is whether such matters have a rightful place in a social studies program—or a school's program. Some individuals argue that the sample questions deal with things that students will (or should) learn from their parents (or from day-to-day life), and that for schools to get involved in such matters would be an invasion of the rights and responsibilities of the home. Other individuals, ourselves included, would disagree. Although such questions and concerns cannot, and indeed should not, be the sole basis for social studies programs, there are legitimate roles that they can play.

Our intent throughout this book is to provide a basis for critically examining the activities and practices associated with teaching social studies in elementary and middle schools. Included in that examination are activities and practices that you will be expected to follow, such as lesson planning and evaluation, as well as numerous activities and practices that you could employ with children as you see fit. At various points throughout the book, we may take an occasional potshot at some of the things that are done in the name of teaching social studies, but our intent is to be critical in the spirit of critical thinking. *Critical* in this sense does not mean "finding fault with" in a negative, degrading kind of way. Rather, it means to examine analytically in an effort to develop a balanced, reasoned, and practical approach to social studies instruction.

Identifying what social studies is and what it can be are major thrusts of this book. An equally important concern relates to how one goes about teaching social studies. As we deal with these, our intent is to provide the background, the skills, and the experiences that enable you to plan and teach a dynamic social studies program.

SOCIAL STUDIES AS A SCHOOL SUBJECT

How does social studies compare with other subjects taught in elementary and middle schools? How do students feel about social studies as a subject, and why do they feel as they do? This section is organized around these key questions.

SOCIAL STUDIES AND THE BASICS

The expression "back to the basics" has characterized the educational reform movement for almost a decade, and implies that schools have somehow moved away from an emphasis on teaching basic skills. Although some educators would argue that teachers never *stopped* emphasizing "the basics"—and thus there is nothing to move back from—other Americans seem to believe that schools should exhibit most (but not necessarily all) of the following characteristics: (1) an emphasis on the "three Rs"; (2) strict discipline; (3) promotion from one grade level to the next based on demonstrated achievement (no social promotion); (4) teaching techniques that include drill, recitation, homework, and frequent testing; (5) elimination of "frills," which apparently includes anything that isn't "basic"; and (6) an emphasis on patriotism and other traditional American values (Brodinsky, 1977, pp. 522–23).

When "back to the basics" was beginning to gather steam during the mid-1970s, there was concern that some subjects—social studies and science especially—were being pushed aside in favor of increased attention to reading and language arts (e.g., Shaver, Davis, and Helburn, 1979; Welton, 1978; Gross, 1977). Richard Gross (1977), for example, cited surveys indicating that in some areas social studies was taught for only one hour per week (sometimes even less). When investigators (Davis, Frymier, and Clinefelter, 1977) examined how children actually spend their time in schools, however, the picture did not seem quite as bleak. The researchers "shadowed" sixty-five fifth-grade students for three weeks to determine how often they used different kinds of educational materials. The findings from this study, which are shown in Table P-1, confirm the strong emphasis on language-related subjects. Mathematics and social studies received a somewhat similar emphasis. Had the study examined students at lower grade levels, however, the results might have been quite different. Weiss (1978), for example, reported that two-thirds of the primary-level (K–3—Kindergarten through Grade 3) teachers responding to a survey indicated that the time available for teaching social studies was inadequate, averaging only twenty minutes of instruction per day. Other studies (Stake and Easley, 1978) confirm that in the

TABLE P-1   Curriculum Materials Used by 65 Fifth Graders, by Subject Matter, Percentage of Use, and Percentage of Time

Subject Matter	Number of Times Used	Percentage of Use*	Percentage of Time*
Language-Literature	365	40	39
Aesthetics-Recreation (includes music, recess, and physical education)	152	17	17
Social Studies (includes history, geography, social-behavioral science, philosophy, religion, values, and psychology)	143	16	16
Mathematics	135	15	17
Science (includes biological and physical science/technology)	93	10	11
Not Classified	16	2	—
Total	904	100	100

Source: O. L. Davis, Jack R. Frymier, and David Clinefelter. 1982. "Curriculum Materials Used by Eleven-Year-Old Pupils: An Analysis Using the Annehurst Curriculum Classification System." *Journal of Educational Research,* 75 (July–August), 325–332.
*Rounded

primary grades, more time is likely to be devoted to instruction in reading, language arts, and mathematics—time gained at the expense of social studies and science.

As students move upward through the elementary grades, the amount of time devoted to social studies instruction tends to increase. As Lengel and Superka (1982, p. 33) noted, ". . . in Grades 4–6 social studies does not appear to be an endangered species." By the time students reach middle or junior high schools, where departmentalized organization is the rule (and the day is divided into periods), they typically receive forty to forty-five minutes of social studies instruction each day.

CORE CURRICULUM REQUIREMENTS

Efforts to achieve educational reform are still underway in some areas of the country, so the overall picture is quite varied (Morrissett, 1986). Reforms enacted in some states have already taken effect, whereas in other states, reform legislation is pending. Apparently only a few areas have escaped legislatively mandated changes.

The trend in much of the reform legislation has been toward establishing statewide subject-matter requirements for all subjects, including social studies. For example, in Texas, Virginia, Utah, and several other states, the state boards of education or other governmental agencies have established minimum subject matter requirements that are known as the *core curriculum, essential elements,* or by other similar terms. As part of the "essential elements" legislation in Texas, for example, the knowledges and skills that must be taught in *each* subject area and at *each* grade level have been identified. Teachers in Texas must keep precise records of those essential elements that their students have mastered, and their lesson plans must be keyed to show the elements toward which instruction is being directed. Not all states have such stringent requirements, of course, and some states have moved in the other direction. In Mississippi, for instance, all subject matter requirements for social studies were eliminated (except for instruction in career education) (Morrissett, 1986).

State-mandated requirements clearly limit the freedom that teachers and local schools have traditionally enjoyed to determine what and when something will be taught in the schools. In other words, a major component of instructional decision making in many states now takes place at the state level instead of at the teacher or district level, often with grossly different content priorities. Thus in Texas, for example, latitude and longitude *must* be taught in the fourth grade; decisions to delay such instruction until the fifth or sixth grade—when the students' background in mathematics might better enable them to understand latitude and longitude—are no longer an option. On the other hand, state-mandated requirements may force teachers to devote more attention to social studies than they otherwise would—whether they want to or not. We believe that social studies should be an equal partner in a school program, but we question whether coercion is an appropriate way to achieve that goal.

STUDENTS' ATTITUDES TOWARD SOCIAL STUDIES

Determining how students feel about the subjects they study has intrigued researchers for years (Jersild and Tasch, 1949; Herman, 1963; McTeer, Blanton, and Lee, 1975; Haladyna, Shaughnessy, and Redsun, 1982; Schug, Todd, and Beery, 1984; Shaughnessy and Haladyna, 1985). Spelling and mathematics typically emerge as the subjects students like most, while social studies usually falls somewhere back in the pack. Schug, Todd, and Beery's (1984) findings of children's most- and least-preferred subjects, which are shown in Table P-2, are typical.

Why Students Feel As They Do

The fact that some students rate social studies as their most preferred subject seems to suggest that it is not inherently dull. In fact, the data in Table P-2 indicate that twice as many students dislike mathematics more so than social studies. Despite the small consolation that such findings offer, the number of students who rate social studies among their least-liked subjects is a continuing concern.

To determine why social studies tends to rank among the less preferred

TABLE P-2   Children's Most- and Least-Favorite Subjects, by Percentage
            Selecting

Subject	Most Preferred	Least Favorite
Mathematics	30	33
English	22	24
Social Studies	13	15
Science	11	15
Art	11	*
Industrial Arts	7	*
Reading	7	*
Music	*	7
Other	*	3

Source: Reprinted from *Social Education* with permission of the National Council for the Social Studies.
*=Not rated

subjects, Schug and his colleagues (1984) interviewed a number of sixth- and
twelfth-grade students. Some of the sixth graders said things like the
following:

> [I didn't like] working with the government and ancient things. First of
> all, [the teacher] talks a lot about it. There isn't much work. Every day you
> know you're going to have social studies and just sit there.

> In social studies you mostly stay on a subject for a long time, like a
> month or two months; but in reading you can do worksheets and then you
> have different stories and stuff like that—about different things.

Other sixth graders, however, said things like the following:

> I like learning about Christopher Columbus and the Indians—his sailing
> around the world and finding out the world was round.

> In third grade we talked about tribes and different people. . . . It's really
> interesting to learn about different people who do different things for
> different reasons and compare them to us and see what culture you like
> best. (p. 385)

In summarizing their findings, Schug states, "It appears that social studies is
not perceived as being a particularly enjoyable subject, it is seldom mentioned as
'important,' and it is not considered especially difficult" (p. 384).

Reflect for a moment on your experience with social studies, especially your
elementary school experience (if you can remember it). Do you recall anything that might help to explain why students tend to rank social studies as
they do?

Perhaps children feel as they do because when they study arithmetic or spelling their answers are either right or wrong, whereas in social studies they are never quite sure. Or perhaps it's because in science they deal with butterflies and bugs—real, living things—not with places far removed and people long since dead. Or maybe it's because in reading and language arts they deal with interesting stories—stories with plots—while in social studies the books look like miniature encyclopedias. The list could go on.

Perhaps children feel as they do about social studies because they find the content they study about either irrelevant or obvious. It's the rare child, for example, who hasn't watched with fascination as a fire engine raced down the street, lights ablaze and siren screaming. It's also a rare child who cannot explain what fire fighters do. At the same time, however, some primary-level social studies programs include a lengthy unit on community helpers that deals in part with fire fighters, often in ways that add little to what children already know. In other words, social studies programs sometimes focus on teaching children that milk trucks carry milk when children are well aware of what milk trucks carry.

When social studies programs deal with information that is actually new to children, they may go to the opposite extreme. For example, being asked to identify the six provinces of Australia can pose a problem for many adults, to say nothing of children. Although such information might be new, neither children nor adults may care much about learning it. The tendency of some programs to deal with content (information) that children don't see the need for is, we think, one reason that social studies tends to get such low ratings.

A second reason for both the high and low ratings almost certainly involves *how* social studies is taught. Some teachers seem able to make the most lifeless material interesting and worthwhile. Others get stuck in a read and then answer-the-questions-at-the-end-of-the-chapter routine that becomes monotonous at best. Techniques for developing vibrant and appealing social studies programs are something we deal with throughout this book.

Motivation

Telling children that they should care about information they're not interested in is seldom an effective motivator. Even phrases such as "You are going to need to know this" lose their potency after a while, especially after children discover that it's often easier to learn what they need to know when they *really* need to know it. Students' comments such as "This is dumb," and "Whatta we gotta learn this stuff for?" are usually symptoms of a problem that pervades all education; namely, the tendency to provide answers *before* students have asked the questions. Thus, another purpose of this book is to help you avoid situations where social studies becomes a process of memorizing answers to questions that students have not asked. It is not essential that children come away liking social studies, although we would be extremely pleased if they did, but rather that they care about it and see it as worthwhile.

The social sciences offer a wealth of information about the human experience that children can use to interpret and to make sense of the world. (© *Elizabeth Crews*)

SOCIAL STUDIES AS SOMETHING ONE DOES

It is important to distinguish between liking a subject and caring about it. Some of us don't like arithmetic, for example, yet we care about it. Arithmetic has utility; it is something all of us must do from time to time, and this alone may be sufficient to make us care about it. By contrast, social studies tends to be something one *knows* but seldom does. Even the terminology, *doing* social studies, sounds foreign (except in instances such as "doing one's social studies homework").

Subjects that we use or "do," such as arithmetic, can be described as *skills* (or skill subjects). These subjects have a strong knowledge base but they go a step further; skill subjects require you to apply what you know in problem-solving situations. It is in the application—in knowing what you should do when—that the actual skill enters the picture. The ultimate test of your arithmetic ability lies not in your knowledge of the number system or the additive principle, but in your ability to apply your knowledge in a problem-solving situation. The fact that some of us occasionally bounce a check at the bank isn't necessarily an indication of our lack of arithmetic knowledge (although it can be); it's more likely to be an indicator of carelessness or of our inability (or unwillingness) to apply what we know. Indeed, most of us know our arithmetic facts (2 + 2 = 4, etc.); it's just that some of us don't "do" them very well!

Is it possible to teach social studies in many of the same ways that arithmetic is taught—as something children know *and* do? We don't advocate throwing out all of the traditional "knowing about" elements of social studies—that would be throwing the baby out with the bath water. Rather, we believe the social sciences offer a wealth of information about the human experience that children can use to interpret and make sense of the world we live in. Our aim is to strike a balance between the factual knowledge traditionally associated with social studies and opportunities for students to apply that information—that is, to create situations in which students can actually *do* social studies.

SUGGESTED ACTIVITIES

1. "Well I taught it, they just didn't learn it" is a remark heard in schools across the country. Try wrestling with the question of whether teaching can take place in the absence of learning.

2. Classifying all subjects taught in elementary schools according to the criteria of "to do" and "to know" should enable you to generate an interesting perspective on the curriculum as a whole. For example, was handwriting (penmanship) something you were expected to know? Or was it something you were expected to do? Classify the subjects listed below into one of the two categories. (Note that we've separated language arts, science, and social studies into some of their major components, e.g., grammar, spelling, history, chemistry. We realize that few elementary schools have a separate course entitled "Chemistry"; nevertheless, elements of chemistry are taught under the more general label of "science.")

Subjects

Anthropology	Geology	Physics
Arithmetic	Grammar	Poetry
Art (drawing)	History	Political science
Astronomy	International relations	Reading
Biology	Literature	Social psychology
Botany	Music (vocal/instrumental)	Sociology
Chemistry	Penmanship	Spelling
Economics	Physical education	Zoology
Geography		

12

Subjects One "Does" *Subjects One "Knows"*

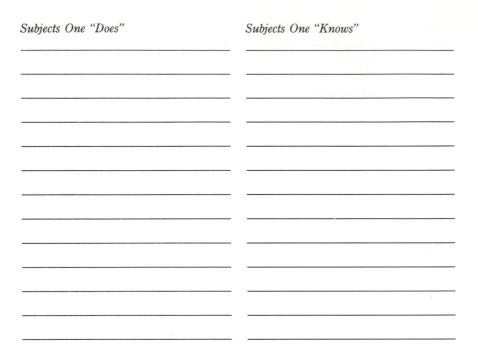

3. Although the "Joan of Arc" syndrome may well be responsible for the inclusion of some things in the social studies curriculum that might not be necessary, the reverse is probably just as true; some of the things presently taught as social studies should continue to be taught as such. Identify and place in rank order at least five major ideas or topics that you feel should continue to be taught in social studies programs. In a small group, use your rankings as a basis for developing a single list that incorporates all suggestions.

REFERENCES

Brodinsky, Ben. 1977. "Back to the Basics: The Movement and the Meaning." *Phi Delta Kappan,* 58 (March), 522–26.

Davis, O. L., Jr., Jack R. Frymier, and David Clinefelter. 1982. "Curriculum Materials Used by Eleven-Year-Old Pupils: An Analysis Using the Annehurst Curriculum Classification System." *Journal of Educational Research,* 75 (July–August), 325–332.

Gross, Richard E. 1977. "The Status of the Social Studies in the Public Schools of the United States: Facts and Impressions of a National Survey." *Social Education,* 41 (March), 194–200.

Herman, Wayne L., Jr. 1963. "How Intermediate Children Rank the Subjects." *Journal of Educational Research,* 56 (April), 435–36.

Haladyna, Thomas, M., Joan Shaughnessy, and A. Redsun. 1982. "Correlates of Attitudes Toward Social Studies." *Theory and Research in Social Education,* 10 (1), 1–25.

Jersild, Arthur, and Ruth Tasch. 1949. *Children's Interests and What They Suggest for Education.* New York: Bureau of Publications, Teachers College, Columbia University.

Lengel, James G., and Douglas P. Superka. 1982. "Curriculum Patterns." In *Social Studies in the 1980s,* ed. Irving Morrissett. pp. 32–38. Alexandria, Va.: Association for Supervision and Curriculum Development.

McTeer, J. Hugh, F. Lamar Blanton, and H. Wayne Lee. 1975. "The Relationship of Selected Variables to Student Interest in Social Studies in Comparison with Other Academic Areas." *Journal of Educational Research,* 68 (February), 238–40.

Morrissett, Irving. 1986. "The Status of Social Studies in the Mid-1980s." *Social Education,* 48 (April/May), 303–10.

Schug, Mark, Robert J. Todd, and R. Beery. 1984. "Why Kids Don't Like Social Studies." *Social Education,* 48 (May), 382–87.

Shaughnessy, Joan M., and Thomas M. Haladyna. 1985. "Research on Student Attitude Toward Social Studies." *Social Education,* 49 (November/December), 692–95.

Shaver, James P., O. L. Davis, Jr., and Suzanne W. Helburn. 1979. "The Status of Social Studies Education: Impressions from Three NSF Studies." *Social Education,* 43 (February), 150–53.

Stake, Robert E., and Jack A. Easley. 1978. *Case Studies in Science Education.* Washington, D.C.: National Science Foundation.

Weiss, Iris R. 1978. *National Survey of Science, Mathematics, and Social Studies Education.* Washington, D.C.: National Science Foundation.

Welton, David A. 1978. "A Brief Pause for Station Identification." *The Social Studies,* 69 (January/February), 12–13.

CHAPTER 1

The Dynamics of Social Studies

"Citizenship education has been the central goal of social studies for at least the last century."   Hazel Hertzberg

KEY QUESTIONS

☐ What is social studies and why is it taught?

☐ What is citizenship education?

☐ How does one *do* social studies?

KEY IDEAS

☐ Social studies is characterized by multiple goals and purposes.

☐ The overarching aim of social studies is citizenship education.

☐ Contemporary social studies programs place more emphasis on individual involvement, decision making, and acquiring skills, and less emphasis on memorized information.

INTRODUCTION: The Social Studies Family Tree

Social studies is an offspring of the social sciences. Prior to its creation over seventy years ago, what we now call social studies usually referred to just two subjects, history and geography, both of which were taught as separate courses. At that time, some of the social science disciplines, such as sociology and psychology, were still in their infancy, and some psychologists and other social scientists occasionally found themselves defending their disciplines as legitimate fields of study.

Today, the social studies family tree has grown to include (1) history and the major social science disciplines of geography, political science, anthropology, sociology, and psychology; (2) a variety of specializations within the different disciplines, such as archaeology and cultural anthropology; and (3) elements from related disciplines, such as psychiatry and law. With that kind of background, it's not surprising that social studies has developed a varied character. In fact, because its character is so varied, there are different views of what social studies is and why it should be taught. A few of those views, which deal primarily with why students should study history or geography, existed before social studies was created, and some of them persist today. We have used the term *dynamics* in the title of this chapter to indicate that social studies has been and continues to be an exciting and evolving field of study.

When you were an elementary student, you undoubtedly had teachers who held somewhat different views of social studies as a subject area. Some of those teachers probably emphasized the need to learn names and dates, the so-called facts of history, while others more or less ignored such things and emphasized main ideas, basic concepts, self-awareness, and so forth. You probably were not privy to the decisions your teachers were making about what social studies was and how it would be taught; in fact, you may have been wholly unaware that such decisions even existed. Yet, the social studies that you studied clearly resulted from them. Our intent in this chapter is to clarify some of the options that your teachers may have considered in determining what social studies is and why it should be taught, considerations that will ultimately influence the kind of social studies program you provide for your students.

SOCIAL STUDIES: THE STUDY OF THINGS SOCIAL

Social studies is a composite subject area drawn primarily from (1) the social science disciplines; (2) the findings (or knowledge) that the social science disciplines have produced; and (3) the processes that social scientists use to produce their findings. Defined in its briefest and most cryptic form, *social studies is a composite subject area based on findings and processes drawn from history and the social science disciplines.*

As a subject, social studies is an American invention (Hertzberg, 1982). Schools in other nations—most notably Canada, Australia, and some of the emerging nations in Africa—also combine the social science disciplines into composite courses, but elsewhere in the world, especially in Europe, the disciplines are still taught separately. In other words, there are many places in the world where, were you to mention "social studies," people wouldn't know what you are talking about.

Even in America, social studies tends to be a phenomenon of the elementary and middle school experience. You tend *not* to find the subject "social studies" in American high schools and colleges; at those levels the social science disciplines are typically offered in separate courses. It's true that high school teachers sometimes use the generic label "social studies teacher" even though they teach courses in the separate disciplines, but college teachers almost always use disciplinary labels to refer to themselves—historians, economists, etc.

In elementary and middle schools, the findings and processes from the social science disciplines are intermingled or merged together into what we call "social studies." Sometimes history or geography are dominant, but elements from the other disciplines are usually there too. The purpose for merging several disciplines into a single course, which is called a *broad fields* approach to curriculum, is to help students see relationships that might not be evident if the disciplines were taught separately. Note that the same broad fields format is also used for elementary language arts and science programs.

The social science disciplines furnish much of the content for social studies, but other sources are also used. These include the humanities and aspects of law (jurisprudence) and medicine, as we will see in later chapters. Social studies also draws on the media—newspapers, TV, etc.—both as a source of data and for current events. Perhaps most important of all, however, social studies draws on children's experiences, both as a source of content to be studied and as a way to bring meaning to what might otherwise be abstract events and ideas. It is the intermingling of these components, which can be accomplished in different ways, that sets social studies apart from its parent social science disciplines.

The following model student activity illustrates how the focus of several social science disciplines and your own experiences can be intermingled to create a social studies experience.

MODEL STUDENT ACTIVITY

Who Is Qualified for the Presidency?

(*Introductory Note: This is the first of many model student activities you will find throughout this book. Most of these activities have been used successfully with children in the form they are presented here. More importantly, however, these activities are presented as* models—*as exemplary lesson formats that can be adapted and modified for other topics or content areas.*)

OVERVIEW

In this decision-making activity, you (or better yet, a small group of students) are asked to identify which one of eight candidates is best qualified and which is least qualified to be president of the United States. Biographical data on the candidates, all of whom are (or were) real people, are presented on cards. Their names and sex have been omitted, however.

All of the candidates meet (or met) the three constitutional qualifications for the presidency; that is, they are all natural-born citizens, at least thirty-five years old, and have resided in the United States for at least fourteen years prior to a presidential election.

POTENTIAL OBJECTIVES

1. Given the constitutional qualifications for president, the individual will (1.1) identify any additional qualifications he or she feels to be appropriate, (1.2) determine if these are acceptable to a group of peers, and (1.3) defend or modify the selection of a potential candidate to reach group consensus.

2. Upon completion of this activity, each individual will list at least seven factors that might influence voters in deciding upon a candidate's qualifications for the presidency.

PROCEDURE

In using this activity with students, Phases One and Two should be done in small groups. The discussion questions in Phase Three can be considered in small groups, and then summarized in a teacher-led large-group activity.

Phase One—Additional Qualifications

Before considering the candidates, identify any additional qualifications (beyond those identified in the Constitution) that a president of the United States should possess. For example, should a president be a college graduate? Should he or she have had prior political experience?

Phase Two—Selection

Using the data cards on the following pages, identify the individuals you feel would be (1) *best* qualified and (2) *least* qualified to be president of the United States. (The candidates' identities appear in Appendix A.)

   [*Note:* "Age as of this date" on the data cards refers to the point in each candidate's career at which he or she had accomplished all of the activities listed on the card. For those candidates who served as President, for example, the date used was just prior to their election to office.]

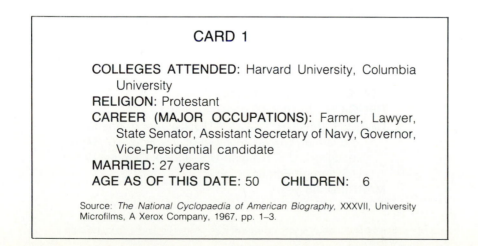

CARD 1

COLLEGES ATTENDED: Harvard University, Columbia
      University
RELIGION: Protestant
CAREER (MAJOR OCCUPATIONS): Farmer, Lawyer,
      State Senator, Assistant Secretary of Navy, Governor,
      Vice-Presidential candidate
MARRIED: 27 years
AGE AS OF THIS DATE: 50   CHILDREN: 6

Source: *The National Cyclopaedia of American Biography*, XXXVII, University Microfilms, A Xerox Company, 1967, pp. 1–3.

CARD 2

COLLEGE ATTENDED: None
RELIGION: Protestant
CAREER (MAJOR OCCUPATIONS): Investor, Druggist, Bookseller, Brigadier General in U.S. Army
MARRIED: 1st spouse: 5 years until spouse's death; 2nd spouse: 1 year
CHILDREN: 3 by first marriage
AGE AS OF THIS DATE: 38

Source: *Dictionary of American Biography,* Charles Scribner's Sons. 1928, pp. 362–67.

CARD 3

COLLEGES ATTENDED: Morehouse College, A.B. and L.H.D., Crozer Theological Seminary, B.D., University of Pennsylvania, Boston University, Ph.D., D.D., Harvard University, L.L.D., Central State College, Morgan State College
RELIGION: Protestant
CAREER (MAJOR OCCUPATIONS): Protestant minister, Teacher of Philosophy at Harvard, President of a civil rights organization, 1 of 10 outstanding men for the year according to *Time* magazine, Nobel Prize winner, Noted public speaker
MARRIED: 15 years
AGE AS OF THIS DATE: 37   **CHILDREN:**   4

Sources: *Current Biography Yearbook 1965,* H. W. Wilson Co., 1966, pp. 220–23; *Current Biography Yearbook 1968,* H. W. Wilson Co., 1969, p. 457.

CARD 4

COLLEGE ATTENDED: None
RELIGION: No specific denomination
CAREER (MAJOR OCCUPATIONS): Land speculator and farmer, Lawyer, Member of U.S. House of Representatives, U.S. Senator, U.S. Judge, Commander of U.S. Armed Forces
MARRIED: 38 years
AGE AS OF THIS DATE: 62   **CHILDREN:**   none

Source: *Dictionary of American Biography,* IX, Charles Scribner's Sons, 1932, pp. 526–31.

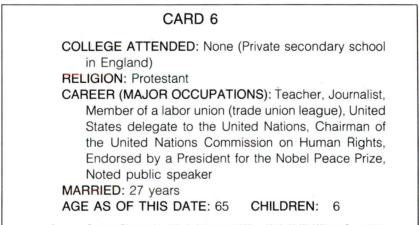

CARD 5

COLLEGE ATTENDED: Columbia University
RELIGION: No specific denomination
CAREER (MAJOR OCCUPATIONS): Writer, Served as Lieutenant Colonel in Army, Lawyer, Member of a congress, Member of a constitutional convention, Secretary of the Treasury
MARRIED: 24 years
AGE AS OF THIS DATE: 47   **CHILDREN:** 8

Source: *Dictionary of American Biography,* VIII, Charles Scribner's Sons, 1932, pp. 171–79.

CARD 6

COLLEGE ATTENDED: None (Private secondary school in England)
RELIGION: Protestant
CAREER (MAJOR OCCUPATIONS): Teacher, Journalist, Member of a labor union (trade union league), United States delegate to the United Nations, Chairman of the United Nations Commission on Human Rights, Endorsed by a President for the Nobel Peace Prize, Noted public speaker
MARRIED: 27 years
AGE AS OF THIS DATE: 65   **CHILDREN:** 6

Source: *Current Biography: Who's News and Why, 1949,* H. W. Wilson Co., 1950, pp. 528–32.

CARD 7

COLLEGE ATTENDED: University of Alabama
RELIGION: Protestant
CAREER (MAJOR OCCUPATIONS): Lawyer, State Assistant Attorney General, State legislator, U.S. Judge, State Governor, Party Candidate for Presidency, Served in U.S. Air Force, Noted public speaker
MARRIED: 1st spouse: 26 years until spouse's death; 2nd spouse: 3 years
CHILDREN: 4 by first marriage
AGE AS OF THIS DATE: 55

Sources: *Who's Who in America,* II, Marquis Who's Who, Inc., 1972, p. 3300; *Current Biography, Yearbook 1963,* H. W. Wilson Co., 1964, pp. 454–56.

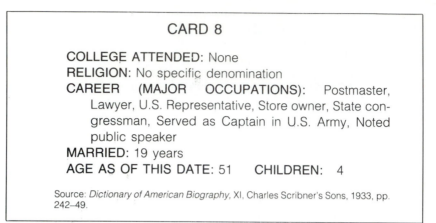

Phase Three—Summary

Questions

1. To what extent did your choices reflect the qualifications you listed in Phase One? Would you modify your list in any way?

2. Which of the following factors, if any, should be considered in selecting a presidential candidate?

   2.1. Age
   2.2. Religion
   2.3. Sex
   2.4. Educational background
   2.5. Number of children

   2.6. Previous occupation
   2.7. Personal appearance
   2.8. Personality
   2.9. Ethnic background
   2.10. Marital status

3. Should other factors be considered? Physical health?

4. What qualifications are most important? Least important?

Optional Extending Activities

1. Examine the candidate's identities as shown in Appendix A. Would you change your selection? Why or why not? Does the new information influence your conclusions about the necessary qualifications?

2. Are your qualifications representative of the beliefs of most individuals in your community? In your class? Identify a plan for determining how you could find out.

Source: Adapted from Marsha Hobin, "Clarifying What Is Important," in Allan O. Kownslar, Ed., *Teaching American History: The Quest for Relevancy.* Copyright 1974 by National Council for the Social Studies. Reprinted by permission of Allan O. Kownslar and NCSS.

"Who Is Qualified for the Presidency?" which is adapted from Marsha Hobin (1974), illustrates two techniques that help to enhance student interest and involvement. Briefly, those techniques are (1) *creating mystery-type situations,* which in this case was achieved by intentionally limiting the amount of infor-

Instructional activities dealing with particular social phenomena—such as selecting a presidential candidate—can involve aspects of many of the different social science disciplines. (© *David S. Strickler/The Picture Cube*)

mation available (the candidates' names and sex were omitted), and (2) *providing alternatives for students to choose among.* Separately, the creation of puzzle- or mystery-type situations and providing opportunities for realistic decision making are excellent interest-arousing techniques; but when combined, as they were in this activity, they become especially powerful.

"Who Is Qualified for the Presidency?" focused on several elements that included the qualifications of the chief executive and factors that may influence the electoral process. These elements typically fall within the realm of political science. However, those factors that influence group behavior and that might affect a decision about which candidate certain groups might support fall within the realm of sociology. Although the activity itself did not present findings from either political science or sociology, a teacher could follow up the activity by presenting information about factors that influence the electoral process (from political science) or the voting behavior of various groups (from sociology).

Other social science disciplines in addition to political science and sociology could also appear in the presidency activity. Consider the following statements, each of which reflects the focus of a social science discipline, and determine which of them could play a role in the presidency activity.

Yes   No

_____ _____   The use of historical data (history)

_____ _____   The interaction of people and their physical environment (geography)

_____ _____   Systems of trading and distributing resources (economics)

_____ _____   Elements of government and political behavior (political science)

_____ _____   Individual and group values, and group behavior (sociology)

_____ _____   The study of cultures and cultural change (anthropology)

_____ _____   The study of human relationships and interpersonal affairs (social psychology)

To a greater or lesser degree, at least five social science disciplines can play a role in the presidency activity. They are history, anthropology, social psychology, and the aforementioned political science and sociology. Although the activity could be used as part of a lesson in any of these disciplines, it was not created as a history lesson, a sociology lesson, or a political science lesson. Rather, it was created as an instructional activity that deals with a particular social phenomenon—selecting a presidential candidate. This means that whatever label you might want to apply to the activity (history activity, political science activity, etc.) would depend on how you wanted to use it. In other words, social experiences are part of our everyday life; how we decide to label those experiences (should we wish to do so) can come afterward.

In the next section, we examine some of the ways in which social studies and its parent disciplines have evolved over time.

SOCIAL STUDIES: PERSPECTIVES

None of the social science disciplines has a monopoly on studying social behavior. Each discipline offers a different perspective from which to examine the human (social) experience. The fact that a phenomenon such as voting behavior can be the focus of several disciplines suggests that the boundaries that separate one social science discipline from another are sometimes fuzzy. Actually, determining the location of those boundaries is seldom a problem for teachers or students, and, frankly, even most social scientists don't worry much about them. Rather, most social studies programs focus on a certain social phenomenon and the processes used to study that phenomenon, not the disciplinary label we might attach to it. In fact, as John Dewey noted in 1938 (p. 367), "in the proper emphasis upon social studies, the primary problem . . . is to determine the scope and range of the subject matter designated 'social.' "

Historical Perspective

Edgar Wesley produced one of the most widely quoted answers to the question "What is social studies?" when he said, "The social studies are the social sciences simplified for pedagogical [instructional] purposes" (Wesley and Wronski, 1958, p. 3). This definition is most applicable to the high school level, where social studies courses tend to be simplified versions of similar social science courses taught at the college level. Prior to about 1920 and in selected instances since that time, Wesley's "simplified social sciences" definition would also have applied to elementary social studies. As we noted earlier, what is now called "social studies" once referred to two separate subjects, history and geography, both of which were simplified for presentation to elementary children.

Until the early decades of this century, the study of history and geography was thought to (1) provide a form of religious and moral training and (2) inspire patriotism. Similar reasons are sometimes used to justify teaching history and geography today, but at that time another reason was often cited—namely, (3) for the "mind training" or mental discipline those subjects offered. It was widely believed that the human mind was like a muscle that needed to be trained or disciplined through mental exercise, in somewhat the same manner that athletes train their bodies through physical exercise. For students, that mental training often consisted of long—sometimes deliberately prolonged and distasteful—lessons. In other words, an activity such as memorizing the Roman Emperors in order was supposedly good for students because of the mental effort it required.

Mental discipline's demise as a learning theory was hastened when psychologists discovered that "training the mind" in one subject did not transfer to other subject areas. Memorizing page after page of Latin, for example, had no influence on a student's performance in history, and vice versa. A similar fallacy of the mental-discipline approach was its tendency to equate memorization with understanding. The error in equating the two is illustrated by children who may be able to recite the Pledge of Allegiance flawlessly, but haven't the faintest idea what "one nation, indivisible" really means.

By the early decades of this century, mental-discipline approaches to teaching had been discredited, but they did not (and have not) disappear entirely. Even today some teachers require students to memorize the Gettysburg Address or the presidents of the United States, in the name of patriotism and mind training. It's true that some children seem to enjoy the challenge that memorizing poses, but other children despise such activities with equal passion.

Despite the decline of mental discipline, history and geography continued to play a major role in most schools. However, the reasons for teaching them tended to become more utilitarian. By the 1920s, the study of history and geography were thought to produce individuals who were more socially intelligent and historically minded (Wehlage and Anderson, 1972). This shift, slight as it was at the beginning, was further intensified during the 1930s and 1940s, by an increased emphasis on "education for life adjustment." Instead of teaching subjects for their intrinsic value, teachers were increasingly called upon to provide schooling that addressed practical problems that students would encounter in the real world.

The emphasis on education for life adjustment influenced social studies teaching to the extent that it was no longer widely assumed that there were bodies of knowledge from the disciplines that had to be taught for their own sake—history as history, and so forth. Agreement on this point was not universal, however, and it still isn't. With the current "back to the basics" emphasis, arguments that certain subjects should be taught for their intrinsic value seem to be enjoying renewed popularity. From the 1930s through the 1950s, however, the emphasis on helping students cope with problems they might encounter in the real world was accompanied by a corresponding de-emphasis on teaching the social science disciplines separately. In place of separate subjects, elements from geography, history, economics, political science, and the other social science disciplines were increasingly merged into "social studies."

Unified Studies

In elementary and middle schools today, social studies typically reflects a *unified studies,* or integrated, approach. In a unified studies (or broad fields) approach, topics rather than separate disciplines are the focal point. In an integrated studies approach to a topic such as "England," for example, elements of English history and geography, England's form of government, its economic and educational systems, and a study of English culture might be considered within a single course. Conversely, when the social science disciplines are the focus, one might study British history in a history course, English geography in a world geography course, the British form of government in a political science course, and so forth.

The practice of intermingling elements from various social science disciplines into integrated units is not without its critics. For example, some individuals question the relative emphasis given to the various disciplines. In the process of selecting new social studies textbooks, someone might argue that a certain book has "too much history and not enough economics." In a unified studies approach, the degree to which the various disciplines are drawn upon can differ considerably, and there are no clear criteria on which to base the "drawing." Other individuals (to whom we referred earlier) object to any kind of integration; they want the "pure" disciplines retained so that "history can be taught as history, economics as economics," and so forth. They sometimes equate "integration" with "simplification," and may even use arguments such as "the more difficult (the subject), the better"—arguments that harken back to a time when mental discipline was in vogue.

Over twenty years ago, Shirley Engle summed up the situation that still prevails today in the following way:

> **There is confusion, if not open disagreement, about the nature and hence the purpose of the social studies. On the one hand are those, principally academicians, who see the term social studies as no more than a**

general name of [for] a collection of separate but somewhat related disciplines—history, sociology, economics, political science, etc. To many at this extreme, the very name "social studies" is anathema because it does not refer to a particular subject. At the other extreme are those who see social studies as a discipline in its own right, intermingling knowledge from all of the social science disciplines and dealing directly with social ideas and problems as these occur to the average citizen. (1965, p. 1)

Recent Emphases

From time to time in our recent past, there have been efforts to alter the nature and form of social studies. For example, after the Russians successfully launched their satellite in 1957—thereby leading the United States in the race to space—national attention turned to the so-called crisis in our schools. At that time it was not clear precisely what the schools were doing wrong (that had enabled the Russians to win the space race), but it was clear that America had to do something—if only to salvage its national pride. The solution took the form of massive, federally funded curriculum-development projects, first in the area of mathematics and science, and later in the social sciences and the humanities.

The effort to develop social studies curriculum materials during the 1960s was called "Project Social Studies," and led to something called the "new social studies." Almost all of the teaching materials developed under Project Social Studies shared two characteristics: (1) they focused on a single social science discipline, and (2) they emphasized the techniques and processes used by specialists within that discipline. For example, some of the materials developed by the Michigan Social Science Curriculum Project focused on social psychology, a discipline that had previously received little emphasis in the elementary curriculum. Those materials were part of the *Social Science Laboratory* series (Lippitt, Fox, and Schaible, 1969), a title that reflected the view that classrooms could serve as functioning social science laboratories. A similar emphasis was evident in materials produced by the Georgia Anthropology Project, in which the focus discipline was, obviously, anthropology.

Many of the teaching materials developed under Project Social Studies are dated and out of print, but some of the approaches and techniques have been incorporated into the text materials available from commercial publishers. Note also that the emphasis on techniques and processes that social scientists use to produce and validate their findings still plays a role in social studies programs, although it is somewhat more limited than was true in the 1970s.

As "back to the basics" was gathering momentum in the late 1970s, there were subtle (and some not so subtle) efforts to de-emphasize the processes of social science and to re-emphasize what could be called "the basic nature of the disciplines." In most instances, however, this did not mean a return to the kind of social studies that had been taught at the turn of the century—in part because some of the disciplines themselves had changed.

One of the best illustrations of this change is found in political science. It is oversimplified but essentially correct to say that for many years political science was dominated by an emphasis on "structure." This means that political scientists focused most of their attention on how political institutions were organized. The "structuralists' " interests were reflected in questions such as "How many members are in the United States House of Representatives?" and "How are those seats allocated?" More recently, some political scientists have shifted their attention toward *political socialization*—the ways in which we develop political attitudes and beliefs. Instead of focusing on structure, a political socializationist would be likely to ask, "How does a person become a Republican, a Democrat, or an independent?" This does not mean that political socializationists ignore questions of structure, or vice versa; it's a matter of changing emphases, not exclusion.

Definitions

The dynamic character of social studies is illustrated by changes in what are sometimes referred to as the "official" definitions of social studies. Prior to 1978, for example, the National Council for the Social Studies, the preeminent organization of social studies educators, defined social studies as including "history, economics, sociology, civics, geography, and all modifications or combinations of subjects whose content as well as aim is predominantly social" (NCSS, 1979). This was subsequently changed to the following:

> **Social studies is a basic subject of the K–12 curriculum that (1) derives its goals from the nature of citizenship in a democratic society that is closely linked to other nations and peoples of the world; (2) draws its content primarily from history, the social sciences, and, in some respects, from the humanities and science; and (3) is taught in ways that reflect an awareness of the personal, social, and cultural experiences and developmental levels of learners. (NCSS, 1984, p. 251)**

Several elements of the more recent definition deserve mention. First, social studies is still seen as a composite subject area, but the descriptor "basic" has been added. Second, the phrase "closely linked to other nations and peoples of the world" is a reflection of the global dimension of social studies that has emerged in the 1980s. Finally, the statement recognizes the natural and physical sciences and the humanities as sources of social studies content. We'll examine these recent emphases in later sections.

THE ESSENTIALS OF SOCIAL STUDIES

Many of the changes in social studies are a reflection of changes that have occurred in education itself. From a beginning that focused on history and geography, social studies has evolved to the point that it is sometimes not entirely clear even to experts just how much it encompasses. In other words, to suggest that social studies is concerned with anything and everything "social" covers a very large territory indeed.

In an effort to identify the essential characteristics of social studies (K–12), the National Council for the Social Studies in 1981 issued the position statement that appears below. The intent was to capture both the nature of social studies as a field of study and the purposes for which it is taught.

ESSENTIALS OF THE SOCIAL STUDIES

Citizen participation in public life is essential to the health of our democratic system. Effective social studies programs help prepare young people who can identify, understand and work to solve the problems that face our increasingly diverse nation and interdependent world. Organized according to a professionally designed scope and sequence, such programs:

1. Begin in pre-school and continue throughout formal education and include a range of related electives at the secondary level.
2. Foster individual and cultural identity.
3. Include observation of and participation in the school and community as part of the curriculum.
4. Deal with critical issues and the world as it really is.
5. Prepare students to make decisions based on American principles.
6. Demand high standards of performance and measure student success by means that require more than the memorization of information.
7. Depend on innovative teachers broadly prepared in history, the humanities, the social sciences, educational theory and practice.
8. Involve community members as resources for program development and student involvement.
9. Lead to citizenship participation in public affairs.

In 1979, the National Council for the Social Studies joined with eleven other professional associations to reaffirm the value of a balanced education. We now enumerate the essentials of exemplary social studies programs. Such programs contribute not only to the development of students' capacity to read and compute, but also link knowledge and skills with an understanding of and commitment to democratic principles and their application.

Knowledge

Students need knowledge of the world at large and the world at hand, the world of individuals and the world of institutions, the world past, the world present and future. An exemplary social studies curriculum links information presented in the classroom with experiences gained by students through social and civic observation, analysis and participation.

Classroom instruction which relates content to information drawn from the media and from experience focuses on the following areas of knowledge:

History and culture of our nation and the world.

Geography—physical, political, cultural and economic.

Government—theories, systems, structures and processes.

Economics—theories, systems, structures and processes.

Social institutions—the individual, the group, the community and the society.

Intergroup and interpersonal relationships.

World-wide relationships of all sorts between and among nations, races, cultures and institutions.

From this knowledge base, exemplary programs teach skills, concepts and generalizations that can help students understand the sweep of human affairs and ways of managing conflict consistent with democratic procedures.

Democratic Beliefs

Fundamental beliefs drawn from the Declaration of Independence and the United States Constitution with its Bill of Rights form the basic principles of our democratic constitutional order. Exemplary school programs do not indoctrinate students to accept these ideas blindly, but present knowledge about their historical derivation and contemporary application essential to understanding our society and its institutions. Not only should such ideas be discussed as they relate to the curriculum and to current affairs, they should also be mirrored by teachers in their classrooms and embodied in the school's daily operations.

These democratic beliefs depend upon such practices as due process, equal protection and civic participation, and are rooted in the concepts of:

Justice   Freedom

Equality   Diversity

Responsibility   Privacy

Thinking Skills

It is important that students connect knowledge with beliefs and action. To do that, thinking skills can be developed through constant systematic practice throughout the years of formal schooling. Fundamental to the goals of social studies education are those skills which help assure rational behavior in social settings.

In addition to strengthening reading and computation, there is a wide variety of thinking skills essential to the social studies which can be grouped into four major categories:

Data Gathering Skills Learning to:

Acquire information by observation

Locate information from a variety of sources

Compile, organize, and evaluate information

Extract and interpret information

Communicate orally and in writing

Intellectual Skills Learning to:

Compare things, ideas, events, and situations on the basis of similarities and differences

Classify or group items in categories

Ask appropriate and searching questions

Draw conclusions or inferences from evidence

Arrive at general ideas

Make sensible predictions from generalizations

Decision Making Skills Learning to:

Consider alternative solutions

Consider the consequences of each solution

Make decisions and justify them in relationship to democratic principles

Act, based on those decisions

Interpersonal Skills Learning to:

See things from the point of view of others

Understand one's own beliefs, feelings, abilities, and shortcomings and how they affect relations with others

Use group generalizations without stereotyping and arbitrarily classifying individuals

Recognize value in individuals different from one's self and groups different from one's own

Work effectively with others as a group member

Give and receive constructive criticism

Accept responsibility and respect the rights and property of others

Participation Skills

As a civic participant, the individual uses the knowledge, beliefs, and skills learned in the school, the social studies classroom, the community, and the family as the basis for action.

Connecting the classroom with the community provides many opportunities for students to learn the basic skills of participation, from observation to advocacy. To teach participation, social studies programs need to emphasize the following kinds of skills:

Work effectively in groups—organizing, planning, making decisions, taking action

Form coalitions of interest with other groups

Persuade, compromise, bargain

Practice patience and perseverance in working for one's goal

Develop experience in cross-cultural situations

Civic Action

Social studies programs which combine the acquisition of knowledge and skills with an understanding of the application of democratic beliefs to life through practice at social participation represent an ideal professional standard. Working to achieve that ideal is vital to the future of our society. However, even if excellent programs of social studies education were in place, there would often remain a missing element—the will to take part in public affairs. Formal education led by creative and humane teachers can provide the knowledge, the tools, the commitment for a thoughtful consideration of issues and can even stimulate the desire to be active. But to achieve full participation, our diverse society must value and model involvement to emphasize for young people the merit of taking part in public life.

As we approach the bicentennial of our Constitution and Bill of Rights, is it not time for us to recommit ourselves as a nation to strong education for civic responsibility? (NCSS, 1981, pp. 163–64)

SOCIAL STUDIES: THE QUEST FOR PURPOSE

Students study subjects like reading and arithmetic for reasons that are almost self-evident; such subjects embody skills that students will use throughout their lifetimes. But the reasons for teaching other subjects, such as social studies and science, are not nearly as clear. This section has two purposes: (1) to identify the different purposes that social studies can serve, and (2) to make you aware that you may encounter parents, principals, or other teachers whose expectations of social studies are different from yours.

The overall structure of elementary social studies is illustrated in Figure 1.1. That figure illustrates that the overarching goal of social studies is citizenship education, which means teaching the knowledge and skills that enable individuals to function effectively in whatever settings they find themselves.

FIGURE 1.1   The Organization of Elementary Social Studies

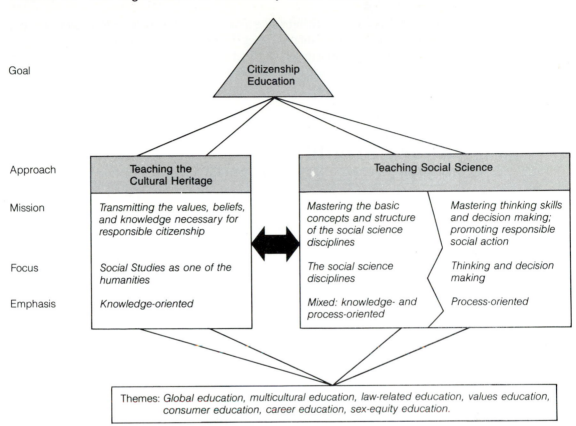

Figure 1.1 also illustrates two approaches or avenues by which social studies can contribute to producing educated citizens: (1) by teaching the cultural heritage and (2) by teaching social science. Within the latter category there are two relatively distinct foci: (1) teaching the social science disciplines and (2) teaching children to think and inquire. Finally, there are several instructional themes, such as global education, multicultural education, and values education, that appear in all of the different approaches.

The two basic approaches to social studies are interrelated, as indicated by the arrow in the diagram. In practical terms, this means that a teacher who focuses on the cultural heritage could shift gears to focus on a specific social science discipline and/or adopt a thinking skills/decision-making emphasis. There is nothing necessarily wrong with such shifting, but making the shift is not as easy as it might seem. This is because the approaches, although interrelated, are not interchangeable. You cannot select a mission from one approach and a focus from another without wreaking havoc on the overall approaches as we have described them.

Rather, most teachers focus their efforts on the approach with which they feel most comfortable.

In the balance of this chapter, we look first at the purpose for teaching social studies—citizenship education—and at the different approaches for reaching that goal. We then take a brief look at two instructional themes, multicultural education and values education, that influence social studies instruction regardless of the approach a teacher uses.

SOCIAL STUDIES AS CITIZENSHIP EDUCATION

The purpose of social studies, like the purpose of schools themselves, has been and continues to be to educate children and youth in the attributes of good citizenship. But training someone to be an effective citizen takes in virtually everything schools teach: English, social studies, science, thinking—everything! Because citizenship education is a shared goal, the appropriate question here is, "What can social studies contribute to the education of effective citizens?"

From time to time, various individuals and groups have tried to answer that question by identifying desirable attributes of citizenship; that is, the skills and behaviors that effective citizens should demonstrate. The results of two such efforts, one from the 1950s and one from the 1980s, are shown on page 33.

The attributes identified by Edwin Carr and Edgar Wesley, which were published in the 1950s, reflect a relatively broad definition of citizenship. The attributes from the 1980s (Remy, 1980) reflect a somewhat narrower, more politically oriented view of citizenship. The latter view is sometimes described as *civic education* or political education (Patrick, 1977). The two lists are presented side by side in Table 1.1 to facilitate comparison, but because they reflect somewhat different views of citizenship, the entries are not intended to represent matched pairs.

The attributes of citizenship identify competencies or behaviors that students are expected to demonstrate *after* instruction. However, they do not identify the subjects that should be taught to produce such competencies. In other words, nothing on either list indicates specifically that students should study something such as history—a subject common to social studies programs everywhere. Because a course of study that would produce the desired attributes is not stated, it is necessary to infer what subjects should be taught. This is where the different approaches to social studies (as shown in Figure 1.1) enter the picture. All of the approaches contribute to producing responsible citizens, but each reflects a somewhat different view of *what* students should be taught and *how* they should be taught so as to achieve that goal.

(Don't be too hasty to fault the specialists for not providing a course of study to accompany their attributes of citizenship; you can be almost certain they have one. The reason they provide only the attributes, we suspect, is "political" and

TABLE 1.1   Basic Competencies of Citizenship

A responsible citizen is one who: Carr and Wesley	Remy
Is skillful in securing, sifting, evaluating, organizing, and presenting information.	Is competent in acquiring and processing information about political situations.
Respects the rights and opinions of others.	Is competent in assessing one's involve-ment and stake in political situations, issues, decisions, and policies.
Assumes social and civic responsibility.	
Becomes a judicious consumer.	Is competent in making thoughtful de-cisions regarding group governance and problems of citizenship.
Uses basic social studies skills.	
Exercises critical judgment.	
Gets along with individuals and groups.	Is competent in developing and using stan-dards such as justice, ethics, morality, and practicality to make judgments about peo-ple, institutions, policies, and decisions.
Makes intelligent adjustments to change.	
Acts in accord with democratic principles and values.	
Understands principal economic, social, and political problems.	Is competent in communicating ideas to other citizens, decision makers, leaders, and officials.
Understands and promotes social progress.	Is competent in cooperating and working with others in groups and organizations to achieve mutual goals.
Understands the interdependence of people and groups.	
Learns about vocational activities and oppor-tunities.	Is competent in working with bureaucra-tically organized institutions in order to promote and protect one's interests and values.
Becomes a happy member of the home.	

Sources: Adapted from "Social Studies" by Edwin R. Carr and Edgar B. Wesley. Reprinted with permission of Macmillan Publishing Company from ENCYCLOPEDIA OF EDUCATIONAL RESEARCH, 2nd Edition, Walter S. Monroe, Editor. Copyright © 1950, 1978 by American Educational Research Association; and Richard C. Remy. *Handbook of Basic Citizenship Competencies.* Copyright © 1980 by the Association for Supervision and Curriculum Development. All rights reserved. Reprinted with permission of the Association for Supervision and Curriculum Development.

involves the different approaches to social studies we noted above. Many in-dividuals so strongly favor one approach over the others that they virtually reject the other approaches. Rather than risk having their attributes rejected because their proposed course of study favors a different approach, the specialists often follow a safer course and present only the attributes. An individual can then decide if the approach that he or she favors will "fit" the desired outcomes.)

APPROACHES TO INSTRUCTION

The approaches to social studies differ in terms of (1) what a teacher might hope to accomplish (the *mission*), (2) the kind of content the teacher might employ (the *focus*), and (3) the elements within that content the teacher might emphasize (the *emphasis*) and, ultimately, expect children to be able to do as a result of instruc-tion. The elements within each approach are interrelated, but not interchangeable.

An introductory example from American history may illustrate the difference among the different approaches. American history is both a repository of our cultural heritage and a social discipline [although the latter point is disputed by some authorities (c.f., Krug, 1967)]. Thus, on the surface it would seem that teaching American history kills two birds with one stone. But the situation is not so simple. Since the mission of the Cultural Heritage approach is to *transmit* knowledge (and beliefs and attitudes), its emphasis would be on having students know American history—in much the same manner as you were expected to know it in most of the courses you've taken. You undoubtedly had to do some thinking, of course, but most of the emphasis was on mastering a body of knowledge.

The main mission of the Social Science–Disciplines approach is to help students master the concepts and structures of the social science disciplines. Our example gets a little shaky in this approach, however, because there is no agreed-upon list of major concepts in American history that students should know. (The courses in the separate social science disciplines that you took in high school or college— economics, sociology, political science, etc.—are better examples of the Disciplines approach.)

Teachers who follow the Disciplines approach to American history might teach many of the same things that are taught in the Cultural Heritage approach, but they would do so for a different reason. Strictly speaking, teachers would teach the content—in this case American history—*because it is part of the discipline* in question. Students would learn this historical information to better comprehend the essence of what history is.

A major component of history—but not all history courses—is the processes that historians use to produce new knowledge—namely, historiography. Because historiography is an integral part of history, students in the Social Science– Disciplines approach would learn how historians produce (or discover) new historical knowledge. Formal historiography would be difficult for young children, of course, especially those who can't read. However, a teacher could help young children deal with oral history in the form of stories told by grandparents or other elders that students have tape-recorded. The point of this example is to show that the emphasis in the Disciplines approach is mixed; students are expected to know the major elements of American history, and they are also expected to know the processes that historians use to produce and validate their knowledge.

The main mission of the Social Science–Thinking/Decision-Making approach is to help children master information-processing skills (thinking skills) and decision making. The approach here is quite different from the others, because teachers would not attempt to cover the scope of American history—as teachers in the other approaches might do. Instead, they would select and use content from history (and possibly the other social science disciplines) in ways that help children to develop their thinking and decision-making skills.

The "Who Is Qualified for the Presidency?" activity (pages 16–20) is characteristic of the emphasis associated with this approach (although it could certainly be used in the other approaches as well). In using that activity, the teacher would help children focus on (1) the decision-making processes they used to determine the most- and least-qualified candidates and (2) the additional qualifications that people might look for in a president.

The historiography and oral history elements that we noted in the Social Science–Disciplines approach would also be appropriate in this approach because of their emphasis on helping students process information. What you would *not* find in the Thinking/Decision-Making approach is a heavy emphasis on the so-called facts of history. The major exception to that rule involves those elements of history that must be taught by law, and which we explain in the next section.

The point here is that content from American history could be used within each of the different approaches to social studies. However, it would not always be exactly the same subject matter (content), nor would it necessarily be used in the same ways or with the same emphases. Rather, the teachers' overall approach will be reflected in their decisions regarding *how* and *why* they will use certain content—which mission and which focus they are seeking to fulfill. The reverse is also true; that is, if teachers know what overall approach they wish to adopt, whether it be teaching the cultural heritage or teaching social science, their mission, focus, and emphasis will usually reflect that decision.

TEACHING THE CULTURAL HERITAGE

Mission: The *transmission* to children of selected knowledge, values, and attitudes that are drawn from the total fund of human knowledge and experience.

In nations where governments have been thrown from power, one of the new government's first actions is to order that the history books be rewritten. From the government's perspective, it is important that future citizens get the "correct" view of their nation's history. It doesn't take much imagination to determine which government is depicted in the most favorable light.

Schools everywhere are concerned with producing good citizens, no matter how that expression is defined. In fact, one of the few things common to schools everywhere is the expectation that they teach how their respective societies came into being. Thus, Russian children study Russian history, British children study British history, American children study American history, and so forth around the globe.

Legal Requirements

Before states began enacting more rigid requirements, most curriculum regulations were fairly general; although they identified certain content to be taught, they typically did not specify precise topics or the grade level at which the subject should be taught. In most areas, for example, the study of American history is required by law, and in some states it is required before students leave elementary school. Such general regulations, which were referred to as "Spirit of '76" laws, still prevail in some parts of the country, but the trend in the 1980s has been for states to increase the number of topics/subjects that schools are required to teach (Morrissett, 1986). In addition to American history, some states require consumer education, career education, or, more recently, geography. Other states require that the study of democracy or free enterprise precede the study of communism, socialism, or other governmental forms.

Legal requirements identify certain subjects or topics that state governments, and presumably the people they represent, want taught in the schools. Although most existing regulations indicate what social studies are to be taught, none of the legal requirements that we know of specify which approach a teacher should take. In other words, teachers still have some latitude in determining *how* they teach.

Scope

Legal requirements notwithstanding, teachers who favor the Cultural Heritage approach have a massive amount of potential content to deal with. Our collective heritage extends beyond national history to encompass the origins of human civilization, the development of cultures throughout the world, and the different ways we have devised to explain our place in the universe. A teacher would not be expected to cover all of that information in a single year, of course. Indeed, the scope of our cultural heritage is so wide that it would take years to cover it all.

The mission of the Cultural Heritage approach is to *transmit* elements of that heritage to the young. To accomplish this goal, many teachers treat social studies as one of the humanities, as we explain in the next section.

Social Studies as Humanities

The humanities refer to *those bodies of knowledge concerned with people and their culture, including literature, philosophy, and the fine arts, as opposed to the sciences and technical crafts.* To state it another way, the humanities deal with things human. If you were to take a catalog from a liberal arts college and eliminate all of the humanities—courses that deal with people and their culture—relatively little would remain. We are not being critical of the sciences or technical crafts here, but as a category of knowledge, the humanities is very broad indeed.

The humanities represent those bodies of knowledge that students *could* learn about people and their cultures. The curriculum identifies what students *should* learn about people and their cultures. In other words, the curriculum is intended to reflect the community's decision about what subjects students should know and study.

Questions about whether a subject is useful or has practical value are *not* the issue here. At some point, an individual, group, or organization determined that certain subjects should become part of the school curriculum. That is why many of us spent time in school reading works of literature such as *The Illiad, A Tale of Two Cities, Silas Marner,* or *The Red Badge of Courage,* and studying ancient Egypt or the Middle Ages, even though there was no readily apparent connection between those topics and our daily lives.

Unfortunately, it is not always clear why some subjects and topics were originally included in the curriculum. Perhaps the subject was practical at the time, as was true when colonial schools taught surveying and navigation. Or perhaps it was thought that the subject would prove useful to students in the future. Then, too, perhaps utility was not a factor, and the subject was simply something that people thought should be part of a citizen's general fund of information. Regardless of the original reasons for its inclusion, once a subject gets into the curriculum it is very difficult to remove (the Joan of Arc syndrome).

In this regard, consider why you may have studied about ancient Egypt, Greece, Imperial Rome, or Hannibal crossing the Alps. Would your life today be any different if you had not studied the pharaohs and ancient Egypt? If you are leaning toward "no," consider that in addition to expanding your general fund of knowledge, your study of ancient Egypt, the Middle Ages, or even the westward expansion of the United States may have influenced the way in which you view the world and how you define what it means to be a civilized human being. Admittedly, that influence could be so subtle that you may be unaware of it, but when subjects are treated as part of the humanities, certainty about their inclusion and influence can be elusive.

Every society and culture establishes its own definition of what it means to be a civilized human being. In most societies, including ours, those expectations are reflected in the customs and mores of the people rather than in written form. That is how, for example, our culture has identified a generally agreed-upon way to do such a simple thing as place silverware on a table. If you were to place the dinner fork on the right side of the plate (instead of the left), you might notice a few raised eyebrows, but you would probably not be ridiculed—at least not openly. In many Middle Eastern societies, however, reaching into a common food pot with one's left hand (instead of one's right hand) is considered vile and uncivilized behavior and can even lead to banishment.

Our culture's definition of a civilized and educated person typically refers to someone who is knowledgeable, thoughtful, articulate, and widely read. For the most part, our society relies heavily on the school curriculum for decisions concerning what we should be knowledgeable about and what books we should have read. Parents play a role in these decisions, of course, as do teachers and the culture in general, but this is an area where the curriculum plays a significant role.

When social studies is taught as one of the humanities (within the Cultural Heritage approach), the dominant subject is history in its many and varied forms: world history, American history, European history, and so forth. The mission is to transmit that "story"—that knowledge and its associated attitudes and values—to students.

In the Cultural Heritage approach, there are few guidelines as to what knowledge is most important. This can lead to situations in which one person's "essential" knowledge becomes another person's trivia. In the absence of clear guidelines, teachers often find themselves attempting to cover vast amounts of information. Some sixth-grade teachers, for example, are expected to cover the

COMMENTARY: Image of Greatness

Involving students in in-depth biographical studies of prominent Americans from our near and distant past continues to be a thread that weaves through many social studies programs, particularly those with a Cultural Heritage focus. National heroes such as George Washington, Thomas Jefferson, Benjamin Franklin, and Abraham Lincoln have traditionally received extensive treatment. More recently, individuals such as Crispus Attucks, George Washington Carver, Susan B. Anthony, and John Glenn have been added to the list.

To explain why these individuals play such a prominent role in social studies programs, Donald Oliver (1960) identified what he called the "image of greatness" technique. The rationale, according to Oliver, "is to provide young people with inspiring symbols which dramatically present basic human problems and the particular cultural solutions of our society." Through narrative history, the hope is that children will project themselves into situations that bind them to their compatriots in the past.

Expecting children to mimic American heroes is probably not very realistic, especially because the society in which most of these people achieved prominence is not the one we live in today. Nevertheless, the fact that they were (and are) real people, and the fact that narrative history tends to focus on concrete events (as opposed to analytic history's tendency to focus on abstract trends and issues) helps to make the "image of greatness" technique something children can relate to.

scope of world history—from the Ice Age to the Atomic Age—in one semester, an almost impossible feat. Then, too, students do not necessarily enjoy studying topics from a humanities focus simply because they are expected to know about them. In these situations, a teacher's *method* of instruction can be extremely important. We present a number of techniques throughout this book which, although they may not enhance the perceived utility of various topics, can at least make them more interesting.

TEACHING SOCIAL SCIENCE

As we noted earlier, the Social Science approach is made up of two related approaches, one that focuses on the social science disciplines and one that focuses on thinking and decision-making skills.

The Social Science–Disciplines Approach

Mission: Helping children to master the structure, concepts, and the processes of the social science disciplines.

A persistent criticism of traditional social studies programs is that they emphasize isolated bits and pieces of information without providing a structure that enables children to organize that information into a meaningful whole. Without such a framework, social studies can indeed become a collection of random information.

The structures that would enable children to "put it all together" already exist, it is held, in the form of the social science disciplines. By teaching the disciplines to children, they would have the structures to deal with information. Barr, Barth, and Shermis (1977) captured the essence of this approach as follows:

> **The various social science disciplines . . . offer not only the most reliable, responsible, and precise way of knowing the world, they also guarantee that the knowledge that students learn will not be obsolete in a few years. That is, as students learn the process by which social scientists function, they will be gifted with a *way of knowing* that will endure. They will understand the world in the deepest meaning of the term *understand;* and they will thereby become better citizens, capable of making decisions about problems around them. (p. 6)**

The main elements of the Social Science–Disciplines approach are (1) the structure (or organization) of the various disciplines and (2) the findings from the social sciences—the facts, concepts, and generalizations that social scientists have produced in their quest for knowledge. A third component, the processes and techniques that social scientists employ to produce and validate their findings, may also be introduced but it is seldom as prominent as the other elements.

As we noted earlier, high school and college-level courses are among the best examples of this approach, because the social science disciplines are typically taught as discrete bodies of knowledge. In elementary and middle schools, various aspects of the disciplines may appear in textbooks under headings such as "An Investigation." First-grade students, for example, may be asked to gather data on their physical characteristics—height, weight, hair color, etc.—and then present that information in a simple graph or chart form. An equally common technique is a straightforward presentation of information about what social scientists do. This is usually presented in sections of the text with titles such as "What Do Archaeologists Do?" The intent of the Social Science–Disciplines approach is to make the social science disciplines an integral part of the elementary classroom.

The Social Science–Disciplines approach has been criticized on several grounds, among the most prominent of which is the claim that elementary schools should not be in the business of producing miniature historians, sociologists, and so forth. A related criticism involves the contention that most of us deal with events holistically; that is, we deal with human encounters in their totality—in terms of what our senses and experiences tell us is most appropriate—and not, say, as a sociologist might.

At the heart of the Social Science–Thinking/Decision-Making approach is the development of critical thinking skills such as hypothesizing, classifying, inferring, and identifying relevant information. (© *Paul Conklin/Monkmeyer*)

The Social Science–Thinking/Decision-Making Approach

Mission: Helping children to master thinking and decision-making skills (reflective inquiry), and promoting responsible social action.

The Social Science–Thinking/Decision-Making approach focuses on the development of skills that students could use with any kind of data they encounter. These include hypothesizing, identifying relevant information, hypothesis testing, and generalizing, and may be referred to collectively as *critical thinking, reflective inquiry, problem solving* or, simply, *inquiry*. A representative list of these skills is presented under the heading "Thinking Skills" in the "Essentials of the Social Studies" statement (see pages 28–29).

Before thinking and decision making can take place, students must have something to think about. In the Thinking/Decision-Making approach, the "raw material" typically consists of items/elements drawn from the social science disciplines, as illustrated by the "Who Is Qualified for the Presidency?" activity, or from experience. In the Thinking/Decision-Making approach, the social science disciplines are not regarded as bodies of knowledge that must be learned as such, but as repositories of information that teachers and students can *draw upon* as needed.

The late Hilda Taba was an influential advocate of using elementary social studies to teach thinking skills. Taba expressed her position this way: "One of the most widely accepted (and highly questionable) assumptions is that thinking cannot take place until a sufficient body of factual information has been accumulated to 'think with' later" (1967, p. 27). All of us have encountered teachers who said something to the effect of "first, we need some background information about 'X'." However, after they got done presenting the information, there was seldom time left to *do* anything with it. In this context, Taba went on to say, "Teaching that follows this assumption stresses coverage of factual knowledge, thus burdening the student's memory with an unorganized, perishable, and obsolescent collection of facts."

The Social Science–Thinking/Decision-Making approach is seldom criticized for its mission; teaching thinking and decision-making skills is something few individuals oppose. Instead, the criticism may be in terms of what the approach does *not* do. Since the emphasis of this approach is not on factual knowledge as such, those who believe the purpose of social studies is to teach factual knowledge can usually identify certain facts that students will not have learned. In other words, the overall approach (and teachers who adopt it) may be criticized because students cannot name Belgium's major export, the geographic regions of Mexico, or other similar facts. Teachers who favor the Thinking/Decision-Making approach often find themselves balancing the knowledge expectations associated with traditional social studies teaching with an instructional approach that emphasizes providing students with the skills needed to deal with any kind of information they may encounter.

COMMENTARY: Is Thinking Really Valued?

Few people argue against teaching children to think effectively; it's the kind of thing almost everyone favors. However, in traditional social studies programs, thinking skills seldom receive very much attention. We think there are some important though usually unstated reasons for this. What do you think?

1. *Thinking skills are not really valued (despite what people may say to the contrary).*   Imagine yourself in the following situation: You have been accused of a crime and have been offered two methods of trial. One is by a jury of your peers; the other is by a computer, that is, a computer that is accurately programmed to analyze all of the available information and to render a verdict wholly consistent with the data.

   Which option would you choose—the jury of your peers or the computer? Would it make a difference if you were guilty? Or innocent?

2. *Thinking skills are difficult; they are too much work, and besides, the kids can't do them.*   If students could apply thinking skills prior to instruction, there would be little need to teach them. But the fact that children may have difficulty recognizing an underlying assumption or distinguishing between a fact and an opinion, for example, is not a sufficient basis for avoiding such skills. Applying thinking skills is sometimes difficult; it can be hard work. It's a curious kind of logic, however, that uses this as a basis for not teaching such skills.

   The situation is further complicated by a comment that you've undoubtedly heard from time to time: "Don't bother me with all of *that,* just tell me the answer." Our concern for getting answers—the quicker the better—and our corresponding lack of concern for the processes used to produce those answers, may help to explain why thinking skills don't get more attention than they do.

3. *Thinking skills are cold, abstract, and impersonal.*   Thinking is one of the few quiet activities (sleeping is another one) children engage in. You can't necessarily tell when it is taking place. Indeed, thinking can be a highly personal kind of thing. It's doubtful, however, that thinking skills are any more abstract than, say, the skills involved in long division. They may be more difficult at times, but not inherently "colder" or lacking in emotion. Were some people more intimate with thinking skills, perhaps they would become more personal and less "distant."

Thinking and Social Action   The interesting thing about thinking is that it is not an end in itself. To have a child say, for example, "Okay, I've thought about it"—period—should leave you dangling as it does us. The question is, "Now that you've thought about it, what's going to happen?" In other words, what will be the visible result—the product—of that invisible process called "thinking" that (supposedly) went on inside a child's head? Unless thinking results in some kind of action, in the child's doing something visible, the effort may be regarded as a kind of academic exercise.

What children do with the results of their thinking has two situational dimensions. The first occurs in the classroom, where the children must somehow demonstrate that they have thought—that they are able, for example, to distinguish between a fact and an opinion or to identify the central issue in a problem or argument. The second dimension is displayed in a broader societal context, where students, because they have been trained to think effectively, can be expected to engage in some type of social action. As a committee for the National Council for the Social Studies (1962, p. 318) put it, ". . . the purpose of teaching skills in social studies is to enable the individual to gain knowledge concerning his [or her] society, to think reflectively about problems and issues, and *to apply this thinking in constructive action*" (italics ours).

Student councils are sometimes cited as appropriate avenues of constructive action for elementary students. As a form of social action, student councils are generally controversy-free. The anti-nuclear protests of the 1980s can also be viewed as civic or social actions, but they are certainly far from controversy-free. One of the dangers in any civic or social action, in schools or beyond, occurs when individuals move into action without analyzing the alternatives open to them. In other words, constructive action should be the result of thought—of intelligent, reflective thinking. If it isn't, we invite a form of chaos.

INSTRUCTIONAL THEMES

In Figure 1.1, we identified multicultural education and values education as examples of instructional themes that influence all of the approaches to social studies. In practical terms, this means that regardless of which approach you favor, the tenets of multicultural education, for example, will affect *how* you and your students deal with certain kinds of subject matter—and even what subject matter you select. The other themes—global education, law-related education, career education, and sex-equity education—can have the same effect—even if, at this point, you are not certain what those terms refer to.

The instructional themes are so broad that we cannot deal with them in detail in this chapter. Two brief examples of multicultural education and values education are presented below. More detailed examinations of values education and the other themes are presented in Chapters 6 and 7.

MULTICULTURAL EDUCATION

The basic premise of multicultural education is that the "melting pot" notion that was once thought to characterize American society is no longer applicable. Instead of a single, monolithic culture, we are—as the term *multicultural* suggests—a nation of many different cultures, each of which has contributed to our contemporary way of life.

This premise necessitates that all groups be treated in a manner that recognizes and respects their dignity and their contributions to society. It also means that teachers must be especially sensitive to the way various groups are treated in both the literature and in their classrooms. To denigrate a culture or minority group because its members eat different or unusual foods, for example, is as wrong as praising the Anglo culture simply because it is dominant. The main concern in multicultural education is that all cultures and groups be treated equitably.

VALUES EDUCATION

What things are most important to you? What kinds of things do you prize, cherish, and value? When faced with decisions like selecting a college, a wardrobe, or even a mate, what things do you consider? Providing students with a basis for answering such questions is a major thrust of values education.

First of all, it is impossible for teachers not to teach values (as we describe in detail in Chapter 6). When a teacher decides to teach something, for example, he or she is in effect saying, "This is important and worth knowing." From the students' point of view, if something were not important and worth knowing, teachers would not spend time teaching it. In addition, every action teachers take, every behavior they model, serves as an implicit indicator of ways students should conduct themselves. In other words, teaching values is an inescapable fact of classroom life.

As a theme in social studies, values education has two dimensions: (1) determining *which* values should be taught explicitly and (2) providing children with techniques for identifying and clarifying the values they already hold. The first dimension can be a sensitive issue, particularly because the school is only one of several institutions—including the home and the church—associated with teaching values. Moreover, it is one thing to teach that democracy is one of several governmental forms, for example, but quite another to teach that democracy is the *superior* form. The latter reflects a value judgment which, when presented uncritically and as if everyone believed it were true, represents a form of indoctrination.

When teachers consciously, explicitly, and uncritically set out to teach certain values, e.g., "democracy is the superior form of government," they enter the arena of indoctrination. Despite this recognition, many people believe that teaching children to believe in the core values of a democratic society is an important component of social studies. Indeed, in the Cultural Heritage approach to social studies, one is expected to transmit those core values, which include a belief in the dignity and equality of the individual, a belief in the value of hard work (the "work ethic"), and allegiance to democratic principles. Values are implicit in the other approaches too, such as "Be suspicious of information until you know its source"—a value associated with the Thinking and Decision-Making approach to social studies.

Teaching the core values of a democratic society isn't likely to raise many eyebrows—even if values are presented uncritically and as something children should (or must) believe in. It usually isn't long, however, before teachers enter areas that are not so clear. Abortion and euthanasia are only two extreme examples. The question of which values to teach is fraught with moral overtones, making it a very sensitive issue. Barr, Barth, and Shermis (1977, p. 16) captured the matter as follows: "By far the most important issue in social studies has been the question of indoctrination. No other single issue has so dominated discussions and debates in the field."

THEMES AND CITIZENSHIP

Instructional themes, such as multicultural education and values education, are broader than special units or courses. In other words, although it would be possible to teach a unit on something such as multicultural education, the multi-cultural-education perspective influences social studies teaching throughout the entire curriculum. Actually, the instructional themes identify desirable character-istics, attitudes, and beliefs that all citizens should demonstrate. However, the overall responsibility for developing these characteristics is something that social studies shares with other subject areas.

COPING WITH THE KNOWLEDGE EXPLOSION

Among the more perplexing things that all teachers face is the problem of "coverage," of getting everything in. It matters not which approach to social studies you lean toward, there are simply more skills and more information that should be taught than there is time to teach them. This situation is perhaps best illustrated in American history courses in which many teachers, faced with encyclopedic textbooks, are seldom able to get beyond World War II. It is the rare history course that can devote significant attention to the Vietnam conflict or the civil rights movement of the 1960s, all of which have had—and in some instances are still having—an impact on American life. The problem here is created by the fact that the school year has remained an almost-constant 180 days, whereas history just keeps rolling along. A teacher in the early 1940s had nearly fifty fewer years of history to deal with, and the events that affect us today were somewhere in the distant future.

Sooner or later every teacher must make decisions about how he or she (and the students) will approach a subject area. Those decisions typically take one of four forms, as illustrated below. Assume that you are teaching fifth-grade Amer-ican history here, and determine which of these seems most advisable to you.

_____ *Decision One*   Skim over the entire textbook, attempting to give relatively equal treatment to everything within the time available and recognizing that it may be necessary for students to accept awareness rather than understanding.

_____ *Decision Two*   Select certain topics—such as Columbus, the Constitution, and the Civil War—that you wish to emphasize, then skim over the balance of the text. In so doing, you accept the fact that simply making students aware of some topics is sufficient because you hope to achieve greater understanding of those topics that will be studied in depth.

_____ *Decision Three*   Study only those topics—possibly including the Constitu-tion, the Civil War and Reconstruction, and the civil rights movement—that you feel warrant in-depth study and understanding. You believe that it is not necessary to read and study every chapter in the text.

_____ *Decision Four*   I prefer to reserve my decision until I have more infor-mation.

We have problems with the first alternative, for reasons that will become evident as we go. On the other hand, we recognize that teachers in states that

COMMENTARY: Selective Neglect and Postholing

One solution to the problem of coverage is what we call "selective neglect." This means that teachers identify topics that they do *not* plan to deal with—topics they intend to neglect. This enables them to devote more time and attention to the topics they do plan to cover. Even so, the teachers are apt to feel constant pressure to move on.

Another related option is called *postholing*. Teachers who use this technique identify topics that they and their students will study in depth (similar to Decision Three above). With postholing, you really "dig into" a topic. In the social studies program called "Man: a Course of Study," for example, students spend almost an entire semester studying the Netselik Eskimos. For some students, studying Eskimos for an entire semester is a case of going too far overboard in the other direction.

have mandated learning outcomes, and where, for example, students must pass a competency test to proceed to the next grade level, may be forced to accept Decision One, even though they might prefer another alternative. Because of the situations those teachers find themselves in, the best alternative they can hope for is probably Decision Two. Our preference, however, is for Decision Three. We believe the textbook is a resource to be used *with* a social studies program; it is not the program itself.

The widely heralded "knowledge explosion" influences every subject taught in schools today. Some subjects, such as history and the sciences, are more susceptible to it than others, such as arithmetic. You've undoubtedly heard various estimates of how quickly the amount of knowledge available to us is doubling; sometimes it's said to double every ten years, for example. Whatever the exact figure may be, the point here is that, compared to fifty years ago, we have a tremendously expanded reservoir of knowledge today, a situation illustrated in pictorial form in Figure 1.2.

If it were possible to "pump" the entire reservoir of knowledge into children, even in small doses, they would probably drown. If it were possible to deal only with the smaller (older) reservoir of knowledge, selecting what to teach might be less of a problem. There is simply less of it. But information in the new reservoir—new knowledge—often causes us to alter our view of the old information. Our knowledge about the Viking presence in North America, for example, is much more recent than most of our information about Christopher Columbus—and more recent information has altered the traditional view of Columbus's landfall (Judge, 1986). Not everything has changed of course, but trying to teach the totality of either reservoir of knowledge to children is clearly impossible—there's just too much of it.

As teachers, we are forced to select from the reservoir the knowledge we

FIGURE 1.2   The Knowledge Explosion

RESERVOIR OF KNOWLEDGE

Total amount of knowledge   Amount of knowledge generated
prior to 1925   during last fifty years

intend to pass on to children. We want to select the knowledge that will best serve children in the future. But more important than teaching knowledge itself, we think, is providing children with the skills that will enable them to deal with the reservoir of information on their own.

SUMMARY

If it wasn't clear when we started, it is probably very clear now that describing the nature of social studies can be a complex and possibly confusing matter. Social studies is a composite subject based on findings and processes drawn from the social science disciplines.

The overarching goal of social studies is citizenship education. However, educating responsible citizens is one of the reasons, if not the main reason, we have schools. In other words, citizenship education is an all-school enterprise, not the responsibility of social studies alone.

The two dominant approaches to social studies are (1) teaching the cultural heritage and (2) teaching social science. The latter approach has two components, one that emphasizes teaching the social science disciplines and one that focuses on teaching thinking skills (reflective inquiry) and responsible social action.

In the Cultural Heritage approach, social studies is often treated as one of the humanities. From this perspective, knowledge, attitudes, and values are not taught for their practical value, but rather because they are something we as intelligent, educated citizens are expected to know. The expectation that students learn certain information or read certain books—neither of which may have any direct bearing on the student's daily life—is often part of the culture's definition of what it means to be an "educated person." However, because that definition is agreed upon only in the most general way, it is difficult to identify precisely what students should know. As a consequence, what students should learn as social studies is open to a number of differing interpretations.

In the next chapter we take a detailed look at the social science disciplines, the kinds of human endeavor they study, and, perhaps most importantly, how those disciplines go about studying our collective human experience.

SUGGESTED ACTIVITIES

1. Stuart Chase has said that "formal history, with its Caesars and Napoleons, tends to be a record of the abnormal, the geniuses, sports, freaks, and misfits; the glandular cases of mankind" (*The Proper Study of Mankind,* p. 65). How would you react to Chase's contention in light of your own experience?

2. In the 1981 definition (NCSS, 1981), social studies was described for the first time as a "basic" subject. Considering that "back to the basics" was in full swing when this definition was agreed upon, speculate on the motives that might have led the NCSS to use *basic* as a descriptor.

REFERENCES

Banks, James A. 1984. *Teaching Strategies for Ethnic Studies.* 3rd ed. Boston: Allyn and Bacon.

——. 1978. "Multiethnic Education Across Cultures." *Social Education,* 42 (March), 177–87.

Barr, Robert D., James L. Barth, and S. Samuel Shermis. 1977. *Defining the Social Studies.* Bulletin 51. Washington, D.C.: National Council for the Social Studies.

Carr, Edwin R., and Edgar B. Wesley. 1950. "Social Studies." In *Encyclopedia of Educational Research,* rev. ed., ed. Walter S. Monroe. New York: Macmillan.

Dewey, John. 1938. "What Is Social Study?" *Progressive Education,* 15 (May), 367–69.

Engle, Shirley H. 1965. "Objectives of the Social Studies." In *New Challenges in the Social Studies: Implications for Research,* eds. Byron G. Massialas and Frederick R. Smith. Belmont, Calif.: Wadsworth.

Fitzgerald, Frances. 1979. "Onward and Upward with the Arts: Rewriting American History—II." *The New Yorker,* (March), 40–92.

Hahn, Carole L. 1984. "Promise and Paradox: Challenge to Global Citizenship." *Social Education,* 48 (April), 240–43.

Hammond, D. Rosalind, et al. n.d. "Reducing Prejudice in the Classroom." How to Do It Series Four, Number 2. Washington, D.C.: National Council for the Social Studies.

Hartoonian, H. Michael. 1985. "The Social Studies: Foundations for Citizenship in Our Democratic Republic." *The Social Studies,* 76 (January/February), 5–8.

Hertzberg, Hazel W. 1982. "Social Studies Reform: The Lessons of History." In *Social Studies in the 1980s,* ed. Irving Morrissett. pp. 2–14. Alexandria, Va.: Association for Supervision and Curriculum Development.

Hobin, Marsha. 1974. "Clarifying What's Important." In *American History: the Quest for Relevancy,* ed. Allan O. Kownslar, 169–87. Washington, D.C.: National Council for the Social Studies.

Judge, Joseph. 1986. "Where Columbus Found the New World." *National Geographic,* 170 (November), 566–71.

Kniep, Willar M. 1986. "Defining a Global Education by Its Content." *Social Education,* 50 (October), 437–46.

Krug, Mark M. 1967. *History and the Social Sciences.* Waltham, Mass.: Blaisdell.

Morrissett, Irving. 1986. "The Status of Social Studies in the Mid-1980s. *Social Education,* 48 (April/May), 303–10.

National Council for the Social Studies. 1962. "The Role of the Social Studies." *Social Education,* 26 (October), 318–25, 327.

⸻. 1979. *The Social Studies Professional,* 52 (September), 8.

⸻. 1981. "Essentials of the Social Studies." *Social Education,* 45 (March), 162–64.

National Council for the Social Studies Task Force on Scope and Sequence. 1984. "In Search of a Scope and Sequence for Social Studies." *Social Education,* 48 (April), 251.

Oliver, Donald W. 1960. "Categories of Social Science Instruction." *High School Journal,* 43 (April), 387–97.

Patrick, John J. 1977. "Political Socialization and Political Education in Schools." In *Handbook of Political Socialization Research,* ed. Stanley Renshon. New York: Free Press.

Remy, Richard C. 1980. *Handbook of Citizenship Competencies.* Alexandria, Va.: Association for Supervision and Curriculum Development.

Taba, Hilda. 1967. "Implementing Thinking as an Objective in Social Studies." In *Effective Thinking in the Social Studies,* eds. Jean Fair and Fannie Shaftel. Yearbook 37, 25–49. Washington, D.C.: National Council for the Social Studies.

Wehlage, Gary, and Eugene M. Anderson. 1972. *Social Studies Curriculum in Perspective: A Conceptual Analysis.* Englewood Cliffs, N.J.: Prentice-Hall.

Wesley, Edgar B., and Stanley P. Wronski. 1958. *Teaching Social Studies in High Schools.* Boston: D.C. Heath.

SUGGESTED READINGS

Robert D. Barr, James L. Barth, and S. Samuel Shermis. 1977. *Defining the Social Studies.* Bulletin 51. Washington, D.C.: National Council for the Social Studies. As Shirley Engle noted, this book has managed "to clarify the lines of battle between the competing philosophies of the social studies and to point up the irreconcilable nature of the issues that separate them" (p. 103). For a more concise treatment, see James L. Barth, and Samuel Shermis. 1970. "Defining the Social Studies: An Exploration of Three Traditions." *Social Education,* 34 (November), 743–51.

Frances Fitzgerald. 1979. *America Revisited.* Boston: Little Brown. This popular bestseller provides a lively, detailed account of how social studies textbooks treat various topics, and how those treatments have changed over the years.

John D. Hass. 1977. *The Era of the New Social Studies.* Boulder, Colo.: ERIC Clearing-house for Social Studies/Social Science/ and the Social Science Education Consortium, Inc. This superb, thoroughly documented and detailed account traces the rise and fall of the so-called new social studies.

Maurice P. Hunt, and Lawrence Metcalf. 1968. *Teaching High School Social Studies.* (2nd ed.) New York: Harper & Row. Despite the fact that its title indicates its orientation, this book's treatment of reflective thinking, "closed areas," and the techniques of value analysis is excellent.

Howard D. Mehlinger, and O. L. Davis, Jr., eds. 1981. *The Social Studies,* Eightieth Yearbook. Chicago: National Society for the Study of Education. This scholarly collection is probably the best statement on the current state of social studies education.

Richard C. Remy. 1980. *Handbook of Basic Citizenship Competencies.* Alexandria, Va.: Association for Supervision and Curriculum Development. At 108 pages, this is one of the briefest and most practical treatments of the most recent thinking on citizenship education.

CHAPTER 2

Social Studies and the Human Experience: The Disciplinary Foundations

"History is

 . . . the story of man." Samuel Eliot Morrison

 . . . a fable agreed upon." Napoleon

 . . . bunk." Henry Ford

KEY QUESTIONS

☐ What have we learned from the human experience, and what implications does this have for social studies education?

☐ How does an *analytic* discipline, such as mathematics, differ from *synthetic* disciplines, such as social studies, and what does this mean for anyone who will teach them?

☐ What are alternative ways one might approach social studies content?

KEY IDEAS

☐ Humans have the potential to learn from experience—individual and collective.

☐ The human experience is the source of content for social studies programs.

☐ Different ways of examining the human experience have emerged over time, ways that collectively constitute the social science disciplines.

☐ The nature of social studies differs considerably from an analytic discipline, such as mathematics. To approach them as similar is to misunderstand their nature.

☐ Findings (concepts and generalizations) drawn from the social science disciplines are the primary basis for social studies content.

INTRODUCTION: On Studying Ourselves

We humans are really a remarkable species; we devote lifetimes to collecting things. Some of us, like pack rats, gather artifacts from the past, artifacts which, once they have aged properly, we call "antiques." This permits us to sell them for three times what we paid for them or, in some cases, three times what they're worth.

Others of us literally risk our lives collecting information about ourselves and our habitats. In fact, some of us question the sanity of those individuals who risk life and limb to stand on the South Pole. Yet others regard such actions as "brave," "courageous," and "dedicated to the cause of science."

Some of us, though, neither collect antiques nor feel sufficiently curious to seek out new, and in some cases original knowledge. Still we are, from birth onward, collectors, repositories, and processors of information about our individual and collective selves. We may not have the training of professional anthropologists or sociologists, but all of us nevertheless engage in a lifelong study of human behavior and the human experience.

Our purpose in this chapter is to examine the human experience, to consider how we have devised increasingly specialized ways of looking at it, and to see what has been found as a result of that examination. Finally, we look at what this means in terms of those portions of the human experience we select to pass on to the young—what we call social studies.

SOCIAL SCIENCE AS A WAY OF STUDYING HUMAN EXPERIENCE

During our undergraduate days, we took an introductory psychology course in which the professor spent three lectures defending psychology's qualifications as a science. At the time, it seemed odd to us that someone would devote so much effort to defending a field of study when most of us (as students) approached psychology as another body of information to learn, another course to pass. Most students in that class, we suspect, were not aware of who could be attacking psychology in a way that justified such a vigorous defense. It certainly wasn't the students.

Hindsight has enabled us to put that teacher's behavior into perspective; apparently her concern was with the academic respectability that a particular way of examining the human experience gains when it matures to the point where it is regarded as valid. We discovered that, at one time, psychologists were frowned upon, regarded as upstarts who really had nothing to contribute to the fund of human knowledge. Today, however, we doubt that anyone would take three class periods to defend psychology's qualifications as a legitimate body of knowledge. In fact, we suspect that today you will find the even more specialized areas of psychology—such as psycholinguistics, the study of language as a reflection of one's attitudes and values—vying for increased recognition as legitimate ways for studying the human experience.

We are suggesting two things: first, that various ways of looking at ourselves tend to gain respectability and acceptability over time, and, second, that we have evolved ever more specialized ways for examining the human condition. At one time, for example, there was just anthropology—the study of cultures. Today there is cultural anthropology, economic anthropology, physical anthropology, social anthropology, and applied anthropology, as well as archaeology, ethnography, and ethnology, each of which looks at a specialized facet of the cultural experience.

SCIENCE AS A WAY OF KNOWING

The social science disciplines focus on social phenomena, just as the natural science disciplines, such as botany and biology, focus on natural phenomena and the physical science disciplines, such as physics, focus on physical phenomena. The two terms common to these descriptors, *science* and *discipline,* should be clarified lest the balance of this chapter (and book) prove unnecessarily confusing.

It is important to recognize that *science* has two meanings. The first and most obvious refers to courses, such as biology and chemistry, that all of us have taken at one time or another. As we noted earlier, most science courses in elementary and middle schools are—like social studies—based on the broad-field (unified studies) approach, in which the topics are drawn from the different science disciplines. That's why in teaching science you might deal with a weather unit drawn from meteorology, followed by a unit on plants that is drawn from botany, and then a unit on sound that is drawn from physics.

The second definition of *science* is as a way of knowing; that is, as a basis for saying that we know something. Faith affords another way of knowing; that is, you accept some things to be true on the basis of faith, the belief that they are true. Science as a way of knowing also encompasses a set of procedures and processes for dealing with information. It is this latter element, the systematic procedures for securing and processing information, that all scientists (social, natural, and physical) have in common.

Among the most important aspects of science (as a way of knowing) is the process of proof. If someone were trying to convince you that the moon was made of green cheese, for example, you would probably ask for proof. If the individual says, "Because I say it is," you have the option to accept that argument on faith, ask for more information, or dismiss the contention entirely. Unless that person can provide more information, he or she will probably *not* have met the requirements of science.

When scientists present their findings, the processes of science require that they provide, openly and in public, empirical evidence that supports their findings. Scientists who lack supporting evidence for their theories are free to state them, of course, but they must present them as theories, not facts. They must also include phrases similar to "*I think* the moon is made out of green cheese" to indicate they are stating a theory and not presenting new knowledge. Our main point here is that it is not the hardware—the test tubes, the computers, the white coats, or other paraphernalia—that makes someone a scientist; rather it is the rigorous, disciplined way the individual secures and processes information in order to produce new knowledge.

When you see the term *science* throughout most of this book, think *process,* not courses. When we refer to science courses, we will make it clear that we are referring to the alternative definition. In addition, when you see expressions such as "a process emphasis" or "process-oriented," they refer to the processes of science and to the ways in which children can be involved in some of the same processes and procedures that scientists use.

Discipline, as in social or natural science discipline, refers to a branch of knowledge. In educational circles, *discipline* usually pertains to behavior or, in some instances, to what happens to you when you misbehave. Up to this point in this book, we have used *discipline* in its body-of-knowledge sense. We will make it clear when we use that term in its behavioral sense.

The Scope of Science

Young children like to create neat, well-organized categories for dealing with their world. From a child's point of view, for example, individuals may be considered either "good guys" or "bad guys"; there is no middle ground. Among the subjects they study in school, children often say such things as "this is reading" and "that is social studies," as if there were no relationship between the two. As one matures, the distinctions that were once so vivid tend to become less and less clear.

In the same vein, we used to think we could clearly distinguish between the social and natural sciences. Today we are far less certain. You have undoubtedly heard, for example, about "genetic surgery," which makes it possible to alter the genetic structure of an embryo and, ultimately, produce clones. Is this a biological (or medical) procedure that has social implications, or is it a social issue with technological and scientific implications? The answer depends on how you look at the problem, and on how you view science itself.

Although natural science and social science are usually regarded as distinct categories, the view of science shown in Figure 2.1 indicates that the two are functionally related. Findings from the natural sciences influence social science methodologies and findings, just as findings from the social sciences influence the methodologies and findings of the natural sciences.

Consider the following ideas that derive from Figure 2.1:

Science is an offspring of philosophy. At the time of the Greeks, science was equated with moral philosophy.

The basic tools and procedures of science are applicable to both natural and social science. In other words, all scientists have certain rules of procedure that they must follow in conducting an investigation.

FIGURE 2.1 The Fields of Science

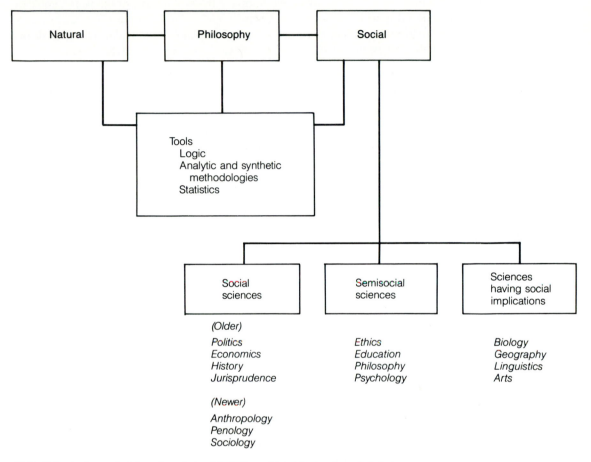

(Note: Natural science disciplines [e.g., botany] have been deleted for brevity and clarity.)

The extent to which a particular discipline uses (1) the tools of science and (2) is committed to the systematic use of observation and measurement influences its classification within the social sciences.

Education is classified as a semisocial science. This is because some processes and procedures in education are based on scientific findings, whereas other educational procedures may be based on faith, folklore, or sources unknown.

THE SOCIAL SCIENCE DISCIPLINES

When individuals talk about the social sciences, they usually mean the so-called major disciplines, such as anthropology, economics, geography, political science, psychology, and sociology. Actually, any field in which the processes of science are applied to social phenomena qualifies as a social science. This means that a field such as psychiatry, which we normally think of as part of medicine, could be considered a social science (see below).

The following listing of social science disciplines and subdisciplines is drawn from the *International Encyclopedia of the Social Sciences* (Sills, 1968).

Anthropology—including cultural, economic, physical, political, social, and applied anthropology as well as archaeology, ethnography, ethnology, and linguistics.

Economics—including econometrics, economic history, the history of economic thought, economic development, agricultural economics, industrial economics, international economics, labor economics, money and banking, public finance, and certain aspects of business management.

Geography—including cultural, economic, political, and social geography (but not physical geography).

History—including the traditional subject matter fields of history and the scope and methods of historiography.

Law—including jurisprudence, the major legal systems, legal theory, and the relation of law to the other social sciences.

Political Science—including public administration, public law, international relations, comparative politics, political theory, and the study of policy making and political behavior.

Psychiatry—including theories and descriptions of the principal mental disorders and methods of diagnosis and treatment.

Psychology—including clinical, counseling, educational, experimental, physiological, social, and applied psychology.

Sociology—including economic, organizational, political, rural, and urban sociology; the sociologies of knowledge, law, religion, and medicine; human ecology; the history of social thought; sociometry and other small-group research; survey research; and such special fields as criminology and demography.

Statistics—including theoretical statistics, the design of experiments, nonsampling errors, sample surveys, governmental statistics, and the use of statistical methods in social science research.

Statistics?

The inclusion of statistics in the above list may seem a little unusual, especially to individuals who associate it with mathematics. The rationale for including it here apparently reflects the fact that most findings about human and social behavior are probability statements. For example, a finding might indicate that "During periods of war, a people's sense of patriotism *tends* to increase." It does not say that patriotism *will* increase, just that it is likely to.

COMMENTARY: The Behavioral Sciences

Some scholars suggest that several of the disciplines listed under the social sciences could be clustered under the label "behavioral sciences," a phrase that gained popularity when the Ford Foundation sponsored a Behavioral Science Program during the 1950s.

The *behavioral sciences* typically refers to disciplines such as psychology, psychiatry, and to a lesser extent, sociology and anthropology, which tend to focus more directly on the behavior of individuals. This distinction sets the behavioral sciences apart from the other social science disciplines, such as anthropology, political science, and economics, which tend to focus on studying the behavior of larger groups, including nations and cultures.

We suspect that the expression *behavioral sciences* might gain wider usage and acceptance were it not for its manipulative connotations—"I don't want any behavioral scientists studying me. Whaddaya think I am, crazy or something?" In light of this, it may be some time before the legitimacy of the behavioral sciences extends very far beyond the academic community.

When scientists decide to investigate a phenomenon, they cannot study everyone or everything. In studying people, for example, there are just too many of us to study everyone. Therefore, scientists select and observe a small sample which they believe to reflect the larger population. Statistics enters the picture as mathematical tools that scientists employ to determine the probability that whatever phenomena they observe in a sample of the population is a reflection of how the entire population would respond, and not simply a random or chance occurrence. In other words, scientists use statistics to test the probability that a finding is valid.

All scientists (social, natural, or otherwise) use statistics extensively. Statistical procedures are part of the processes of science that we have referred to on several occasions earlier. However, we believe that identifying statistics as a social science discipline in its own right is questionable, and that it is more appropriate as a tool that all scientists use—as shown in Figure 2.1.

THE SCOPE OF THE HUMAN EXPERIENCE

To say that you as a prospective teacher have been charged with the responsibility for interpreting and transmitting the human experience to the young of our culture has a grandiose, almost pompous, ring to it. But once you get beyond the mechanics—the how-to-do-it of schooling—that's the name of the game. Admittedly, the schools share some of the responsibility with other institutions in our culture—the family, the government, etc.—but a significant role in the transmis-

FIGURE 2.2   The Sequence of Inventions

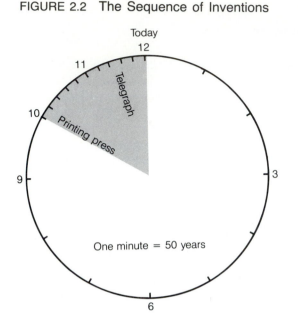

sion and interpretation of the human experience has been relegated to the schools, and to you as a prospective teacher in those schools.

Actually our efforts to pass on our cultural legacy have been indelibly inscribed in the annals of history. First through word of mouth and then through written history, we have transmitted portions of our collective social and cultural heritage to the young. But cast against the backdrop of historical time, our efforts to systematically examine the human experience are comparatively recent. In other words, we managed to govern ourselves well before there was something called political science, and we functioned in groups well before there was something called sociology. Indeed, it is only relatively lately that we have been afforded the luxury and security of devising ever more specialized ways for studying ourselves.

It can be helpful to look at our experience through the metaphor of a clock. (This material is adapted from Postman and Weingartner [1969].) So imagine, if you will, the face of a clock on which every minute represents fifty years, substantially the best part of an individual's lifetime. On such a scale, the printing press would have been invented about nine minutes ago (Figure 2.2). And in medicine, it would have been only about three minutes ago that doctors began to be able to cure people of a variety of illnesses. In fact, in the sweep of medical history, it has been only seconds since medicine achieved some of its most significant developments—organ transplants, laser surgery, and some of the other things we take for granted today.

The same scenario can be replayed for other areas. In the field of communications, for example, imagine what life would be like if we didn't have television. Not only would we be denied almost instantaneous access to events in the world (and beyond) but, with the television set gone, many of us would find ourselves rearranging the living room furniture so as not to be facing a blank spot on the wall (or, more importantly, attending to nourishing primary relationships).

Despite our penchant for the past, we are suggesting that many of those things that afford us our current life-style are of comparatively recent origin. Similarly, much of what we know about ourselves is also of comparatively recent origin. It is only recently that we have had a sufficient grasp of our experience to recognize that our view of what it means to be human has changed over time. The information in Table 2.1 is oversimplified to some extent, but it reveals some of those changes.

TABLE 2.1 What It Means To Be Human: A Historical Perspective

When	Conceptual Framework	Implications
Ancient	Without necessarily making any reference to the real world about them, human beings were believed to be able to use their "unique" mind to reason about their condition.	The world was what human beings said it was. Humans were unique and set apart from the rest of the world. The concept of science at this time was the application of reason to morality and virtue.
Early Christian Era	Religious frameworks found men and women to be part of a larger scheme and to serve purposes for existence that transcended their earthly experience. The application of the human mind and reasoning ability found rational reasons for following reasoned authority and authorities.	Mind was pure and good and physical needs and desires were viewed as evil. Humans were seen as having two dimensions—the soul and the body. Men and women were born in sin and human effort was directed toward redemption and the "other" world.
Renaissance	The political framework found men and women recognizing social realities found in existing social conditions. Power, control, leadership, and forms of social organization were based on political realities. Machiavelli's precepts emerge. Note: some argue that Machiavelli was the first political *scientist*—a scientist because he built his framework by observing and generalizing from the real world.	Beginning of the nation state and nourishment of loyalty to earthly concerns now ran parallel to religious ideals. Beginning to use observed and observable information upon which to build ideas, people started to become increasingly aware of the complexity of their world. This movement modified their "way of knowing."
18th and 19th Centuries	The economic framework emerged. The human condition began to focus on industrializing, on ideological justifications for property, and the accumulation/distribution of wealth. The industrial revolution was under way. Adam Smith, Karl Marx, and others observed and interpreted the human experience as basically economic. Economic activity was part of the "natural" world. Human behavior was subject to "laws" just as the natural world was.	There was a definite relationship between people's "daily bread" and their larger conceptual frameworks of politics and religion. Class distinctions emerged, and economic mobility was related to social mobility. The organization and rules for economic activity fed nation-state rivalry, the need for justifying imperialism, and the need for explaining differing economic "levels." Natural laws pertaining to government, economics, and social class emerged as "right" when viewed as a larger, observed pattern of human experience. This led to a view of natural progress that human beings couldn't control.

TABLE 2.1 *(continued)*

When	Conceptual Framework	Implications
Early 20th Century	The psychoanalytic conceptual framework found men and women at the mercy of their subconscious and deterministically influenced by experiences. The framework reintroduced the individual and raised concern with ego, superego, and id. Each individual was a product of his or her environment—especially the early environment that acted in screening subsequent experiences. Freud's interpretation helped sharpen this framework.	The primary focus appeared to be on the individual, and this seemed compatible with political and economic world views that seemed to carry weight. Emphasis was *not* on the individual deliberately interacting with experience but on the impact of early experiences that "conditioned" the psychological sets an individual carried through life—stress was on the inner person and the psychological impact one's life history carried.
Middle 20th Century	The physical sciences had struggled into maturity. The social sciences commenced to scientifically (empirically) study human behavior. Instead of emerging with set and unchanging "laws" of human behavior, the social sciences, through systematic research, came up with findings stated in "if . . . then . . ." terms—findings stated in probability rather than certainty. Aspects of human behavior became the provinces of specific disciplines, as potential sources for understanding and explaining the human condition. The proper study of man was man. Previous conceptual frameworks that focused on absolution external to human beings became challenged through the application of a maturing science to the area of human behavior.	The social science concept of man freed people from any sort of absolute determinism. It portrayed human beings as organisms interacting with man-made and natural environments. Rational applications of social science findings again brought focus to Homo sapiens as a learning/teaching and valuing species. Social concern moved from "other worldliness" to the human condition on this planet. Ways of "knowing" shifted from logic and reason to observable human phenomenon. With a continuing struggle, men and women assumed responsibility for their life chances. As John Dewey maintained, the purpose of life is life. Social science provided different information with which to help adapt and control. The choices, difficult as they are, are ours to make.

Jacob Bronowski, in *The Ascent of Man,* indicated that the human experience has provided us with important lessons, the most fundamental of which he called the "principle of tolerance." Bronowski stated that:

> **There is no absolute knowledge. And those who claim it, whether they are scientists or dogmatists, open the door to tragedy. All information is imperfect. We have to treat it with humility. That is the human condition. (1973, p. 20)**

MAJOR FINDINGS FROM THE SOCIAL SCIENCES

What have we learned from the human experience? from the social science disciplines? The following are some general findings that apply to human beings and human activities regardless of social situations, cultural backgrounds, or geographic locations. Ultimately, these findings, which are stated in nonacademic terminology, serve as a foundation (or part of one) for virtually every social studies program.

A. People all over the world are the same in some ways and different in other ways. People respond to the same problems. The ways people respond may differ.

B. Human beings *learn* to behave the way they do. The ways human beings think and act depend more on their experiences than on being born with differences.

C. Most human beings learn social habits. Some of these habits are performed automatically and without thought. When people behave in habitual ways, there are patterns to their behavior; these patterns help others to predict how people will behave.

D. Most people think that their own way of doing things and their own ways of thinking are "natural" and right.

E. Every habit, pattern of behavior, and idea people have makes "sense" to them and to their living situation. The habits, behaviors, and ideas of other people not in the same life situation may *not* make the same sense.

F. All people have the ability to learn from past experience; people can accept or change their ways of living.

G. When a change takes place in one part of a person's life, it is likely to make changes in other parts of his or her life. Some intended changes bring about unintended changes.

H. People usually respond to what they *think* things are and not to what things really are.

I. Most people live in group settings. A person may live in a number of different group settings at the same time. This may cause conflict for a person, especially if different groups expect opposite kinds of behavior.

J. Most people carry a "map" of their social worlds in their mind. This helps make social living different from just being in the physical presence of others.

K. Most groups in which people live are dependent upon other groups (in which they don't live). This can lead to cooperation or conflict.

L. People learn to play certain roles. Other people expect the roles to be played in certain ways. The roles a person plays (and the rewards and punishments that go with the roles) may change over time and with new situations.

M. A person seldom behaves in a certain manner for only one reason. Why individuals behave as they do usually involves a number of factors. Behavior is not a simple thing to understand.

N. Most human behavior is done to satisfy some purpose. Humans behave in order to achieve goals.

O. All human beings are born with the same physical needs. Ways of satisfying these needs differ from one person to another, from one group to another.

P. A person's personality is usually made up of physical traits, life experiences, and the physical setting in which the person lives.

Q. Individual human beings differ from each other in what they value and in how they behave. People living in the same group have a tendency to share values and behaviors that are quite similar.

R. The groups in which people live have definite ways to teach group members what to think and how to behave. Most people both influence others and are influenced by others.

S. Every human group has some way of handling how people work, how resources are used and distributed, and how the group's "wealth" is to be managed. All this is related to what the group values.

T. In most groups, individual group members depend upon one another for satisfying needs and wants.

U. How people use their physical environment depends upon what is available, what is wanted, and how the group manages itself. How people use their physical and social environments depends upon their value system.

V. How people think and behave depends, in part, on past experience. People can use past experience a number of ways: (1) to learn how and when to change, (2) to find reasons for continuing certain things, (3) to provide answers to problems, and (4) to make people feel unique and part of a common, shared past.

W. All people live under some form of control. There are basic rules of behavior and basic ways of enforcing the rules. In all groups of people there are rules for individual behavior and rules for group behavior. How rules are made and enforced often depends upon what people value.

X. In all human groups there are ways of handling disagreements.

Y. In order for human beings to live with one another, there is need for a common language that allows peoples to share ideas in ways that allow understanding.

Z. Most people and groups of people believe in myths and legends that help them interpret the world and that help them make sense of their own world.

These findings could become the content around which social studies instruction is organized. In this instance, we are using *content* to refer to two different but mutually supporting ideas: (1) the information and ideas contained in a particular subject area, such as social studies, and (2) the subjects or topics that matter in a specific field of study. If you think about the two different meanings, a rather crucial aspect of social studies teaching begins to emerge: being a teacher is different from being a scholar. Teachers must identify and use specific information and ideas to ensure that *others* learn to identify and use information and ideas, whereas scholars usually identify information and ideas to be used in developing more content and more effective modes of inquiry.

We are not suggesting that scholars can't teach, nor are we suggesting that teachers cannot also be scholars. Our point is that while teachers have some dependency upon the scholars' work, teachers and scholars may view content from different perspectives.

To a large extent, the social (and behavioral) sciences are constructs developed to aid in the scholarly pursuit of knowledge. Yet in a very basic sense, the information and findings from the academic disciplines become the raw materials upon which social studies programs are built. How one chooses to select, organize, and use this raw material will determine the nature of that program.

TEACHING IMPLICATIONS FROM THE DISCIPLINES

As we suggested earlier, findings from the social science disciplines can take many different forms. In some instances, they may be presented in the form of generalizable statements that apply at all times and in all places. For example, we know that *all* cultures develop a means for social control, for governing the conduct of their members. Every culture holds certain expectations of how its members should behave. We also know that when two cultures come into contact, a certain amount of change and diffusion will occur.

Still other data about the human experience exist in the form of probability statements, which, as we noted earlier, identify how people *tend* to behave. Thus, we know that the members of a group will *tend* to perceive the group's collective opinion as closer to their own than it actually is (Berelson and Steiner, 1964, p. 336). By knowing this, we have a basis for anticipating and interpreting the behavior of others. But because some findings are based on tendencies, not absolutes, we know that some of our predictions may not be valid.

In many (some will say *too* many) cases, social studies information consists of factual data—uninterpreted, documentary information. You could, for example, determine how many acres of farmland were harvested in 1957 or how many bushels of wheat were produced in Kansas in 1987—assuming you have a need for such information. In other instances, social studies information takes the form of reinterpretations of previously existing information. This might include a reconsideration of the role that slavery played as a cause of the Civil War or a new explanation for why the food problem in India might be further complicated if the Indians were to eat their sacred cows.

We will consider the different forms of social studies information in greater detail in the next chapter. Our purpose here is to highlight the nature and form of different kinds of information that we might teach students.

THE NATURE OF SCHOOL SUBJECTS

When curriculum developers convert bodies of knowledge or scholarly disciplines into school subjects, they sometimes act as if all bodies of knowledge were similar; that is, they act as if the major difference between subjects like social studies and arithmetic, for example, is the content. We suggest that to approach a subject such as social studies as you might approach arithmetic is to misunderstand the nature of the beast. Further, we suggest that arithmetic is an example of an *analytic* discipline, whereas social studies (and quite a few other subjects) is a *synthetic* subject area, as we describe below.

Analytic Disciplines

Mathematics is perhaps the best illustration of a school subject (discipline) that has a preexisting structure: it has a number of identifiable elements that, once you learn them, will enable you to move through the structure and to communicate accurately and correctly in mathematical terms. Further, arithmetic has an identifiable hierarchy and, thus, a sequence that will present problems for the learner if one gets things out of order. Ask yourself, for example, why most schools don't teach long division to first graders. Then ask yourself what a first grader must understand before he or she can "do" long division. Addition and multiplication are helpful, to be sure, but if you can't subtract, you cannot do long division successfully.

The basic structure of arithmetic is sufficiently clear that it can be analyzed in order to identify what a child must know to enter the system. Somewhat the same situation exists in instrumental music; if you don't understand the concept of "staff" and don't know what those little markings stand for, reading music is an impossibility.

We refer to disciplines and subjects such as mathematics and instrumental music as *analytic* disciplines. Once you have learned the discipline, you can then analyze what a learner needs to know in order to learn it also. By contrast, the structure and hierarchy of *synthetic* disciplines, such as social studies and science, are much less apparent if they exist at all. Think about what information, if any, children *must know* before they can study American history. Note that we are referring here to legitimate prerequisites which, if children don't know them, would make learning history impossible. Note also that we said *information,* not skills; the ability to read is a skill. You should find that unlike mathematics, social studies (and especially history) seldom have prerequisites—other than vocabulary.

Most analytic disciplines share the following characteristics:

1. The entire scheme of the discipline rests upon abstract rules and constructs.

In arithmetic, one learns that all circles, by definition, have 360 degrees, and that a degree is 1/360 of a circle. There are no equivalents for a degree in the real world, and thus no one has ever seen one; rather, we must rely on our mental image of what a degree is (which is why it is an abstraction). Using degrees as a unit of measurement for circles is simply part of the abstract structure of mathematics.

2. The products and processes of the discipline are governed by principles, rules, or axioms that are logically related and given.

In fractions, such as ¾, the bottom number always refers to the units into which the whole has been divided, and the top number refers to the number of portions; these are givens. Were you to violate these givens and reverse the two numbers, the result is certain disaster. Further, we cannot add $\frac{3}{4} + \frac{2}{3}$ until we do something to make them more alike ($\frac{3}{4} + \frac{2}{3} = \frac{9}{12} + \frac{8}{12} = \frac{17}{12} = 1\frac{5}{12}$). In other words, if the elements in arithmetic are not related, we must do something to them—as in identifying a common denominator—that makes them logically related, and that then permits us to perform additional operations.

3. After students have learned the rules of an analytic discipline, they should be able to manipulate abstractions to arrive at predetermined, right answers.

The answers are correct because they are based on the total system.

Teachers often use concrete objects to teach arithmetic principles initially, but sooner or later students must move into the realm of abstraction. In that realm, most of us could correctly compute a problem such as "7,000,000,000 + 4,000,000,000 = ?" even if we have never seen a billion units of anything.

The implications for teaching and learning in analytic disciplines include:

The existence of correct procedures for finding answers.

The presence of predetermined correct answers.

A structure within which most aspects of a procedure are dependent upon preceding aspects, and which necessitates teaching and learning the content in sequence. That sequence is imposed largely by the nature of the subject matter.

Once you understand the structure and processes of an analytic discipline, you can make relatively precise judgments about how well a student is learning it. The processes and procedures of arithmetic, for example, are clear and, up to a point at least, agreed upon by almost everyone. Furthermore, the structured nature of analytic disciplines provides a relatively secure basis for saying that one knows something. Most of us can say, for example, "I know (or don't know) mathematics" with greater certainty than is true of the more synthetic subjects, like social studies or science.

Synthetic Subjects

Each of us adds something to the human experience, and each of us tends to look at the human experience a little differently. As a consequence, each of us builds or synthesizes a personal view of the world we live in. Despite differences in the ways we perceive our world, it is difficult to say that a particular view is "wrong"; different, yes, but not necessarily wrong.

We indicated earlier that social studies is a composite subject area. This means that unlike the analytic subjects (like arithmetic), which have a predetermined conceptual structure, social studies can be (and is) assembled or synthesized in different ways. Lest we create the wrong impression here, it should be noted that much of elementary and middle school social studies follows a fairly standard format, and the differences between most programs are not of earth-shaking proportions. Nevertheless, in terms of the sources and referents upon which social studies is built, the potential exists for programs to be quite different and still remain within the social studies domain.

Because there are no general rules for determining correct answers in synthetic subjects like social studies, the correctness of each element must be judged separately. (© *Janice Fullman/The Picture Cube*)

Synthetic subject areas can be described as follows:
1. The basis of the subject area (discipline) rests on phenomena that have been observed in the real world.

Mental constructs or generalizations are then developed based on what has been observed. Thus, students are *not* confined to working with abstract constructs that have no necessary basis in real-world or observable phenomena.
2. The concepts, generalizations, and findings of synthetic disciplines are determined after the fact (after observation), not given (in the philosophical sense) beforehand.

There are not necessarily any predetermined logical relationships among the findings. Field studies in anthropology, for example, indicate that all cultures, no matter how primitive, have some form of economic system and some form of religion. However, because a culture has a certain kind of economic system does *not* mean that it must have a certain religion; the two elements are not necessarily logically related.
3. The findings in a study are judged in terms of the procedures used to identify those findings; answers cannot be determined in advance.

In synthetic disciplines, investigators use logic, analysis, and other skills to conduct systematic inquiries into a variety of phenomena. To be acceptable, they must submit both their findings and procedures to public scrutiny.

The implications for teaching and learning in synthetic subject areas include:

A limited view is taken of a "correct" answer. There are correct answers in social studies, of course, but they are seldom part of a larger system (as is the case of analytic subjects). Paris is the capital of France, for instance, not because it is part of a system for naming national capitals, but because of a unique decision made within the French government. Because there are no general rules for determining correct answers in social studies, the correctness of each element must be judged separately. This is why your ability to identify the capital of Norway (Oslo) is of no assistance in learning the capitals of Sweden (Stockholm) and Denmark (Copenhagen); all are separate and unique elements that must be treated and learned accordingly.

There are valid procedures to follow, and these can be evaluated as such.

Generalizations and findings are less hierarchical, and thus are less dependent upon students having learned a highly structured network of previous findings and generalizations. Consequently, the content need not be learned in a pre-established sequence, nor does the discipline readily lend itself to task analysis. (We describe task analysis in Chapter 3.)

The structure of the subject is created and organized by individuals rather than imposed by the discipline. As a consequence, it can be modified and changed.

Although most of social studies reflects the characteristics of a synthetic subject area, the element of map skills, especially latitude and longitude, more nearly reflect the characteristics of an analytic discipline. Latitude and longitude are part of a mathematical system for determining locations and measuring distances on a sphere. Unfortunately, some social studies programs attempt to teach longitude and latitude without attending to their underlying mathematical base. Without that basis, students often find themselves memorizing what seems to be an arbitrary system. Inasmuch as no one has ever seen the lines that represent parallels of latitude and meridians of longitude in the real world (they are found only on maps and globes), latitude and longitude are indeed abstractions.

We are not suggesting that the inherent structure of analytic disciplines makes them superior to the less clearly structured, synthetic subject areas. They are—simply—different. What makes this excursion through these differences necessary is the fact that some curriculum developers and teachers are either unaware of or ignore them. Those individuals seem to act as if all school subjects were based on an analytical-discipline model, and that there are certain things about the subjects that require them to be sequenced and learned in certain ways. What is true for mathematics, however, is not necessarily true for social studies or science or literature—as we have tried to illustrate here. In fact, because the structure of social studies (and science and literature) imposes fewer inherent

TABLE 2.2   Alternative Ways of Looking at Social Studies

Objects of Study	Disciplines	Major Findings and Ways of Knowing	Instructional Purposes
the community	anthropology	value statements	miniature scholars
native Americans	economics	descriptions	cognitive skill development
area studies	geography	nonempirical-based feelings	accumulation of knowledge
the United States	history	principles (analytic or empirical)	concept development and testing
non-Western civilization	philosophy	generalizations based on observations and probability	creative use of individual and collective experience
the environment	political science		indoctrination
change processes	psychology		social control
minorities	sociology		
local, state, and national government			
citizenship			
consumer economics			

constraints, teachers and curriculum developers have greater latitude to use other factors—including students' interests and skill levels—as a basis for selecting and sequencing content.

The synthetic nature of social studies actually makes possible a number of different entry points to the human experience. Some of these possibilities are illustrated in Table 2.2.

By using listings from the various columns in Table 2.2 as entry points, over three thousand alternative configurations of social studies content are possible, each of which reflects a different orientation and a different blending of content and instructional purpose. When we suggested that social studies could be approached in a number of different ways, we doubt that you anticipated quite this many possibilities! Consider also that the listing in Table 2.2 is not exhaustive, and that by adding the social science subdisciplines, such as paleontology and archaeology, the number of possible configurations would double once again. With so many possibilities, it's little wonder that some individuals go to the other extreme; they define social studies simplistically—as history and geography, period. Yet to do so is to deny the nature of the human experience.

SOCIAL STUDIES OR SOCIAL SCIENCE EDUCATION

During the 1970s, a popular textbook series was titled *Social Science: Concepts and Values*. That carefully selected title was intended to reflect the fact that, in addition to traditional social studies content, these texts emphasized the processes by which social scientists produce and validate information. The texts indicated that *social studies* and *social science* were not synonymous. Unfortunately, that textbook series became a victim of the back-to-basics emphasis on a more traditional education. In addition, countless teachers didn't understand the process emphasis and yearned to return to the kind of social studies program with which they were more familiar. With these two elements working against it, the publisher dropped the process emphasis and returned to a more conventional approach.

Distinguishing between *social studies education* and *social science education* is not really the academic hairsplitting it might seem, for the two terms can describe quite different programs. "Social studies" is the more commonly used expression by far, and refers primarily to programs that emphasize our cultural heritage and prior achievements. Thinking and decision-making skills may be incorporated into social *studies* programs, but most of the emphasis is on developing knowledge of and appreciation for social, political, cultural, and technological achievements. If it is not already apparent, the humanities emphasis that we described in the last chapter is predominant in most social studies programs.

To be considered a *social science program,* the processes of science must be present. This means that much of the emphasis will be on incorporating the application of science as a way of studying social phenomena and the human experience. Considerable attention will also be devoted to helping children develop the skills that social scientists use to produce and validate information. This does *not* mean that social science education rejects the goals of social studies education—far from it. Rather it is a matter of emphasis, of orientation. It is oversimplified but essentially correct to say that social science education adds an information-processing emphasis to more knowledge-oriented social studies programs.

How you go about teaching the human experience will depend on many factors, obviously. These may include the resources you have available, the community's expectations, mandated requirements, your own background in the social sciences, and whatever curriculum guide your school district uses. If most of your course work and experience has been in the humanities, you may very well feel most comfortable with that approach to social studies. We favor the social science emphasis because we believe that information-processing and decision-making skills provide children with tools they can use outside of school. However, we don't reject the other approaches. In fact, we would be remiss if, in the balance of this book, we did not present activities and materials that you could use or modify regardless of your orientation.

SUMMARY

What do we know about ourselves? How can and should we go about selecting and teaching what we know about ourselves? Our intent in this chapter has been to blend these two questions in an examination of the human experience, that colossus from which all social studies stem.

We looked first at some of the ways in which we examine the human experience; namely, the social science disciplines. We focused particularly on the ways in which information gleaned from the social science disciplines differs from other disciplines, such as mathematics. We suggested, also, that while differentiating between analytic and synthetic disciplines could very well be meaningless for students, it has some important ramifications for those of us faced with teaching those disciplines. Finally, we differentiated between social studies education and social science education, and suggested that traditional social studies instruction has reflected a humanities approach, one that does not give primary emphasis to the processes of science. We also suggested that the way most teachers approach social studies reflects, to one degree or another, a blending of social studies and social science.

REFERENCES

Berelson, Bernard, and Gary A. Steiner. 1964. *Human Behavior: An Inventory of Scientific Findings.* New York: Harcourt, Brace and World.

Bronowski, Jacob. 1973. *The Ascent of Man.* Boston: Little Brown.

Postman, Neil, and Charles Weingartner. 1969. *Teaching as a Subversive Activity.* New York: Dell Publishing.

Seligman, Edwin R. A. 1930. "What Are the Social Sciences?" In *Encyclopedia of the Social Sciences.* Vol. 1, ed. E.R.A. Seligman, pp. 3–7. New York: Macmillan.

Sills, D. E. 1968. "Introduction." In *International Encyclopedia of the Social Sciences.* Vol. 1, ed. D. E. Sills. New York: Macmillan.

SUGGESTED READING

Stuart Chase. 1967. *The Proper Study of Mankind: An Inquiry into the Science of Human Relations.* rev. ed. New York: Harper & Row. Long one of our favorites—we have difficulty keeping a copy around. An excellent introduction to how the social sciences look at experience.

CHAPTER 3

The Nature of Social Ideas

"A concept . . . is something about an idea expressed in the words of our language." Myles M. Platt

KEY QUESTIONS

☐ What is a social idea?

☐ How are social ideas related to facts, concepts, and generalizations?

☐ What role do these elements play in teaching social studies?

☐ How do descriptive and prescriptive (value) concepts differ?

KEY IDEAS

☐ An idea is a mental image, a thought, a conception.

☐ A concept is a cluster of related ideas.

☐ Concepts are the means by which we organize ideas and prior experiences; in that role, concepts are a kind of mental organizer.

☐ *Social ideas* refer to mental conceptions (ideas) that pertain to human activity, past or present, as opposed to ideas that involve nonsocial phenomena.

☐ Ideas vary in terms of their nature and the functions they serve. In other words, some ideas are more useful than others.

☐ Teachers select the ideas they wish to emphasize with students.

INTRODUCTION: The Facts of Life, Broadly Speaking

For most children, a *party* is a celebration, and a *wing* is something a bird flies with. But in social studies, such terms have meanings far different from the concrete representations children know so well. Sooner or later, of course, we learn that a *party* refers to a more or less identifiable group that shares similar political beliefs, and a *wing* describes individuals within a group—usually a party—

who favor certain political positions. Yet among children who have great difficulty determining what it means to be a Republican or a Democrat, you can imagine the problems they have with expressions like "She's a left-wing Democrat."

None of us has ever seen a political "party" (a political convention is only a representative sample) or a political "wing," because both are ideas, both are abstractions that we can describe with words but for which there are no visible physical manifestations. This is what makes something abstract; it cannot be seen, felt, or touched in the real world. Abstractions—like ideas—exist only in our individual and collective intellects. Language permits us to talk about abstractions; in fact, it is through language that abstractions become real.

Social studies textbooks are filled with terms such as *party* and *wing*, all of which require children to leave the concrete world with which they are familiar and enter the realm of abstraction. Consider the following passage from a fifth-grade social studies textbook as an example. For emphasis, we have italicized the ideas (concepts) that children must understand for the passage to be meaningful.

> **Little by little, *Canada* won its *freedom* from *Great Britain*. By 1949, Canada was *fully independent. Canadians control* their own *country*. They also choose their own *leaders*. (McAuley and Wilson, 1985, p. 41) [Emphasis added.]**

The passage is short, yet the number of concepts and ideas that children must know in order to understand it is significant. Notice that the authors have attempted to describe one concept, "fully independent," by providing examples of that idea in the following sentences. In other words, the authors have used somewhat less abstract ideas (control, leaders) to describe a more abstract concept (fully independent). In such instances, the degree of abstractness is determined by the likelihood that the child has had previous experience with the ideas in question.

With experience, each of us learns that words and expressions may have multiple meanings. We become aware that terms such as *capital, marginal utility,* or even *wing* can have specialized meanings. Through the medium of language, we can describe phenomena that are either real or abstract. Sometimes we experience a certain phenomenon first, such as a compelling desire for water or other liquids, and then learn the term (or label) to describe that sensation—*thirst.* In other instances, we become aware of a word, such as *democracy,* and then learn the phenomena to which it refers. Regardless of how we learn to connect words with the experiences or things to which they refer, most of us continually engage in the process of refining those connections to explain ourselves and the things we experience more precisely.

Think of what life would be like if each of us did *not* develop systems for organizing and making connections between and among the things we have experienced. We would have millions of tidbits of information floating randomly inside our heads. This doesn't happen, of course, because all of us develop schemes for organizing ideas and events—the things we think about and the things that have happened to us—in personally meaningful ways.

This chapter focuses on a metaskill that cuts across all levels and types of thinking behavior, and that enables individuals to make sense of and deal with their experiences. That process is called *conceptualizing*. It is impossible to talk about thinking or conceptualizing without also considering the ideas and concepts we think with. All of us have millions—perhaps even billions—of ideas in our intellects. We use the term *social ideas* in this chapter to designate those mental notions and concepts that have something to do with social (human) endeavors, and that would reasonably fall within the domain of social studies. We have no idea how many social ideas there are; our intent is merely to designate a category of ideas that relate to human activities, and to set them apart from ideas that deal with nonsocial phenomena—such as the flow of electrons (otherwise known as *electricity*) or the speed of light.

Concepts and conceptualizing are not unique to social studies, of course. Thinking is relevant to all subjects and virtually every aspect of the human experience. We call special attention to these elements here (1) because social studies contains such a vast amount of information that forming concepts to organize that information and make it meaningful is essential; (2) because social studies programs tend to emphasize certain kinds of ideas at the expense of others; and (3) because social studies sometimes deals with ideas that are well beyond a child's actual experiences.

CONCEPTS AND CONCEPTUALIZING

No one has even seen an idea or a concept. Both are mental constructs that we presume to exist because we see their effects in what people say and do. Were it not for concepts, we would have nothing with which to organize the vast array of ideas and experiences that each of us encounters.

The organizing function of concepts can be illustrated through a vastly oversimplified example in which the human memory is thought of as a complex conglomeration of mental pigeonholes, not unlike a kind of postal sorting system. Each of the mental pigeonholes is labeled with something—usually called a *concept*—with which we organize, identify, and cluster the ideas, information, experiences, memories, feelings, and whatever else we choose to place in that mental category. Each of the separate ideas—each piece of information, each experience, each feeling, etc.—that we associate with a concept is referred to as an *attribute*. "Dryness in the throat," for instance, is an attribute of *thirst*.

To explain how individuals bring meaning to the words on a printed page, researchers in reading education have directed considerable attention to the mental system that we described above (Rummelhart, 1980; Anderson and Pearson, 1984). They use *schemata* to refer to the mental structures (pigeonhole systems) that we alluded to, and the singular form of that term, *schema*, in reference to the individual pigeonholes. To ensure some consistency between

The more frequent and varied the experiences students are able to participate in, the greater the opportunity they will have to develop richer and deeper concepts. (© *Susan Lapides 1987*)

subject areas, and because these terms will reappear when we examine reading skills (in Chapter 9), we will occasionally use that terminology in this chapter.

All of us develop schemata through experiences. For example, each of us has had a host of color-related experiences that we cluster with something called red (or blue, or green). Also included in that cluster is the three-letter word *red*, which describes and has come to be associated with that color. To eliminate some potential confusion later on, it is important to note that the word itself is *not* a concept; it is simply a symbol or label that has come to stand for the cluster of ideas that exists in our intellect. The concept is that cluster of ideas within the pigeonhole (or schema), all of which in this instance have something about redness associated with them. The point here is probably best exemplified by the blind, who have heard and learned the word *red* but lack the visual referents and experiences that permit the sighted to build a concept with which red can be associated. As a result, the blind may associate *red, blue, green,* etc., with something called *color* on an abstract level, but it's doubtful they can go much beyond that.

Early on you attained your concept of red—and we say "your concept" advisedly because concept formation is a personal thing that takes place inside one's head.

Despite that highly personal nature, concepts do have a public dimension. Many of us share common attributes for a concept, in this case, redness; otherwise, communication would be impossible. In any event, once you thought you understood "redness," you probably tested your discovery by pointing to something, a fire truck perhaps, and saying "red?" The resulting expression of approval (from an adult perhaps) confirmed the fact that you had attained the concept, even though you certainly didn't think of it in those terms.

The typical concept of "red" describes things that have some quality of "redness" about them. After attaining that initial concept, however, we often discover that some ideas related to *red* just don't fit our existing schemata. In other words, as we gain experience we realize that our existing conceptual pigeonholes are inadequate and must be reorganized to accommodate the new ideas. For example, a figurative expression such as "seeing red" is only distantly related to color, whereas referring to a person as "a Red" doesn't seem to fit at all. The condition whereby new information or experiences do not "fit" into our existing schemata is called *cognitive dissonance.* When individuals say, "I don't understand this," they are probably indicating that their existing mental schemata—their pigeonhole systems, if you will—cannot accommodate the new information. To continue our example of redness, it is doubtful whether children will understand expressions such as "seeing red" or "redneck" *until* they have expanded their color-related concept to accommodate the new ideas. At the same time, they may also need to rearrange, re-cross-reference, or possibly create new mental categories (schemata) to further accommodate the new information. In so doing, they may add a new idea, "seeing red," to their existing concept of "anger," and their schema for "Communist" (assuming they had such a concept to begin with) may have grown to incorporate "Red."

The process of rearranging our mental pigeonholes to absorb new experiences and ideas is what Piaget called *accommodation.* Not all learning takes place this way, but accommodation is obviously an essential dimension. Incidentally, if one is unable to accommodate new information, learning is impossible.

Our schema typically includes an affective (or feeling or attitude) component. These attributes too are highly personal. For example, when someone says "Communist," your immediate and implicit reaction may be akin to "Ugh!" Similarly, a cat lover's concept of *cat* almost certainly includes feelings of affection. An avid dog lover's schema for *cat* undoubtedly has an emotional component too, but it may not include feelings of affection.

An individual's attitude toward a concept is probably a result of his or her prior experiences with it. In some instances he or she may feel strongly; in other instances, positively neutral. For example, you may have strong feelings—either positive or negative—about something like geometry, but be quite neutral about circles, squares, and rectangles. It is this affective component that helps to set your personal schemata apart from the more objective attributes that you could otherwise find in a dictionary.

All of us are living proof that humans can learn to think and conceptualize, even in the absence of concept-based teaching. But confronted with an ever-expanding body of knowledge about the human experience, we believe that social studies teaching should be organized in ways that promote the conceptualization process.

SOCIAL IDEAS: FORM AND FUNCTION

Social studies is loaded with ideas. Those ideas usually fall into one of three broad categories: (1) ideas that *describe* how things are or were (or will be), (2) ideas that *prescribe* how things should be, and (3) ideas that identify *procedures* or techniques for dealing with information or other ideas.

From a child's point of view, most of the things he or she learns in school are "facts." At times, children may inherently understand that some ideas are more important than others and that some ideas are different from others, but they are usually unable to differentiate among them. Teachers, on the other hand, have an obligation to understand the kinds of ideas they are teaching to children. In this section we examine some of the different kinds of ideas that you and your students could (and probably will) encounter in social studies.

Note that when an idea (a mental notion) is written down, it takes the form of a statement. When you incorporate a written statement into your intellect, it takes the form of a mental image or idea. Because we are limited to the printed page, we must necessarily present ideas as written statements. To indicate that we were referring to ideas as mental notions, we considered calling these written statements "idea statements," but that seemed too cumbersome. Therefore, when we use the terms *statement* and *concept* in the balance of this section, think of them as mental notions or ideas in written form.

An assortment of statements (ideas) commonly associated with social studies is presented below. The three categories (descriptions, prescriptions, and procedures) that we identified above are represented here, but only two of the statements are "facts" in the traditional sense of that expression. Can you identify them?

1. The British burned Washington, D.C., during the War of 1812.
2. Patriotism.
3. Pharaoh: A king of ancient Egypt.
4. People should be good neighbors.
5. Large amounts of statistical information should be shown on a graph or table.
6. Dr. Martin Luther King, Jr., was assassinated in Memphis, Tennessee.
7. If a change in one aspect of life occurs, (then) other changes are likely to occur.
8. A good citizen is one who votes.
9. Community.

10. To determine the distance between two cities on a map, one must locate the scale of miles.

11. During periods of inflation, prices tend to rise.

12. Community needs are met by groups of people engaged in many related fields.

13. Economics is the study of how resources are allocated.

14. GM builds the best cars on the road today.

15. Good student.

DESCRIPTIVE STATEMENTS

There are several different kinds of descriptive statements in the list above. Indeed, we have evolved lots of different ways to describe things. Some of the statements describe phenomena very precisely, whereas others provide a more general description. We will begin with the most specific.

Facts (UN Statements)

What people call *facts* can include a variety of descriptive statements. Consider the following illustration of the characteristics of facts:

1. Complete the following line:

   I, _____, was born on _____ _____ _____.
   (name)   (month) (day) (year)

2. Now, compare your statement with the following:

   The Declaration of Independence was signed in 1776.

3. What similarities do you notice?

Both statements describe *unique* events, neither of which will occur again in exactly the same form. In other words, both statements describe phenomena that are nonrepetitive. Such statements reflect what Mallan and Hersh (1972) call *UN concept statements:* they describe an event or experience that is *unique* (U) and *nonrepetitive* (N)—something that happened once and will not happen again.

Numbers 1 and 6 in the previous list are facts (UN statements). As such, they are precise descriptive statements. Actually, the precision of facts can vary from the extremely precise statements, such as Numbers 1 and 6 above, to somewhat more general statements, such as "The Civil War was fought between the Union and the Confederacy," or "The Amazon is the longest river in the world." However, the dominant characteristics of these statements are the UN features we noted above. Note that if you find our reference to UN statements (as facts) troublesome, it is not essential that you adopt our terminology as long as you understand the characteristics of the ideas that fall into this category.

Defined Statements (Definitions)

Statements 3 and 13 reflect descriptive ideas presented in definition form. A definition captures and describes the essential characteristics of the phenomenon it refers to. Although children often treat definitions as "just more facts to learn," we consider defined statements as separate from facts because we are categorizing ideas in terms of their function (what they do).

You have had enough experience with learning definitions to know that unless you (or the student) understand *all* of the component ideas in the definition, the entire statement will remain meaningless. In our example "Economics is the study of how resources are allocated," the child must have the schemata to understand *study, resources,* and *allocation* before the definition can be meaningful. If the schemata do not exist, the student will be forced to resort to memorizing—assuming, of course, the individual cares enough to make that effort.

We will return to definitions in the context of cue concepts below.

Generalizations (GR statements)

UN statements (facts) describe phenomena precisely. For example, the Declaration of Independence was signed on July 4, 1776, not July 5. Generalizations are at the other end of the continuum; they describe more general, repetitive phenomena—things that may occur again and again, and that may apply at many different times and in different places.

Descriptive statements such as "Living people breathe," and "All societies develop a means for governing and judging the conduct of their members," are examples of generalizations. As such, these statements (and Statements 7 and 12 on pages 76–77) clearly represent broad and very basic descriptions about the human condition. Such statements have two key characteristics: (1) they can be *generalized* (G), that is, they can be applied to phenomena in many different settings; and (2) they are *repetitive* (R), that is, the phenomena they describe can occur again and again. These characteristics are what led Mallan and Hersh (1972) to identify such ideas as *GR concept statements.*

Conditional (Cause-Effect) Statements

Many descriptive generalizations can be phrased in a cause-and-effect (or conditional) form, as reflected by Statements 7 and 11. Such statements are *conditional* because they contain (or imply) the notion that *if* some condition is present, *then* something will occur. For example, Statement 7, "If a change in one aspect of life occurs, other changes are likely to result," describes a functional relationship between the elements to which it refers. In other words, "*If* a change in one aspect of life takes place, *then* . . ." something else is going to happen. We cannot say precisely what is going to happen nor can we say that a change in one aspect of life will always lead to other changes. A change in one thing will usually cause other changes—other *effects*—but not always. This is why *likely* is included in the statement; in fact, if it were omitted, the entire statement would be inaccurate. Note that the terms *if* and *then* may be implied as is the case for Statement 11.

When descriptive statements are stated in the conditional, "if-then" form, they can become powerful tools for interpreting, analyzing, and predicting the outcomes of the situations and decisions we face every day. This function can be illustrated by your ability to complete the effect portion for some or all of the following if-then statements:

"If I spend all of my money on bubble gum, then. . . ."

"If I change my classroom routine, then I can anticipate. . . ."

"If I don't study for the test, then. . . ."

Your experience should enable you to predict what could happen if, for example, you choose not to study for a test. Your experience may not be the same as everyone else's, however, and your "thens" (effects) are likely to differ somewhat. This is where the social sciences enter the picture. Findings from the social sciences permit us to predict the effects with greater consistency than if we relied solely on our own experiences. Based on those findings, for example, we can say with some assurance that "If you institute a change in your classroom routine, (then) communication among your students will increase—communication designed to provide mutual emotional support." True, your students might just sit there, apparently doing nothing, but findings from the social and behavioral sciences indicate a high *probability* that your students will talk about the changes among themselves—even if you tell them not to.

Cause-effect statements have a larger probability element than other descriptive generalizations. For example, in a generalization such as "All living humans breathe," probability does not enter the picture at all. Where probability is a factor, however, as in our "change" examples above, "if-then" statements can serve as hypotheses to be tested, confirmed, denied, or modified as they apply to specific situations. You might very well find instances when, for example, a change in one thing does *not* lead to other changes. Such exceptions do not deny the validity of the generalization; rather, they illustrate the variability of the human character.

Cue Concepts

Just before a television newscast begins, someone standing next to the camera will count down the number of seconds remaining. After "four, three, two, one," the individual points at the reporter to cue him or her to begin.

We are using *cue* in its figurative sense here as referring to a word or phrase that points us to a particular cluster of ideas. When someone says "dog," for example, you think immediately of the cluster of ideas and feelings you have about those furry, four-legged creatures. As we noted earlier, your concept refers to the *cluster* of ideas and feelings (about dogs or anything else), *not* the word itself.

Words or short phrases such as *dog, good citizen, patriotism,* or *community* (Statements 2 and 9 on page 76) merely cue (or point) us to an idea cluster.

A question such as "What is your concept of community?" asks an individual to go into his or her intellect (their mental pigeonhole system, if you will) to retrieve the ideas that are clustered around "community." Often the individual's response to the question will be a statement that captures the essential characteristics or qualities of the concept, such as "It's an area where people live." In other words, the verbal rendering of the attributes of a cue concept may take the form of a *definition.*

The relationship between descriptive (UN and GR) statements and cue concepts is illustrated in Figure 3.1. An individual's existing concept of *community,* for example, may or may not include ideas associated with common interests, as in "farming community" or "community of scholars." If you have not heard a university referred to as "a community of scholars," then you might add that idea to two of your existing concepts, *university* and *community.* If those ideas are already part of your conceptual schema, you can relax and do nothing.

Defining Cue Concepts   So much of social studies depends on learning the meanings for cue concepts such as "economy" or "capital" (to name just two), that instruction often begins with a definition-learning session. The approach is similar to that found in many reading lessons: "Here is a new word, and this is what it means." If the terms are abstract, however—as in the case of "wing," "party," or "fully independent"—you could find yourself defining one abstract term with other terms only slightly less abstract.

Helping children to deal with abstract terms can be difficult, as well you might imagine. For some terms, especially those associated with history, there may be very few concrete examples available. This is because much of history is pre-

FIGURE 3.1   Relationship of Facts, Concepts, and Generalizations

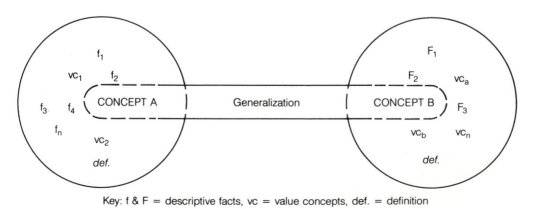

Key: f & F = descriptive facts, vc = value concepts, def. = definition

sented in the form of UN statements. The *pharaohs,* for example, were unique to ancient Egypt, so you simply don't find them elsewhere. You could liken pharaohs to certain medieval kings, who were also absolute monarchs, but your students could find the concept "absolute monarch" equally foreign, perhaps more so. It might be easier to compare and contrast the pharaohs with other monarchs in a unit titled "How the Rulers Governed"—a unit that examines the pharaohs, selected medieval kings, and Chinese and Roman emperors—but most current social studies programs are not organized in this manner. Without that option, you may be forced to employ role playing, sociodrama, or one of the other techniques we describe later in this book to provide concrete or semi-concrete experiences for what would otherwise remain abstract concepts.

One technique for dealing with defined ideas is to *build* a definition from examples (as opposed to teaching it by telling). This technique is illustrated in the following material drawn from S. I. Hayakawa's *Language in Thought and Action* (1964). In this illustration, the object in question is a *shrdlu*. Note that the idea here is to develop a comprehensive definition, not to identify a one-word synonym.

1. **He was exceptionally skillful with a shrdlu.**
2. **He says he needs a shrdlu to shape the beams.**
3. **I saw Mr. Jenkins buying a new handle for his shrdlu.**
4. **The steel head of Jenkins's shrdlu was badly chipped.**
5. **Don't bother with a saw or an ax; a shrdlu will do the job faster and better.**

Definition: A *shrdlu* _____

By generating a definition from examples, you are in effect building a concept—a cluster of related ideas—that can be associated with a certain event or phenomenon, in this case a *shrdlu*. (A shrdlu is apparently an ax-like tool used for shaping and dressing wood, probably very similar to an adz.)

In an article provocatively titled "Beyond the Rattle of Empty Wagons," Parker and Perez (1987) suggest a second technique for dealing with cue concepts. The authors contend that most vocabulary learning in social studies is an intellectually passive activity in which students dutifully memorize words and definitions, such as " 'Interdependence' means being mutually dependent" and " 'Democracy' means the rule of the people by the people themselves," but with little or no thought about the ideas these cue concepts stand for. As Parker and Perez note, "Hilda Taba called this superficial approach to concepts 'the rattle of empty wagons': the empty wagons are unexamined concepts, and the rattle is the ambiguous chatter of concept *labels*." [Italics in original.]

To deal with this problem, Parker and Perez recommend the following activity in which students identify labels (cue concepts) for existing concepts.

MODEL STUDENT ACTIVITY

Inventing Words: A Sudden Turn for the Good

DAY ONE: INVENTING THE WORDS

On the first day, the teacher explains a concept for which there is not presently a single word in English. The idea of "a sudden turn for the good" (the antonym for "catastrophe") works well. The teacher asks, "If peace broke out around the world tomorrow, what word could we use to describe this sudden turn for the good?" Other possibilities can include "the (empty) space within a bottle that contains no liquid" or "the interior surface of a hole," both of which are concepts for which we have no cue concept labels.

Students are then assigned to small groups of three to five. The teacher explains one of the following methods for making new words:

1. New combinations of existing words. Examples include *teenager*, *ethnocentric*, and *chairperson.*

2. Expanding old words to cover new meanings. Examples include *stereotype*, *culture, hip* and *bad* (slang for "good" or "great").

3. Create new words by adding affixes to existing words. Examples include *brown-bagging, coolest*, and *centaphobia* (fear of pennies).

Task   Create or invent three new words that might be good labels for "a sudden turn for the good."

DAY TWO: ANALYZING THE WORDS

Copies of each group's invented words are distributed to everyone. Using all of the lists, each group should decide the following:

1. the word(s) most likely to become popular with the public

2. the word(s) least likely to be widely used

3. the word(s) that best capture the concept

DAY THREE: DISCUSSION

The teacher may pose the following open-ended questions:

1. What part of the activity did you find most interesting? Why?

2. Does the fact that there is no single word in English for "a sudden turn for the good" mean that we expect the worst?

3. What happens to an idea when we name it?

4. What other concepts do you know of for which we need a word?

5. Who invented the words you use?

6. What do a society's words tell us about its way of life?

(*Note:* A recommended cue concept label for "a sudden turn for the good" is "benestrophe." *Bene* is Latin for "good"; *strophe* is from the Greek and means "to turn.")

Source: Reprinted (adapted) from *Social Education* with permission of the National Council for the Social Studies.

PRESCRIPTIVE STATEMENTS

Statements 4 and 8 on page 76, "People should be good neighbors" and "A good citizen is one who votes," describe desired or valued behaviors. Statement 4 is likely to be found among the ideas associated with the value concept *good neighbor,* and Statement 8 could be found among the attributes of the value concept *good citizen.*

Value Concepts

A descriptive cue concept, such as *citizen,* changes considerably when an additional descriptor, such as "good," is added—thus producing *good citizen.* It is clearly not the same concept; the attributes of *good citizen* have a qualitative and prescriptive dimension not always associated with *citizen.* Many attributes of *good citizen* consist of statements of belief concerning how individuals should behave and conduct themselves, e.g., good citizens are loyal to their nation, a good citizen is one who votes, etc. Admittedly there is a kind of generalized agreement about what the concept means because most Americans agree on how good citizens should behave. However, because the majority of the attributes involve desired or valued behaviors, we refer to these as *value concepts.* In other words, value concepts are a type of cue concept in which the attributes usually involve "shoulds" as opposed to descriptive statements of "what is."

Statement 15, "Good student," in the list on page 77 is an example of a value concept, as is the notion "good neighbor" in Statement 4.

Value Statement

Statements 4, 8, and 14 on pages 76–77 are value statements. Notice that all of them have a prescriptive quality that indicates how individuals should behave. The level of prescriptiveness can vary, however, from the specific behavior identified in "A good citizen is one who votes" to an implied message as illustrated by Statement 14, "GM builds the best cars on the road today." The latter statement describes a personal judgment, preference, or opinion that may be associated with a value concept but could just as likely be free-standing. In other words, a value statement such as "I hate brussel sprouts" need not be part of a value concept (e.g., "things I dislike"), although it could be. There is nothing very prescriptive about indicating your dislike for brussel sprouts, unless your intent is to convince someone else to hate them too.

Value statements are not facts—even though they are sometimes presented as if they were—because they do not fit the U (unique) N (nonrepetitive) criteria we established earlier. Value statements are not generalizations either, although they may be generalized and, to some extent, repetitive. GR statements are objective descriptions of social phenomena based primarily on findings from the social and behavioral sciences, whereas value statements identify what someone or some group believes is desirable or ought to be.

Value statements typically involve subjective elements. Because of this, identifying complete and agreed-upon definitions for value concepts such as "good citizen" or "good student" is difficult and sometimes impossible. We may agree, for example, that "a good citizen is one who votes," but we think the statement reflects an excessively limited and even simplistic view of citizenship. In other words, voting is certainly not the only thing that makes one a good citizen.

Our point here is not to argue about what is or is not a good citizen, a good neighbor, a good student, or whatever, but to identify characteristics of the different kinds of ideas you may be expected to teach—value statements among them. As we indicated in Chapter 1, you will be expected to teach the core values of our society—an allegiance to democratic principles, the dignity and worth of the individual, etc. We believe in these values, indeed, we think most Americans do, but simply because many of us agree with and believe in certain values or value statements does not make them "facts."

Ethical problems can arise when teachers make value statements such as "Democracy is *the* superior form of government," or "Good neighbors are people who mow their lawns and keep their yards neat." Both are declarative statements which, from the students' point of view, may seem similar to other UN statements they have previously encountered. The problem here is that qualifying phrases, such as "Many people believe that . . ." or "I think," are absent. Without such phrases or something similar, a teacher could be presenting a prescriptive idea as if it were a descriptive idea. Should the students leave a discussion of "good neighbors" believing it to be a descriptive cue concept characterized by lawn mowing and keeping one's yard neat, the teacher has practiced a form of indoctrination. The extent to which teachers should be expected to indoctrinate students is an issue we consider in Chapter 7.

PROCEDURAL STATEMENTS

Statements 5 and 10 on pages 76–77, "Large amounts of statistical information should be shown on a graph or table" and "To determine the distance between two cities on a map, one must first locate the scale of miles," describe rules or procedures that are used in creating and interpreting knowledge. Procedural ideas, which we call "skill rules," refer to the techniques and procedures we learn for handling, manipulating, and even creating different kinds of information.

All of us have learned procedural ideas, but it is unlikely that we thought of

TABLE 3.1 Terminology Review

Terms	Referents
Descriptive Statements	
Facts (UN statements)	Statements describing unique, nonrepetitive phenomena, e.g., "The first American flag had thirteen stars"; "Abraham Lincoln was born on February 12, 1809."
Cue concept (also known as concepts or subconcepts)	A word or phrase that identifies a mental class, a mental construct, or cluster of related phenomena, e.g., patriotism, interdependence, subsistence farming.
Definition (also a defined statement)	A written or verbal rendering of a concept that expresses its attributes or characteristics, e.g., *bank:* the funds of a gambling establishment.
Generalization (GR statements, also known as understandings, organizing ideas, and unifying generalizations)	A statement that describes primary (basic) relationships among generalized and repetitive phenomena, e.g., "Change has been a universal condition of human society."
Conditional (cause-effect statements, also known as "if-then" statements, principles, laws, and theories)	A subcategory of generalizations in which the relationship is stated in an "if-then," cause-and-effect format, e.g., "A change in one thing is likely to result in other changes"; "If a nation has few resources, (then) it will be more dependent upon other nations."
Prescriptive Statements	
Value concept	A specialized type of cue concept in which the attributes are largely prescriptive (rather than descriptive), e.g., "good student," "good citizen."
Value statement	A statement expressing a desired behavior, judgment, or opinion that may or may not be associated with a value concept, e.g., "Democracy is the superior form of government"; "A good student should walk quietly in the hall."
Procedural Statements (also known as skill rule)	A rule or procedure for testing, interpreting, or acting upon other ideas or information, e.g., "To identify the location of an unknown city on the map, first locate the index."

them as such. As a simple example, in the process of learning to read you undoubtedly learned the rule that states, "When two vowels go walking, the first one does the talking." You learned this first as an idea—as knowledge—and then as something that you applied or used when you came upon a word you didn't know. In other words, the procedural idea provided a technique that you could apply when you encountered an unknown word. Unfortunately, that skill rule doesn't apply all the time, as in the case of words such as *great* and *chief,* but it is still taught in classrooms across the country.

A second example of procedural rules occurred as you learned subtraction (in mathematics, such rules are called *algorithms*). You learned that in setting up an addition problem, it does not make any difference whether the top number is larger or smaller than the bottom number. But you learned that in setting up a subtraction problem, it makes a great deal of difference where you place the two numbers.

Our point here is that all of us learn procedural ideas. These ideas function as rules that we employ when we encounter certain kinds of information or certain problems. In other words, *skill rules* tell us how to proceed. Skill rules (or procedural ideas) are one part of *skills*—they are the knowledge component that indicates what we should do. Skills also have an application component that tells us how we should go about following or applying the rule. Note that if you find the skill rule concept difficult, simply think about how you would teach a child to set up a subtraction problem.

It was necessary to derive our examples of skill rules (procedural ideas) from the areas of reading and arithmetic because social studies is so seldom taught from a skills emphasis. There is one notable exception, however: map and globe skills (which we examine in Chapter 11). Most of us know the skill rules for locating a city on the map by using the index, for example, but many of us are less familiar with the skill rules that apply to other forms of knowledge. What, for example, are the skill rules for testing a theory? That question is usually difficult to answer, despite the fact that many of us informally formulate and use theories every day. Every time you say "I wonder what would happen if . . .?" you are positing a hypothesis—even if you don't think of it in that way. A second and equally valid question concerns whether children should be involved in theorizing and theory testing at all? We'll return to such questions at the end of this section.

TEACHING IMPLICATIONS

One reason for this lengthy excursion is to identify the different kinds of ideas that teachers and students must deal with. A second and equally important reason is to call attention to the idea that teachers, curriculum developers, and textbook authors have a choice about which ideas they emphasize. That choice is not completely open, to be sure. Traditional curriculum guides, instructional materials, and other guidelines often support a social studies program that emphasizes descriptions (descriptive ideas), definitions, and prescriptions (value concepts and statements). Such a program may neglect some of the other kinds of ideas, especially conditional and procedural ideas. This does not mean that there is necessarily a conscious effort to exclude the other kinds of social ideas; it could be a matter of benign neglect. At the same time, however, one reason prospective teachers may have difficulty understanding conditional ("if-then") and procedural (skill rule) ideas could lie in their inexperience with them. If a teacher's only experience with procedural ideas is in the context of map and globe skills, he or she probably has a right to feel uncomfortable.

Of the different ideas you will encounter in teaching social studies, descriptive generalizations will be among the most abstract. Generalizations always contain at least two cue concepts—usually more—that are also abstract. This means that before your students could possibly deal with a generalization such as "Subsistence farming is common in less developed nations," they must understand at least three cue concepts: *subsistence farming* (farms that produce little or no products to sell), *less-developed,* and *nations.* As we noted earlier, if students are unable to bring meaning to any of these concepts, the entire GR statement will remain meaningless.

Most generalizations are so complex that teachers and (and textbooks) must employ a carefully structured building process that begins with experiences aimed at helping students understand the various cue concepts they contain. That building process was illustrated in Figure 3.1, on page 80.

A particular problem with the generalization cited above is the inclusion of the relational concept "less-developed." A *relational* concept is always cast in terms of another concept. In this instance, before children could understand "less developed," they would need to understand the concept "developed nation." Since many children may not be clear about "nation," to say nothing of "less-developed nation," a teacher might wish to approach this generalization as if it were a definition—one in which subsistence farming is treated as a characteristic of less-developed nations. Regardless of how the teacher decides to approach this, it is almost certain that students will need many additional experiences before they can bring meaning to the generalization.

CONCEPTS AND GOALS

We have placed so much emphasis on ideas, concepts, and concept formation because (1) they are the building blocks from which generalizations are created; (2) students will be unable to understand a generalization until they have had sufficient experience with its component concepts; and (3) they help individuals organize masses of separate facts into usable bunches.

Students in the primary grades usually don't care about a generalization like "Regional specialization encourages interdependent trade relations among nations." Such a statement is just too far removed from their experience, as we describe in the next section. However, children can gain meaningful experience with some of its component concepts, such as *interdependence* and *specialization,* and perhaps even *regional specialization.* All of that experience need not (and perhaps should not) occur in a single lesson or unit; in fact, it could occur over a period of years. The concept of *interdependence,* for example, could be introduced through a discussion of the relationships among the members of a family, a school, a club, a community, and so forth. By beginning with these less complex and more immediate examples, children may begin to deal with *interdependence* in a meaningful way well before they encounter the more complex generalization stated above.

The point here is that most concepts fit into a number of generalizations. Interdependence, to pursue the example a bit further, can appear in several contexts that might include those identified below:

As specialization increases, interdependence also increases.

The members of a family are interdependent.

The members of a community are interdependent.

Helping children build GR statements that explain the human experience is a goal of social studies instruction. However, the route from facts through concepts to generalizations is neither straight nor level. Sometimes it is clearly an uphill struggle. The reason many social studies programs spend so much time sightseeing in the concepts neighborhood is that, by nature, a single concept can mark the beginning of progress toward a number of generalizations.

WHAT MAKES SOMETHING DIFFICULT?

Every student knows that some things are easier to learn than others. The question for us as teachers is *why?* What makes some things easy to learn and other things more difficult?

Teachers can make almost any subject difficult, depending on what they choose to emphasize. Yet even students who are expected to recite the middle names of U.S. presidents in order probably face an easier time of it than students asked to explain $e = mc^2$ (Einstein's general theory of relativity). The nature of the ideas inherent in $e = mc^2$ make it much more difficult to explain than memorizing the fact that the *K* in James K. Polk stands for *Knox* (his mother's maiden name).

To illustrate why some ideas are more difficult than others, we used to ask our classes "What president of the United States wore wooden false teeth?" Their responses were always quick and certain: "George Washington!" We then asked them to identify three points from Washington's Farewell Address. The response: silence. (For the record, we have since learned that Washington's false teeth were made from ivory and bone, not wood, so what we thought was an accurate response to our first question is now inaccurate.)

Our students' responses (or their inability to respond) illustrate some of the elements that affect the apparent difficulty of a concept or concepts. We examine those elements in the following sections.

Scope

The fact that George Washington wore false teeth is characterized by its simplicity. As a simple UN statement, there is nothing complicated about it. On the other hand, the task of identifying the main points from Washington's Farewell Address involves several related concepts. First, the number of elements increase, from one (teeth) to three (major points), but more importantly, each of the major points involves several related concepts. Just one of Washington's points, the need "to avoid entangling foreign alliances," for example, may require considerable explanation before children understand "entangling," "foreign," and "alliances." Even when children understand those terms taken separately, however, that does *not* mean they will understand the concept of "entangling foreign alliances" when the terms are taken together. The point here is that the concept of "entangling alliances" has a much broader scope than false teeth.

Concepts that are broad in scope involve a larger number of related ideas and, thus, are more difficult to manage than concepts that involve fewer ideas. They are more complex than narrow-scope concepts.

The scope and complexity of concepts can range along a continuum from narrow to broad, as illustrated below.

Scope

Less difficult	*More difficult*
Narrow scope involving few concepts [Examples: false teeth	Very broad scope involving many concepts entangling foreign alliances]

Distance

Although Washington's false teeth are a part of history, they are also something most children can relate to vicariously; all of them have teeth—although usually not false teeth—and most remember well their visits to the dentist. Young children's fascination with Washington's dental problems also reflects their inherent but highly personal interest in the past (Elkind, 1981). On the other hand, the concept of "entangling foreign alliances" is more distant from either the direct or vicarious experience of most children and, as a consequence, it is not something they relate to readily.

The aspect of conceptual difficulty we are dealing with here is *conceptual distance*. It refers to the degree to which the attributes of a concept are related to a child's experience. The closer the attributes are to children's experiences, the easier they can deal with the concept in question; the more distant the attributes, the more abstract and difficult the concept.

When conceptual distance is depicted on a continuum, the result is this:

Distance
Least difficult   *Most difficult*

Within the child's direct experience (concrete) [Examples: the dentist	Within the child's vicarious experience Washington's teeth	Beyond direct or vicarious experience (abstract) foreign alliances]

Drawing continuously on young children's experiences for concrete examples of concepts is sometimes impossible; most children simply have not lived long enough to have a sufficient body of experience upon which to draw. Because of this, one alternative teachers can employ is an appeal to the child's imagination. By creating mental images so vivid they cannot be ignored, it's sometimes possible to create experiences that children can relate to vicariously—as if they were really happening and the children were actually participating in them. The key to doing that, in a word, is *details*.

The role that factual details play is perhaps one of the most widely mis-understood aspects of social studies instruction. In the creation of vicarious experience, details can provide the basis that enables children to build vivid mental images. Consider the following statement as it might appear in a textbook as an example: "In 218 B.C., Hannibal left Cartegena with an army of over 100,000 soldiers, crossed the Alps, and then met the Roman legions in what is now Italy." Although accurate, the statement doesn't really capture the imagina-tion. It takes details, such as the fact that Hannibal's thirty-seven elephants had been trained to terrorize enemy soldiers (they practiced on prisoners), and that the elephants had to be lured onto sod-covered rafts before they could cross the Rhone River, to create a sufficiently vivid visual image that students can relate to. Individually, and in the sweep of human experience, each detail may be in-significant, but collectively, they play a significant role in the creation of vicarious experience.

Unfortunately, some teachers use the child's ability to remember details as an indication of his or her knowledge of historical incidents. By asking a test question such as "How many elephants did Hannibal have?" for example, the teacher is changing the role and function of factual details. Instead of using the details to build vivid mental images of events far distant from children, the teacher is in effect telling them that details are important—that details are something the children must remember. The children, in turn, may focus their attention to trying to learn the vast array of details instead of focusing on the overall incident, which is what the details are intended to help them do.

Two elements of conceptual difficulty that are not readily evident in our false-teeth example but which may influence students' ability to deal with other concepts are *stability* and *open-endedness*.

COMMENTARY: On Outlines

To reduce the number of concepts that children must deal with, common sense might suggest that we give them an outline of the material they should learn. However, this is an instance where a commonsense solution could create more problems than it solves.

On occasions in the past, for example, there have been efforts to make American history more understandable to slow learners by providing them with simplified outlines of major events. In other words, the students were taught an even more abbreviated form of American history than was usually the case. The effort was well intended; just provide the children with the "big ideas" and eliminate the details. But to the teachers' surprise, the students experienced more problems working with the outlines than they had with the traditional instruction.

This effort backfired because the outlines proved to be too abbreviated. They lacked the factual details that provided a context for children to use in relating major events. Without the details with which to build meanings and associations, the students found themselves memorizing a list of isolated events.

This experience with American history is not too dissimilar from many students' experiences with research papers and outlines. Instead of doing the outline first, as most teachers request, many students—perhaps yourself included—make an outline *after* they have written their paper. The reason for that, and part of our point here, is that an outline is a tool for organizing information. Students must have information in their possession before they can either construct an outline or make any sense of the information in an outline.

Stability

As an element of conceptual difficulty, stability is illustrated by the fact that, while every state has a governor, not every city as a mayor. Even in cities that do have mayors, the mayor is not always the chief executive. Some cities are run by city managers or administrators with other titles. It is easier for children to handle stable concepts in which certain attributes are universally present, such as governors, than to handle concepts that deal with probabilities or tendencies.

On a difficulty continuum, the stability dimension appears as follows:

Stability

Less difficult	*More difficult*
Attributes always present [Examples: governor, dog	Attributes sometimes present mayor, conflict]

Open-endedness

Consistency and certainty also play a role in what can be called the *open-endedness* of concepts. For example, you will not get much argument about whether or not something is a dog, an apple, a table, or a farm. These cue concepts can be considered relatively closed, and therefore less open to misinterpretation. But concepts such as "democratic citizenship," "patriotism," or "Republican (or Democrat)," are more open, subject to more interpretation, and consequently less reliable for communicating the same thing to different individuals. As a rule, the more open-ended the concept, the more difficult it is for a child to handle.

On a continuum, this dimension becomes

| *Open-endedness* | |
Less difficult	*More difficult*
"Closed," extremely reliable	Open to interpretation, less reliable
[Examples: car, false teeth	Democrat, foreign alliances]

These facets of conceptual difficulty suggest that familiarity, stability, and simplicity contribute to ease of understanding, while distance, instability, and complexity contribute to the difficulty of a concept. Unfortunately, some teachers mistakenly assume that children must deal with simple, more familiar, closed concepts before they can deal with more complex, less familiar, more open-ended concepts. This is not the case, however. In a study of young children in Australia, Stevens (1982) found that children were often capable of handling more sophisticated social studies content than they were being exposed to in most classrooms. Our point here is that it is not entirely a matter of "easy" before "difficult," but of meshing concepts with the children's experiences to as great a degree as is possible.

Reducing Conceptual Complexity?

Simplifying complex concepts so children can understand them more readily may seem to be an admirable idea, but a note of caution is warranted. The simplification of a complex (broad-scope) concept by omitting some of its component ideas can create a situation where the teacher presents misinformation. For example, to teach the concept *family* as consisting of the so-called nuclear family—Mom, Dad, and the kids—is incomplete and, thus, misleading. To avoid overwhelming children, you might teach the nuclear family in one or two lessons, but in the interest of accuracy and completeness it is imperative that you deal with the extended family and the single-parent family in other lessons.

In cases where presenting all of the attributes of a complex concept might overwhelm children, it is certainly reasonable to focus on one or two attributes at a time. However, it should be understood that such simplification *is only temporary,* and that other attributes will be examined in subsequent lessons. Wherever possible, complex concepts should be simplified by presenting numerous concrete examples of the component attributes, not by omitting those ideas.

SELECTING CONCEPTS TO TEACH

With a universe of things to teach at their disposal, most teachers discover that there just isn't time to teach everything they would like to, want to, or should. As a result, they are forced to make choices, deciding which concepts they are going to teach and which they are not. In other words, teachers are forced into the role of selector, whether they want that role or not.

Developmental Considerations

The kinds of previous experiences your students have had, combined with the ideas they have derived from those experiences, will play a significant role in determining the concepts they can deal with in meaningful ways. But while experiences are important, a growing body of research suggests that developmental considerations also play a role in children's understanding. We know, for example, that young children (below six or seven) move easily between a fantasy world and the real world, but may have difficulty in separating them (Egan, 1979). As a consequence, young children may believe that political leaders wield almost unlimited power, as do the kings in some fairy tales; e.g., that the president owns all the property, makes all the laws, and tells everyone what to do (Stevens, 1982). In other words, young children begin to explain their worlds, both fantasy and real, by overgeneralizing from and elaborating on their personal experience (Furst, 1980). Young children are subject to daily control by authority figures—parents, teachers, and other adults—but they have no means for determining where that adult authority ends. It is reasonable, then, for children to view authority figures as having authority over *everything*. When asked why they believe this is so, the typical response is a simple "Because!" On other occasions, children may believe that things are caused by magic. Neither response is very satisfying for most adults, but they are clearly sufficient for many young children.

As children gain increased experience with their world(s), they begin to establish simple connections between events (Furst, 1980). At this stage, which usually extends into the early elementary years and includes most seven- and eight-year-olds, children typically become aware that separate events may be linked together. This awareness, however, is usually at a very simple and observable level. For example, it is common among children at this level to believe that adults "get" money simply by writing a check. The idea that one must deposit funds in one's account *before* writing a check isn't even considered until children begin to move into a third phase, in which they develop simple cause-effect systems for interpreting events. At this stage, they may not know (or care about) why one must deposit funds in a checking account, for example; it's just something one must do to write checks.

By the time children reach age eleven or twelve, they have usually begun to

As children develop and mature, their capacity to understand the world, to see relationships, and to make connections among ideas also expands and matures. (© *Elizabeth Crews*)

develop increasingly systematic and logical frameworks for interpreting events (Furst, 1980). Children at this stage understand, for example, that one must earn the money that one spends—it does not come from heaven, nor do employers "give" money to their employees—and that one must place money into a checking account before it can be withdrawn. However, "plastic money" (credit cards), loans, and other financial transactions are often unexplainable.

The developmental research described above has some rather profound implications for what is taught in schools, for when it is taught, and for reasonable expectations for what students should be able to do as a result of that instruction. For example, attempting to teach a logically based concept, such as latitude and longitude, to first or second graders is almost certain to be an exercise in frustration for teachers and students. It is not a matter of providing students with sufficient experiences with latitude and longitude because, from a developmental perspective, the students would not understand those experiences anyway. Students at that level are still in the process of linking and interpreting simple events that they have experienced personally—and you can be certain that latitude and longitude are beyond the personal realm of most young children.

What about moving latitude and longitude to fourth grade, as the curriculum requirements in states such as Texas require? *Some* students at this stage may be starting to develop more systematic frameworks for interpreting events, but these by no means approach the abstract frameworks that adults use. The result, again, is apt to be frustration—as many fourth-grade teachers (and students) in Texas will attest. Based on findings from the developmental research, about the earliest one could teach latitude and longitude with a reasonable expectation for success is fifth grade, and even then it can be risky.

A second implication from the developmental research is that instruction in the early grades especially can be directed toward providing children with alternative explanations for the phenomena they have encountered, explanations that correct their existing misconceptions. The intent here is not to destroy the child's fantasy world, for that will disappear on its own, but to provide alternative ways for explaining how things happen. Whether the explanation should extend to *why* things happen depends on the complexity of the concept in question.

A third implication of the developmental research highlights the vital role that children's experiences play at the elementary school level. In this context, it is important to note that what are sometimes viewed as deficiencies, as in a child's inability to identify cause-and-effect relationships, for example, may be of developmental origin. In other words, children who believe that parts of the world are inhabited by gentle purple monsters may be developmentally incapable of identifying complex cause-and-effect relationships. Given sufficient experience and appropriate instruction, most normal children are eventually able to develop such abilities. From a developmental perspective, the problem may be with the expectation—with expecting too much understanding too soon—and not with what the child is actually able to do.

Schooling practices in the past have tended to ignore much of what we know about how children learn and view their world. For example, and despite everything we know to the contrary, many individuals persist in viewing children as if they were miniature adults. Children don't look like adults, they don't act like adults, and as we have suggested here, they certainly don't think like adults. Throughout the balance of this book, one of our goals is to provide social studies instruction that is appropriate to the ways in which children actually view their world.

Concept Selection

Any selection process involves the identification of selection criteria. The developmental considerations we described above provide one set of criteria.

Unfortunately, another significant criterion—your students' skill levels—is probably unknown at the moment. You probably don't know, for example, whether you will have a class of gifted readers, a mixed group, or whatever. As a result, certain decisions must be deferred until that information is known.

Students' skill levels provide a basis for determining the kinds of teaching materials to use with them. Students with reading difficulties, for example, may experience problems when building concepts from reading-based materials—a rather obvious statement to say the least. However, your students' abilities to handle different kinds of teaching materials may be developed by having them use certain materials under your guidance. Then, too, a teacher might employ role playing, sociodrama, or some of the other nonreading techniques we describe in the second half of the book.

Other general criteria for concept (content) selection, some of which are patently obvious, include the following:

interest—yours and your students'

values—what you and the community in which you teach think is important

the *sophistication* of your students—which is probably related to their prior experiences

the *difficulty* (complexity) of the concepts—as identified in the previous section

These general concept-selection criteria apply to all subject areas. Criteria that pertain to the social sciences specifically are reflected in *The Ten Guidements of Science* below.

Ten Guidements of Science

I. One should not make wild claims about human behavior or the nature of social environments.

II. One should not pretend to "know" or cheat.

III. One should not use information solely for the purpose of persuading others.

IV. Beliefs and knowledge claims should not appeal to prejudice or private authority.

V. One should not "hide" from others that which is not known.

VI. "Truth" should be established with evidence and logic, not hopes and feelings.

VII. One should communicate the processes and evidence upon which one's knowledge is based.

VIII. One should use empirical (verifiable) evidence as the prime basis for knowing.

IX. One should honor and respect those who question one's thoughts and thinking with more effective thoughts and thinking.

X.   One should live with humility and in an appreciation of tolerance.

(Adapted from Bronowski, 1964.)

The Ten Guidements suggest that concepts and materials selected for use with children share the following characteristics:

1. They have an empirical base (that is, they are based on evidence gathered from our environment and are verifiable).

2. They do not rely on authority ("Because *I* said so") or private knowing as the basis for proof.

3. They do not use emotion- or value-laden words (e.g., conservative, Progressive, etc.).

4. They could be useful as tools in the further study of human behavior.

Which of the following statements meet all four criteria noted above? (Check those you think do.)

A. _____ It's raining.

B. _____ Iranians are weird.

C. _____ A stitch in time saves nine.

D. _____ As unemployment rises, different types of crime also rise.

E. _____ Franklin D. Roosevelt was our finest president.

F. _____ In some cultures, wealth is determined by the number of children one has.

[*Analysis:* A does not meet #4; B violates #3; C violates #2 as stated, but would be acceptable if presented as a hypothesis; D and F meet all criteria; E would be acceptable if presented as a hypothesis, but violates #3 as stated.]

EXEMPLARS OF CONCEPT-BASED INSTRUCTION

The following exemplars illustrate how you might go about managing concept-based instruction. The first activity identifies several techniques that might be used to help children understand relatively simple, low-level concepts. In the second exemplar, which is based on the work of the late Hilda Taba (1967), children are asked to identify groups or categories of items of a similar nature. The third exemplar illustrates how concept-oriented teaching can be accomplished using information from a magazine advertisement.

DIRECT INSTRUCTION

When you suspect that children do not understand a relatively low-level concept, such as *isthmus,* you have several fairly obvious options. First, you can simply *define* it for them: "An *isthmus* is a narrow strip of land between two bodies of water." The impact of your words will be enhanced by *illustrating* the concept by using a picture, a map, or other illustration. You might also use an *analogy;* e.g., "An *isthmus* is a kind of 'land bridge,' a skinny piece of land that connects two larger land masses." That analogy might be part of a larger explanation in which you use a *synonym or antonym;* e.g., "An *isthmus* is like a strait, except it's land instead of water." Your explanation for some concepts, such as *peninsula,* might include a description of the origin of the expression: " 'Peninsula' comes from the Latin—*pene* for 'almost' plus *insula* for 'island.' In other words, a *peninsula* is almost an island."

Having students use a dictionary or glossary is clearly another option, but making them copy the definition is no assurance that they will understand what it means. For many students, copying definitions from the dictionary is tantamount to punishment. Dictionaries and glossaries are useful for identifying low-level concepts that have concrete referents, such as *isthmus* and *peninsula,* but when it comes to abstract cue concepts, such as *capitalism* or *imperialism,* the definitions themselves are typically so abstract that they are meaningless to young children. The nature of abstract concepts imposes similar limitations on the other techniques we have identified thus far.

A direct technique that can be employed with a wide range of concepts, including more abstract ones, involves having students distinguish between examples and nonexamples of the concept. This can be done in discussions in which students identify the critical attributes of a concept, and then identify examples and nonexamples. Obviously, students cannot identify examples of a concept *unless* they know something about the concept itself, so some type of prior instruction or study is usually required. Distinguishing between examples and nonexamples can also be presented in a game format as illustrated in the Model Student Activity below.

MODEL STUDENT ACTIVITY

The "Family" Game

In the family game, students must identify the common characteristic among several examples and nonexamples of a concept. To play the game, students pose questions in the following form: "Is (an element) in the family?" Correct examples are listed in the "In" column; incorrect items are added to the "Out" column (see below). Students should not call out the name of the quality that the elements have in common (the "family"); their contributions must be posed as a question.

The teacher begins by drawing a simple diagram on the chalkboard and then entering examples in the appropriate columns as shown below.

Phase One

In	Out
Boston	Dallas
Springfield	New Orleans
Salem	

From the entries in Phase One, it's apparent the family (the concept) has something to do with cities. But what is the pattern? Perhaps the family is "cities in Massachusetts." To test that hypothesis, a student might ask "Is Plymouth in the family?" Another student might have no idea what the family is, but ask "Is Chicago in the family?" Simply to gain more information. The results are shown in Phase Two.

Phase Two

In	Out
Boston	Dallas
Springfield	New Orleans
Salem	*Plymouth*
	Chicago

The game continues as students try different options. . . . Omaha, Sacramento, Austin, and Atlanta. These results are shown in Phase Three.

Phase Three

In	Out
Boston	Dallas
Springfield	New Orleans
Salem	Plymouth
Sacramento	Chicago
Austin	*Omaha*
Atlanta	

In this example, the "family" is state capitals. When most students are able to add additional family members, the teacher can indicate the family accordingly.

The possible families for this activity are almost endless. In fact, every concept is a potential family. The family can be fairly simple, as in our example above, or more esoteric, such as spouses of leaders (Prince Phillip, Mary Todd Lincoln, Nancy Reagan, etc.) or the names of nations that end in a vowel (Saudia Arabia, China, Morrocco, etc.). Consider the following:

Example Two		Example Three	
In	Out	In	Out
Snake	Canada	police	taxi
Colorado	Florida	fire	electricity
Columbia	Philadelphia	sewer	banks
Mississippi	Alabama	street	supermarkets

(The family in Example Two is "rivers"; in Example Three it is "services provided by local government.")

CONCEPT FORMATION: THE TABA MODEL

Taba's concept-formation strategy is based on a three-step sequence illustrated in Table 3.2. Students are first asked to identify and enumerate items, then to find a basis for grouping or clustering them together, and finally to identify a label for the items they have clustered. The way in which the three phases might be conducted for a second-grade class is illustrated in the following Model Student Activity, including a discussion provided by Taba (1967, pp. 95–99).

Taba's concept-formation model has been criticized by some authorities (see, e.g., McKenzie, 1979, p. 42) on the basis that it does not teach children a skill but rather tests their existing skills. That criticism seems warranted if teachers attempt to elicit the various categories from children solely through questioning. However, we see no reason the teacher cannot suggest additional categories that the children might not think of, including "things that are hard," "things that are natural," "things found in a supermarket," and so forth.

TABLE 3.2 Taba's Concept Formation Strategy

Phase	Overt Activity	Covert Mental Operations	Eliciting Questions
One	Enumeration and listing	Differentiation	What did you see? Hear? Note?
Two	Grouping	Identifying common properties, abstracting	What belongs together? On what criterion?
Three	Labeling, categorizing	Determining the hierarchical order of items; super- and sub-ordination	What would you call these groups? What belongs under what?

Source: Hilda Taba, Mary Durkin, Jack R. Frankel, and Anthony McNaughton. *Teacher's Handbook for Elementary Social Studies.* 1967. Addison-Wesley Publishing Company. Reprinted by permission.

MODEL STUDENT ACTIVITY

Taba's Concept-Formation Strategy

Teacher: Let's start listing on the board the things that you would buy if you went to the store.

David: Apples.

Paul: I'd buy a steak.

Randy: Shrimp.

Denny: I'd buy a puppy.

Teacher: A puppy is different, isn't it?

Mike: Watermelon.

Carla: Candy bar.

Ann: Scooter.

Teacher: Scooter, that's something different again, isn't it?

Teacher: We've almost filled up our board with things that we would buy. What can we do with these things? Do some of them belong together? Which ones belong together? Which ones could you find in the same place?

Denny: You can buy a doll and scooter in the same place.

Teacher: You would buy them in a toy shop, wouldn't you? Let's pick the ones that you might buy in a toy shop. What else would you buy in a toy shop?

Ricky: Squirt gun.

Teacher: All right, we would buy a squirt gun in the toy shop. What else would we buy in the toy shop?

In Phase Two (Grouping), students continue to suggest different (and multiple) groupings for some items, such as "Steak and watermelon—things at a cook-out," or "Shrimp and steak, because both are meats." Students may or may not identify a category "Food" for items such as apples, watermelon, steak, and shrimp. After the larger clusters have been identified, the teacher can move to Phase Three (Labeling and Categorizing), by asking "What would you call these groups?" Responses may include "Things you can buy in a store," "Things we eat," "Things we use," etc. As Taba (1967, p. 94) noted, it is important for students "to discover that any item has many different characteristics and therefore can be grouped in many different ways. Each of the multiple qualities can be used as a basis for grouping."

USING ADVERTISEMENTS FOR CONCEPT-BASED INSTRUCTION

Our final exemplar is intended to illustrate that concept-based teaching can be based on materials from quite different sources. In this instance, we were reading a magazine one evening and happened across an airline advertisement that we thought had some potential for helping children engage in the process of conceptualizing—of building and testing relationships among specific facts. We tried it and it worked, hence its inclusion here.

MODEL STUDENT ACTIVITY

Flying to South America

PHASE ONE

The following information appeared in a magazine advertisement. Although we have changed the name of the airline, the balance of the data is accurate.

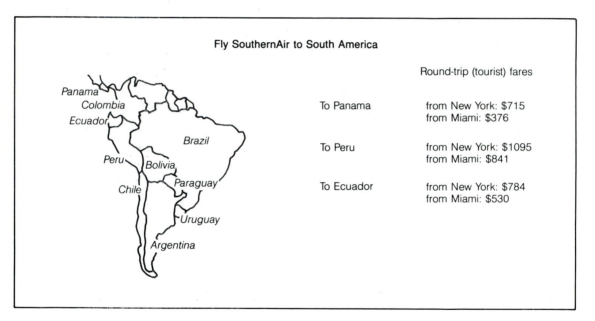

Fly SouthernAir to South America

Round-trip (tourist) fares

To Panama	from New York: $715 from Miami: $376
To Peru	from New York: $1095 from Miami: $841
To Ecuador	from New York: $784 from Miami: $530

Task One: Identify the facts.
Students listed the following:

1. The cost from New York to the other countries:

New York to Panama:	$715
New York to Peru:	$1,095
New York to Ecuador:	$784

2. The cost from Miami to the other countries:

Miami to Panama:	$376
Miami to Peru:	$841
Miami to Ecuador:	$530

Task Two: What patterns do you find?
(Students were asked to identify preliminary findings):

Finding It costs more to go from New York to Peru than it does to go from New York to Panama.

Finding It costs more to go from New York to Peru than it does to go to any of the other countries.

Finding Peru is a greater distance from New York than are the other countries.

Task Three: Is there a pattern or order in this information?
Students produced two lists that went from least to most: least in cost to most in cost, least in distance to most in distance, as follows:

Costs	*Distance*
Panama	Panama
Ecuador	Ecuador
Peru	Peru

(*Skill rule:* data is more easily interpreted if it is organized in a consistent pattern.)

Task Four: Does the information in these lists go together somehow?
From this effort, students identified the following GR statement:
   The longer the distance, the higher the travel cost (or as the students put it, "the longer you fly, the more it costs."

Comment: Notice the ordering of events thus far. The students went from unordered facts to low-complexity concepts about what the facts meant, to ordering (categorizing) the facts, to recognizing a relationship between the categories, and then to developing a generalization that explained what the relationship meant. Note also that GR statements can serve as hypotheses that are subject to change in light of additional information, as is illustrated in Phase Two.

PHASE TWO

The following additional information was provided:
   After the students added the new information to their cost/distance chart, they found that their earlier GR statement was no longer accurate: flying to Argentina at the special discount fare cost no more than flying to Brazil at the discount fare, even though Argentina is much farther from New York City. In other words, it became necessary to restate their GR statement as follows: The greater the distance you fly, the more it costs, unless you can find a discount fare.

BRAZIL		ARGENTINA	
$2105	Regular round trip air fare from New York	$2307	Regular round trip air fare from New York
$1807	Regular round trip air fare from Miami	$2135	Regular round trip air fare from Miami
Special discount		*Special discount*	
$1468	From New York	$1468	From New York
$1296	From Miami	$1296	From Miami

COMMENTARY: Some Concept Statements About Concept Statements

A concept is an idea about some social phenomenon or process or object.

Concepts reflect the ways individuals have organized their previous experiences. They, in turn, have a bearing on subsequent experiences.

Each concept statement involves a number of related concepts.

Concept formation (conceptualizing) is sometimes random.

Different kinds of ideas serve different functions. UN statements permit us to describe unique and nonrepetitive phenomena; GR statements permit us to describe phenomena that are generalizable and repetitive; value statements permit us to express judgments and opinions.

Concept statements based on the social and behavioral sciences describe human behavior; those descriptions are based on empirical (observed) information.

Most social studies concepts are, by definition, abstractions; they are based on empirical information but are not themselves observable.

Empirical information (data) from the social sciences can become the building blocks for concept-based instruction.

Concept-oriented teaching focuses on building and testing different types of social ideas.

WHERE DO TEACHERS FIND CONCEPTS?

The most obvious place to look for concepts is in curriculum guides provided by textbook publishers, some school systems, and a few of the state education agencies. Don't be too surprised, however, if your search proves frustrating, even futile. The title of this section implies that all sorts of different concepts exist somewhere "out there," and that all one has to do is discover them. While concepts exist everywhere, you also need to know what you are looking for.

As part of the planning process, which we examine more closely in the next chapter, teachers may be given a curriculum guide that identifies the topics to be covered, and probably a textbook. Neither the curriculum guide nor the textbook may refer to concepts as we have described them in this chapter. It is almost as if someone has fiendishly hidden the concepts away somewhere. Should you find yourself in this situation, and you very well might, it may become necessary to identify concepts based on the topics and materials you have available. In other words, you may need to identify or construct the concepts to be taught.

Concepts are built from experiences. There's a teachable concept somewhere in every experience. What so often happens, however, is that we don't look for the transferable or generalizable relationships in our experience. When we go to the store, for example, we don't usually think of shopping in terms of "meeting our needs" (physical, social, or psychological), even though that's often what it is. When we read a magazine, the ads may be perceived of as just that—ads—and not as potential teaching vehicles. To the question, "Where do teachers find concepts?" the most appropriate response may be "Where they look for them." Unsatisfactory as that response may seem, the sources of content from which you can derive concept statements are many: text materials, observations, films, talk, television, experience, etc. All can serve as vehicles for bringing content to the student. But obviously they can serve as sources only when you know what you're looking for. Identifying concepts requires that one look beneath the surface of an experience in order to identify relationships that can explain what's actually happening and bring greater meaning to that experience.

SUMMARY

An idea is a mental notion or image. A concept is a mental construct, a cluster of related ideas (mental images) with which we organize the knowledge, experiences, and events we encounter. Within a given concept, each of us determines the common qualities and the basis we use to relate one idea with another. When we encounter ideas and experiences that don't fit our existing conceptual schemes, we reorganize and restructure our mental constructs through a process called *accommodation*.

We identified three categories of ideas that one typically encounters in teaching social studies: (1) *descriptive*, (2) *prescriptive*, and (3) *procedural*. Some of the different kinds of descriptive ideas we identified were as follows: (1) *facts* (UN statements), which describe unique (U) and nonrepetitive (N) events and phenomena; *cue concepts,* which are either words or short phrases, such as *community* or *dark horse,* that cue (or point) us to certain idea clusters; and (3) *generalizations* (GR statements), which describe behaviors or events that are generalizable (G) and repeatable (R). UN statements are very precise descriptions, whereas GR statements enable us to make very broad and general descriptions of the ways in which humans are likely to behave in a variety of situations. We also noted that some GR statements can be phrased in an "if-then," cause-and-effect format; these statements enable us to describe the possible effects that could occur if a particular cause is present, e.g., "If a change occurs, (then) other changes are likely."

Value concepts and value statements *prescribe* certain desirable or undesirable behaviors. *Good citizen* is an example of a *value concept,* that is, a short phrase that refers to a cluster of ideas regarding the way in which an individual, in this case a "good citizen," should behave. Within a value concept are a cluster of *value statements,* such as "A good citizen is one who votes," and "A good citizen is patriotic," each of which identifies a desired behavior. The subjective nature of value concepts is reflected by the fact that some Americans will argue that protesting an unjust law, for example, is *not* an attribute of the cue concept *patriotism,* while others will insist as vehemently that it is.

Procedural ideas identify rules or procedures for manipulating, interpreting, or otherwise acting upon other information or ideas. We identified these ideas as *skill rules;* that is, they are ideas that specify procedures to follow in testing a theory, identifying a city on a map, using a dictionary, or any other instance in which we must apply what we know.

What do concepts do? We've suggested the following functions:

1. They help to organize data (information and experience) into more meaningful relationships.
2. They assist in developing more effective questions (because every question suggests an underlying conceptualization).
3. They provide guides for planning and designing student activities.
4. They serve as "tools" for
   a. using facts in different ways
   b. analyzing new situations
   c. organizing and ordering new data
   d. recalling important facts more effectively
   e. continually building ever more inclusive concepts.

There's little question that concepts enable us to think more efficiently and effectively. But concepts are double-edged swords. Unless we are aware of the evidential base for concepts, the nature of concepts, the processes used in developing and testing concepts, and the transfer limitations of a particular concept, we are at the mercy of habit. Such habits can severely limit a person's ability to take advantage of life's opportunities. For example, to treat UN statements (facts) and GR statements (generalizations) as if they were similar is to misunderstand their nature and function. Facts describe phenomena very narrowly, whereas GR statements (generalizations) help us to explain and understand the human condition.

How does all of this relate to teaching social studies? As John Michaelis (1968, p. 73) put it:

> **There is general agreement that fragmented knowledge, isolated facts, and descriptive information should be replaced by a cohesive set of ideas. The learner can use such a set of ideas to organize information, recall facts as needed, and add new concepts as they are discovered.**

The relationships among ideas, concepts, and elementary social studies are fundamental to our concern for helping children to organize and make manageable what would otherwise be random bits of information. Confronted with an ever-expanding body of knowledge about the human experience, we believe that social studies teaching should be organized in ways that aid the conceptualization process.

SUGGESTED ACTIVITIES

1. Do a frequency count of the different types of concepts found in selected chapters from two social studies textbooks for the same grade level. For comparability, try to select chapters on similar topics. Note the number of cue and value concepts, and GR and value statements. Form a hypothesis regarding the type and level of social ideas emphasized in the different texts.

2. Assume that you are considering taking your students on a field trip to the local fire station. Try to determine what kinds of concepts might be associated with this experience.

3. Select a cue concept, such as interdependence, community, or democracy, that appears in an elementary social studies textbook. Design a strategy for use with your students that includes as many concrete experiences as you can identify.

4. Using Hayakawa's teaching model as a basis, develop three language-related learning activities that would be appropriate in a social studies program.

REFERENCES

Anderson, R. C., and P. D. Pearson. 1984. "A Schema-theoretic View of Basic Processes in Reading Comprehension." In *Handbook of Reading Research,* ed. P. D. Pearson, pp. 255–91. New York: Longman.

Berelson, Bernard R., and Gary Steiner. 1964. *Human Behavior: An Inventory of Scientific Findings.* New York: Harcourt, Brace & World.

Bronowski, Jacob. 1964. *Science and Human Values.* rev. ed. New York: Harper & Row.

Egan, Kiernan. 1979. "What Children Know Best." *Social Education,* 43 (February), 130–34.

Elkind, David. 1981. "Child Development and the Social Science Curriculum of the Social Studies." *Social Education,* 46 (October), 435–37.

Furst, Hans. 1980. *The World of Grown-Ups: Children's Conception of Society.* New York: Elsevier North Holland.

Hayakawa, S. I. 1964. *Language in Thought and Action.* 2nd ed. New York: Harcourt, Brace & World.

Mallan, John T., and Richard Hersh. 1972. *No G.O.D.s in the Classroom: Inquiry into Inquiry.* Philadelphia: W. B. Saunders.

McAuley, Karen, and Richard H. Wilson. 1985. *The United States Past to Present.* Lexington, Mass.: D.C. Heath.

McKenzie, Gary. 1979. "The Fallacy of Excluded Instruction." *Theory and Research in Social Education,* 7 (Summer), 35–48.

———. 1980. "The Importance of Teaching Facts in Elementary Social Studies." *Social Education,* 44 (October), 494–98.

Michaelis, John. 1968. "Social Studies." In *Using Current Curriculum Developments.* Alexandria, Va.: Association for Supervision and Curriculum Development.

Parker, Walter, and Samuel A. Perez. 1987. "Beyond the Rattle of Empty Wagons." *Social Education,* 51 (March), 164–66.

Rummelhart, D. E. 1980. "Schemata: The Building Blocks of Cognition." In *Theoretical Issues in Reading Comprehension,* eds. R. J. Spiro, B. C. Bruce, and W. F. Brewer, pp. 33–58. Hillsdale, N.J.: Lawrence Erlbaum Associates.

Stevens, O. M. 1982. *Children Talking Politics: Political Learning in Childhood.* Oxford, U.K.: Martin Robertson and Co., Ltd.

Taba, Hilda, Mary Durkin, Jack R. Frankel, and Anthony McNaughton. 1967. *Teacher's Handbook for Elementary Social Studies.* Introductory ed. Reading, Mass.: Addison-Wesley.

West, Edith. n.d. "Concepts, Generalizations, and Theories." Background Paper No. 3. Minneapolis, Minn.: University of Minnesota.

SUGGESTED READINGS

Barry K. Beyer and Anthony Penna, eds. 1972. *Concepts in the Social Studies.* Washington, D.C.: National Council for the Social Studies. Although this volume is now fairly old, it is still one of the best collections on concepts and concept-based teaching.

Hans Furst. 1980. *The World of Grown-Ups: Children's Conception of Society.* New York: Elsevier North Holland. This book identifies the different developmental stages that children go through in terms of how they perceive their social world.

S. I. Hayakawa. 1964. *Language in Thought and Action,* 2nd ed. New York: Harcourt, Brace & World. This volume is an old but extremely interesting and well-written examination of how language influences thought and vice versa.

John T. Mallan and Richard Hersh, 1972. *No G.O.D.s in the Classroom: Inquiry into Inquiry.* Philadelphia: W. B. Saunders. This three-volume publication was the first to use the UN-GR approach to concepts. Loaded with practical examples and student activities.

PART TWO

Social Studies: An Instructional Framework

CHAPTER 4

Planning for Instruction

"When in charge, ponder; when in trouble, delegate; when in doubt, mumble." (Unknown)

KEY QUESTIONS

☐ How does one plan social studies lessons and units?

☐ How do teachers deal with the complex aspects of planning?

☐ Where do teachers find goals and objectives?

☐ How do teachers *use* content?

KEY IDEAS

☐ Planning is a systematic process in which each aspect interacts with every other aspect.

☐ Planning is complex because of the number of elements that must be considered, but it is not inherently complicated.

☐ Effective planning hinges on what students should be able to do *after* instruction.

☐ Goals and objectives reflect different levels of specificity; goals are general, objectives are more specific.

☐ Social studies content is something that teachers *use,* not simply something students are expected to know.

INTRODUCTION: Beginning at the End

The natural place to start something—whether it's teaching, reading this chapter, or anything else—is at the beginning. Such an obvious statement hardly demands elaboration, but when it comes to instructional planning, things are not as obvious as they seem. At some point, teachers must decide what their students will do on the first, second, or third day of class, of course. But the planning process itself begins at the "end," at the destinations that teachers want students to reach. In other words, the first phase of planning focuses on what students should be able to do *after* instruction.

In actual teaching, the planning process is reversed. Through instruction, teachers help students to reach the destinations—the goals and objectives—they identified in the planning process. However, a significant amount of planning also takes place during teaching itself. Sometimes things don't go as originally planned, for example, which may make it necessary to present the lesson a second time from a different angle. Then too you might feel that redoing the lesson wouldn't be worth the time and effort, and decide instead to make some adjustments in lessons planned for tomorrow or for next week. Such decisions are an ongoing aspect of teaching.

On the surface, planning appears to involve three elements: identifying where you want to go (and why you want to go there); deciding on how you will get there; and determining how well you got to wherever you were going. Although these elements are accurate enough, the perspective is focused entirely on the teacher. Planning is something that teachers do, of course, but their motive is to help students develop new knowledges, skills, and attitudes. Thus, a more accurate planning model consists of the following elements:

1. identifying *what* students should be able to know or do after instruction;
2. identifying *how* students will achieve those aims; and,
3. identifying *how well* students have achieved what you expected of them.

All three components of planning are essential, but the key to the process is the first element. Unless you identify clear objectives for what students will be expected to accomplish, you could very well teach something irrelevant or perhaps even nothing at all. In other words, like Robert Mager's fabled sea horse described below, you need to know where you are going before you begin.

THE FABLE OF THE SEA HORSE

Once upon a time a Sea Horse gathered up his seven pieces of eight and cantered out to find his fortune. Before he had traveled very far he met an Eel, who said,

"Psst. Hey, bud. Where 'ya going?"

"I'm going out to find my fortune," replied the Sea Horse proudly.

"You're in luck," said the Eel. "For four pieces of eight you can have this speedy flipper, and then you'll be able to get there a lot faster."

"Gee, that's swell," said the Sea Horse, and paid the money and put on the flipper, and slithered off at twice the speed. Soon he came upon a Sponge, who said,

"Psst. Hey bud. Where 'ya goin'?"

"I'm going out to find my fortune," replied the Sea Horse.

"You're in luck," said the Sponge. "For a small fee I will let you have this jet-propelled scooter so that you will be able to travel a lot faster."

So the Sea Horse bought the scooter with his remaining money and went zooming through the sea five times as fast. Soon he came upon a Shark, who said,

"Psst. Hey, bud. Where 'ya going?"

"I'm going out to find my fortune," replied the Sea Horse.

"You're in luck. If you'll take this short cut," said the Shark, pointing to his open mouth, "you'll save yourself a lot of time."

"Gee, thanks," said the Sea Horse, and zoomed off into the interior of the Shark, there to be devoured.

The moral of this fable is: if you're not sure where you're going, you're liable to end up someplace else—and not even know it. (Mager, 1984, preface)

In the balance of this chapter, we examine the planning process and the products—the lesson plans and units—that result from it. The emphasis in the first section is on identifying and stating goals and objectives. We then examine how instructional goals and objectives may be influenced by different kinds of content—whether from textbooks or elsewhere—that you might use with children. Finally, we examine a sample unit and lesson plan, and consider the kinds of decisions that must be considered in developing them.

We consider the second element of planning, determining *how* to reach your goals and objectives, only briefly in this chapter. That element is another way of saying "selecting and developing instructional activities," which we deal with throughout the balance of the book. Likewise, we don't deal extensively with evaluation—with determining *how well* you and your students have reached your goals and objectives—because that aspect of planning is the focus of Chapter 16.

MANAGING MULTIPLE GOALS AND OBJECTIVES

Typically, at least three expectations are held for children who have studied social studies (or anything else): they will be expected to *know* something about social ideas—the facts, concepts, and generalizations of social studies; they will be expected to apply *skills* that enable them to use the knowledge they have acquired; and they will be expected to acquire certain *attitudes* and beliefs that society feels are important for citizens to share. Children will, for example, be expected to know something about history, geography, and human behavior, just as they will be expected to read a map or to distinguish between statements of fact and opinion. Above all, they will be expected to feel a commitment to using their knowledge and skills to be effective, responsible citizens.

Associated with the three categories of expectations (knowledge, skills, and attitudes) will be a variety of statements that describe them with varying degrees of precision. Some of those statements, such as "to produce effective citizens," will be stated in broad, very general terms, whereas others will be much more specific—e.g., "to name forty-five of the fifty state capitals." The first statement is an example of a general goal or aim, while the other is a specific objective. Both types of statements have a role in teaching social studies, but they serve quite different functions.

GOALS

Broad statements such as "producing effective citizens," or "understand American history" identify long-term goals or aims. Goals establish a general direction toward which teaching should be aimed.

Because goals are stated in general terms, it is usually difficult to tell when they have been achieved. Though we might want to say, for example, that by virtue of their social studies experience children will "understand American history," we also witness historians for whom "understanding American history" is a life-long quest. The point here is that goals reflect relatively long-term statements of intent. The length of the term may vary; some goals may apply to a unit of study, as in having students "understand the Civil War," others may apply to courses, such as "understand American history," and still others are school or lifetime goals, such as "understand and appreciate the human experience." The different levels of goals (and objectives) are shown in the list that appears at the end of the next section.

OBJECTIVES

At the opposite end of the spectrum from goals are specific objectives such as "From memory, the child will name forty-five of the fifty state capitals." Unlike goals, objectives precisely specify the behaviors a child is to exhibit. Because such statements describe how the child is expected to perform or behave, they may be referred to as *performance objectives* or *behavioral objectives*. In addition, and because objectives state a criterion that the child is expected to meet—in this instance, "forty-five of the fifty state capitals"—the term *criterion-referenced objective* is sometimes applied. (This is one of those possibly frustrating instances where there are at least three terms to describe essentially the same thing.)

The distinction between goals and objectives is illustrated in the following conversation, which we have titled, "I Want To Be the Best Archer in the World."

Robin: Some day I'm going to be the best archer in the world.
Mr. Hood: That's great son, but how will you know when you are the best?
Robin: (scratching his head) What do you mean Dad? By practicin', I guess.
Mr. Hood: Okay. But how will you know when you have become the world's best archer?
Robin: C'mon Dad. Even Coach says I'm good.
Mr. Hood: I mean *specifically*. Give me something that I can see, something so that I'll know when you've reached your goal.

Robin: Ya' mean like hitting the target most of the time?

Mr. Hood: Don't give me any of this "most of the time" business. How many times do you need to hit it?

Robin: Say, like ninety-nine times out of one hundred tries?

Mr. Hood: Now that's more like it. That's your objective!

Robin: But some people can hit the target one hundred times in one hundred tries.

Mr. Hood: In that case, maybe you'd better change your objective to, say, nine hundred ninety-nine times out of one thousand. Maybe that's closer to your goal.

Robin: Or maybe I could win an Olympic gold medal.

Mr. Hood: That sounds good to me, son. Your objectives are measurable and you'll know when you've reached them. But can you do it? Are they reasonable?

Robin: Hmmmm.

Performance (behavioral) objectives, such as "The child will, from memory, name forty-five of the fifty state capitals," reflect the following characteristics; they identify

1. an *object* of instruction (state capitals)
2. a *condition* under which the behavior will be demonstrated (from memory)
3. a *standard [criterion* or *performance level]* (forty-five of fifty) that the student must demonstrate
4. an identifiable *task* or *behavior* (to name)

The accountability and assessment programs in some school districts demand *very* precisely stated objectives. In addition to the elements noted above, such objectives may include (1) the *time* at which the behavior will be demonstrated (such as "after instruction," or "at the end of the unit"); and (2) the *population* (such as "the students reading on grade level") to whom the expectation applies. This specificity is not necessary under most circumstances, especially when the population, time, conditions, or performance level are obvious. An objective such as "The student will explain the significance of Abraham Lincoln's actions during the Civil War" usually conveys the expectation clearly.

If disagreements arise about whether a student has accomplished an instructional aim, you are probably dealing with a goal, not an objective. In other words, "to *really* understand" something implies a greater depth of comprehension than simple "understanding," but in the absence of more specific indicators for either term, both would function as goals. What it all boils down to is the specificity of the verbs used in stating the goal or objective.

Below we have provided two lists of verbs. In one of them, the terms are more precise and therefore more closely associated with objectives. In the other, the verbs are more global, more open to differing interpretations. Which list would you associate with goals? With objectives?

List 1	*List 2*
to grasp the significance of	to write or list
to really understand	to illustrate
to recognize	to define
to appreciate or to enjoy	to predict or to suggest
to believe or to have faith in	to name or identify
to comprehend or to understand	to locate or to rate
to know (or to know thoroughly)	to restate or to tell why
to be aware of	to distinguish or to discuss
to esteem or to take satisfaction in	to differentiate or to ask

The terms in List 2 reflect the level of precision associated with objectives, whereas List 1 reflects the more general terms associated with aims or goals. Actually, the precision of goals and objectives varies according to the functions they serve. As illustrated in the list below, the objectives for a particular lesson may be more specific than the objectives for a unit or a semester, and the goals for a course may be more specific than a school or lifelong goal.

Levels of Specificity for Goals and Objectives

Objectives

Level 1: Very Explicit. Example: Given a state highway map, the student will be able to use the index to locate five towns or villages. (Specific Lesson Objective)

Level 2: Specific. Given a limited amount of information about unknown nations, the students will be able to identify plausible hypotheses that describe life in those nations. (Unit or Course Objective)

Goals

Level 3: General. The student will understand how technology has influenced our way of life. (Course Goal)

Level 4: Very General. Example: The student will be able to cope with the problems of life. (School/Lifelong Goal)*

After having read the preceding discussions, do you think you can tell a goal from an objective? In the following exercise, place a *G* in the space provided for statements that are goal-related, and an *O* for those that are objectives.

_____ 1. The student will list, in chronological order, the full names of the four U.S. presidents whose last names begin with the letter J.

_____ 2. The student will really understand "critical thinking."

*Adapted from Sawin, 1969. Reprinted with permission of the author.

_____ 3. Given the following concept statements, the student will circle each statement that is testable in the form presented.
  3.1. Capital punishment deters homicide.
  3.2. Individuals who oppose nuclear energy are unpatriotic.
  3.3. Most societies have a code that determines acceptable and unacceptable behavior.

_____ 4. The student will identify one assumption in each of the following statements:
  4.1. People without children should not pay school taxes.
  4.2. One person's opinion is as good as another's.
  4.3. Teachers should not be permitted to strike.

_____ 5. The student will form a hypothesis using the following information:
  5.1. Boston is located on the Charles River.
  5.2. Moscow is located on the Volga River.
  5.3. London is located on the Thames River.
  5.4. Cincinnati is located on the Ohio River.
  5.5. Paris is located on the Seine River.
  Hypothesis: _____

_____ 6. Using the hypothesis developed in Task 5, the student will identify one exception to that hypothesis.

_____ 7. The student will demonstrate proper respect for the rights and opinions of others.

_____ 8. The student will grasp the significance of any three of the following holidays:
  8.1. Thanksgiving
  8.2. Christmas
  8.3. George Washington's Birthday
  8.4. Memorial Day
  8.5. The Fourth of July*

*(*Note:* Statements 2, 7, and 8 are goals.)

STATE MANDATES

As we noted in the Prologue, recent legislation in several states has rendered much of the previous discussion academic; in those states, the instructional goals and, in some cases, the objectives are prescribed. Teachers in those areas often find themselves designing and formulating lessons that will enable children to reach the predetermined goals and objectives.

Below are the core curriculum goals for third-grade social studies for the state of Utah. These goals and objectives are very similar to the essential elements or core curricula of other states that have such requirements. Most states employ a numbering system, such as that shown below, for record-keeping purposes. For brevity, we have reproduced the objectives portion for only one goal statement.

Goal 01   The students will practice a variety of listening, speaking, writing, and reading skills in completing social studies activities. [Note that this goal remains constant throughout the elementary grades, but the specific objectives become more complex at the higher grade levels.]

Goal 02   The students will understand the cultural and historical development of their local community.

Goal 03   The students will understand that people use natural resources to meet their basic needs and these resources must be protected and conserved.

Goal 04   The students will understand geographic concepts.

Goal 05   The students will understand the interplay of economics in their daily lives.

> *Objectives*
> 0501   Define wages, prices, producer, consumer, specialization, division of labor, profit, loss, and productivity.
>
> 0502   Explain reasons for spending and saving money.
>
> 0503   Identify the relationship between supply and demand and its effect on the price of a product.
>
> 0504   Identify the advantage of division of labor (job specialization which increases productivity and creates interdependence).
>
> 0505   Identify the natural resources that determine the types of jobs in your community in the past, present, and future.
>
> 0506   Identify the role of profits as being the primary reason for production.
>
> 0507   Identify how inventions influence change in society.

Goal 06   The students will understand that the purpose of government is to protect and serve the needs of citizens in their community.

State-mandated goals and objectives eliminate one portion of a teacher's planning burden. In fact, in some respects they may force teachers into a technician role. Although the goals and objectives are standardized and predetermined, teachers must still identify ways to reach them that are meaningful to children. In other words, the teacher does not begin with Objective 1 for Goal 1 and then move sequentially through the list, for to do so would undoubtedly result in disjointed, fractionalized instruction. Instructional activities often have multiple outcomes and may relate to two or more objectives, as we illustrate later in this chapter. We are suggesting that simply because certain goals or objectives appear first in a listing does not mean that they must be taught in that order.

Although planning a lesson does not have to follow a step-like, linear sequence, the planning stage is one of the most important in the development and instruction of any lesson. (© *Jean-Claude Lejeune*)

SYSTEMATIC PLANNING

A particularly troublesome notion for prospective teachers is the belief that the planning process follows the same linear, step-like sequence in which written lesson plans and units are often presented. Most published units, for example, are presented in the following order: (1) the theme or topic, (2) a list of goals, (3) a list of concepts or generalizations, (4) a list of performance objectives, (5) suggested student activities, and (6) a sample test or suggested evaluation activities. The planning process can follow the same sequence but it does not need to. In fact, it's doubtful that most unit developers actually produced the elements of their plans in the sequence in which they are published. In the same way, after you have identified your instructional intent, whatever planning sequence you follow is not terribly important; what is most important is that everything is logical and "hangs together" when you are done.

  To illustrate our point here, think back to those times just before the first test in some of the classes you have taken. Didn't you sometimes find yourself wondering what questions the instructor would ask? After that first test, when you had a better idea of what was expected, you probably approached the second test with considerably greater confidence. From a planning perspective, consider that every test question reflects an objective; every question represents something the child is expected to know. By analyzing a teacher's test questions, you can readily identify at least some of that teacher's instructional objectives.

Once you have determined the goals for your unit or lesson, you could begin your more specific planning by constructing a preliminary version of the final test. If you have twenty questions on that test, you should have the basis for about twenty objectives. We will examine evaluation in Chapter 16; in the meantime, consider that developing a test need not be the last element of planning—it could be among the first.

At times in your planning, you may identify or design a student activity for a particular goal or objective. At other times, you may put your initial emphasis on identifying possible learning activities and *then* develop objectives and evaluation strategies to fit them. Once you are satisfied that you have dealt with your goals, you can evaluate your plan in terms of its overall consistency. The basic question at this point is, does your plan accomplish what you started out to do?

Determining your instructional intent is the appropriate starting point in planning. This usually takes the form of identifying instructional goals. Thereafter, we suggest that planning becomes an interactive system in which the different elements interact with each other, and in which there is no preestablished sequence that determines the order in which things must be considered. If this sounds complicated, it really isn't. In the last part of this chapter, we will walk you through the process, step-by-step.

In the balance of this section, we first consider overall goals for instruction. We then look at the relationship between objectives and instructional activities, simply because the two go hand-in-hand. Finally, we will consider some criteria for judging the appropriateness of objectives and activities.

GOALS

Goals provide a general direction for teaching. However, from a planning perspective, goals such as "understand interdependence" or "provide training for effective citizenship," are so general that they may leave one wondering where to begin. Because of this, we have found it helpful to create somewhat more specific goals statements that reflect the different approaches to social studies (that we identified in Chapter 1). These intermediate-level goal statements—although not as specific as objectives—can provide some guidance for identifying instructional objectives, unit objectives, and even course objectives.

We suggest the following intermediate-level goal statements, each of which corresponds to one of the approaches to social studies that we described in Chapter 1:

A. A goal of social studies is to provide children with knowledge and attitudes that are part of our cultural heritage. (Cultural Heritage approach)

B. A goal of social studies is to provide children with knowledge of the structure, findings, and processes associated with the social science disciplines. (Social Science–Disciplines approach)

C. A goal of social studies is to provide children with ideas about the social nature of human activity; these ideas should be transferable to the contemporary scene and should provide children with skills that enable them to make effective decisions and to build, test, and use other ideas. (Social Science–Thinking/Decision-Making approach)

These goal statements can provide a standard for determining the relative merit of potential objectives and activities. The standard in Goal C, for example, is to have children learn ideas that are directly related to the social aspects of human activity. This suggests the kind of content that children might deal with. However, it does *not* provide a developmental standard of appropriateness; that is, it does not indicate whether a particular objective (or activity) is suitable for a particular group of children. The latter standard is something teachers must decide when the characteristics of their students become known.

An illustrative planning framework related to Goal C would be as follows:

Goals: "To produce effective citizens"
"To build and test social ideas and provide opportunities for students to learn and use skills"

General Objective: "To provide appropriate materials that permit cognitive skills to be developed and applied as children build and test specific social ideas"

Specific Objective (sample): "The child will identify three statements of fact and three statements of opinion from a presidential speech."

Other instructional goals, such as "understand American history" or "know American geography," define certain kinds of content—in this case, American history and geography. The idea, then, is to identify those elements from American history or geography that students might be expected to know, and which, collectively, would constitute an "understanding." To accomplish this, a teacher would probably turn to textbooks, curriculum guides, or other resources for assistance in narrowing down the possibilities. In other words, some of the teacher's objectives may be derived from textbooks or other resources. Note that the teacher's intermediate-level goals would also influence *how* he or she approached American history or geography, as we described in Chapter 1, and would be reflected in the kinds of objectives identified.

OBJECTIVES AND ACTIVITIES

From an instructional perspective, *an objective must be considered in relation to the learning activities that are designed to teach it.* The objective "name forty-five of

FIGURE 4.1 Planning—An Interactive Process

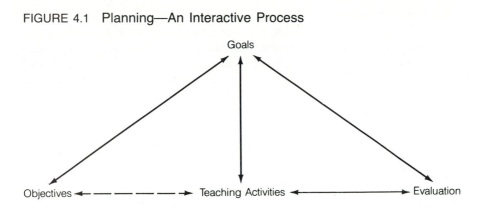

the fifty state capitals from memory," for example, implies that the teacher will do something to help students attain that objective. The objective does not say what a teacher will do—and there are quite a few different activities that a teacher could use with children—but the implication is that the teacher must do something.

Rather than beginning with general goals and then identifying specific instructional activities, the research suggests (Zahorik, 1975; Morine-Dershimer, 1978; Yinger, 1979) that many teachers plan in the opposite direction; they identify possible learning activities to use with children and then derive their objectives from those activities. We suspect that those teachers have general goals in mind when they plan, but their procedure highlights the interactive nature of the planning process, as shown in somewhat simplified form in Figure 4.1.

As Figure 4.1 illustrates, once the instructional intent (the goals) has been identified, the balance of the planning can be dealt with as an interactive system; the objectives will suggest certain teaching activities, the activities will suggest other possible objectives, the objectives (and activities) will be considered in relation to evaluation, and so forth.

Appropriateness

The components of instructional planning must be judged in terms of their consistency and appropriateness. For example, simply because objectives are stated in behavioral form does not necessarily mean they are appropriate for classroom use. In other words, although a statement such as, "Students will be able to name forty-five of the fifty state capitals from memory" illustrates a properly stated objective, that alone is not sufficient. Objectives must also be judged in terms of (1) whether or not students can realistically achieve them, which may depend on students' grade level and maturity *and* (2) whether they are logically consistent with the goals to which they relate.

Students often enjoy instructional activities that challenge their abilities. Challenging activities—and the objectives associated with them—are fine as long as the children have a reasonable chance of meeting those challenges. Based on the developmental research we noted in Chapter 3, however, expecting first-grade children to understand the language and structure of the U.S. Constitution, for example, would be unreasonable. On the other hand, with considerable practice most first graders could probably memorize the states and capitals. But because children *could* achieve an objective does not mean that they *should* attempt to do so.

There must also be a clear and logically consistent relationship between the objective and the goals to which it relates. In other words, one needs to judge whether an objective, such as memorizing the state capitals, will necessarily contribute to one's goal, such as "understanding United States geography." If it does, the objective meets the *appropriateness* criterion; if not, it is probably inappropriate and should be discarded. Determining the relationship between goals and objectives is often a judgment call.

Your judgment about the appropriateness of the state-capitals objective we have been using here will undoubtedly be influenced by your own ability to achieve it, and possibly by your sense of parental or community expectations. The point is that simply because an objective meets certain technical specifications (conditions, performance level, etc.) does *not* mean that it is automatically appropriate for use with students. If the objective is inappropriate, the activity designed to teach that objective probably needs to be discarded too.

Limitations

Teachers are generally expected to state their expectations as precisely as possible. However, this does not mean that *everything* must be stated in *behavioral* terms. Some experienced teachers think about objectives in behavioral terms, but what they write in their lesson plans is in a much more abbreviated form. Some teachers, for example, operate on the basis of a mental image of their plan (Morine-Dershimer, 1979). In other instances, it is virtually impossible to specify behavioral indicators for certain types of activities, especially creative, open-ended activities for which there are no right answers. The same may be true for objectives pertaining to attitudes or higher-level thinking skills, such as analysis and synthesis.

Our point here is that not everything teachers do need necessarily be stated in a performance-objective format. Nevertheless, we recommend that you identify your expectations as precisely as possible. The more precisely objectives are stated, the easier it is to evaluate how well they have been met.

GOALS AND OBJECTIVES FOR THINKING AND FEELING

To better enable teachers to describe and deal with the different kinds of thinking and feeling they might expect from their students, Benjamin Bloom and his associates developed a system for organizing and classifying educational objectives. This landmark work, the *Taxonomy of Educational Objectives: The Classification of Educational Goals,* is divided into three parts, each of which deals with a different domain of behavior. The two parts we deal with here are *Handbook I: Cognitive Domain* (Bloom, 1956) and *Handbook II: Affective Domain* (Krathwohl, 1964).

A *taxonomy* is simply a hierarchical classification scheme, of which the phyla in biology is perhaps the best example. Each level of a taxonomical scheme builds upon and is more complex than the previous level.

THINKING: THE COGNITIVE DOMAIN

The *cognitive domain* refers to activities that involve different kinds of thinking and remembering. The major categories of the cognitive domain, which are shown in Table 4.1 (Gronlund, 1985), are organized in terms of the complexity of the thinking skills involved. Thus, when you hear people refer to "higher-level

TABLE 4.1 The Cognitive Domain of the *Taxonomy of Educational Objectives* (Bloom, 1956)

Descriptions of the Major Categories in the Cognitive Domain	Illustrative General Instructional Objectives	Illustrative Behavioral Terms for Stating Specific Learning Outcomes
Knowledge is defined as the remembering of previously learned material. This may involve the recall of a wide range of material, from specific facts to complete theories, but all that is required is the bringing to mind of the appropriate information.	Knows common terms Knows specific facts Knows methods and procedures Knows basic concepts Knows principles	Defines, describes, identifies, labels, lists, matches, names, outlines, reproduces, selects, states
Comprehension is defined as the ability to grasp the meaning of material. This may be shown by translating material from one form to another (words to numbers), by interpreting material (explaining or summarizing), and by estimating future trends (predicting consequences or effects). These learning outcomes represent the lowest level of understanding.	Understands facts and principles Interprets verbal material Interprets charts and graphs Estimates future consequences implied in data Justifies methods and procedures	Converts, defends, distinguishes, estimates, explains, extends, generalizes, gives examples, infers, paraphrases, predicts, rewrites, summarizes
Application refers to the ability to use learned material in new and concrete situations. This may include the application of such things as rules, methods, concepts, principles, laws, and theories. Learning outcomes in this area require a higher level of understanding than those under comprehension.	Applies concepts and principles to new situations Applies laws and theories to practical situations Constructs charts and graphs Demonstrates correct usage of a method or procedure	Changes, computes, demonstrates, discovers, manipulates, modifies, operates, predicts, prepares, produces, relates, shows, solves, uses

TABLE 4.1   (continued)

Descriptions of the Major Categories in the Cognitive Domain	Illustrative General Instructional Objectives	Illustrative Behavioral Terms for Stating Specific Learning Outcomes
Analysis refers to the ability to break down material into its component parts so that its organizational structure may be understood. This may include the identification of the parts, analysis of the relationships between parts, and recognition of the organizational principles involved. Learning outcomes here represent a higher intellectual level than comprehension and application because they require an understanding of both the content and the structural form of the material.	Recognizes unstated assumptions Recognizes logical fallacies in reasoning Distinguishes between facts and inferences Evaluates the relevancy of data Analyzes the organizational structure of a work (art, music, writing)	Breaks down, diagrams, differentiates, discriminates, distinguishes, identifies, illustrates, infers, outlines, points out, relates, selects, separates, subdivides
Synthesis refers to the ability to put parts together to form a new whole. This may involve the production of a unique communication (theme or speech), a plan of operations (research proposal), or a set of abstract relations (scheme for classifying information). Learning outcomes in this area stress creative behaviors, with major emphasis on the formulation of *new* patterns or structures.	Writes a well-organized theme Gives a well-organized speech Proposes a plan for an experiment Integrates learning from different areas into a plan for solving a problem Formulates a new scheme for classifying objects (or events, or ideas)	Categorizes, combines, compiles, composes, creates, devises, designs, generates, modifies, organizes, plans, rearranges, reconstructs, relates, reorganizes, revises, summarizes, writes
Evaluation is concerned with the ability to judge the value of material (statement, novel, poem, research report) for a given purpose. The judgments are to be based on definite criteria. These may be internal criteria (organization) or external criteria (relevance to the purpose), and the student may determine the criteria or be given them. Learning outcomes in this area are highest in the cognitive hierarchy because they contain elements of all of the other categories, plus conscious value judgments based on clearly defined criteria.	Judges the logical consistency of written material Judges the adequacy with which conclusions are supported by data Judges the value of a work (art, music, writing) by use of internal criteria Judges the value of a work (art, music, writing) by use of external standards of excellence	Appraises, compares, concludes, contrasts, criticizes, describes, discriminates, explains, justifies, interprets, relates, summarizes, supports

Source: From TAXONOMY OF EDUCATIONAL OBJECTIVES: *The Classification of Educational Goals: HANDBOOK I: COGNITIVE DOMAIN* Copyright © 1956 by Longman Inc. Reprinted (abridged) by permission of Longman Inc.

thinking skills," they are in all likelihood referring to skills reflected in the higher and more complex levels of the *Taxonomy* (application, analysis, synthesis, and evaluation). Illustrative general objectives as well as potential terms for stating specific learning outcomes are also shown in Table 4.1.

Formulating Cognitive Objectives

Formulating knowledge-level objectives is relatively easy, especially if you use the descriptors in Table 4.1. You must first identify the information students will be expected to know and then state the *conditions* and the *performance level* under which they will be expected to know it. In an exemplary objective such as "The child will, from memory, identify two ways in which housing in a desert area is similar to and different from housing in a mountainous region," the phrase "from memory" indicates the condition under which the behavior will be demonstrated. Other conditions might include "without notes," "after instruction," or any other phrase that accurately reflects the conditions under which the expectation will be demonstrated. The phrase "two ways" identifies the performance level expected. If there are actually five differences in types of housing, identifying just two is not an especially rigorous criterion. The point here is that a teacher can consider any number of factors, such as the students' abilities and the nature of the task or activity, in determining the desired performance level.

ATTITUDES AND VALUES: THE AFFECTIVE DOMAIN

Attitudes and values, which involve one's feelings and emotions, fall within the *affective domain.* For analytical and planning purposes, it is possible to deal with the cognitive (knowing) and affective (feeling) domains separately, but in practice the two tend to merge together. This becomes evident in instances where a teacher's attitudes and feelings about certain subject matter may come across as strongly as the subject matter itself.

A significant part of social studies is directed toward affective expectations, as reflected in goal statements such as "Develop respect for the American way of life," "Develop an appreciation for American history," or "Become responsible school citizens." The problem here is that it's one thing to state a desired attitude or behavior—such as "being a good classroom citizen"—but it is quite another to identify specific behavioral indicators for such a generalized notion. We could indicate, for example, that a "good school citizen" is one who pays attention, turns in work on time, etc., but it soon becomes difficult to avoid stating behaviors that a student should *not* exhibit—does not interrupt, never gets out of seat, etc. But when such potential affective objectives are phrased as positive statements, such as "The student will stop interrupting the teacher whenever the teacher is talking," they can take on a "Have you stopped browbeating your spouse yet?" flavor. As you see, developing effective affective objectives is no easy feat.

Handbook II: Affective Domain (Krathwohl, 1964) of the *Taxonomy* offers a system for organizing and making sense of affective objectives. The major categories of the affective taxonomy, as well as illustrative objectives and descriptive terms, are shown in Table 4.2 (Gronlund, 1985).

The hierarchy for the cognitive domain was based on the complexity of the thinking skills involved at each level. The taxonomy of the affective domain uses a different basis; namely, the degree to which an individual has internalized an

TABLE 4.2   The Affective Domain of the *Taxonomy of Educational Objectives* (Krathwohl, 1964)

Descriptions of the Major Categories in the Affective Domain	Illustrative General Instructional Objectives	Illustrative Behavioral Terms for Stating Specific Learning Outcomes
1. *Receiving.* Receiving refers to the student's willingness to attend to particular phenomena or stimuli (classroom activities, textbook, music, etc.). From a teaching standpoint, it is concerned with getting, holding, and directing the student's attention. Learning outcomes in this area range from the simple awareness that a thing exists to selective attention on the part of the learner.	Listens attentively Shows awareness of the importance of learning Shows sensitivity to human needs and social problems Accepts differences of race and culture Attends closely to the classroom activities	Asks, chooses, describes, follows, gives, holds, identifies, locates, names, points to, selects, replies, uses
2. *Responding.* Responding refers to active participation on the part of the student. At this level he [or she] not only attends to a particular phenomenon but also reacts to it in some way. Learning outcomes in this area may emphasize acquiescence in responding (reads assigned material), willingness to respond (voluntarily reads beyond assignment), satisfaction in responding (reads for pleasure or enjoyment), or seeking out and enjoying particular activities.	Completes assigned homework Obeys school rules Participates in class discussion Completes laboratory work Volunteers for special tasks Shows interest in subject Enjoys helping others	Answers, assists, complies, conforms, discusses, greets, helps, labels, performs, practices, presents, reads, recites, reports, selects, tells, writes
3. *Valuing.* Valuing is concerned with the worth or value a student attaches to a particular object, phenomenon, or behavior. This ranges in degree from the more simple acceptance of a value (desires to improve group skills) to the more complex level of commitment (assumes responsibility for the effective functioning of the group). Valuing is based on the internalization of a set of specified values, but clues to these values are expressed in the student's overt behavior. Instructional objectives that are commonly classified under "attitudes" and "appreciation" would fall into this category.	Demonstrates belief in the democratic process Appreciates good literature (art or music) Appreciates the role of science (or other subjects) in everyday life Shows concern for the welfare of others Demonstrates problem-solving attitude Demonstrates commitment to social improvement	Completes, describes, differentiates, explains, follows, forms, initiates, invites, joins, justifies, proposes, reads, reports, selects, shares, studies, works

4. *Organization.* Organization is concerned with bringing together different values, resolving conflicts between them, and beginning the building of an internally consistent value system. Thus the emphasis is on comparing, relating, and synthesizing values. Learning outcomes may be concerned with the conceptualization of a value (recognizes the responsibility of each individual for improving human relations) or with the organization of a value system (develops a vocational plan that satisfies the need for both economic security and social service). Instructional objectives relating to the development of a philosophy of life would fall into this category.

Recognizes the need for balance between freedom and responsibility in a democracy

Recognizes the role of systematic planning in solving problems

Accepts responsibility for his [or her] own behavior

Understands and accepts his [or her] own strengths and limitations

Formulates a life plan in harmony with his [or her] abilities, interests, and beliefs

Adheres, alters, arranges, combines, compares, completes, defends, explains, generalizes, identifies, integrates, modifies, orders, organizes, prepares, relates, synthesizes

5. *Characterization by a Value or Value Complex.* At this level of the affective domain, the individual's having a value system that has controlled his [or her] behavior for a sufficiently long time for him [or her] to have developed a characteristic "life-style." Learning outcomes at this level cover a broad range of activities, but the major emphasis is on pervasive, consistent, and predictable behavior. Objectives concerned with the student's personal, social, or emotional adjustment would be appropriate here.

Displays safety consciousness

Demonstrates self-reliance in working independently

Practices cooperation in group activities

Uses objective approach in problem solving

Demonstrates industry, punctuality, and self-discipline

Maintains good health habits

Acts, discriminates, displays, influences, listens, modifies, performs, practices, proposes, qualifies, questions, revises, serves, solves, uses, verifies

Source: From TAXONOMY OF EDUCATIONAL OBJECTIVES: *The Classification of Educational Goals: HANDBOOK II: AFFECTIVE DOMAIN* by David R. Krathwohl et al. Copyright © 1964 by Longman Inc. Reprinted (abridged) by permission of Longman Inc.

attitude or value. In other words, the affective taxonomy is based on how strongly individuals feel about and are willing to fight for what they hold dear. Thus, an individual who is just becoming aware of the issues surrounding a topic such as abortion, for example, might willingly listen to different points of view (Receiving), whereas someone at the more advanced stage of Valuing might be more inclined to organize a peaceful demonstration or protest.

Formulating Affective Objectives

Using the terms in Table 4.2 as a guide, it is possible to state affective objectives for most of the different levels of the affective domain, although seldom as precisely as for the cognitive domain. The following are sample objectives for the goal "demonstrates appreciation for the democratic process."

1. The students will *listen attentively* to teacher-led discussions of the democratic process.

2. The students will *share their opinions* (respond to) about elements of the democratic process.

3. When given an opportunity to choose among several possible procedures, the students will *select* the most democratic.

4. The students will *explain* how the democratic process imposes responsibilities that may impinge on other freedoms.

We are unable to provide a sample objective for Stage 5, Characterization by a Value, because the behavior, which is illustrated in a statement such as "The student's belief in the democratic process is reflected in his or her life-style," would require observation for years into the future. As such, it is more characteristic of a long-range goal than an objective.

The reference to *time* in the descriptor for Stage 5 highlights another element that influences the entire affective domain. We know, for example, that most attitudes reflect behavior patterns that have developed over time. Likewise, we know that most attitudinal changes, whether among children or adults, also occur over time. Developing affective objectives that call for dramatic shifts in a student's attitudes or feelings, and then expecting these changes to take place after one or two activities or lessons—or even a three-week or six-week unit—is probably unrealistic.

We discuss instructional techniques for modifying attitudes and values in detail in Chapter 6. Suffice it to say that consistency between desired attitudes or values and the behaviors that a teacher *models* is essential. For example, a teacher who mouths the need to respect the rights and opinions of others but who also, perhaps unintentionally, "puts Sarah down" every time Sarah says something, exhibits an inconsistent behavior pattern that children will detect very quickly. In the long run, the day-in-and-day-out behavior that teachers model may be more crucial than every affective objective ever created.

OBJECTIVES AND QUESTIONS

Precisely stated objectives indicate the types of thinking skills a teacher wants children to demonstrate. Some objectives will deal with remembering, others should involve higher-level thinking skills. However, objectives themselves do not cause children to think; a teacher's questions posed in the course of a lesson or activity do that. In other words, an objective identifies the desired kind of thinking, and the teacher's questions are posed to get children to produce it. Thus, the three elements—objectives, thinking, and questions—are interrelated, as shown below:

$$\text{Objectives} \longleftrightarrow \text{Questions} \longleftrightarrow \text{Thinking}$$

A mismatch can occur when any one of the elements gets out of synch. For example, an objective may call for children to explain the significance of Abraham Lincoln's activities during the Civil War, a task that calls for comprehension-level thinking skills. The teacher's question "What was important about Lincoln's activities?" would be consistent with the desired outcome—assuming the children can answer it, of course. But questions such as "Where was Abraham Lincoln born?" or "How many children did Abraham Lincoln have?"—both of which require only knowledge-memory skills—would constitute a mismatch. We treat questioning strategies in considerably more detail in Chapter 6.

In the next section, we examine content and some of the different ways content can be used in planning and instruction.

CONTENT UTILIZATION: A DIFFERENT PERSPECTIVE

Traditionally, social studies content has been regarded as what teachers teach and children are expected to know. Unfortunately, that view seldom reflects the dual role that social studies content can play. From a teaching perspective, content can be something that teachers *use,* something they teach with. In other words, content can be regarded as something teachers teach (and students learn) *and* as something teachers use to teach. The idea that content can serve as a vehicle to reach certain objectives (as opposed to serving as an end in itself) is critical to instructional planning. From our perspective, a basic ingredient in the know-how of teaching lies in knowing how to approach and use social studies content in different ways and for different purposes. We examine this perspective on content in the following section.

KEY ELEMENTS OF CONTENT UTILIZATION

Figure 4.2 is an illustration from the delightful children's book *Mike Mulligan and His Steam Shovel* (Burton, 1939), in which Mike's steam shovel, Mary Anne, is nearly sent to steam shovel heaven because the new, engine-powered shovels are getting most of the jobs. In the story, Mike and Mary Anne agree to dig the cellar of the new town hall. They also agree to finish the job in just one day, or else they won't get paid. By digging furiously, they manage to complete the job within a day—except for one thing. In their haste, Mike forgets to leave a way to get Mary Anne out of the cellar. So there she sits, quietly belching smoke, at the bottom of the hole they dug.

An argument between Mike and a member of the town council follows. Because Mary Anne is still sitting in the cellar, the councilor argues that the job isn't finished (and Mike should not be paid). The day is saved, however, when a little boy suggests that they build the new town hall around Mary Anne and make her its new furnace. And Mike? He could become the new janitor.

Although *Mike Mulligan and His Steam Shovel* is not the kind of content one might normally associate with social studies, a teacher could use that story to illustrate the concept of structure and function. That cue concept reflects the fact

FIGURE 4.2   Children's Book Illustration

(Source: Virginia Lee Burton, Mike Mulligan and His Steam Shovel. *Copyright © 1939 by Virginia Lee Demetrios. Reprinted by permission of Houghton Mifflin Company.)*

that a particular structure, such as a steam shovel, could be used to serve a number of different purposes or functions (such as a hole digger, a *very* slow form of transportation, or even a furnace).

Children at the earliest primary levels can readily handle the idea of structure and function. For example, when we asked a group of first graders to indicate the different functions a twelve-inch ruler could serve, here's what they suggested:

1. to measure
2. to make straight lines
3. to spank someone
4. to stir something
5. to mark your place when reading
6. as wood to build something, like a birdhouse
7. to dig holes with
8. to prop up something (like a window)
9. to use when hanging things like mobiles when you can't reach
10. as a weapon
11. as a stake in a garden
12. you could carve it and make things
13. as a perch in a birdcage

14. as a pointer when talking at the board

15. as a number line for doing math

16. as a pattern for making a ruler of your own

17. as a turner when cooking

18. as a paint stirrer

19. tie a cloth around it and use as a shoeshiner

20. use it to jam something closed (like a door)

21. put under the corner of a table to stop it from wiggling

22. cut in two lengthwise and use the parts to make a kite

23. as drumsticks

You could undoubtedly add several more functions to the students' list. The problem for most of us, however, is that our culture and our previous experiences tend to limit the way we view certain structures. For example, in our culture dogs are used as pets, not as sources of food. Likewise, horses, which could readily serve as sources of protein, are typically used for work or pleasure when alive, and for dog food when dead. Moving to an educational context, we find that content—subject matter—is usually viewed as having a single function, as something that "teachers teach and children are expected to know." Content utilization has three key elements:

1. *purposes* for which you intend to use the content

2. *selection* of the content to use with students

3. *use* of the content (how you plan to go about dealing with it)

All of these elements are interrelated. If you selected one of the goal statements we identified earlier, that element is already determined. If not, you will need to determine a suitable goal. How you decide to use a particular content selection will depend on your goals, just as the materials you have available will largely determine which ones you use with students. If your only resource is a textbook, you obviously don't have much to select from, a situation that probably explains why teachers often become collectors on a grand scale. As we illustrated in Chapter 3, even an airline ad can furnish potential content.

CONTENT UTILIZATION AND PLANNING

One of the best ways to illustrate the nature of content utilization and its relationship to instructional planning is to actually do some planning. To plan a segment of a skills-oriented unit of study, we have selected a content vehicle that isn't commonly associated with social studies teaching: two cans of Green Giant Niblets corn (see Figure 4.3).

Why corn? Why not a more common topic such as community helpers? Our reasons are threefold. First, we can avoid that "it's something that every child

FIGURE 4.3   The Basis for the Corn Curriculum

(Source: Art based on Green Giant Company logo. Actual label © Green Giant Co. The Pillsbury Company.)

should know" syndrome that so often influences what is taught as social studies. There is probably nothing about two cans of corn that students should know. They certainly are not significant components of our cultural heritage, nor are they components of the social science disciplines. Our second purpose is to illustrate that it is quite possible to teach legitimate skills by using neutral—even mundane—content. Our third purpose is to illustrate that our content—mundane as it is—could also be used in other subject areas as well. Throughout this section, you need to recognize that the corn serves as a vehicle, nothing more.

Our immediate task is to *use* the two cans of corn as a basis for questions which, as students try to answer them, could serve as vehicles for teaching a variety of skills and ideas. As an alternative to posing possible questions, you could identify potential activities, like "Design a new label" or "Try to determine a more appealing color scheme for the existing label." Or you could do both. We find it useful to begin with key questions because they provide a focus for potential lessons and activities. In other words, posing a question such as "How many words can be made from the word *niblets?*" clearly implies an activity that students could do. In presenting that activity to students, it is not essential that the question be asked. Rather, the teacher could say something such as "Let's see how many words we can make from the letters in *niblets.*" Because some teachers bombard students with questions throughout any given day, it is some-times preferable to present an activity as a task, not as yet another question. Our point is that key questions underlie most instructional activities, regardless of subject area.

For the purposes of this activity, try your hand at brainstorming two or three key questions or potential student activities *in each of the major subject areas taught in elementary schools:* language arts (including reading), mathematics, science, and social studies.

We have suggested some potential key questions and activities below. Note that as you identify questions, it is *not* essential that you be able to answer them in advance. In fact, some of the best questions may be those you can't answer. Questions like "Why do most cans have ridges (or rings)?" can serve as un-knowns, as things to inquire about. Concern for the answers to those questions can come after your students (or you) have inquired.

Language Arts

How many different words can you make from the letters in *niblets?*

Write a story entitled "The Day the Green Giant Turned Blue" (creative writing).

Create a new advertising jingle for Green Giant products.

Classify the words on the label beginning with *G* as nouns, verbs, or adjectives. Star those that fit into more than one category.

Other Language Arts Questions/Activities

_____

_____

Mathematics

Identify three different ways to determine the number of kernels in the large can. Then determine which way is the most accurate.

How could you measure the length of the label without taking it off the can?

When would purchasing the large can be a bad buy?

Other Math Questions/Activities

_____

_____

Science

What else is in these cans besides corn? How could you find out? Why would this be important to know?

Does "net weight" include the liquid the corn is packed in? How could you find out?

Are tin cans really made from tin? How could you find out?

Other Science Questions/Activities

_____

_____

Social Studies

Do most of the people in this class prefer canned corn or frozen corn? How could we find out?

What information on the label is there by law? When did labeling laws come into effect? Why?

When were safe canning processes developed? How did they change our way of life?

What role does corn play in our diet? How could we find out?

How many different occupations are involved in getting corn from the Giant's valley to us?

Other Social Studies Questions/Activities

_____

_____

Questions such as "How could you find out?" and "How do you know?" serve to shift the focus of an activity from a concern for the answers to a concern for *finding* the answers. Realistically, the answers to many of these questions, such as "What else is in these cans besides corn?" (water, salt, etc.), have little utility in the child's day-to-day life. However, their transfer value may lie in the processes that students use to arrive at their answers—processes they could employ to solve other problems they may encounter. Indeed, how could you find out what is in these cans besides corn?

In their present form, the questions and/or potential tasks we've just developed are simply an amorphous collection. There is no sequence to most of them, so it is not essential that students complete one activity before moving on to another. Note, however, that were we to use some of the mathematics activities, we would need to be very sensitive to the prerequisite knowledge they might require. Note also that simply because we have identified possible questions and activities does not mean they are all worth using with students; some may have very limited value and should be discarded. Thus, the planning problem we face is selecting among and organizing these elements in a way that makes sense, both to us as teachers and for our students.

As an overall organizer for individual lesson plans, a unit is a way of ensuring that a teacher's day-to-day activities will come together to form meaningful experiences for students. (© B. Griffith 1982/The Picture Cube)

ORGANIZING FOR INSTRUCTION

The intent of all planning is to determine what students should do, and then to identify courses of action that will permit them to do it. The result of a teacher's planning—their unit or lesson—typically consists of a series of learning experiences that have a common theme or focus. Sometimes that theme is phrased as a question, such as "How do people manipulate the behavior of others?" More typically, the activities and experiences deal with selected aspects of a topic: "transportation," "community helpers," "life in Colonial America," etc.

Unit teaching, which is the practice of organizing instruction around selected themes, questions, and topics, is such a well-entrenched practice that the terminology should be familiar. The units you experienced as students were, as the term implies, a series of learning activities and experiences related to a common focus. As students, you were on the receiving end of a *teaching unit*. What you experienced were the activities and materials that your teachers used with your class. Your teacher, however, may have selected those activities and materials from a larger, more encompassing resource unit. A *resource unit* is a planning aid that teachers develop for themselves and that includes possible learning activities, materials to support those activities (lists of films, filmstrips, and other teaching aids and resources), as well as references or background material.

If a teacher wanted to develop a teaching unit on canned corn, he might create a file that would ultimately become the basis for his resource unit. Every time that teacher happened upon an article about corn, canning, or anything related to the topic, he might clip it and add it to the resource file. If that article were usable by children or could be rewritten for them, it might one day be incorporated into the teaching unit. Until then it would remain a part of that teacher's resource unit.

Unit planning is a way of ensuring that a teacher's day-to-day activities will come together to form a meaningful experience for students. As such, the unit serves to provide an overall organizer for the individual lesson plans from which it is built. In fact, the overall organization that a detailed unit plan provides usually eliminates the what-am-I-going-to-do-tomorrow dilemma teachers might otherwise face. Teachers must, of course, plan on a day-to-day basis, making adjustments in tomorrow's lesson based on what happened today. But with a unit to provide a long-range plan, those daily adjustments will be minor, especially compared with what is involved in planning from scratch. In the absence of long-range plans, one continually faces the question of what to do tomorrow.

UNIT PLANNING

Our purpose in this section is to work through some of the phases of the unit-planning process. Unfortunately, developing a unit in the absence of a group of children lends an air of artificiality to this activity. For our purposes here, we have assumed that we are teaching at the primary grades and that our students are poor-to-average readers. This assumption does not change the way we would plan, but it does mean we cannot use activities that depend heavily on reading.

Identifying a Purpose

For this activity, we will adopt the purpose associated with the Disciplines approach to social studies. This means that our purpose is to provide children with knowledge of the structure, findings, and processes of the social science disciplines. We have selected this purpose because of its relative clarity and simplicity. Because we are preparing a unit for primary-level children, our treatment of the discipline(s) will necessarily be simplified. If we were teaching in a state or school district with mandated curricula, we would have to select a goal from the list provided.

Identifying a Focus

For the purpose of this illustration, we have elected to follow up on our previous example that dealt with canned corn. A unit on corn is not something you would normally find in most elementary schools, of course, but by using it as our vehicle we are able to illustrate aspects of the planning process—particularly the principles of content utilization—with greater clarity than would be true using a more traditional topic. If the curriculum guide had called for us to focus on Eskimos or some other content source, we would follow those guidelines. However, because we are building this unit from scratch, we have the luxury of making decisions that might otherwise be made for us by the curriculum guidelines within a state or school system.

One of the most important decisions in unit planning concerns what direction we should take with our vehicle—in this case, corn. Our purpose is to teach ideas associated with one or more of the social science disciplines, but which discipline and what ideas should we focus on? In the next couple of pages we elaborate some of the elements to consider in developing this unit. Understand that until we decide on a course of action, none of this would be written down except as brief notes or reminders.

Exploring Alternatives   Should we focus on the governmental regulation of food products (labeling laws, etc.), the development of food processing (canning, freezing, etc.) and its influence on our way of life, or should we examine the relationship between transportation and trade (the various aspects of shipping and selling corn)? Of the many possible ways to go, two factors will influence our decision: (1) what students already know about these topics and (2) the skills that may be required to complete potential learning activities. In the case of governmental regulation of the food industry we can be fairly certain that we are dealing with something unknown to most primary-age students. If we are uncertain about that, a pretest should remove any doubt. Then, too, government regulations could be something students don't care about. If that's a problem, which it could very well be, we'll need to pay particular attention to developing activities that spark their interest.

Studying how the government regulates the food industry could be a way of helping students broaden their awareness of government itself. However, if this were to become one of our goals, there are probably better vehicles than canned corn to help teach it. Besides, potential learning activities relating to governmental functioning and food regulation would likely involve considerable reading. For these reasons, we can discard the government-regulation focus.

The different modes of transportation involved in producing canned corn might be an appealing focus, especially because we could devise some nonreading (pictorial) activities dealing with trucks, trains, ships, and other forms of transport. On the other hand, most primary-level students are aware of trucks, trains, ships, etc., and unless we are careful, we may find ourselves boring students with discussions about how milk trucks carry milk.

Primary-level students are probably not aware of how heavily any kind of trade depends upon transportation. Should we decide to pursue this focus, we would need to do the same type of *task analysis* as we did for government regulation of the food industry. We need to determine what children must understand before they can deal with the role of transportation in any kind of trade. An obvious prerequisite here is the need to understand the notion of trade as the exchange of goods and services. Then students must understand the notion of transportation, not solely in terms of trucks and trains, but also in terms of its function—the movement of goods and people. And if students are to understand why things are transported, they must also understand why goods are traded. These understandings involve difficult concepts of self-sufficiency and interdependence.

If all of this seems to have become very complex, you're right. Our task analysis reveals a host of difficulties. Just in terms of potential cue concepts we have identified the following: trade, transportation, self-sufficiency, interdependence, goods and services, exchange, and communication. Separately, none of these concepts is beyond the grasp of primary children; in fact, some of them are on the mandated list for third grade that we illustrated earlier (page 119). But when it comes to helping children understand how these ideas are interrelated, we seem to have tackled something much more complicated than we bargained for, something unnecessarily complex for exemplary purposes.

We have taken you through this possibly tedious example that has gotten us nowhere to illustrate a common phenomenon that almost no one talks about: the need to back up and start over. If everything went well on the first try, planning would be far less time-consuming.

Among the key questions we posed earlier was one about the type of corn that most people buy (canned or frozen). That question might serve as the keystone for a unit that follows a more manageable tack. Implicit in that question is the concept of *choice:* the fact that people satisfy their wants and needs in different ways. By expanding that idea to a context that goes beyond consumers' decisions, it becomes apparent that many choices (decisions) were made in the production of the canned corn. These extend to a farmer's decision to grow corn instead of something else, and to the fact that the wood from which the paper label was made could have been used for something else (or not used at all).

From a specific instance, the choice of what kind of corn to buy, we have worked backward to a generalization: the allocation and use of human and natural resources is based on decisions. In other words, the two cans of corn can serve as visible indicators of resources that were allocated and used in particular ways. By considering corn and other products, we should be able to develop a teaching unit that illustrates how people make decisions to use resources to satisfy their needs. In this instance, our focus discipline will be economics—*very simplified* economics.

Up to this point, we have determined that our unit will focus on the cue concept "resource utilization." Notice also that we have identified some potential goals. These include (to cite just two) the desire to have students understand that (1) human and natural resources are allocated and (2) the way in which resources are used involves a variety of decisions.

A lot of cue concepts would need to be dealt with before primary-age children could begin to comprehend some of the goals stated above. These include *resources, natural resources, needs, allocation,* and the like. By making a list of cue concepts as we go, we can review the learning activities we will develop to see that we are not overloading children with unfamiliar terms. In some instances, we may be able to reduce the conceptual load by using terms such as "divide up" instead of *allocation.* In the other cases, we will also state the cue concept in sentence form, e.g., a *resource* is a supply of something that we can draw on when we need; a *need* is something we must have or would just like to have, etc.

There are several different routes we could follow in developing our unit from this point, such as identifying instructional objectives more precisely. We could indicate, for example, that "the student will identify, from memory, three examples of natural resources" or that the student "will distinguish between a human and a natural resource." Note that our request for "three examples of natural resources" in the objective above is arbitrary (and tentative). Note also that each cue concept indicated above may suggest one or more additional objectives. Sooner or later we must identify all of our objectives, but some of them will evolve from the kinds of activities we develop. So, at this point in the unit, we prefer to identify additional key questions, simply because they tend to lend direction and specificity to our unit. Some of those key questions are as follows:

1. What resources were used to produce the two cans of corn?
2. What resources are used to produce other common products?
3. What other things could be produced from those same resources?
4. What are resources, and where do they come from?
5. How are resources used differently?

These questions are not necessarily in the order we may finally put them in, nor is it essential that we deal with all of them. Notice, also, that the questions suggest additional objectives, e.g., "The student will identify at least four resources that were used to produce a can of corn," etc.

In the course of this unit, the children should come to appreciate the fact that although humans may have an almost unlimited supply of needs and desires, our supply of resources is limited. The need to allocate scarce resources wisely is also something that students should understand and appreciate. In so doing, we have implicitly identified two affective (attitudinal) goals for our fledgling unit: (1) an appreciation of the scarcity of resources and (2) an appreciation for the need to allocate them wisely.

After a couple of false starts, we have finally laid the foundation for our unit. Although our planning is far from complete, we have tentatively identified the following elements, presented as a progress report below.

PLANNING: PROGRESS REPORT

Unit Development

Unit title: Undecided

Grade level: Primary (Third)

Unit focus: Resource utilization

Generalization: The allocation and use of human and natural resources is based on decisions.

Major vehicle: Canned corn

Unit Goals:
Cognitive: The child will understand the nature of resources. The child will understand that the use of resources always involves choices and decisions.

Affective: The child will appreciate the scarcity of resources, our widespread dependency on them, and the need to use resources wisely.

Cue Concepts:
resources, natural resources, human resources, wants, needs, allocation, scarcity

Objectives:
(Sample, tentative)

The student will identify, from memory, three examples of natural resources.

The student will distinguish between a human resource and a natural resource.

The student will identify three alternative uses for a particular resource.

Skill Focus:
To be determined in activities

Learning Activities:
(Yet to be decided)

Formulating Objectives and Activities

Notice that we have established a basic structure for our unit without referring to any activities; we have established where we are going, but we have not identified how we will get there. Our planning problem now becomes one of filling in the gaps. Recognize that there isn't necessarily any one best way to proceed from this point. Some teachers may prefer to specify objectives with greater clarity, some may wish to identify potential student activities, and others may wish to identify possible resources and teaching materials. Instead of working with just one element at a time, some teachers shift back and forth, working on the various components simultaneously.

Our preference is to identify a way to initiate the unit, a way that not only grabs the students' attention but also helps establish a direction for the activities that

FIGURE 4.4   A Family Tree for a Can of Corn

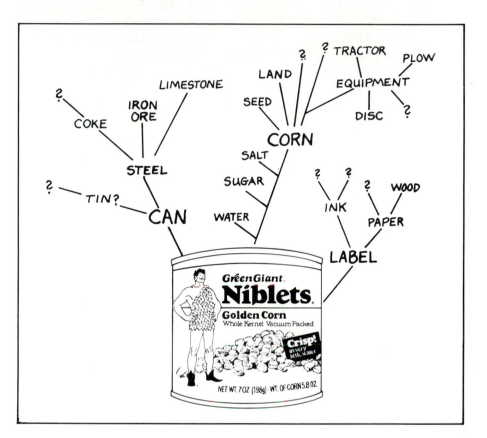

follow. It has been our experience with both unit planning and daily lesson plans that if we can get an activity or lesson off to a good start, and if we know what that activity or lesson should lead to, then the middle will almost sustain itself.

Of the several possible ways to initiate this unit, our first decision is *not* to begin with the usual defining of terms. We'll need to deal with definitions eventually, of course, but beginning with them is about as dull a way of starting a unit that we can think of. Our inclination is instead to begin the unit by identifying the resources that went into producing the cans of corn. (Note that we're using adult language here, not necessarily what we'd use with students.) Presenting a list of "things" (resources) that went into producing the canned corn is one alternative, or we could develop a kind of "family tree" for canned corn as is illustrated in Figure 4.4.

Choosing between starting with a list, the family tree, or something else is just one of the countless decisions that planning requires. In this instance, we would use the family tree activity because it illustrates both the resources used in producing canned corn and their sequence of use. Also, in our judgment, it's a more appealing format for presenting data. Finally, developing a family tree for canned corn in a whole-class setting could serve as a model for follow-up activities in which small groups of students could create similar charts for other familiar products—furniture, clothing, agricultural products, or almost anything else. Note that our reason for going into such detail here is to indicate some of the factors we considered in arriving at our decision. Of course, if the notion of a family tree is totally foreign to our students, a preliminary activity in which students learn to create their own family trees may be advisable. This decision would hinge on our awareness of our students' previous experiences (with family trees), which is something teachers gain simply by working with their classes. Since the students' experiences are unknown to us here, we are forced to make assumptions. If we assume incorrectly or don't make provisions (emergency plans) for instances where we have assumed improperly, we may find ourselves in serious trouble. Enough said about the important role that students' past experiences play.

After students have identified some of the natural resources used to manufacture various products, they could compare their charts to determine what resources are common among the products. They could then produce pictorial charts (pictures cut from magazines, perhaps) or murals showing the different products produced from a particular resource, with titles such as "Things Made from Wood." These activities would rely primarily on children's prior experiences and could be construed as a kind of test unless we add new sources of information. To do this, we would use some of the numerous films and filmstrips that deal with how we use natural resources. A particularly good film, for example, is *The New House: Where It Comes From* (Coronet Films). Other films and filmstrips, some with generic titles such as *The Story of . . . (Bread, Wood, Steel,* etc.) might also be suitable.

Thus far, we have begun to identify a rough sequence of potential learning experiences. We have also tried to show that the progression of unit planning moves from the "whole," the unit, to the "parts," or specific teaching activities, and then back to the "whole."

A special note about the role of daily lesson plans in unit planning is in order here. You will notice below that we have presented our teaching episodes on an activity basis, not on a lesson-plan basis. The reason for this is that each activity is intended to reflect a meaningful learning episode. However, until we actually try the activities with students, we can't tell how long each activity will take. Some may require a day, some two days, and some considerably longer. Because the unit plan provides the overall framework, the daily lesson plans will merely indicate where the class is in relation to the overall plan. In such a case, a teacher's daily plans might read, for example, "Continue Activity Two." Teachers who do not use unit planning must necessarily employ a more elaborate daily planning procedure.

Developing and sequencing learning activities is neither more nor less important than any other aspect of planning. Unfortunately, we know of no formula or procedure to help you do it. In most instances, it seems to be a matter of what makes the most sense to an individual teacher. Below we have indicated a sequence of activities that we could use, but this certainly is not the only way that such a unit could be organized or taught.

A SAMPLE UNIT PLAN

The following activities are described in adult terms, not necessarily as we would present them to children. In developing your own units, you may wish to include key questions in the language you would use with students.

As you proceed through the sample unit, you will note that not all of our objectives are stated in behavioral terms. In most cases, this will be because the students are involved in group activities that do not focus on the skill levels of individual students. We do not mean to imply that behavioral objectives are incompatible with group activities. They are not. Because we do not plan to assess the performance of each student, it doesn't seem reasonable to state objectives in behavioral terms. When we evaluate the group activities, however, the results for students who do not fare too well may indicate a need for additional activities or experiences for which behavioral objectives would be appropriate.

Be advised that as complex as the sample unit plan below may seem, it represents a very basic organizational structure. As such, we have not indicated provisions for individualized instructions nor have we dealt extensively with assessment and evaluation, which we consider in Chapters 14 and 16. The skill areas that we identify for each lesson are also treated in later chapters.

UNIT PLAN

"Using Resources Wisely"

Grade level: Primary (Third)

Generalization: The allocation and use of human and natural resources is based on decisions.

Goals:

Cognitive: The child will understand the nature of resources. The child will understand that the use of resources always involves choices and decisions.

Affective: The child will appreciate the scarcity of resources, our dependency on resources, and the need to use them wisely.

INITIATING ACTIVITY

Objective: Working in small groups, students will identify the components of canned corn.

Description: Phase One. Divide the class into small groups and, if possible, provide each with an identical can of corn. Ask each group to identify as many "things" as possible that went into making the corn, can, and label. Gauge the length of time spent on this portion of the activity by the students' interest; five minutes or less may be sufficient.

Phase Two. Have the various groups report their findings. List the components on the chalkboard as each group reports. Probe, cajole, and stimulate as necessary. After the groups have gone as far as they seem able, ask if any of the items seem to go together. Follow the Taba concept-building procedure (pages 100–101). Note that some items may go into more than one category.

Skill areas: Observing, analyzing, inferring, classifying

ACTIVITY TWO: BUILDING A FAMILY TREE

Objectives: Working together in a large group, the teacher and students will develop a model "family tree" for canned corn.

Based on experiences in the group, the child should be able to explain the process for making a "family tree" (pedigree) chart.

Description: Working with the list of "things" previously identified, the teacher and students will locate components on a "family tree" chart similar to the one illustrated in Figure 4.3. As a group, students will identify all of the "things" (not yet identified as resources) they can think of that were involved in producing the cans of corn. Have a good reader read the label. Items the students identify should be listed on the board, and may include such things as *farmer, metal, paper, ink,* etc. Don't push too far here. For example, accept *paper* without going into paper's components (wood, etc.) unless the children insist on it. This will be picked up again in Activity Three.

Skill area: Recording data

Optional initiating activity. If students are unfamiliar with a family tree chart, the unit could be begun by having students make family tree charts of their own, using snapshots if available or simply names of relatives.

ACTIVITY THREE: PAPER

Note that Activities Three, Four, and Five each follow a similar format. The children should tentatively identify the resources and process that go into producing the various components of the cans of corn—paper, metal, etc. Their suggestions should be treated as hypotheses—things they think go into the component, but about which they may not be sure. In these activities, the students' hypotheses are tested against data (on paper making, etc.) provided through films, filmstrips, or other media.

The exact nature of these activities and the length of time they take will depend on the materials and resources available.

Objectives: The student will identify a natural resource as something from our environment that people may use.

The student will describe the process for making paper.

Description: The intent of this activity is to test and then validate the children's ideas about the resources used in making paper. Key question: What do you think paper is made from?

Phase One. List responses to the key question on the chalkboard. Then follow up with any of the following materials:

Encyclopedia articles

Film: *Paper and Pulp Making* (Coronet)

Film loop (8 mm.): *Products from Trees* (Doubleday)

Phase Two. Review the elements the children hypothesized originally. Add the resources to the master family tree chart.

Phase Three (optional extending activity). Making paper. Follow instructions for making paper in *Teaching Social Studies in the Elementary School* by Ralph Preston and Wayne L. Herman, Jr., 3rd ed. New York: Holt, Rinehart, and Winston, 1974, pp. 568–570.

Skill areas: Hypothesizing, hypothesis testing

ACTIVITY FOUR: TIN CANS

Objective: The student will identify the major components in metal cans.

Description: Follows the same format as Activity Three. Key question: What are tin cans made from? Possible materials include the following:

Films: *Tin from the Malayan Jungle* (International Film Bureau); *Steel & America* (Disney Productions)

Filmstrip: *Rocks, Minerals, and Mining* (Encyclopaedia Britannica Films)

Encyclopedia articles

Skill areas: Hypothesizing, hypothesis testing

ACTIVITY FIVE: CORN

Objectives: The student will identify the major steps in the production of corn.

   The child will name at least five resources used in the production of canned corn (for Activities Three, Four, and Five collectively).

Description: Follows same format as Activities Three and Four. Key question: What elements are involved in producing corn?

   Possible materials include the following:

Encyclopedia articles

Films: *Farmer* (Encyclopaedia Britannica Films); *Farmer Don and the City* (Film Associates)

Filmstrips: *Farming in Indiana* (Jam Handy); *Where Food Comes From* (Encyclopaedia Britannica Films); *The Corn Belt* (Society for Visual Education)

Skill areas: Hypothesizing, hypothesis testing

Optional activities: Children can consider and investigate the nature of salt, ink, or any other component as interest warrants. Follow same format as Activities Three, Four, and Five.

ACTIVITY SIX: WHERE DO THINGS COME FROM?

Objective: Given a common object or article, the student will identify either (1) the components (resources) that were used to produce it or (2) the steps involved in its production.

Description: Each child (or small group) will select a common object or article and make a family tree chart for it (similar to the one done for the corn). For some materials, such as articles of clothing, this may involve identifying the steps in its production.

   Children should explain and display their charts.

Skill areas: Observing, inferring

ACTIVITY SEVEN: MINI-SYNTHESIS

Objectives: The student will identify at least five resources originating in the land.

   The student will distinguish between a human resource and a natural resource.

   The student will distinguish between wants and needs.

Description: Using the corn chart and the materials the children constructed for Activity Six, develop a discussion-oriented activity that will help the children to recognize that (1) the "things" (materials) that went into making the canned corn all ultimately originated in the land, (2) all goods ultimately have their origin in the land, and (3) people are involved at every step along the way. If the occasion has not arisen previously, the term *resources* can be identified as a label for "things," and the term *goods* associated with objects or products produced from natural resources.

Key questions include the following: (1) Do you notice anything about those "things" our cans of corn were made from? (2) Can you think of anything that does not come from the land?

Possible materials include:

Film: *Man's Basic Need: Natural Resources* (Encyclopaedia Britannica Films)

Film loop: *Our Productive Resources* (Doubleday)

Cue concepts: Resources, natural resources, human resources, wants, needs, goods

Skill areas: Classifying and labeling, inferring

ACTIVITY EIGHT: WHAT WOULD HAPPEN IF?

Objective: The students will speculate on how things might be different if certain products were not available.

Description: This discussion activity is based on the key question, What would happen if we didn't have any wood? electricity? water? bicycles? corn?

Skill areas: Hypothesizing/speculating

ACTIVITY NINE: WHAT WE DO WITH WHAT WE'VE GOT

Objective: Given a picture of one product or basic natural resource, the student will identify at least seven other pictures of that resource being used in different ways.

Description: The intent of this activity, which may take several days, is to extend the idea that goods and basic resources are used in different ways. For example, a tree, while reflecting the use of the land in a particular way, can itself be used in different ways.

Provide individual students or groups with labeled pictures (cut from magazines, etc.) of various resources—land, a tree, water, etc. The students are then asked to make a collage of pictures that illustrate different ways in which the product or resource might be used. The teacher should also make a collage showing land being used in different ways—for a playground, for growing crops, for housing, for parks, for parking lots, etc.

Instruct students *not* to include their original picture in their collage until after the class has had an opportunity to identify what resource each collage depicts.

Skill areas: Observing, interpreting, inferring

ACTIVITY TEN: WHAT COULD WE DO WITH THE PLAYGROUND?

Objective: The students will identify at least three factors that might influence the ways in which resources are used.

Description: This activity is intended to illustrate that people have decided to use a particular piece of land, the school playground, in a certain way. In other words, if oil were discovered beneath the playground, the land might be used for other purposes—in this case, to hold an oil well. How the playground is used is subject to certain limitations, including the presence of mineral resources.

Certain value issues also enter the picture. For example, if gold or oil were discovered on the school playground, it could be turned into a gold mine or an oil field; but *should* it? The physical determinants—climate, etc.—should be dealt with first through questions such as "Could our playground be used as an orange grove? a tree farm?"

Value considerations can then be introduced through role playing. For example, the following situation could be presented to students.

Gold Discovered on School Playground

"Gold has been discovered on the _____ School playground. The Acme Mining Company wants to buy the playground and build a gold mine there. They are willing to pay a lot of money for the property."

The key question is, What should the school do?

Skill areas: Inferring, identifying alternative explanations

CULMINATING ACTIVITIES

Objectives: The student will, from memory, (1) identify the primary decision makers (the farmer, the lumberman, etc.) involved in the production of the canned corn and (2) identify at least one alternative decision those individuals might have made in terms of the way they used the resources available to them.

Given a series of pictures of people in different occupations (a machinist, a dairy farmer, a baker, etc.), the student will identify (1) the goods or services being provided and (2) the natural resources being used.

Description: Return to the master family tree chart (for corn) and help the children identify the individuals noted in the first objective above. Then provide a series of pictures as suggested by the second objective.

Culminating activities provide students with opportunities to apply and extend some of the ideas previously dealt with in different contexts. In the sample unit above, we began with the canned corn as a primary vehicle and then returned to it in the culminating activity. It was not essential to do that, but it seemed to round things out rather nicely. It is helpful, though not essential, if the culminating activities provide a bridge to the next unit, which might focus on conservation (the use and abuse of resources), the role of tools in using resources to produce goods and services, or perhaps the role of money as a medium for allocating resources.

Once teachers have decided how they will culminate their unit, a vital phase of planning still remains. Having dealt with the various parts of their unit, it now becomes important to examine the whole, to go back over what they've developed to see that it does what they hoped it would do. To facilitate this preliminary review, we have developed the following Unit Plan Checklist. We suggest that you use it to evaluate the unit we've just developed. If you can't answer "yes" to every criterion, we apparently have left some planning undone.

General

Yes	No	Goals
_____	_____	Have we identified in general terms what students should know at the end of this unit?
_____	_____	Have we identified in general terms what skills students should be able to demonstrate at the end of this unit?
_____	_____	Have we identified affective goals for this unit?
_____	_____	Have we identified what should be done for students who cannot demonstrate what is indicated above?

		Unit Objectives
_____	_____	Have we identified cognitive and affective objectives for this unit?

Specific

Yes	No	
_____	_____	Have we identified a vehicle or focus for the unit?
_____	_____	Have we identified a main idea or generalization for the unit?
_____	_____	Have we task-analyzed the elements of this unit in terms of prerequisite understandings?
_____	_____	Have we stated instructional objectives in performance terms?
_____	_____	Have we identified and sequenced learning activities?

Yes	*No*	
_____	_____	Have we identified guiding (key) questions a. for planning purposes? b. for instructional use with students?
_____	_____	Have we identified teaching materials and resources?
_____	_____	Have we identified a way to initiate the unit?
_____	_____	Have we identified the means for student evaluation?
_____	_____	Have we devised a means for evaluating the unit for internal and external consistency (such as this checklist)?
_____	_____	a. Do the various sections of the unit "fit together"; e.g., no "hidden objectives" (internal consistency)?
_____	_____	b. Is the unit, as a whole, justifiable? Can it be defended as worthy of being studied (external consistency)?

LESSON PLANNING

With unit plans to provide the overall organization, lesson planning is seldom a tedious task. Without a unit plan, however, lesson planning requires that you duplicate much of what you might otherwise have done in preparing a teaching unit.

In developing daily lesson plans, we suggest that you *not* succumb to the practice of listing every question you might ask of students in the sequence in which you plan to ask them. No matter how logical it might seem, when teachers do this, their questions—not the students' responses—tend to become the focal point of the lesson. When this happens, the possibility of building on a student's previous response is often lost. Thus, listing your questions in the sequence in which you plan to ask them could very well limit your ability to respond to changes in direction suggested by the students' responses. Our experience indicates that if you know where a lesson should go and what it's leading to, then four or five key questions are sufficient.

For prospective teachers, it's important to recognize that lesson plans are not for your use alone. Often, those plans must communicate what you intend to do to your cooperating teacher, a college supervisor, and sometimes even the principal (some of whom collect daily or weekly lesson plans from all of their teachers). This sometimes results in lesson plans that are, in our judgment at least, more detailed than they would otherwise need to be for effective teaching. Recognize, though, that the length and scope of your lesson plans may be a function of the dual purpose they serve: (1) as a plan for the students you teach and (2) to communicate your intent to those who observe you.

The following is a sample daily lesson plan in a format that should enable you to deal effectively with students *and* communicate your intent to those who evaluate your planning. In this instance, our example comes from Activity Nine, "What we do with what we've got," from our unit plan.

EXEMPLARY LESSON

Daily Lesson Plan

Unit generalization(s): Resource utilization results from choices among alternatives, choices made by human beings. (It is helpful, though not essential, that generalizations be repeated on each lesson plan.)

Lesson focus: Alternative utilization of resources and goods.

Objective: To extend the notion that basic resources and goods are used in different ways.

Performance objective: Given a picture of one product or basic natural resource, the student will identify at least seven pictures of the product or resource being used in different ways.

Advance preparation:
1. Locate pictures of products or basic resources—farmland, a tree, water, an ingot of iron, etc. Label these appropriately.
2. Gather needed materials: magazines (you'll need a variety, and lots of them); tagboard, large newsprint, or colored paper (on which to mount the collage); scissors (if the children don't have their own); rubber cement (for mounting pictures without wrinkling).

Procedure: Distribute pictures and then identify the students' task: "Make a collage showing different ways in which the product or resource shown on your picture is used." (If students have not made collages previously, you may need to show them a sample—such as the one you are making for land usage.) (Reminder: Be sure to tell students not to mount their original pictures on their collage. They should keep them "hidden.")

Follow-up: Have children share their collage with the rest of the class. When the product or resource has been identified, add the original picture to the collection.

Evaluation: Conducted during activity as pre-performance objective

SUMMARY

Planning isn't complete until teachers see their plans come to fruition. Yet even then the planning process continues, usually in the form of day-to-day adjustments. Additional planning may also take place after instruction, as teachers decide what should be changed when (and if) the unit is taught again.

In this chapter, we identified the various components of planning and illustrated how those components fit together. Goals were identified as statements of intent that indicate a general direction that teaching should take. Examples of goals include statements such as "appreciate the contribution of American patriots," or "understand the impact of technology on contemporary American life." Instructional objectives, on the other hand, describe specific behaviors that students will demonstrate. Statements such as "The student will, from memory, identify three factors that led to the Civil War" and "Given a list of statements, the student will identify those that are facts and those that reflect opinions" are examples of instructional (behaviorally stated or performance) objectives. We noted that just because objectives are phrased in behavioral terms, it does *not* necessarily mean they are good and worthy of instruction. Rather, teachers must evaluate potential objectives—no matter how they are stated—in terms of their students' ability to achieve them and in terms of the goals to which they relate.

We indicated that after identifying your instructional intent, instructional planning becomes a systematic, interactive process—as opposed to a series of discrete steps that one follows in a certain sequence. For example, objectives may imply or suggest certain instructional activities, just as activities may suggest or imply certain objectives. We also suggested that the way teachers approach and use social studies content plays an important role in the planning process. *Content utilization* refers to the fact that teachers and students can use content in different ways and for different purposes. We are not suggesting that you should develop a unit on canned corn, as we did in this chapter, although you might wish to do so if it were appropriate. Rather, our intent was to illustrate how canned corn could serve as a *vehicle* that might enable us to reach our goals.

SUGGESTED ACTIVITIES

1. Most colleges of education maintain collections of social studies curriculum guides and textbook series. If not, the local school system might loan you copies. Where possible, get two different curriculum guides or texts (preferably teacher's editions) *for the same grade level.* Compare and contrast them in terms of the following:
   a. the nature and clarity of their goals and objectives
   b. the relationship of suggested student activities to the stated goals and objectives
   c. the similarities and differences in format, suggested topics, and suggested teaching approaches.

2. Occasionally schools in some parts of the country periodically suspend their regular curriculum for a day. In place of it teachers develop variations on the "can of corn" curriculum we dealt with in this chapter. On those days, the entire curriculum is developed around a single vehicle, such as apples, pumpkins, breakfast cereals, sports, or almost anything you could imagine (including corn). You may never be called upon to teach "apple math" or "soccer social studies," but the prospect can be intriguing.

   Using the procedures we suggested earlier (pages 135–136), try your hand at identifying possible questions and student activities for each subject in the curriculum for the topic/vehicle of your choice.

3. Sequencing activities to be accomplished in order to complete a larger, more encompassing task is an established part of planning. A newspaper recently ran an article on how to filet fish—a step-by-step approach that "even a novice can master." After purchasing unassembled toys, one is often faced with a series of steps that must be followed in sequence. Try to locate some directions that require "taxonomic" steps to complete, and then break them down into even easier steps.

4. Using the descriptive statements of the various categories of the *Taxonomy* for the cognitive domain that appear in this chapter, try to form some different categories than the ones offered by Bloom and his colleagues. Is it possible that there are different ways of looking at and classifying knowledge?

REFERENCES

Bloom, Benjamin S. et al. 1956. *Taxonomy of Educational Objectives: The Classification of Educational Goals: Handbook I: Cognitive Domain.* New York: Longman.

Burton, Virginia Lee. 1939. *Mike Mulligan and His Steam Shovel.* Boston: Houghton Mifflin.

Gronlund, Norman E. 1985. *Stating Objectives for Classroom Instruction.* 3rd ed. New York: Macmillan.

Krathwohl, David R. et al. 1964. *Taxonomy of Educational Objectives: The Classification of Educational Goals: Handbook II: Affective Domain.* New York: Longman.

Mager, Robert F. 1984. *Preparing Instructional Objectives.* 3rd ed. Palo Alto, Calif.: Fearon.

Morine-Dershimer G. 1978. "Planning and Classroom Reality: An In-Depth Look." *Educational Research Quarterly,* 3, 83–89.

Preston, Ralph C., and Wayne L. Herman, Jr. 1974. *Teaching Social Studies in the Elementary School.* 3rd ed. New York: Holt, Rinehart, and Winston.

Sawin, Enoch I. 1969. *Evaluation and the Work of the Teacher.* Belmont, Calif.: Wadsworth.

Yinger, R. J. 1979. "Routines in Teacher Planning." *Theory into Practice,* 18, 163–69.

Zahorik, J. A. 1975. "Teacher's Planning Models." *Educational Leadership,* 33, 134–39.

SUGGESTED READINGS

Christopher M. Clark, and Penelope L. Peterson. 1986. "Teachers' Thought Processes." In *Handbook of Research on Teaching,* Merlin C. Wittrock, ed. 3rd ed. pp. 255–96. New York: Macmillan. This chapter summarizes most of the recent research on how teachers plan for and think about teaching.

James E. Davis, and Frances Haley, eds. 1977. *Planning A Social Studies Program: Activities, Guidelines, and Resources.* Boulder, Colo.: ERIC Clearinghouse for Social Studies/Social Science Education/Social Science Education Consortium, Inc. This is an eminently practical guide to developing or modifying a social studies program. It's probably the finest publication of its type that we've seen.

Every social studies methods text deals with planning in one fashion or another. Some that complement your text in this area are listed below:

William Joyce, and Janet Alleman-Brooks. 1979. *Teaching Social Studies in the Elementary and Middle Schools.* New York: Holt, Rinehart and Winston.

Peter H. Martorella. 1985. *Elementary Social Studies.* Boston: Little Brown.

John U. Michaelis, and Haig A. Rushdoony. 1987. *Elementary Social Studies Handbook.* San Diego: Harcourt Brace Jovanovich.

CHAPTER 5

Social Studies Programs: Who Teaches What, When?

"In some areas, textbooks supplement the curriculum; in other areas, they *are* the curriculum."   Robert Zais

KEY QUESTIONS

☐ What is taught when in social studies?

☐ What is the typical pattern for organizing elementary social studies programs?

☐ How important is *sequence* to a social studies program?

KEY IDEAS

☐ For years, the dominant pattern among elementary social studies programs has been the "expanding-environments" approach.

☐ Developmental considerations, including how children develop concepts of time, space, and distance, influence the organization of social studies programs.

INTRODUCTION: Program Planning

Developing a social studies curriculum is much like unit planning but on a *much* larger scale. Many of the activities essential to unit planning, such as identifying goals and specifying objectives, also apply in curriculum development. However, instead of deciding on the sequence of activities within a unit, the concern in program planning shifts to identifying those topics that will be taught in a given year or at a particular grade level, and the sequence in which they will be presented. Of equal concern is how what is taught during one year relates to what was taught the previous year, and with what will be taught the following year. Just as the elements of unit planning—the goals, objectives, teaching activities, and the like—must fit together into a cohesive whole, so too must the elements of curriculum planning fit together into a meaningful social studies experience.

The major focus in this chapter is on social studies programs—how they are organized, and the factors that influence them. Throughout the chapter, you will notice that we use the terms *program* and *curriculum* interchangeably. Authorities sometimes distinguish between the two, with *curriculum* being the broader framework within which teachers develop their own programs. However, in schools you often hear expressions such as "our social studies program" or "our career education program." Those references are usually to an existing curriculum for several grade levels—typically K through 6—that the teachers in a school or district have modified or adapted for their use. Inasmuch as *program* seems to be edging out the more formal *curriculum* in common usage, we have opted to follow that convention in this chapter.

ORGANIZING SOCIAL STUDIES PROGRAMS

The essential aspects of any educational program are captured in four little words: *what, why, when,* and *how.* You could actually add a fifth word, *where,* but that has generally been assumed to be "in school." Teaching is not restricted to classrooms, of course, but there hasn't been a stampede to take advantage of the alternatives.

What should be taught? *Why* should something be taught (and, why should it be taught instead of something else)? *When* (in what sequence) should something be taught? And, *how* (in what manner) should something be taught? These are the four basic questions of curriculum planning. In slightly altered form, they become the following:

1. *Scope*   What segments of the universe of social studies knowledge will be taught? In other words, what should the breadth or *scope* of the subject matter be? On a practical level, the question is one of whether a unit on "farms" or "desert communities," for example, will or will not be included in a social studies program (K–6).

   Questions related to scope must always be considered in relation to the question of *why* (or why not).

2. *Rationale*   Why is something to be included in (or excluded from) a social studies program? The question *why* functions as a request for a rationale—a reasoned and thoughtful statement of justification. When students ask "What do we have to study this stuff for?" they are asking for a justification of why something is worthy of being studied. Because students are so close to the program, they tend to ask the "why" question more often than parents or other individuals further removed from the classroom. Nevertheless,

a rationale is a reasoned statement of justification that should satisfy anyone who asks why something is (or is not) being studied.

Curriculum guides almost always indicate what should be taught, but they seldom indicate why it should be studied. Somewhere along the line, that question was addressed, but the reasons certain content was selected are not often conveyed to teachers. Because of this, teachers may find themselves creating their own rationales after the fact. Whether their justifications resemble the original rationale simply cannot be determined.

3. *Sequence*   After determining which topics should be taught and why, it becomes necessary to determine when—at what time and in what order or *sequence* those topics should be taught. The matter of sequence has two dimensions: (1) determining at which grade level (what time within the total school program) something will be taught and, once that question has been answered, (2) determining when it should be taught within that grade. For example, having decided that a unit on "the farm" should be included in a social studies program, the between-grade question is "At which grade level should it be taught?" The placement of topics or units at certain grade levels can be influenced by many factors, which we will examine shortly.

The within-grade-level question is concerned with the sequence of units within a single grade level. For example, having decided that Greece, Rome, and ancient Egypt should be taught at a certain grade level (usually Grade 6), the within-grade sequencing question concerns the *order* in which those topics will be taught. Sometimes the decision is arbitrary, but at other times it may be based on a logical progression, such as from simple to complex. Whenever history is involved, as in this example, the sequence is almost always based on chronology. On that basis, ancient Egypt would be taught first. Which would come next—Greece or Rome?

4. *Synthesis*   This aspect of program planning is concerned with *how* everything will be pulled together into a meaningful whole. To illustrate how important the synthesis dimension can be, consider a social studies program that asks you to teach the following sequence of topics to a third-grade class:
a. explorers
b. the history and geography of Australia
c. community helpers
d. transportation
e. the Civil War

If there is something—a theme, an approach, anything—that can pull these topics together so that they make sense, it isn't readily apparent. The list is seemingly a disjointed collection of discrete topics. Whoever determined the scope of that program may have had good reasons for including what they did, but they seem to have some odd ideas about the how and why of sequencing. There probably isn't any one best basis for sequencing social studies programs, but, as should be evident from the example above, the program must be organized around something.

Among the guidelines established by the National Council for the Social Studies are
the principles that the social studies program should deal with the real social world
and that it should be drawn from valid knowledge of human experience and culture.
(© *Jerry Howard 1982/Positive Images*)

From time to time, the National Council for the Social Studies (NCSS) has
identified a set of guidelines for developing social studies programs. Highlights
from the most recent effort are reproduced below.

1. **The social studies program should be directly related to the age, maturity, and concerns of students.**

2. **The social studies program should deal with the real social world.**

3. **The social studies program should draw from currently valid knowledge representative of human experience, culture, and beliefs.**

4. **Objectives should be thoughtfully selected and clearly stated in such form as to furnish direction to the program.**

5. **Learning activities should engage the student directly and actively in the learning process.**

6. **Strategies of instruction and learning activities should rely on a broad range of learning resources.**

7. **The social studies program must facilitate the organization of experience.**

8. **Evaluation should be useful, systematic, comprehensive, and valid for the objectives of the programs.**

9. **Social studies education should receive vigorous support as a vital and responsible part of the school program. (NCSS, 1979, pp. 261–73)**

FIGURE 5.1   Expanding-Environments Approach to Social Studies (K–6)

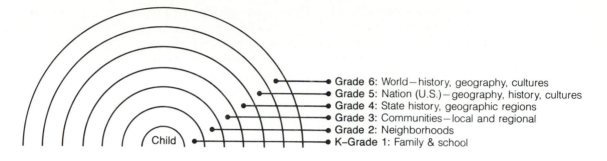

Grade 6: World—history, geography, cultures
Grade 5: Nation (U.S.)—geography, history, cultures
Grade 4: State history, geographic regions
Grade 3: Communities—local and regional
Grade 2: Neighborhoods
K–Grade 1: Family & school

Child

EXPANDING ENVIRONMENTS

Figure 5.1 illustrates an organizational approach to social studies that was created in the mid-1920s, became popular during the 1930s, and continues to dominate elementary social studies programs throughout the country today. You may find occasional variations, to be sure, but the *expanding-environments* approach is virtually a national curriculum (see Superka and Hawke, and Morrissett, 1980). This organizational pattern is sometimes referred to as *expanding horizons, widening horizons,* or *expanding communities of man,* all of which refer to essentially similar programs.

The organizing principle for the expanding-environments approach is a mixture of physical and conceptual *distance.* The sequence of topics begins with environments (or communities) that are closest to the child—the home, school, and neighborhood—and then moves in an apparently logical progression through environments that are successively more distant from the child—the local community, the state (or region), the nation, and finally the world. All of us live in these environments simultaneously, of course, so the assignment of certain environments to certain grade levels is done for instructional purposes.

The expanding-environments pattern for sequencing topics ends at Grade 6; it is strictly an elementary (K–6) program (as its developer, Dr. Paul Hanna, a professor at Stanford University, originally intended). The grade-to-grade sequence in secondary (7–12) social studies programs is also topical, but the basis for sequencing the topics at that level is not readily apparent. For example, seventh graders typically study either world geography or world history, which are extensions of what was studied in Grade 6. In many areas, however, seventh graders study state history, which is an extension of their studies in Grade 4. Eighth graders usually study American history, but without the emphasis on geography that occurred in Grade 5.

Virtually every elementary social studies textbook series currently being published follows the expanding-environments pattern. Our experience with several major textbook publishers indicates that although they readily acknowledge the existence of other organizational patterns that *might* prove educationally and financially successful, the publishers are unwilling to abandon the dominant pattern. Indeed, with development costs for a social studies textbook series easily exceeding $5 million, significant deviations from the expanding-environments pattern would necessarily expose publishers to considerable financial risk. The situation is further complicated by the fact that some states—such as California, Texas, and about a dozen others—adopt textbooks on a statewide basis. Trying to convince a state textbook committee that it should adopt a textbook series that takes a "deviant" or untried approach to social studies can be challenging, and can elicit examples of the "Joan of Arc" syndrome from even the most liberal committee members.

Despite its popularity, the expanding-environments approach is not without some problems. For example, we know that most kindergarten and first-grade children are not aware of, much less do they understand, the overall sequence of environments that they will study over the next six years. They do not concern themselves with the "whole," with how one topic relates to the other topics they study; their concern is with the "parts," with what they are studying today. At the other end of the program, it is not clear whether sixth graders understand the organizational pattern of social studies that they have been exposed to for six years. But perhaps children do not need to understand the overall pattern of what they study; that's a question researchers have yet to investigate. Nevertheless, in the next section we examine some factors that may influence how students view both the expanding-environments and other types of social studies programs they might experience.

Expanding Environments Reconsidered

The idea that children should study nearby environments before they study more distant environments seems to make eminent sense. In other words, the logic of the expanding-environments sequence is readily apparent to most adults. Through an adult's eyes, each environment seems to be built upon the previously studied environment. Children, however, do not view their world through an adult's eyes. What seems so logical to adults may be totally lost upon children for whom tomorrow is the immediate future and next week is "way off" in the distant future. Most first graders, for example, haven't the slightest interest in what they will be studying in fifth or sixth grade or, for that matter, in what they will be studying next month. Whether these students *should* be concerned with what they will study in the future is not the issue here; their concern *is* with the present, and not with something they may need next month or next year.

The expanding-environments pattern seems to reflect the educational principle of "beginning with the concrete and moving to the abstract." The fact that families (Grade 1) and neighborhoods (Grade 2) are more concrete for most children than states (Grade 4) or the nation (Grade 5) is certainly true. However, take note of what happens between Grades 3 and 4. In third grade, when children study their community, they are learning about something fairly concrete, something most children have experienced simply by having lived in a community. By looking out the classroom window, they can see at least a portion of the reality they are studying. When they study "the state" in fourth grade, however, children move to something that often is not part of their view of the world. Despite the fact that states have physical dimensions—such as boundaries, a capitol, etc.—the state is actually a phenomenon of political organization. It is lines on a map—lines that can't be seen anywhere except on a map.

Even though the state is a smaller, less distant environment than the nation (which children will study in fifth grade), and while children may indeed live in "the state," these factors do not make it any less an abstraction. Likewise, fifth-grade children cannot "see" the United States, except by looking at a map that is itself an abstracted representation of our country. Neither can we expect that world history or the geography of the Eastern Hemisphere will be any closer to a sixth grader's view of reality. The point here is that abstraction is determined by conceptual distance—the extent to which a phenomenon is within or beyond a child's realm of experience—not physical distance. From this perspective, the expanding-environments approach is not so much a logical progression from concrete to abstract as a confusing "quantum leap" that occurs after third grade.

The expanding-environments sequence is based primarily on physical distance; each environment is farther removed from the child. In this age of modern communication, however, children are likely to have seen pictures of Rome, Italy, or Athens, Greece, on television. Although children may regard them as "cities somewhere else," they probably have had more experience with them than, say, Rome, New York, or Athens, Ohio (except, of course, if they've visited the latter places). To put it in slightly different terms, Rome, New York or Athens, Ohio may be more abstract for children who have not been there, than either Rome, Italy or Athens, Greece.

We are suggesting that the sequence in which children study different environments is neither as rigid nor as important as it might seem. It is not necessary, for example, that primary-level children study their families (or *the* family) before studying the (their) neighborhood. Neither is it necessary for children to study the American family prior to studying Russian families, simply because Russian families are more physically distant. Rather, if the family is the focus of study, an appropriate way to study it is by examining various families both in the neighborhood and in other nations.

We have several motives for challenging the expanding-environments pattern. First, as we noted in Chapter 2, social studies is a synthetic discipline that lacks the preestablished structure found in subjects such as mathematics. Yet the expanding-environments pattern imposes a math-like sequence that makes it appear as if social studies is an analytic discipline (based on prerequisite learning). Such a sequence ignores the very nature of social studies. (We also suggest that teachers who insist on following a rigid sequence in social studies may be fulfilling their own need for organization rather than something that stems from the children as learners.)

Our second motive is to indicate that although most textbook series follow the expanding-environments pattern, teachers occasionally find deviations they have difficulty explaining. For example, a popular textbook for fourth grade deals with regions of the United States. Within each unit, however, there is a chapter that deals with a foreign region or nation. The "mountain regions" unit, for example, focuses on Colorado, but includes a chapter on Switzerland—a chapter that doesn't seem to "fit" the expanding-environments pattern. Some teachers skip those seemingly alien chapters, but they are included so the children can compare and contrast life in the regions in the United States with similar regions elsewhere.

The expanding-environments pattern is one of many ways in which social studies can be organized and sequenced. We examine some of the other possibilities later in this chapter, but because the expanding-environments pattern is so dominant, most of the balance of this book is geared to it.

DEVELOPMENTAL CONSIDERATIONS

Pressure to Perform

Most historians agree that childhood is a luxury—indeed, a healthy luxury—that less advanced societies are sometimes unable to afford. All humans go through a period of infancy, childhood, and adolescence, of course, but children in less advanced societies are sometimes unable to experience the freedom and the absence of responsibility that we typically associate with childhood. In less advanced societies, the family's survival may hinge on treating children as "miniature adults." This phenomenon is not limited to less advanced societies, however. The survival of some families in America, including the families of migrant farm workers, demands that children work alongside their parents in the fields. In those families, childhood is something children squeeze in whenever they can, whenever they are free from other more pressing responsibilities.

In *The Hurried Child,* David Elkind (1982) argues that children from middle- and upper-class families in this country are being pressured to adopt the trappings of adulthood before they are either prepared to or need to deal with them. Such children, Elkind claims, are often dressed in miniature adult costumes (many with designer labels), are expected to cope with a bewildering array of behaviors (e.g., the violence and sex they see on television), and are judged by how early and how quickly they can acquire academic skills in school. Such expectations, combined with a tendency to treat children as miniature adults, have, Elkind suggests, created unnecessary levels of stress among many children.

The pressures that schools place on children may have unwittingly been increased by two apparently unrelated phenomena: (1) the flurry of reports, such as *A Nation at Risk* (Gardner, 1983) that severely criticized the state of American education and (2) some relatively recent studies that are commonly referred to as "effective teaching" research.

Schools have always taught the work ethic—that work is good and that "idle hands are the devil's playground"—but the spate of critical reports suggested that there was too much wasted time in schools and that children (and teachers) were not producing or working hard enough. The essential recommendation was that "teachers need to become more effective, and children needed to work harder in school."

Time on Task

At roughly the same time that schools were being criticized for their lack of productivity, the findings from earlier research on learning and academic achievement conducted by Rosenshine (1979) and others (e.g., Rosenshine and Berliner, 1978) were receiving widespread attention. The researchers had found that student achievement was related, in part, to the amount of time they were actively engaged in learning tasks. Although these findings are hardly earthshaking, the way they were misinterpreted in some schools is almost beyond comprehension.

In their quest to improve academic achievement, some schools began to define "time on task" (and in some instances, "good teaching") in terms of the amount of time children had their noses stuck in a book or had pencils in their hands. For example, we have visited elementary schools where recess and breaks have been eliminated (or where teachers get a morning break but students don't); where students are permitted twenty-seven minutes of "free time" for lunch; and where, as we entered classrooms, the teacher would say "I'm sorry, I'm giving the children some free time." We also visited schools where students were copying pages from the glossary at the end of the textbook or, if they erred in answering the questions at the end of a chapter, they had to recopy the entire page. Such activities were conducted under the auspices of "time on task," which had become a sword held over the heads of teachers and students alike. In some instances, children had less free time during the school day than did adults working on an assembly line. The most unfortunate dimension of this situation was the singular focus on time and the almost total disregard for a second component of the time-on-task research; that is, the *quality* of the task itself. In other words, *what* children spend their time doing is at least as important as *how long* they work at a particular task.

In the 1980s, some elementary and middle schools have become high-pressure, learning factories where, if students are not visibly working, something is "wrong." These are often environments in which "quality" or "excellence" is sought by having students learn materials at ever-earlier ages—where most second graders, for example, are expected to read at a third-grade level or higher, and where second graders who actually read at the second-grade level are thought of as "average" (as if being average were a problem). We are committed to excellence in American education, indeed we applaud intelligent efforts toward that end. However, we have problems with those who look for simplistic solutions to complex problems, and who, in their efforts to hurry children along, seemingly ignore the developmental considerations that affect how children learn.

Time

Have you noticed that your birthdays seem to come around faster than they did when you were younger? Do you remember the day of Halloween or Christmas Eve when it seemed as if it would never get dark? Childhood is a period when time seems to creep along. Time hasn't speeded up in the intervening years, of course, but the way we perceive time has certainly changed.

It isn't entirely clear how children develop a sense of time. Apparently the ability to deal with time, especially historical time, develops so gradually that children are quite unaware of what is taking place. The evidence suggests that very young children begin to perceive their world in terms of polar opposites such as "hot-cold," "now-then," "good-bad," etc. (Levi-Strauss, 1966, and Egan, 1979). At first, things are either "hot" or "cold." As children gain experience, they seem to gradually differentiate and refine the opposites in order to form a continuum. They learn that "warm" lies somewhere between "hot" and "cold," and that *very* hot" and *very* cold" become new ways for expressing the extremes of temperature.

In much the same way, conceptions of time apparently develop from an initial "now-then" orientation to the world. "Now" is the easier for children to deal with, because it refers to the present moment. "Then" usually refers to anything not happening "now," and thus includes both past and future. If lumping the past and future together seems illogical to us as adults, it also serves to illustrate that logic itself is a learned behavior.

In the child's world of "here and now"—a world in which time just creeps along—it seems to take considerable experience for the child to differentiate between "then-future" and "then-past." Logic suggests that conceptions of "the past" should be easier for children to deal with because their past is made up of events the child has already experienced. "The future," on the other hand, hasn't happened yet and is further removed from present reality and, hence, more abstract. Logical or not, both "past" and "future" are difficult concepts for young children.

By the time children enter elementary school, they have a fairly secure conception of "yesterday." However, something that happened to them two years ago is thought of as happening "a long time ago"—somewhere in a distant, undifferentiated past. But then, events that occurred two weeks ago or two months previous are *also* regarded as having taken place "a long time ago."

The fact that young children cannot differentiate the time span of events in the past does *not* mean they have forgotten what happened. Children can often describe events—vacations, birthday parties, and other experiences—in amazing, even excruciating, detail. Although they can tell you what happened, they typically cannot provide an accurate time frame for when those events took place.

At about age ten or eleven, children seem to have developed a sense of time

(Source: Charles M. Schulz, © 1956. United Features Syndicate. All Rights Reserved.)

that permits them to feel some awareness (but not necessarily a complete understanding) of the historical past. Until that time, teaching about something that happened two centuries ago, for example, may be as frustrating as teaching the concept of "snow" to someone from Jamaica. This does *not* mean that history must be totally ignored, however. Young children can often relate vicariously to the individuals and events of history, particularly if they are presented in story form (in image-of-greatness fashion). Emphasizing historical time frames, however, could go over their heads.

The way children develop a conception of the future seems to be similar to how they develop notions of the past. Just as past events may be regarded as "a long time ago," young children tend to view events that are two weeks or two months away as being somewhere in the distant future. Because of this, primary teachers learn *not* to respond to a child's request for help with "I'll be there in a minute." From a child's perspective, a minute is an eternity. Ten seconds or so later, the student will probably be back asking, "Will you help me now?" From that student's perspective, the minute has passed. Such situations can be avoided (although this is no guarantee) if the teacher avoids potentially confusing time referents and says, instead, "I'll be with you as soon as I can."

Space/Distance

Children's conceptions of space—how they fit into their environment—and distance (physical remoteness) seem to develop in the same way as their conception of time. Initially, distance is measured by the number of *fars* they attach to *away*. As any young child can tell you, "far, far away" is much farther than plain old "far away."

Eventually children's conceptions of time and space do indeed develop. In some instances, it may be possible to speed up the children's acquisition of time concepts, but the question is, should we bother? Sooner or later children gain the experiences that enable them to develop concepts of time, space, and distance; it's something all of us do—simply through the process of living. Like David Elkind, we feel that pressures within the society make children grow up fast enough, and that attempting to speed up a process that will occur normally is not a particularly good investment of a teacher's time. Instead of trying to hasten the way children perceive time, we feel that educationally valuable things can be achieved that do not require children to alter the way they view their world.

Intellectual Development

How children develop conceptions of time and space appear to be closely related to their overall intellectual development.

Some of the most substantive research on the development of children's thinking was conducted by the late Swiss psychologist Jean Piaget. Piaget's early interest was in zoology, particularly snails, clams, and other mollusks, but he shifted to children after he began working with Alfred Binet, the developer of the first intelligence tests. Binet wanted to determine how children of various ages responded to the questions on his test, and he hired Piaget to do the research. Piaget's early training in zoology led him to adopt the distinctive research method—observing children in natural settings—that marks his research.

After working with several hundred children, Piaget observed that children at certain age levels would consistently use quite different reasons to justify their answers. Four-year-olds would respond quite differently from eight-year-olds, whose answers would be different still from responses provided by teenagers. When children between the ages of two and seven were provided with three objects of different shapes labeled "A," "B," and "C," those children could almost always point out which object was the tallest. But when confronted with a hypothetical proposition such as "If A is bigger than B but smaller than C," those children could almost never tell which item was the largest. In fact, Piaget found that children could not deal with such a problem until about age eleven. Actually, their responses were so consistent that Piaget was able to predict how children of certain ages would respond to specific questions. From these observations, Piaget developed his basic theory of how children's thinking develops.

Piaget identified four developmental stages that all children progress through as they mature. These stages are illustrated in Table 5.1. Piaget also determined that all children pass through each of the four stages in order—from sensorimotor to preoperational to concrete operations to formal operations—with each stage serving as a basis for the next. There is nothing hard and fast about the age range for a particular stage; the onset of each stage is age-related, but not

TABLE 5.1   Stages of Cognitive Development as Described by Piaget

Stage and Age Range	Description
Sensorimotor (Birth to 2 years)	Children learn what things are like through their senses, through what they touch, feel, taste, smell, and manipulate. If they can't see, feel, or touch an object, they believe it doesn't exist.
Preoperational (2–7 years)	Children in this stage gradually acquire the ability to think of more than one thing at a time (decenter). They also begin to master symbols that permit mental manipulation. However, reasoning is still dominated by perception. For example, children in this stage will maintain that a tall, thin tumbler holds more liquid than a short, fat glass even if shown that they hold the same amount. Language is egocentric; words have unique meanings, which limit children's ability to consider others' points of view.
Concrete Operations (7–11 years)	Children are able to decenter, conserve (understand that two differently shaped objects may have the same volume), and reverse (understand that a ball of clay that's been rolled into a long snake, for example, can be reformed into the original ball). Such thinking is limited to concrete objects, however, with little or no ability to generalize beyond them.
Formal Operations (11 years and older)	Children are able to consider the hypothetical, things that don't exist except as mental abstractions. They also become increasingly capable of dealing with propositional thinking and of developing hypotheses.

age-determined. Children tend to move from stage to stage in a gradual progression that is unique to each child. However, unlike Bloom's cognitive *Taxonomy*, Piaget's stages are a true linear sequence; children never skip a stage.

Implications

To the extent that space (geographical place) and historical time involve the ability to deal with abstractions, Piaget's research suggests that most children are able to comprehend these concepts at about fifth or sixth grade—age ten or eleven. But for the majority of their years in elementary school, children function at the concrete-operational level. Likewise, the majority of primary-age children probably operate at the preoperational level.

The National Council for the Social Studies captured the implications of this situation when it stated

> **. . . The social studies curriculum should *not* move sequentially from topics that are near at hand to those that are far away for the purposes of expanding the environment. The purpose of extending content outward, away from a self-centric focus, is to illustrate how people and places**

interact; how people of different areas depend on each other; how people are part of interlocking networks that sustain life in modern societies; and how people and places everywhere fit into a global community. . . .

Most important to sequence is not the "what" but the "how" of teaching. Developmental research suggests that as children's capabilities develop, particular types of learning activities are most suitable. For example, young children learn best through concrete experience, manipulation of materials, and observation of their environment. Similarly, perspective-taking abilities can be developed in middle childhood (after around age ten) through practice. . . . [I]deas should initially be introduced to young children as concrete and simple. Then they should be continually reinforced and applied—extending, expanding, and illuminating in more depth, taking advantage of the student's development. (NCSS, 1984, pp. 252–53)

Individuals who regard children as "miniature adults"—and there are more of them than you might suspect—tend to ignore the developmental considerations that should influence the design of educational programs. These people often argue that most programs are too babyish—too simplistic. Despite those claims, we must be careful that we do not provide social studies programs which make sense to us as adults, but which impose intellectual demands on children that go beyond their abilities. Eventually, children must (and will) be able to look at the world from an adult perspective. However, by attempting to force this perspective too soon, we risk winning the battle and losing the war—and producing children who hate social studies (or school) in the process.

ORGANIZATIONAL PATTERNS AND THEMES

In this section, we take a detailed look at the expanding-environments approach to social studies, which is the organizational pattern you are most likely to encounter. We then examine several alternatives to the dominant theme, elements of which may appear in some programs.

THE DOMINANT THEME

The expanding-environments pattern, which we discussed briefly at the beginning of this chapter, is so dominant that it is virtually a national social studies curriculum. Countless studies (e.g., Lengel and Superka, 1982) have also shown that social studies textbooks, virtually all of which follow the expanding-environments pattern, continue to be the dominant instructional resource that teachers employ.

At one time, many school districts created their own social studies programs and then sought textbooks that met their needs. Some schools still do this, but developing such programs has become increasingly costly, in part because basic curriculum-development activities are typically seen as beyond a teacher's daily responsibilities. Many curriculum-development activities today are conducted by groups of teachers hired for extra pay during the summer. The cost of program development, the growing number of state mandates, and several other factors that we note in the next section have combined to create a situation where it is often easier and less expensive (and sometimes more politically expedient) to make textbooks the basis for a social studies program.

Basing social studies programs on a textbook series may be a lesser evil, but it does not ensure a consistent, integrated program. Recent studies (e.g., Woodward, Elliot, and Nagel, 1986) suggest that current social studies textbook series are collections of loosely related volumes. There is no assurance that a fifth-grade textbook, for example, will necessarily complement its fourth- or sixth-grade companion text. Despite these shortcomings, the nature of the social studies programs in many areas is determined by textbooks.

The composite social studies program illustrated in Table 5.2 is based on five social studies textbook series. It shows the common topics, the typical sequence of units, and social science discipline(s) emphasized within the units. At the lower grade levels especially, the units are truly composite; that is, the various disciplines are integrated throughout. Because no single discipline is emphasized in those instances, we have indicated either "None" or "None/Integrated," whichever was most appropriate. Trends and occasional exceptions for each grade level are noted below.

Kindergarten Most kindergarten programs are designed to familiarize children with their developing selves and their new environment, the school. Because most kindergarten children cannot read, the texts necessarily rely heavily on pictures and photographs. Sometimes a teaching kit, containing pictures, cards, and other resources, is used in place of a text as such. No particular social science discipline predominates, and there is no particular logic for the sequence of topics. Note that the "Special Days" unit is listed last in Kindergarten (and Grades 1 and 2), but teachers almost always draw on it from time to time throughout the year.

Grade 1 First-grade social studies programs focus on elements in the local area: the family, the school, the neighborhood, etc. The social science disciplines are treated in an integrated fashion, although consumer economics gets somewhat more attention than the others. Note the continuing emphasis on holidays.

Grade 2 Although second-grade programs traditionally focus on neighborhoods, this is often broadened to a community focus. This shift is, in part, a reflection of ways in which neighborhoods have changed. Fifty years ago, many of a neighborhood's residents were of similar ethnic origin, and neighborhoods themselves were characterized by stable populations and well-established social and economic systems. When a family moved into (or out of) the neighborhood, it was a major event. In the last half of the 20th century, however, our highly mobile population has destroyed much of the stability that neighborhoods once enjoyed so that, in many areas today, a neighborhood is simply a place where one lives.

TABLE 5.2 Composite Social Studies Curriculum (K–6)

Grade Level	Focus/Title	Typical Sequence Unit Topics	Dominant Discipline
K	*Getting Started*	Learning About My World	None—the social science disciplines are integrated throughout all units.
		Families	
		Community Helpers	
		Transportation and Communication	
		From Farm to Table	
		Weather and Seasons	(Science)
		Special Days	None
One	*Families, Homes and Neighborhoods*	Our Earth	Geography/Map skills
		Families Meet Their Needs: Food, Clothing, Shelter	None—the social science disciplines are integrated throughout all units.
		Families at Work	
		The Neighborhood	
		Schools: Places Where We Learn	
		Farms and Factories	None/Integrated
		The Shopping Center	None/Integrated
		Holidays Around the World	None
Two	*Neighborhoods and Communities*	Exploring Our Earth	Geography/Map skills
		Living and Working in Communities	None—the social science disciplines are integrated throughout all units.
		Urban, Suburban, and Farm Communities	
		Communities—Today and Yesterday	
		Living in Our Country	None/Integrated
		Transportation and Communication	None/Integrated
		Communities Celebrate Holidays	None
Three	*Communities and Resources, Here and There*	Map and Globe Skills	Geography/Map skills
		Living in Different Communities	None/Integrated
		Governing Communities: Making Rules and Laws	Political Science
		Building Cities	None/Integrated
		Small Communities	None/Integrated
		How Communities Change	None/Integrated
		Farm and Ranch Communities (Dairy Farm, Wheat Farm, etc.)	None/Integrated
		Communities Around the World (Desert, Forest, Grassland)	Geography/History
		Working Together	Economics
Four	*Regions Near and Far*	Our Earth	Geography/Map skills
		Regional Studies Emphasis: Units on Forest Regions: e.g., The Pacific Northwest	Geography

Grade Level	Focus/Title	Typical Sequence Unit Topics	Dominant Discipline
		Plains Regions: e.g., The Central Plains	
		Mountain Regions: e.g., The Rocky Mountains, Switzerland	
		Desert Regions: e.g., The Southwest, etc.	
		Working Together Around the World	Economics
		State History Emphasis:	
		Major Resources and Landforms	Geography
		Early Settlements	History
		Governing Our State	Political Science
		Citizens Who Helped Our State Grow	History
		Our State Today	None/Integrated
Five	*Our United States*	Map and Globe Skills	Geography/Map skills
		Founding the New World	History
		The American Colonies	History
		Building a Nation (through Revolutionary War)	History
		Establishing a Government	History/Political Science
		A Divided Nation (Civil War)	History
		Our Nation Expands (Westward Movement)	History
		Age of Inventions	History
		Our Nation Today	History
		Regional Geography of the United States: Units on New England, the Middle Atlantic States, the Southeast States, the Central States, the Mountain States, the Pacific States	Geography
		Canada and Latin America	Geography/History
Six	*Our World Today*	Map, Globe, and Graph Skills	Geography
		World History Emphasis:	
		Classical Civilizations: Egypt, Greece, Rome	History
		The Middle Ages	History
		Our Changing World (Industrial Revolution through Twentieth Century)	History
		Eastern Hemisphere Emphasis:	
		Our World Today: Units on Western Europe, Eastern Europe, the Soviet Union, North Africa and the Middle East, Africa South of the Sahara, Asia, Australia, and the South Pacific	Geography and history throughout all units.
		Western Hemisphere Emphasis:	
		Early Beginnings: Inca, Aztecs	
		Our Neighbors to the South: Units on Mexico, South American nations, Central American nations, the Caribbean Basin	History and geography are integrated throughout all units.
		Our Neighbors to the North: Units on the St. Lawrence Seaway, the Prairie Provinces, etc.	Geography and history throughout all units.

The focus in second-grade programs is on examining different kinds of neighborhoods/communities—rural, urban, and suburban. Identifying connections between the students' local community and communities elsewhere in the nation or world is often the focus of the last unit.

Grade 3   After an obligatory first unit on maps and globes, the emphasis in third-grade programs turns to communities in a generic sense of the term. The initial focus on communities in different environments typically shifts to an emphasis on political, economic, and social aspects of community life. Selected cities, both contemporary and historic (e.g., Washington, D.C., Tenochtitlan), are often presented as case studies. At some point in the year, at least one unit on the local community is common.

Grade 4   Nationally, social studies programs focus on geographic regions of the United States. Regions in this country are usually compared with similar regions elsewhere in the world. Geography, and especially the subdiscipline economic geography, tend to be the dominant social science disciplines, but history and economics are also prominent.

In many states, the regional focus is either supplemented or replaced entirely by a state history/geography emphasis. Because most textbook series are distributed nationally, and thus do not treat individual state histories, schools that follow the state-history emphasis must turn to materials published by local or regional publishers.

Grade 5   The historical emphasis of fifth-grade programs is clearly evident in Table 5.2. The geographical emphasis in Grade 5 depends in part on the program for Grade 4. In areas where state history is emphasized in Grade 4, a regional-geography emphasis is usually incorporated into Grade 5. However, if regional geography is treated in Grade 4, the historical emphasis becomes the focus in Grade 5.

Grade 6   The scope of sixth-grade programs is exceedingly broad. Of the three emphases shown in Table 5.2, a relatively common pattern is to devote the first semester to the world-history emphasis, and the second semester to a study of the history and geography of nations in the Eastern hemisphere. In a typical ninety-day semester, it is impossible to do justice to world history, much less the history and geography of nations of the Eastern hemisphere. Even if sixth-grade teachers practice selective neglect and postholing (as described in Chapter 1), they can easily find themselves in a race to cover topics before the school year ends.

Variations in sixth-grade programs usually hinge on the nature of the program for Grade 7. Where world history or world geography are taught in Grade 7, those emphases *may* be reduced or eliminated in Grade 6. In those cases, the sixth-grade program often follows the Western hemisphere emphasis. However, when state history is taught in Grade 7, the world history/Eastern hemisphere program is typically taught.

Grades 7 and 8   Although Grades 7 and 8 were not illustrated in Table 5.2, we summarize them briefly here because they may have an impact on the elementary program, as we described above.

There is more variability at Grade 7 than at any other level. State history, for example, is sometimes taught as a one-semester course. The other semester may be devoted to an anthropological study of world cultures, or world geography or world history. In year-long courses, any of these topics may be the focus.

In Grade 8, the study of American history is almost universal. The only significant deviation at this level occurs when American history is treated over a two-year period. In those instances, the eighth-grade program may focus on American History through 1877 (or some other convenient date), and the "second half" is treated at another grade level (usually Grade 9 or 11).

Program Components

This section is a summary of selected components and features from all levels of the composite program illustrated in Table 5.2. They are as follows:

1. *Large increases in the grade-to-grade scope of the program*   Primary-level social studies programs have sometimes been faulted for dealing with a limited range of material. At the same time, the intermediate-grades (4–6) program can be faulted because the scope is so broad. The scope at Grade 6 is often so massive that it easily exceeds the scope (although not the depth) of many high school and college courses.

2. *A first unit on map and globe skills at most grade levels*   Map and globe skills are vital components of social studies programs. However, when they are presented in isolation, map and globe skills are abstract and, quite frankly, dull. Rather than being taught as a separate unit at the beginning of the year, we strongly recommend that map and globe skills be integrated into lessons taught throughout the year, primarily in contexts where those skills provide information that children can use.

3. *An emphasis on developing a global view*   This emphasis is not readily apparent from the list of topics, but is reflected by the number of units that have an "our world" perspective in their titles. The idea here is that children should understand that many problems—such as providing food and shelter, and maintaining world peace—are common to people around the globe. We deal with global education as a theme in Chapter 6.

4. *The continuing presence of the "holiday" curriculum*   This element is easy to overlook because it is often presented as a single unit (and stated last in the Kindergarten and Grade 1 programs). Nevertheless, much of the primary (K–3) curriculum is devoted to observing and celebrating the holidays and festivals that occur throughout the year. This long-standing practice has added life and color to classrooms for many years, and has been the reason for holding countless parties. However, the holiday curriculum sometimes gets so much emphasis that it overwhelms everything else.

In the next section, we examine alternative approaches to elementary social studies.

VARIATIONS ON A THEME

The popularity of the expanding-environments approach has not stopped various groups and individuals from proposing alternative elementary programs. One such proposal developed by the NCSS Task Force on Scope and Sequence (1984) is shown in Table 5.3.

The NCSS alternative is not a radical departure from the existing program shown earlier in Table 5.2. Indeed, although it claims different motives (see statement on pages 169–170), the proposal closely resembles the expanding-environment pattern.

Whether the NCSS proposal has any chance of being accepted is difficult to determine because it really isn't clear who does the "accepting." Aside from legally authorized agencies (school boards, etc.), there is no organized group that dictates what the social studies will or will not be. In addition, and no matter how persuasive the arguments for a change might be, powerful forces tend to maintain the status quo. It is appropriate to pause briefly to examine some of the factors that limit curricular change and innovation in social studies.

TABLE 5.3 A Proposed Social Studies Program (NCSS)

Grade Level	Content
Kindergarten	Awareness of Self in a Social Setting Socialization experiences to bridge home life with life in schools
Grade 1	The Individual in Primary Social Groups: Understanding School and Family Life Specialized roles, family structure, interdependence, the need for rules and laws
Grade 2	Meeting Basic Needs in Nearby Social Groups: The Neighborhood Social functions including education, production, consumption, communication, and transportation within a neighborhood context
Grade 3	Sharing Earth Space with Others: The Community Same social functions of Grade 2 except in the context of the community in a global setting
Grade 4	Human Life in Varied Environments: The Region Geographic and cultural regions; the state as a political region, as may be required
Grade 5	People of the Americas: The United States and Its Close Neighbors Emphasis on the development of the United States; core values; significant individuals; history and geography of Canada and Mexico
Grade 6	People and Cultures: The Eastern Hemisphere Major geographical regions, historic and economic development, political and value systems

Forces That Inhibit Innovation

Availability of Materials   Teachers are often encouraged to alter or even delete entire lessons or units in day-to-day instruction with their children. When it comes to making changes at the program level, however, even seemingly minor variations can lead to major problems. For example, when Texas instituted its educational reforms in the early 1980s, the fourth-grade program was changed to a year-long study of state history. Most of the commercially available materials emphasized the regions of the United States and did not provide sufficient state-history content for an entire year. Until local and regional publishers stepped in to fill the need, the *availability of materials* posed a major problem.

Cost   During the fourth-grade crisis referred to above, many teachers and some school systems exercised the obvious option; they adapted and developed their own teaching materials. Some teachers used computerized word-processing equipment, but even on a small scale the expense was considerable. Local publishers produced materials that could meet the demand, but these had to be paid for from local school budgets, not from state-adopted textbook funds. Again, cost became a factor. The Texas market for educational materials is so large that some of the national publishers will produce special Texas editions of their fourth-grade materials. If such a program change had been proposed by the Muleshoe Local School District—with its population of sixty-four fourth graders— it's doubtful the commercial publishers would have been quite so eager.

Tradition   What we have referred to as the Joan of Arc syndrome plays a role in inhibiting curriculum change. Just as parents expect that certain things will be taught at certain grade levels, teachers also develop an affinity for certain topics or units. When teachers enjoy teaching something, and when they do an effective job, the question is "Should they be forced to change?"

State or Local Mandates   Virtually all of the essential elements and core-curriculum mandates that we referred to earlier are keyed to the expanding-environments organizational pattern. In addition to those statewide requirements, a growing number of school districts have established *competency testing* require-ments that students must pass before they can proceed to higher grade levels. The tests, like the state mandates, are typically geared to the expanding-environments approach.

Standardized Achievement Tests   Students in districts that do not have state or local mandates are typically required to take standardized examinations at specified intervals. Most tests of this nature use the expanding-environments pattern as the basis against which progress is measured.

Although achievement tests supposedly measure students' performance *after* something has been studied, they also identify what students are expected to know. Instead of testing what has been taught, some teachers invariably find themselves teaching what will be tested. When this is combined with the fact that students' achievement-test results are sometimes used as a measure of teaching quality—which is theoretically inappropriate but not all that uncommon—the mandated tests can pose a potent inhibiting factor.

Taken individually, there are options for dealing with most of the factors that inhibit program innovation. It should be apparent, however, that even minor changes in a social studies program necessitate a number of other changes. When taken collectively, we sometimes wonder how teachers and other curriculum developers have accomplished as much as they have.

VARIATIONS ON DIFFERENT THEMES

In this section, we examine three elements which, when incorporated into a social studies program, have produced something quite different from the programs we have dealt with thus far. Those elements are (1) the use of content as a vehicle (which we examined in the context of planning), (2) the nature of spiral curricula, and (3) concept-based approaches to social studies.

Content Utilization—Contrast

Consider the following statement:

The Eskimos have over thirty words for snow.

On face value, this statement could be simply another piece of factual trivia. Or you could conclude that snow must be very important to Eskimos; otherwise, they would not bother to describe it so precisely. Consider, then, another statement:

The Arabs have over forty words for camel.

More trivia? Apparently camels are to Arabs as snow is to Eskimos—important. The point here relates not to what these statements indicate about either the Eskimos or the Arabs, but to what these statements tell us about ourselves and our language. Despite the fact that language is an intimate part of our daily lives, most of us are quite unaware of its characteristics and limitations—as reflected by the fact that we have so few ways to talk about snow or camels. On the other hand, of course, we may not need to talk about snow or camels any more precisely than we already do. Nevertheless, the information that the two statements convey can provide a new awareness of Eskimos, Arabs, *and ourselves.*

We are dealing with a kind of anomaly here: things that we are extremely close to—such as our family, our language, or ourselves—are more difficult to study than things that are more distant from us. Our families, for example, are so much a part of our everyday lives that we tend to take them for granted. We have a vast body of feelings and information about families in general and our own family in particular—about what they are and what they should do. By virtue of our upbringing and our prior cultural experiences (enculturation), most of us (including children) have developed perceptual blinders that keep us from thinking about families objectively. The same is true of our language. In fact, individuals who study foreign languages often find they learn a great deal about their native language—and especially its grammar—from such studies. Unfortunately, some individuals regard our inability to describe snow as precisely as the Eskimos as a criticism (of our language or culture, or both) when it is, in fact, nothing more than a descriptive statement. At the same time, most of us are unaware of things we can describe with a precision that rivals the Eskimo's description of snow or the Arab's description of camels. In most instances, however, those things are so much a part of our culture that we just don't think about them. Consider, for example, that to Peruvians in the remote reaches of the Andes, a car is just that—a car. Most of us, on the other hand, are able to describe cars with a precision—Mustangs, Cougars, and a variety of letters such as 280 ZX and 914—that would confound the uninitiated. The point here is that information about (or from) other cultures and languages provides a basis for *contrast* that forces us to relate the unfamiliar with phenomena that we know extremely well.

What does all of this have to do with social studies programs? It should begin to explain why, in their study of families, you may find first graders studying the Japanese family. Consider that most children are quite aware of what families are—or so they like to think. First graders sometimes study the Japanese family *not* because there are things about those families that everyone should know, but because of the contrast with American families that such a study can provide. In other words, first graders can study American families by using the Japanese family as a *vehicle,* in much the same fashion as the canned corn was used as a vehicle in the sample unit on resource utilization.

Man: A Course of Study   An especially effective use of contrast is found in "Man: A Course of Study" (hereafter referred to as MACOS), a fifth- or sixth-grade social studies program used in some schools during the 1970s. The MACOS program was produced during the era of the "new social studies," that is, the federally funded movement during the mid-1960s that (1) led to the development of new teaching materials that used innovative teaching strategies, (2) made greater use of raw social science data and source material, and (3) emphasized some of the so-called neglected disciplines, such as anthropology, economics, sociology, and social psychology. The materials produced were certainly "new" at the time, but the term *new social studies* is still used to describe a movement that took place over two decades ago.

MACOS is organized around three key questions. In adapted form, they are

What is human about human beings?

How did they get that way?

How can they be made more so?

In MACOS, animals are used as a vehicle for learning about human beings. In fact, the entire first semester is based on animal studies—the salmon, Herring gulls, and a fascinating unit on baboons—which are intended to help children identify those qualities that set humans apart from animals. In the second half of MACOS, children engage in a semester-long study of the Netselik Eskimos. The intent, again, is not to have children accumulate factual information about Eskimos, because the Netselik are merely a vehicle for helping children to find out more about our own culture and the things that make us human. For example, the children learn that in the absence of a written language, the Netselik control themselves through an elaborate system of unwritten myths, beliefs, practices, and traditions that are handed down from one generation to the next. This information provides a basis for children to examine our culture to determine which behaviors are governed primarily by written laws and those things that are governed by myth, belief, or tradition. Throughout their study, children actually learn a great deal about the Netselik even though the objective is to learn about human behavior in general.

Once an idea or concept is introduced, it is built upon and expanded throughout the MACOS program. One of the first such ideas is that of "life cycle," the notion that significant events—birth, death, reproduction, etc.—occur in the life of almost every member of a species, human or animal. "Life cycle" is presented first in the introductory lessons, reintroduced and expanded upon as children study the salmon, and then further developed in the study of the Herring gulls, the baboons, and eventually the Netselik. In this process, children discover that although individual lives are certain to end, life itself goes on.

The cue concept *learning* is studied in a similar manner. It is continually expanded and built upon throughout the course in a kind of spiral fashion (see Figure 5.2). In studying the salmon, for example, students find that after the eggs are fertilized, both the male and female salmon die. Of the five to six thousand eggs produced by an adult pair, only two or three offspring are likely to survive

FIGURE 5.2   Development of the Concept *Learning,* Based on Man: A Course of Study

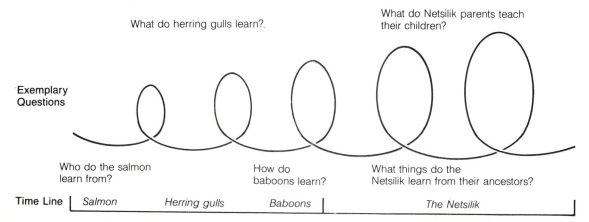

In a spiral curriculum, concepts and generalizations are introduced in simple, concrete terms in the primary grades and then continuously expanded as the children progress from grade to grade. (© *Freda Leinwand/Monkmeyer Press Photo Service*)

until maturity. The purpose of this information is to get children to ponder the questions "If the adult salmon are dead, how do baby salmon learn?" and "Who do they learn from?"

The emphasis in MACOS is on having students raise their own questions. After the learning question is raised from their study of the salmon, for example, students move to a study of Herring gulls. In a film on Herring gull behavior, children find that adult birds do not feed their young until the chicks peck at a small red spot on the side of the adult gull's beak. If the chicks don't peck at the red spot, they starve. The question this leads up to is "How do baby Herring gulls learn to peck at that red spot?" The teacher then provides MACOS student booklets on innate and learned behavior. Afterward, the focus temporarily shifts from learning but returns to it again when students study baboons, and then again as they study the Netselik.

There are two main points here. First, in MACOS, the information about animals and the Netselik is not important in and of itself. Rather, it is used as a vehicle to enable children to say something about the nature of human beings. Second, the study of the unfamiliar can provide the *contrast* necessary for us to examine that which is very familiar.

Spiral Curricula

Simply stated, the basic premise that underlies a spiral curriculum is "Once students learn an idea, let's continue to build upon what they already know by introducing new and different dimensions of the concept, and by expanding their ideas to new situations." The way the cue concept "learning" was treated in MACOS is an example of this approach to instruction.

The idea of helping students apply ideas to new situations is hardly unique. However, the problem students often encounter is that the ideas they learn are left in isolation, and they have nothing to connect them to.

Figure 5.3 shows an example of the spiral development of a generalization as described by Hilda Taba (1967). The essential thing to note about this spiral is that it focuses on the development of generalizations (as opposed to a sequence of expanding environments). For example, the notion that geography and natural resources influence how people live and what they do is first introduced in the primary grades and then expanded upon in different contexts at higher grade levels.

Concepts and generalizations are introduced in simple, concrete terms in the primary grades and then continuously expanded upon as the children progress from grade to grade. The key in that expansion process is not simply to present new applications of the idea, lest the student treat them as totally new ideas. Rather, it is often necessary to help students understand how a new application of the idea is connected to an earlier application.

Concept-based Programs

In traditional, topic-based social studies programs, the major emphasis is on learning information associated with the topic itself. If the topic is China, for example, you would usually study things associated with Chinese agriculture, its climate, its government, its resources, and other aspects of life in that nation. Then, if the next unit were Japan, you would go through the same process again, this time studying Japanese agriculture, Japanese government, and so forth. This situation is illustrated in Figure 5.4.

The premise in a concept-based approach is that it is not necessary to study every country in the world in order to say something about how nations organize their governments, or practice agriculture, or conduct whatever else we might want to examine. It is possible to establish a pattern among nations by study-ing only selected nations, not the entire universe of nations. Figure 5.5 illustrates that we may be able to identify a general pattern in agricultural practices by studying agriculture in China, India, Japan, the Soviet Union, and the United States.

In a topic-to-topic approach, students tend to become so concerned with the "parts"—the climate, the government, the customs, etc.—that they tend not to see the "whole." In a concept-based approach, the focus shifts to "the whole,"

FIGURE 5.3 The Spiral Development of a Generalization

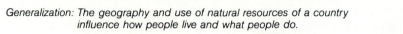

Generalization: The geography and use of natural resources of a country influence how people live and what people do.

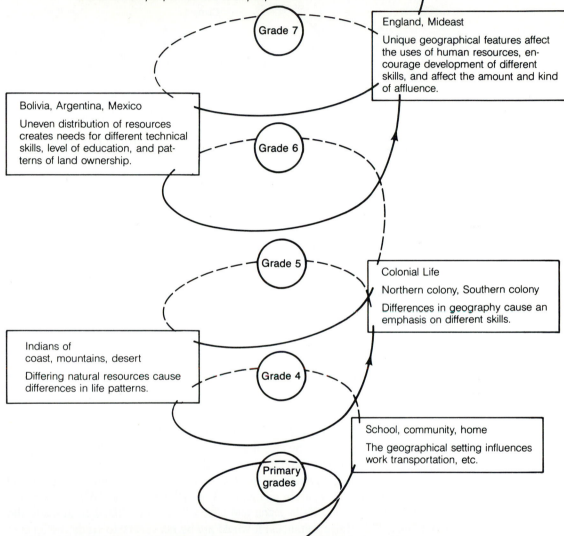

(Source: Hilda Taba: TEACHER'S HANDBOOK FOR ELEMENTARY SOCIAL STUDIES, 1967. With permission of Addison-Wesley Publishing Company.)

and the parts—in this instance, individual nations—become vehicles that enable children to see the whole.

The parts/whole emphasis is illustrated by the kinds of major questions associated with each approach. In a topic-to-topic approach, as illustrated in Figure 5.4, at least seven questions would be generated, all of which would follow the general

FIGURE 5.4   A Traditional, Topic-to-Topic Approach

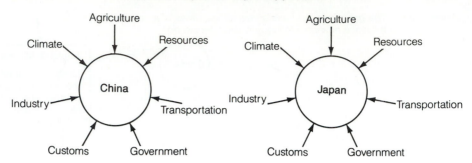

(Source: Adapted from Hilda Taba: TEACHER'S HANDBOOK FOR ELEMENTARY SOCIAL STUDIES, 1967. With permission of Addison-Wesley Publishing Company.)

FIGURE 5.5   A Concept-based (Selected-Dimensions) Approach

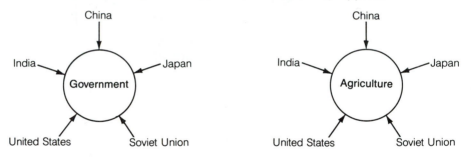

(Source: Adapted from Hilda Taba: TEACHER'S HANDBOOK FOR ELEMENTARY SOCIAL STUDIES, 1967. With permission of Addison-Wesley Publishing Company.)

form of "What is Chinese _____ (agriculture, transportation, etc.) like?" The same questions would then be asked about Japan. The end result—assuming you get answers—would be fourteen or so unrelated pieces of data.

In a concept-based approach, as illustrated in Figure 5.5, the questions would focus on patterns, not separate elements. A question might be "What is common about agricultural practices in Japan and China?" or "the United States and the Soviet Union?" In these instances, it would *not* be necessary to study the form of government in any of the countries unless you suspected that there was something about the government that might influence agricultural practices. Such an examination would have fewer questions, each studied in greater depth.

The customs and rituals of a culture is an area where the topical approach may be more appropriate than a concept-based approach. This is because customs and rituals tend to be unique to a particular culture. In other words, if your interest is in Japanese customs, it will be necessary to study Japan. On the other hand, if you were interested in determining if there were customs common to the nations in

FIGURE 5.6   An Approach to the Concept *Social Control*

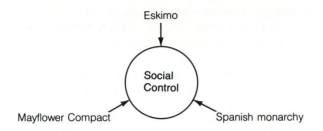

the Far East (which strikes us as a rather interesting question), you would need to study several Far Eastern nations to decide. That question also identifies the kind of information you would be after, which means you would not be particularly interested in data on resources, transportation, and the like.

We suspect that one reason concept-based instruction has not been more successful is that teachers have tended to approach it as if it were a topic-to-topic approach with which they were more familiar. In one concept-based third-grade program, for example, the children study the Spanish monarch, the Mayflower Compact, and the Eskimos. From a traditional perspective, these would be seen as three separate and unrelated topics. However, as Figure 5.6 illustrates, the focus is the cue concept *social control*.

The Mayflower Compact, as you may recall, was produced by the travelers on the good ship *Mayflower*, who agreed in writing to govern (control) themselves for the common good. The Eskimos, as we noted earlier in this chapter, govern themselves by elaborate but unwritten laws and traditions. The Spanish monarch served as an exemplar of absolute control based on the divine right of kings. The fact that these three forms of social control differ so vastly is intended to provide the basis for contrast.

Concept-based programs may sometimes seem a little piecemeal, especially to individuals who are familiar with more traditional topic-oriented approaches. Some teachers provide occasional in-depth case studies of a single culture, subculture, or nation to provide an example of instances in which several separate cue concepts are integrated. The point here is that concept-based approaches offer an avenue to enable children to learn about human behavior in general, rather than a mass of unique and nonrepetitive (UN) ideas about lots of different subjects.

SUMMARY

Most elementary social studies programs are based on the expanding-environments (expanding-horizons) approach. We indicated that although the traditional program is both logical and sequential from an adult perspective, its logic and sequence may be much less evident to children. We also examined some of the most significant variations found among the new social studies programs, especially those that follow a spiral, or a concept-based approach, and those such as *Man: A Course of Study,* in which the content (subject matter) functions as a vehicle that allows children to contrast new information with something from their own experience.

The notion that information isn't necessarily important in and of itself is often difficult to accept, especially for those who place a premium on information retention. Indeed, the idea that low-level information can be used as a vehicle to get to higher-level, more useful information hasn't been encountered extensively in practice, at least not in our experience. However, we've tried to illustrate some elementary social studies programs that are based on just such an idea.

The research on how children develop concepts of time and space, particularly historical time and geographical space, suggest that they are better able to handle these concepts after they have moved to Piaget's stage of "formal operations," which is somewhere around the age of eleven. How, then, are primary children able to deal with something, such as the Japanese family, that reflects a culture far removed from theirs? First, Japanese families (or families from any other culture) are used for their contrast with American families, and second, the Japanese family is made as concrete and real as possible. Teachers use films, stories, pictures, or anything they can get their hands on to bring the Japanese family within the scope of the child's experience. Third, how far away a Japanese family lives, as well as Japan's location on a map or globe, are secondary if not incidental to the entire study. For primary-level students, the fact that Japanese families live "far, far away" is usually sufficient. The day-to-day activities and the structure of the Japanese family are what's important, especially as they help to clarify the day-to-day activities and the structure of American families.

We indicated also that to expect children to "know themselves" before studying others is tantamount to putting the cart before the horse. Those things that we are extremely close to and intimate with, including our families, our language, and ourselves, are very difficult to study objectively or effectively. Therefore, the way to find out about ourselves is by watching and studying others—our friends, our families, and individuals from other cultures. This phenomenon suggests multiple purposes for virtually all social studies content: as information (about families, cultures, communities, history, geography, etc.) that students can be expected to know, and as a means of finding out about ourselves.

SUGGESTED ACTIVITIES

1. Do you think it makes any difference for children to understand the logic (the "why") of what they are studying? In math? In social studies? In anything?

2. What type of social studies program do you feel is preferable—one based on adult logic, such as expanding environments, one based on the ever-changing interests and abilities of children, or some combination of these?

3. Since most elementary children are in Piaget's concrete-operations stage, what does this suggest about teaching strategies for elementary schools? About social studies in particular?

4. Go to your curriculum library or resource center and get at least three or four texts, each for the same grade level but from different textbook series. Do a content analysis of these, comparing the topics they cover, the approach they take, and the things they do and do not emphasize. If you work in a small group of six or eight members, and each takes a different grade level to study, you will have a composite of the similarities and variations among textbook series, any one of which you might find yourself teaching from.

5. Assume that you are teaching in a school that uses MACOS. A small group of individuals has charged that you are not teaching social studies anymore. They say you are teaching about fish, birds, and monkeys, and, as anyone knows, that's science. How would you respond to them?

6. Review the assumptions upon which the expanding-environments approach to social studies is based—for example, that children should be exposed to the world by Grade 6, etc. Then, in small groups, outline the characteristics of a K–8 social studies program that follows alternative assumptions of your choosing.

REFERENCES

Egan, Kiernan. 1979. "What Children Know Best." *Social Education,* 43 (February), 130–34.

Elkind, David. 1982. *The Hurried Child.* Reading, Mass.: Addison-Wesley.

Gardner, D. P. 1983. *A Nation at Risk.* The National Commission on Excellence in Education, U.S. Department of Education.

Lengel, J., and D. Superka. 1982. "Curriculum Patterns." In *Social Studies in the 1980s,* ed. Irving Morrissett. Alexandria, Va.: Association for Supervision and Curriculum Development.

Levi-Strauss, Claude. 1966. *The Savage Mind.* Chicago: University of Chicago Press.

National Council for the Social Studies. 1979. *Revision of the NCSS Social Studies Curriculum Guidelines.* Washington, D.C.: NCSS.

National Council for the Social Studies Task Force on Scope and Sequence. 1984. "In Search of a Scope and Sequence for Social Studies." *Social Education,* 48 (April), 249–62.

Piaget, Jean. 1950. *The Psychology of Intelligence.* New York: Harcourt Brace and World.

Rosenshine, B. 1979. "Content, Time, and Direct Instruction." In *Research on Teaching: Concepts, Findings and Implications,* ed. P. Peterson and H. Walberg. Berkeley, Calif.: McCutchan.

Rosenshine, B., and David Berliner. 1978. "Academic Engaged Time." *British Journal of Teacher Education,* 4, 3–16.

Superka, D., and Sharryl Davis Hawke. 1980. "Social Roles: A Focus for Social Studies in the 1980s." In *Social Studies in the 1980s,* ed. Irving Morrissett. Alexandria, Va.: Association for Supervision and Curriculum Development.

Taba, Hilda, Samuel Levine, and Freeman F. Elzey. 1964. *Thinking in Elementary School Children.* U.S. Office of Education Cooperative Research Project No. 1574. San Francisco: San Francisco State College.

Taba, Hilda. 1967. *Teacher's Handbook for Elementary Social Studies.* Introductory Ed. Menlo Park, Calif.: Addison-Wesley.

Woodward, Arthur, David L. Elliot, and Cathleen Carter Nagel. 1986. "Beyond Textbooks in Elementary Social Studies." *Social Education,* 50 (January), 50–53.

SUGGESTED READINGS

Social Studies Materials and Resources Data Book. Boulder, Colo.: Social Science Education Consortium. Annual volumes. Editors will vary. Formerly known as the *Social Studies Curriculum Materials Data Book* and published in cooperation with the ERIC Clearinghouse for Social Studies/Social Studies Education (now at Indiana University), this ongoing series of publications offers the most complete set of descriptions and analyses of social studies materials to be found anywhere. A "must" for every curriculum library.

Donald H. Bragaw, ed. 1986. "Scope and Sequence: Alternatives for Social Studies," *Social Education,* 50 (November/December), 484–542. This special theme section presents a variety of alternative scope and sequence proposals for social studies by noted authorities in the field.

John Jarolimek. 1985. *Social Studies in Elementary Education.* 7th ed. New York: Macmillan. This well-established methods text provides an excellent description of the organization of elementary social studies programs.

William W. Joyce and Janet Alleman-Brooks. 1979. *Teaching Social Studies in the Elementary and Middle Schools.* New York: Holt, Rinehart, and Winston. This methods text focuses on life-long roles that students might play, including citizen, family member, avocation, and personal efficacy.

CHAPTER 6

Instructional Themes

"The values and related lifestyles of ethnic communities . . . constitute their essence, not chow mein, basket weaving, sombreros, or soul food."   James A. Banks

KEY QUESTION

☐ What are instructional themes, and when does one teach them?

KEY IDEAS

The following instructional themes are broad topics and concerns that influence the entire (K–12) social studies curriculum.

☐ *Global education* is intended to help children understand the complexities of citizenship in a world community.

☐ *Multicultural education* is intended to develop a sense of pride, understanding, and respect for the various groups that make up our society.

☐ *Law-related education* is intended to help children understand the influence of law in our daily lives.

☐ *Consumer education* is intended to help children understand the role that consumers play in the marketplace.

☐ *Career education* is intended to help children understand how economic factors and career choices affect people's lives.

☐ *Sex-equity education* is intended to foster equality among all Americans, regardless of gender.

INTRODUCTION: "Do You Have Toes?"

Several years ago, one of us (Welton) had the privilege of accompanying a delightful Nigerian lady, Ms. Katherine Abeyta, as she visited schools in several areas of the country. Dressed in a long, flowing native costume and armed with lots of artifacts, Ms. Abeyta spoke to elementary and middle school classes on the Nigerian culture.

On one memorable occasion, we were visiting a kindergarten class in a middle-class suburb of Cleveland, Ohio. Ms. Abeyta told the group about some of the foods unique to Nigeria, which brought forth the usual "ughs" and facial grimaces to which she had grown accustomed. She then explained how members of the Ibo tribe sometimes discriminated against members of the other two dominant tribes in Nigeria. The thought of blacks discriminating against blacks gave most of those children a new (although perhaps not entirely welcome) perspective on the world.

Upon finishing her short presentation, Ms. Abeyta asked if there were any questions. One little boy's hand shot up, Ms. Abeyta nodded in his direction, and he asked, "Do you have toes?"

The question was as innocent and sincere as only a child's question can be. The teacher was aghast, of course, but none of the children laughed or even giggled; they were clearly interested in what to them was a serious matter. Ms. Abeyta smiled, lifted her gown a few inches off the floor, slipped off her shoe, and proved conclusively that people from Nigeria did indeed have toes.

I did not think about it at the time—probably because the expression had yet to become popular—but Ms. Abeyta had contributed to those children's *global education.* In fact, by her seemingly small action, Ms. Abeyta may have made a major contribution to those children's understanding that despite their apparent differences, people around the globe share many things in common—including toes.

The global education of the children in this incident was only beginning; their understanding of problems and characteristics common to people around the globe will be built upon and added to throughout their school career and, in many instances, their lifetimes. The same is true of multicultural education, law-related education, and the other instructional themes that we introduced initially in Chapter 1 (see Figure 1.1) and that we explore in more detail in this chapter and the next. These themes, including values education (which we consider in the next chapter), are reflected in all of the approaches to social studies and appear at grade levels throughout the entire curriculum.

GLOBAL EDUCATION

Those of us who inhabit planet Earth face common problems as we journey through the cosmos. Those problems—which include pollution, overpopulation, discrimination, and the denial of human rights (to cite just a few)—are to one degree or another shared by everyone everywhere. Understanding and dealing effectively with such complex problems demands that schools prepare citizens who have a global view—one that permits them to live in a pluralistic and increasingly dependent global society. This is the goal and rationale of global education.

The need for developing a sense of world-mindedness (a global perspective) has become apparent with the emergence of two opposing trends in American society. On the one hand, the United States is being drawn into an increasingly interdependent stance with other nations. Throughout the 1980s, for example, we have imported more products than we exported, thereby creating a cumulative trade deficit in the billions. Most of the VCRs, cameras, and many of the cars purchased by American consumers are made in Japan. Meanwhile, there is growing concern about foreign investments in the United States. More and more Americans are, as *Newsweek* (1987) put it, "employees of Japan, Inc." Likewise, a growing proportion of American farmland is owned by foreign investors. Ownership aside, the fact that our government must subsidize American farm products to make them competitive on the world market underscores the intensity of our economic relationships with other nations.

Some Americans seem to ignore the fact that our "backyard" is the world. Those individuals would prefer that we turn inward, become less internationally minded, and focus on problems in our literal backyard. Thus for many people, the idea that they should identify themselves as Americans *and* citizens of a global society is decidedly "un-American." In other instances, some conservative groups oppose global citizenship on the grounds that it will lead to what they call "one-world government" (Jenkinson, 1987). It is not entirely clear how they arrive at that conclusion. Although authorities such as Collins and Zakariya (1982) have indicated that ". . . common citizenship in the world community does not mean that we must repudiate our national identities," it is clear that agreement on the desirability of a global perspective is not universal.

TEACHING FOR GLOBAL AWARENESS

Kniep (1986) has noted that the content of global education is drawn from the historical realities that define and describe the world as a global society. Kniep goes on to identify four elements of study basic to global education.

The study of diverse human values—with an emphasis on the commonalities (housing, food, dress, tools, etc.) that transcend the diversity.

The study of global systems—economic, political, ecological, and technological.

The study of global issues and problems—particularly problems related to peace, security, development, the environment, and human rights.

The study of global history (*not* histories of Western civilization) that can help students understand the conditions that underlie issues and problems in the world today.

Global education does not seek to make children experts in world affairs by the time they leave elementary or middle school. Indeed, the extremely broad perspective of global education can pose problems for children who view themselves as members of their families and their classes at school, but who do not yet think of themselves as functioning members of the other communities (state, nation, world, etc.) in which they live.

Teachers can help build a basis for global education by highlighting the international or global dimensions of topics typically studied in elementary and middle schools, but that might otherwise go unmentioned. Global education in Grades K–8 need not try to answer complex questions of international relations, which can be dealt with when children are older, but should address such simple things as the ways in which all people everywhere satisfy their common needs for food, housing, and a sense of safety.

Older elementary and middle school students are often better able to deal with issues that have international dimensions than students in the primary grades, but even then a note of caution is warranted. Overemphasizing global problems, such as overpopulation, terrorism, or the possibility of nuclear war, can create what has been called the "Doomsday" effect; students come away with the impression that world problems are unsolveable and that Doomsday is inevitable. The other extreme, oversimplification, is equally undesirable. For example, for children to say something like "We wouldn't have airline hijackings if someone would just shoot 'X' (the leader of a nation in the Middle East)" vastly and inaccurately oversimplifies a complex problem. Either extreme can be misleading, even irresponsible. A balanced approach that recognizes that global education is a complex and long-term undertaking is essential.

Johnson and Benegar (1983) suggest three phases in the process of global education: (1) developing global awareness, (2) developing a sense of global interdependence, and (3) developing cross-cultural acceptance and understanding. Johnson and Benegar also recommend the following student activity as a means for developing global awareness.

MODEL STUDENT ACTIVITY

Our Shrinking World

PURPOSE
To explore how changes in the technology of transportation have affected the world and people's perceptions of it.

MATERIALS NEEDED
"Our Shrinking World" handout, paper, crayons, pencils, or markers.

Our Shrinking World
As the speed of transportation increases and travel time decreases, the relative size of the world continues to shrink.

1750: The best average speed of horse-drawn coaches on land and sailing ships at sea was approximately 10 miles per hour.

1850: Steam locomotives averaged 65 steamships averaged 36 mph.

1950: Propeller-driven aircraft averaged 300–400 mph.

1980: Jet passenger aircraft averaged 500–700 mph.

2000: The next step in transportation systems (?)

PROCEDURE

1. Distribute copies of the handout. Explain that as transportation systems have improved over time, both the speed at which people can move over the earth and the distances they can easily cover have increased dramatically. The handout shows the development from the 16th century to the 1980s.

2. Ask students to speculate about or brainstorm a list of new developments in transportation systems that might take place in the 21st century (for example, spaceships for extraterrestrial travel).

3. Ask students to list some of the changes that advances in transportation have brought about in the world. How have people's views of the world been changed by the development of faster means of transportation? What is meant by the term "shrinking world" or "global village?" Do we know more about our planet and the people on it than people knew in the past?

4. As a follow-up, have students do one of the following:
   a. Investigate the changes over time in methods of communication (for example, from cave drawings to satellite transmission). How has the speed of communication changed?
   b. Bring in examples of other items that they use or see around them which might illustrate changes in technology or ways that we are becoming more connected to the rest of the world.
   c. Make a visual time line or chart showing changes over time in the various means of transportation.

This activity is based in part on information published in *World Facts and Trends,* by John McHale (New York: Macmillan, 1972).
Source: Reprinted from *Social Education* with permission of the National Council for the Social Studies.

GOALS

The long-term nature of global education is reflected in the following goals, which are adapted from Herman (1983). Because these goals apply throughout the K–12 curriculum, elementary and middle school children would not be expected to achieve all of them.

Summary of Goals for Global Education
The students will

1. view themselves as members of (1) a family, (2) other groups, (3) the nation, (4) the human species, and (5) as inhabitants of the planet.

2. identify basic human commonalities. Some of these include a common dependence on the biosphere, similar human needs/desires, similar but diverse cultural adaptations, and other common problems, such as population expansion, resource depletion, and pollution.

3. describe interconnections between their lives and the society in which they live, and their impact on global conditions, and vice versa.

4. practice the skills required to participate in and to shape a global society, including communication, problem solving and conflict resolution, and functioning in a group.

5. analyze events from a global perspective.

6. demonstrate empathy for the perspective with which others view the world.

MULTICULTURAL/MULTIETHNIC EDUCATION

Near the turn of the twentieth century, a play entitled *The Melting Pot* was staged in New York City. That play, according to Banks (1984), captured an ideology common in America at the time. Our collective view was that the cultures brought to this country by immigrants from around the world were somehow to be merged and melded together, in a big pot so to speak. The school was expected to do most of the cultural melding because it was the institution that most immigrants dealt with on a regular basis. What supposedly came out of the schools were individuals who reflected *the* American culture and value system.

TEXTBOOK TREATMENTS

Social studies textbooks have long been a major vehicle for projecting what it means to be an American. For example, Fitzgerald (1979) indicated that prior to the mid-1960s, textbooks depicted America as populated by two kinds of people: "we Americans" and "the immigrants." The process of turning immigrants into Americans was depicted as "a problem."

Prior to the mid-1960s, black Americans were mentioned infrequently in social studies textbooks, and when they were, it was as "the slaves"—as individuals who appeared here after a harrowing voyage in the hold of a slave ship. Few women, aside from Jane Addams and Dolley Madison, were even mentioned, while the Spanish colonizers of Mexico and the Southwest were typically cast as gold-hungry villains. In short, the American history presented in social studies textbooks was almost exclusively an Anglo-Saxon, male-dominated enterprise.

In the aftermath of the civil rights movement of the 1960s, most textbooks ceased distinguishing between "we Americans" and "the immigrants." As Fitzgerald (1979, p. 49) noted, "The country they [the textbooks] had conceived of as male and Anglo-Saxon turned out to be filled with blacks, 'ethnics,' Indians, Asians, and women. . . . The country also turned out to be filled with Spanish-speaking people who had come from Mexico, Puerto Rico, and other countries of the Caribbean basin."

A MULTICULTURAL VIEW

The multicultural-education theme reflects the fact that we are a multicultural, multiethnic society. Associated with this theme is the contention that because so many ethnic groups have retained the customs and traditions of their respective cultural heritages, the "melting pot" metaphor is inaccurate and inadequate. Instead, it would be more accurate to describe our society as a "salad bowl," as a melange of ethnicities, cultures, and traditions that are intermingled together.

For most purposes, *multicultural education* and *multiethnic education* are synonymous. Both share a common goal of sensitizing students to the heritages, cultures, and contributions to our society of blacks, Hispanics, Native Americans, and other ethnic groups. One technique for achieving that goal, particularly at the high school and college levels, is through *ethnic studies;* that is, in separate courses in black history or Spanish-speaking cultures, etc. Such separate courses are seldom found at the elementary and middle school levels, where the components of multicultural education are typically integrated in existing materials.

Children's literature affords an excellent vehicle for integrating a multicultural/ multiethnic focus into social studies. Children's books, such as *Annie and the Old One* by Mishka Miles (1971), *The Great Gilly Hopkins* by Katherine Paterson (1978), and *The Sign of the Beaver* by Elizabeth George Spears (1983), all portray strong characters from a variety of ethnic and socioeconomic backgrounds.

To assist teachers in selecting children's literature appropriate to this or some of the other themes in this chapter, a joint committee of the National Council for the Social Studies and the Children's Book Council evaluates children's books that are useful in teaching social studies. Each spring, an annotated listing of their selections, "Notable Children's Trade Books in the Field of Social Studies," is published in *Social Education,* the journal of the National Council for the Social Studies.

NEGATIVE STEREOTYPES

Multicultural activities must be conducted with sensitivity and caution lest they do more harm than good. An occasional ethnic meal, a day set aside to honor a certain cultural or ethnic group, and even some art-related activities can unintentionally convey inaccurate information and negative stereotypes. For example, we once witnessed a group of kindergarten children who, in studying a unit on Native Americans, had dyed pieces of macaroni with red, orange, yellow, green, and blue food coloring. After the macaroni had dried and was strung on strings, the children proudly displayed their "Indian necklaces." Be advised that no self-respecting Native American wears a necklace made from colored macaroni!

The problem here was not the construction of the necklace itself, which is an interesting craft activity, but the fact that it was done in the context of studying Native Americans. In addition to their necklaces, the children had constructed a large tepee from brown wrapping paper. We left that classroom wondering how many of those children think that "All Indians lived in tepees" (when only the Plains Indians did) or that "Native Americans live in tepees today," which is not the case at all.

The occasional ethnic day to honor a particular culture as well as food-related experiences must also be approached with sensitivity, no matter how enjoyable such activities might seem on the surface. For example, students who dress in sombreros and serapes for "Mexican Day" would be in for a rude disappointment were they to visit Mexico City and expect to see such costumes. Likewise, eating tacos or tamales does not help children "appreciate Hispanics" any more than eating chitterlings (deep-fried pig intestines known as "chitlins") helps children to appreciate or understand black culture. What children learn from such experiences may have nothing to do with the underlying culture, but rather may involve whether they like tacos, tamales, or chitlins. Activities of this kind can easily lead to what James Banks (1976) has described as "the chitlins and tepee approach" to multiethnic education.

Teachers who have their students build a tepee, for example, should make certain that the children clearly understand they are recreating a historical event, and rather imperfectly at that. The problem can be even further compounded by the way textbooks and other materials depict historical events. In the context of teaching the westward expansion of the United States, for example, which of the following is "correct?"

"The Native Americans were hostile savages who preyed on enterprising settlers."

   or

"The Native Americans were merely defending their tribal lands from greedy landgrabbers."

   or

"Both the Native Americans *and* pioneers believed they were in the right."

Unless children are exposed to various points of view—even if some are not particularly popular by contemporary standards—the potential for negative stereotyping and teaching misinformation looms large. The multicultural-education theme demands unusual sensitivity to the peoples of all nations and cultures.

GOALS

The following list of goals and objectives for multicultural education is adapted from Herman (1983). Because these are long-term (K–12) goals, children would *not* be expected to demonstrate all of these competencies by the end of elementary or middle school.

Summary of Goals/Objectives for Multicultural Education
The students will

1. improve their self-identity, self-concept, and self-understanding.
2. understand the cue concepts of *race, culture, ethnicity,* and *self-determination.*
3. identify and develop an appreciation for other people's contributions to culture and society, including contributions from individuals different from themselves.
4. define the concept of *racism,* and identify its forms and effects on American society.
5. recognize individuals of complex ancestry (e.g., blacks who are part Native American, and vice versa).

LAW-RELATED EDUCATION

If your experience was anything like ours, you probably sat through your share of boring lessons on such topics as "How a Bill Becomes a Law" or the legal distinction between felonies and misdemeanors. You may also remember when your teachers tried to explain the reasons behind school rules. The fact that some lessons were boring or the justification for school rules sometimes went over the students' heads does not negate a long tradition of teaching about the courts and the legal system in general. How is law-related education any different from what schools have been doing all along?

The current interest in law-focused education is in part a response to both the rising crime rate and a general ignorance of the practical operation of the legal system, as well as a reaction against the traditional approach to law as a body of theoretical concepts and principles. Law-related education does not deny the need for students to understand traditional law-related topics, such as the structure of our legal system or the lawmaking process. The goal of law-related education is to move beyond these "parts"—the structural components—to develop an understanding of the basis of law (or jurisprudence) and the vital role it plays in our daily lives.

The ultimate objective of law-related education is to help students understand that the basis for law rests in morality, and not the other way around. Laws that punish murderers, for example, are a reflection of the moral principle involving the sanctity of human life. The law itself does not make murder a crime; rather, our sense of morality makes murder a criminal act. Likewise, the "wrongness" of stealing does not grow out of laws that punish those who steal; it stems from the violation of a moral principle. Because people sometimes violate moral principles, our society has created laws that deal with these situations.

TEACHING IMPLICATIONS

It is difficult for children to deal with abstract concepts involving the law. No matter how much time teachers spend telling children about the possibility of hurting someone if they run in the hallway, for example, the children usually translate this into what will happen to them if they get caught. The punishment is something children can deal with, something they can feel—perhaps painfully at times.

Despite the difficulty that young children experience in dealing with abstractions, there are a host of law-related concepts that they can deal with—if not in their entirety, at least in part. Even very young students have well-developed concepts of fairness, which they are quick to demonstrate if they feel they are being treated unfairly. Initially, a young child's concept of fairness has a "me-oriented," egocentric perspective, as in "Why can't I do what you are letting her do?" or "Why does he get a candy bar and I don't?" The task with young children then, is to extend their me-oriented sense of fairness to a "we" orientation. In addition to fairness, other law-related concepts that can be built upon include authority, equality, freedom, honesty, participation, property, privacy, responsibility, and tolerance.

Children's literature often provides an excellent vehicle for treating law-related concepts. For instance, you may remember the classic tale *The Little Red Hen,* in which a hen finds several grains of wheat. Her pleas for assistance in planting and harvesting the wheat and grinding it into flour are ignored, and she is forced to do everything herself. When her loaf of bread finally comes out of the oven, she discovers that lots of volunteers are willing to help her eat it. But since nobody helped her do the work, she decides to eat it herself. And she does!

Instead of moralizing about the story, a teacher could work toward building upon the children's concept of fairness by asking, "Was the little red hen fair to the others?" "Was she fair to herself?" Because good discussions among primary-level children (to whom such stories are usually told) are difficult to conduct, consider using stories like *The Little Red Hen* with older students, even sixth graders. You may be quite surprised at how well they respond.

Widespread interest in law-related education has yielded a wealth of resources and teaching materials. Among the best resources in this respect are *Law in the Classroom: Activities and Resources (Revised)* by Mary Jane Turner and Lynn Parisi (1984), which is available from the Social Science Education Consortium, 855 Broadway, Boulder, CO 80302, or The American Bar Association Youth Education for Citizenship Committee, 750 N. Lake Shore Drive, Chicago, IL 60611. Law-related education projects also exist in over a dozen states.

GOALS

Goals for this instructional theme, like those for other themes presented in this chapter, should be viewed as long-term expectations. In fact, one way of looking at them is as part of a continuum. The summary below states each goal as a continuum.

Summary of Law-Related Education Goals

Children move away from	*Children move toward*
perceiving law as restrictive, punitive, immutable, and beyond the control and understanding of the people affected	perceiving law as promotive, facilitative, comprehensible, and alterable
perceiving people as powerless before the law and other sociocivic institutions	perceiving people as having the potential to control and contribute to the social order
perceiving issues of right and wrong as incomprehensible to ordinary people	perceiving right and wrong as issues all citizens can and should address

Source: Charlotte C. Anderson. "Promoting Responsible Citizenship Through Elementary Law-Related Education." *Social Education* 44 (May 1980), pp. 383–386.

perceiving social issues as unproblematic	perceiving the dilemmas inherent in social issues
being impulsive decision makers and problem solvers who make unreflective commitments	being reflective decision makers and problem solvers who make grounded commitments
being inarticulate about commitments made or positions taken	being able to give reasoned explanations about commitments made and positions taken
being unable to manage conflict in other than a coercive or destructive manner	being socially responsible conflict managers
being uncritically defiant of authority	being critically responsive to legitimate authority
being illiterate about legal issues and the legal system	being knowledgeable about law, the legal system, and related issues
being egocentric, self-centered, and indifferent to others	being empathetic, socially responsible, and considerate of others
being morally immature in responding to ethical problems	being able to make mature judgments in dealing with ethical and moral problems

CAREER EDUCATION

Among the uninformed, career education is sometimes erroneously assumed to be another way of saying "vocational education." This it is not! Vocational education is a much narrower concept that refers to the practice of providing students with the skills and training needed to enter a specific vocation or occupation. Career education, on the other hand, is a much broader concept.

An expression that often goes hand in hand with career education is "education for the world of work." Here, too, *work* is defined not in terms of one's job or occupation but in a larger societal context. Patrick Good et al. (1977) identify seven characteristics associated with work as it is seen from a career-education perspective. In addition to producing income, these characteristics include: occupying oneself in an interesting way, helping to maintain or increase one's social status, fostering satisfactory social interaction, providing a sense of self-identity, supplying necessary goods and services, and providing opportunities for creative expression and self-fulfillment (Good et al., 1977, p. 136).

If you consider that schools have long acknowledged a responsibility for helping to prepare students for the world of work, why then should career education receive so much attention today? Several possible explanations have emerged. First, some authorities suggest that schools hadn't done an adequate job in preparing students for the world of work and thus renewed their emphasis on this goal. A second motive becomes apparent in Hoyt's (1977) effort to further clarify career education, when he describes it as "an effort *aimed at refocusing American*

One possible means of developing career awareness within a career education theme would be to take students to visit local industries and commercial establishments in the community. (© *Ellis Herwig/Taurus Photos*)

education and the actions of the broader community in ways that will help individuals acquire and utilize the knowledges, skills, and attitudes necessary for each to make a meaningful and productive and satisfying part of his or her way of life" [emphasis added] (Hoyt, 1977). Using career education as a vehicle to change educational practices was further reflected by Sidney Marland, then U.S. Commissioner of Education, who stated, "If there is a central message in our conception of career education, it is to cry out against this absurd partitioning of the house of education, this separation of subject from subject, of class from class, this false and destructive distinction between the liberal academic tradition on the one hand and the utilitarian-vocational tradition on the other" (Marland, 1973, p. 501). One of the things Marland was referring to, apparently, was the "we teach 'grasslands' in fourth grade" phenomenon often found in the topic-to-topic approach to social studies. A topic like "the grasslands" may be assigned to a grade level, and then once taught there, seldom dealt with again. By defining career education broadly, it can't be dealt with as an isolated topic.

Career education is not a topic, nor is it a course, although it is sometimes approached as such. Neither is career education the sole responsibility of social studies (although it is sometimes approached that way too). It is, as we indicated previously, an emphasis that transcends the entire school program.

How does one approach career education with students who, when asked what they'd like to be when they grow up, respond in terms of locomotive engineers, firefighters, nurses, or pilots? The dominant approach in elementary schools seems to be aimed at developing *career awareness*. There are over twenty thousand different occupations in this country, many of which are beyond the child's scope of experience. At times throughout the year and as appropriate, teachers can draw attention to some of the different occupations (though certainly not to all twenty thousand), thereby building an awareness of the different career choices the children may have open to them. After identifying occupations, teachers can then move on to the skills and/or special training they require. In a unit on transportation, for example, students could investigate the skills required of an intercity truck driver. The teacher could then follow up by inviting a truck driver to talk with the class, preferably a female trucker who, without saying a word about it, can help to destroy the sex-role stereotyping often associated with this particular career. The same holds true for female doctors and male nurses. In our judgment, such approaches can do more to dispel sex-role stereotyping than all the words a teacher might utter. We also hasten to add that integrating career education into an ongoing social studies program is a planned, not an incidental, activity (though don't pass up those spur-of-the-moment opportunities either).

GOALS

As was true of the other themes in this chapter, the goals for career education, which are adapted from Herman (1983), are long-term expectations. Once again, children would *not* be expected to demonstrate all of them by the end of elementary or middle school.

Summary of Goals for Career Education
The student will

1. describe how economic factors and career choices affect people's lives.
2. describe how the role of work has changed over time, and how labor contributes to American society today.
3. describe the positive aspects of differences among individuals.
4. explain the relationship between and among economics, life-styles, occupational roles, and the interdependence of various factors such as goods and services, organizations, and societies.
5. define and give examples of the concept "wise use of leisure time."
6. practice decision-making skills and act responsibly in making career choices.

CONSUMER EDUCATION

Compared with career education, consumer education is a considerably narrower, more manageable concept. The goal of consumer education is to provide individuals with knowledge and skills that enable them to understand the nature of the marketplace and to make intelligent decisions in it.

By asking yourself what it takes to be a shrewd buyer, two of the major thrusts of consumer education should become apparent. They are helping students recognize a bad deal when they see one, and making students aware of what they can do if they feel they've been taken advantage of. Helping students to become aware of fraudulent or questionable business practices extends the scope of consumer education to include the study of advertising and product-packaging techniques, product evaluation (such as that found in *Consumer Reports*), warranties and guarantees, and consumer protection agencies.

Consumer education extends beyond recognizing the "traps" that buyers should beware of to include aspects related to intelligent money management, such as budgeting, and aspects related to building an understanding of the consumer's role in the marketplace. For example, helping children understand how consumers' decisions can influence the price of an article or service is an important element of consumer education. Helping children to achieve that understanding, however, also demands an understanding of rudimentary economics. Unfortunately, economics is not a strength of many elementary teachers; many still regard it as "the dismal science." As a result, we suspect that the economic role consumers play sometimes gets less attention than it merits.

In dealing with topics like misleading advertising or fraudulent business practices, it often takes considerable skill not to project the image that all business people and advertisers are crooks who try to relieve the unwary of their hard-earned money. This is particularly important in teaching primary-level children who tend to think in either-or categories. After examining techniques that advertisers use to manipulate potential buyers, for example, it's all too easy for students to get the impression that consumers are "good" and that all advertising is "bad," as are the businesspeople who advertise their products. Because of this "good guys-bad guys" phenomenon, teachers' statements to the effect that not all advertising is misleading should be accompanied by appropriate examples.

The financial aspects of consumer education can also present potential problems, especially for teachers at the primary level again, because of the way in which children perceive money. When asked to choose between a stack of fifteen pennies or a stack of four quarters, primary-level children often select the pennies; from their perspective the taller stack is "bigger" and is thus worth more. And when asked to deal with large sums of money, such as $100 (or in some cases, $20) many primary-level children have little comprehension of what that amount will buy. These problems are further complicated by the common misconception that banks "give" people money.

On one hand, children's perceptions and their inexperience and inability to deal with large dollar amounts are consistent with Piaget's findings on cognitive reasoning. On the other hand, correcting misconceptions (about banks, etc.) could very well take place in a consumer-education context. Primary-level children are able to deal with simple comparisons, for example, particularly if the elements being compared are within their realm of experience. More sophisticated analyses, however, may be better left until the intermediate grades or later, when students have achieved a better grasp of the prerequisite understandings.

GOALS

As was true for the other themes in this chapter, children would *not* be expected to demonstrate all of these consumer-education goals by the end of elementary or middle school.

Summary of Consumer-Education Goals
The students will

1. develop an understanding of the role consumers play in the economic market-place.
2. identify techniques used to influence people, including an analysis of misleading and nonmisleading advertising.
3. identify techniques and processes for evaluating products.
4. become aware of fraudulent and/or questionable business practices (e.g., bait-and-switch sales techniques, deceptive packaging).
5. identify techniques associated with intelligent money management (budgeting, etc.).
6. identify consumer protection agencies (including their scope and authority).

SEX-EQUITY EDUCATION

The first illustration in a twenty-year-old, first-grade social studies book from a major publisher shows a neatly dressed, aproned woman standing on the front steps waving good-bye to her children as they board the bus to school. Several pages later, after the children have reached school, the pictures show that the teacher and nurse are female, and the principal and custodian are male. Somewhat later in the book, a briefcase-carrying male wearing a suit and tie arrives home from work (according to the text), and is then shown, his feet on the ottoman, reading the newspaper. In the same illustration, the woman (whom we know by then is the wife and mother) is shown preparing dinner in the kitchen. When the family goes on a trip—which they do quite often in first-grade books—guess who drives?

Think for a moment about the subtle messages such illustrations can convey to children. They begin with "A woman's place is in the home" and go on from there. Not only are such messages simplistic and sexist, they inaccurately depict and limit the roles and responsibilities of women and men in modern society.

Recent social studies textbooks are far less guilty of such treatments. Current texts, for example, are likely to depict single-parent families, women in roles traditionally viewed as male, and males in roles traditionally viewed as female. In the decades to come, we expect that roles will be increasingly identified in a gender-free manner, and that expressions such as "traditionally viewed as male (or female)" will become meaningless. In the meantime, we must be sensitive to instructional materials that may still present forms of sex-role stereotyping. The depiction of characters in storybooks and some of the older basal readers warrant

Exposing students to carefully-chosen storybooks that contain balanced and equitable story lines, characters, and illustrations is one way of helping students to dispel stereotyped thinking about sex roles. (© *Susan Lapides 1987*)

particular attention. Any number of studies (see e.g., Ferguson and Smith, 1976) indicate that male characters were often depicted as clever, adventurous, and brave, whereas female characters were more likely to be shown as passive, domestic, and dependent on males for success. This does *not* mean that the wealth of children's literature must be abandoned; rather, teachers must exercise care in *selecting* stories in which the treatment of characters is balanced and equitable.

Sex-equity education places stronger demands on the teacher than perhaps any of the other instructional themes. One reason for this is the almost complete absence of specific teaching materials. High school sociology texts may contain a chapter on sexism, but at the elementary and middle school levels, instructional materials that deal explicitly with sex-equity education are almost nonexistent. The lack of materials is in part a reflection of the fact that there is not a large body of sex-equity content that children are expected to learn. In other words, sex-equity education focuses primarily on helping children develop a way of looking at the world—and at how individuals are treated within that world—rather than on having children learn a predetermined body of factual information. Teachers play a key role in that process, especially as they call attention to the inequitable treatment of individuals of either gender in whatever situations or materials the children encounter.

GOALS

The overall goal of sex-equity education is to eliminate sexism and sex-role stereotyping in order to foster equality among all Americans regardless of gender. This includes developing a sensitivity and awareness among children regarding the equitable treatment of individuals of either sex, in both life situations and in instructional materials. The long-term goals of sex-equity education, which are adapted from Herman (1983), are summarized in the list below.

Summary of Goals for Sex-Equity Education
The students will

1. identify instances of sexism in their lives.
2. describe the socialization process that initiates and maintains sexism.
3. Identify sex-bias in textbooks and instructional materials.
4. Identify policy issues that are sex discriminatory.
5. Identify and appreciate the need to eliminate practices that prevent women from growing intellectually, socially, and physically.

COMMENTARY: Is This Censorship?

After surveying forty contemporary social studies textbooks for Grades 1–4, Paul Vitz (cited in Glenn, 1987), in *Censorship: Evidence of Bias in Our Children's Textbooks,* claims that in the texts' treatment of families:

the words *husband* and *wife* never occur.

"not one of the many families described in these books features a homemaker—that is, a wife and mother—as a model . . ."

there is not one portrayal of a contemporary American family that clearly features traditional sex roles.

the words *marriage* and *wedding* do not occur in an American context.

Whether contemporary texts are as biased in one direction as older texts were in another direction depends upon your view of reality. In their effort to right past wrongs, have the textbook publishers gone overboard, as Vitz claims?

SUMMARY

In this chapter we have examined several instructional themes that cut across the entire social studies (and school) curriculum. Individually and collectively, these themes reflect beliefs or positions that are thought to be desirable for children (and adults) to hold. For example, the goal of global education is to help children see themselves as citizens in a world community, and to understand that problems in one part of that community affect individuals in other parts of the globe.

A knowledge and a value component is associated with each of the themes. The knowledge components include such things as understanding the nature of interdependence in a world community (global education), identifying contributions to our society from various cultural groups (multicultural education), and understanding the pervasiveness of law in our daily lives (law-related education). The value component is reflected by the fact that not everyone agrees about the desirability of all the themes. Opponents to sex-equity education may argue, for example, that it is intent on destroying traditional sex roles in American families and could destroy the family as we know it. On the other hand, proponents argue that sex-equity education is intended to reflect changes that have already taken place or are currently underway in both families and the larger society. Regardless of whether your personal view leans toward the opponents or the proponents, the fact that you have a personal viewpoint further reflects the value base that underlies each of the themes in this chapter.

SUGGESTED ACTIVITIES

1. Select two social studies texts for the same grade level and examine how they treat the topic *family*. Determine if the texts promote a particular bias, as Vitz has suggested.

2. Assume that you are teaching in a community that has a relatively small but vocal segment of the population that belongs to very conservative, fundamentalist religious groups. Classify the instructional themes treated in this chapter into one of two categories: those that are more likely to arouse active opposition from this segment of the population and those less likely to arouse such opposition.

3. Obtain a fifth-grade social studies text. Using the index entries for "Native Americans" and any other identifiable ethnic group as a guide, assess the overall balance of the way the two groups are treated.

REFERENCES

Anderson, Charlotte C. 1980. "Promoting Responsible Citizenship Through Elementary Law-Related Education." *Social Education,* 44 (May), 383–86.

Banks, James A. 1984. *Teaching Strategies for Ethnic Studies.* 3rd ed. Boston: Allyn and Bacon.

————. 1978. "Multiethnic Education Across Cultures." *Social Education,* 42 (March), 177–87.

————. 1976. "Multiethnic Education: Practices and Promises." Paper delivered at the Annual Meeting of the National Council for the Social Studies, Washington, D.C.

Collins, H. Thomas, and S. B. Zakariya. 1982. *Getting Started in Global Education: A Primer for Principals and Teachers.* Arlington, Va.: National Association of Elementary School Principals.

Ferguson, P., and L. C. Smith. 1976. "Treatment of the Sexes in Instructional Materials: Guidelines for Evaluation." In *Teaching About Women in the Social Studies,* NCSS Bulletin No. 48, ed. Jean Grambs. Washington, D.C.: National Council for the Social Studies.

Fitzgerald, Frances. 1979. "Onward and Upward with the Arts: Rewriting American History—II." *The New Yorker* (March), 40–92.

Glenn, Charles L. 1987. "Textbook Controversies: A 'Disaster for Public Schools'?" *Phi Delta Kappan,* 68 (February), 451–55.

Hahn, Carole L. 1984. "Promise and Paradox: Challenge to Global Citizenship." *Social Education,* 48 (April), 240–43.

Hammond, D. Rosalind, et al. 1985. "Reducing Prejudice in the Classroom." How to Do It Series Four, Number 2. Washington, D.C.: National Council for the Social Studies.

Herman, Wayne L. 1983. "What Should Be Taught Where?" *Social Education,* 47 (February), 94–101.

Hoyt, K. B. 1977. *A Primer for Career Education.* Washington, D.C.: U.S. Government Printing Office.

Jenkinson, Edward B. 1987. "The Significance of the Decision in 'Scopes II.'" *Phi Delta Kappan,* 68 (February), 445–50.

Johnson, Jacquelyn, and John Benegar. 1983. "Global Issues in the Intermediate School." *Social Education,* 47 (February), 131–37.

Kniep, Willard M. 1986. "Defining a Global Education by Its Content." *Social Education,* 50 (October), 437–46.

Marland, Sidney P. Jr. 1973. "Career Education, Not Job Training." *Social Education,* 37 (October), 500–04.

Miles, Mishka. 1971. *Annie and the Old One.* Boston: Little Brown.

Newsweek. 1987. "Working for Japan, Inc." 109 (February 2), 42–46.

Patterson, Katherine. 1978. *The Great Gilly Hopkins.* New York: Crowell.

Remey, Richard C. 1979. *Handbook of Citizenship Competencies.* Alexandria, Va.: Association for Supervision and Curriculum Development.

Rosenzweig, Linda W. 1982. "Law-Related Education and Legal Development." In *Developmental Perspectives on the Social Studies.* NCSS Bulletin No. 66, ed. Linda Rosenzweig. Washington, D.C.: National Council for the Social Studies.

Scott, Kathryn P., guest ed. 1982. "Sex Equity in the Elementary School." *Social Education,* 46 (January), 44–57.

Spears, Elizabeth George. 1983. *The Sign of the Beaver.* Boston: Houghton Mifflin.

Wheeler, Ronald. 1980. "Law-related Education." *Social Education,* 44 (May), 381–97.

SUGGESTED READINGS

James A. Banks. 1984. *Teaching Strategies for Ethnic Studies*. (3rd ed.) Newton, Mass.: Allyn and Bacon. This was one of the first books on multicultural/multiethnic education, and it remains one of the best.

Willard M. Kniep. 1986. "Global Education: The Road Ahead." *Social Education*, 50 (October), 415–46. This special section addresses the notion that the social studies agenda must reflect a commitment to global education.

Gerda Lerner. 1979. *The Majority Finds Its Past: Placing Women in History*. New York: Oxford University Press. This excellent volume describes the evolution of women's history.

Dorothy Lungmus, Frances Haley, G. Dale Greenawald, and Jerry Forkner. 1980. *Consumer Education Sourcebook*. Boulder, Colo.: Social Science Education Consortium/ERIC Clearinghouse for Social Studies/Social Science Education. An excellent resource for descriptions, analyses, and sources of consumer-education materials.

Sheila M. Rothman. 1978. *Women's Proper Place: A History of Changing Ideals and Practices, 1870 to the Present*. New York: Basic Books. An excellent analysis of changes in society's attitudes toward women.

Mary Kay Thompson Tetreault, ed. 1987. "Women, Gender, and the Social Studies." *Social Education*, 51 (March), 167–213. This special section takes the perspective that by making women an integral part of social studies education, we change the way we think about both men and gender.

Mary Jane Turner and Lynn Parisi. 1984. *Law in the Classroom: Activities and Resources, Revised*. Boulder, Colo.: Social Science Education Consortium. This four-part volume provides an overview, lesson materials, a handout, activities for specific law-related areas, and a directory of additional resources.

CHAPTER 7

Values Education

"Men assert most confidently when they have the least grounds." Montaigne

KEY QUESTIONS

☐ How do we identify the values we hold?

☐ How sensitive must teachers be to parental and community expectations?

☐ How can we teach values systematically, and should we?

KEY IDEAS

☐ The school's role in teaching values continues to be the source and subject of controversy. Nevertheless, all teachers do teach values, whether implicitly or explicitly.

☐ Community expectations concerning values education are seldom consistent, nor, in most cases, are they known in advance.

☐ The key components of values education are (1) values themselves and (2) a process of valuing. General agreement as to the specific nature of these components does not exist.

☐ Four major approaches to values education are (1) inculcation, (2) values clarification, (3) moral reasoning, and, (4) values analysis.

☐ Whenever teachers select something to teach, they are in effect reflecting a value position, one that their students may be quite unaware of.

INTRODUCTION: On Teaching Values

It is impossible to avoid values and values teaching, even if a teacher wanted to. Everything teachers say and do—what they choose to study and discuss in class, and how they operate their classrooms—implicitly reflect value positions. By their actions and deeds, teachers indicate to children what is important, valuable, and worthwhile, as well as what is not. For those of us who intervene in the lives of children, values teaching is an inescapable fact of life.

Before the turn of the century, a major mission of schools was to mold recently arrived immigrants into the mainstream of American society. At that time, values teaching was usually called *character education* (Pietig, 1983). By modeling desired behaviors, by preaching, and occasionally by mocking children who deviated from what was expected, teachers were expected to instill certain core values such as honesty, truthfulness, promptness, obedience to and respect for one's elders, and beliefs in the dignity of the individual and the value of work. The school's success was judged by the extent to which the core values were incorporated into students' belief systems, and ultimately their behavior.

Whether values are something that should be taught—systematically and intentionally as in the past—or treated more casually—as something students should be exposed to—is still an issue today. Some individuals believe, for example, that schools and teachers have an obligation to teach values through any means available. Others believe that the complexity of our society and of the choices citizens must make demands that children be taught a process for analyzing value questions and issues. Still others believe that any attempt to influence what children believe and value smacks of brainwashing or indoctrination, neither of which have any place in schools today.

In light of these different positions, consider what you would do if a child asked the apparently innocent question, "Where did people come from?" (in the historical, not the biological-sexual, sense). Which of the following would you select?

_____ Indicate that the question is something that should be dealt with at home, not in school.

_____ Indicate that the Biblical (Adam-and-Eve) view is the most widely accepted.

_____ Briefly explain the concept of evolution.

_____ Present both the Biblical and evolutionary explanations.

_____ Indicate that people answer the question differently, without further elaboration.

_____ Indicate that people answer the question differently, and then provide examples.

_____ It depends. (Note: This answer is unacceptable unless you are also willing to indicate *what* it depends upon.)

The Biblical and evolutionary views of creation are not values; they are different explanations of an event. Values enter the picture to the extent that some parents value one explanation more highly than others. In fact, some parents prefer that certain explanations about our origins be withheld from their children, thereby tacitly and sometimes openly supporting a form of indoctrination. The issue is easier to deal with in parochial schools, primarily because parents send their children to such schools expecting that certain points of view will be presented. In public schools, however, parental expectations are more varied and considerably less clear.

When students ask questions about emotion-charged topics like creation, abortion, or AIDS, you seldom have the luxury of contemplation. In what amounts to a split second, you must respond in a way that is factually accurate, satisfies your student's curiosity, and respects parental expectations, yet doesn't compromise your personal beliefs on the matter. Treading such a fine line is clearly among the more difficult tasks a teacher faces.

Value issues are so pervasive that they extend to the fundamental goals of the school. The goal that children should arrive at certain value decisions through rational means, for example, reflects a value position. Why "rational?" Why not something else? Why not let students operate on the basis of faith, hunches, or intuition, as many of us do anyhow? Michael Scriven's eloquent statement is perhaps the best response we've seen. He said:

Moral reasoning and the moral behavior it indicates should be taught and taught about, if for no other reason than it is immoral to keep children ignorant of the empirical and logical bases behind the law and institutions which incorporate this country's virtues and permit its vices. But in addition to this intellectual payoff is the practical benefit to society of possessing members who are skilled in making value judgments. Such a society becomes a moral community offering important benefits to all of its members. (Scriven, 1966, p. 2)

Scriven's statement was written in the mid-1960s, a time when America was going through a turbulent period of introspection and social turmoil. The 1960s, and much of the 1970s, was a period when civil rights had come to the forefront, when the motives of political leaders were suspect, and when our continuing involvement in the Vietnam War led to protests and riots. It was a time when cherished values, such as patriotism, took on new meanings. No longer was patriotism uniformly viewed as support for "our nation, right or wrong." For many Americans, their sense of patriotism demanded that they protest America's involvement in what they considered an unjust war. Other Americans, however, followed the more traditional view of patriotism and criticized the protesters' actions as "unpatriotic."

The purpose for this excursion into recent history is to establish a context for the values dilemma that schools faced during the 1970s and throughout the 1980s. That dilemma is perhaps best captured by the question "Are the schools 'wrong' in teaching patriotism, honesty, responsibility, and other core values to children?" That question reflects the fact that, in the aftermath of the turbulent Vietnam era, long-standing practices had become debatable propositions, and there were no clear guidelines on how schools should proceed.

When you cut through the flowery language of philosophy statements, the real purpose of schools is to help students become "smart" and "good" (Ryan, 1986). Indeed, to suggest that a society would support schools that help children become "dumb" and "bad" is unthinkable. Schools have traditionally approached the "good" aspects of education by transmitting the culture's cherished values. But when those values began to be questioned, as they were in the 1960s and 1970s, schools and teachers began to shy away from issues of right and wrong or good and bad, and began concentrating on the knowledge component of education—on transmitting "smartness."

By the mid-1980s, many schools had attempted to become value-neutral; that is, they avoided explicit instruction in moral and ethical principles to whatever extent they could (see Sizer, 1985). In some instances the explicit avoidance was total. In other cases, however, attention turned to helping students develop strategies for arriving at value judgments on their own, strategies that we examine later in this chapter. At the same time that schools have attempted to adopt a value-neutral stance, more and more authorities have begun calling for schools to return to their former role (see Kohlberg, 1980; Shaver, 1985). In fact, as Ryan (1986) noted, by *not* treating values explicitly, schools are doing only half their job.

In 1981, over 70 percent of the parents responding to a poll (Gallup, 1981) on education favored the teaching of morals and values. Nevertheless, there is still lingering doubt and confusion among parents, teachers, administrators, and even students concerning how schools should accomplish that task. As a consequence, you may find teachers who take an absolutist approach (Beane, 1985/86) to values training; that is, they attempt to inculcate or instill certain values in their students. Other teachers take a more developmental approach to values education. Some of them emphasize helping students to clarify and become aware of the values they already hold, while others focus on helping children to improve the quality of their moral reasoning. Teachers in the latter group place special emphasis on the different ways children justify their actions and decisions. Still other teachers focus on helping students analyze the issues and consequences associated with value questions such as "Is it okay to make copies of someone's computer program?" You will also find teachers who intermingle absolutist and developmental approaches as they see fit.

Values education is the explicit attempt to teach about values and the process of valuing. Because it can take so many different forms (as we noted above), values education is a multidimensional movement, not a predetermined unit or program. The overall goals of values education include helping children (1) to become aware of the core values within our culture, e.g., honesty, truthfulness, etc.; (2) to become aware of the values they already hold; (3) to identify and analyze the value questions involved in an issue; and (4) to act in accordance with what they know. We examine four major approaches to values education in the next section.

APPROACHES TO VALUES EDUCATION

No one has ever seen a value. Like other concepts and ideas, value concepts exist only in our minds. As Fraenkel (1973) has noted, values are standards of conduct, beauty, efficiency, or worth that individuals believe in and try to live up to or maintain. Honesty and truthfulness, for example, are standards that can (but don't always) govern an individual's behavior. Even though we cannot see an individual's values, we can see the individual's behavior. Thus, when people say that "Honesty is the best policy" and then proceed to lie and cheat whenever it is to their advantage to do so, there is an obvious discrepancy between their actions and what they say; their value claims don't "fit" the behavior we see. The cliche that actions speak louder than words might be trite, but when it comes to values, one's actions are excellent indicators of the standards one tries (or says one tries) to live up to.

In dealing with values, standards for determining beauty are usually treated separately from standards of conduct. What we enjoy and find beautiful, such as the sun setting in the west, is said to reflect *aesthetics,* while determining whether one's conduct is "right" or "wrong" from a moral standpoint is reflected in the study of *ethics.*

Because schools deal with both aesthetics and ethics, distinguishing between the two provides a basis for determining the kind of values a teacher is attempting to influence. Most of the approaches to values education that we deal with in this chapter are more amenable to ethical questions or issues involving the moral standards or principles that influence one's behavior. Aesthetics can influence one's behavior, to be sure, but it more often involves matters of personal preference and individual prerogative, and for which there are few (if any) clear standards. Whether or not you like Picasso's paintings (or rock music), for example, is a matter of personal taste, and for someone to suggest that you *must* like Picasso's work (or rock music) could be viewed as an imposition on your personal prerogative. Arguments involving matters of aesthetics may be passionate (and loud), but they seldom have the moral implications associated with ethical issues.

An overview of four approaches to values education is provided in Table 7.1.

INCULCATION

Throughout human history, inculcation has been a frequently used technique for molding human behavior. As an approach to values education (or to all human behavior for that matter), *inculcation* refers to the process of making an impression on the mind through frequent repetition or insistent urging. In other words, inculcation is based on the premise that if you tell someone something often enough, sooner or later he or she will believe it (and behave accordingly).

Inculcation is a two-phase process that consists of (1) identifying the desired standard or value and (2) providing appropriate and consistent reinforcement, either positive or negative. In phase one, an adult might indicate a desired

TABLE 7.1 Overview of Approaches to Values Education

Approach	Purposes	Possible Methods
Inculcation	To instill or internalize certain values in students To change the existing values of students so they more nearly reflect certain desired values	Modeling; positive and negative reinforcement; mocking, nagging; manipulating alternatives; providing incomplete or biased information; games and simulations; role playing
Clarification	To help students become aware of and identify their own values and those of others To help students use rational thinking to examine feelings, values, and behavior patterns	Role-playing exercises; contrived or real value-laden situations; in-depth self-analysis exercises; sensitivity exercises; small-group discussion; simulation
Moral Reasoning	To help students develop more complex moral reasoning patterns	Moral-dilemma episodes with relatively structured and argumentative small-group discussion
Analysis	To help students use logical thinking and scientific investigation in conceptualizing their values and in deciding about value issues and questions	Structured, rational discussions that demand application of reasons as well as evidence; testing principles; analyzing analogous cases; debate; research

Source: Douglas P. Superka et al., VALUES EDUCATION SOURCEBOOK: CONCEPTUAL APPROACHES, MATERIALS ANALYSES, AND AN ANNOTATED BIBLIOGRAPHY. Boulder, Colo.: Social Science Education Consortium, and ERIC/CHESS, 1976, pp. 4–5. Adapted with permission.

standard such as "Children should respect their elders." In this case, the standard would probably be expressed verbally, but in other instances, adults could very well establish the expectation through modeling or other nonverbal means.

Reinforcement (phase two) can take a variety of forms—verbal, nonverbal, or physical action. In the case of respecting one's elders, children may learn what that standard is through negative reinforcement. Adult statements such as "How many times have I told you not to talk back to your elders?" (which isn't really a question), or "If you sass your father again you'll get a spanking" are examples of negative reinforcers. Observing another child being chastised for being disrespectful of an elder might also serve the same purpose. Adults may supply appropriate nonverbal reinforcement as well—a nod, a smile, etc.—but they sometimes neglect to provide positive verbal reinforcement. In other words, adults are often quick to deal with "bad behavior" but may neglect to supply positive verbal reinforcement for desired behavior, such as "You were very respectful of your grandfather." This may help to explain why children sometimes look upon desired behaviors as things they should do *because they will be punished if they don't.* Instead of regarding the behavior from a positive frame of reference—such as "respecting one's elders is good"—children sometimes adopt a negative view, as in "If I'm not respectful of my elders I'll be punished."

The Hidden Curriculum

The nature of teaching puts you in a position to inculcate values, either directly or indirectly. But in addition to what you say and do as a teacher, you are likely to have some help from the teaching materials you use, from the way schools are structured, and from the process of schooling itself.

The *hidden curriculum* refers to the multitude of things that schools (and teachers) convey to children, almost all of which are not part of the formal school curriculum. For example, most schools "teach" that meaningful work can be accomplished only in silence—complete silence—despite the fact that you know people who work well with a stereo going full blast. You have also encountered teachers who devoted much effort to catching students who talked at the "wrong" time, and you've learned that despite what some teachers said to the contrary, asking a question in their class was clearly an interruption, bordering on misconduct. (Sometimes it depended on the specific question and the context in which it was asked, of course.) You also discovered that learning in school was something that could be measured by the number of products (worksheets, reports, etc.) you completed, and that putting an incorrect heading on an otherwise perfect paper could produce devastating results. These cases could all be considered examples of incidental learning, yet they may be just as important as some of the subject matter that you were expected to learn formally but have long since forgotten. Incidental or not, teachers "taught" them and you learned them.

Curriculum and teaching materials usually focus explicitly on subject matter, but they too can have their more subtle, hidden agendas. For example, Nelson (1987) describes a fifth-grade social studies textbook which, for a section describing the development of the Constitution, uses the subhead "A Wise Plan of Government." We, like Nelson, agree with the description. Notice, however, that it is a value-concept statement, not a descriptive fact. As Nelson asks, "How can a student discuss *any* problems with the U.S. Constitution after reading that it is a 'wise plan of government'?" (page 78).

The degree to which teaching materials directly or indirectly inculcate values is sometimes a criterion by which they are judged. Many individuals want students to believe that our form of government was a wise choice, for example, and they are not overly concerned about the means used to instill that belief. From this point of view, a textbook that posed the question "Did the United States make a wise choice of government?" could be censored simply because it raises a question about our form of government—even if the ultimate answer to that question is "Yes." Likewise, a textbook that treats the question "Is it okay to lie sometimes?" could find itself under attack because it invites children to consider circumstances in which lying could be acceptable behavior. Because of this, the text (or teacher) could be accused of encouraging dishonesty. Such attacks may come from individuals who readily admit that they lie sometimes, but who argue that the question is something for adults to deal with, not children.

Be especially cautious of teaching materials that emphasize only positive virtues, such as honesty or truthfulness, but which exclude any mention of dishonesty or cheating. That seemingly innocent "emphasize the positive" approach could create an unintended credibility gap. Even kindergarten children know that not everyone is honest, and to pretend that dishonesty does not exist can create a credibility gap—if not in kindergarten then elsewhere in school. No

COMMENTARY: How Real Should Social Studies Be?

Elementary social studies programs have sometimes been criticized for presenting an idealized conception of the world. Sometimes those criticisms appear in unlikely places, as in Robert Goldhammer's supervision text entitled *Clinical Supervision: Special Methods for the Supervision of Teachers,* published by Holt, Rinehart and Winston, Inc., in 1969. Here's what Goldhammer said about social studies:

Imagine a unit of study somewhere in the primary grades, on "The Family . . ." How is "family" generally represented in the early grades?

The houses in which families live never, as far as we are told, include toilets. Members of the family never scratch themselves, utter obscenities, cheat on their wives, fix traffic tickets, drink beer, play the horses, falsify their tax returns, strike one another, make love, use deodorants, gossip on the telephone, buy on credit, have ulcers, or manifest a million other signs of life that even the most culturally deprived child knows about in the most intimate detail. . . .

Certainly at their dinner tables, no textbook fathers talk about having out-bargained that New York Jew, about the niggers who are trying to take over the neighborhood, the cops, . . . and so on. On the contrary, one may safely expect the textbook family to be disembodied, apolitical, generally without a specific ethnic identity or religious affiliation, free of social prejudice, innocent of grief, economically secure, vocationally stable, antiseptic and law-abiding straight down the middle. It occupies a universe from which disaffection, divorce, cynicism, loneliness, neurosis, bastardy, atheism, tension, self-doubt, wrecked cars, and cockroaches are inevitably absent.

Unless he is downright dull, it is impossible to imagine that at some level of experience the child is not aware of the thundering disparity between the real world and the school's priggish, distorted, emasculated representations of that world. It seems reasonable to suspect that the child's knowledge almost certainly includes the realization that, in plain language, the curriculum is phony, at least in relation to the example we have considered.

What reactions would you anticipate if textbooks actually presented what Goldhammer criticizes them for not presenting? From students? Parents? Teachers?

matter how desirable it may seem on the surface, trying to inculcate values by presenting a desired but one-sided view of human interaction can yield results far different from those you might expect.

VALUES CLARIFICATION

Most people, we suspect, are so close to themselves that they really don't know themselves—a statement which, though it may seem to contradict itself at first, should take on additional clarity as we go. We contend that you are so close, so intimate with yourself that you are unable to stand back and take a completely objective look at yourself. In fact, we suggest that the major way in which you learn about yourself is by watching others. For example, have you ever found yourself observing someone and then saying to yourself "Hey, that's me! I do that too" or "I would never want to be like *that*"?

Or consider what often happens when you are asked to describe yourself. Once you get beyond a physical description, which astute observers don't need anyway, and once you get beyond your hobbies, interests, and talents, you will ultimately arrive at your values. And upon being asked what moral characteristics you exhibit, the result is apt to be a watered-down version of the Scout law—trustworthy, loyal, helpful, . . . and obedient (at times). To that, you'll usually encounter the request to "be honest." You may then respond with a statement such as "Well, I'm a little lazy, and I tend to put things off until the last minute."

Thus far, with the exception of your talents, interests, and possibly your hobbies, you've probably described a typical American. What you are not likely to have described are the norms—values, if you will—that are unique to you and set you apart from others. You—and many Americans like you—are so close to yourself that you are probably not aware of what some of your own norms and values actually are—until, that is, you are confronted with situations that force you to act on them. Values clarification is an approach to values education that is intended, in part, to do just that—help individuals clarify what their values are in a rational and justifiable way.

The values-clarification approach to values education is usually associated with the book *Values and Teaching,* by Louis Raths, Merrill Harmin, and Sidney Simon (1978). A variety of teaching activities is presented in *Values Clarification: A Handbook of Practical Strategies for Teachers and Students,* by Sidney Simon, Leland Howe, and Howard Kirschenbaum (1972).

The Approach Defined

Values clarification is considered a value-neutral approach. That means it does not try to instill a particular value or set of values, as is the case in inculcation, but rather advocates a seven-phase valuing process, as follows:

Choosing
  1. **Encourage children to make choices, and to make them *freely*.**

2. Help them *discover alternatives* when faced with choices.

3. Help children *weigh* alternatives thoughtfully, reflecting on *the consequences* of each.

Prizing

4. Encourage children to consider what it is that they prize and *cherish*.

5. Give them opportunities to *affirm their choices* to others.

Acting

6. Encourage them to act, *behave,* live *in accordance with their choices.*

7. Help them be aware of repeated behaviors or patterns in their life (Raths et al., 1978, pp. 28, 38). [Emphasis added.]

Why should people be clear about the values they hold? Raths et al. (1978, p. 10) indicate that "It seems to us that the pace and complexity of modern life has so exacerbated the problem of deciding what is good and what is right and what is desirable that large numbers of children are finding it increasingly bewildering, even overwhelming, to decide what is worth valuing, what is worth their time and energy." Kirschenbaum further elaborated on the major hypothesis of values clarification by stating, "If a person skillfully and consistently uses the 'valuing process' [outlined above], this increases the likelihood that the confusion, conflict, etc., will turn into decisions and living that are both personally satisfying and socially constructive" (Kirschenbaum, 1977, citing Kirschenbaum, Harmin, Howe, and Simon, 1975, p. 398).

Values clarification is an *orientation,* not a set formula, that teachers adopt to help students employ the valuing process outlined above. Values clarification is not something that must be done on a whole-class basis, although teachers may do so if they wish. In many instances, values clarification can be appropriate for interacting with a single student.

The Clarifying Response

Whether used with individual students or an entire class, the clarifying response is a key element of the values-clarification approach. The nature of the clarifying response is illustrated in the following exchange:

Teacher: Bruce, don't you want to go outside and play on the playground?
Student: I dunno. I suppose so.
Teacher: Is there something that you would rather do?
Student: I dunno. Nothing much.
Teacher: You don't seem much to care, Bruce. Is that right?
Student: I suppose so.
Teacher: And mostly anything we do will be all right with you?
Student: I suppose so. Well, not anything, I guess.
Teacher: Well, Bruce, we had better go out to the playground now with the

As part of the values clarification approach, a teacher can use the clarifying response in which he or she encourages students to examine and think about their ideas but does not hold up one "right answer" to them. (© *Elizabeth Crews*)

others. You let me know sometime if you think of something you would like to do. (Dialogue adapted from Raths et al., 1978, p. 55.)

As this exchange illustrates, the intent is not to get the child to adopt the seven-step values-clarifying process in a single fifteen-second exchange. That's a long-range goal, to be accomplished over a period of time. The intent of the clarifying response is to encourage students to look at their ideas and to think about them without moralizing, criticizing, evaluating, or otherwise suggesting that you, as the teacher, have a "right answer" in mind (Raths, 1978, p. 55). If the whole exchange isn't genuine, it will fall flat on its face.

Productive clarifying responses may include the following:

Is this important to you?

Are you happy about that?

Did you think of other (alternative) things you could do?

Would you really do that or are you just talking?

What other possibilities are there?

Would you do the same thing over again?

Is it important enough that you would be willing to share your idea (project, experiences, etc.) with the others? (Raths et al., 1978, pp. 59–63)

Students often find whole-class or small-group values-clarification activities to be particularly engaging. The following student activity is adapted from one entitled "The Miracle Workers," which appears in *Values Clarification*.

MODEL STUDENT ACTIVITY

The Miracle Workers

Begin by telling students "Several world-famous experts have agreed to provide their services to this class. Their skills are so effective that they are considered miracle workers by the people who have used their services. You can be 100 percent sure that they can do what they say they will. However, their services are in such demand that you must choose only those three workers whose gifts you would most like to receive. You should also choose those three workers who are least appealing to you—the ones whose services you don't think you (or other members of the class) will want or need. After you have identified your choices, we will do the same thing in small groups."

Then present the following list.

_____ Dr. Face Lift—a famous surgeon who, by using a new painless technique he has invented, can make you look the way you have always wanted to look. If you want more muscles, he can do that. If you want to be taller, thinner, or to change the color of your eyes, hair, or anything, he will do it for you.

_____ Abby Landers—Her advice will help you be well liked by everyone. Your life will be filled with good friends.

_____ Madame Xavier—You will never have a question about the future and what it holds for you if you select this expert's services.

_____ Dr. Gannon Welby—You will never need to worry about sickness or injury if you select this expert. Perfect health will be yours!

_____ Dr. I.Q.—The world-famous thinker will make you brilliant. You might never need to study (or do homework) again.

_____ Mr. Yule Makamint—Wealth—all the money you ever dreamed of—will be yours if you select this expert.

_____ Olive Branch—Peace and harmony will be yours. This expert will stop all fights—on the playground, at home, or anywhere in the world.

_____ Chunky Goodbar—This expert will provide you with a free, lifetime supply of candy, gum, ice cream, and potato chips. He will also make sure you have no cavities on your next ten trips to the dentist.

_____ Ima Starmaker—Did you ever dream of becoming a Dan Marino, a Michael Jackson, or a Chris Evert? Well, you can, and for any sport you choose. Just make Ima Starmaker one of your first three choices.

Procedure

1. Have the students rank choices individually, then in small groups.

2. Groups should then record choices on chart paper or on the board.

3. Compare groups' choices, both most favorable and least favorable, in terms of similarities and/or unusual choices. Discuss feelings and reactions.

4. As an optional step, present students with another candidate—such as Dr. Liva Longlife as shown below. Ask them to go through the first three steps again to determine whether the additional candidate caused them to alter their selections.

_____ Dr. Liva Longlife—This expert has the secret of eternal youth and can help you live as long as you wish. His treatment is painless, and some of his previous patients have lived to be over 200 years old.

Source: Reprinted (adapted) by permission of DODD, MEAD, & COMPANY, INC. from VALUES CLARIFICA-TION: A HANDBOOK OF PRACTICAL STRATEGIES FOR TEACHERS AND STUDENTS by Sidney B. Simon, Leland W. Howe, and Howard Kirschenbaum. Copyright © 1972, 1978 by Hart Publishing Company, Inc.

Note how adding a tenth candidate (Dr. Liva Longlife) in the activity above increases the number of alternatives to choose among. This addition could well force individuals to change their priorities—or at least to reexamine them. Each time an alternative is added or removed, the "Miracle Workers" becomes a different activity. Because of that, students' selections (priorities) are likely to change accordingly. Altering the activity in this way illustrates two aspects of values clarification that have come under criticism: (1) it suggests that the merits of a particular value position depend on the situation (or what is called "situational ethics") and (2) that in the absence of clear "right answers," one value or value system is as good as another.

What Critics Say About Values Clarification

Values-clarification activities have sometimes generated enough controversy that their use has been either severely restricted or banned in some school systems. These actions have been largely the result of parental objections, the basis for which should be apparent in the following episode.

In a school system in the Southwest, a sixth-grade teacher had decided to use an activity entitled "The Cave-In," which appeared in *Values Clarification* (Simon et al., 1972). As the instructions for the activity directed, the desks had been moved out of the way and the class was seated on the floor around a single lighted candle. The class was then told that while they were exploring an underground cavern, an earth tremor had caused a cave-in. Only a narrow pathway to the outside world remained, but other rocks loosened by the tremor were expected to fall momentarily. The teacher then informed the class that, in order to escape, they must form a single line. Individuals at the head of the line would be most likely to get out safely, while those at the end of the line faced almost certain death. The students had to decide among themselves which places in the line they should be entitled to. Those students who agreed to go toward the end of the line were, in effect, agreeing to die.

The instructions for this activity contained a cautionary note to the teacher indicating that this was a powerful activity that should only be used with students who had developed a high mutual-trust level and who were experienced in values-clarification activities. Since the teacher had already used several other values-clarification activities with the class, he apparently thought these criteria were met.

When the activity got underway, several students said "I pass," which was a recognized way for them to indicate that they didn't want to participate in the activity. For a while, nobody said very much, until one boy rose and stated, "I can't do anything right; I guess I deserve to die," and walked to the end of the line. The class was dumbfounded, as was the teacher, who wisely ended the activity immediately and attempted to counsel the boy individually.

Several parents heard about what had gone on and protested to the teacher, the principal, and the school board. The teacher agreed that things hadn't gone as planned and that he wouldn't use the activity again. However, some parents indicated that they didn't want their children placed in such a situation—ever—and to ensure that they were not, the parents requested that such activities be banned from that school system. The school board agreed.

In this case, and in other instances like it, the positive benefits that might result from other, less potent values-clarification techniques have been condemned (and banned) through guilt by association. Nevertheless, two questions must still be asked: (1) to what extent should the positive benefits of values clarification be weighed against the potential of doing psychological harm to a child; and (2) should elementary and middle school students be confronted with situations where they must participate in making life-and-death decisions?

Privacy   Much of the criticism directed against values-clarification activities has focused on the use of techniques that can jeopardize students' rights to privacy, such as requiring students to state their beliefs publicly. It's almost impossible to clarify your values publicly without disclosing personal information about yourself and your relationships with others, including your family. Thus the very nature of values clarification can constitute a threat to the privacy rights of students and their families. This may be further compounded by explicit questioning techniques that may ask students to identify such things as who in their family brings them the greatest sadness, or by projective techniques that ask students to complete sentences that begin "If I were a dog . . .," for example.

Students often voluntarily reveal their innermost fears and secrets to teachers, which then places the teacher in the role of amateur psychologist and counselor. When students do this voluntarily, the role is imposed upon teachers. But many values-clarification activities are specifically designed to elicit students' feelings, beliefs, and fears. Imagine, for example, what you would say to the boy who said that he couldn't do anything right and decided to go to the end of the line in the episode described above. Would you cajole him, reassure him, or what? Notice also that the clarifying responses shown on page 220 are deceptively benign. Those responses and questions are much like the ones trained counselors and psychologists use in group-therapy sessions. Asking a question like "Is that

COMMENTARY: Privacy and the Hatch Amendment

All of the developmental approaches to values education (values clarification, moral reasoning, and values analysis) offer opportunities for children to reflect on their beliefs and attitudes. As we noted earlier, when children share their feelings publicly, the possibility exists that the child's privacy (or the family's privacy) could be invaded.

To protect the students' privacy in school settings, Congress enacted the Hatch Act in 1974. That Act ensured the right of parents and guardians to review the instructional materials used in federally supported research and experimental programs. In 1978, the Hatch Act was amended to include parental review of any testing and treatment that could cause children to reveal their political affiliation; any potentially embarrassing mental or psychological problems; sexual behavior and attitudes; any illegal or antisocial behavior; critical appraisals of close family members; and other information of a personal nature (see, e.g., Greene and Pasch, 1985/86). Note that the Act does not prohibit discussions that might involve such information, but rather makes such "treatments" subject to parental review.

The Hatch Amendment applies to federally funded programs. However, some groups have interpreted the Act as if it applied to everything done in schools. The types of activities for which parental approval may be required is mind boggling. These activities include role-playing situations involving moral issues; education pertaining to alcohol and drug abuse; death education, including education about suicide and abortion; instruction in nuclear war and nuclear policy; and education in interpersonal relationships.

The types of activities that might be subject to review and possible restriction illustrate that the school's role in moral education is a matter of continuing debate. However, because a teacher's activities *could* become controversial does not mean that they *will* become so. Our purpose is not to suggest that you avoid values education but rather to highlight the fact that moral education is an area that involves deeply held and sometimes conflicting beliefs.

important to you?" is easy enough, but you may get answers that you are not trained to handle. If that happens, stop everything before you get in over your head.

Moral vs. Nonmoral Issues   Values clarification has also been criticized for its failure to distinguish between moral (ethical) and nonmoral (aesthetic) value issues. Some values-clarification activities, for example, ask students to identify their favorite foods, their hobbies, and the like—things that are largely a matter of personal taste. Obviously, there's nothing immoral or unethical about disliking mushrooms. But in activities like the "Cave-In" simulation, moral issues are clearly involved. Helping children decide how they will spend their allowance, and helping them decide which individuals should be permitted to live and which should die, are clearly not issues of equal magnitude. Indeed, unless you are prepared to help students deal with the issues underlying life-or-death decisions, we suggest that you avoid such activities entirely.

Another criticism that has been leveled at the values-clarification approach is that it tends to promote *ethical relativism*. Ethical relativism refers to the belief that individuals' actions are governed by the situations in which they find themselves—by what is practical or expedient, for example—rather than by overarching moral principles, such as the dignity of the individual and the sanctity of human life, that should apply in all situations. This criticism seems to stem from the fact that there is no justification phase in the seven-step valuing process (pages 218–219). Because students are neither asked nor required to justify or defend their decisions, they could come away with the impression that one person's views are as good as anyone else's, *regardless* of the situation.

It's true that in some values-clarification activities, such as "The Miracle Workers," one person's selection of "experts" isn't necessarily any better or worse than someone else's; the selection can legitimately be a matter of personal taste. However, upon moving to activities where moral questions are involved, as in "The Cave-In" simulation, it seems almost irresponsible to suggest that life-and-death issues should be settled as a matter of personal opinion.

In summary, the major criticisms directed toward the values-clarification approach concern the following:

1. the use of techniques (such as stating beliefs publicly) that could jeopardize the student's right to privacy
2. the reliance on techniques and methods that sometimes place teachers in the role of a psychological therapist (or psychiatrist)
3. the failure to distinguish moral from nonmoral issues
4. the tacit acceptance of all value beliefs as being equally valid (ethical relativism) (Lockwood, 1977)

In addition to the criticisms noted above, researchers (Lockwood, 1978; Leming, 1985) have raised serious questions about the overall effectiveness of values clarification as a teaching technique. For example, after reviewing over seventy-five studies conducted between 1976 and 1984, Leming (1985) found that values-clarification techniques seldom produced the kinds of attitudinal or behavioral changes that the researchers had anticipated. In light of such dismal findings, Leming suggests that the continued popularity of this approach may be the result, in part, of the wide assortment of values-clarification activities available for classroom use.

MORAL REASONING

The *moral-reasoning* approach to values education is closely associated with the work of Lawrence Kohlberg, the late Harvard psychologist. Kohlberg and his associates first developed a theory dealing with how children learn to reason morally, and then developed a teaching strategy to help children improve the quality of their moral reasoning. In order to determine what makes one kind of moral reasoning "better" than another it's necessary to understand the theory on which Kohlberg's teaching strategy is based.

In many respects, Kohlberg's research is similar to that of Jean Piaget, which we presented in Chapter 5. Piaget was interested in how children learn to think and reason, while Kohlberg narrowed that focus to the question "How do individuals develop the ability to reason morally (to justify their actions)?"

After investigating moral reasoning among individuals of various ages and from various cultures, Kohlberg found sufficient similarities to be able to identify a Piaget-like developmental sequence, which is shown in Table 7.2. Note that at one time there were six stages in the developmental sequence, but after further research, Kohlberg redefined his model so that Stage 5 now incorporates what was formerly in Stage 6.

Sooner or later almost everyone reaches Piaget's last developmental stage, formal operations. Kohlberg has found, however, that fewer than 25 percent of American adults ever reach Stage 5 (Principled Level); the rest of us consistently operate at lower stages. If you consider that the moral basis of the Bill of Rights reflects Stage 5 reasoning, Kohlberg's findings suggest that we may be living in a society where the majority of citizens neither understand nor appreciate the fundamental moral principles upon which the society was founded. This may also explain why fifth- and eighth-grade teachers often find that teaching a required unit on "the Constitution" is so frustrating; the majority of their students may be operating at Stage 3, the level at which their primary interest is in gaining the social approval of others. In many instances, students are quite unable to deal with the Stage 5 reasoning on which the Constitution is based.

In Kohlberg's scheme, as in Piaget's, each stage serves as a basis for the next. But while Piaget was able to link age and stage and say, for example, that children around the age of eleven or twelve should begin to be able to deal with mental abstractions, the age-stage relationship is less evident in moral reasoning. As Lickona has noted, "In general . . . Stages 1 and 2 dominate in the primary school years and persist in some individuals long beyond that. Stage 3 gains ground during the upper elementary grades and often remains the major orientation

TABLE 7.2 Kohlberg's Stages of Moral Development

Level	Stage	Characteristics
Principled: Concern for fidelity to self-chosen moral principles	5	*Motivator:* Internal commitment to principles of "conscience"; respect for the rights, life, and dignity of all persons. *Awareness:* Particular moral/social rules are social contracts, arrived at through democratic reconciliation of differing viewpoints and open to change. *Assumption:* Moral principles have universal validity; law derives from morality, not vice versa.
Conventional: Concern for meeting external social expectations	4	*Motivator:* Sense of duty or obligation to live up to socially defined role and maintain existing social order for good of all. *Awareness:* There is a larger social "system" that regulates the behavior of individuals within it. *Assumption:* Authority or the social order is the source of morality.
	3	*Motivator:* Desire for social approval by living up to good boy/good girl stereotype; meeting expectations of others. *Awareness:* Need to consider intentions and feelings of others; cooperation means ideal reciprocity (golden rule). *Assumption:* Good behavior equals social conformity.
Preconventional: Concern for external, concrete consequences to self	2	*Motivator:* Self-interest: what's in it for me? *Awareness:* Human relations are governed by concrete reciprocity; let's make a deal; you scratch my back, I'll scratch yours. *Assumption:* Have to look out for self; obligated only to those who help you; each person has own needs and viewpoints.
	1	*Motivator:* Fear of getting caught; desire to avoid punishment by authority. *Awareness:* There are rules and consequences of breaking them. *Assumption:* Might makes right; what's regarded by those in power is "good"; what's punished is "bad."

Source: Based on material in Thomas Lickona, "How to Encourage Moral Development," *Learning,* 5 (March 1977), pp. 37–42.

through the end of high school. Stage 4 begins to emerge in adolescence. Only one in four persons moves on in later adolescence or adulthood to Stage 5" (1977, p. 39).

The situation is further complicated by the fact that although individuals may be capable of reasoning at higher levels, they sometimes use lower-level reasoning to justify their actions. Consider, for example, those people who feel that the 55-mph speed limit (on other than rural interstate highways) is an unjust law and therefore one they can break as a matter of principle. That's Stage 5 reasoning (unless, of course, they are using the "matter of principle" as a rationalization for their real belief that they should be able to drive as fast as they want to—in which case it would be Stage 1 throughout). Yet those same individuals will not exceed the speed limit, even as a matter of principle, if there is a chance they might be caught. Self-interest, then, appears to be a confounding factor. To the extent that Kohlberg's stages provide rough—and we emphasize *rough*—indicators of the types of moral understanding you can expect from students, the question then becomes one of how you get students to move to higher levels of moral reasoning.

The following statements reflect different stages of moral reasoning. Can you identify what the stages are?

How Do You Justify Your Actions?

Statement	Stage
1. "I don't oppose busing (for the purpose of integrating the schools) because it's the law."	_____
2. "I never run in the hall because . . .	
a. I'll be punished if I get caught."	_____
b. someone might get hurt, especially me."	_____
c. it's against the rules."	_____
3. "The only way to make it in a dog-eat-dog world is to cover your flank."	_____
4. "All of us, as individuals, are entitled to certain rights."	_____
5. "I do what every good teacher should do; I keep my students in line and I don't rock the boat."	_____
6. "I never exceed the speed limit because I might get caught—I even bought a radar detector."	_____

(Answers: No. 1, 4; No. 2a, 1; No. 2b, 2; No. 2c, 1; No. 3, 2; No. 4, 5; No. 5, 3; No. 6, 1.)

Using Moral Dilemmas

The intent of this approach to values education is to help students move toward more complex (higher-stage-level) patterns of moral reasoning. Justifying one's value orientation, which was not a critical phase in values clarification, becomes a critical element in moral reasoning. This is because the way individuals justify a course of action reflects their stage (or level) of moral development.

Kohlberg's research indicates that students will be stimulated to move to the next stage of moral development upon repeated exposure to higher levels of moral reasoning. Such exposure can be gained by helping students work with moral dilemmas—stories or situations in which conflicting moral principles are involved—that require students to identify and evaluate alternative courses of action. Note that a dilemma is a situation in which the alternative courses of action are either desirable or undesirable, but not both. When the two elements are mixed, there is no dilemma; the individual merely follows the most desirable course of action.

A simple moral dilemma might involve a seven-year-old girl named Holly who comes upon a small boy whose kitten is stranded in a tree. Tears stream down the boy's cheeks as he pleads with Holly to rescue his kitten. Although Holly is sympathetic, the last time she climbed a tree she fell and sprained her wrist. After that incident Holly promised her father she wouldn't climb any more trees. What should Holly do? (Lickona, 1977, p. 37)

Holly could do a number of things, including trying to get help from an adult. Or she could break her promise to her father. By exploring such alternatives in group settings, moral dilemmas are intended to provide students with exposure to different (and hopefully higher) stages of moral reasoning. For younger children, the dilemmas should be fairly simple; they should involve relatively few characters and moral principles (obedience to authority vs. helping a friend in need, for instance). Note also that changing just one element in a moral dilemma, such as changing the kitten in a tree to a kitten trapped on a telephone pole, alters the entire situation.

For older students, the moral dilemmas can be much more complex. The Model Student Activity below involves the question of whether a young German girl should hide her Jewish friend from the Nazi Gestapo.

MODEL STUDENT ACTIVITY

Helga's Dilemma

Helga and Rachel had grown up together. They were best friends despite the fact that Helga's family was Christian and Rachel's was Jewish. For many years, this religious difference didn't seem to matter much in Germany, but after Hitler seized power, the situation changed. Hitler required Jews to wear armbands with the Star of David on them. He began to encourage his followers to destroy the property of Jewish people and to beat them on the street. Finally, he began to arrest Jews and deport them. Rumors went around the city that many Jews were being killed. Hiding Jews for whom the Gestapo (Hitler's secret police) was looking was a serious crime and violated a law of the German government.

One night Helga heard a knock at the door. When she opened it, she found Rachel on the step huddled in a dark coat. Quickly Rachel stepped inside. She had been to a meeting, she said, and when she returned home, she had found Gestapo members all around her house. Her parents and brothers had already been taken away. Knowing her fate if the Gestapo caught her, Rachel ran to her old friend's house.

Now what should Helga do? If she turned Rachel away, the Gestapo would eventually find her. Helga knew that most of the Jews who were sent away had been killed, and she didn't want her best friend to share that fate. But hiding the Jews broke the law. Helga would risk her own security and that of her family if she tried to hide Rachel. But she had a tiny room behind the chimney on the third floor where Rachel might be safe.

Question: *Should Helga hide Rachel?*

Procedure

1. Ask students to identify what should be done and why. "What should Helga do?"

2. Divide the class into small groups, either in terms of those who support a particular course of action or at random, and then ask them to discuss their reasons and justify the course of action they have chosen. "Why should Helga do what you think she should do?"

3. Permit groups to summarize and clarify their positions.

4. Ask additional probing questions. "Is the welfare of one's relatives more important than the welfare of one's friends?"

Students should be encouraged to express reasonable value positions, though it is not necessary that they arrive at consensus.

Source: Social Studies Curriculum Center, Carnegie-Mellon University. "Helga's Dilemma" also appears in Galbraith and Jones (1975, p. 18).

─────────────────

How students justify what Helga should or should not do will identify their level of moral reasoning, as Galbraith and Jones (1975, p. 20) illustrate in the following:

Stage 1: "If Helga lets Rachel in she might also get into trouble with the Gestapo."

Stage 2: "Helga shouldn't let her in because Rachel probably wouldn't let Helga in if she got into trouble with the Gestapo."

Stage 3: "Helga has an obligation to her family. She will really let them down if she gets them in trouble."

Stage 4: "Helga has an obligation to obey the laws of her society."

Stage 5: "**Friendship is not the issue. If Helga was really concerned about the problem in her society, she should be helping all the Jews in order to protest the government action. She should not hide Rachel unless she intends to hide other Jews and to make a public protest in opposition to putting Jews in concentration camps.**"

The small-group decision making and the extended discussion of complex issues associated with moral dilemmas can demand a level of experience and sophistication that younger children simply cannot handle. In light of this, an appropriate alternative for younger children (and older children too) is role playing.

The following Model Student Activity presents a brief example of how a teacher might use role-playing for a value-related issue. For illustrative purposes, we have used the "Holly and the Cat in the Tree" dilemma.

MODEL STUDENT ACTIVITY

"Holly and the Cat in the Tree"— A Procedure for Young Children

Introduce the Situation
Teacher: "One day, a little girl named Holly was walking down the street . . ."

Role Playing
Teacher: We need someone to play Holly and the little boy. James? Do you want to play Holly?
James: I'm not playin' no girl.
Teacher: Sure you can, James. We're just role-playing.
James: (Shakes his head, no.)
Teacher: Okay, Merryl . . .
(Two students role play a possible solution for the incident.)

1. Mini-discussion
   Teacher: Did they manage to solve the problem?
   (Brief discussion ensues. If a child wants to suggest a different solution, move to part (2) immediately. If not, the teacher suggests another solution, secures new role players, and the incident is reenacted again.)

2. Role play another alternative.
   Continue (1) and (2) until children are satisfied they have identified the possible alternatives.

Debriefing
1. Review briefly.
   Teacher: "Let's see. In the first incident, Holly disobeyed her Daddy and

climbed the tree. In the second, she went to get somebody else to help. What happened in the third incident? . . ."

Louise: "Holly made the boy get someone else to help."

Teacher: "Thanks, Louise. Then in the fourth incident . . ."

2. Evaluate alternatives.

Teacher: "Were some solutions better than others? And do you think Holly's father should punish her for disobeying?"

Students' responses will vary.

Teacher: (Summarizing) "It's good to help a person in need. But we should obey our parents too. Sometimes we need to look for a way to do both things. It's hard, sometimes, isn't it?" (More discussion may ensue.)

The debriefing is not intended as an opportunity for the teacher to moralize or present "right" answers. Rather, the pluses and minuses of each alternative should be summarized.

What the Critics Say About Moral Reasoning

Much of the criticism directed toward the moral-reasoning approach has questioned either the adequacy of Kohlberg's theory or the contention that higher-stage reasoning is necessarily better than lower-stage reasoning. An earlier question about whether discussing moral dilemmas results in movement from one stage to the next has largely been resolved. Leming (1985) states that "unlike the values-clarification approach, the weight of the evidence supports the claim . . . that the discussion of moral dilemmas can stimulate development through the stages of moral reasoning" (p. 131). However, the research suggests that for this to occur, the discussions must take place over a period of time, not just once or twice during a semester.

Because most criticism of moral reasoning involves the more theoretical aspects of moral development, we recommend that you examine the publications listed in the "Suggested Readings" section at the end of this chapter.

VALUES ANALYSIS

"Is it morally right for missionaries to introduce new technology into a primitive culture when to do so may cause serious disruptions in that culture's way of life?"

This question is an outgrowth of a situation we shall describe in greater detail in Chapter 8, and it also serves as an example of the kind of value issue that can be attacked through values analysis. Recognize, however, that with a couple of minor changes, the question could change to "Should missionaries introduce new tech-

In the values analysis approach, students must not only gather and organize evidence but also choose among possible solutions and decide what appropriate action should be taken in a particular situation. (© *Steve Takatsuno*)

nology into a primitive culture when they know, in advance, that to do so may cause serious disruptions in that culture's way of life?" Voilà! Here's a moral dilemma amenable to the procedures we noted in the previous section.

In the values-analysis approach to values education, the emphasis is on *analysis*—careful, deliberate, discriminating analysis. The idea is to examine value questions as rationally and unemotionally as possible. Whereas the moral-reasoning approach would have students take a position and then justify it, values analysis would have students refrain from taking a position until they have analyzed the issued involved.

The following tasks are essential to the analysis of any value question or issue:

1. Identifying the issue
2. Clarifying the value question

3. Gathering and organizing evidence

4. Assessing the accuracy and relevance of the evidence

5. Identifying potential solutions

6. Identifying and assessing the possible consequences for each solution

7. Choosing among the alternatives

8. Deciding and taking appropriate action

There is no "best" way to get students involved in these processes. Any means the teacher can use to get them involved (except browbeating and coercion, of course) is acceptable. Ultimately, the intent is to wean students from the teacher's influence so that they are able to follow the processes on their own.

What the Critics Say About Values Analysis

The critics don't have much to say about values analysis, at least as far as we can determine. However, because some elements of this valuing process are similar to those found in values clarification, some of the same cautions may be in order. Notice also that elements of values analysis (and the other approaches to values education) rely heavily on teachers asking a series of questions. In some instances, it may be necessary for a single student to respond to a sequence of three or four questions (or more if elaboration is required). In a class of twenty-five students, a teacher could find herself engaged in what amounts to a dialogue with one student. Hopefully the other twenty-four children will be interested enough to pay attention, but the longer the mini-dialogues go on, the more likely young children are to become disinterested. In light of this, several cautions (which also apply to discussions in general) seem apparent:

1. Teachers should be especially sensitive to the interest level of students who are not participating actively.

2. When possible, the approaches should be used in a small-group format.

3. When student interest begins to sag, summarize, and then move on to something else.

SUMMARY

Values underlie *everything* a teacher does. It is simply impossible (and inadvisable) to sterilize lessons to make them value-free. Under the principle of academic freedom, teachers have the right to teach the truth as they know it, even if their views differ from the prevailing community sentiment. However, academic freedom does not entitle teachers to knowingly violate state laws or to ignore direct orders from principals, superintendents, or other duly constituted authorities, for to do so could constitute insubordination. In communities where school boards have limited the use of values-clarification activities, for example, the situation is relatively clear. Barring these limitations, teachers are generally free to teach and to approach values education as they see fit.

In this chapter we have tried to do three things: first, to examine the roles that values and value conflicts play in the context of teaching; second, to identify four approaches to values education—(1) inculcation, (2) values clarification, (3) moral reasoning, and (4) values analysis; and, third, to identify some criticisms leveled against each of these approaches.

If our treatment of values education has made you a bit cautious about attempting some of the strategies we've described in this chapter, we have succeeded in meeting one of our objectives. Don't misunderstand us; we think values education is important—vitally important. At the same time, it is (1) an area that may require skills that exceed those provided in most teacher training programs, skills similar to those used by trained and licensed psychotherapists, and (2) an area that has the potential to violate the student's right to privacy, no matter how noble our motives. The final chapter on the appropriate role of values education has yet to be written. It's still a matter of concern and, in some cases, controversy. To the extent that moral dilemmas play a significant role in values education, so too is there a dilemma of sorts about values education itself.

SUGGESTED ACTIVITIES

1. Select and examine at least one chapter in a social studies textbook for any grade level. Determine the extent to which statements within the chapter, such as "A Wise Plan of Government," reflect a value-based agenda.

2. If you are one who likes the challenge of a difficult activity, attempt to identify behavioral (performance) objectives for "The Miracle Workers" or for "Helga's Dilemma."

3. Select an elementary social studies text for the grade level you'd like to teach. For any section of the book you choose, indicate how you might incorporate values education into your approach to teaching that segment.

REFERENCES

Beane, James A. 1985/86. "The Continuing Controversy Over Affective Education." *Educational Leadership,* 42 (December/January), 26–31.

Coombs, Jerrold R., and Milton Meux. 1971. "Teaching Strategies for Value Analysis. In *Values Education: Rationale, Strategies, and Procedures,* ed. Lawrence E. Metcalf. Yearbook, 41, 29–74. Washington, D.C.: National Council for the Social Studies.

Davis, E. Dale. 1984. "Should the Public Schools Teach Values?" *Phi Delta Kappan,* 65 (January), 358–60.

Fraenkel, Jack. 1977. *How to Teach About Values: An Analytic Approach.* Englewood Cliffs, N.J.: Prentice-Hall.

Galbraith, Ronald E., and Thomas M. Jones. 1975. "Teaching Strategies for Moral Dilemmas: An Application of Kohlberg's Theory of Moral Development to the Social Studies Classroom." *Social Education,* 39 (January), 16–22.

Gallup, George H. 1981. "Gallup Poll of the Public's Attitudes Toward the Public Schools." *Phi Delta Kappan,* 63 (September), 33–47.

Goldhammer, Robert. 1969. *Clinical Supervision: Special Methods for the Supervision of Teachers.* New York: Holt, Rinehart, and Winston.

Greene, Bert I., and Marvin Pasch. 1985/86. "Observing the Birth of the Hatch Amendment Regulations: Lessons for the Education Profession." *Educational Leadership,* 42 (December/January), 42–48.

Hersh, R. H., J. P. Miller, and G. D. Fielding. 1980. *Models of Moral Education: An Appraisal.* New York: Longman.

Kirschenbaum, Howard, Merrill Harmin, Leland Howe, and Sidney B. Simon. 1975. *Phi Delta Kappan,* 56 (April), 743–46.

Kirschenbaum, Howard. 1977. "In Support of Values Clarification." *Social Education,* 41 (May), 401–02.

Kohlberg, Lawrence. 1980. "High School Democracy and Education for a Just Society." In *Moral Education: A First Generation of Research and Development,* ed. R. D. Mosher. New York: Praeger.

Leming, James S. 1985. "Research on Social Studies Curriculum and Instruction: Interventions and Outcomes in the Socio-Moral Domain." In *Review of Research in Social Studies Education, 1976–83,* ed. William B. Stanley. Washington, D.C.: National Council for the Social Studies, and Boulder, Colo.: ERIC Clearinghouse for Social Studies/Social Science Education, and the Social Science Education Consortium.

Lickona, Thomas. 1977. "How to Encourage Moral Development." *Learning,* 5 (March), 37–43.

———. 1980. "Beyond Justice: A Curriculum for Cooperation." In *Development of Moral Reasoning,* ed. D. B. Cochrane and M. Manley-Casimir. New York: Praeger.

———. 1983. *Raising Good Children: Helping Your Child Through the Stages of Moral Development.* New York: Bantam.

Lockwood, Alan L. 1977. "What's Wrong with Values Clarification." *Social Education,* 41 (May), 399–401.

Nelson, Murry R. 1987. *Children and Social Studies.* New York: Harcourt, Brace, Jovanovich.

Oliner, Pearl. 1983. "Putting Compassion and Caring into Social Studies Classrooms." *Social Education,* 47 (April), 273–76.

Pietig, Jeanne. 1983. "Values and Morality in Early 20th Century Elementary Schools: A Perspective." *Social Education,* 47 (April), 262–65.

Raths, Louis E., Merrill Harmin, and Sidney B. Simon. 1978. *Values and Teaching.* 2nd ed. Columbus, Ohio: Charles E. Merrill.

Reimer, J., D. P. Paolitta, and R. Hersh. 1983. *Promoting Moral Growth: From Piaget to Kohlberg.* 2nd ed. Reading, Mass.: Addison-Wesley.

Rest, James. 1983. "Morality." In *Handbook of Child Psychology,* ed. P. Hussen. Vol. 4. New York: Wiley.

Ryan, Kevin. 1986. "Doing Half the Job." *Houghton Mifflin/Educators' Forum.* (Fall), 12.

Scriven, Michael. 1966. "Values in the Curriculum." *Social Science Education Consortium Newsletter,* 2 (April), 1.

Shaver, J. P. 1985. "Commitment to Values and the Study of Social Problems in Citizenship Education." *Social Education,* 49 (March), 194–97.

———, and W. Strong. 1982. *Facing Value Decisions: Rationale Building for Teachers.* 2nd ed. New York: Teachers College Press.

Simon, Sidney, Leland W. Howe, and Howard Kirschenbaum. 1972. *Values Clarification: A Handbook of Practical Strategies for Teachers and Students.* New York: Hart Publishing.

Sizer, Theodore. 1985. *Horace's Compromise.* Boston: Houghton Mifflin.

Superka, Douglas. 1974. "Approaches to Values Education." *Social Science Consortium Newsletter,* 20 (November), 1–4.

Superka, Douglas P., Christine Ahrens, Judith E. Hedstrom, with Luther J. Ford and Patricia L. Johnson. 1976. *Values Education Sourcebook.* Boulder, Colo.: Social Science Education Consortium/ERIC Clearinghouse for Social Studies/Social Science Education.

SUGGESTED READINGS

Richard S. Hersh, J. P. Miller, and G. D. Fielding. 1980. *Models of Moral Education: An Appraisal.* New York: Longman. This 200-page book provides an overview of the different approaches to values education.

James S. Leming. 1985. "Research on Social Studies Curriculum and Instruction: Interventions and Outcomes in the Socio-Moral Domain." In *Review of Research in Social Studies Education, 1976–83,* ed. William B. Stanley, pp. 123–213. Washington, D.C.: National Council for the Social Studies, and Boulder, Colo.: ERIC Clearinghouse for Social Studies/Social Science Education, and the Social Science Education Consortium. This chapter provides an excellent analysis of the existing research on all forms of values and moral education.

James P. Shaver and William Strong. 1982. *Facing Value Decisions: Rationale Building for Teachers.* 2nd ed. New York: Teachers College Press. This book combines theory with lots of practical examples.

CHAPTER 8

Teaching Strategies: From Exposition to Inquiry

"The First Commandment of Teaching: Thou shalt not bore."
David Kellum

KEY QUESTIONS

☐ What teaching strategies work best for which objectives?
☐ What's the difference between teacher-centered and student-centered teaching strategies—in action, that is?
☐ How do teachers decide which questions to ask and when to ask them?
☐ What is inquiry, and how does it differ from discovery learning and problem solving?

KEY IDEAS

☐ Teaching techniques—lectures, discussions, etc.—are the stuff from which teaching strategies are built. Teaching strategies reflect overall plans into which the parts (techniques) fit.
☐ Some teaching strategies are more appropriate than others for reaching certain kinds of objectives. (Although there may be many ways to skin a cat, not all are equally effective.)
☐ The heart of any teaching strategy lies in the questions a teacher asks.
☐ Underlying every question a teacher asks is a purpose for asking it. These purposes may be as varied as the questions.
☐ Teacher-centered strategies tend to be more appropriate for conveying information; student-centered strategies tend to be more appropriate for developing information-processing skills.

238

INTRODUCTION: Symptoms and Ailments

Somewhere in your educational experience, you probably encountered teachers who, even when they resorted to a lung-busting "All right, people! Shut up!" didn't phase kids in the slightest. Substitute teachers are especially prone to such problems, we suspect, because they really don't have much influence on the long-run payoff for students. They may penalize students, to be sure—a list of misdeeds reported back to the regular teacher or even an occasional trip to the principal's office—but these penalties would tend to be short-run, spur-of-the-moment affairs not likely to result in serious consequences like a failing grade, immediate expulsion from school, or, most important of all to children, rejection by their peers.

Prospective teachers sometimes experience a haunting fear that they too will suffer the same fate so often met by substitute teachers—being ignored by students. When student teachers ask "How can I get the children to stop talking?" for example, we suspect that at least part of their concern is motivated by the substitute-teacher syndrome. It should be readily apparent that if you can't get children to pay attention today, you're probably on the brink of even bigger problems tomorrow.

Getting children to pay attention is sometimes difficult, to be sure, but the apparent problem could actually be a symptom of an even more basic problem. In this instance, the underlying problem could result from any number of things: the lack of clear ground rules in the classroom, or ground rules that are not consistently adhered to (in which case the problem is inconsistency)—or it could be that the children don't see much point in studying whatever it is they won't pay attention to. If they have already completed thirty worksheets during a particular week, for example (which is considerably *fewer* than some students actually complete during a week), you can be assured that students are not anxiously awaiting the thirty-first, no matter how interesting it may be. In this case, continued talking could simply be a stalling tactic intended to avoid additional work.

When an entire class is demonstrating an undesirable behavior, don't be too hasty to place all of the blame on the students. There are occasional "bad kids" to be sure, but when an entire class is showing similar symptoms, the teacher would be well advised to examine his or her own behavior for possible causes. It could be, for example, that some discipline problems are the result of having students complete in excess of thirty worksheets every week. In other words, some discipline problems may unwittingly result from the kind of teaching strategy that the teacher is employing.

This chapter focuses on teaching strategies, those patterns of daily lessons and activities that teachers design to enable their students to reach certain learning outcomes. Just to be clear, the purpose of a teaching strategy is to promote students' learning, not to avoid discipline problems. As a consequence, we deal with discipline only incidentally in this chapter. We also examine the different

Depending upon his or her approach to and beliefs about instruction, a teacher may organize (or direct) the instructional activities within the classroom in a variety of ways. (© *Joel Gordon 1987*)

kinds of questions that teachers might pose, and which are an integral part of an overall teaching strategy.

TEACHING STRATEGIES

The term *strategy* can have manipulative, even devious, overtones. It sometimes conjures up images of football coaches developing their "game plan" or of politicians devising strategies for an upcoming campaign. Despite these connotations, the planning processes that coaches, politicians, and teachers follow are often markedly similar.

In coaching, the ultimate goal is clear: winning the game. To accomplish this, coaches first analyze the strengths and weaknesses of the opposing team (and their own). The information gleaned from this analysis provides the basis for developing an overall strategy. For example, if the opposing team has a weak

FIGURE 8.1   Components of a Teaching Strategy

Short-range techniques
Various combinations of

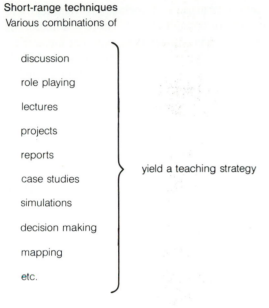

discussion

role playing

lectures

projects

reports

case studies   yield a teaching strategy

simulations

decision making

mapping

etc.

defensive line and a good pass defense, the coach's game plan (strategy) will probably revolve around keeping the ball on the ground (running plays) and involve relatively little passing. However, if things don't go as planned when the game is actually played, the coach will undoubtedly make some adjustments or, possibly, revise the game plan entirely.

In teaching, the purpose is also clear: to promote learning by helping students attain desired goals and objectives. To accomplish this, most teachers employ the planning procedures outlined in Chapter 4. The teacher's unit plan—his/her overall strategy—is roughly equivalent to a coach's game plan. Once the goals have been determined, the teacher then plans certain lessons (plays) that are intended to help students achieve those outcomes. The individual lessons will undoubtedly reflect a variety of teaching techniques—different day-to-day teaching activities such as role playing, discussions, and the use of films and filmstrips—which fit together to constitute an overall teaching strategy. The relationship between a teaching strategy and teaching techniques is shown in Figure 8.1.

TEACHING VERSUS LEARNING STRATEGIES

Teachers who base their teaching strategy on a single instructional technique, such as lecturing—day after day of lecturing—can probably anticipate problems from elementary-age students. The same could be true of a teacher whose strategy is designed around worksheets, as we described earlier. The question, then, is "How do you develop a teaching strategy that doesn't rely too heavily on a particular technique?" The answer to this question is conditioned by a subtle yet crucial aspect of teaching, namely, the tendency to confuse teaching strategies with learning strategies.

A learning strategy refers to the combination of techniques that learners employ as they deal with whatever they are trying to learn. There are numerous ways to learn something—memorization, drill, association, deriving ideas from experiences, etc. The point here is that how you go about teaching something is not necessarily the way your students will learn it; a teacher may be engaged in quite different behaviors than his or her students.

The distinction between teaching and learning strategies is probably most apparent in the stereotypical college class where the professor's teaching strategy consists of a single technique—lecturing—repeated over and over again. As the professor lectures, students are usually engaged in note taking, and ultimately in memorizing or otherwise comprehending what the professor has said. Thus the students' behavior is likely to differ considerably from the professor's teaching behavior.

COMMENTARY: There Is Nothing Like a GOOD Lecture

In some educational circles there prevails a notion that lectures are inherently bad and that, should you choose to lecture, you will be committing a grievous sin. (Ironically, it is often in a bad lecture that we are told how bad lecturing is as a teaching strategy.) At the same time, you've undoubtedly witnessed some extremely good lectures in your career as a student—some of which even made eight-o'clock classes worth getting up for. Thus we find ourselves in a situation where on one hand we may be told that lecturing is evil, while on the other hand we have experienced some excellent lectures by superb lecturers.

Our experience indicates that the quality of a lecture depends heavily on the ability of the person doing the lecturing. Good lecturers, we've found, must demonstrate most of the following characteristics.

1. They must be extremely well versed in their subject. Good lecturers stand at the opposite end of the continuum from students whose reports to the class often reflect the total scope of their knowledge on a topic. Subject-matter expertise is a necessary but not sufficient qualification, however, since on more than one occasion we have heard subject-matter experts—nationally known specialists in their fields—deliver some abominable lectures.

2. They must have mastered the skills of acting. Good lecturers must be sensitive to timing, pacing, form and style of expression—when to raise their eyebrow or change their tone of voice. The importance of these elements—the "show-biz" aspects of lecturing—were illustrated in what has been called "The Doctor Fox Effect." To determine if the way a lecture was presented made any difference in how students reacted to it,

continued

two researchers hired a Hollywood actor, whom they called Dr. Fox, to present six different types of lecture. The actor first memorized the scripts for three different lectures on the same topic. Each lecture differed in the amount of information it contained; one had a very high content, another had some content, while the third contained a lot of verbiage but very little information. The actor then presented each lecture to different groups of students in one of two ways. For one presentation of each type of lecture, Dr. Fox really hammed it up, using gestures, humor, movement, vocal inflection, and considerable enthusiasm. For the second set of lectures, all of the expressive embellishments were omitted and the actor virtually read from the prepared script.

What happened? According to Williams and Ware (1977), students who had experienced the highly expressive presentations did significantly better on achievement tests about the material than did students who had experienced the less expressive presentations. In addition, the students almost always rated the expressive presentations as "more effective" than the less expressive lectures, regardless of the content they contained. The implication, then, is that even if you have little to say on a topic, you should say it with gusto!

Lecturers who have mastered the skills of acting and who have subject-matter expertise are likely to have captured the best of both worlds. Subject-matter expertise is gained through study, while acting skills are developed through practice.

IDENTIFYING TEACHING STRATEGIES

Teachers are responsible for the activities that occur in their classrooms. If that statement seems obvious, our point is that all classrooms are teacher-directed. However, the ways in which teachers organize (or direct) the instructional activities within their classrooms can vary considerably. The teaching strategies they adopt may range from almost complete teacher domination at one extreme to almost complete student involvement at the other. Most teachers probably fall somewhere between these extremes.

Teachers who approach instruction almost wholly in terms of their own actions, and who believe that learning results from a teacher's direct action upon students, tend to fall toward the left of the continuum shown in Figure 8.2. Those teachers' strategies reflect *teacher-centered instruction* and are usually characterized by a "telling" (or expository) orientation. To put it in slightly different terms, the emphasis in a teacher-centered classroom is on what the teacher is doing and secondarily on what students are doing because of the teacher's actions.

FIGURE 8.2   A Teaching Continuum

Teacher-centered	(Mixed)	Student-centered

←——→

Exposition		Problem-solving/Inquiry

Teachers who strive for a high level of active student involvement fall toward the right of the continuum. Those teachers' strategies are *student-centered;* that is, they focus primarily on what students are (or will be) doing and secondarily on the teacher's actions that caused children to become involved in certain activities. Student-centered strategies are characterized by a problem-solving or inquiry orientation. Teachers who use such strategies influence instruction more indirectly than do teachers who employ teacher-centered strategies.

Students are the ultimate benefactors of whatever instructional strategy a teacher employs. However, teachers who tend to approach instruction as something they do *to* students, as in the case of lecturing for example, would favor more direct, teacher-centered instructional strategies. On the other hand, teachers who approach instruction as something that teachers *do with* or *draw from* children would favor a more indirect, student-centered teaching strategy. Still other teachers, perhaps even the majority of them, employ strategies that combine elements of teacher-centered and student-centered instruction, and thus lie somewhere in the middle of the continuum.

TEACHER-CENTERED INSTRUCTION

Teacher-centered instructional strategies usually follow a Read-Recite-Lecture-Test format. The recitation phase, which is an oral test of retained information, is sometimes omitted, especially at the college level. Occasionally, the teacher may reverse the format and talk about material prior to having students read it. On other occasions, additional elements may be added—films, discussions, demonstrations, student reports, or current events periods, for example. Such variations notwithstanding, the dominant feature of a teacher-centered strategy is its emphasis on "telling" or giving information—through lecture, demonstrations, or other expository techniques—that students are expected to learn. In other words, the goal of such expository teaching strategies is to present information to students as quickly and as efficiently as possible.

When teachers conduct a question-and-answer session to determine how well students have retained information, they sometimes mistakenly refer to those sessions as *discussions.* Doing so may sound less formal and imposing than the correct term, *recitation,* but the two terms are not synonymous. The distinction between *discussion* and *recitation* is based on the purpose of the activity. A discussion can serve multiple purposes, including sharing different points of view on an issue, motivating students or developing interest in a topic, generating ideas, synthesizing ideas, or providing closure to an activity. The purpose of recitation is to test (orally) how well students have understood and retained prior information.

Despite the bad reputation sometimes associated with teacher-centered strategies, there are times when lecturing (or telling) can be extremely useful. When students are not fully aware of the issues associated with a topic, for example, so-called discussions can become futile exercises in shared ignorance. At other times, students may find themselves floundering hopelessly because their teachers—who favor an inquiry or discovery approach to teaching—mistakenly believe that students can discover *everything,* including the information needed to discover whatever they are supposed to discover. These problems can be avoided if the teacher gives a short presentation or mini-lecture that brings fresh information to bear on the points in question. We don't advocate presenting a daily diet of half-hour speeches by any means, but there are countless instances where mini-lectures are a wholly appropriate teaching activity.

A Model for Effective Instruction

Over the last twenty years, researchers have focused intense interest on the relationship between teachers' strategies and students' academic achievement. One of the most consistently successful instructional sequences for dealing with *certain kinds of subject matter* was described by Rosenshine and Stevens (1986). It is referred to as the "direct-instruction model," and is described below.

Begin the lesson with a short review of the previous day's work, reteaching if necessary.

Provide an overview and a short statement of objectives for the lesson.

Present new content/skills, usually in small steps and at a rapid pace; provide opportunities for student practice after each step.

Give clear and detailed instructions and explanations.

To check for comprehension, ask a lot of questions and try to obtain responses from all students.

Provide opportunities for students to practice under the teacher's guidance.

Provide systematic feedback and correctives, reteaching if necessary.

Provide independent practice until students' responses are firm, quick, and automatic.

Provide weekly and monthly reviews. (pp. 377 and 379)

Rosenshine and Stevens indicate that this teacher-centered model for instruction is most appropriate for subjects that they call "well structured," that is, subjects that have a learning hierarchy in which later learning depends upon earlier learning (p. 377). As we pointed out in Chapter 2, most of social studies is a synthetic subject area that lacks a clear learning hierarchy. Learning that

Copenhagen is the capital of Denmark, for example, has almost no connection to anything else about Denmark that children might study. On the other hand, map-reading skills and a very few other elements of social studies have a defined structure with which this model might work well.

Major Techniques and Purposes, Summarized

Technique	Purpose(s)
Lecture	To present information
Recitation	To test, orally, retained information
Discussion	Multiple purposes:
	To motivate or generate interest
	To share points of view on an issue
	To generate ideas or identify new applications for ideas
	To synthesize ideas
	To bring closure to an activity

"MIXED" INSTRUCTION

"Mixed" teaching strategies reflect a blend of teacher-centered and student-centered teaching techniques. Just how those techniques are blended will vary from teacher to teacher and, in some cases, from topic to topic.

The further a teacher moves away from the more clearly defined roles of the teacher-centered strategy, the more difficult it becomes to describe his or her behavior precisely. When the focus shifts to a student-centered teaching strategy, the attention necessarily shifts from one individual, the teacher, to the teacher *and* the students.

STUDENT-CENTERED INSTRUCTION

The goal of student-centered (inquiry/problem-solving) teaching strategies is to develop the students' ability to manipulate and process information from a variety of sources—academic, social, and experiential. In a student-centered strategy, teachers act as guides to assist students in identifying problems, generating possible answers, testing those answers in the light of available data, and in applying their conclusions to new data, new problems, or new situations. In other words, the focus is on the *skills* of inquiring and processing information instead of on learning the *products* of someone else's information processing—as is more typical of a teacher-centered strategy. The point here is that teacher-centered strategies tend to be more appropriate for transmitting information, whereas student-centered strategies tend to be more appropriate for developing information-processing skills.

In the next section, we examine the nature of inquiry and its relationship to student-centered teaching strategies.

The Nature of Inquiry

In an educational context, *inquiry* is both an act and a process. Like problem solving and even memorization, inquiry affords a way in which students and adults can go about solving problems or processing information. But what, specifically, does someone who uses inquiry do?

The scholar in the following example (Olsvanger, 1947; Ausubel, 1948) is an inquirer. Without speaking a word, he identifies the gentleman sitting across from him in a railroad coach. There is no trick to this example, even though it may seem that way at first. As you read it, determine *how* the scholar identified the man sitting across from him. Note that we are asking you to describe the various phases of the process here, and not simply label it (e.g., "by deductive reasoning," etc.).

"IT WAS OBVIOUS"

A Talmudic scholar from Marmaresch was on his way home from a visit to Budapest. Opposite him in the railway carriage sat another Jew, dressed in modern fashion and smoking a cigar. When the conductor came around to collect the tickets the scholar noticed that his neighbor opposite was also on his way to Marmaresch.

This seemed very odd to him.

"Who can it be, and why is he going to Marmaresch?" he wondered.

As it would not be polite to ask outright he tried to figure it out for himself. "Now let me see," he mused. "He is a modern Jew, well dressed, and he smokes a cigar. Whom could a man of this type be visiting in Marmaresch? Possibly he's on his way to our town doctor's wedding. But no, that can't be! That's two weeks off. Certainly this kind of man wouldn't twiddle his thumbs in our town for two weeks!

"Why then is he on his way to Marmaresch? Perhaps he's courting a woman there. But who could it be? Now let me see. Moses Goldman's daughter Esther? Yes definitely, it's she and nobody else . . .! But now that I think of it—that couldn't be! She's too old—he wouldn't have her, under any circumstances! Maybe it's Haikeh Wasservogel? Phooey! She's so ugly! Who then? Could it be Leah, the money-lender's daughter? N—no! What a match for such a nice man! Who then? There aren't any more marriageable girls in Marmaresch. That's settled then, he's not going courting.

"What then brings him?

"Wait, I've got it! It's about Mottell Kohn's bankruptcy case! But what connection can he have with that? Could it be that he is one of his creditors? Hardly! Just look at him sitting there so calmly, reading his newspaper and smiling to himself. Anybody can see nothing worries him! No, he's not a creditor. But I'll bet he has something to do with the bankruptcy! Now what could it be?

"Wait a minute, I think I've got it. Mottell Kohn must have corresponded

with a lawyer from Budapest about his bankruptcy. But that swindler Mottell certainly wouldn't confide his business secrets to a stranger! So it stands to reason that the lawyer must be a member of the family.

"Now who could it be? Could it be his sister Shprinzah's son? No, that's impossible. She got married twenty-six years ago—I remember it very well because the wedding took place in the green synagogue. And this man here looks at least thirty-five.

"A funny thing! Who could it be, after all . . .? Wait a minute! It's as clear as day! This is his nephew, his brother Hayyim's son, because Hayyim Kohn got married thirty-seven years and two months ago in the stone synagogue near the market place. Yes, that's who he is!

"In a nutshell—he is lawyer Kohn from Budapest. But a lawyer from Budapest surely must have the title 'Doctor'! So, he is Doctor Kohn from Budapest, no? But wait a minute! A lawyer from Budapest who calls himself 'Doctor' won't call himself 'Kohn'! Anybody knows that. It's certain that he has changed his name into Hungarian. Now, what kind of a name could he have made out of Kohn? Kovacs! Yes, that's it—Kovacs! In short, this is Doctor Kovacs from Budapest!"

Eager to start a conversation the scholar turned to his traveling companion and asked, "Doctor Kovacs, do you mind if I open the window?"

"Not at all," answered the other. "But tell me, how do you know that I am Doctor Kovacs?"

"It was obvious," replied the scholar.

The Inquiry Process

In this section, we examine the inquiry process that the Talmudic scholar used in "It Was Obvious" (some elements of which may be far from obvious).

The process the scholar used was very systematic. First, he observed the situation—a cigar-smoking, modernly dressed man going to Marmaresch. On the surface there seems nothing unusual about this, but to the scholar, "this seemed very odd." We are not told why the scholar found the situation odd, just that it was. *Something* just didn't fit, and thus became a *discrepant event*, which the scholar then tried to explain.

1. *Awareness of a Possible Problem*   One's awareness of a discrepant event results from a kind of mental "disturbance" called *cognitive dissonance*. If you've ever heard a clarinet "squeak," you've experienced dissonance; something was out of harmony, musically speaking. A cognitive (or mental) parallel to musical dissonance occurs when you hear a child counting "One, two, three, four, five, seven, eight," for instance. Cognitive dissonance exists when you sense that something is "wrong," or out of harmony with your existing ideas. Upon hearing the child skip the number six, an adult may sense that something is "wrong" (even if the child doesn't) and go back over what was said to determine what the problem was.

Our journey into the nature of cognitive dissonance and discrepant events is intended to emphasize how crucial this phase—awareness of the problem—is to the inquiry process. If the scholar had not sensed a problem there would have been nothing to inquire about, and the story would have ended in the first paragraph. Likewise, if students don't sense that a discrepant event exists, they have nothing to explain. The clear implication is that teachers who wish to use inquiry-oriented teaching strategies may need to structure activities in which they intentionally create cognitive dissonance that provides students with a *motive* for inquiry.

2. *Defining the Problem*   The scholar in the example is obviously a curious individual who enjoys an intellectually challenging activity. Perhaps that's what makes him a scholar. For others of us, however, dissonance can so disturb our equilibrium that we must somehow resolve the problem. For the Talmudic scholar, explaining the discrepant event became his *problem*, which he immediately broke down into two more manageable problems: "What can it be," and "Why is he going to Marmaresch?"

3. *Reviewing the Data*   Once the problem was identified, our Talmudic scholar reexamined his data—modern dress, cigar-smoking, etc.—and then restated his problem in a way that may be more easily managed: "Whom could a man of this type be visiting in Marmaresch?" Since the scholar has a great deal of information about Marmaresch, he in effect rephrases his question to state, "What's going on in Marmaresch that would bring a man like this to town?"

4. *Hypothesizing*   "The town doctor's wedding?" That's a possibility—*a hypothesis,* a tentative answer, an educated guess. But the scholar knows that the wedding is two weeks away, and such an early arrival just doesn't seem very logical. So the scholar rejects Hypothesis 1 and returns to a restatement of his problem, "Why, then, is he on his way to Marmaresch?"

5. *Testing Hypotheses*   "Courting a woman?" Hypothesis 2. But what woman? Esther Goldman (Hypothesis 2.1)? The scholar's interpretation of Esther's age suggests she would be inappropriate for his railway-carriage companion. Hence, Hypothesis 2.1 is rejected.

   But what about Haikeh Wasservogel (Hypothesis 2.2)? Both Haikeh and "Leah, the money-lender's daughter" (Hypothesis 2.3) are rejected. Since there are no more marriageable girls in Marmaresch, Hypothesis 2 is totally rejected. The scholar has exhausted the possibilities, at least as he interpreted them. Note that the scholar is assuming that he and his traveling companion share similar views about the desirability of the women in Marmaresch.

6. *Concluding, Tentatively*   After rejecting Hypothesis 2, it's back to the problem once again: "What then brings him?" In a flash of intuition, the scholar decides it has something to do with the bankruptcy case (Hypothesis 3). He tests, rejects, or modifies various subhypotheses until he *concludes,* "In a nutshell—he is Lawyer Kohn from Budapest."

His conclusion, though, is *tentative*, subject to change in light of any additional data. And change it the scholar does. It finally becomes "Doctor Kovacs from Budapest." Now the scholar has an "answer" he can live with. But, is it the right one?

7. *Testing the Conclusion*   He *tests* his conclusion by asking to open the window. Based on his companion's response, it may be possible to determine if his answer was right. But was it?

In the previous episode, the scholar's problem-solving behavior occurred in a number of distinct phases (not steps), all of which reflect the inquiry process. In summary form, they are listed below.

The Inquiry Process, Summarized

1. Becoming aware of a discrepant event (1.1), which then became a problem to be solved (1.2)
2. Identifying hypotheses (possible explanations or tentative answers)
3. Testing the hypotheses in light of the data
   3.1. If a hypothesis is rejected, the problem may be restated for clarity, and the inquirer goes to Phase 2 again.
   3.2. If the hypothesis is accepted (not rejected), the inquirer proceeds to Phase 4.
4. Modifying the hypothesis, which has become a tentative conclusion, in light of additional data until satisfied that it is a plausible explanation
5. Testing the tentative conclusion (Does it fit? Does it explain the discrepant event?)

The Challenge of Inquiry Teaching

It would be misleading to suggest that every inquirer follows these procedures in precisely the order identified above. People just don't think that way. Identifying a problem must come first, of course, because otherwise there would be nothing to inquire about. But thereafter students' educated guesses or bright ideas can serve as legitimate shortcuts. Students, like the Talmudic scholar in our example above, may shift from trial and error to gradual analysis, and then be suddenly inspired by a flash of insight or intuition. Because none of these methods is necessarily wrong, inquiry-oriented teachers have no guarantee that all students will approach the inquiry process in the same way.

Because the inquiry skills that students use in their everyday lives are informal, helping them to become aware of the formal process—problem awareness, hypothesizing, testing tentative answers, etc.—is not without some practical problems. This is especially true for primary-level students who have not yet made the transition to Piaget's stage of formal operations.

Even very young children can become aware of discrepant events, particularly if those events do not involve abstract thought. But apparently because there are so many discrepant events in a young child's life—things that are unexplained—

children tend to react to them in one of two ways: either they become so interested in something that they insist on sticking with it until it's resolved to their satisfaction, or they dismiss it immediately and for no apparent reason. Unlike many adults, young children do not feel compelled to explain everything and can often live quite happily with things that they don't understand.

Older students, on the other hand, sometimes jump on the first explanation (hypothesis) they create, and cling so tenaciously to it that they ignore other possibilities or data to the contrary. It sometimes becomes a case of "I've already made up my mind, so don't bother me with information!" There's some ego involvement too, we suspect. In a child's world, where things are clearly "right" or "wrong," the very idea of rejecting a tentative answer because the data doesn't support it can be construed as being *wrong* (when it is actually *right* to reject it). Even though teachers may say things like "You're not wrong," such statements may not carry much weight if a child is concerned about losing status and prestige for having identified what others regard as an incorrect answer. It takes considerable sophistication to understand why identifying a hypothesis that must be rejected because the data doesn't support it ("He's going to Marmaresch to get married") is a perfectly acceptable, even essential element of inquiry.

The problems associated with inquiry teaching are a challenge, not a basis for avoidance. We have suggested, however, that (1) conducting full-blown inquiry lessons on a whole-class basis may prove difficult, particularly in the primary grades; and (2) helping children develop information-processing skills such as analyzing, inferring, observing, in small segments can equip thcm to inquire more effectively when they feel the need to do so.

TEACHING STRATEGIES REVISITED

On the surface it might appear that your task is simply to pick a teaching strategy and go to it. If only it were that simple! The decision ultimately involves your conception of what it means to teach.

The teacher's role is critical to any teaching strategy, but it is especially so in an inquiry-oriented classroom. Skeel and Decaroli (1969, p. 547) captured part of the issue as follows:

> **Inquiry falters if a teacher views his position as that of a central figure from which knowledge, ideas, value judgments, and conclusions spew forth to be absorbed by young minds. A teacher abdicates this position in an inquiry-centered classroom to accept the less prominent but equally important role of guide.**

While teacher-centered strategies are most frequently concerned with transmitting large bodies of information to students, those students obviously require skills for dealing with that information. As a result, to say that teacher-centered strategies are concerned only with knowledge transmission is probably inaccurate.

Despite the fact that student-centered (inquiry) teaching strategies focus on information-processing skills, such skills cannot be developed in a void; students must have data to work with. In that context, inquiry strategies are necessarily concerned with both the kinds of information that children work with and the skills they apply to that information. In moving from a teacher-centered to a student-centered teaching strategy, what changes is not the existence of data, knowledge, or skills, but the *role that information and skills play in the strategy* itself.

COMMENTARY: Inquiry, Discovery, and
_____ Problem Solving

When teachers talk about the instructional strategies they use, it's not uncommon to hear some say "I use a discovery approach," others say "I use inquiry," and still others say "I prefer a problem-solving approach." Because universally accepted definitions for inquiry, discovery, and problem solving don't exist, you would need to visit these teachers to find out how they actually teach. You might find that, despite the different terminology, the three strategies are more similar than they are different.

The most striking similarity among these approaches is their emphasis on thinking processes and skills. In one form or another, all of them ask students to piece together several items of information in order to identify or discover relationships that may exist among those items. Literally, *discovery* refers to the moment a student perceives a relationship among various data—when the student says "Aha, I've got it!" The teacher's main role in discovery teaching is creating situations and an environment where students are encouraged to discover and test ideas on their own. If this role sounds like the one we described for inquiry-oriented teachers, it is; a discovery approach is part of a larger process that is similar to the inquiry processes that we outlined earlier.

Problem solving can be confusing because the expression may refer to two somewhat different types of activities. One of these, which is probably the most common, refers to what students do as they answer the problems in a math text. All of us have done this type of relatively short-range problem solving at one time or another. A second type of problem solving involves more complex, longer-range concerns (problems), such as "How could you determine the favorite soft drink in your class?" or "How is a Republican different from a Democrat?"—that tend to be more closely associated with social studies.

Until the experts straighten out the terminology, suffice it to say that discovery, inquiry, and problem solving all refer to teaching strategies that involve students in the process of search—a search for relationships between and among data.

Difference Splitting

Rather than associate themselves with either a teacher-centered or a student-centered strategy, some teachers hope to select from both strategies in unique, eclectic ways. However, what might seem to be a safe, middle-of-the-road position has some hazards. As Rogers (1970, p. 74) stated,

> **The notion of inquiry is an intriguing one, and it conjures up images of deeply involved, questioning, bright-eyed children who have finally been rescued from the drudgery of "traditional" classroom teaching. One does not—one cannot—simply insert inquiry lessons, projects, or programs into a framework that in its totality is organized to defeat the purposes of the inquiry approach. The situation is analogous, perhaps, to the rejection of a transplanted organ in the human body. The new heart may be perfectly sound, but its new environment is hostile, so it is in fact rejected.**

Where do you as a social studies teacher wish to place your emphasis? As we have indicated, the decision is a question of emphasis, not exclusion.

Dimensions of Teacher-Centered and Student-Centered Strategies

A teacher-centered strategy requires that the teacher have

1. a command of the subject matter
2. the ability to organize subject matter in a way that is understandable to students

A student-centered strategy requires that the teacher have

1. a command of the subject matter
2. an understanding of the nature of inquiry
3. the ability to relate subject matter to a student's process-skill levels

An essential difference in all of these strategies lies in their sources. The source of a teacher-centered strategy lies primarily in *content*—in the subject matter. The teacher's role is primarily one of helping the children learn the subject matter. Students' needs and skills are an obvious consideration as teachers go about fulfilling that role. The source of a student-centered (inquiry-oriented) teaching strategy, on the other hand, lies primarily in the students' ability to *process* information—to solve problems. The teacher's role is primarily one of selecting and using subject matter (as a vehicle) in a manner that facilitates student skill development.

QUESTIONING STRATEGIES

As every student knows, questions are a teacher's stock in trade. From a student's point of view, teachers always have more questions than they have answers. Our concern here is not with answers but rather with the kinds of

Posing good questions is an important part of effective teaching, for every question that a teacher asks should have an underlying purpose that relates directly to the content being taught. (© *Susan Lapides 1986*)

questions that teachers ask, and the relationship between those questions and a teacher's teaching strategy.

The relationship between the questions that teachers ask and their teaching strategy is so close that the two are almost inseparable. A teacher who, for example, continually poses questions that begin with "Who" or "What," such as "Who was Henry Hudson, what was the name of his ship, and on what river did he sail?", will have implicitly indicated what he or she thinks is important for children to know. The question itself does not determine the teacher's strategy. In fact, any teacher might have reason to ask about Henry Hudson, his ship, and where he sailed. The point is that teachers who continually pose questions of this nature are more likely to employ a teacher-centered teaching strategy within which the emphasis is on having students learn the subject matter—in this case, information related to Henry Hudson.

Another teacher might ask "How can we find out who Henry Hudson was and what he did?" In this instance, the emphasis has shifted from the information itself to a concern for "finding out." Of course, if this were the only kind of question the teacher asked, the students would probably go a little crazy—"All he ever does is say 'How can we find out?' " The point is that this type of question reflects a concern for processing information that is more closely associated with a student-centered (inquiry-oriented) teaching strategy. The second point is that through the questions they ask, these teachers have indicated two quite different purposes.

FOR EVERY QUESTION THERE IS A PURPOSE

For every question teachers ask, there is (or should be) an underlying purpose, something the teacher is trying to get at. By analyzing a teacher's questions, we should be able to infer what those purposes are. The reverse is also true: if you know what a teacher's purposes are, you should be able to suggest several questions or activities that will contribute to achieving them. (If you can't do that right now or if this seems a bit theoretical, take heart, some specific examples are forthcoming.)

Questioning, in the sense of deciding what questions to ask and how to ask them, is at the heart of every teaching strategy. Before we can ask a single question, however, we need something to ask questions about—some kind of content. We also need a purpose; in fact, once we have a purpose for using certain content, the questions follow naturally.

To put it algebraically, the issue would be one of

$$\text{Purpose} + \text{Content} = \text{Questions}$$

Even that is not quite accurate, however, since you may be forced into the situation of determining purposes for using predetermined content such as that found in a social studies textbook. Or, you may have a purpose in mind, such as improving your students' library research skills, but need to identify content on which their research can focus. This will influence the kinds of questions you pose to the students. Thus, the following statement more accurately depicts the situation most teachers face:

$$\text{Purpose} \leftrightarrow \text{Content} = \text{Questions}$$

Question posing acts as a system of relating purposes and content—a key factor in any teaching strategy. As we suggested in the heading for this section, "For every question there is a purpose." The reverse of that is equally true—for every purpose there is a question. In either case, however, we need some content to ask questions about. The following material drawn from Stuart Chase's *The Proper Study of Mankind* (1963, pp. 112–13) should serve that purpose. As you read it, attempt to identify at least four different kinds of questions (or tasks) you might pose to students.

"STONE AXES"

On the northern coast of Australia lives a tribe of hunters and fishermen called the Yir Yoront. Like most primitive Australians, the tribe enjoyed great stability; they had almost no contact with other cultures. In fact, before the tribe would accept any changes in their beliefs and customs, a myth had to be invented which proved that one's ancestors did things that way, and that the change really wasn't a change at all.

In many ways the tribe was still living in the Stone Age. One of their most important tools was a short-handled stone ax—something they used to build huts, cut firewood, and make other tools for hunting, fishing, and gathering wild honey. The stone heads came from a quarry 400 miles to the south and were obtained from other tribes in an annual fiesta. There, handles were fitted to the axheads with great skill and care. Once finished, the axes were more than just a tool but came to stand for a symbol of being a man; they were something to be treated with great care, handed down from father to son, and almost never loaned to someone else. Not only was the stone ax useful, it became the center of the Yir Yoront belief system.

Just before World War I, missionaries visited the tribe and began distributing steel axes as gifts and rewards. If a man worked very hard he might get an ax, and so might his wife or son. By using the axes as gifts, the missionaries hoped to get the tribe to plant gardens and improve their diets.

New steel axes had an interesting effect on the tribe. Certainly they could cut down trees much faster, but men also lost their importance and dignity. Women and children who had their own axes became independent and disrespectful. The entire tribe was thrown into confusion. The fiesta was no longer held. Crime increased.

The "Stone Axes" material is not very long, yet there are enough possible tasks or questions that we must look at them in terms of categories, not individual questions. As a consequence, you will need to determine how your questions fit into one or more of our categories, which are based on and identified in terms of the thinking skills that students must use to answer them.

Categories of Questions

Memory-Recall   Among the most obvious possible questions are those that follow the form of "What is the name of the tribe living on the northern coast of Australia?" or "How far from the tribe's home was the stone quarry?" The purpose of this type of question is to determine if students can recall factual information. There is little concern with inferring, evaluating, or speculating here; rather, the focus is on the facts and whether or not the students know them.

Questions in this category require *memory-recall* skills and are classified accordingly.

Descriptive-Interpretive   Examples of a second category of possible questions are "Describe in your own words what happened to the Yir Yoront when the missionaries began distributing steel axes" and "Explain why you think the missionaries acted as they did." From these examples, it should be apparent that *descriptive-interpretative* questions are often expressed as tasks, not as direct questions.

Questions/tasks in this category require that students go beyond the memory-recall level to describe, interpret, or otherwise explain events or actions. In addition, the description or interpretation must be in the student's own words. This is intended to assure that the response is the student's own, and not a memorized rehash of someone else's description.

Application-Synthesis   Another category of questions requires that students identify relationships and draw conclusions, bringing in other information as it is appropriate. Examples of questions in this category are "How would you sum up what happened to the Yir Yoront in general terms (or in as few words as possible?)" and "What general statement could you make about the Yir Yoront's experience?" Because questions of this kind require that students put things together (synthesize) in order to identify relationships or generalizations that go beyond a specific event, the category is labeled *application-synthesis.*

In most instances, application-synthesis questions must be preceded by lower-level questions; otherwise they may seem to come from nowhere. For example, a teacher might state that the introduction of steel axes was a change that affected the Yir Yoront, then ask "What other changes resulted, either directly or indirectly, from the introduction of steel axes?" This question would fall into the descriptive-interpretive category. After students respond, the teacher might summarize by stating, "Introducing the steel axes caused all of these other changes." The teacher could then use an application-synthesis question like "How would you complete a statement that began, 'If one thing changes, then _____ (other changes are likely to occur).' " In this example, the teacher is clearly leading students toward making a general statement about the nature of change. You might accomplish the same thing with less leading by asking either of the exemplary questions for this category noted above.

Evaluative-Judgmental   Examples of another category of possible questions are "Were the missionaries right to introduce steel axes into the Yir Yoront way of life?" and "Did the Yir Yoront culture advance after the introduction of the steel-axe technology?" These questions require that students produce an evaluation or render a judgment and, thus, fall into the *evaluative-judgmental* category. A distinguishing characteristic of evaluative-judgmental questions is that students must identify the *criteria* they will use in reaching their evaluation. Thus, an evaluative question might be phrased more accurately as follows: "According to what criteria would you decide that the missionaries were either right or wrong?" Even though this might seem to be an unnecessarily long-winded way to pose a question, our intent is to emphasize the need to specify clearly, and in advance, the criteria by which something is being judged. If the evaluative criteria are not explicit, a student's response would be purely personal opinion.

Speculative-Heuristic   A final category of questions asks students to speculate in a hypothetical mode. Examples of questions in this category are "What might have happened to the Yir Yoront if the missionaries had never come?" and "What if the missionaries had chosen to use beads, mirrors, or objects other than steel axes?" The "what-if" form evident in the examples above is characteristic of questions in the *speculative-heuristic* category.

Speculative-heuristic questions are excellent for generating inquiry, promoting divergent thinking, and getting students to speculate on and analyze alternative courses of action. They also allow students to formulate their own questions, such as "How do missionaries elsewhere get people to change?" and "Where can we find more information on _____?" Once students begin to pose their own questions, you have two options: (1) attempt to answer them as best as you can—*if* you can; or (2) guide students in finding answers on their own. The latter option, while preferable in many instances, also requires your judgment as to whether the students' curiosity has been sufficiently aroused to counteract the frustration they may encounter in finding an answer. You'll also need to determine if a student's question is significant enough to warrant a search. For example, a student question such as "What did the steel axes look like?" is a kind of dead-end question. Finding an answer—if that is possible—might lead to satisfaction on the student's part, but very little else.

Caution: speculative-heuristic questions should be used judiciously. Three "what-if" questions in a row may be enough to confuse even your most sophisticated students. Instead of speculation, their response may be "Who cares!"

Levels of Questions

The various categories of questions described above are illustrated in summary form in Table 8.1. These categories correspond, albeit roughly, to the levels of the *Taxonomy: Cognitive Domain* (Bloom, 1956) that we described in detail in Chapter 4. In terms of the *Taxonomy,* a descriptive-interpretative question such as "In what country did the Yir Yoront live?" would be referred to as low-level, while a speculative-heuristic question such as "What do you think happened to the Yir Yoront after the missionaries left?" would be considered higher-level.

The basic criterion for distinguishing between low-level and high-level questions is complexity—more specifically, the complexity of the cognitive (thinking) skills required to complete the task or answer the question. In other words, higher-level questions are believed to require more complex cognitive skills than lower-level questions.

TABLE 8.1   Types of Questions by Category and Purpose

Type of Question	Purpose
Memory-recall	To determine if students can recall previously learned information
Descriptive-interpretive	To describe, interpret, and/or explain events or actions in the students' own words, including reasons (non-speculative) for why individuals acted as they did
Application-synthesis	To identify relationships and to form and draw reasonable conclusions that go beyond the particular action or event
Evaluative-judgmental	To render an evaluation or judgment as to actions or events in light of explicit, previously identified criteria
Speculative-heuristic	To encourage divergent thinking and to speculate on and analyze alternative courses of action

Other Questions

The categories of questions outlined above were based on the skills required of students in order to answer them. In this section we consider three other categories of questions that are not directly linked to thinking skills but which teachers sometimes employ. Two of these categories, rhetorical and probing questions, are fairly common, while the third, multi-focus questions, is relatively uncommon and should remain so.

Rhetorical questions are actually statements, phrased as if they were questions but for which the teacher really doesn't expect an answer (or for which the teacher supplies the answer). A statement (rhetorical question) such as, "Let's see now, what happened to the Yir Yoront? The missionaries came and . . ." could be used to (1) summarize, (2) refocus, or (3) restructure the lesson in a direction the teacher wishes to pursue.

Probing questions enable the teacher to explore a student's previous responses in greater detail or to bring out elements not previously identified. Examples of probing questions are "Can you elaborate on that in greater detail?" and "I'm not sure I understand what you just said; can you give an example of what you mean?" Probing questions can also be used to extend discussion or to elicit responses from other students, such as "Does anyone else have anything to add to what Steve just said?"

Multi-focus questions should be avoided. The only reason we even mention them is so that you can recognize a multi-focus question when you see (or hear) one. An example of a multi-focus question is "What differences did you find in the patterns of government and trade in South America and what is similar about these differences?" Formulating the question isn't too difficult, but trying to formulate an answer is something else again; it demands that too many thinking processes be used simultaneously. But that's only one of the things wrong with multi-focus questions. As Taba noted, such a question

. . . asks the pupil to make several differentiations simultaneously on several levels: (1) differentiation between trade and government; (2) identification of patterns of government for each country; (3) contrasting trade patterns between three countries, which involves three pairs of contrasts; (4) contrasting governmental patterns in three countries, calling for three pairs of contrasts; (5) isolating the differences in governments from the similarities; and (6) generalizing what is similar about these trade patterns on one hand and governmental patterns on the other. (Taba, 1967, pp. 120–21)

After having done all of this—assuming that you understand what must be done *and* can do it—you may be ready to answer the question. The obvious implication

---

COMMENTARY: On the Multiple Uses of Social Studies Content

We illustrated in Chapter 4 that two cans of corn could be used as the basis for a variety of legitimate instructional activities. In this chapter we have suggested that the Stone Axes material could also be used in several different ways—ways determined largely by how a teacher might wish to use it, and by the kinds of questions he or she asks about it. In both instances, the principle we are illustrating is that of *content utilization,* the fact that content can be used in a variety of different ways.

How might you use the Stone Axes material? Consider the following: (1) as an informal diagnostic reading test (which really isn't social studies); (2) as an ethnographic case study of a primitive tribe; (3) as an example of what may happen when one isolated group comes into contact with another culture, or when a technological innovation is introduced into a culture; (4) as a data base to test previously identified hypotheses (e.g., "Is a change in one thing likely to cause other changes?"); (5) as a vehicle for teaching cognitive skills—hypothesizing, analyzing, inferential thinking, etc.; (6) as a source of speculative-heuristic questions to initiate student inquiry; (7) as a situation or vehicle for asking students to make evaluative judgments (e.g., "Were the missionaries right?"); and (8) as a springboard for further inquiry and research.

When students *use* social studies content, they also learn the content in the process. Students cannot, for example, analyze the Stone Axes material without learning something about what happened to the Yir Yoront. In other words, even though we used "Stone Axes" as a vehicle for illustrating the different levels of questions you could ask, you undoubtedly *learned* something about it as well. Were your students to use the Stone Axes material as a source for generating hypotheses, for example, they would actually be learning to use social studies content as they go along.

is that before asking a question—*any* question—it's essential to consider the skills the students must employ to produce an answer.

QUESTIONS AND THINKING PATTERNS

The relationship between teachers' questions and children's thinking patterns was the focus of some significant educational research noted earlier, that of Hilda Taba and her associates. One of Taba's contributions is the technique of *cognitive mapping,* a way of graphically illustrating the thinking processes that children use in approaching content. For example, when third-grade children were confronted with the heuristic question, "What would happen to the way of life in the desert if sufficient water became available?" the following discussion ensued.

Sequence	Speaker	
1	Teacher	Think about the boys and girls of the desert and the big changes that might happen if they had water.
2	Gary	Lots of people will start moving there.
3		They would have a big city with schools.
4		They would have machines and streets and cars.
5,6		They won't need the animals, because the people will go to school and learn how to drive cars.
7	Mary	When they have cars and everything they would be more like our country.
8		They could learn from the things that we do.
9	Alan	If they have streets like we do, we could teach them some of our sports.
10	Andria	They could have better schools, bigger playgrounds, and better books to read. They could have a new type of arithmetic. (Taba, 1967, p. 67)

This discussion excerpt was then depicted in graphic form (Figure 8.3), with the innermost horizontal representing the most immediate consequences or predictions (e.g., "people will move in") and the most distant horizontal lines reflecting higher levels of cognitive thought, that is, predictions that are several causal leaps beyond the more immediate ones.

In random discussions, where individuals share opinions but the discussion never seems to lead anywhere, a teacher's questions aren't especially important. But in discussions that are intended to help move children from Point A to Point B or Point C, the kinds of questions you ask, as well as the pace or speed at which you ask them, become much more critical. For one thing, there is a tendency for teachers to move to higher levels of questioning once they've received a desired response to a lower-level question. A problem can arise when only one student

FIGURE 8.3   Translation of a Discussion Excerpt into a Cognitive Map
(Grade 3)

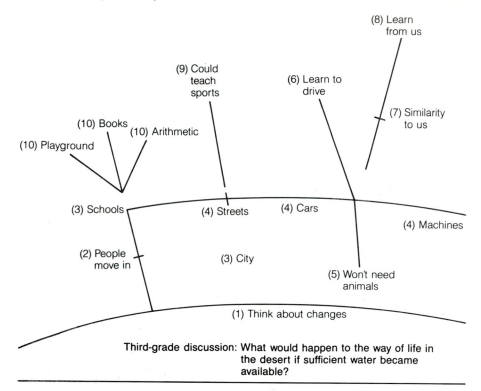

(8) Learn
from us

(9) Could
teach
sports

(6) Learn to
drive

(7) Similarity
to us

(10) Books
(10) Arithmetic

(10) Playground

(3) Schools

(4) Streets

(4) Cars

(4) Machines

(2) People
move in

(3) City

(5) Won't need
animals

(1) Think about changes

Third-grade discussion: What would happen to the way of life in
the desert if sufficient water became
available?

(Source: Hilda Taba: TEACHER'S HANDBOOK FOR ELEMENTARY SOCIAL STUDIES, 1967. With permission of Addison-Wesley Publishing Company.)

(the one who answered the lower-level question) is ready to move on to a higher level; the rest of the class may be lost. As Taba (1967, p. 123) observed, "The decision about how much time to spend on each level—pacing—must take into account the necessity for allowing at least the majority of the class to participate. . . ."

Sequencing Questions

The question many prospective teachers ask is "What questions should I ask when?" There are no hard-and-fast answers, but Taba (1967) has suggested a practical, three-question sequence that is applicable to many situations. The questions are "What?" "Why?" and "What does it mean?"

We have applied this questioning sequence in the example that follows. The purpose of each question is indicated in italics. Notice especially that the questions are *not* asked one after the other, in rapid-fire order, but follow the overall "what-why-what-does-it-mean?" pattern. Note also that we have omitted the student responses for brevity and because our focus is on the functions these questions serve in the lesson.

> *T:* **What happened in *this* incident [the Stone Axes material]?**
> *(Function: Focusing—What?)*
> *S:* Response
> *T:* **Did anyone notice anything else?**
> *(Function: Eliciting and extending thought at same level)*
> *S:* Response
> *S:* Response
> *S:* Response
> *T:* **Is there anything else we've missed?**
> *(Function: Eliciting and extending)*
> *T:* **OK. But why did this happen?**
> *(Function: Lifting thought to another level—Why?)*
> *S:* Response
> *S:* Response
> *T:* **You mean you think the missionaries were responsible?**
> *(Function: Clarifying and extending)*
> *S:* Response
> *T:* **But do you think the missionaries were responsible for increased crime?**
> *(Function: Lifting thought to another level)*
> *S:* Response
> *T:* **What caused the problems—the steel axes or the missionaries?**
> *(Function: Clarifying and extending)*
> *S:* Response
> *T:* **Anyone else have a different idea?**
> *(Function: Extending thought at the same level)*
> *S:* Response
> *S:* Response
> *T:* **OK, but what does all of this mean?**
> *(Function: Lifting thought to another level—What does it mean?)*
> *S:* Response
> *S:* Response
> *S:* Response
> *T:* **Well, then, are you suggesting that a lot of changes resulted from this one intervention?**
> *(Function: Clarifying and extending)*
> *S:* Response
> *T:* **If the missionaries were coming anyhow, what might they have used other than steel axes?**
> *(Function: Refocusing)*
> *S:* . . . .

The questions you ask will depend on the function you want them to serve; it should be apparent that questions can serve several functions. Those we've used are based primarily on Taba, but we've added some of our own.

One of the most important functions questions serve is that of *focusing*. Such questions set the stage for whatever is to follow. The question "What?" serves this function, as well as serving to make certain that students understand the facts of the situation.

The questions "Why?" and "What does it mean?" serve to shift the thinking

COMMENTARY: Wait Time

"Whenever we have a discussion, the same kids participate all of the time and the rest of the class just sits there. Sometimes the students that do talk don't have much to say—it's all very superficial. I don't know. I'm about ready to give up on discussions."

Frustrated teachers have been echoing complaints like this for years. Yet a potential solution to their problem is so simple that it's easily and often overlooked. The solution, which takes no special skills and has achieved dramatic results where it's been employed, is: Doing nothing. Well, almost nothing.

In some fascinating research, Mary Budd Rowe (1969) examined the relationship between a teacher's wait time and the quality of classroom discussions. *Wait time* refers to the period of silence between the end of a teacher's question and the teacher's next statement or question. Rowe found that most teachers are apparently unwilling to tolerate silence during a discussion, because their average wait time was only nine-tenths of a second. No wonder students didn't participate! They didn't have time to think before the teacher went on with another comment or question.

After Rowe informed teachers just how short their wait time was, they decided to double it—at least to two seconds. Awkwardly at first, the teachers waited the allotted time. For some of them it seemed like an eternity, but they waited, all two seconds. The results? The number of students participating in class discussions improved dramatically, as did the quality of their contributions. When teachers also lengthened the period of silence between a student's response and the teacher's next comment or question—what Rowe called "Wait Time II"—the results were even more impressive. Even more students responded, including some who almost never participated, while the quality of the discussions improved as well.

The implication is clear: if your discussions don't go well and the same students participate all the time, try lengthening your wait time. If you do that and your discussions still don't go well, you may need to reexamine the kinds of questions you are asking.

from one level to another. In the Stone Axes example, the question "Why?" lifts the level from the enumeration of facts to a consideration of why the events took place. The *why* question also asks students to analyze the interaction between the events that took place. Finally, the question "What does it mean?" asks students to assess the significance of the incident or events, and may also lead to a generalizable statement such as "A change in one thing may cause lots of other changes."

SUMMARY

A *teaching strategy* refers to a teacher's overall plan of organization. Teaching *techniques* refer to the day-to-day instructional activities (recitations, discussions, etc.) that teachers use in interacting with students. On any given day, a teacher might use several teaching techniques such as showing a film, directing a discussion, and presenting a mini-lecture. However, developing a teaching strategy is not simply a matter of mixing together a series of interchangeable teaching techniques. Rather, teacher-centered and student-centered teaching strategies embody different assumptions and somewhat different activities on the part of both teachers and students. Teacher-centered strategies tend to emphasize "telling" or exposition, whereas student-centered strategies tend to be inquiry or problem-solving oriented and encourage active student involvement.

The more student-centered the strategy a teacher develops is, the more important that teacher's questions become. We identified five categories of questions that teachers might ask, all of which were identified in terms of the skills they require of students in order to answer them. Those categories are memory-recall, descriptive-interpretive, application-synthesis, evaluative-judgmental, and speculative-heuristic. We also identified two other categories of questions which, although not keyed to thinking skills, a teacher might ask in the course of a lesson. Those categories of questions are rhetorical and probing. (We identified a third type of question—multi-focus—which should be avoided; the questions are too confusing for students to handle.)

In addition to the key role they play in most teaching strategies, the questions teachers pose largely determine the way students will use social studies content. If most questions are of the memory-recall type, for example, the teacher's emphasis will be on having children know the content itself, not use it. Higher-level questions—that is, higher in terms of their level on the *Taxonomy of Educational Objectives*—are more likely to demand that your students use content. This doesn't make lower, knowledge-level questions "bad," however. Memory-recall-level (knowledge-level) questions can be used to determine if students have desired information in their possession. The goal, in most instances, however, is to move beyond the knowledge level.

The essence of teaching social studies—or any subject area—is not defined solely in terms of *what* one knows, but also in terms of how one *uses* what one knows. We can't be guaranteed that as students use social studies content in the classroom, they will automatically transfer this use to their outside activities—factors beyond our control will influence that action. However, the hope is that we will have provided students with the skills and training that enable them to make that transfer.

SUGGESTED ACTIVITIES

1. Select teacher's editions of a first- or second-grade and a fifth- or sixth-grade social studies text. Then, using Bloom's *Taxonomy* as a basis, analyze the recommended questions or tasks for one unit in each book. Determine what proportion of questions/tasks reflects each of the six levels of the *Taxonomy*.

2. Observe a children's television program, such as *Sesame Street, The Electric Company,* etc., and determine what teaching strategies are *used most often.*

3. Using the *Taxonomy: Cognitive Domain* presented in Chapter 4 (pages 125–126), determine the taxonomic category for the following questions/tasks, all of which are based on the Stone Axes material.

   3.1. What has happened in other societies in which technological changes have been introduced?
   3.2. In your own words, describe what happened to the Yir Yoront.
   3.3. What do you think happened to the Yir Yoront after the missionaries left?
   3.4. Devise a plan that might avoid the negative consequences that resulted from the missionaries' actions.
   3.5. Were the missionaries right in doing what they did?
   3.6. In what country did the Yir Yoront live?

4. The more student-centered a teacher's strategy, the more important that teacher's questions become. Although their questions are important, inquiry-oriented teachers may actually ask fewer questions in the course of a lesson than teachers who employ other teaching strategies. How would you explain this?

REFERENCES

Beyer, Barry K. 1971. *Inquiry in the Social Studies Classroom.* Columbus, Ohio: Charles E. Merrill.

Bloom, Benjamin S. 1956. *Taxonomy of Educational Objectives: Classification of Educational Goals: Handbook I: Cognitive Domain.* New York: Longman.

Chase, Stuart. 1963. *The Proper Study of Mankind: An Inquiry into the Science of Human Relations.* New York: Harper & Row.

Olsvanger, Immanuel, ed. 1947. *Royte Pomerantsen.* New York: Shocken. English translation from Nathan Ausubel. 1948. *A Treasury of Jewish Folklore.* New York: Crown.

Rogers, Vincent R. 1970. "A Macrocosmic Approach to Inquiry." *Social Education,* 34 (January), 74–77.

Rosenshine, Barak, and Robert Stevens. 1986. "Teaching Functions." In *Handbook of Research on Teaching,* ed. Merlin C. Wittrock. 3rd ed., pp. 376–91. New York: Macmillan.

Rowe, Mary Budd. 1969. "Science, Silence, and Sanctions." *Science and Children,* 6 (March), 11–13.

Skeel, Dorothy J., and Joseph G. Decaroli. 1969. "The Role of the Teacher in an Inquiry-Centered Classroom." *Social Education,* 33 (May), 547–50.

Taba, Hilda. 1967. *Teacher's Handbook for Elementary Social Studies.* Introductory ed. Menlo Park, Calif.: Addison-Wesley.

Williams, Reed G., and John E. Ware. 1977. "An Extended Visit with Dr. Fox: Validity of Student Satisfaction with Instructional Ratings After Repeated Exposures to a Lecturer." *American Educational Research Journal,* 41 (Fall), 449–57.

SUGGESTED READINGS

Bruce Joyce and Marsha Weil. 1980. *Models of Teaching.* 2nd ed. Englewood Cliffs, N.J.: Prentice-Hall. This volume ranks among the landmark texts in education because it was one of the first to reduce the mountain of literature dealing with teaching strategies to manageable terms.

Meredith Gall. 1984. "Synthesis of Research on Teachers' Questioning." *Educational Leadership,* 42 (November), 40–47. This article offers a cogent synthesis of a large body of research on questioning strategies.

Norris Sanders. 1966. *Classroom Questions: What Kinds?* New York: Harper & Row. This elderly but excellent volume was one of the first books to relate classroom questions and tasks to the *Taxonomy of Educational Objectives.* It is still one of the best.

CHAPTER 9

Skills-based Instruction: Access Skills

"Shallow men believe in luck . . . strong men believe in cause and effect."   Emerson

KEY QUESTION

☐ How can teachers help children to use direct and vicarious experience to gain access to information?

KEY IDEAS

☐ Before students can deal with information or experience, they must have effective and efficient access to it.
☐ Access skills, which include reading, observation, and listening, are part of a broader group of information-processing skills applicable to all walks of life.
☐ After children gain access to information, they can use that information to build and tests ideas. Mere access is not sufficient.

INTRODUCTION: Reading Between the Lines

Reading between the lines is something that some of us, like Lucy (see cartoon on page 269), are not very good at. In fact, for some students, reading the lines themselves is a problem, much less reading "between" them. Reading between the lines is actually an information-processing skill that involves taking two or more pieces of information and relating them to produce a third idea that goes beyond the original information. Thus, a comment such as "The author is really saying that . . ." results from a reader having inferred what the writer might have had in mind.

It's no secret that Lucy and a lot of real-life elementary children have difficulty moving beyond a literal, word-for-word restatement of whatever information they happen to be dealing with. At the same time, traditional social studies programs

(Source: Charles M. Schulz, © 1956 United Features Syndicate. All Rights Reserved.)

have also been faulted for never leaving the literal level. Despite some claims to the contrary, a student's major responsibility has typically been to restate whatever the textbook said about a particular topic. Oftimes, students stored the information in their short-term memory, answered the test questions as best they could, and then promptly forgot most of what they had remembered.

In an era when we are bombarded with information from almost every conceivable source, it seems reasonable that we should provide children with skills that enable them to go beyond such literal thinking, skills that enable them to deal with information on their own. Indeed, if social studies is to be a really meaningful component in a child's education, it seems to us that the emphasis must shift to what information means, not just to what it says—and that "reading between the lines" should be a regular feature of social studies teaching.

Reading between the lines is an information-processing skill; it is something one does with (and to) information. Reading in its more generic sense is also an information-processing skill, as are the two other skills that we deal with in this chapter—observing and listening.

This is the first of five chapters that deal with different skill areas. For us to devote such a significant chunk of this book to skills should be a clear indication of where we think the emphasis in social studies should be placed. At the same time, we needed a way to organize and present the various skill areas. Of several plans we could have employed, we decided to deal with skills in terms of their function—in terms of what we use them for. As a consequence, skills used to process information are treated in this chapter and the next. The element that sets reading, observing, and listening (which we deal with in this chapter) apart from the generic information processing skills—such as inferring, classifying, predicting, and analyzing—is the fact that we use reading, observing, and listening to gain access to information and experience, hence the title "Access Skills." In Chapter 11, we consider a group of applied skills that provide access to the specialized information found on maps, globes, charts, graphs, and tables. Finally, it takes two chapters (12 and 13) to treat the social and group-management skills that play such a vital role in teaching.

None of the skill areas noted above are unique to social studies; to one degree or another, they cut across every subject area. Even map reading, which is traditionally associated with social studies, is a recognized component of most reading and mathematics programs. So although many skills themselves are not unique to social studies, students can readily apply them to social studies content and materials.

Clearly, a student's reading skills may influence how well he or she performs in social studies. At the same time, the reciprocal is equally true: working with social studies materials offers countless opportunities for helping students to improve their reading skills. The same principle applies to skill areas such as observing and listening. Thus, an effective vehicle for teaching group interaction skills is having students work together on social studies projects.

In the balance of this chapter, we examine techniques for teaching the access skills of reading, observing, and listening.

COMMENTARY: On the Nature of Skills

When someone asks "How much is 2 + 2?" most of us simply spout out the answer—"4!" The problem is so familiar that determining the answer is less a skill than recalling a piece of knowledge that we drilled into our heads many years ago. However, when someone asks "How much is 72 + 41 + 69 + 85?" most of us don't have that knowledge on the tip of our tongues. But most of us do know the agreed-upon rules or procedures (procedural rules) for adding two columns of numbers. For the second problem, the skill is composed of (1) *knowing* the procedural rules that govern a process or procedure and (2) *applying* that procedure accurately. Both elements of a skill are essential. Merely knowing the procedural rules is insufficient.

Things will get very complex if we give elaborate examples of skills, so permit us another simple illustration. If children demonstrate that they lack the "skills" needed to use an index, for example, what would you teach them? Think of your response in terms of the skill rules that children would need to know. First, the children must (1) know what an index is, (2) know where it is located, and (3) they must know how an index is organized. All of this knowledge is for naught, however, unless the student can apply it to locate the desired information.

continued

We acknowledge that gifted athletes and gifted artists seem to have an inborn talent that permits them to demonstrate extraordinary skills. Such exceptions notwithstanding, our point is that skills have two sequential components: (1) a significant knowledge (skill rule) component and (2) the ability to apply those rules in problematic settings.

This distinction is critical when it comes to diagnosing children's skill deficiencies. The children's problem could lie in the skill-rule (knowledge) component, in the application component, or both. However, because the skill-rule component is a prerequisite for the application component, we suggest that you begin there. We do not mean to oversimplify a complex matter, but the reason that children are unable to determine the distance between two cities on a map, for example, could lie in their lack of familiarity with the scale of miles. Or it could lie in their inability to use the scale of miles to determine distance.

READING

Of all the subjects students study in school, we can think of only one, literature, in which the demands on a student's ability to read may exceed those imposed by most traditional social studies programs. The complexity of the reading skills demanded by social studies texts for a particular grade level almost always exceeds the skills being taught in formal reading classes at that level. Then, too, in most reading classes the students are grouped by ability. This means that teachers can often provide reading materials that are suited to the children's ability levels. However, the content of social studies texts varies markedly from one grade level to the next (as we suggested in Chapter 5). As a result, it is difficult to match a student with a social studies text that covers the same topics *and* that is appropriate to the student's reading-skill level. We don't mean to imply that every student must be on the same page of the text; it's just that without special provisions, most social studies materials don't provide as many options for poor readers as reading materials do.

TEXTBOOKS AND READABILITY

Most of the publishers we've met would like nothing better than to produce a third-grade text, for example, that had a second-grade reading level. However, publishers have also learned that in social studies programs based on the expanding-environments model, there are certain topics at each grade level that textbooks are expected to include. If those topics are not included, the books may not be adopted (or purchased) by states or local school districts.

To understand the abstract cue concepts and generalizations contained in most social studies texts, children typically need concrete examples. This is where another confounding element, *length,* enters the picture. Every example takes space, which adds to a book's length. If the text is too lengthy, it may not be adopted. Thus, to maintain a reasonable length, textbook authors are often denied the opportunity to clarify abstract concepts with enough concrete examples. The result: too many concepts in too few pages, or what is called high *concept loading.*

Social studies (and science) textbooks have often been criticized for having high concept loading, which in turn makes them more difficult to read and understand. In response to these complaints, many publishers have attempted to simplify their materials. However, they have tended to deal with the problem not by attacking concept load directly, which would mean eliminating some abstract concepts and adding concrete examples for others, but by shortening the sentences. In theory, short, simple sentences are easier to read than longer, more complex sentences; an assumption that has been disputed by some recent research in reading. Nevertheless, the clear trend in textbooks is to reduce the length of sentences.

A common technique for determining the difficulty level of instructional materials is to apply a *readability* measure, such as the Fry Readability Graph presented in Figure 9.1. Such measures are usually based on readily quantifiable measures, such as the complexity of sentences as determined by the number of syllables they contain. In light of this, most authors and publishers quickly learn how to "beat" a readability formula in order to make the material appear easier than it actually is. Shortening (or avoiding) complex sentences and saying *big* instead of *enormous* are just two ways of accomplishing this. Unfortunately, none of the readability formulas of which we are aware include concept loading as a component, and that, we think, is part of the larger problem. Placing complex ideas in short sentences does not in itself make those concepts easier to understand.

Individuals in various parts of the country have criticized efforts to simplify and reduce the reading levels in textbooks—a process they sometimes refer to as "dumbing down." It has led, they claim, to textbooks that are dull, completely lacking in style, and so simplified as to be almost simplistic. On the other hand, because readability formulas are often important factors in determining which textbooks a school district may adopt, we can understand why the publishers have acted as they have.

Cloze and Maze Procedures

Two diagnostic procedures that permit you to *estimate* your students' ability to read social studies materials are the *cloze* and the *maze.* The two techniques are similar because they both ask students to supply words that have been systematically deleted from previously unread material. The percentage of words students replace correctly indicates how closely the materials correspond to the students' ability to comprehend them.

A sample reading inventory based on the cloze procedure is shown in Figure 9.2. It was prepared according to the guidelines on page 274.

FIGURE 9.1 Fry Readability Graph

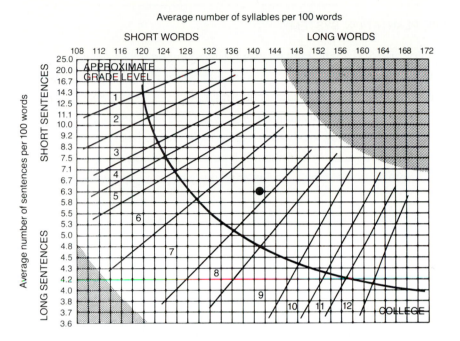

Average number of syllables per 100 words

SHORT WORDS   LONG WORDS

DIRECTIONS: 1) Randomly select three, 100-word passages from the beginning, middle, and end of the material. Count proper nouns, numerals, and initializations as words, e.g., "1980" is one word, as is "NATO".

2) Count the total number of sentences in each passage. Estimate partial sentences to nearest tenth. Average these three numbers as shown in the example below.

3) Count the total number of syllables in each passage. There is a syllable for each vowel sound, e.g., cat (1), bluebird (2), geography (4). Count a syllable for each symbol, e.g., "1980" is 4 syllables, as is "NATO". Note that making a slash mark on scratch paper for each syllable can eliminate confusion as you count mentally. Average the total number of syllables for the three samples as shown below.

4) Plot the average number of syllables and sentences (using the appropriate coordinates) on the graph, as shown in the example. The approximate grade level is represented (roughly) by the area between the perpendicular lines.

Example:	Sentences (per 100 words)	Syllables (per 100 words)
1st Sample	8.2	120
2nd Sample	4.5	149
3rd Sample	11.9	122
Average (total divided by 3)	8.2	130
Readability: Grade Five		

Note: Before concluding that this material is suitable for fifth graders, notice the wide variability in the samples. The second sample, before averaging, is 9th grade level material, while the third sample is at the 2nd grade level. When you find this kind of variability, more samples are called for. You may find that portions of this material are unsuitable for your students.

(Source: Adapted from Fry, 1972.)

FIGURE 9.2 Cloze Inventory Format

"THE PLANTATION SYSTEM"

For over 300 years, farming was the most important way of earning a living. _____ first farms in the _____ were plantations along the _____ rivers. A plantation is _____ large farm that produces _____ or two major crops. _____ plantations specialized in raising _____ . Others specialized in rice, _____ , or cotton. They received _____ from the crops. Then _____ bought the goods they _____ from England. It was _____ to run the plantations. _____ were scarce. It took _____ lot of workers to _____ and weed the big _____ .

In the 1600's, many _____ English colonists came to _____ . They could not pay _____ fare across the ocean.

---

1. Select a representative passage (or passages) of previously unread material, approximately 250 words long.

2. Leave the first and last sentences free of any deletions. For the balance, delete every fifth word until you have obtained fifty blanks. Note that each blank space should be the same size so as to not provide clues to the length of the word. Note also that some authorities (e.g., Feely, 1975) recommend deleting every seventh word in social studies materials. Should you choose to follow this recommendation, which we endorse, you will need to select longer passages in order to provide the necessary fifty blanks. All other procedures remain the same.

3. Assure students that their performance will not be graded. When possible, students may be permitted to score their own inventories. There are no time limits.

4. Provide a key for correct answers. Note that according to established cloze procedures, synonyms are not acceptable. Students must replace each word exactly (a procedure with which we disagree personally).

5. Determine the percentage of correct responses, and based on that percentage, use the following criteria to determine difficulty level:

For Narrative Materials	For Expository Materials	Level
58–100%	54–100%	*Independent level*—students can read on their own.
44–57%	39–53%	*Instructional level*—students can read with assistance.
0–43%	0–38%	*Frustration level*—unsuitable for reading.

These scores should not be treated as rigid cutoff points. However, if the class's median score falls below 39 percent, many of your students may find the materials too difficult to use without revision or other corrective measures.

The maze procedure is similar to the cloze technique except that in place of blanks to be filled in, the student selects the correct word—in multiple-choice style—from three words that are presented. Alternative words are presented in random order and consist of the following: (1) the correct word, (2) an incorrect word of the same grammatical class (by grammatical class we mean noun, verb, preposition, etc.), and (3) an incorrect word of a different grammatical class. A sample maze exercise is shown in Figure 9.3.

Indications are that the maze procedure, while slightly more difficult to construct than the cloze technique, is less likely to produce apprehension among young children. If nothing else, students have at least a 33 percent chance of guessing the correct response. As a consequence, however, the recommended difficulty-level cutoff points for the maze technique are considerably higher than for the cloze.

FIGURE 9.3 Sample Maze Exercise (segment)

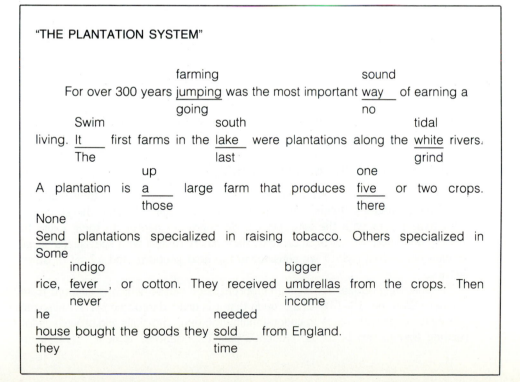

In order to read social studies material fluently and with real comprehension, students must be able to handle specialized vocabulary and must employ many critical thinking skills. (© *Elizabeth Crews*)

Suggested readability levels (Feely, 1975) for the maze procedure are

92% or greater—Independent level

80–91%—Instructional level

75% or less—Frustration level

[Note: This section is based on Lundstrum and Taylor (1977).]

READING COMPREHENSION SKILLS

Whether or not students understand the social studies materials they read can hinge on an amazing number of elements. Some of these include the students' prior experiences with the concepts (as we noted in Chapter 3), their ability to identify unfamiliar words from context, their ability to deal with specialized social studies vocabulary (which we consider in the next section), and a host of other factors.

The following outline of reading comprehension skills—which is adapted from Cooper (1986, pp. 10–13)—is unique in that it is divided into two parts: skills and processes to provide clues to understanding the text, and skills and processes for relating text materials to the student's past experiences. Recent research indicates that the prior experiences (concepts or schema) that students *bring to* reading are just as important as a student's decoding skills (Cooper, 1986).

Reading Comprehension Skills and Processes

I. Skills and processes to provide clues to understanding the text.

  A. Vocabulary skills.

    1. Context clues. The reader uses the familiar words in a sentence or passage to determine the meaning of an unfamiliar word.

      Example: The *fertile* topsoil would grow many different crops.

    2. Structural analysis. The reader uses prefixes, suffixes, inflectional endings, base words, root words, compound words, and contractions to determine word meanings.

      Example: The fertile *topsoil* would grow many different crops.

      The reader should recognize that topsoil is a compound word. Note that meaning may also hinge on an awareness of *subsoil.*

    3. Dictionary skills.

      Exemplary skill rule: When other techniques for deriving meaning for an unknown word are unsuccessful, refer to a dictionary for the meaning.

  B. Identification of relevant information.

    1. Identifying relevant details in expository materials.

      Example: Delaware was the first of the original thirteen colonies to ratify the Constitution.

    2. Identifying the main idea and supporting details.

      Example: Many crops grown in the United States are also grown in Mexico. These include citrus fruits, strawberries, melons, and vegetables such as cucumbers, peppers, and beans. Because Mexico's climate is warmer, the crops can be brought to market before the crops grown here have ripened.

    3. Identifying relationships among ideas found in the following expository structures.

      a. Description: The author presents information about or identifies characteristics of a topic.

      b. Collection: The author presents related ideas in a group; a sequence of ideas is apparent.

      c. Cause and effect: The author relates ideas in such a way that a cause-and-effect relationship is stated or implied.

      d. Response: The author presents a problem, question, or remark that is followed by a solution, answer, or reply.

      e. Comparison: The author asks the reader to note likenesses or differences in two or more objects or ideas.

II. Processes and skills for relating text to the student's past experiences.
   A. Inferencing. The reader uses information stated by the author to determine that which is not stated.

   Example: Farmers in some parts of Sweden used to gather seagull eggs and eat them. The seagulls simply laid more eggs. The farmers solved their problem by gathering and cooking the eggs until they were hard-boiled. Then they put the eggs back into the seagulls' nests.

   The reader must infer that the seagulls were destroying the farmers' crops or doing other kinds of damage.

   B. Critical reading. Readers must evaluate and judge as they read.
      1. Distinguishing between facts and opinions.

      Example: Ronald Reagan was the oldest and best President in American history.

      The "oldest" is fact, the "best" is opinion.

      2. Recognizing bias (the author's feelings for or against something).

      Example: Countries throughout the world should experience the benefits of socialism.

      The author apparently feels that socialism has some advantages that other forms of government do not.

      3. Recognizing assumptions (statements taken for granted as being true).

      Example: "Students today are soft and can't begin to compete with the students that I went to school with."

      The apparent assumption is that schools in "the good old days" were superior to schools today.

   C. Other techniques.
      1. Reading to get a general idea of what an author is saying and what he or she is trying to persuade readers to think.
      2. Looking for techniques, such as those in B. above, that would cause students to question what an author has said.
      3. Comparing what students are reading with what they already know.

   D. Monitoring. Teaching students to check their progress as they go and to determine that what they are reading is making sense.

DEALING WITH SPECIALIZED VOCABULARY

To a large extent, "learning" a subject—any subject—involves learning the specialized vocabulary associated with that subject area. Literature, for example, has its *sonnets* and *metaphors,* science has its *atoms* and *antennae,* and social studies has its *wings,* its *steppes,* and a host of others. Because specialized vocabularies are common to every subject area, the problems students encounter in trying to learn those vocabularies tend to be common too. It doesn't matter if the term is *wing,* as in a branch of a political party, or *wash,* as in a dry streambed, nor does it matter how well or poorly a student reads: when a student's train of thought is interrupted by specialized terminology—such as wings that have nothing to do with birds—the problem becomes one of bringing such usage into the child's realm of experience.

Several types of specialized terminology that may present problems for students were identified by John Lundstrum (1977) and others. These are the following:

Common words that can have multiple meanings   Examples include wing, class, power, bank, bill, branch, fork, wash, and belt. The appropriate meaning of the word must be determined from the context in which the word is being used.

Proper names for historically and/or physically remote personages and places   Many of the terms in this category do not follow the familiar rules for phonic analysis. Examples: Pharaoh, tsar (or czar), Hwang Ho, San Jose.

Regional expressions   In the Middle Atlantic states, a passageway through the mountains is known as a *gap;* in New England, it's a *notch;* and in the West, it's a *pass.* Likewise, a small river may be called a creek, a draw, a run, or a brook, depending upon the region. Other examples include borough, county, parish; tote, carry; pop, soda, tonic.

Terms associated with abstract concepts   Examples include ethnocentrism, political socialization, nationalism, culture, temperate, democracy, and inflation. None of these have concrete referents a child could point to readily.

Figurative expressions   Terms in this category usually take the form of short phrases. Examples: Fertile Crescent, paper tiger, dark horse, cold war, iron curtain, log rolling, etc.

Acronyms   These can often present special problems inasmuch as they are often abbreviations for organizations with which students are unfamiliar. Examples include OPEC, IRS, NSC, FCC, TVA, DAR.

The key to handling specialized terminology lies in anticipating problems *before* students become so frustrated that they want nothing more to do with it. Even if a passage attempts to explain the term in question, or even if the meaning is clear from the context, remember that what may seem perfectly clear to adults doesn't always appear that way to children, especially children with reading problems. Don't get us wrong: we believe that written explanations and context clues are extremely helpful tools for dealing with new vocabulary. However, whenever possible, these techniques should be used to help students relate specialized terminology to their previous experiences. In other words, we don't feel that a child's first encounter with abstract or specialized terminology should be via the printed word; rather, the printed word should cue the child to previous experiences with such terms.

There are several techniques for helping students deal with specialized terminology prior to encountering the terms in their reading material. One of these techniques can be used just prior to reading assigned materials, when the teacher introduces the new term, writes it on the chalkboard, and then defines it for students. Even though this option tends to treat terms out of context, it is often preferable to having students look up new terminology in a dictionary (which can quickly become a meaningless ritual in word copying). A preferable technique, we think, involves integrating social studies vocabulary with other subject areas. Suppose, for example, that *fence* is a word in a current spelling lesson. If you know that your students will encounter the figurative expression *iron curtain* in social studies one or two weeks hence, you could use the spelling lesson (and the word *fence*) for a brief foray into the realms of metaphor. You could muse rhetorically, "What could we call a wooden fence besides a *wooden fence?* Any ideas? How about a wooden wall? What about a fence made of steel? A steel shield? A fence of copper? A copper curtain?" This might open the way for a *brief* explanation of the figurative meaning of *iron curtain,* an explanation that will provide students with an experience they can refer back to later.

Our "iron curtain" example may seem a little contrived, but the key to it lies in brevity: the entire episode need not take any longer than the time it has taken you to read about it. Your tone has to be just right as well, because if you are too serious, too intense, or too long-winded, students may begin to wonder what's going on in the middle of the spelling lesson. On the other hand, if you are too casual, students may pass off the entire episode as unimportant.

WHAT TO DO FOR CHILDREN WHO CAN'T
READ THE TEXT

Based on everything we've said here, you can be almost certain that some of your students will have difficulty reading their social studies text. The first thing to ask yourself when you are confronted by such situations is why the students need to know whatever it is they can't read. "Because they need to know it" really isn't an adequate answer, since it doesn't address the point of the question, which in this case can be rephrased as "What do they need that information for?"

Once you are satisfied that a bona fide need for the information exists, you face a two-pronged course of action. The immediate, short-range action involves getting information from the printed page "into" the child's head. There are several ways to attack this kind of problem, none of them very simple. Perhaps the easiest is to read the selection to those students having difficulty. The problem with that procedure lies in finding something meaningful for the other students to do while you are reading to an individual child or a small group. This can be avoided if you either (1) have an aide or (2) have designed a section of the room as a listening center and have recorded portions of the text on cassette tapes. Teachers who put the text on tape are then free to work with other groups while their poorer readers listen and follow along in their books.

Over a period of time, teachers often build up a tape library to include the entire text. Of course, it doesn't have to be recorded all at once. The tape approach is not quite as massive (and expensive) as it may seem if several teachers at a grade level are using the same texts and are willing to contribute to the recording effort. In addition, since other teachers are undoubtedly encountering the same kinds of reading problems among their students, it isn't likely to take much convincing to gain their help.

A third option involves establishing a cross-age tutoring program in which older students work with younger students on an individual basis. Some school systems have had considerable success with programs in which, for example, a fourth, fifth, or sixth grader works with a younger student.

A fourth option, which can be the most time consuming, involves rewriting the material (or portions of it) in simpler language. It depends on the kind of material you are working with; it isn't especially easy to simplify statistics, for example. For text material, this option is complicated by the fact that texts are generally written at the simplest possible level to begin with. In fact, rewriting is probably a more viable (and necessary) option if you wish to use advanced material, such as that from secondary- or college-level texts or from sources such as *Time, Newsweek,* and the social science journals.

The longer-range course of action involves identifying the problem that's keeping the child from reading the text in the first place. If it's a reading problem, as it will more than likely prove to be, then you will have encountered one of the most fundamental problems in schools today. We, like teachers everywhere, are looking for answers to the reading problem. Until those answers are found, you will undoubtedly be forced to rely on one or more of the alternative strategies described above.

COMMENTARY: Oral Reading and Social Studies

Remember those occasions when your teachers said, "Okay, turn to page so-and-so in your book and we'll begin reading aloud"? If your teacher called on students at random, you had to pay attention in order to know which paragraph you might be asked to read. But if the teacher followed a pattern in calling on students (going around the room in sequence, etc.), you may have found yourself counting the paragraphs until you identified the one that would be yours. Until your turn was imminent, you probably daydreamed or found something else to occupy your time. One thing you probably did *not* do during the interval was listen to whatever was being read by a fellow student.

On rare occasions, such as when you or your students find a short passage in a book or magazine that pertains to what the class is studying, oral reading can be an acceptable way to share information. But as a general rule, most social studies textbooks are abysmally ill-suited to oral reading. Therefore, teachers who think they are killing two birds with one stone—teaching both oral reading and social studies by having students read aloud from the text—are likely to be doing neither very well.

OBSERVATION AND LISTENING

It's said that the way to distinguish an optimist from a pessimist is by having both look at a half-filled glass of water. The pessimist, they say, will describe it as "half-empty," while the optimist will say it is "half-full." This incident illustrates how much our perceptions influence what we see. Both the optimist and the pessimist see the same object, but they perceive it quite differently. This phenomenon is the basis for the distinction between *seeing*, which relates to the physical or sensory aspects of vision, and *observing*, which relates to what people perceive or take special notice of through their visual senses.

Our perceptions and purposes also influence how we describe what we see and observe. Consider, for example, the following descriptions of a plant (Houp and Pearsall, 1980, p. 4).

Example	*Commentary*
. . . the very nice plant my mother had on her table in the front hall	Everyday, homey diction, which depends a great deal on the reader's imagination
. . . properly potted and displayed specimen of the family *begoniacae*	Abstract, general, formal, open to interpretation
. . . in a shaft of yellow sunlight, a white-flowering begonia in a red clay pot	Pictorial, vivid, sensory, "show" rather than "tell about"
. . . a 12-inch, white-flowering begonia propagated from a three-inch cutting; age: 42 days	Specific, technical, factual, empirically informative

Much communication (and observation) is reflected in the first three messages, yet only the last description reflects the results of a verifiable observation. The idea in observing is to produce descriptions that others can employ, not to appeal to one's senses or emotions.

Perceptions also play a role in listening and hearing. Earlier we noted students who can study with the stereo going full blast, whereas other students must have almost complete silence. The stereo users seem not to be bothered by the music because they don't hear it—they "tune it out" in much the same way that children sometimes "tune out" nagging parents (or teachers). Such "selective listening" is sometimes even more apparent than "selective vision," and its existence has led to the distinction between *hearing,* which is what we receive via our ears, and *listening,* which refers to the sound stimuli that we actually perceive and respond to.

How we use information gained via listening and observing is perhaps best illustrated by the ways in which young children acquire language. Consider that a substantial part of a child's language acquisition will have taken place by the time he or she is five or six years old.

Language acquisition involves a number of specific learnings. In summary form, these include (1) learning to separate the language that children hear into separate units of sound and meaning; (2) the discovery of patterns and rules by which units of sound and meaning are combined into sentences (syntax, grammar, etc.); and (3) the identification of context clues (semantics) that guide the social aspects of dialogue (Moskowitz, 1978). By the time children enter school, they have what linguists refer to as a "fully formed grammar and language system." The amount of complex and higher-order learning that occurs through listening and observing (and experimenting) is almost miraculous—as is the fact that virtually all of it takes place without the benefit of formal schooling.

If we were to observe first-hand what children do in the process of language acquisition, we would likely find the following:

Children in all cultures actively reflect upon and analyze what they observe and hear.

Based upon what they observe, children form theories (about language) and then test them in real situations.

Children observe real people in real situations, and use those situations to develop and test theories and revise learning.

A crucial, first step in learning is *over-generalizing*, as in "We 'goed' to the Burger King." In other words, children quickly learn that "ed" (a bound morpheme) means that "something happened in the past." Until they learn the exceptions to that rule, they may add "ed" to verbs of any tense, including "go" or "went."

Children have been observed practicing language learning when they are alone (as in their cribs or playpens).

Clearly, the language-acquisition process, which takes place largely through observation and listening, is not as informal as it might at first appear. Children systematically form and test theories based on the information they gain through their senses.

Teachers can provide instruction in observing and listening by making these skills an integral part of their ongoing activities. The dominant characteristic of observing and listening activities is that they usually involve little if any reading. As a result, these activities are often appropriate for poor readers or students in the primary grades.

OBSERVING ACTIVITIES

Activities that focus on observation skills emphasize things that children can observe; things that can include objects, behaviors, or processes.

```
MODEL STUDENT ACTIVITY
```

The Peanut Butter Study

Consider a bulletin board devoted entirely to the results of a class of students' observations regarding, of all things, peanut butter. In the center of the bulletin board is a newspaper article with the headline "It's as American as Apple Pie." The article also reports the role that peanut butter plays in our nutritional and eating habits. It indicates that

85 percent of American homes have at least one jar of peanut butter on hand at all times.

The average supermarket carries thirty-three brands, styles, and sizes of peanut butter.

Adults tend to prefer crunchy peanut butter; children tend to prefer smooth.

Approximately 1.5 million peanut butter sandwiches are served in school cafeterias every school day, most of them as part of federal lunch programs.

A questionnaire the students developed to use in interviewing other students in their school is also part of the bulletin board. The findings are presented in bar graphs.

To the question "Do you always have a container of peanut butter in your house?" 86 percent of the interviewees said "yes," and 14 percent responded "no."

The favorite brands of peanut butter, in order of popularity, were Peter Pan, 51 percent; Jiff, 17 percent; Skippy, 16 percent; other, 13 percent; and Jelly Mix, 8 percent.

Creamy peanut butter was the preferred form (45 percent), but crunchy was a close second (at 37 percent). Extra crunchy was 13 percent, and Jelly Mix was 5 percent.

Over 31 percent of the students believed that individuals consumed more than eight pounds of peanut butter in one year.

(*Note:* Conducting even simple surveys can entail many details that are easily overlooked. In this instance, there are some additional questions we hope the students considered. For example, how might they explain the results for the favorite-brands question (for which the responses exceed 100 percent). Should we be told how many individuals responded to the survey? Their ages? The number of people in the household?)

Using Pictures and Photographs

Pictures cut from magazines, such as the one shown in the following Model Student Activity, are perhaps the most obvious data sources. In this instance, the picture is mounted on a task card. That picture could also become the basis for a whole-class or small-group activity, as we explain in Chapters 14 and 15.

MODEL STUDENT ACTIVITY

Task Card

Use the following task card as part of a study or learning center set up for students' independent use.

Observing

When you make an observation you record all of the details of what you see. You do not include your personal feelings or opinions unless you indicate that you have done so.

Look at the picture carefully.

Remember than even the smallest detail may be an important one.

Record only what you see on a separate sheet. Do not take anything for granted.

Source: Photo © George Mars Cassidy/The Picture Cube

Just the thought of cutting up a *National Geographic* is more than some people can bear, while actually doing so almost borders on a criminal act. As a result, many teachers leave one of their most potent instructional resources sitting, neatly bound, on their classroom shelf. Actually, there's little reason not to cut up your *National Geographic*s, since almost every school library in the country has a complete set that can be used for reference purposes. If you want to keep your set intact, place a small notice in the school's newspaper; some family is almost certain to be moving to another area and willing to donate their copies to you (thus avoiding the cost of moving them).

What you are after in magazines such as *National Geographic, Smithsonian,* and the like are their spectacular photographs. Mounted on oak tag—the stuff file folders are made from—and *with their captions removed,* those photographs can provide the basis for some remarkably interesting and involving observing and inferring activities. By removing the captions, the photographs become un-interpreted data. The students must interpret the data for themselves in order to determine what the picture is of and what is going on in it. If you haven't already done so, look at the uncaptioned photo on the teacher-made task card above to see just how involving such photos can be. Without captions, there is obviously nothing to read. Because of this, captionless photocards can be used with any age or grade level. An alternative activity can be developed by mounting the caption on a separate "caption card" and then having students match the caption with the appropriate photo.

When pictures or photographs of a particular culture are clustered together, which is the way most *National Geographic* articles are presented, you have what we call *culture cards.* If you organize the photographs (uncaptioned) on some other basis—similar occupations, similar types of homes, etc.—you could just as well call them *picture cards.*

There are several ways that uncaptioned photo cards can be used, as illustrated in the following Model Student Activities. Other uses and sources for instructional photographs are examined in Chapter 15.

MODEL STUDENT ACTIVITIES

Picture and Culture Cards

To develop your own culture or picture cards, we offer the following recommendations:

Mount photographs on standard-size pieces of oak tag or posterboard. We use 7 × 11-inch cards for small pictures and 11 × 14-inch cards for larger ones. The standard sizes simplify storage problems considerably.

Use rubber cement for mounting purposes; it doesn't cause wrinkles. Or if your school has the facilities, you could have your pictures dry-mounted. For durability, you can either cover the pictures with clear Contac paper or have them laminated.

The simplest way to get pictures that are printed on both sides of a page is to order two subscriptions each of *National Geographic* and similar publications. If this isn't feasible, you'll need to learn one of the techniques for splitting a page to salvage the pictures on each side.

1. Prior to studying a culture, the class can be provided with a set of un-captioned pictures of a group of people (Eskimos, the Japanese, or whomever). Using just the pictures, ask students to describe the people as best they

can. The object is *not* to guess who the people are. You can avoid the students' tendency to do that by simply telling the class, "Here are some pictures of . . . and we want to describe them as best we can. How do they live? What kind of area do they live in?" etc.

Some of the descriptions (inferences) the students provide will be inaccurate. These can be corrected as the students move into other materials—texts, filmstrips, etc.—about that particular culture. In other words, their inferences or descriptions can serve as hypotheses to be tested. This suggests a new role for "background information" (see Commentary on pages 292–293).

2. After studying a culture, the students can be provided with a set of uncaptioned cards intermingling photographs from two or three cultures. Their task in this approach is to separate the pictures of the culture just studied from pictures of other cultures.

3. Given a set of randomly assorted culture cards, students can be asked to group them according to either criteria that you supply (family activities, seasons, etc.) or to criteria of their own choosing. This type of classifying activity is an integral part of concept building.

4. As a small-group activity, students can write their own captions for the pictures. They can then compare their captions with the original captions (which are mounted on a separate "caption card").

_____

The following student activity relies primarily on the access skill of observing (and the process skill of inferring). In addition to its skills focus, this activity is representative of a particular type of instructional activity in which students find themselves playing the role of social scientists, in a somewhat simplified form of course. In this activity students find themselves in the position of archaeologists/ anthropologists.

MODEL STUDENT ACTIVITY

Excavating a Wastebasket

STAGE ONE

Materials needed   One full wastebasket from another room—another classroom preferably, or from the teachers' lounge or principal's office. (*Note:* A plastic bag inserted the previous morning can make this activity a lot less messy.)

Procedure
Do NOT indicate which room the wastebasket is from.

1. Place the basket where everyone can see it.

2. Appoint one person as the excavator. That student's job is to take the objects out of the basket, one by one, and describe them carefully.

3. Appoint another child as the cataloger. This job involves drawing a cross section of the wastebasket on the chalkboard and noting the position of the items as they are dug up by the excavator. (Note: Since the "digging" proceeds from the top downward, allow plenty of room to draw an oversized illustration.)

4. Have the rest of the class list the items and describe them briefly on a sheet as follows:

Item	Description
8 milk cartons	empty, from Byrne Dairy, ½ pint
5 plastic straws	red and white striped, about 8 inches long
8 pieces orange peel	different sizes, dry
pencil shavings	yellow, green and blue, mostly yellow, about ¼ cup
one crumpled paper	three-ringed notebook, subject: math, addition problems with three wrong. Name: Sarah Farr

5. Ask the following questions, as appropriate:
   a. What kinds of activities took place wherever this wastebasket came from?
   b. Which took place first? (Those that produced items at the bottom of the basket.)
   c. Can we be sure?
   d. Where did the basket come from?
   e. Which articles give the best clues?
   f. Can we be sure of the significance of some items? (Does the *presence* of orange peel but the *absence* of brown lunch bags and waxed paper indicate that lunch was eaten in the room?)

6. At a prearranged time, appoint a small delegation (of three or four students) to take the findings to the room from which the wastebasket came to check out the accuracy of the students' conclusions. If they are uncertain as to exactly which room it is from, you may need to make some hasty arrangements and have several delegations operating simultaneously.

STAGE TWO: EXCAVATING WASTEBASKETS

Materials needed Full wastebaskets from a variety of places—both in school and out. (You can "load" some with clues if you wish.) Each basket (or plastic bag) should be labeled Exhibit A, Exhibit B, etc.

Procedure Proceed as on the previous day, except this time provide each small group with its own wastebasket.

Their task "Tell as much as you can about wherever this wastebasket came from and what activities took place where it was." Each group should record its findings on chart paper and present them to the class upon completion. Note: Caution each group *not* to indicate where their basket is from until after they have presented their information to the entire class.

Source: Adapted from the MATCH (Materials and Activities for Teachers and Children) Unit, "The House of Ancient Greece" (MATCH 1966). Used by permission.

LISTENING ACTIVITIES

Listening is a combination of what you hear, what you expect to hear, what you observe, and what you recall from your previous experiences. To be an effective listener, you need to be aware of the factors that influence listening. These include (1) thinking ahead of the talker and anticipating the direction of the discourse; (2) assessing the kind(s) of evidence the talker is using; (3) periodically reviewing the talker's points; (4) "Listening between the words"; (5) constructing ideas rather than being satisfied with just picking up facts; and, (6) withholding evaluation of the message until after the speaker is through talking.

Instead of developing thirty- or forty-minute lessons that deal with all six of these skills, we believe that, for elementary children, the skills are best approached as a part of other ongoing activities. For example, on occasions when a speaker is talking to the class, and it's possible to stop the speaker in mid-stream, the teacher can interrupt and ask one or two of the following questions:

a. "What do you think the speaker will say next?"

b. "What has the speaker said up to this point?"

c. "What is the speaker's main idea?"

d. "What things [kind(s) of evidence] has the speaker used to get us to believe what he or she is saying?"

e. "Which parts of what the speaker said were opinion?"

Beware however! When students' (or anyone's) train of thought is interrupted, they may resent the intrusion. Thus you must use your judgment as to when listening-oriented activities such as the one above are appropriate. If students are bored, they probably won't mind the interruption, but then they may not have been listening well enough to answer your questions.

Cassette tape recorders have made it possible to develop homemade listening-oriented activities. By taking a tape recorder with you as you travel, for instance, you can gather interesting materials for listening activities; consider developing a three-minute tape of sounds at a busy intersection, a shopping mall, or a super-market. The idea, initially, is to have students *describe what they hear,* not guess at what they're hearing. If a child says, "I hear a supermarket," for example, he or she is inferring something rather than describing the sounds. Inferring is a logical

If students have planned and structured an oral history interview ahead of time and if they are clear about what they are looking for, the interview will not only go more smoothly but will be more informative. (© *Elizabeth Crews*)

extension of describing—an inevitable extension in most instances—but the students' first focus should be on describing the sounds themselves.

Other listening activities could be based on the following: (1) sound-effects records; (2) commercially available audio tapes; and (3) playing short segments of movies with only the sound turned on (no picture). Note that reversing the procedure for number 3 above—playing short movies with the sound turned off—can provide the basis for an excellent observing activity.

Oral History

The *oral* in "oral history" refers to the spoken word. In more practical terms, oral history refers to a technique for collecting historical information. In the most practical sense, oral-history activities are based on having students plan and conduct tape-recorded interviews with individuals who have firsthand knowledge of a historically interesting event or way of life. The tape-recorded interview is then converted into a word-for-word transcript that, after editing, can provide the basis for a document (probably the only such document of its kind) that may then be placed in the school library.

As a technique, oral history is ideally suited to the study of local history. The actual study can be broken down into subfields such as urban history, minority history, women's history, family history, agricultural history, or even local school history, depending upon the area you live in (you couldn't very well produce an urban history for a rural area, etc.).

A key aspect of doing oral history involves planning and structuring the oral-history interview; otherwise you may end up with several dozen random conversations that are of little or no value. Before they get their hands on a tape recorder, student interviewers must be clear about what information they are after. Their purpose may be to get a local resident's account of the day the old courthouse burned down, someone's views on how population growth has affected the community, or almost anything else that might be of interest. The students' purpose is not just to conduct an interview, as some seem to think, but rather to conduct an interview *about something*. It doesn't matter so much what that "something" is as long as students understand what they are after.

Some guidelines for conducting oral-history activities are the following:

1. The focus should be on one topic, especially in the lower elementary grades.

2. Careful preparation for the interview, including helping students "bone up" on the topic using other sources—wills, diaries, other accounts—is essential. However, don't do so much preparation that the students lose interest.

3. Equipment for the interview may include props like an old photograph or picture, and, of course, a tape recorder. Tape recorders with built-in microphones are the least obtrusive, but those with external microphones often provide better sound quality.

4. Appointments for interviews should be made through official sources so that students don't face the burden of explaining the entire project. Interviews should be restricted to one hour or less.

5. The interviewee should be asked to sign a release form describing the extent to which the taped material may be used. In fact the teacher may wish to interview a lawyer about the legal implications of interviewing (libel, slander, etc.) and play this tape for the class as a model.

6. Send students in interview teams of two or three.

7. Contact the high school typing teacher (well in advance) for possible assistance in typing the transcripts.

The mechanics of producing written transcripts from several dozen tape-recorded interviews can sometimes become so cumbersome that it isn't worth the effort. In that event, the audio tapes can provide the basis for one of the multimedia presentations suggested on the next page.

The logistics of oral history sometimes become so cumbersome that you may wonder whether it's worth the effort. Consider that in doing it students are actually creating history, and may be acquiring the following: listening skills, observing skills, the skill of asking questions, the skills associated with organizing

---

MODEL STUDENT ACTIVITIES

Multimedia Presentations

1. Choose a topic of local concern, such as mine safety, and develop an edited tape on which several people describe the various types of equipment developed during the mine's existence. Exhibit the equipment, using photographs or slides if necessary.

2. Synchronize slides made from old photographs with comments made by eyewitnesses to an important local event—the day the old schoolhouse burned down, for example.

3. Edit a tape of several people describing how an artifact was made—soap, quilts, horseshoes, etc. Pass sample items around the classroom as the tape is being played (if your students won't be too distracted by them).

4. Build a scale model of a local monument. Have "old timers" describe why it was built, how it was funded, and what controversies arose concerning it. (There are always controversies, and these add spice.)

5. Make a movie of the history of the school. If possible, have the oldest living graduates do the narration. Be sure they are interviewed before the final script is written, so that their reminiscences become the focal point of the presentation.

Source: Willa K. Baum, "Oral History," in *Looking At* (September 1975). Boulder, Colo.: ERIC. Used by permission.

---

information, distinguishing fact from opinion and relevant from irrelevant information, and, if nothing else, a better understanding and appreciation of the older generation. The latter alone may make oral history worth the effort.

COMMENTARY: A New Role for Background Information

Traditional social studies teaching so often begins with "a little background information" that the practice has almost become a ritual. There are times when background information is essential, of course, such as in making certain that students have the concepts that enable them to bring meaning to the things they read. On other occasions, however, presenting background information almost becomes an end in itself, and there is seldom enough time remaining for students to do anything with that information.

Notice that in the wastebasket activity, it was *not* necessary to present any background information on what anthropologists do prior to beginning

continued

the activity. The necessary information was inherent in the activity itself. This phenomenon should be evident in most of the student activities we suggest throughout this book.

Background information can add perspectives that might otherwise go unnoticed in an activity. The basic question, however, concerns *when* the background information comes into play. A basic consideration involves the extent to which the students feel the need for additional information. By using uncaptioned culture cards *before* studying a particular culture, for instance, children almost always raise questions—*their* questions—about the culture. They can then attempt to answer those questions through reading. Likewise, after having experienced the wastebasket activity, students should have a feeling for what archaeologists/anthropologists do, which can add to accounts they read about such people.

What we are talking about here is a matter of timing. Engaging students in an activity *prior* to providing them with background information can often create the need for information, thus providing students with a reason to read. This phenomenon sometimes mirrors what teachers notice among nonreading students who are somehow able to comprehend articles on sports, auto mechanics, or the latest hairstyles, but cannot get through the stuff they're "spozed" to read. The implication is that when students want information, they can generally get it. It also suggests that before teachers assign large amounts of material intended as background information, they should consider how they can create a need for such information.

SUMMARY

Before students can develop the skills for using information, they must have access to information. This chapter has identified three access skills: reading, listening, and observing. We also identified techniques that can help you build students' skills in gaining access to information.

No matter how much students may need it, pure skills-based teaching can sometimes become downright dull—for both teachers and students. To offset this, many of the sample activities in this chapter have incorporated elements of mystery or problems to be explained, both of which are intended to enhance student interest (as we noted in Chapter 1). Another technique used by some teachers to counter the groan students emit when they hear "Today we will do another observing lesson" is based on a little harmless subversion. As long as you know what skills you are planning to emphasize in an activity, it isn't necessary to even mention those skills when presenting the activity to students. Thus a statement such as "Describe what you see in these pictures" is not likely to turn students off.

Implicit in this chapter are several teaching guidelines for managing instruction directed toward access skills. They are as follows:

1. Directing at least a portion of almost every social studies activity toward the skills of observing, listening, and reading.

2. Providing individualized instruction (task cards, etc.—see Chapter 14) for students who continue to have difficulty with particular skills.

3. Using social studies content to teach reading skills whenever appropriate. When students' reading skills are so poor that using regular text materials could become an exercise in frustration, consider using nonreading approaches—culture cards, etc.—that draw on the skills of observing and listening.

4. Making skills the explicit focus of activities in terms of your own planning, but keeping them implicit in terms of the way you present activities to your students.

SUGGESTED ACTIVITIES

1. Select two social studies texts for the same grade level. Using material that treats the same topic, compare the two texts in terms of their concept loading. Or, using the procedures described in this chapter, determine the readability level of each.

2. Select an issue of *National Geographic* or a similar publication. Develop a learning activity that is either based on the illustrations from one article or that asks students to do a basic content analysis that involves observation, categorizing, or reporting.

3. Select a location from which you will try to conduct an observation. The intent of this activity is to have you realize first-hand the things that get in the way of effective observation. Note the specific planning that must take place before sound observation can be conducted.

4. As part of a small group, design and conduct a survey on a topic of your choosing (e.g., the favorite soda, the preferred brand of pizza, or perceptions of the nation's foreign policy, etc.). Administer the survey to your class or other representative group. Design a means for presenting your findings graphically.

REFERENCES

Baum, Willa K. 1975. "Oral History." *Looking At,* (September), 1–2. Boulder, Colo.: ERIC Clearinghouse for Social Studies/Social Science Education.

Cooper, J. David. 1986. *Improving Reading Comprehension.* Boston: Houghton Mifflin.

Feely, Theodore M. 1975. "The Cloze and the Maze." *The Social Studies,* 66 (November/December), 252–57.

Fry, Edward. 1972. *Reading Instruction for Classroom and Clinic.* New York: McGraw-Hill.

Houp, Kenneth W., and Thomas E. Pearsall. 1980. *Reporting Technical Information.* 4th ed. New York: Macmillan.

Lundstrum, John P. 1977. "Reading in Social Studies." In *Developing Decision-Making Skills,* ed. Dana Kurfman. pp. 109–40. Washington, D.C.: National Council for the Social Studies.

———— and Bob L. Taylor. 1977. *Teaching Reading in the Social Studies.* Boulder, Colo.: ERIC Clearinghouse for Social Studies/Social Science Education and the Social Science Education Consortium, Inc.

MATCH. 1966. *House of Ancient Greece, Teacher's Guide.* Nashua, N.H.: Delta Education.

Machart, Norman C. 1979. "Doing Oral History in the Elementary Grades." *Social Education,* 43 (October), 479–80.

Metcalf, Fay M., and Matthew T. Downey. 1982. *Using Local History in the Classroom.* Nashville, Tenn.: American Association for State and Local History.

Moskowitz, Breyne A. 1978. "The Acquisition of Language." *Scientific American,* 239 (November), 93–96.

Patton, William E., ed. 1980. *Improving the Use of Social Studies Textbooks.* Bulletin 63. Washington, D.C.: National Council for the Social Studies.

Schneider, Donald O., and Mary Jo McGee Brown. 1980. "Helping Students Study and Comprehend Their Social Studies Textbooks." *Social Education,* 44 (February), 105–12.

Sitton, Thad, George L. Mehaffy, and O. L. Davis, Jr. 1983. *Oral History.* Austin, Tex.: University of Texas Press.

Squire, James R. 1982. "Language Concepts for Application to Social Studies." *Social Education,* 46 (October), 442–43.

Thavenet, D. J. 1981. "Family History: Coming Face-to-Face With the Past." NCSS How to Do It Series, Set 2, No. 15. Washington, D.C.: National Council for the Social Studies.

Wolff, Florence, Nadine Marsnik, William Tracy, and Ralph G. Nichols. 1983. *Perceptive Listening.* New York: Holt, Rinehart and Winston.

SUGGESTED READINGS

J. David Cooper. 1986. *Improving Reading Comprehension.* Boston: Houghton Mifflin. This extremely practical guide to improving reading comprehension does not demand an extensive background in reading.

There are a relatively large number of books available dealing with teaching reading in the content areas. Among those we recommend are Richard Vacca and J. L. Vacca. 1986. *Content Area Reading.* Boston: Little Brown.

George L. Mehaffy, Thad Sitton, and O. L. Davis, Jr. 1979. *Oral History in the Classroom.* How to Do It Series Number 2, Number 8. Washington, D.C.: National Council for the

Social Studies. This eight-page pamphlet provides a step-by-step guide to oral-history activities. Other titles in this series are *Improving Reading Skills in Social Studies; Effective Use of Films in Social Studies; Reach for a Picture; Using Questions in Social Studies; Architecture as a Primary Source for Social Studies;* and *Perspectives on Aging.* Available from the National Council for the Social Studies, 3615 Wisconsin Ave., N.W., Washington, DC 20016.

CHAPTER 10

Skills-based Instruction: Process Skills

"Thinking in its lower grades is comparable to paper money, and in its higher forms it is a kind of poetry." Havelock Ellis

KEY QUESTIONS

☐ What are process skills? How are they related to thinking?

☐ How does one teach students to develop and use process skills effectively and efficiently?

☐ What is decision making? How does it relate to thinking?

☐ How are teaching strategies and process skills connected?

☐ Where do teachers locate materials related to skills teaching?

KEY IDEAS

☐ Skills-based teaching and learning employ a variety of process skills.

☐ Process skills are part of a "family" of skills that individuals use to assess and interpret information and experience.

☐ Process-skill activities tend to be holistic and involve several skills simultaneously.

☐ Information-processing skills can be taught systematically.

INTRODUCTION: On Teaching Thinking

Process skills are operations—mental operations—that we use when we do something with information or our experience. We can do any number of things to information and experience—we can describe it, record it, interpret it, analyze it, or store it away for future reference. The point is that all of us use these skill areas every day, perhaps every waking moment (and sometimes when we sleep). In other words, we *think*.

Thinking is something that all of us learn to do, often without much formal instruction. It's also apparent that some people learn to do it better than others. Because thinking—like observing and listening—is something that seems to happen naturally, we sense a certain willingness among some people to simply stand back and let the natural processes (of thinking) unfold. In addition, for someone to suggest that you could be taught skills to enable you to "think better" can imply that there's something wrong or deficient with the skills that have gotten you where you are today. It's little wonder that people sometimes become defensive at such suggestions.

As we enter the 1990s, we see more and more emphasis placed on teaching children to "know about" subjects, and relatively less emphasis on "knowing how" to think efficiently and effectively. This emphasis is reflected in expectations that children should "know" that the capital of Argentina is Buenos Aires, for example, as opposed to knowing how to locate a capital in an atlas. Our concerns about this change in emphasis are mirrored by the increasing number of articles that stress the need for schools to reemphasize the teaching of thinking skills (e.g., deBono, 1983; Sternberg, 1985; Beyer, 1985).

A growing number of schools across the country have begun to offer "critical thinking" classes in which thinking skills are taught specifically. On one hand we are pleased to see such an emphasis, but we are also concerned that by establishing separate classes, thinking skills could be considered a totally separate subject—as something certain teachers teach at certain times of the day—instead of as something all teachers include in every subject they teach. We believe that teaching thinking skills is like citizenship education: both are all-school concerns, not something taught from 9:05 to 9:47 every Tuesday. On the other hand, we recognize that even some direct teaching of thinking skills done separately is probably better than none at all.

We believe that teaching children how (and when and why) to think effectively and efficiently is among the most important responsibilities—if not *the* most important responsibility—of schools today. Teaching thinking skills is not simply something nice that teachers might do for children. In fact, as Muller noted in *Uses of the Past* (1952) over thirty years ago, teaching future citizens to think well is basic to our morality. Muller's message seems as appropriate today as it was when our parents and grandparents were in school. Indeed, in a society based on the active participation of educated citizens, effective thinking skills are a necessary prerequisite.

We have used the expression "thinking skills" to describe the mental processes that we use to manipulate ideas, but we have done so with caution; the term *thinking* is so global that it is almost meaningless. As a consequence, we have defined these mental processes more specifically, as "information-processing skills." In other words, when we manipulate information we are indeed thinking.

However, we believe the expression *information processing* more precisely defines the kind of thinking we are talking about.

When we think, we obviously need something to think about. In addition to the data that come from books or lectures—the kinds of things one traditionally thinks about in schools—we extend the source of ideas to include experience. For example, once you have the impression that someone is trying to "snow" you, that impression—which you derive from your experience—will influence your future interactions with that individual. Everything he or she says may be regarded with suspicion. In fact, once the specter of doubt is raised, it may take a lot of "nonsnowing" experiences with that person before your trust is restored. But all of this is fairly obvious. Our point is that *experience* can and should serve as sources of data to which you and your students apply process skills.

Welles (1983) summarized much of what the research indicates about thinking skills, and found that

Teaching a general approach to thinking to "average" people over a period of years can drastically improve their thinking.

Students' performance in classrooms is more dependent on the strategies they use to acquire and use information than it is on IQ.

Novice thinkers try to recall every isolated bit of information, whereas experts tend to look for chunks—for patterns and relationships among the information.

Learning thinking skills often involves repetition and practice as well as reworking, organizing, and elaborating on the information.

Thinking involves intuitive, inductive, inferential, and sometimes even illogical components.

A key element of thinking involves learning how to apply and use what is known.

The purpose of this chapter is threefold: first, to identify the information-processing skills that children should develop; second, to examine the interrelationships among those skills; and, third, to present exemplary activities that children can employ to develop their ability to process information effectively and efficiently.

PROCESS SKILLS

Sometimes things that seem simple enough can become more difficult than one might imagine. Tying one's shoes, for example, is so commonplace that most of us do it automatically. But consider what it's like to tell a child how to tie his or her shoelaces.

Enter Christopher, a bright-eyed, four-year-old wearing a pair of dirty white sneakers, one of which has the laces dangling. There are only two ground rules for this activity. First, you are not permitted to use any demonstrations; just *tell*

Christopher how to tie his shoelaces. Second, you are not permitted to practice on your own shoes (assuming they have laces). Because tying one's shoes is something almost everyone knows how to do, you need merely to describe the process from memory. Ready?

If you get very far beyond the stage of "First you put one lace over the other," consider yourself exceptional. Describing how to tie one's shoes is a task so difficult that it almost defies description. And, although shoe tying is a physical (motor) skill, this episode illustrates something that also holds true for information-processing skills. Shoe tying is not complete until one has mastered a whole series of subskills—loop making, pushing one looped shoelace under another (while maintaining tension on the original twist), and so forth. In fact, it is one of those operations in which failing to complete any one of the requisite subskills throws the entire process out of kilter.

The same things can be true for children who, although they are able to identify plausible hypotheses, lack the ability to identify relevant information with which to test them. Hypotheses, no matter how good they are, may be meaningless unless a child is able to test and validate them. The point here is that information-processing skills are part of an interrelated "family" of skills that can be brought to bear on almost any activity.

Because process skills are part of a broader family, you will notice in this chapter—as in the previous chapter—that although some activities may focus on a particular skill area, they seldom stop there. Most process-skill activities are holistic; that is, although they focus on a particular information-processing skill—such as organizing data, analyzing, or inferring—other process-skill areas will almost surely be involved. Process skills, like access skills, just don't work well in isolation.

PROCESS SKILLS IDENTIFIED

When confronted with a problem, most of us more or less follow the inquiry process that our Talmudic scholar employed in Chapter 8; that is, we clarify the nature of the problem, gather additional data (if necessary), identify possible solutions (hypotheses), evaluate or test the alternative solutions to determine which one best fits the situation, and then we take appropriate action. At each phase of that process, we employ one or more of the following skill areas:

1. describing
2. record keeping
3. classifying
4. evaluating (judging)
5. interpreting
6. inferring
7. deducing
8. hypothesizing (predicting)
9. analyzing
10. experimenting
11. planning and designing
12. generalizing

Potential tasks associated with some of these skill areas are illustrated in Figure 10.1.

FIGURE 10.1 Skill Lesson Profile/Checklist

Lesson/Activity/Date Place checkmarks in boxes below to reflect skill focus of each lesson.	Sample 9/11														
ACCESS SKILLS:															
Observing applied to:															
Objects															
Events															
Behaviors	✓														
Processes															
Listening applied to:															
Objects															
Events															
Behaviors															
Processes															
PROCESS SKILLS:															
Gather Data															
Identify amount and kind of information needed	✓														
Evaluate different kinds of evidence															
Design systematic methods for gathering data															
Plan questions to be posed	✓														
Organize Data															
Record data systematically	✓														
Classify/categorize data	✓														
Construct tables															
Analyze Data															
Interpret the following:															
tables															
charts															
graphs															
maps															
Identify relationships among data/events															
Recognize limitations in the data															
Develop hypotheses from data (inductive reasoning)	✓														
Use data to test hypotheses (deductive reasoning)															
Identify factors that may influence the analysis	✓														
Interpret Data															
Understand how data are used to make ideas															
Offer alternative explanations for phenomena	✓														
Identify the need for additional information	✓														

Presenting Process Skills to Children

The above listing of process skills, as well as those provided in Figure 10.1, can be rather imposing. In fact, to say that students "should be able to analyze two or more sources of evidence so as to identify areas of agreement or potential contradiction" can be as imposing (if not more so) as the list above. Despite this problem, all of the information-processing skills can be taught in some form to elementary children. It is true that some children don't have the background or vocabulary to handle some of the more complex forms of analysis, synthesis, or evaluation, but they can often indicate, for example, if something in a story "fits," or whether "something seems wrong." Such simple forms of analysis are well within their ability. The secret, though, may lie in how the task is presented to them.

In many instances, though not all, the form in which information-processing skills are presented for teachers is *not* the form suitable for presenting them to elementary children. The exceptions to this include those processing skills that involve measuring, observing, and describing; elementary children seldom experience unusual problems handling such operations. But for most other skills, you will probably need to translate them into simpler language. Your exact translation will depend on the kind of data or experiences you're using, of course, but some examples of what we mean are illustrated in Table 10.1.

Rather than examine each of the information-processing skills separately, which results in a kind of piecemeal approach, we have organized the balance of this section so that it reflects the holistic way in which process skills are actually used, that is, in relation to the inquiry (problem-solving) process. For example, before students "do" anything with information they must identify the existence of a problem—they must have something to inquire about. Thus, the first subsection deals with how we can go about helping students identify problems. In the following subsections we examine techniques for helping students identify hypotheses and make inferences based on the information they have, how students can gather additional data and then do something with it, and finally, helping students generalize beyond their immediate experience.

IDENTIFYING PROBLEMS

There seems to come a stage in every child's life when the word they most frequently utter is *why*—almost to the point of exasperation. Sometimes *why* comes in the form of "How come?" but the basic thrust—the request for an explanation—is there nevertheless.

"Why do I have to go to bed?"

"How come we can't watch Rambo on cable?"

"Why does it rain?"

"Why" questions usually fall into one of two fairly obvious groups. Children are either asking for a reason or justification for something—"Why can't I go outside and play in the rain?"—or they want an explanation for something they don't

TABLE 10.1 Translating Process Tasks into Children's Language

Task	Adult's Language	Child's Language
Classifying	Classify these into two categories.	Do some of these go together?
	How many different ways could you classify these?	Are there different ways these can go together?
		In how many different ways you can group these?
Hypothesizing and inferring	Develop two hypotheses that might explain this.	How would you explain this?
		Are there some other reasons this might have happened?
	Given data, develop three hypotheses.	What is _____ really like?
Analyzing	Given two sources of data, identify possible contradictions.	Do you notice anything "wrong" or unusual (about these data)?
		Is there anything here that doesn't seem to "fit" right?
	Identify relevant or irrelevant information.	Is there some information here that we don't need?
		Which information is most helpful?
Inductive reasoning	Given two or more data sources, develop an inductive generalization.	Is there an idea that "fits" all of these examples?
Deductive reasoning	Given an idea, can you test its validity?	Given this idea, can you think of other examples it applies to, or examples where it does not apply?
Evaluating	Identify criteria to support your judgment.	Why do you think one is better than another?

understand. In either case, the "why" question indicates that they've identified a problem—their problem—and that a *teachable moment* may have arrived. In other words, by helping children deal with the problem that led to their "Why?" we may, in fact, be teaching them something. Unfortunately, after the tenth (or twentieth) explanation of why the child cannot go outside to play in the rain, one may begin to wonder if the question wasn't just another way of testing adult authority and really had nothing to do with explanations or teachable moments.

Among the thousands of legitimate "why" questions children ask, you will find many that are based on inconsistencies they've observed (without ever being taught how to identify an inconsistency). Consider, for example, how you will react when Laurie announces, "My daddy says that out there it's everyone for themselves, but in school you keep saying that we should cooperate. Who's right?" This is the kind of question some teachers would rather not be asked.

The problem teachers face is to identify ways to translate social studies content into real problems that grab students—and that is no mean trick.

Traditionally, social studies teachers have been so bound by the subject matter they were expected to teach that they had little recourse other than to pose problems to students. In other words, requests to "identify the capitals of the middle Atlantic states" or "trace the sequence of Roman emperors" were actually teachers' problems imposed on students. As such, they then became the students' problems. But even within a fixed curriculum, you can help to enhance student involvement (and a feeling that they are dealing with *their* problems) by the way you present problems to them. These techniques include (1) creating mystery-type situations, where students deal with an unknown element or elements, (2) providing incomplete (limited) information at the outset of an activity, from which students try to "fill in the holes," or (3) using a speculative-heuristic question, for example, "What if you were the fire chief," or "What if you were a member of the Indian Parliament and were facing a request to. . . ." These are still teacher-structured problems, to be sure, but they have a way of involving children to the extent that the problems may become "theirs."

The creation of mystery-type situations often involves intentionally limiting the information you make available to students as you begin an activity. As students work with that information, additional problems sometimes emerge. For example, in the following activity adapted from Mallan and Hersh (1972, pp. 234–35), a *fact sheet* is used to create a mystery-type situation. In this instance, a real country is identified only as "Nation X." Obviously you would not tell your students the real name of Nation X, since to do so would eliminate all traces of "mystery" from the problem. It would also eliminate the need to *use* the information about Nation X; your students could simply rely on what they already know.

This fact sheet is designed so that children must use the information to describe Nation X. However, in our right-answer-oriented society, your biggest problem will be to keep their attention focused on *describing* Nation X. From the outset, they will want to guess which real nation Nation X is. The object is not to establish a guessing game; to permit students to make guesses will limit the usefulness of this activity.

MODEL STUDENT ACTIVITY

Nation X—Using a Fact Sheet

OVERVIEW

Using only the data provided below, students are asked to infer what Nation X is like. As is true of most inferences, these will need to be tested further. Thus, students must then identify whatever additional information they would like, some of which you may have ready in advance. Just how this activity ends depends on how far you wish to take it.

Fact Sheet #1

	U.S.A.	Nation X
Doctors per 100,000 inhabitants	120	20
Dentists per 100,000 inhabitants	50	2
Percentage of population literate	99	18
Radios per 1,000 inhabitants	750	2
Percentage of people living in cities	66	18

Procedure

1. Working either individually or in small groups (you decide in advance), pose the following task: Using just this information, describe Nation X as best you can. What's it like, and what are the people who live there like?

2. List student inferences (in terms of key descriptors) on the board or have small groups list their inferences on chart paper.

3. Summarize inferences, pointing out those that may be contradictory. Note that it is possible to arrive at two wholly opposite inferences. The dentist data, for example, could suggest either that Nation X has poor dental health, or that Nation X has little need for dentists.

4. In summarizing, you may wish to raise questions such as How is literacy defined? How big must a city be to be defined as a city? Is it fair to say that Nation X is poor?

5. (Optional) On an overhead transparency, you may wish to present the class with the following information:

   Nation X has several thousand unemployed college graduates.

   Consider what this information may indicate about (a) the size of Nation X, (b) its educational system, and (c) its way of life.

6. After assessing whether their inferences follow from the data, you can ask students what other kinds of information they might want. (Be prepared for a long list.)

7. Present the following information (on an overhead transparency):

Fact Sheet #2

Nation	Population 1987	Approximate % of world population
China	1,038,000,000	21
Nation X	768,000,000	15
Soviet Union	278,000,000	7
United States	241,000,000	6
Japan	121,000,000	3

Given this data, some students will try to guess the identity of Nation X. Or, they can check population figures in the atlases found at the back of most social studies texts. In any event, maintaining the mystery much longer could prove frustrating, so you can tell the class that Nation X is India. (Knowing that, you can now assess your *own* inferences.)

8. At this point you have the option of pursuing the India study in several different ways. You might wish to do two things simultaneously: (1) have the children use their inferences as research questions to be answered, using whatever resources or references they can garner, and (2) pursue an inference children often make about Nation X, namely, that it is poor. If they don't infer this, you can always build a case for it. Among reasons that will be suggested for India's poverty will be its food problem and, related to that, its health and population problems.

9. You also have the option of confronting the class with a moral dilemma by telling them that they are the Parliament of India and that you are a representative of the World Health Organization. You have come to offer them the services of two thousand doctors who will work, free of charge, to help India alleviate its health problems. Divide the class into small groups and have them consider your offer. Someone is almost certain to discover that those Indians who are kept alive will put an even greater strain on the available food supply. Thus, by saving people, the Indians might be adding to their food-supply problem. The class as a group must then decide whether or not to accept the offer, or whether to attach any "strings" to it, such as an equal number of agricultural specialists.

Caution: The topic of birth control usually arises in discussions related to population. Be prepared to know how you wish to handle the issue—in advance of its coming up.

10. Even if you do not wish to follow the Indian Parliament segment of this activity, you could pursue the poverty issue even further by raising the question, "If most of the people in a country are poor, what does *being poor* mean? Is being poor an average condition? If so, would the average Indian define himself as poor?"

The following information could then be presented to the class (again, using an overhead transparency may be easiest):

Fact Sheet #3

In many places in India, but in rural villages especially, the poorest family is one in which there are no children.

What does this indicate about the Indian value structure? (What does this indicate to you about the lack of success of birth control campaigns in India?)

Source: John T. Mallan and Richard Hersh, NO G.O.D.s IN THE CLASSROOM: INQUIRY AND ELEMENTARY SOCIAL STUDIES, 1972.

A special note is warranted about the kinds of data suitable for fact sheets. Recall that a fact is a statement about a unique and nonrepetitive event or phenomenon. However, some facts are so unique that it's nearly impossible to say anything about them. This became apparent when some teachers modified the "Nation X" format to apply to states; in other words, they developed "State X" fact sheets. On them they included data such as the following: the state bird, the state tree, the state motto (in Latin), a picture of the state flag, and the date of the state's admission to the Union. For the most part, this kind of information—no matter how accurate—is so unique that there is little that can be said about it. To be told that State X's state bird is the cardinal, for example, or that the state tree is the buckeye, tells you little or nothing about the area in question. Rather, it heightens the "guessing game" effect.

Determining Researchable Problems

In the course of most social studies activities, students will generate questions that no amount of research will answer. In the previous activity, for example, an inference that India is poor because the people are bad or lazy is almost guaranteed to lead to frustration and discontent, should your students attempt to research it. It's just not a researchable question as long as *poor, bad,* and *lazy* are left undefined. Even then, establishing causal relationships among these will challenge the best of scholars.

The teaching implication in such cases should be evident: it is necessary to help children examine problems in terms of their researchability. To do otherwise could lead them on a wild-goose chase.

Some of the following statements and problems are based on the student activities we've considered thus far. Others are not. Which of the following statements have potential for further student research or study?

Yes/No   *Problems/Statements*

——— 1. Identify the constitutional requirements for the office of president of the United States.

——— 2. John F. Kennedy and Franklin D. Roosevelt were two of the best presidents the United States has ever had.

——— 3. The best route for a freeway is one that does not destroy a school.

——— 4. The Dutch are an industrious and friendly people.

——— 5. India is unable to employ all of it's college graduates in the kinds of positions for which they were trained.

——— 6. Communications media (radio, TV, newspapers, etc.) in India have not improved over the last ten years.

——— 7. The introduction of new technology into a culture is likely to lead to other changes.

FIGURE 10.2   Cartoon for Inferencing

_____ 8. American farmers today grow more food on larger, more specialized farms than did farmers ten or twenty years ago.

_____ 9. Yuppies are extremely patriotic.

_____ 10. The majority of students in *this* class strongly dislike Italian food.

Researchable problems (hypotheses, inferences, and questions) are like behavioral objectives: they do not use vague terms, yet are specific enough that one need not spend a lifetime in the quest. As such, Statements 1, 5, 6, 7, 8, and 10 are researchable, but Statements 2, 3, 4, and 9 would need greater clarification and specificity before students could deal with them. In the case of Statement 4, for example, it might be possible to define *industrious* and *friendly* but how do you define *the Dutch?* Are the Dutch only those people who live in the Netherlands? Or do they include people of Dutch descent?

HYPOTHESIZING AND INFERRING

Based on the "Help Wanted" cartoon shown in Figure 10.2, which of the following might you reasonably infer?

Yes/No

_____ 1. Business seems to be good.

_____ 2. The cartoon depicts a scene in the United States.

_____ 3. The employer has a bias against women.

_____ 4. Women are not good workers.

Unusual or unknown physical and natural objects, such as the ones students will encounter on a field trip to a museum, offer excellent opportunities for students to develop hypothesizing skills. (© *Elizabeth Crews*)

_____ 5. The sign reflects a basic societal belief that a woman's place is in the home.

_____ 6. The cartoon depicts a scene that might take place today.

That business seems to be good is a reasonable inference, otherwise there would be no "Help Wanted" sign. On the other hand, perhaps working conditions in the plant are so bad that some employees quit after only a few days. If that were the case, the management would continually need additional help just to maintain normal operations. Both are plausible inferences.

If you have no intention of testing which of these inferences is valid, your inference would remain just that—a possible, plausible inference. But when you set out to test whether or not business is good—at least as depicted in the cartoon—your inference then functions as a hypothesis. That is, your inference is a testable proposition: the reason the plant displays a Help Wanted sign is that business is good and the company therefore needs additional employees. To test this you obviously need more data about the events depicted in the cartoon.

You might infer that the cartoon does *not* depict a scene taking place today, because the law forbids discrimination based on gender. The probability of your inference being valid is so high that you might feel little need to pursue the issue further. Thus, your inference would remain just that—a highly probably inference.

All of us infer, almost all the time. We continually attempt to explain events, sometimes without realizing it. If we infer and hypothesize anyway, why should there be such concern for formal hypothesis testing? The answer lies in the fact that what we do in informal situations has application in many more formal situations and with many other kinds of data sources. And, although in informal situations we might be satisfied using impressionistic data—a hunch, a whim, or a feeling—formal hypothesis testing requires that all elements of the process be *public*. In other words, in informal, face-to-face relations, one is relatively free to use whatever information one wants; in more formal, rational, and public data-validating procedures, one must follow the rules. Hence, our distinction between an inference and a hypothesis.

Knowns and Unknowns

When something is known, there's not much left to hypothesize about. A statement such as "Milk comes from cows" isn't very likely to lead to much speculation. But if you ask, "Where does milk come from?" you can get some mighty interesting hypotheses:

From trucks

From dairies

From the supermarket

These are all testable statements in terms of their accuracy, but you must assess whether the children will gain enough from testing these hypotheses to make the effort involved worthwhile. We can test the accuracy of "knowns," but we must hypothesize about things that are unknown or that can be explained only in part.

Physical objects often offer an excellent opportunity for hypothesizing activities, especially when the object and its use are unknown to the children. A colonial bootjack—a forked board used to help remove one's boots—or even a butter churn can lead to creative hypothesizing activities. An antique shop can provide a wealth of objects for potential hypothesizing activities.

Coins, stamps, buttons—almost any physical object—can serve as a basis for hypothesizing and inferring activities. In the case of coins, for example, the student's task can be stated as follows: "Given a half dollar, a quarter, dime, nickel, and penny, what do you know about the people who made them?"

"Buildings seem to be important, as well as eagles."

"Except for one, all of the coins have a man on them."

"They have a letter and number system."

"They have a god in whom they trust."

"They have a language we don't understand, *E Pluribus Unum.*"

Hypothesizing and inferring activities demand something that is unknown to students—objects, events, or whatever. Otherwise there may be little or nothing for children to explain. Indeed, if explanations already exist, there is little one can do other than question their validity. To help children hypothesize and infer, the teacher can provide them with unexplained events—unknowns that, through inferring, hypothesizing, and hypothesis testing, can become "knowns."

MODEL STUDENT ACTIVITY

Teaching Kit: A House of Ancient Greece

An excellent example of a series of activities, most of which focus on hypothesizing and hypothesis testing, can be found in the MATCH unit "House of Ancient Greece." The unit contains a wealth of materials—an authentic Greek coin, filmstrips, pictures, several reference books, etc.—but most intriguing are some photographs and reproductions of artifacts found by a team of American archaeologists, led by Dr. David Robinson, as they excavated the site of the ancient Greek city of Olynthus. All of the kit's artifacts are reproductions of artifacts found in the various rooms of a home that Dr. Robinson named the Villa of Good Fortune. Whether the home's original owners called it that 2,300 years ago is unknown. (Dr. Robinson's name was derived from a translation of the mosaic found on the floor in one of the villa's rooms.)

As best they could, the archaeologists developed a floor plan for the villa. In adapting the floor plan for the MATCH kit, the rooms were labeled Alpha Room, Beta Room, etc., as illustrated below:

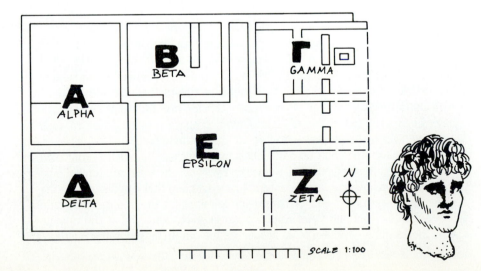

SCALE 1:100

In the MATCH kit, artifacts from each room are packaged separately. The class is divided into teams, one team for each room in the villa. The objective is for each team to identify (1) what the various artifacts are, (2) what they might have been used for, and (3) the nature of the room from which they came. Artifacts from the Beta Room are shown below:

After describing what they think they have found, the children have the opportunity to check their findings with Dr. Robinson's. His findings for the Beta Room are listed in the materials included with the unit. (We have printed Dr. Robinson's findings at the end of this chapter, on page 329.)

Source: Map adapted from MATCH unit, "House of Ancient Greece," Teacher's Guide, p. 23. Objects illustration from MATCH kit, "House of Ancient Greece." Used by permission of Delta Education.

COMMENTARY: When Museums Take the Labels Off

Remember when you went on a field trip to a historical museum and viewed collections of articles, each properly labeled with its name, purpose, and year of manufacture? Everything you wanted to know about the item (and sometimes more) was provided for you. Increasingly, however, museums are providing exhibits without such labels, exhibits that provide children with opportunities to infer what various articles are and what they might have been used for. Some museums even prepare a printed key to such exhibits, which the children can use to check themselves.

Even if museums don't take the labels off, you can—by building your own collection. Instead of building a display by yourself, your students could furnish unusual objects (even contemporary articles) that could serve as the basis for "What is it?" and "What do you know about the people who made it?" exhibits. Although your students are likely to know what the objects are, the exhibits could serve as resources for other classes in the building.

DATA GATHERING AND PROCESSING

Before anyone bothers to gather and process data, it's only common sense that they have previously identified a purpose for that information. Gathering information in the absence of a problem isn't very productive unless, of course, you have an obsession for trivia. Learning that English muffins were invented in America, for example, or that when the story of Hansel and Gretel is told in parts of Africa, the witch's house is made of salt, not cake, may be interesting enough, but is the information useful?

From your experience as a student, you undoubtedly remember teachers who, when they said that they wanted you to gather information, really meant that they wanted you to absorb information from some source, usually a textbook. Your problem—your *real* problem—probably had little to do with data gathering; it was more likely a case of remembering all of that information until the test. On other occasions, however, gathering data was something you did in response to a problem, *your* problem, not one imposed upon you by an upcoming test. Undoubtedly the most universal example of this is the way you learned about sex. Think back to your childhood experiences to see if at some point you didn't overhear some whispered discussions among some interested groups of adults or among some of your peers. This may have occurred after several early experiences where it was indicated that "Nice people don't talk about *that.*" In some cases, your curiosity may have been whetted because the discussions took place under clandestine circumstances that lent a sense of intrigue to the entire matter. In other cases, you may have found that your peers who had more information about the topic were accorded more prestige in the group. Thus, if you got the necessary information, you might share some of that prestige.

Whatever the incentive, your problem was to get more information. The important thing here is that it was *your* problem, although undoubtedly one you shared with many other children. In any event, you gathered a great deal of information—some of it misinformation—and probably from a remarkable variety of sources. For some, it was the first time they had ever used the dictionary voluntarily! By the time you were fourteen or so, you probably had a veritable wealth of data, though not necessarily the means to determine what was accurate and what wasn't. That would come as you applied your information in still other circumstances.

Because students and teachers may perceive data gathering quite differently, you need to ask yourself two key questions: What's my motive (as a teacher) for having students study this?" and "What are my students' motives for dealing with this information?" Motivation then, is a process of identifying the best possible match between your motives as a teacher and the motives of your students.

Successful data gathering depends upon three interacting elements: (1) a precisely stated problem, (2) an awareness of the specific information needed, and (3) the ability to deal with data presented in different forms (narratives, charts, graphs, etc.). Most important of these, we think, is stating the problem precisely. This was driven home to us on an occasion when we made our students "ambassadors" and had them do written reports on various countries around the world. At the time, we neglected to take into account the fact that a precisely stated problem provides criteria for determining what information should be included or excluded. Without those criteria, students put anything and everything even remotely related to the country into their reports. The student who "did" Scotland, for example, brought her report to class in a large carton. Reading those reports became a nightmare, and like it or not, grading was based on a subjective mixture of quality and weight. And even though our first students were proud of the tall stacks of data they had gathered, the next year we spent considerable time narrowing their topics down to a more manageable size.

Many teachers seem to equate data gathering with "library research," as we did above, thus neglecting data that can grow out of students' experiences. Even primary children, many of whom are unable to use library sources to begin with, can get involved in data-gathering procedures. Conducting surveys to determine favorite TV shows or the time at which most second graders go to bed are possible topics for data collection by surveying.

A primary teacher planned a lesson along similar lines. She felt that her pupils were addicted to television commercials and that they tended to accept advertising claims as fact. The teacher wanted children to understand that although there may be some truth in what commercials say and show, this does not mean that all claims are true. To accomplish this, the teacher developed the lesson illustrated in the activity below.

MODEL STUDENT ACTIVITY

The Detergent Survey

1. Gather information. The information will relate to different laundry detergent products that students see and hear about on TV commercials.
2. Students bring in samples of detergents used at home.
3. Students then determine a way to test the commercials' claims. Pieces from a cotton sheet are marked with different stains—crayon, dirt, paint, grease, chalk, etc.
4. Identify things (variables) to consider: (1) water temperature, (2) same kind of stained material, (3) amount of detergent used, and (4) length of washing time.
5. Read the directions on the detergent package to students.
6. Wash materials and record observations on the chart below: happy face, stain removed; sad face, stain not removed; question mark, stain partially removed.

7. Students add the number of happy faces in each column to determine which detergents removed all or some of the stains.

8. Discuss values such as the ethics involved when you give your word that something is true.

Stains	Detergents			
	1	2	3	4
crayon	☹	☹	☹	☹
dirt	☹	☹	☹	☹
paint	☹	☹	☹	☹
grease	☹	☹	☹	☹
chalk	☺	☺	☺	☺
magic marker	☹	☹	☹	?
pen	?	?	?	?
total				

Based on the disappointing results, the teacher initially judged the activity to be a failure. Although everything didn't work out as planned, the concept of "failure" holds only if the students and the teacher have not learned from the experience. A few changes, such as fewer detergents, fewer stains, better control over washing time, and a more precise way of measuring stain removal, might have ensured a more successful outcome. But whether or not the experiment succeeded is not entirely the point. In fact, despite the unsuccessful outcome, the students learned how *not* to conduct an experiment. The point here is that the activity provided students with an opportunity to use and apply skills—which was the focus of the activity. To sum it up, a skills-oriented activity can be judged a failure only if students do not learn something from it.

Organizing Data

Skill-oriented lessons focus on systematically planned activity sequences. At the minimum they involve (1) specific data to work with, (2) a problem, and (3) procedures or rules for processing the information. In the sample lesson shown in the Model Student Activity that follows, the general strategy follows the inquiry mode. The discussion phase permits students to share and reflect on how they went about completing the activity.

MODEL STUDENT ACTIVITY

Organizing Data

PROBLEM: DO DOCTORS (M.D.s) TEND TO LIVE IN A CERTAIN AREA OF THE CITY?

Format

Students are provided with data from a local telephone directory, including a map of the telephone exchange areas. During the discussion phase, the intent is to distinguish between effectiveness and efficiency in organizing information.

Objectives

The students will

1. construct a table on which the information is organized

2. explain how they organized the information to answer the problem

3. distinguish between information presented effectively and information presented efficiently

Skill Rules

Rules for organizing and processing data:

1. Eliminate unnecessary data.

    1.1 Determine criteria for determining necessary and unnecessary data.

2. Where possible, replace narrative information with numerical equivalents.

3. Identify why individual responses may have limitations.

Data (sample)

Holbrand, Peter A.	902-8865
Hulverin, Carl	902-1622
Issacs, A. S.	901-0075
Indehenturio, August	902-2212
Iverson, Charles, M.D.	903-3437

Jacobs, Henry	903-1128
Jacobsen, Arlene, M.D.	903-5358
Jacobsen, Arthur A.	901-9002
Jensen, Peter M., M.D.	903-7542
Johnson, Elizabeth	903-8144
Maroney, Paul S., M.D.	903-6161

Procedure

1. Ask students to organize and present the data above in the most effective and efficient table form.

2. Provide an opportunity for students to make their tables. Leave the specific format up to students.

3. After they have developed their tables, ask students to share them with the class.

Note: Anticipate that most of the tables will be accurate, and will communicate the information effectively. However, some tables will communicate the results more efficiently than others. If some of the following tables seem confusing, remember that (1) the problem was to determine if doctors tended to live in certain areas of the city and (2) students don't always put clear headings on their tables.

4. Ask students to explain, step by step, the thinking involved in deciding how to analyze and present the data.

5. Ask students to judge the different tables in terms of efficiency and effectiveness.

6. Review the skill rules to determine which were used in constructing the tables.

Note: All three tables communicate essentially accurate information, but one is more efficient (easier to read and comprehend) than the others.

Sample Students' Table 1

Doctors	Area
1	3
2	3
3	3
4	3

Sample Students' Table 2

Name	901	Area 902	903
Holbrand		x	
Hulverin		x	
Issacs	x		
Indhenturio		x	
Dr. Iverson			x
Jacobs			x
Dr. Jacobsen			x
Jacobsen	x		
Dr. Jensen			x
Johnson			x
Dr. Maroney			x

Sample Students' Table 3

Doctors	Phone Area
Iverson	903-3437
Jacobsen	903-5358
Jensen	903-8144
Maroney	903-6161

Data: Forms Suitable for Processing

Some kinds of information (or data) better lend themselves to information processing than other forms of data. For example, if your intent is to help children process information, your main focus should be on providing them with unprocessed information—raw data—that they can work with. Generally, that information should be presented in uninterpreted form to permit students to do the interpreting.

Children are limited in the amount of processing they can do when the data are presented in the form of conclusions. For a statement such as "Nation X is a poor, underdeveloped country," the conclusion has already been presented, and there is little left for children to do—other than to remember it. In the materials provided in this chapter, note that the information was preselected, but it was not preprocessed. No one told you what to conclude about Nation X, for example. You had to reason inductively, piecing together information, to arrive at your own interpretations. So it is with uninterpreted data.

Some contemporary social studies programs place considerable emphasis on helping students work with information from primary sources. Such programs lean heavily on uninterpreted information, some of which (as in the case of surveys) the children gather firsthand. Note that *primary* in this sense refers to firsthand accounts, not to a particular level of schooling. Likewise, *secondary accounts* refers to sources of already-interpreted information.

As a kind of self-check, determine which of the following sources are more likely to provide primary (firsthand) accounts (use a *P*) and those that are more likely to contain secondary (previously interpreted) accounts (use an *S*). Use a *?* if you are not sure.

_____ Aerial photographs   _____ Lectures

_____ Advertisements   _____ Letters (personal)

_____ Artifacts   _____ Magazine articles

_____ Atlases   _____ Maps

_____ Census reports   _____ Paintings

_____ Diaries   _____ Photographs

_____ Directories   _____ Reports

_____ Documents   _____ Survey reports

_____ Encyclopedias   _____ Textbooks

_____ Interviews

Of the items on this list, the secondary sources are fewer in number. They include encyclopedias, lectures, magazine articles (and *some* journal articles), reports, and textbooks. Some sources, such as advertisements, may be questionable, especially since the way data are used in advertisements is often questionable. Interviews might also be questionable to the extent that interviewees sometimes give the answer they think is anticipated by the interviewer. Maps can also fall into the questionable category, since someone had to transform (i.e., process) data into map form. Thus, maps could be considered secondary sources, while aerial photographs, from which some maps are made, would be considered primary sources. For all practical purposes, though, it is safe to regard most maps (and the balance of the items on this list) as primary sources. It is to them you could turn as some of your best resources for process-based activities.

GENERALIZING

One of the more challenging aspects of teaching is helping students to identify patterns or relationships among otherwise unconnected events or pieces of data. That challenge, expressed in a word, is *generalizing*.

We suspect that teachers have sometimes been unjustly faulted for not helping students to generalize from their own experiences. It's not that teachers haven't tried this, we think, but that they have tried and failed. If you look at what is involved in generalizing—making general statements based on patterns among specific events—it actually requires that children leave the comfort of concrete experience and move into the realm of abstraction. As Jean Fair (1977, p. 39) has noted, "Generalizations, like concepts, are abstractions." Dealing with abstractions is something that students are often reluctant, and in some cases unable, to do. Even some adults have difficulty standing back from specific situations so they can analyze what is actually taking place. In the Stone Axes study, for example, it is not immediately apparent that the introduction of steel axes into the culture constituted a change, and that because one thing changed, other changes were likely to occur. As adults we often get wrapped up in the specifics, the details or content of situations themselves, and then deal with the details separately. Note that we are not talking about the *need* to generalize here, for that clearly exists. Our focus is on the *willingness* to move into the realm of abstraction, which is something that even adults, who are better able to handle abstractions, are sometimes reluctant to do.

Generalizing reduces the disorder and confusion of otherwise isolated bits of experience. That reduction is achieved by organizing experiences into classes and categories by forming concepts. Generalizing, then, involves making statements about classes or categories of objects or events.

To build a class or category requires at least two events or situations. This means that a single event, such as the Stone Axes material in Chapter 8, is insufficient as a basis for generalizing. We need something else to compare and contrast with the Stone Axes study. To be able to say something about how technological innovations affect us, for example, we would need to compare the impact of introducing steel axes with the impact and changes resulting from the introduction of the telephone, the automobile, or any other innovation we select. If we pursue this by examining the impact of the telephone on American society, for example, we would need to identify some of the changes resulting from it. These could include new jobs, faster communication, fewer letters being written, and the like. At this point, by asking students to identify how the two events were similar—the introduction of steel axes and the telephone—we have a basis for generalizing in an "if-then" concept-statement format: "A change in one thing is likely to lead to other changes."

A teaching strategy for generalizing is summarized in Table 10.3.

Notice that while comparing two events or phenomena in terms of their similarities can yield warranted generalizations, comparing them in terms of differences—things that are not similar—can yield testable propositions. For instance, introducing the steel axes into the Yir Yoront society ultimately led to an increase in crime. We have no evidence, however, that the introduction of the telephone has led to a higher crime rate in our society. An appropriate question then is "Do most technological innovations lead to a higher crime rate?" Questions such as these can serve as the focus for further investigations.

Data Banks

Organizing and keeping track of skills-based teaching materials can easily become a problem for teachers, which may help to explain why some turn to those old standbys, workbooks. If nothing else, having everything bound into one volume eliminates the need to manage a file full of worksheets. The management problem

TABLE 10.3 Questioning Sequence for Generalizing

Phase	Questioning Sequence	Purpose
One	What do you notice? See? Find? or What do these events, incidents, etc., have in common? How are they different?	To elicit elements or patterns that will provide a basis for making general statements. Note that the items mentioned should be made accessible to participants by listing them on the chalkboard or through other appropriate means.
Two	Why do you think this happened? or How do you account for these differences?	To elicit explanations or inferences and to clarify these as needed.
Three	What do these tell you about . . .?	To elicit general statements (generalizations). Seek additional clarification as needed.

Note: This pattern may be repeated and expanded upon to include more aspects of the data and to reach more abstract generalizations.

Source: Adapted from *Development of a Comprehensive Curriculum Model for Social Studies for Grades One Through Eight, Inclusive of Procedures for Implementation and Dissemination* by Norman E. Wallen, Mary C. Durkin, Jack R. Fraenkel, Anthony H. McNaughton, Enoch I. Sawin. Final Report, Project No. 5–1314, U.S. Office of Education (Washington, D.C., Oct. 1969), p. 17.

FIGURE 10.3   Sample Data-Bank Card (5 × 8 Format)

Skill: Generalizing from data

<table>
<tr><td align="center"><u>Data</u></td><td align="center"><u>Possible Uses</u></td></tr>
<tr><td>Boston is on the Charles River.</td><td>1. Check accuracy of each statement.</td></tr>
<tr><td>Moscow is on the Volga River.</td><td>2. Identify two variables at work in each statement.</td></tr>
<tr><td>London is on the Thames River.</td><td rowspan="2">3. Make a general statement, about both variables, that would include all statements given.</td></tr>
<tr><td>Cincinnati is on the Ohio River.</td></tr>
<tr><td>Paris is on the Seine River.</td><td>4. Identify/locate three other cities that would fit under the broad general statement.</td></tr>
<tr><td></td><td>5. Identify one "major" city that appears to be an exception.</td></tr>
<tr><td></td><td>6. Formulate three possible explanations for the exception in number 5.</td></tr>
</table>

---

need not become overwhelming, however, if you are willing to develop a data bank.

Data banks can take a variety of forms. Some teachers prefer to use 8½ by 11 inch sheets while others, ourselves included, prefer 5 by 8 inch index cards, like the one illustrated in Figure 10.3. The data bank should include two elements: (1) sets of data for students to work with, which may include extrapolated raw data, charts, graphs, tables, figures, maps, and, if necessary, hypothetical data; and (2) notations regarding different ways in which students can use the data.

When potential teaching materials are organized in data-bank form, the following things should become apparent.

Teachers need not use all of the data on a card, especially if students might find it overwhelming. Rather, they can select the kind and amount of data to be included in a student activity.

When teachers provide the data for students to work with, the nature of student activities tends to change. Less student time is spent on data gathering and significantly more time is devoted to developing other process skills.

The availability of skill data banks can help the teacher accommodate a wide range of pupil skill levels, be they remedial, practice, or enrichment.

Data banks are, in fact, content banks, but are organized in such a way that content or information acquisition is not separated from skill development.

Posing situational dilemmas to students and encouraging them to make choices
and solve problems is a means of helping students develop decision-making skills.
(© *David S. Strickler/The Picture Cube*)

DECISION MAKING

Much of the attention focused on information-processing skills is based on the
premise that, once they leave school, children will be confronted with a myriad of
problems and dilemmas that will demand decisions *and* some kind of action.
Decision making calls for skill usage. By focusing social studies teaching on
information-processing skills, children can gain experience with the various data-
handling processes associated with rational decision making, and thus will have a
model to use when they leave school.

   Decision making is the process of making reasoned choices from among alternatives, choices that are consistent with the decision maker's values (Cassidy and
Kurfman, 1977, p. 1). In social studies, however, decision making is referred to in
two senses, one of them broad and the other narrow. In the broad sense,
Theodore Kaltsounis (1979), Cassidy and Kurfman (1977), and many others use
decision making to describe a total approach to social studies, one that incorporates all the skills we have dealt with (or will deal with) in this book. In its

narrower sense, decision making is used to describe instructional activities that ask children to apply decision-making skills. Our concern in this section is with decision making in the narrower, "activities" sense of the term.

A classic decision-making activity is based on a situation in which a rocket ship has crashed on the moon. Students, who take the part of surviving crew members, must rank the articles that were not damaged in the crash in terms of their usefulness. Note that in this and many other decision-making activities, participants must first make decisions on an individual basis, then reach consensus in a small-group setting.

MODEL STUDENT ACTIVITY

Lost on the Moon

Provide the following information to students:

You are a crew member of a spaceship that has just crashed on the moon. You were originally scheduled to rendezvous with a mother ship located on the lighted surface of the moon, two hundred miles away. However, the crash has ruined your ship and destroyed almost all of the equipment on board. Only the fifteen items listed below survived the landing undamaged.

The survival of your crew depends on reaching the mother ship. However, since you can't take everything, you must choose the most important articles to bring along on the two-hundred-mile trip. Your task is to rank the fifteen items in terms of their importance for your survival. Place number 1 by the most important item, number 2 by the second most important, and so on through number 15, the least important.

Your Rank		Group's Rank
_____	Box of matches	_____
_____	Food concentrate	_____
_____	Fifty feet of nylon rope	_____
_____	Parachute silk	_____
_____	Solar-powered portable table heating unit	_____
_____	Two .45-caliber pistols	_____
_____	One case of dehydrated Pet milk	_____
_____	Two 100-lb. tanks of oxygen	_____
_____	Stellar map (of the moon's constellations)	_____
_____	Self-inflating life raft	_____

_____   Magnetic compass   _____

_____   Five gallons of water   _____

_____   Signal flares   _____

_____   First aid kit containing injection needles   _____

_____   A solar-powered FM receiver-transmitter   _____

PROCEDURE

Each student should first complete this activity individually. Then, in groups of four to seven, students should share their individual solutions. They will need to agree on one ranking that best satisfies all group members. Of course, everyone in the group may not be completely satisfied, but group members should try to come as close as they can to a consensus in reaching their decisions. As much as possible, they should avoid using mathematical averaging, majority votes, or flipping a coin.

The answers and reasons are shown in Appendix B.

Source: Special permission for reproduction of the above material is granted by the author, Jay Hall, Ph.D., and publisher, Teleometrics International. All rights reserved.

———————————

"Lost on the Moon" is based on a forced-choice format similar to that of "Who Is Best Qualified for the Presidency?" Notice that, had the activity been left open-ended, students would have been free to identify any items they wished (from whatever they think might have been aboard a spacecraft), and the nature of the activity would have changed markedly. Instead of choosing and ranking specified items, the activity's emphasis would be on creating and identifying items from a universe of possibilities. In the forced-choice format, however, individuals are afforded a common basis for comparing their decision-making efforts. Note also that there is nothing magic about the number of items students rank—it could be more than fifteen, or less.

"Lost on the Moon" is an atypical decision-making activity in that it includes previously established "best" answers. Without them, it wouldn't be possible to develop numerical scores, nor would there be a basis for determining statistically that when dealing with an unknown, a group's decision will usually be superior to the decisions of individuals acting alone. Among teacher-made decision-making activities, there are typically no previously established "best" answers. Instead, the answers (actually, the best decisions) are determined by the individual or group.

A model for forced-choice decision-making activities is based on two components: (1) a problem statement based on a speculative-heuristic question ("What if you were . . .?") and (2) a limited number of choices.

The following student activity is based on the forced-choice model. In it, children are asked to decide which items they would take with them on a voyage to the New World. Except for the fact that this activity has no previously established answers, it closely follows the "Lost on the Moon" format.

MODEL STUDENT ACTIVITY

Voyage to the New World

Provide the following information to students:

You are about to leave your home in England on a one-way voyage to the North American colonies. You have decided to give up your old friends for a new life in the Plymouth Colony in New England. The colony has been settled for only five years, but your family really wants to go despite the hardships they may meet.

You will be traveling aboard the good ship *Daffodil*. However, because quite a few other people will be making the trip, storage space has become a problem and each family is permitted to take only eight items.

Below is a list of things you might find useful in the New World. Number in order of importance the eight items you want to take with you.

Ranking		Items	Ranking		Items
Your's	Group's		Your's	Group's	
_____	_____	Folding cot	_____	_____	Suit of warm clothes
_____	_____	Hunting knife	_____	_____	Fishing pole
_____	_____	Party dress	_____	_____	Candles
_____	_____	Camera	_____	_____	Flint and tinder
_____	_____	Bible	_____	_____	Surf board
_____	_____	Vegetable and grain seeds	_____	_____	Ax
_____	_____	Musket and powder	_____	_____	School books
_____	_____	Table and chairs	_____	_____	Iron pot
_____	_____	Shovel	_____	_____	Dog
_____	_____	Barrel of flour	_____	_____	Sewing kit
_____	_____	Flower seeds	_____	_____	Dishes (fine china)
_____	_____	Wool blanket	_____	_____	Medicine kit

Procedure
Working individually, students should rank the eight items they would take with them. They should then do the same thing in groups of four to six students each.

Have each group list their choices, in order, on the chalkboard (or on chart paper). Then, have the groups classify and label the items to determine what *type* of item appears most often (tools, essentials, luxury items, etc.).

Decision-making activities like "Voyage" work well as introductions to areas with which children are unfamiliar, particularly since they raise questions as to what an area is (or was) like. The nature of the problems you pose can be shifted to almost any area or historical period. For example, "If you were Marco Polo . . ." or "If you were part of a family going from Connecticut to California in 1849 . . . what would you bring with you?"

Should you use "Voyage to the New World" with your students, be advised that they will almost always take the dog (as one of the items), even if it means leaving something like the ax behind. This illustrates an important facet of decision-making activities. In defining decision making, we noted that decisions should be consistent with the decision maker's values. Recall also that as the American pioneers moved westward, they sometimes discarded useful items—shovels, plows, etc.—but saved items that were less essential, like a grandfather clock or a piano. Our point here is to indicate that the *values* component of decision making is vitally important and should not be treated lightly. As Cassidy and Kurfman (1977, p. 5) noted, decision making "always entails a value judgment, whereas scientific inquiry reaches conclusions using criteria of validity and reliability. Science [though value-based] is concerned with establishing truth, not deciding the best thing to do." As a consequence, in dealing with decision-making activities, we suggest that you (1) avoid arguing that "the dog" is necessarily a poorer choice than "the ax," for example, and (2) avoid conveying the impression that the most frequently chosen items are better than the less frequently chosen items. In other words, decision-making activities may involve elements of values clarification and should be treated accordingly.

DEVELOPING AND USING DECISION-MAKING ACTIVITIES

One key to developing decision-making activities lies in limiting the problem to something that is both real and manageable for students—otherwise they'll have no basis for considering the alternatives. For most elementary students a question such as "Which had a better organizational basis—the League of Nations or the United Nations?" really isn't a manageable problem for a decision-making format: it would be better suited as a high school or college debate question. As a general rule, decision-making activities for elementary students should afford more immediate access to the information on which their decisions will be based.

Decision-making activities can serve as a focus for information-processing skills. However, unless teachers continually stress rational information processing such activities can degenerate into arguments of "My opinion is as good as yours." In decision-making activities, attention must be focused on the *processes* children use in arriving at their decisions and not just on the decisions they reach.

Decision-making activities require that students *use* information, as do other process-oriented activities—fact sheets, surveys, problem situations, etc. Unfortunately, teachers whose only exposure has been to traditional social studies programs have been known to relegate process-oriented decision-making activities to a secondary and often trivial role—as something to do on a Friday afternoon or during a rainy recess. In addition, instead of serving as the heart of a social studies program, information-processing and decision-making activities are sometimes treated as gimmicks—neat, prepackaged activities that will keep students busy. Unless the focus is kept on *using* information and on the rational processes that go into decision making, such activities can indeed become very gimmicky. In the final analysis, only you can assess the balance you want to maintain in your classroom between process-oriented social studies and a more traditional knowledge orientation.

SUMMARY

In this chapter we have presented some activities that can help you manage process-oriented skill instruction. For the sake of organization, we identified skills that were part of the inquiry (problem-solving) process. We also suggested that process skills are part of a "whole" and that they cannot be held in isolation for very long. Hypothesizing, for example, is a process skill, but it can't end there; once students hypothesize, they must do something with those hypotheses. Otherwise they will be left hanging.

One key to developing many information-processing and decision-making activities, we suggested, is in limiting the information available to students at the outset. Paralleling that was the suggestion that students are not likely to do much processing with information that has been preprocessed. Thus a second key factor involves selecting unprocessed (raw) information with which students can work. Finally, we suggested that process-oriented and decision-making activities can be misused or become "gimmicky" if a focus on rational information processing is not maintained.

REFERENCES

Beyer, Barry K., ed. 1985. "Critical Thinking Revisited." *Social Education*, 49 (April), 268–310.

Cassidy, Edward W., and Dana G. Kurfman. 1977. "Decision Making as Purpose and

Process." In *Developing Decision-Making Skills,* ed. Dana Kurfman. pp. 1–27. Washington, D.C.: National Council for the Social Studies.

deBono, Edward. 1983. "The Direct Teaching of Thinking as a Skill." *Phi Delta Kappan,* 64 (June), 706–09.

Fair, Jean. 1977. "Skills in Thinking." In *Developing Decision-Making Skills,* ed. Dana Kurfman. pp. 29–70. Washington, D.C.: National Council for the Social Studies.

Fraenkel, Jack R. 1973. *Helping Students to Think and Value: Strategies for Teaching Social Studies.* Englewood Cliffs, N.J.: Prentice-Hall.

Kaltsounis, Theodore. 1979. *Teaching Social Studies in the Elementary School: The Basics for Citizenship.* Englewood Cliffs, N.J.: Prentice-Hall.

Mallan, John T. 1986. *Thinking About Thinking: Teaching Cognitive Skills in the Classroom.* Syracuse, N.Y.: Syracuse University.

———, and Richard Hersh. 1972. *No G.O.D.s in the Classroom: Inquiry and Elementary Social Studies.* Philadelphia: W. B. Saunders.

Muller, Herbert J. 1952. *The Uses of the Past.* New York: Mentor Books.

Sternberg, Robert J. 1985. "Teaching Critical Thinking, Parts 1 and 2." *Phi Delta Kappan,* 67 (November and December), 277–80.

Taba, Hilda. 1967. *Teacher's Handbook for Elementary Social Studies,* Introductory ed. Palo Alto, Calif.: Addison-Wesley.

Welles, Chris. 1983. "Teaching the Brain New Tricks." *Esquire,* 99 (March), 49–54.

SUGGESTED READING

Barry K. Beyer, ed. 1985. "Critical Thinking Revisited," *Social Education,* 49 (April), 268–310. This special theme section provides an excellent review of recent advances in teaching critical thinking skills. Two articles in this section, "Critical Thinking in Elementary School Social Studies" by Mary McFarland, and "Helping Students Ask Their Own Questions" by Francis P. Hunkins, are especially useful.

ANSWERS TO BETA ROOM ACTIVITY

The objects pictured on page 312, from left to right, are as follows:

Owl cup. Typical of many found in Greece, these cups were made of reddish clay and baked. Then black paint was applied to create the design.

Spoon. In ancient Greece, most people ate with their fingers, so a spoon like this was probably used in the kitchen to dish up soups and gravies.

Mortar and pestle. These objects were used to grind nuts, small grains, spices, etc. A household was likely to have a variety of different-sized mortars and pestles.

The room is obviously the kitchen. In a villa of this size much of the cooking was probably done by slaves.

CHAPTER 11

Skills-based Instruction: Maps, Globes, Graphs, and Other Media Forms

I hear and I forget;
I see and I remember;
I do and I understand. Chinese Proverb

KEY QUESTIONS

☐ How can students use maps, charts, and other kinds of social studies information?

☐ How can mathematics be used in social studies?

KEY CONCEPTS

☐ Maps, globes, graphs, and charts are specialized forms in which information is presented.

☐ When students have difficulty gaining access to some specialized forms of information, part of the problem may be their lack of understanding as to how the information got into that form in the first place.

☐ Although most of social studies is synthetic in nature, map and globe skills are clearly analytic. There is an identifiable sequence of skills and knowledge necessary to interpret information in these forms.

☐ The specialized knowledge and skills needed to deal with maps and globes—specifically, latitude, longitude, and scale—are founded in mathematics, not in social studies, and should be treated accordingly.

The skill of reading and using maps, which are challenging abstract devices, includes numerous subskills such as interpreting symbols, knowing cardinal directions, and working with concepts of distance and scale. (© *Michael Goss Photography*)

INTRODUCTION: The Specialized Access Skills

Maps and globes, and to a lesser extent, charts, graphs, and tables, have always been an integral part of social studies education. However, it's important to recognize that there is nothing inherently "social" about a map, graph, chart, table, or globe—despite the role they play in social studies. Collectively, they are specialized ways for presenting information, nothing more.

The nature of maps, globes, graphs, charts, and tables becomes more apparent if you consider that the information they deal with could be presented in other forms. An aerial photograph, for example, can convey at least as much (probably more) information than many landform maps. Likewise, the information on a chart or table could also be presented in a written description. However, written descriptions of the information presented in income tax tables, for example, would undoubtedly be so complex that they might be incomprehensible.

Gaining access to the information presented on maps, charts, or in graphic form requires specialized skills and knowledge. Map, chart, and graph reading all demand decoding skills not unlike those required to read information presented in narrative form (as you are doing now). True, the symbols are different—dots on a map, for example, may stand for something different than squares—but the process of bringing meaning to these symbols is clearly a form of decoding.

Reading plays such an important role in gaining access to the information on maps, graphs, charts, and tables that our approach in this chapter is borrowed from the language-experience approach to teaching reading. This approach is based on the premise that if children see their speech being translated (encoded) into written symbols (words), they will be better able to read (or decode) those symbols. This means that teachers who use the language-experience approach spend considerable time encoding (writing down) stories that children dictate to them, which the children then decode (or read) at a later time.

Our approach in this chapter is also based on the premise that one reason children may have difficulty with map reading, for example, is that they don't understand how the information got *into* that form. Likewise, if children have difficulty decoding charts and tables, the problem may lie in their inability to understand how information was encoded into the chart or table form. This should explain our emphasis on encoding—on map making, table making, chart making, etc.—as a necessary balance for decoding experiences—map reading, table reading, chart reading, etc.—that have traditionally played a starring role in social studies programs.

In the first section of this chapter, we examine map- and globe-related skills and identify several exemplary activities you might use to teach such skills. Tables, graphs, charts, and other quantitative date forms are considered in the following sections.

MAPS AND GLOBES

Maps are among the most abstract devices used in teaching social studies. Most maps leave out more information than they include and then use symbols to describe the information that is included. The abstract nature of maps is well illustrated in Figure 11.1. What may look to us like a random collection of sticks and shells makes perfect sense to a mariner from the Marshall Islands. The sticks represent consistent wave patterns, while the shells mark reefs and islands. With maps like this one the Marshall Islanders navigated their way across empty stretches of the Pacific.

For children who are in Piaget's concrete-operations stage of development, the notion that a map "stands for" something can be especially difficult to grasp. Indeed, as Figure 11.1 illustrates, most maps are models—theoretical models, if you will—of things that most of us have never seen, and, in many cases, never will.

FIGURE 11.1   A Mariner's Map

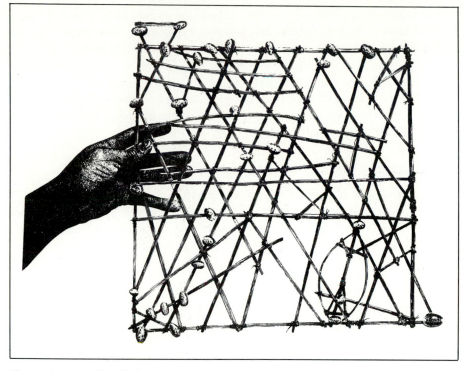

(Source: Artwork by Paul M. Breeden, © National Geographic Society.)

What adds to the abstract nature of most maps is the rapidity with which they lose one-to-one correspondence. On most maps, trees and buildings are the first things to disappear. Cities become dots or squares that look nothing like the areas represented, and, on some maps, some dots (for small cities) may not even appear. Thus, what children know to exist in reality may not appear on many maps.

Maps also demand that we look at things from a different and unusual perspective. Except for astronauts, few of us have had the luxury of viewing the world while suspended in space. (Landstat maps made from satellite photographs have helped considerably in this respect—see page 340.) Maps demand that we assume the perspective of "looking down on" or what, in children's terms, can be described as a bird's-eye view.

To help children gain experience with the perspective from which maps are made, we suggest that you provide several "bird's-eye view" activities. Here are some suggestions.

1. Draw a picture of your shoe. (If the heel is visible, it's not a bird's-eye view.)

2. Hold a "bird's-eye view contest." Have students draw and identify pictures of various objects as they would be seen from a bird's-eye view. Some examples are pictured in Figure 11.2.

3. Place a ladder somewhere in the classroom and then place various objects underneath it (model cars, etc.). Have children draw only what they see from the ladder. *Note:* This may be very difficult for young children who, because they know that a model car has wheels, for example, may draw them in regardless of whether they can be seen from a bird's-eye view.

4. Have students work with a computer program, such as "Bird's Eye View" (Hartley). As illustrated in Figure 11.3, children first move an animated bird around the computer screen to view various objects from the bird's point of view, and then determine their relative position in space, e.g., near, far, beneath, between, etc.

MAP MAKING

Map making refers to activities in which children transform or encode a scene into map form. In other words, the students actually produce a map. That automatically excludes a variety of map-copying activities (which are sometimes called "map making") in which children color in and correctly label a blank outline map.

FIGURE 11.2 Common Objects Seen from a Bird's-eye View

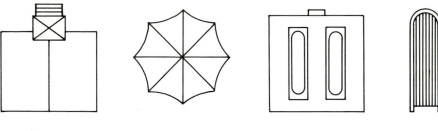

CHURCH   UMBRELLA   TOASTER   BOOK

FIGURE 11.3 Sample Screens: "Bird's-eye View" Computer Program

(Source: Courtesy of Hartley Courseware, Inc., 1987.)

Copying an existing map may be useful in helping to fix areas in a child's mind, but it teaches little or nothing about what a map is or about the purposes that maps serve. In many instances, map-copying lessons focus on the artistic dimensions of mapping, especially if children use colored glitter, spangles, or other unusual materials to depict different areas. Indeed, such maps should probably be judged on an aesthetic basis—as works of art, rather than as a way to depict certain types of information.

Map making in the encoding sense requires an area to be mapped. Beginning with bird's-eye views of various objects, students may move to increasingly larger areas—their classroom, the school building, the neighborhood around the school, or other areas of the community. Aerial photographs, which are available from the United States Department of Agriculture (try the Soil Conservation Service Office first) or NASA, can prove invaluable, especially because most maps are made from aerial photographs anyhow.

The objective of initial map-making activities is to help children visualize the local environment from a bird's-eye (or spatial) perspective and to help them understand that when anything is reduced in size—as maps are in relation to the areas they depict—some things must be omitted. Children should consider on what basis some things are kept in and others left out.

Relief Maps

If your school is located on the plains of West Texas, making a relief map of the area is probably pointless; the terrain is as flat as a tabletop. In most other areas of the country, however, relief maps can show hills and valleys, thus illustrating yet another type of map making. But beware! Making accurate relief maps can be a time-consuming, painstaking, and often messy process.

MODEL STUDENT ACTIVITY

Relief Maps

To build relief maps of small areas, such as the immediate neighborhood around a school, you might have students actually measure changes in elevation. But because doing that is more difficult than you might imagine, we recommend that you use topographical maps from the U.S. Geological Survey. They show changes in elevation while maintaining one-to-one correspondence by showing buildings and other features not found on many maps.

If it is necessary to enlarge a small map (or a portion of a map) in order to provide an area large enough for children to work on, you can do so by placing the original in an opaque projector and then tracing the enlarged image on posterboard. This procedure is suitable for enlarging almost any kind of map, and also preserves the colors. If your original map is small and you are also willing to sacrifice color, you can make an overhead transparency of the map and then enlarge it using an overhead projector.

Relief maps can be constructed from a variety of materials, the least messy but most costly of which is clay—pound after pound of clay. Recipes for other relief-map making materials are as follows:

1. *Papier-mâché*   Tear newspapers into strips and soak in water overnight. Mix wheat paste (wallpaper paste) with warm water to the consistency of thin cream. Squeeze water out of the newspaper strips, dip into the paste, remove the excess, and then apply to the map form.

2. *Salt and flour*   Mix four cups flour, two cups salt, and approximately two cups of water. Knead thoroughly. Food coloring may be added to the water, or tempera paint can be kneaded into the mixture. The mixture may require two to three days to dry completely.

3. *Sawdust and glue*   Mix slightly thinned white glue with dampened, fine sawdust until it reaches a workable consistency.

Relief maps, except those of undried clay, can be coated with a thin mixture of plaster of Paris and water. If allowed to dry overnight, this coating will keep paint from soaking in as much as it otherwise would.

Scale

In map making, it usually isn't very long before a question arises as to whether or not maps should be drawn to scale. For primary-grade children, the answer is generally no; not-to-scale drawings will usually suffice. For the intermediate grades, it depends. That isn't much of an answer until you find that what it depends on is the math program your students are using.

The notion of scale, like latitude and longitude, is mathematically based. And scale, perhaps better than anything else, reflects the zenith of representational thought. In this case, one thing is said to equal something else. For elementary students, the notion that "one inch can equal one foot (or one mile or ten miles)" can present some of the same difficulties that many algebra students encounter when they find that "x can equal anything."

Even some adults have difficulty with the way scale can be presented, especially if it is identified by a representative ratio such as 1:10,000. This means that 1 unit of *anything* on the map equals 10,000 of the same units on the ground. To the extent that 10,000 inches may not mean much even to you, we suggest that only those with masochistic tendencies should try to teach this form of scale to most elementary children.

The notion of scale is so integral a part of maps and map making that it cannot be dealt with casually. By the end of the intermediate grades, for example, Hanna et al. (1966, p. 25) have suggested that children have had experience with some of the following ideas related to scale:

Scale is the relation of distance on the map to the distance it represents on the ground.

The scale of a map is large or small in relation to the object it represents.

The use of a large scale for a map enables the mapper to show many details about a small area.

The use of a small scale for a map enables the mapper to show a large area but fewer details.

Scale on the globe may be used to measure the distance between two points on the earth's surface.

The scale on one part of a map may be different from the scale on another part (an inset map, for instance).

You may have to be satisfied that most of your students can, for example, use the scale on a map to calculate the distance between two points. A more complete understanding of scale may come only after they've had more experience with higher mathematics. However, many modern math programs introduce representational thought, and even the notion of scale, much earlier than they used to. As a result, we recommend that you correlate your map-making activities with your math program, which may even introduce "scale" in the primary grades.

Translation Mapping

Translation is a major subdivision of the comprehension category of the *Taxonomy of Educational Objectives,* and is defined as changing data from one form to another. This is, in fact, what map making is all about—depicting real areas or phenomena in more abstract map forms. Using this definition as a basis, it's possible to create activities based on translating, some of which, though not especially thrilling, will be educational. For example, you could have students engage in the activities described below.

MODEL STUDENT ACTIVITIES

Translation Mapping

1. Produce a written description of information contained on a chart or table (educational, but not too thrilling).

2. Produce a map of a nation, such as Japan, from a written or verbal description. (This activity is a lot more interesting than it may seem and produces some very interesting maps—inaccurate but interesting.)

3. Produce and translate a map. (In this activity, one group of students produces a map and another group uses it to locate an object—interesting, though the instructions are more complex than the activity.)

The class is divided into teams of two. Each team then locates an object somewhere around the school grounds (lavatories are off limits), returns to the classroom, and provides a verbal description to another team, which then produces a map from that description. Finally, the maps are given to yet another team, which must retrieve the object. As a follow-up, share the various problems the teams encountered in either making or using the maps.

WHEN SHOULD MAP AND GLOBE SKILLS BE TAUGHT?

There is no single established sequence for map and globe skills for the elementary grades. Sometimes first graders will be expected to know and locate the major continents and oceans, for example, while in other instances, this is not dealt with until Grade 3 or later. In other words, there is often considerable variation from one social studies program to the next.

From time to time, various individuals and groups have identified desirable scope and sequence for teaching map and globe skills. The sample scope and sequence presented in Table 11.1, which was developed by the Joint Committee on Geographic Education of the National Council for Geographic Education and the Association of American Geographers (1984), is an example of one such effort.

TABLE 11.1 Suggested Scope and Sequence for Map and Globe Skills

Grade Level	Recommended Learning Outcomes
Kindergarten	1. Knows and uses terms related to location, direction, and distance (up/down, left/right, here/there, near/far).
	2. Recognizes a globe as a model of the earth.
	3. Recognizes and uses terms that express relative size and shape (big/little, large/small, round/square).
	4. Identifies school and local community by name.
	5. Recognizes and uses models and symbols to represent real things.
Grade 1	1. Knows geographic location of home in relation to school and neighborhood.
	2. Knows the layout of the school campus.
	3. Uses simple classroom maps to locate objects.
	4. Identifies state and nation by name.
	5. Follows and gives verbal directions (here/there, left/right).
	6. Distinguishes between land and water symbols on globes and maps.
	7. Relates locations on maps/globes to locations on earth.
	8. Observes, describes, and builds simple models and maps of the local environment.

Grade Level	Recommended Learning Outcomes
Grade 2	1. Makes and uses simple maps of school and home neighborhoods.
	2. Interprets map symbols using a legend.
	3. Knows and uses cardinal directions.
	4. Locates one's community, state, and nation on maps and globes.
	5. Identifies local landforms.
	6. Differentiates between maps and globes.
	7. Locates other neighborhoods studied on maps.
	8. Traces routes within and between neighborhoods using a variety of maps and models.
	9. Compares pictures and maps of the same area.
Grade 3	1. Uses distance, direction, scale, and other map symbols.
	2. Compares own community with other communities.
	3. Compares urban and rural environments.
Grade 4	1. Interprets pictures, graphs, charts, and tables.
	2. Works with distance, direction, scale, and map symbols.
	3. Relates similarities and differences between maps and globes.
	4. Uses maps of different scales and themes.
	5. Recognizes the common characteristics of map grid systems (map projections).
	6. Compares and contrasts regions on a state, national, or world basis.
Grade 5	1. Recognizes distance, direction, scale, map symbols, and the relationship of maps and globes.
	2. Works with longitude and latitude.
	3. Uses maps, charts, graphs, and tables to display data.
	4. Discusses location in terms of where and why.
	5. Maps the correspondence between resources and industry.
	6. Maps physical and cultural regions in North America.
Grade 6	1. Improves understanding of location, relative location, and the importance of location.
	2. Uses maps, globes, charts, and graphs.
	3. Readily uses latitude, longitude, map symbols, time zones, and basic earth-sun relationships.
	4. Gains insight about the interaction of climate, landforms, natural vegetation, and other interactions in physical regions.
	5. Maps trade routes, particularly those connecting developed and developing nations.
	6. Plots distributions of population and key resources on regional maps.

Source: Abridged and adapted from Joint Committee (1984).

USING MAPS AND GLOBES

With satellite photography, it is now possible to illustrate the earth in a manner previously possible only with a globe. Today, Landstat satellites circle the earth sending back color photographs of remarkable clarity. The Landstat map shown in Figure 11.4 is of New York City, Long Island, and the New Jersey coast. Although our sample is reproduced in black and white, it should give you some idea of the potential this innovation has for map-related instruction.

FIGURE 11.4   Landstat Map of New York City, Long Island, and New Jersey Coast

(Source: Courtesy of Community and Education Services Branch, Public Affairs Division, National Aeronautics and Space Administration.)

Landstat maps notwithstanding, the globe is still one of the most accurate tools for helping children orient themselves to the planet on which we live. It can help them distinguish between land and water areas, and, when its use is begun in the primary grades, it can help to correct the commonly held notion that "up" on a map is north and "down" is south. Children may still use those expressions, but at least they will know that up is away from the center of the earth and down is the reverse. With a globe, they can also learn that north is toward the North Pole and south is toward the South Pole, something almost impossible to illustrate clearly on a wall map.

To show the relative roundness of the earth as well as basic directions, teachers can simply refer to a globe. But when it comes to locating specific places on the globe, two problems often emerge. To avoid the problem of having students line up and file past the globe, some schools purchase classroom sets of eight- to twelve-inch globes, which are kept on a cart and wheeled from classroom to classroom as needed. The second problem is more a function of the globe itself, or, more accurately, of its size. On a twelve-inch globe, for example, the United States measures approximately four inches from west to east. On an average wall map, the United States measures approximately four feet from west to east, thus permitting the presentation of considerably more detail. Of course, some schools have a *very* large, 36-inch globe available, often as the focal point of a library or learning center, but even such large globes are limited in the amount of detail they can present. The globe is still the best geographic tool for most purposes, but when it comes to detail, you'll probably need to turn to a wall map.

Wall Maps

Getting a round earth to fit onto a flat map has perplexed cartographers for centuries. The classic example of peeling an orange and then trying to make the peel lie flat, or of doing the same with a rubber ball, illustrates the essence of the problem. In cartographic terms, it is a question of "projection." Projecting rounded surfaces onto a flat map in different ways will yield the images shown in Figure 11.5.

The distortion on most wall maps is greatest at the high latitudes, as illustrated by the different ways in which a human head is depicted in Figure 11.5. Such distortion is responsible for the question "Why isn't Greenland a continent?" It's really a very logical question for a child to ask, since on many maps Greenland appears to be two to three times the size of Australia, which is a continent. When children look on a globe, however, they will find that Australia is three times larger than Greenland—Australia has 2,975,000 square miles vs. Greenland's 840,000 square miles. Explaining to students how some maps make small things appear larger than they really are is no small feat! For very small areas, of course, the distortion created by different map projections is usually negligible. But for large land masses, we recommend that a globe be used in conjunction with wall maps.

FIGURE 11.5   Distortions Created by Different Map Projections

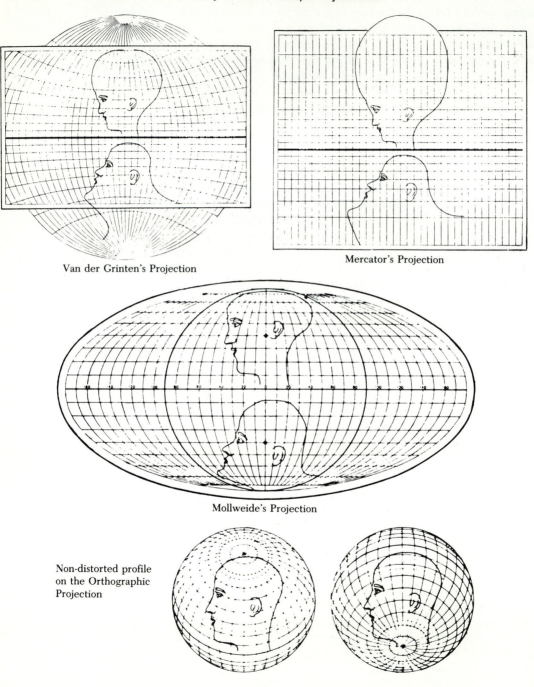

Van der Grinten's Projection

Mercator's Projection

Mollweide's Projection

Non-distorted profile
on the Orthographic
Projection

To avoid the "north is up" phenomenon, we suggest that you occasionally lay wall maps on the floor. Some teachers have gone even further; they have their students paint huge outline maps on the school parking lot or playground (after securing appropriate permission, of course). Such large-scale maps should be accurate in direction and as accurate as possible in scale. For example, an outline map of the United States that is drawn on a parking lot or playground located to the south of the school building would present a northern perspective when viewed from the school building. It's the perspective you would get by turning a wall map upside-down. The objective in doing such large-scale maps is to depict the earth accurately, even if that means creating maps that look different from the ones we're used to seeing.

LATITUDE, LONGITUDE, AND OTHER GRID SYSTEMS

Most map and globe skill programs from fourth grade upward call for instruction in latitude and longitude. One of the more difficult ideas for children to grasp is the fact that while most parallels of latitudes are lines, 90° North latitude and 90° South latitude are not lines, they are points (or, in mathematical terms, poles). Almost equally difficult is the idea that while the meridians of longitude are of equal length, the parallels of latitude get shorter as one moves away from the equator. We suspect that one reason children find these ideas so hard to grasp is because latitude and longitude are often taught as arbitrary systems rather than as part of circular or spherical measurement. And for children who think degrees are units for measuring temperature, you have another key to why latitude and longitude can present difficulties for them.

A related problem is that many social studies programs call for instruction in latitude and longitude in Grade 4 or earlier, while students often don't encounter circular or spherical measurement in their math programs until about Grade 7. Thus, social studies teachers are faced with the dilemma of either teaching the fundamentals of circular and spherical measurement, which would permit children to see the logic of latitude and longitude—and it is an extremely rational and logical system—or teaching latitude and longitude as an arbitrary system, which children may become adept at using but really don't understand.

In its simplest terms, teaching latitude and longitude in elementary social studies programs can be reduced to three components:

1. Use of *a* grid system (any grid system)
2. Use of *the* grid system (longitude and latitude)
3. Understanding the basis for longitude and latitude

Even primary children can become adept at using *a* grid system, especially those involving a combination of letters and numbers. Math texts frequently include an assortment of grid-related activities, sometimes more so than social studies texts. The beauty of many gridding activities is that they can quickly be made into games that kids love to play. A classic is Battleship, in which one student locates his navy on a simple grid, then another student tries to sink that navy by calling out the various squares on the grid. You could also obtain classroom sets of state road maps from one of the petroleum companies and create a version of Cops and Robbers or the FBI and the Crooks. In small groups, the "crooks" identify a quadrant on the map, then the rest of the children ask them questions such as, "Are you in a square near a large city?" In other words, it is the detective game adapted to a map, in which the "crook" must be asked questions that can be answered only by a yes or no. Note that this activity serves several purposes: it provides experience in using a grid system for locational purposes; it helps children formulate questions; and it also provides greater familiarity with state geography. The road map game will prove very popular even after the skills you're teaching are learned.

After your students have had experience using a grid system, the basis for latitude and longitude and its relationship to the globe can be explained. In this case, your task will become one of *applying* a system that children have already worked with to the globe. If you opt to present latitude and longitude through an expository teaching strategy, you will find yourself doing two things at once—explaining both the system and its application to the globe. Whatever approach you finally use to teach longitude and latitude, or any grid system for that matter, we make the same recommendation that we did for teaching the concept of scale: correlate latitude and longitude with whatever math program you are using.

MAP READING (DECODING MAPS)

Students who have had rich and varied map-making (encoding) experience should find that map reading is considerably easier to cope with. Realistically, however, children will be expected to use a wider range of maps than most of them will have had experience making. Making a classroom-by-classroom, population density map of the school, for example, where each dot represents one student, can be a reasonable map-making experience. But making a population density map for large areas, such as the United States or Europe, is such a laborious, time-consuming, and boring activity that it could well lead to a passionate hatred of any kind of map making. (If you insist on having students make population density maps of very large areas, consider doing Antarctica or Greenland!)

By the time children leave elementary or middle school, they will generally be expected to be able to apply the skills required to answer the questions on page 345, all of which are based on the sample map illustrated in Figure 11.6. These questions are similar to those found on standardized achievement tests. Note that we are doing two things here: (1) illustrating how your students' ability to deal with map and globe skills is likely to be measured and (2) identifying what those skills are. Accordingly, you should (1) attempt to answer the questions (all are answerable) and (2) identify, in the space provided, the skill or skills required to answer the question.

FIGURE 11.6 Pleasure Island Map

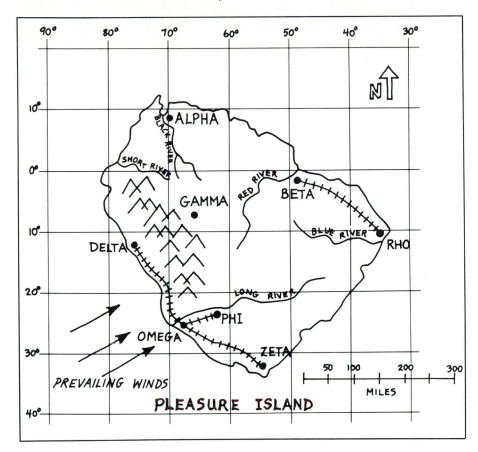

Questions

1. What is the northernmost city on Pleasure Island?
   A. Beta   B. Alpha   C. Gamma   D. Zeta

   Skill: _____

2. How far is it from Delta to Rho?
   A. 250 miles   B. 550 miles   C. 750 miles   D. 900 miles

   Skill: _____

3. Which river flows toward the Northeast?
   A. Long River   B. Blue River   C. Black River   D. Red River

   Skill: _____

4. What is the busiest port city on Pleasure Island?
   A. Beta   B. Gamma   C. Omega   D. Phi

   Skill: _____

5. What city gets the least rainfall?
   A. Beta   B. Gamma   C. Delta   D. Can't tell
   Skill: _____

6. What city lies closest to the equator?
   A. Beta   B. Alpha   C. Rho   D. Can't tell
   Skill: _____

7. In what hemisphere is most of Pleasure Island located?
   A. Northern   B. Eastern   C. Southern   D. Can't tell
   Skill: _____

(Answers: 1. B; 2. B; 3. D; 4. C; 5. B; 6. A; 7. C)

Few map skills consist of single-step procedures; in fact, most are complex chains of steps that must be followed in sequence. If any step is omitted or if the sequence of steps is confused, students are likely to fail. For example, in order to identify the hemisphere in which Pleasure Island is located (Question 7 above), the student must know that the equator is 0° latitude, and that as one moves southward, the degrees of latitude increase in number until one reaches 90° South latitude, the South Pole. The student must then apply this knowledge to the information provided on the map. As a further example of this, identify what you must know and be able to apply to determine whether Pleasure Island is in the Eastern or Western hemisphere.

Task Analysis

Many map skills are more complex than they first appear. However, the analytic (math-like) nature of map skills also permits *task analysis;* that is, map skills are amenable to being analyzed so that you can identify precisely what students must know and be able to do to achieve success. For example, to determine the distance from Delta to Rho (Question 2), the student must know the following skill rules: (1) that all maps have a scale, (2) that the scale indicates real distances in shortened form, (3) that by using a measuring device (a ruler, etc.) one can convert the distance on a map to the real distance, and so forth. All of this could become too abstract, however, if the student does not know that cities on a map are usually shown with a dot, or if he or she is unable to locate the two cities in question. All of these elements must be brought to bear on the problem in the correct sequence; otherwise, failure is almost guaranteed.

If students have used symbols, scale, and directions in making maps, they should have fewer problems when they encounter these elements in map reading. But when students encounter problems, we suggest that you plan a teacher-directed demonstration lesson focusing on the skill. To help students find the distance from Delta to Rho, for example, we would make an overhead transparency of Figure 11.6, and then demonstrate the process in a simple, step-by-step fashion. No elaborate questioning procedure is necessary. In fact, since most map and globe skills yield a single correct answer (such as the distance between two

Map-based activities such as those that involve actual manipulation of blocks and other materials can help children develop map-reading skills. (© *Delta Education, Inc.*)

cities) it will not inhibit your students' creativity if you show them an efficient process for finding that answer.

MAP-BASED ACTIVITIES

Some of the most effective and interesting map-related student activities begin with a heuristic question such as "If you were the town council, where would you build the new incinerator (or park, or shopping center, or apartment complex)?" and use maps as the main data source. One such activity comes from the MATCH Unit, "The City," and focuses on the problem of where a new freeway should be built in a town called "Five Corners, U.S.A."

MODEL STUDENT ACTIVITY

Five Corners, U.S.A.

OVERVIEW
A new highway is being constructed and is complete except for a small section that is to pass through part of the city of Five Corners. Students, each of whom is

either a resident or a business person, must decide where the unfinished portion of the road should go.

MATERIALS

Desk maps of Five Corners

Procedure

1. Assign or permit children to choose one of the residences or businesses as their own. Write their names on the small maps or on a master map if you use the latter. (All plots need not be assigned.)

2. Tell the children that the finished highway must be at least as wide as the two unfinished sections, and that the final route cannot have very sharp bends in it. Considering these limitations, each child (or small group of children) should select a tentative route for the highway.

    Solutions involving tunnels, bridges, the moving of buildings, or an elevated highway are all permissible. You may, however, wish to refrain from suggesting these in advance and let the children arrive at possible alternatives.

    Note: In the MATCH Unit, it's suggested that Step 2 be done as homework. A note is printed on the back of each map explaining the problem and the idea of the activity to parents. Help from the student's family is encouraged.

3. Working either individually or in small groups, the class should try to agree upon a route for the highway.

4. Have the class, either individually or in groups, present the proposed plans. Bring out the implications of the different plans, help clarify choices, and break deadlocks if necessary. How complex you should get depends on your students and their abilities.

5. Try to reach one solution. However, it is permissible *not* to arrive at a solution, a situation that may teach children more than would a hastily arrived-at solution.

VARIATIONS ON THIS ACTIVITY

You could have the children represent special interest groups (a business association, the town council, etc.) instead of individual property owners. This variation would also introduce a political dimension, especially if the town council had the final say.

VARIATIONS ON THE MODEL

Map-based activities of this kind are easy to vary; in fact, if you teach in a suburban or urban school you could create a mythical freeway-type situation using a map of an area near the school. In rural settings, the location of a freeway probably has less human impact—at least fewer buildings need to be destroyed and families moved—so in such instances you might wish to

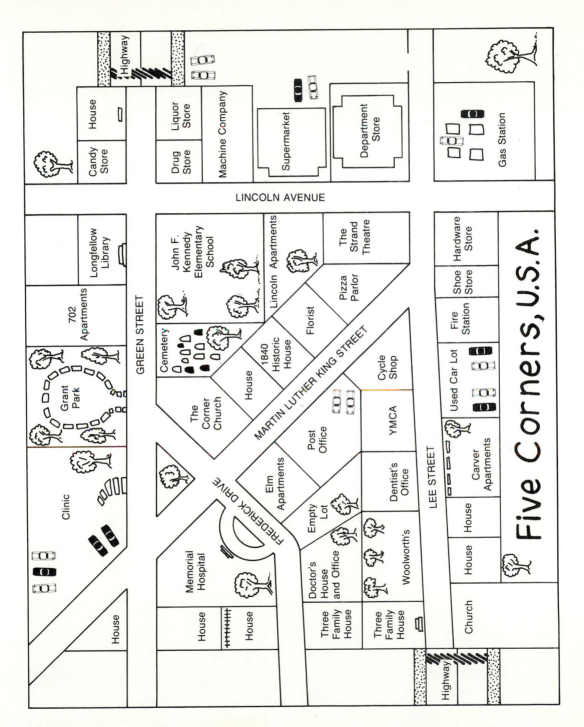

Five Corners, U.S.A.

focus on the ecological impact that freeways can have. Thus, your question could become "Should the proposed freeway be built through a wildlife preserve?"

Source: Map and Activity-MATCH unit, "The City," Teacher's Guide, p. 52. Used by permission of Delta Education, Inc.

Another kind of map-related activity is based on presenting students with a sequence of maps, each of which adds its own kind of specialized information. In the following activity, students are asked where they would locate a city on a mythical island. Then, in succession, additional information on terrain (landforms), vegetation, and rainfall is provided, each on a separate map.

MODEL STUDENT ACTIVITY

Where Would You Locate Your City?

OVERVIEW

The object of this activity is to determine whether students will change their original decision in light of new information.

PROCEDURE

Provide students with a copy of Map 1. Ask where, with just the information they have, they would locate a city if they were prospective settlers. The area is, of course, otherwise uninhabited. Permit them to discuss their choices in small groups, and then have each group present their choice to the entire class. Then provide each group with copies of Maps 2, 3, and 4, one at a time, permitting discussion and explanations (as warranted) after each one is distributed.

Map 1

Scale:1 inch = 50 miles

 sea water

 rivers

 lakes

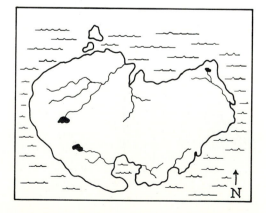

Map 2: Landforms

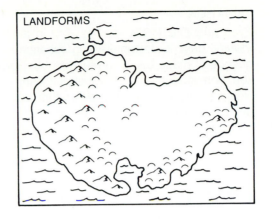

Map 3: Vegetation

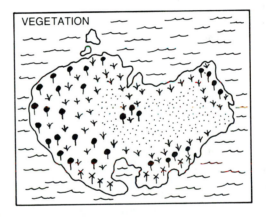

Map 4: Rainfall (average yearly amounts)

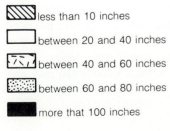

VARIATION

Ryan and Ellis (1974, pp. 41–42), in their book *Instructional Implications of Inquiry*, describe an interesting variation on this activity. It uses a similar sequence of maps but for a real country. However, the identity of that country is kept from students—it's just called "Country X"—until they determine where they would locate a major city within that nation. After students have made their decisions, they can turn to their atlases and compare their selections with the actual location of major cities in the country.

GRAPHS, TABLES, AND CHARTS

For some teachers and students, graphs, tables, and charts are the "bad breath" area of social studies. Teachers sometimes avoid working with apparently lifeless statistical information unless forced to do so, whereas students often regard it as something they can skip over, thus shortening their reading assignment. It is true that quantitative or statistical data can seem imposing, but they are by no means impossible if they are approached from a *use* perspective. Indeed, unless students actually do something with the information on a graph, table, or chart, it can easily degenerate into more "stuff" to memorize.

Two aspects of quantitative or statistical data deserve special mention. First, statistics are, by nature, uninterpreted information. This means that in most instances, individuals must interpret (or process) the data in order to draw their own conclusions. It takes a certain amount of mental effort to draw conclusions, for example, which may account for some of the "bad breath" feelings associated with this kind of information. Too many students (and teachers), we think, find it easier to memorize someone else's conclusions, such as those found in many textbooks, than to process information and draw one's own conclusions.

A second aspect of quantitative data reflects the fact that graphs, tables, and charts are extremely efficient forms for presenting information. They can present large amounts of information in very little space. In fact, graphs, tables, and charts are so efficient that it isn't long before students suffer from information overload; they find themselves faced with too much information too quickly, and they often lack the means to process it. Common sense indicates that students are not likely to *use* data, whether presented in a graph, table, or some other form, when they are reeling under a vast chunk of information that they cannot make sense of. The fact that some teachers expect children to memorize such information may only compound an already difficult situation.

FACT SHEETS

To avoid information overload, and thus better enable children to use information, the clear implication is that *the amount of data that children are expected to handle at the outset of an activity should be limited*. Once students have a grasp of the original data, you are free to add as much additional information as they are able to handle; the limited-information restriction applies only at the beginning of an activity. This means that rather than presenting students with a page full of statistics, for example, it may be necessary to select portions of that information and provide it in much smaller doses, on what are called "fact sheets."

The fact sheet illustrated in Figure 11.7 was produced by a fourth-grade teacher who was teaching a unit on farming in the United States. Although the information on it is limited, it still proved to be too much for her students. She then had them fold the paper so that only Part I was visible.

As she used the American Farmer Fact Sheet, the teacher alternated between questions designed to determine that the children could read the charts and graphs, and interpretive questions that were intended to elicit meaning. During the lesson, the students developed a remarkable body of tentative conclusions about farming in the United States today. On page 354, you have the opportunity to interpret the data in the same sequence as the fourth graders.

All of the following questions refer to the American Farmer Fact Sheet.

1. What does the information contained in Part I suggest to you (interpretative)?

_____

_____

2. What does the information in Graph 1 indicate?

_____

_____

3. What does the information in Graph 2 indicate?

_____

_____

4. What does the information in Graphs 1 and 2 suggest about American farms today (interpretative level)?

_____

_____

5. What does the information in Graph 3 indicate?

_____

_____

(Note: It could mean that farm machinery is more expensive than it used to be.)

6. What does the information in Graph 4 indicate?

_____

_____

FIGURE 11.7   Model Fact Sheet Format: The American Farmer

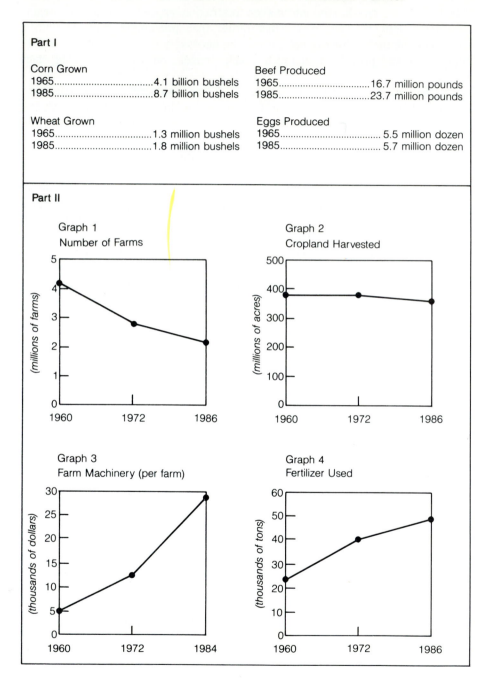

Part I

Corn Grown
1965.................................4.1 billion bushels
1985.................................8.7 billion bushels

Wheat Grown
1965.................................1.3 million bushels
1985.................................1.8 million bushels

Beef Produced
1965.................................16.7 million pounds
1985.................................23.7 million pounds

Eggs Produced
1965................................. 5.5 million dozen
1985................................. 5.7 million dozen

Part II

Graph 1
Number of Farms
(millions of farms)
1960   1972   1986

Graph 2
Cropland Harvested
(millions of acres)
1960   1972   1986

Graph 3
Farm Machinery (per farm)
(thousands of dollars)
1960   1972   1984

Graph 4
Fertilizer Used
(thousands of tons)
1960   1972   1986

7. What is the relationship, if any, between the information in Graphs 3 and 4 and your answer to Question 4 (interpretative)?

_____

_____

The students concluded that, although there are fewer farms in the United States, the amount of food produced on those farms has increased. They also concluded that since fewer farmers (Graph 1) were farming about the same number of acres as in the past (Graph 2), the average size of a farm is larger today than it was in the past. Furthermore, for fewer farmers to grow more food on about the same amount of farmland, the students concluded this was possible because of the increased use of machinery (Graph 3) and fertilizer (Graph 4). They also suggested that there could be other reasons for this (better weather, etc.), but that they didn't have enough information to be certain of these causes.

By using just the information on the American Farmer Fact Sheet, students developed their own conclusions about the changing nature of American farming. Of course, a teacher could approach the topic by having students read a section in the textbook, a section that, in all likelihood, would begin: "American farms today are larger than they used to be. Farmers also use more machinery and. . . ." In this instance, however, students would be reading _someone else's conclusions_ about farming instead of using information to build their own.

ENCODING QUANTITATIVE DATA

Before children can use information on a graph, table, or chart, they must be able to handle that information at the literal level. If children cannot, for example, read Graph 1 on the American Farmer Fact Sheet in order to make statements such as "There were about four million farms in the United States in 1960," then it may be necessary to back up and show them how the information was translated (or encoded) into graph form.

Our premise in this section is the same as the one we suggested for map-related activities; just as map making (encoding) may provide students with a better basis for map reading, encoding quantitative data (graph making, table making, and chart making) can provide students with a better basis for graph, chart, or table reading activities.

As a general rule, encoding experiences for primary-level students should involve simple examples and small quantities. This can be as simple as tallying the number of girls and boys in a classroom, as illustrated in Figure 11.8. Note also that until students are able to deal with representational thought, it is probably wisest to maintain one-to-one correspondence; that is, where one symbol on a table represents something the child can see in reality. In Figure 11.8, each symbol stands for one classmate. As students grow progressively more able to

FIGURE 11.8 Sample Table Encoded by Students

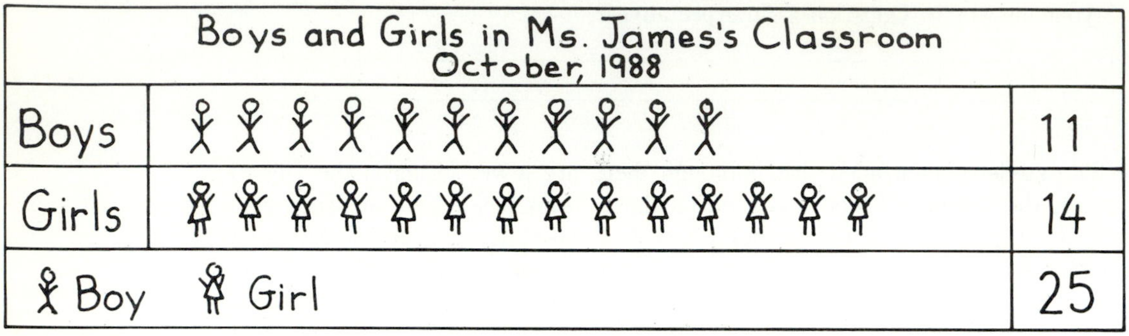

Boys and Girls in Ms. James's Classroom October, 1988		
Boys	♂ ♂ ♂ ♂ ♂ ♂ ♂ ♂ ♂ ♂ ♂	11
Girls	♀ ♀ ♀ ♀ ♀ ♀ ♀ ♀ ♀ ♀ ♀ ♀ ♀ ♀	14
♂ Boy ♀ Girl		25

FIGURE 11.9 Traffic Survey Conducted by Fourth Graders

Traffic Survey

Time: 11:00-11:30   Day: September 28
Surveyors: Roger, Debbie, Susan
Number of
Cars 32
Trucks 14
Station Wagons 12
Vans 9
Cars with whitewall tires 27
People who waved 39

handle representational thought, as when one symbol equals five classmates, for example, their encoding experiences can become increasingly complex.

Simple surveys can provide a wealth of information for encoding activities. That's what the teacher who developed the American Farmer Fact Sheet used when her students had graph reading problems. Small groups of students surveyed the traffic passing by the school at different times of day. They counted

FIGURE 11.10   Bar Graph Made from Traffic Survey Data

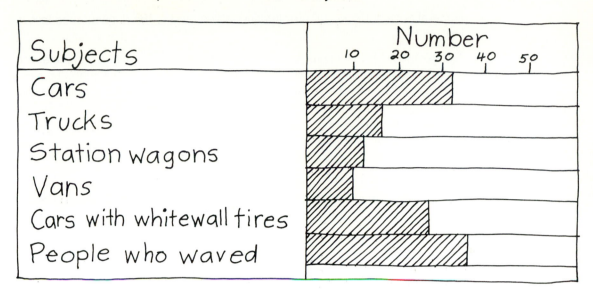

the number of cars and trucks, the number of station wagons, the number of vans, the number of cars with whitewall tires, and the number of people who waved back at them (Figure 11.9). Then, with the teacher's help, each group put its information onto a bar graph. The result of one group's efforts is illustrated in Figure 11.10. Rather than leaving it at just a frequency count, the various bar graphs were hung around the room to provide a basis for comparison. In addition to determining that traffic passing the school varied with the time of day (and was often heaviest when students were going to or leaving school), students also discovered some problems in the kinds of questions they had asked. Since vans are cars, for example, should they put down two tallies, one under cars and one under vans? Or, did *cars* mean non-station wagons and non-vans? To deal with these questions, each group had to review its tallying procedure.

Making Tables

Once data have been gathered, they must be presented in a readily understandable form. One such form, a table, is intended to communicate the relationships between the data. The Model Student Activity that follows shows general guidelines for table (and graph) construction, some sample data from Andrews and Blickle (1978) in a partially organized form, and the same data in table format.

Constructing a Table

General considerations for constructing tables (and graphs) include the following:

Tables should be self-sufficient. That is, a table should give a complete and understandable message: what is being related; the form in which the relationship is established; source of information—everything needed to help readers make their own interpretations.

All rows and columns must have clear headings that follow an identifiable pattern, e.g., high to low, alphabetical, geographic, etc., and, where appropriate, indicate the measure being used—percentages, thousands, square miles, etc.

The source of the data should be included in a footnote.

The table title should make clear what information is being related and in what terms.

Following these guidelines and using sample data such as that shown below, your class could construct a simple table like the one illustrated here.

SAMPLE DATA

Temperature and Snow Report, Week of January 9–15

Monday's high temperature was 30°. Tuesday's high was 25°. Wednesday's high was 28°, followed by 32° on Thursday, 35° on Friday, 37° on Saturday, and 30° on Sunday. The average high temperature for the week was 31°.

The snowfall for the week totaled 14 inches. It did not snow on Wednesday, Friday, or Saturday. It snowed 4 inches on Monday, and 7 inches on Tuesday, for a total of 11 inches for the first two days. Average snowfall was 2 inches a day for the week.

These data were then converted into table form, as shown in the table below.

Temperature and Snow Report, Week of January 9–15

Day	High Temperature (F°)	Snow (inches)
Monday	30	4
Tuesday	25	7
Wednesday	28	0
Thursday	32	1
Friday	35	0
Saturday	37	0
Sunday	30	2
Average high 31		*Total snowfall* 14
		Average daily snowfall 2

Source: Personal measurements.

DECODING GRAPHS AND TABLES

Before children are able to do anything with the information on a graph or in a table, they must gain access to that information. Fortunately, the process of decoding information presented on a graph or in a table is amenable to task analysis (as was the case for map reading). Probably the easiest way to go about this is to ask yourself two related questions: (1) what must the student know (and in what sequence?) to gain access to the information and (2) at what points might students experience problems?

Some of the knowledge components needed to decode the data on the sample task card illustrated in Figure 11.11 are readily evident. For instance, unless students can bring meaning to cue concepts such as "population," "racial minorities," "unemployment," etc., the data will be meaningless. Likewise, the student must be able to interpret extremely large numbers (e.g., 11.4 million), a task that may be further complicated by the use of decimal points. Because even some adults can have difficulty determining what 0.4 million means, we recommend that large numbers be rounded whenever possible. Finally, skill rules peculiar to tables and graphs are necessary to decode the information in Figure 11.11. In other words, unless the student knows that all of the data in the column headed *Chicago* pertains to that city, the table will remain meaningless.

Our point in analyzing graph and table reading as thoroughly as we have is to identify possible problems that students may encounter. Further, when students come to you with a graph or table they can't deal with, the complaint is apt to be vaguely stated, as in "I don't understand this." If you ask "What don't you understand about it?" the response is likely to be "The whole thing" or

FIGURE 11.11   Sample Task Card

Data			Tasks
	Tokyo, Japan	*Chicago, Illinois*	
Population	11.4 million	3 million	*Using just this information, identify three hypotheses:*
Racial Minorities	Koreans	Blacks, Spanish-Americans Native Americans	1. _____ 2. _____
Cases of Murder	213	810	3. _____
Gun Control	Small arms banned	Small arms registered	
Unemployment	Low	High	
Family Structure	Strong	Loosening of family ties	

"I just don't get it." In the final analysis, you will probably find yourself doing a task analysis, much as we have here, to identify where the child is having difficulty.

In light of the problems noted above, we do not recommend using indirect or discovery strategies for teaching the specialized skill rules associated with table or graph reading. There are just too many points at which students might encounter problems. Thus, this is another instance where direct, step-by-step instruction is wholly appropriate.

CHARTS

We suspect that in the days before overhead projectors became widely available, chart making was more common than it is today. With current technology, it is a relatively simple process to place a small-size chart in a thermofax machine; a few seconds later, you'll get an overhead transparency that, when projected, is readily visible to everyone in the class. A problem with overhead transparencies, however, is that once the projector is turned off, the image is gone. A poster-size chart displayed somewhere in the classroom, on the other hand, offers students the opportunity to have repeated visual contact with whatever the chart depicts. The issue then is one of deciding whether you want to settle for a fleeting visual image or sustained visual contact.

An endless variety of things can be depicted in chart form. If you were to enlarge a table (without *increasing* the number of elements) you would have a *tabular chart*. Or if you were to present a schematic drawing of the structure of an organization such as the U.S. Congress you would have an *organizational chart*. And if you were to outline the steps a bill passes through in Congress en route to becoming a law, for example, you would have a *flowchart*. Virtually any process—the production of steel, bread, or whatever—can be illustrated either in pictures, short narrative descriptions, or a combination of the two on a flowchart. The chart illustrating the "family tree" of a can of corn (Figure 4.2, p. XX) is a kind of flowchart, but because it showed the origin of the various products that went into making the canned corn (as opposed to emphasizing the steps in the process), it technically would be considered a *pedigree chart*.

Charts on which students classify or categorize various kinds of data can be especially helpful in the concept-building process. Consider how you might go about classifying the following terms, for example: *pond, lake, brook, run, river, ocean, stream, sea, pool, tank, basin, creek, bayou.* Since all of these have something to do with water—including *tank*, which is used throughout the West to describe a small pond—your *classification chart* might have two headings: (1) terms that describe bodies of water and (2) terms that describe flowing water.

All charts summarize whatever they depict. They are like outlines in that they highlight major points or phases while omitting details. For example, you probably would not include definitions for the terms listed on the classification chart described above, because to do so would present so much information that the major elements would be obscured. Such inclusions would probably defeat the purpose for putting information in chart form in the first place. However, the need to summarize information can be an asset when you have students engage in chart making, because summarizing forces them to identify the information—the main ideas—that they should put on their chart. In this way, chart-making activities can force children to differentiate between main ideas and supporting details. In this context, chart making can be an effective culminating activity for small group work, because it demands that students review what they did and what they found.

MODEL STUDENT ACTIVITY

Linear Charting

As an alternative to making charts on poster-size pieces of tagboard, consider using another technique to accomplish some of the same purposes. For lack of a better term, we call this technique *linear charting.* It consists of having students attach pictures or short descriptions of a process in the correct sequence on a piece of string or yarn. A linear chart for the production of bread is illustrated here:

Note that, although this may not sound like an exciting activity, actually doing it may prove otherwise. Consider, also, that linear charting can be used for more than just social studies activities. For example, instead of traditional book reports you might have students illustrate the significant scenes or events in a book and then attach those pictures, in the correct sequence, to a piece of yarn. Then, when students present their reports, the rest of the class can refer to a visual representation of the book's events, rather than strictly listening to a verbal presentation.

SOURCES OF QUANTITATIVE DATA

The reference rooms of most libraries are filled with sources of quantitative data, but since such sources are not usually selected for casual reading, we decided to include this section. If you have no intention of developing a fact sheet, or if you are not keen on reading a list, you might skip this section and go on to the summary.

The most readily available sources of quantitative data are the variety of almanacs and encyclopedias found in most libraries. In the case of encyclopedias, it is sometimes necessary to extract quantitative data from the narrative of an article. Other sources, organized by the types of data they present, are listed below. All are published annually unless otherwise indicated.

Sources for International Data

Europa Yearbook. London: Europa Publications Ltd.

Facts on File: World News Digest. New York: Facts on File, Inc.

Food and Agriculture Organization of the United Nations. *Trade Yearbook* and *The Production Yearbook.* Rome, Italy: The FAO Press.

Mitchell, B. R., ed. *European Historical Statistics, 1750–1970.* New York: Columbia University Press, 1975.

New York Times Index. New York: New York Times, Inc. Published quarterly.

United Nations. *Demographic Yearbook.* New York: UN Press.

————. *Statistical Yearbook.* New York: UN Press.

World Health Organization. *World Health Statistics.* Geneva, Switzerland: WHO Press.

Sources for Data about the United States

Most of the quantitative data about the United States is collected and published by the U.S. government. The amount is massive. Two sources to help you deal with all this data are *American Statistics Index: Annual, A Comprehensive Guide and Index to the Statistical Publications of the U.S. Government* (Washington, D.C.: Congressional Information Service); and *A Guide to the National Archives of the United States* (National Archives and Records Service, General Services Administration, Washington, D.C.).

U.S. Department of Commerce, Social and Economic Administration, Bureau of the Census. *Census of Agriculture.* Washington, D.C.: The Bureau of the Census. Issued every ten years.

————. *Census of Transportation*. Washington, D.C.: The Bureau. Issued every five years.

————. *Historical Statistics of the United States. Colonial Times to 1970.* Washington, D.C.: The Bureau, 1976.

SUMMARY

This chapter has suggested some approaches for helping children gain access to specialized forms of information, namely, maps, globes, graphs, and tabular data. For each of these forms, we have suggested that *encoding* experiences, which include map, graph, table, and chart making, can help children understand how information gets into a particular form. Such encoding experiences may provide students with a better basis for decoding or gaining access to information displayed on maps, graphs, tables, and charts.

Unlike some of the other areas social studies encompasses, map, table, and graph reading (decoding) involve an identifiable sequence of the knowledge and skills necessary for gaining access to information. As in analytic subject areas, if any step is omitted, or if the sequence of steps is confused, the student is likely to fail. To avoid failure and the sense of frustration that can accompany it, we recommend that you "task analyze" what the student is being asked to do by identifying the knowledge and skills required to complete the task. This analysis can provide the basis for step-by-step instruction as you guide your students through the decoding process.

Once students have gained access to information, the next phase is a "natural": they need to do something with it. It becomes almost a circular process when you recognize that what students *do* with information can provide a reason for them to get (and want) access to it.

SUGGESTED ACTIVITIES

1. Design a map-based decision-making activity that deals with a problem presently confronting the community you are living in, or, as an alternative, use a hypothetical community.

2. It is sometimes argued that much of the time devoted to instruction in longitude and latitude is wasted and could be better spent on something else. That argument is based on the claim that, while latitude and longitude are concepts many Americans know, they rarely, if ever, use them. Develop a response to that argument.

3. Review the instructional activities presented in this chapter and identify those that teach and those that test a student's preexisting skills.

4. Design a fact sheet that could serve as the basis for a lesson on any of the following topics: immigration, health care, education, community, or industrialization.

5. Obtain two social studies textbooks for the same grade level but from different publishers (your curriculum library or learning-resource center should have copies available). Compare the two books in terms of the map reading skills they require of students. Also compare them in terms of the quantitative data skills they require, if any.

REFERENCES

Andrews, Deborah C., and Margaret D. Blickel. 1978. *Technical Writing: Principles and Forms.* New York: Macmillan.

"Bird's Eye View." 1987. Dimondale, Mich.: Hartley Courseware, Inc.

Frazee, Bruce M. 1984. "Foundations for an Elementary Map Skills Program." *The Social Studies,* 75 (March/April), 79–82.

Hanna, Paul R., et al. 1966. *Geography in the Teaching of the Social Studies: Concepts and Skills.* Boston: Houghton Mifflin.

Hawkins, M. L. 1980. "Graphing: A Stimulating Way to Process Data." NCSS How to Do It Series 2, No. 10. Washington, D.C.: National Council for the Social Studies.

MATCH. 1965. "The City." *Teacher's Guide.* Nashua, N.H.: Delta Education.

Muir, Sharon Pray. 1985. "Understanding and Improving Student's Map Reading Skills." *The Elementary School Journal,* 86 (2), 207–16.

Joint Committee on Geographic Education. 1984. *Guidelines for Geographic Education.* Washington, D.C.: National Council for Geographic Education and the Association of American Geographers.

Ryan, Frank, and Arthur Ellis. 1974. *The Instructional Implications of Inquiry.* Englewood Cliffs, N.J.: Prentice-Hall.

SUGGESTED READINGS

Arthur K. Ellis. 1981. *Teaching and Learning Elementary Social Studies.* 2nd ed. Boston: Allyn and Bacon. This methods text has an excellent chapter on making and interpreting maps.

Bruce Frazee, ed. 1986. "Teaching Map Reading Skills." *Social Education,* 50 (March), 199–211. This special section presents some of the most recent research on teaching map skills.

Marion J. Rice and Russell L. Cobb. 1978. *What Can Children Learn in Geography? A Review of Research.* Boulder, Colo.: ERIC Clearinghouse for Social Studies/Social Science Education, and Social Science Education Consortium, Inc. For all the years that map skills have been associated with social studies, you would think there would be a tremendous amount of information available. There isn't. This volume, however, provides an analysis of the research available.

James E. Harf and Anne R. Peterson. 1977. "The Quantitative Perspective on Inquiry in the Social Studies." In *Practical Methods for the Social Studies,* ed. M. E. Gilliom. Belmont, Calif.: Wadsworth. Once again, this volume is aimed toward the secondary teacher. Nevertheless, you should find its treatment of quantitative data techniques of considerable value.

PART THREE

Social Studies: Management and Organization

CHAPTER 12

Managing Group Dynamics

"Committee: A group that succeeds in getting something done only when it consists of three members, one of whom happens to be sick and the other absent." H. W. Van Loon

KEY QUESTIONS

☐ When and why should teachers use small groups?

☐ How large should groups be?

☐ How does one determine group membership?

☐ What is process observation, and how does it work?

☐ How do you get children to examine their behavior?

☐ How do you conduct a classroom meeting?

KEY IDEAS

☐ Almost anything you wish to do with a large group can be done with small groups, although the reverse is not necessarily true.

☐ Teacher feedback is one of the more critical components of effective group management.

☐ In observing group activities, the tendency is to get involved in the content of the group's discussion and neglect the processes used in dealing with that content.

☐ The classroom (and school) can become a functioning social studies laboratory in which behavior is an object of study.

INTRODUCTION: To Group or Not to Group?

Parent: What did you do at school today?

Child: Oh, the teacher put us into groups and we just talked.

Parent: Well, what did you learn?

Child: Nothin'!

Therein lies the beginning of some students' negative feelings about small-group work. Other experiences can contribute to those feelings, of course. For example, you may recall occasions when everyone on your committee got the same grade, but you did all the work. At other times, your group may have spent forty minutes just trying to get organized when you could have completed the entire job in twenty minutes or less. There were probably other times when how you worked in a group didn't make any difference because your grades were based solely on tests and individual projects.

Experienced teachers may have similar feelings about using small-group instruction, sometimes for similar reasons. Determining which student did what in a group and then grading that performance fairly, for example, can be challenging. Small-group work can also consume significant amounts of classroom time—time that some teachers feel could be spent more profitably in teacher-directed instruction.

Clearly, small-group work can be a hassle, both for teachers who lack the skills to use the technique effectively and for students who think of small-group work as something they must endure until they can get back to some "real" instruction. On the other hand, consider that working in small groups is directly related to the overall goal of social studies teaching—promoting the skills of citizenship education. For example, it is difficult, perhaps even impossible, to learn to work cooperatively with others if students experience only large-group (whole class) instruction. Likewise, it is almost impossible for students to demonstrate their willingness to respect the rights and opinions of others if they experience only large-group instruction in which most students seldom get the opportunity to express an opinion.

Consider that almost everything you do with large groups (of twenty to thirty students) can also be done in small groups. Indeed, you could even lecture to two students if you wanted to. But the reverse of that usually does not hold true. In other words, what you can do with small groups is not always possible with large groups. A discussion involving twenty-six students, for example, is less likely to be successful than a discussion involving a group of five to seven students, simply because the participants in a large-group discussion usually have to wait too long before they get a chance to speak. The point here is that although both large- and small-group instruction present challenges to a teacher, we have opted to focus on small groups in this chapter because of their potential for promoting active involvement among students and for enhancing children's citizenship skills.

In the first portion of this chapter, we examine several problems that may be associated with small-group instruction, as well as some techniques that could help you deal with those problems. In the second part of the chapter, we consider elements from the social and behavioral sciences that may help you to maintain an effective learning environment.

For students, learning to work effectively and cooperatively within small groups is directly related to their developing the skills of citizenship, the overall goal of social studies instruction. (© *Elizabeth Crews*)

MANAGING GROUP-BASED INSTRUCTION

Every bad experience you may have had with small-group work can imply a factor that must be considered before you begin group work with your students. For example, before you begin you need to determine if students' performances in small-group work will be graded, and if so, on what basis. Will it be based on letter grades, points, anecdotal records, tests, or what? You also need to determine how the groups will be created. Will you let children choose the individuals with whom they will work or will you do the selecting? And if you do the selecting, will you put two students who are known to dislike each other on the same committee? Or, will you put a low social-status child in a group with high social-status children (or vice versa)? We will deal with these questions throughout this chapter, but suffice it to say here that high- and low-status children can often work together successfully in the same group. It is much rarer, however, that the relationship between two children who actively dislike each other will be improved by working together in a group—primarily because most groups don't deal with the causes of their disenchantment.

THE DYNAMICS OF SMALL GROUPS

In whole-class instruction, the sheer logistics of managing twenty to twenty-five (or more) individuals limits your instructional options. Almost of necessity, you—the teacher—become the focal point. Indeed, it is difficult, though not impossible, to make large-group instruction anything other than teacher-centered. There are times when teacher-centered large-group instruction is wholly appropriate, of course, but you can also anticipate that much of your time will be devoted to managing procedures and maintaining order.

By dividing your class into small groups, the proportion of each student's responsibility to the group increases dramatically. Instead of representing one twenty-sixth of a class of twenty-six, the student represents one-fourth of a group of four. No longer must that student wait for twenty-five other potential contributors to have their say before she or he can become involved in an activity. From one perspective, small groups offer far less chance for students to sit back passively and watch events pass in review. Or from a more positive perspective, students in small groups have considerably more opportunity for active involvement, simply because the structure of the setting encourages it. This does not mean that all students in a small group will be actively involved; it just means that you will have eliminated some of the structural barriers to that involvement.

The formula for determining the number of possible interactions in small groups is illustrated in Figure 12.1. So, how large will your groups be? If you have eight people in a group, there are fifty-six possible interrelationships. A group of this size doing library research will probably spend as much time checking among themselves (and duplicating their efforts) as they will in doing the research itself. Thus, the question of how large a group should be must be determined in relation to its purpose. For most purposes, three to eight students per group is generally acceptable.

It is interesting to note that some sizes of small groups appear to have particular properties, as follows:

Groups of two High tension and emotion, tendency to avoid disagreement, high exchange of information, high potential of deadlock and instability, high differentiation of role with one person the active initiator, the other the passive controller (with veto). . . .

Groups of three Power of the majority over the minority of one, usually the two stronger over the weakest member; most stable, with shifting coalitions. . . .

Odd versus even groups More disagreement in even groups (4, 6, 8) than in odd (3, 5, 7), due to the formation of subgroups of equal size. The

FIGURE 12.1   Formula for Group Interaction

(Number of persons in the group − 1) × number of persons in the group =
the number of interactions (Np − 1) NP = Ni

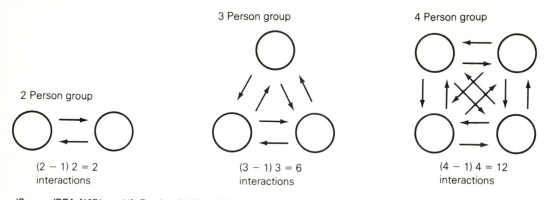

(Source: IDEA [1971, p. 11]. Reprinted with permission of the Institute for the Development of Educational Activities, Inc., an affiliate of the Charles F. Kettering Foundation.)

> **personally most satisfying size seems to be five—ease of movement with-**
> **in; 2:3 division provides support for the minority members; large enough**
> **for stimulation, small enough for participation and personal recognition.**
> **(Berelson and Steiner, 1964, p. 360)**

Groups and Purposes

You can establish groups for any number of purposes, but four of the most
common to social studies instruction are (1) to discuss issues or events, (2) to
engage in decision-making activities, (3) to provide small-group instruction, and
(4) to research or investigate problems or questions. Characteristics of the more
common groups are summarized below.

Discussion Groups

Purpose   To provide children with opportunities to express and clarify their
points of view on issues pertinent to their interests.

Size   Two to six (enough children to stimulate interaction but not so many as to
overwhelm or restrict the flow of discussion).

Comment   From your own experience, you know that discussion groups can
easily degenerate into rap sessions of questionable value. To help keep discussion
groups on track, consider establishing a task for the group—a conclusion, a verbal
report, or a summary—to be presented at the end of the group's deliberations. It
may also be necessary to provide preprinted questions or other guides to help the
groups structure their discussion.

Potential problems Because the teacher cannot be present in each group when several are operating simultaneously, the student who is elected or appointed as the discussion leader has a critically important role. When in doubt, appoint the discussion leader. It may also be necessary to select group members rather than allow children to form their own groups.

Decision-Making Groups

Purpose To provide children with experience in group consensus, and in considering alternatives and arriving at a decision.

Size Three to seven.

Comment The life of most decision-making groups is of fairly short duration. Seldom does it exceed an hour, and it is typically far shorter than that. As a result, the social status of discussion-group members is less critical than for longer-range tutorial or research groups. Students can form their own decision-making groups or members can be selected at random.

Potential problems Some decision-making and discussion groups invariably finish before others. You may need to have a couple of related questions or issues on hand to pose to the early finishers. As a less desirable alternative, you can even join the group and/or turn it into a discussion group. Although seeing you working with one group may have the effect of speeding up the other groups, it may also take the steam out of the intergroup discussion that follows when everyone is finished.

Tutorial Groups

Purpose To provide individual help or advanced work to a small group that might most need or benefit from it.

Size Two to nine.

Comment Tutorial groups provide teachers with an opportunity for more immediate, direct feedback than is possible in large-group settings.

Potential problems The rest of the class will need to be kept busy with meaningful activities while you work with a tutorial group. Also, despite the best of intentions, a social stigma may be associated with students in remedial, tutorial groups.

Research Groups (Investigative)

Purpose To provide individuals with an opportunity to solve a problem, research a question, pursue a line of inquiry, or prepare a project.

Size Two to four.

Comment The limitation on group size as noted previously should be observed. Also, you may need to spend considerable time providing explicit instructions and helping the group organize itself.

Potential problem Care must be taken to see that the mechanics and incidentals of the research or project do not prove more time-consuming than the investigation itself.

Determining Group Membership

Assume that you are going to ask your students two questions: "Which individual in this class do you like best?" and "Which person in this class would you most like to work with?"

Do you think most children would cite the same individual in both instances? That is, do you think they will most often choose their best friend as the person with whom they would like to work? Yes or No?

In some cases they will, of course, but in many instances they will not. When confronted with an activity demanding a lot of reading, for example, and in a case where their best friend is not very adept at reading, children often realize that they would be wiser to choose to work with a better reader. To do so might very well enhance their own performance, a subtlety not lost to most students.

Research suggests that children are cognizant of both a social dimension and a "work" dimension operating in their classroom. It suggests, further, that a child may rank differently in each dimension. And so, for example, you may find boys or girls in your class who, because of their athletic prowess, are social leaders but, maybe because of a skill deficiency, are ranked somewhat lower on the "who I'd like to work with" scale. Similarly, low-status children on the social scale may be ranked somewhat higher in the "work" dimension.

You have undoubtedly had enough experience as a student to know what to look for in identifying the social pecking order in a classroom—the child who is ignored by most other students, or high-status individuals who command almost instant respect from others. By observing the interaction patterns within a classroom—especially who talks with whom when no one is supposed to be talking—it is relatively easy to determine the high- and low-status children. Identifying those individuals in the middle range is often more difficult.

Sociograms   In addition to observation, one means of identifying the social status pattern in your classroom is through a sociometric technique, a sociogram. Gathering the data for a sociogram is fairly simple. You ask students to respond (either verbally or in writing) to a question such as "What person in this classroom do you like best?" You can be more subtle about it by asking "If you could ask only one person in this room to go to the movies with you, who would you invite?" or "Who would you most like to sit next to?" or something similar. But if you are interested in social status, be careful not to ask, "With whom would you most like to work in a group (or on a committee)?" This is a legitimate question for identifying status in the "work" dimension, but it may not accurately reveal the social dimension. If you ask both questions, plan on plotting the responses on two separate target diagrams. If you try plotting them on one diagram, you will face the biggest mess you have ever encountered—and it may not tell you very much anyway.

Caution: Although sociogram questions can be posed in a group setting, students must be able to respond individually. Above all, students' responses must be held in the strictest confidence.

The data are processed by making a list of the students in the class, counting the number of times each one was chosen, and then noting by whom. This information can then be transferred to a target diagram such as the one illustrated in Figure 12.2, which will provide you with a graphic display of the status choices.

The high-status individuals, the *stars*, will be located toward the center of the diagram, while low-status individuals, the *isolates,* will fall outside the circle. The critical question teachers face concerns the degree to which they should intervene by placing low-status students with higher-status students. To do so may not alter the lower-status students' ranking in the overall social ordering, but it might make them feel a lot better about themselves. On the other hand, some isolates are quite content with their loner role and might just as well be left undisturbed. For

FIGURE 12.2 A Target Diagram of Social Relationships

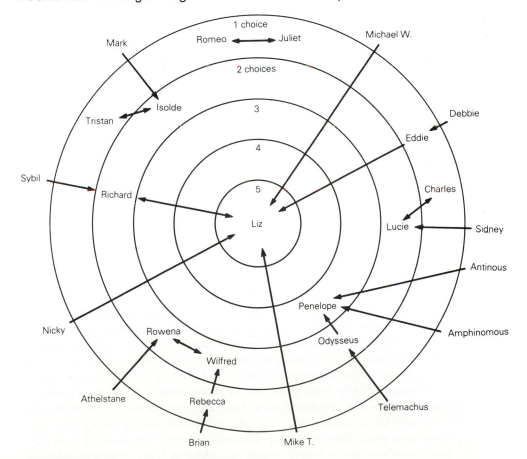

(Source: Biehler [1974, p. 139]. Adapted from Northway [1940]; reprinted by permission of the American Sociological Association.)

these kinds of judgments, only you will have the necessary data about your students on which to base your decisions.

Knowing which students would rather *not* work together is probably as important in terms of structuring groups as knowing which would. However, the negative consequences that can result from gathering such information through sociometric means may outweigh its potential value. In other words, by asking the question "With whom would you least like to work?" you could probably produce a "hatred" scale, and a very accurate one at that. But imagine also the dynamics that will go on in your class as the children discuss whom it is they like least.

How, then, do you select which students will work in what groups? Probably the most equitable way is through a combination of their choices and your judgment. You can inform them in advance of any extensive committee or group work and then have them identify, in writing, the two or three individuals with whom they might like to work. You can then use your own judgment as to whether the groups will work well together or whether you need to make any adjustments.

THE DYNAMICS OF GROUP WORK

Herbert Thelen, who has written extensively about groups and group interaction, describes two group-work situations that beautifully illustrate some of the pitfalls and successes associated with groups. In the first instance, an investigative group of second graders was working on a unit on how different people live. Their task was to select a group of people, find out how they live, and then present a play based on their information. The teacher in this case had considerable information on the Algonquin Indians, so she tried to steer the children in that direction. Undaunted by her efforts, the students, some of whom had recently seen one of Walt Disney's True Life Adventure films, decided that they were going to study prairie dogs. It really didn't matter if prairie dogs weren't people; they were going to study prairie dogs, period! Thelen (1960, pp. 142–43) described what they did:

> **They started their study by naming the characters for the play they would write, and of course the characters turned out to be baby, chicken, mother, father, farmer's boy, snake, etc. They made lists of questions to be answered: What do prairie dogs eat? Where do they live? What do they do with their time? How big are their families? Who are their enemies? etc. Individuals sought answers to questions from science pamphlets, books, the science teacher, officials of the local zoo, and I have no doubt at least a few of them talked to their parents to be taken to see the Disney opus. They reported their findings in compositions during the writing lessons. The plot of the play gradually took shape and was endlessly modified with each new bit of information. The play centered around family life, and there was much discussion and spontaneous demonstrations of how various members of the family would act. Most of these characterizations actually represented a cross-section of the home lives of seven-year-old**

children, as perceived by the children. But each action was gravely discussed and soberly considered, and justified in terms of what they knew about the ecology of prairie dogs.

They built a stage with sliding curtains and four painted backdrops—more reference work here to get the field and farm right. The play itself was given six times, with six different casts, and each child played at least two different parts. There was never any written script; only an agreement on the line of action and the part of it to occur in each scene. And after each presentation the youngsters sat around and discussed what they had been trying to communicate, and how it might be improved.

If all groups worked as well as this one, there would be fewer complaints about group work. But contrast the prairie dog example with one in which a high school social studies class attempted to produce a television series on the history of their community. Thelen (1960, pp. 143–44) described the situation this way:

Harry and Joe took pictures of an Indian mound, left there by original settlers. They took it from the south because the light was better that way; and they never discovered the northern slope where erosion had laid bare a burrow full of Indian relics. Mary and Sue spent two afternoons on a graph of corn production in the region; the graph was in a geography book the teacher gave them and the time was mostly spent in making a neat elaborately lettered document for the camera. The narrators were chosen for their handsome appearance, and much of the staging of the show (which used reports mostly) centered around deciding the most decorative way to seat the students. A lot of old firearms and household implements were borrowed from a local museum and displayed with a sentence or two of comment for each.

In this instance, the students learned a great deal about the mechanics of production—lettering signs, taking photographs, etc.—but relatively little about the history of their community. Indeed, the incidentals of producing the show distracted their attention from the focus of their study. The moral? When you consider group activities, such as presenting a play on Mexico or holding a Greek Olympics Day, be certain that collecting sombreros and sarapes, making the scenery, or building chariots does not overshadow everything else. It very quickly can.

Inquiry vs. Activity

The prairie dog and TV production examples illustrate a key difference between inquiry and simple activity. In the prairie dog study, the children identified questions they wanted answers for, did whatever research was necessary to answer the questions, and then incorporated what they found into their play. In other words, the inquiry process the children followed in the prairie dog study was *purposeful* and *systematic*. In the case of the TV production, however, the end product—the TV show—became the overriding concern and the inquiry process got lost in the shuffle. To produce the TV show, everyone more or less "did their own thing." An inquiry is purposeful and systematic; in simple activity the behavior is often random and the end product takes precedence over the inquiry process.

The irony of inquiry and activity is that students often "feel good" about both. That is, the students who studied prairie dogs probably felt good about what they had accomplished. In fact, if they hadn't enjoyed what they were doing, their study probably wouldn't have been as thorough and all-encompassing as it was. But then the students who made the TV presentation probably felt good about their efforts too, even though they didn't learn much about their original topic. Similarly, participants in "rap sessions" also often enjoy themselves, if for no other reason, because they've sounded off—often at length. But feeling good, by itself, is hardly a sufficient criterion for judging the quality of a learning experience.

True, kids (and teachers) need to feel good about what they're doing or what they've done. If they don't, they probably will not realize the learning potential an activity presents. In fact, if students are not intrigued with continuing an inquiry, it may be necessary to interrupt with another activity intended to raise their sagging interest level. For example, if your class is getting bogged down with library research, you may wish to insert an activity—a game, a short decision-making exercise, even a film on a totally different topic—just to provide a change of pace and renew their interest in the longer-range activity. In other words, your objective may be to present an activity intended to raise your students' "feeling" level so that they are willing to continue their original inquiry. Note, however, that activities that lack significant learning outcomes are suitable *only* when the dynamics of a group indicate that interest is sagging and/or that a change of pace is warranted. Otherwise, activity for activity's sake is not warranted. If you are able to develop motivational activities that also have significant learning outcomes, you will have captured the best of both worlds.

SOCIAL SKILLS AND FEEDBACK

It is often claimed that when children work together on group projects, they are learning social skills—how to cooperate, how to get along with one another, etc. Some of these claims should probably be viewed with suspicion. Because children are placed in a situation that requires cooperation, for example, does not mean that they will necessarily learn anything about cooperation per se. It may simply mean that students cooperated because they were placed in a situation that demanded it.

When problems within small groups become apparent, it is sometimes difficult to know how to respond adequately. For example, assume that you are confronted by a group of three students to whom you have given an assignment similar to the prairie dog study described by Thelen. But in this instance, let's assume that two students want to study the Algonquin Indians while a third, Jamie, wants to study prairie dogs. One of the students comes to you and says,

"Jamie won't cooperate. We want to study Algonquin Indians and he wants to study prairie dogs." How would you respond?

Will you agree that Jamie is not cooperating, which in this instance means not going along with the will of the majority? Or would you ask Jamie his reasons for wanting to study prairie dogs, knowing full well that they are not people and technically don't fit the intent of your assignment? Or would you let Jamie go off on his own (where he need not cooperate with anyone) and study prairie dogs to his heart's content?

The answer—and there really isn't one best answer—probably depends on information you don't have—specific data on Jamie. Is he the type of child you can cajole into going along with the majority? Or is he the type who, if forced to do something he is not really interested in, will engage in a little subtle sabotage along the way? Without more data, these are imponderables. But imagine also that at a parent-teacher conference you have the opportunity to mention that "Jamie doesn't cooperate well with others" and his mother or father responds, "Yes, we know. What do you suggest we do about it?" You may be hard put to come up with specific suggestions.

The problem with information such as "Jamie doesn't cooperate well with others" is that it lacks specificity. True, it may be an accurate description of Jamie's behavior, but at that level of generality there isn't much either Jamie, his parents, or you can do about his apparent lack of cooperation. What typically happens next is that someone says something to the effect that "Jamie, the next time you work in a group, I want you to cooperate." The assumptions implicit in

COMMENTARY: What Teachers Say and What They Really Mean

What the parent hears	What the teacher means
Jamie often exhibits a lack of cooperation.	Jamie is stubborn as a mule.
Cynthia doesn't always respect the rights and property of others.	Cynthia steals like crazy.
John has proven to be a real challenge.	John is a spoiled brat who is driving me up the wall.
Harriet has an especially vivid imagination and tends to exaggerate at times.	Harriet lies constantly.
Claude has problems with social adjustment.	The kids all hate Claude.
Judy is exceptionally mature socially.	Judy is the only fourth grader who wears eye shadow and smokes in the john.

the request are that Jamie (1) is aware of how *and* when he has failed to cooperate and (2) is able (and wants) to do something about his apparent problem. If either of these assumptions is not valid, then telling Jamie to cooperate in the future is likely to be as effective as spitting into the wind.

So how can you deal with Jamie or with students who display similar problems—students who dominate groups, who don't respect the rights and opinions of others (both behaviors reflect a form of noncooperation), or who are unwilling to accept their share of the work? In general, you should provide them with feedback in a form that they—either individually or as groups—can do something with (or about). What we are suggesting here is that the kind of feedback you provide your students, whether in large groups, small groups, or as individuals, will help determine your success or failure as a teacher.

Characteristics of Effective Feedback

Specificity/Descriptiveness   Effective feedback is specific; that is, it describes a specific behavior that the child can modify or do something about. Statements such as "You are not smart enough to be in this group" or "You two don't care about this group" are judgments, not descriptions, and in addition to being unnecessarily cruel, they fail to indicate what the child should do to correct the problem. On the other hand, a statement such as "Before you proceed you need to check your source of information" provides specific information that the child can take action on.

Positive feedback, such as "That was a good report" or "This group is really working well together," is usually music to the ears of anyone—even if it is more judgmental than descriptive. Adding more description yet, such as "You really integrated the material well in your report," is just that much more icing on the cake. But negative feedback is quite another matter. To say to Jamie (from our earlier example) that "You are not a good group member," for example, is likely to evoke Jamie's ego-defense mechanisms, especially if it is stated publicly. Perhaps the only time that such a statement will not cause problems is if Jamie values the fact that he is *not* a good group member.

Normally, negatively oriented feedback will force one to defend oneself and, whether we like it or not, can lead to latent hostility that may surface in the future. To avoid these consequences, feedback should be presented descriptively, non-judgmentally, and as your reaction. Examples:

Poor: "Jamie, you are not cooperating."

Better: "You did not seem to listen to what the others were saying."

Poor: "This group does not work well together."

"You two don't care about this group."

Better: "It seems to me that this group is having difficulty deciding what information is important enough to include in the presentation."

"I get the feeling you aren't interested in what we are doing because neither of you have said anything."

Timing   Feedback is usually most useful immediately after the given behavior has taken place. Under certain circumstances, however, you may need to delay feedback until you can deal with the student on an individual basis. For example, if Jamie (from our earlier example) or some other student is upset about something—a fight with his sister, the death of a grandparent, or almost any of a thousand other things—it obviously may not be the time to criticize his willingness to cooperate; he's got more important things on his mind. Likewise, if you are upset about something, the form of your feedback may serve your needs but not the student's. For example, a sharp "Jamie, you should go along with the majority" may give you a chance to vent your feelings, but it could compound Jamie's problem.

Clarity   From time to time, it may be necessary to determine if students are receiving the same message that you are sending. At times, for example, a student may interpret a teacher's description of a group problem as if it were his or her fault (when it is indeed a group problem). To determine that the communication is clear, the teacher can simply ask the receiver to rephrase the feedback.

Feedback that exhibits the characteristics we have identified here is appropriate for both small-group work and handling discipline problems (see, e.g., Schmidt and Friedman, 1987). In other words, a statement such as "Jamie, stop misbehaving" might be more effective if it were phrased "Jamie, your persistent talking is bothering me and the people around you. Please stop." The rephrased statement identifies (1) the specific behavior in question, (2) the effects that behavior is producing in others, and (3) an appropriate course of action ("stop talking") that can eliminate the problem. Such a statement is specific, descriptive, clear, and delivered with appropriate timing—all elements of effective feedback.

PROCESS OBSERVATION: THE GROUP THAT STUDIES ITSELF

Groups almost always study something—that's why most groups are created. Almost never do groups study themselves; that is, almost never does a group look at how it is operating as a group. At one time or another, all of us have been in groups that seemed to get nowhere—fast—and we have been vaguely aware that something was amiss. Seldom was that problem regarded as a legitimate matter for the group to consider, however. Most groups seem to get so involved in *what* they are considering—in the content they are dealing with—that *how* they are operating often gets lost in the shuffle. Indeed, it takes considerable conscious effort to divorce oneself from the content of a group's discussion in order to take note of the group's functioning, but that is what is required to observe the group process.

The concern for how groups function has led to the development of a technique called *process observation*. Because a group's discussion can become all-involving, an individual—the process observer—is appointed to observe the group process but *not* to participate in the group's deliberations. Rather, the process observer focuses on how the group is functioning, how it is dealing with problems and issues. From time to time, the process observer reports back to the group, which, in turn, provides the group with an opportunity to focus on *how* they are proceeding.

What do process observers look for? First, they note the general sequence of events. When a group first meets, for example, does everyone sit around looking at each other, waiting for someone to take charge? Or do group members begin by voicing their opinions on the issue, without any consideration of how they will operate as a group? And after they have resolved one issue, do they move on to the next or do they keep coming back to reexamine their original decision? The process observer's concern for sequence is broader than, say, the group secretary's, since the observer is concerned with how a group handles the options open to it, not simply with reporting the chronology of group action.

Second, process observers examine how group members handle the things that have been identified as common problems groups are likely to encounter. These include the following:

1. *Terminology*   Terms such as *democracy, evaluation,* etc., often mean different things to different people. Do members of the group clarify their terminology? Do all members of the group use the same words in the same way? What happens when someone tries to clarify terminology?

2. *Respect for the rights and opinions of others*   Does everyone's opinion get a fair hearing?

3. *Willingness to compromise, cooperate*   When the British compromise, they feel they have resolved a problem fairly. When Americans compromise, they often feel as if they've lost the battle—and a little of their integrity with it. Are there members of this group who are not going to compromise on anything? Are there members of this group whose minds are made up and who will "lose" if they must change their position (and "win" if their view becomes accepted)?

4. *Support of others*   Do the various members of this group support other individuals with positions similar to theirs? Or do they let others go out on a limb and fight the same "battle" without support?

5. *Willingness to listen*   Does it appear that the members of this group are more interested in talking than in listening to what others have to say? Are their responses intended to clarify what the previous speaker has said? Do they really *listen* to the opinions of others?

6. *Confront conflict*   When one or more people take conflicting positions, do they avoid dealing with the conflict? Do they operate as if they agreed? Do they bring the issues on which they disagree out into the open for discussion?

Third, the process observer may also identify the various roles or functions that group members play. These could include

Initiating—suggesting new ideas, questions

Clarifying—making the meaning of ideas clear

Elaborating—expanding concepts presented

Integrating—summarizing ideas and helping the group move along

Fact seeking—asking questions to bring out facts

Encouraging—giving encouragement to the other members

Appreciating—modifying one's point of view in terms of what others have said

Self-discipline—keeping one's ideas under control, not talking too much

Affirming—supporting another's contributions or maintaining one's own commitments

When reporting to the group, observers should present their observations as descriptively and nonjudgmentally as possible. This need not be a blow-by-blow account nor a long speech; the observations should focus on a few of the most important events the group may wish to consider further. The following are examples of three considerably different reports for the same group, only one of which really deserves to be called "process observation."

OBSERVER'S REPORTS

(**Context:** The following reports are read aloud after a fifteen-member group has been working for twenty minutes.)

Case No. 1 Report: Paul called the group to order. He told the group what it had to do. Bill asked how much time they had. Sue asked if the group shouldn't break into smaller groups. Paul said no. Dorothy gave three examples of where other attempts had failed. John suggested. . . . Paul said. . . . Then Bill and Paul debated. . . . Sue made another suggestion. . . .

Case No. 2 Report: You should have listened to Paul. You'll never get anything done this way. I saw some things . . . but best I not share them at this time. Sue, your personal needs come through loud and clear . . . if you're not happy at home, don't take it out on the group. If I were you, I would have taken John's suggestion . . . what did you have to lose? Bill, in this particular case, Paul is right. . . .

Case No. 3 Report: Paul spent ten minutes going over the task. During this time four members of the group read the memo given out last week, and two members carried on a side conversation. Paul received little supportive feedback, and I had a feeling that he just kept going with the hope that someone would nod, or something. [Laughter. Paul nods his head affirmatively. John comments that the memo had already spelled out what Paul was repeating.] When Paul finished, there was an extended silence: Bill asked about time, and for fifteen minutes the time factor become a major concern. Sue's suggestion was "denied" by Paul—were there special reasons for keeping the total group together?—and when Bill and Paul had the dialogue, no one else seemed to be attentive. This took five minutes. . . .

The report in Case 1 is simply a recounting of events, with no attempt to indicate how those events influenced the group's functioning. There is no indication, for example, of how Paul's response to Sue's question (about breaking into smaller groups) influenced the group's operation. It could be that his action introduced a dynamic that should be dealt with after the observer's report. In this case, however, the report doesn't provide enough information to determine that.

The report in Case 2 illustrates almost everything a process observer should *not* do—present blatantly evaluative judgments, play "junior psychiatrist," and try to manipulate the group so it will follow the observer's suggestions, etc. It is not the intent of process observation to tell groups what they should or should not do, but rather to provide them with information on what they have done. This distinction is crucial. Once a group receives the information, members can deal with it as they see fit. It is not the observer's role to sit in judgment.

Neither are process observers interested in identifying the underlying causes for events—something that distinguishes process observation from group therapy. The focus of process observation is on the effects of various individuals' contributions to the group, and *not* with the motivation that might underlie those contributions. Thus, the observer's remark about Sue's personal problems at home, even if accurate, is not appropriate data for a process-observation report. If this were a counseling or therapy group, which most school groups definitely are *not*, then the underlying causes for certain behaviors would be appropriate concerns.

The report in Case 3 presents information and raises questions that the group can address, should it see fit. In addition, the contrast between the reports in Cases 2 and 3 should be vivid enough to illustrate the difference between observational data and personal judgments. Personal judgment is so inappropriately in evidence in Case 2, whereas observational data are almost completely lacking in Case 1.

We are not suggesting that elementary children need to be trained as process observers, although some, at the intermediate and middle school levels especially, can become quite adept at it. What we are suggesting is that you will need to become fairly proficient at process observing yourself to be able to diagnose the problems that groups in your class encounter. We are suggesting further that the kinds of process problems that groups encounter should also be legitimate topics for them to consider in addition to the content they are addressing. Indeed, if Jamie, to return to an earlier example, does not cooperate or proves to be a group "blocker," this information may be dealt with by the group. However, *it is critical that it be presented as a difference of opinion between group members,* and not as a problem with Jamie or as Jamie's problem. What the group should consider are alternative ways to deal with the differences of opinion. In fact, the interests of cooperation may be advanced if "win-lose" situations are avoided (where Jamie may view it as losing if he gives in to the Algonquin proposal) and the group decides to study neither Indians nor prairie dogs but rather a third topic such as Eskimos.

In sum, a process observer is

1. A group member who observes and reports elements that seem to influence the group, but who does *not* participate in the group's deliberations

2. A source of information on how the group is proceeding, but *not* a spy, a judge, or a self-proclaimed psychiatrist

3. A hypothesis-poser whose report may stimulate the group to consider *how* it is working, but *not* as a referee, a manipulator, or a "hidden" leader

RECOMMENDED GROUP MANAGEMENT PRACTICES

To summarize this section on group dynamics, we offer the following recommendations:

1. Begin long-term group work only after you feel confident that (a) you can manage several groups operating simultaneously and (b) the individuals in each group are able to work together with minimal problems.

2. You can get some idea of how individuals work together by beginning with clearly defined, short-range group assignments.

3. Identify a clearly defined task for each group. In addition, each group should produce some kind of product (a report, a display, etc.) that they can share upon completing their task. However, it may be necessary to remind the groups to focus on their tasks, not the final product (lest you duplicate the TV-show production we described earlier).

4. Present common group tasks on a large-group basis. Presenting tasks to each group separately may invite problems for the group that have nothing to do until you get around to them.

5. Consider alternative ways in which groups can present the results of their efforts—murals, skits, plays, charts, pictures, film, etc. Long, dull reports leave a lot to be desired. However, be certain that the mechanics of the presentation do not overwhelm the report itself and turn legitimate inquiry into mere activity.

6. Make it clear that both group-process and content-related (but not interpersonal) problems are "fair game" for consideration by small groups or the class as a whole, and allow time accordingly. But obviously, direct and immediate intervention is recommended *before* a group begins to flounder.

7. Establish reasonable deadlines; you can always extend them if necessary. Without deadlines, groups working on even the simplest of tasks have been known to drag on forever. Similarly, have something prepared for those groups that finish early.

8. Decide how you plan to evaluate group work before you begin, and then make this information known to your students. If you plan to grade their reports or presentations, tell them the criteria you intend to use. You can be assured they will listen intently.

MANAGING BEHAVIOR—A PERSPECTIVE ON DISCIPLINE

Thus far in this chapter, we have examined elements that can influence the dynamics of working with small groups in your classroom. These elements, such as the feedback you provide to students or small groups, are but one aspect of managing behavior in the larger, more generic, classroom management sense of the expression. Many of the elements that go into effective classroom management are beyond our scope here—things like establishing a record-keeping system or a classroom schedule. Our purpose in this section is to look at some of the other elements from the social and behavioral sciences that may prove helpful as you go about managing your classroom.

Consider the following dialogue:

Novice: I'm worried about discipline. What do I do?

Expert: Stop worrying about it. Otherwise it's likely to become a self-fulfilling prophecy and you *will* have the problems you are worrying about. The basic rule is that you must be friendly, firm, and confident. You have to radiate confidence so the children know who is in charge.

Novice: But I'm *not* confident . . . not confident at all!

Expert: Then you had better act as if you are. If you seem unsure of yourself, you'll probably be in for trouble.

Novice: Won't the children see through it? Most children are very perceptive . . . won't they be able to tell that I'm just acting?

The novice teacher has raised a good point, even though there is nothing inaccurate about the expert's advice. Part of the problem here is that by providing such general responses, the expert has violated the guidelines for effective feedback that we noted earlier. It would probably be more helpful if the expert responded something like this:

"The confidence you reflect is probably proportional to the security you have in knowing precisely what you intend to say and do, and in knowing exactly what you are going to ask students to do. In other words, if you know that one of the first things you plan to have your students do is write one of those time-worn essays on 'What I did during my summer vacation,' and if you've decided in advance on the general form you want their papers to follow, you can anticipate the kinds of questions that are bound to come up. You know the kind—'Do I have to do it in ink?' 'How long is it s'posed to be?' and so forth. Having done that kind of preplanning, you'll be able to establish the students' task and answer their questions confidently—without acting. And although this may not alleviate your long-run worry, it should meet your immediate problem."

The nature of expert advice notwithstanding, consider that the findings from the social and behavioral science disciplines may permit you to anticipate the ways in which individuals—in this case, your students—are likely to respond to situations that invariably arise in any classroom. Because of this, we are suggesting that some elements of classroom management can be viewed as a kind of applied social science.

DISCIPLINE AND RESPONSIBILITY

Discipline is traditionally seen as something that teachers establish and/or impose on students. In other words, discipline can be an *external* control system imposed on students by a higher authority, usually the teacher. Realistically, findings from the social and behavioral sciences suggest that the typical response to externally imposed control systems—regardless of whom they are imposed by—often takes the form of that well-known game called "beating the system." The nature of that game, when cast as a generalization, becomes: *for almost every system of control, human beings can (and will) develop even more effective systems of evasion.* As is true of most generalizations, you can't be guaranteed that evasion will occur, but we challenge you to find more than one or two events throughout history in which this principle was not operational. Should your discipline ever break down, as almost everyone's can on occasion, the evasion systems will have "won" once again. When this happens, the question that needs to be asked is "What are they evading?" In some cases, it may simply be "more work," which, unfortunately, is probably antithetical to your overall objective as a teacher.

As we see it, a primary objective of classroom management is to replace external control systems with an *internal* control system, usually called self-discipline (on your students' part), which is roughly equivalent to what is often called *responsibility.* Of course there's no denying that internal control systems can be evaded too, perhaps more easily than externally imposed ones: that's something we all have to deal with. But when it comes to helping children accept responsibility for their actions, the goal can often be achieved by your consistent and often implicitly conveyed expectation that your students can and will accept such responsibility. Likewise, if you expect students to misbehave, they are likely to fulfill your expectation.

Preaching about discipline and responsibility (or the lack of it) isn't apt to be especially effective, we've found, unless your actions consistently reflect your expectations. Further, the ultimate goal of classroom management is to develop a situation where external control systems step in *only* when internal control systems fail. In other words, it is not a case of one or the other, but a matter of balancing the two.

BEHAVIOR AS AN OBJECT OF STUDY

Teachers typically think of discipline as the means for maintaining a safe learning environment, controlling disruptive behavior, and teaching students how to conduct themselves in group settings. Although these views are wholly accurate, suppose we were to view discipline in a different way. Consider that the purpose of discipline is to help students better understand:

1. the reasons for their own behavior
2. how their behavior (and the behavior of everyone else for that matter) is a kind of transaction between the individual and the environment
3. how to manage their own immediate needs within a group context
4. how they influence and are influenced by others
5. how to develop empathy for others and to assume at least partial responsibility for the behavior of others

Helping students achieve these understandings is not something one accomplishes in a week, a semester, or even a year. Indeed, there are times we suspect when all of us—even as adults—may be a little fuzzy about our motives for acting as we do or about how we influence others—as noted in items 1 and 4 above. In other words, helping children develop such understandings is a goal to build toward.

When incorporating behavior as an object of study, a teacher must avoid focusing on any individual student's motives, intent, and especially any student's personal predispositions. To become involved in such matters would force teachers to play the role of counselor—a role you may sometimes find yourself playing whether you want to or not. Rather than focusing on individual student's motives, teachers should stress generalized concepts from the social and behavioral sciences that relate to human behavior in general, and that can be transferred to classroom settings. In other words, the intent here is to use social studies content as a way to help students better understand—and possibly change—their behavior.

Opportunities to employ this kind of descriptive (nonpsychoanalytic) approach are illustrated in the following examples.

1. When studying a unit in which the concept of change is involved, one of the key concepts might be *A change in one thing may bring about a number of other changes*. Although the unit vehicle might initially involve, say, the Revolutionary War, the Constitution, or an invention, the students *could* be asked to trace the consequences of a change that took place in the classroom or school. Ultimately, students might find themselves working on the following related generalizations:
   a. Solving one problem often creates other new and unexpected problems.
   b. People who have the most to lose from a change will often find ways of resisting it.

2. When studying historical content, such as the Lewis and Clark expedition (which, on the surface, doesn't appear to be related to behavioral science concepts), an alert teacher could use President Jefferson's orders to the explorers to develop the following concepts:

   a. People in all cultures judge what other people do. When people judge, they often measure others against what they, themselves, are like and believe.

   b. Judging others and being judged ourselves may influence what we think and how we behave.

   c. If judging is important to both the judge and the individuals being judged, then the evidence one uses as a basis for judging becomes important.

   d. Facts don't speak for themselves; usually people interpret the facts.

   Students can involve themselves with the same types of study that Lewis and Clark used in studying Native Americans. For example, how are students judged when in school and in the classroom? By teachers? By fellow students? On what basis? How do the different types of judging and judgments influence behavior in the classroom? What kinds of evidence are used when one judges another person?

3. One of the most obvious ways to incorporate discipline into an ongoing social studies program is to approach it through the study of the manipulation of people, especially since that's what many acting-out behaviors are intended to do—manipulate the behavior of others. We accidentally got into such a study with our own elementary students when we had occasion to describe what in psychology would be called *ego defense mechanisms*. Although our students weren't familiar with the term *ego,* they certainly recognized many defensive behaviors (displacement, projection, etc.). We had learned during our first year of teaching that teachers seldom pass up opportunities to investigate areas in which their students demonstrate abnormally high interest (with some taboo areas excluded, of course). As a result, we soon found ourselves involved in what grew to be a three-week unit on "Protecting Oneself and Dealing with Others." Incidentally, since we didn't have prepared materials (or time to purchase any), we used what resources we had available; we rewrote the section from our college-level Introduction to Psychology text. Terminology wasn't a problem in this instance, because most students were already familiar with the behaviors associated with defending one's ego.

Classroom meetings also provide a legitimate vehicle for bringing discipline problems to the surface and making them an object of study, especially if you happen to be teaching something far removed from the specific discipline problems you may be encountering in your own class. In other words, although you can bring out the behavioral flavor of almost any social studies topic, sometimes it isn't all that easy or relevant. The classroom meeting serves other purposes too, however, and these are described in the next section.

CLASSROOM MEETINGS

The following describes a classroom-meeting strategy devised by Dr. William Glasser, a psychiatrist and author. (It is further elaborated in his book *Schools Without Failure.*)

SCENARIO

It's 11:00 A.M. and the students have drawn their chairs into a circle. For the next thirty to forty-five minutes (or until lunch), this group will hold its daily class meeting. It is a time when the curriculum and predetermined objectives are set aside so that students and teacher can engage in an honest, open, freewheeling discussion of the problems (personal, behavioral, or academic) that concern them. Before beginning, the teacher makes sure to sit in a different place from yesterday (so as not to show favoritism). The teacher may also discreetly make some seating adjustments, such as separating two boys who are prone to nudge each other and carry on their own conversation.

Some days the teacher introduces a topic or question, some days a student will do the introducing, and some days the class will pick up on a topic left over from a previous meeting.

What topics might a class meeting consider? Here are a few:

Are children people?

Does everyone have to like everyone?

If you are really afraid of something, what should you do about it?

If your little brother or sister got hurt while you were taking care of him/her, what would you do?

Why do people die?

Do students really have any rights?

What does freedom mean?

What does it mean to be responsible?

What makes you someone special?

Of course, class meetings as such are hardly innovations in elementary schools. Seldom have those we've seen reflected the characteristics of a class meeting à la Glasser, however, and almost never were they concerned with the kinds of topics noted above. Rather, they tended to be ritualistic affairs, sometimes conducted by class officers who, though they had certain jobs to perform, never had any real power or authority.

The classroom meeting is an opportunity for children to engage in problem exploration and group problem solving. As Glasser (1969, pp. 122–23) states:

When children enter kindergarten, they should discover that each class is a working, problem-solving unit and that each student has both in-

Whether the topic at hand has been introduced by the teacher or by the students themselves, a classroom meeting can provide an opportunity for children to engage in problem exploration and group problem solving. (© *Susan Lapides 1984*)

dividual and group responsibilities. Responsibility for learning and for behaving so that learning is fostered and shared among the entire class. By discussing group and individual problems, the students and teacher can usually solve their problems within the classroom. If children learn to participate in a problem-solving group when they enter school and continue to do so with a variety of teachers throughout the six years of elementary school, they learn that the world is not a mysterious and sometimes hostile and frightening place where they have little control over what happens to them. They learn rather that although the world may be difficult and that it may at times appear hostile and mysterious, they can use their brains individually and as a group *to solve the problems of living in their school world.*

Assuming that you would be willing to consider conducting a classroom meeting as a part of teaching, there are several things to keep in mind. These include the following.

Guidelines for Classroom Meetings

1. Arrange the seating in a large circle. Although moving chairs may be a bit cumbersome, it is essential that everyone be able to see everyone else. Being forced to look at the back of someone else's head (as you would in rows) is not conducive to good group interaction.

2. Meet regularly—at least once a week or even daily if possible—but keep the meetings short. As a general rule, twenty-minute meetings may be a maximum for primary-grade children, but this can be expanded to forty-five minutes for intermediate children.

3. Be as nonjudgmental as humanly possible—verbally and nonverbally—especially in the first few meetings. Remember that you are trying to establish an open, sharing climate.

4. Accept occasional bad grammar and poor usage without correction. To do otherwise may halt future contributions from children who have difficulty expressing themselves. At the other extreme, for children who talk on forever, it may be necessary to interrupt and suggest that they hear from someone else for a while. If you assure the talker that you'll come back to him or her, and then do come back, it should not be interpreted as a put-down.

5. Be open to all legitimate topics. Primary-age children especially may introduce very personal topics, some of which might ordinarily be considered private. In such cases, the other children's responses should be considered before changing the subject, since it may be only you—the adult—who is anxious. On the other hand, if the discussion moves in a direction that might unduly invade the child's privacy (or that of the child's family), you may wish to shift the discussion focus accordingly.

   Older children may be suspicious of your motives for initiating class meetings, and may intentionally introduce risque topics—sex, etc.—to test the ground rules. If you are unwilling to consider, honestly, problems that are real to students, then you probably ought not to be conducting a class meeting to start with. But if you suspect that you are being "tested," you may wish to (a) say nothing until other student responses have attested to the legitimacy of the problem, (b) introduce a topic you would like to discuss, or (c) respond honestly that you think you are being "tested," and then wonder aloud what it is that makes some subjects (topics) "good" and some "bad." If you suspect that you are being manipulated by students, you may wish to introduce "people manipulation" as a topic to consider at the next class meeting.

Good classroom meetings have the potential to offer students an opportunity for genuine involvement within settings where most things—like their choice of curriculums or teachers—are beyond their control. Classroom meetings are also a mechanism through which students can develop a sense of responsibility—for their own actions and for the actions of the group as a whole. It is perhaps the latter dimension—responsibility—that can help children function successfully in their world, and ours.

SUMMARY

In this chapter we have focused on basic considerations and strategies related to managing successful small-group instruction, and on using findings from the social and behavioral sciences as a way to help students develop self-discipline and responsibility. You should find the criteria for teacher feedback helpful whether you are dealing with a group or an individual. Process observation—the strategy for observing the processes that a group uses to deal with content—can also provide remarkable insight into a group's functioning. Classroom meetings, as described by William Glasser, provide opportunities for students to deal with problems that concern them.

In the next chapter we consider group-based teaching activities. As your students engage in dramatic play, role playing, simulations, or other expressive and enactive experiences, you should have plenty of opportunities to apply the small-group management strategies we have considered in this chapter.

SUGGESTED ACTIVITIES

1. Process-observe a group that is working on any of the decision-making activities included in this book: "Five Corners, U.S.A.," etc. Provide feedback that follows the guidelines suggested in this chapter.

2. In a small group, address the question of whether or not a child's participation in group activities should be part of his or her grade. In other words, should group work "count"? If you think it should, identify clear guidelines for incorporating group work in a grading procedure. If you think it should not, indicate why.

3. While engaged in group work, many teachers find themselves confronted with an interminable line of students waiting to talk with them. How would you account for this?

REFERENCES

Berelson, Bernard, and Gary A. Steiner. 1964. *Human Behavior: An Inventory of Scientific Findings*. New York: Harcourt, Brace, and World.

Biehler, Robert F. 1974. *Psychology Applied to Teaching*. 2nd ed. Boston: Houghton Mifflin.

Glasser, William. 1969. *Schools Without Failure*. New York: Random House.

IDEA. 1971. *Learning in the Small Group*. Dayton, Ohio: Institute for Development of Educational Activities.

Northway, M. L. 1940. "A Method for Depicting Social Relationships Obtained by Sociometric Testing." *Sociometry*, 3, 144–50.

Schmidt, Fran, and Alice Friedman. 1987. "Strategies for Resolving Classroom Conflicts." *Learning 87,* 15 (February), 40–42.

Thelen, Herbert A. 1960. *Education and the Human Quest.* New York: Harper.

SUGGESTED READING

Richard A. Schmuck and Patricia A. Schmuck. 1983. *Group Processes in the Classroom.* 4th ed. Dubuque, Iowa: William C. Brown Publishers. This book provides a thorough, scholarly look at group processes, but there is still plenty of material for application.

CHAPTER 13

Managing Group-based Activities

"Youngsters who have spent four years in straight rows with their noses stuck in books they couldn't read, do not automatically take to group responsibilities or open-ended discussion."   John R. Lee

KEY QUESTIONS

☐ What is dramatic play?

☐ Why involve students in role playing?

☐ What are simulations and how do they differ from games?

☐ How does one modify an existing group-based activity?

KEY IDEAS

☐ Most group-based activities are intended to bring reality, albeit simplified, into the classroom.

☐ Group-based activities provide children with a common experience, which can then be analyzed.

☐ Almost every group-based activity can be modified or adapted to fit certain teaching objectives.

☐ The analysis and evaluation that follow a group-based activity are as important as the activity itself.

INTRODUCTION: The Empty-Chair Technique

Context: **An intermediate-level class has been studying Abraham Lincoln and his involvement in the Civil War. On this occasion, the teacher has placed an armchair in the front of the classroom facing the class.**

Teacher: Let's pretend that this chair is Abraham Lincoln [touching the chair with empathy]. He is a tall, bearded man with many interests and lots of problems. How might he be dressed?

Children: . . . [Fill in how you think children might respond].

Teacher: What do you think he is like? How might he be feeling?

Children: . . .

Teacher: Well, let's pretend that Jefferson Davis has just walked into the room. He has heard that Mr. Lincoln, here [pointing to the chair], is going to free the slaves. Does anyone want to be Mr. Davis? Okay, Gerry, you be Jefferson Davis. I'll play Mr. Lincoln's part.

Allison: . . .

Teacher: Okay, Allison. You can be Mr. Lincoln.

Allison: . . .

Gerry: . . .

Context: A primary classroom in which the children have been studying community helpers.

Teacher: Let's pretend this chair is a police officer. How might he be dressed?

Children: . . .

Teacher: What kind of person [moving toward the chair] should this police officer be? What might he be like?

Children: . . .

Teacher: Okay. Now let's put our officer at the corner of Main and First [or two streets the children are familiar with] directing traffic. He sees a young child [about the age of the children in the class] running out of a store with three candy bars clutched in his hand. Close behind him is the store owner, yelling "Stop that boy!"
    What do you think the police officer might be thinking?

Children: . . .

Teacher: How do you think he might be feeling at that moment?

Children: . . .

Teacher: Does anyone want to play the police officer's role? . . . Johnny?

Johnny: . . .

Teacher: Okay, Johnny, you can be the boy. And Debbie, you can be the store owner. I'll be the officer.

We have just illustrated the introductory moments of two role-playing episodes that use the "auxiliary-chair technique" developed by Rosemary Lippit (1958). As indicated, a chair is placed at the front of the classroom, assigned human characteristics, and then the children interact with it as they might interact with a person who has those characteristics.

The empty-chair technique focuses the children's attention on the chair, not on the person playing the character in the chair. This protects the "player" from the psychological stress sometimes associated with drama-oriented activities. It also avoids a problem common to more typical role-playing episodes; when, for example, a girl plays what may be perceived as a male role, students' attention is drawn away from the episode itself.

Not illustrated in our two examples is the post-role-playing discussion, analysis, and evaluation of what took place. In the Lincoln episode, the activity would not end with the enactment of the Jefferson Davis–Lincoln discussion. It would continue with a discussion of the portrayal and a consideration of how the "players" felt at various points in the enactment; it may even include one or more reenactments involving different players and revised roles. Without this kind of follow-up, role playing is not complete.

The purpose of role playing and the other group-based instructional activities that we consider in this chapter is to recreate reality—or at least a slice of reality—in the classroom. Once that reality has been established, the children can then examine, analyze, and hopefully get a handle on the "real" reality they will face outside the classroom.

The activities for recreating reality range from the simple to the complex. We begin with dramatic play, move to a variety of role-playing activities, and then consider games and simulations. Finally, we consider expressive and enactive experiences, activities through which children express themselves (through drama, etc.) or within which students construct or build things (models, Oriental meals, etc.).

When we distinguish among the various group-based activities in this chapter, we do so to help you decide which of these activities might be most suitable for the instructional outcomes you have in mind. Under no circumstances are we suggesting that the structural differences in the activities be taught to children. In using any of these activities with children, the focus should be on the goals and objectives they are intended to serve. In many instances, in fact, it is not necessary to identify to the children which kind of activity (e.g., dramatic play, role playing, etc.) they are engaging in.

DRAMATIC PLAY

Dramatic play involves the spontaneous acting out of real-life situations. It can focus on ships in a harbor, pioneers moving westward in the 1800s, or almost any other situation you can think of.

Dramatic play differs from the random play children engage in daily in that it is intentional; it is designed to lead to something. This is illustrated in the following Model Student Activity, which is a description of a dramatic-play activity dealing with ships and ports.

MODEL STUDENT ACTIVITY

Dramatic Play

ARRANGING THE ENVIRONMENT

On a Friday afternoon, you have the class strip the bulletin boards, put away all old displays, and take all used books back to the library. The class leaves for home. You are about to create an arranged room environment.

Everything in this new environment will have some relationship to ships and ports. One bulletin board is filled with pictures of ships. Underneath goes a strip of tagboard on which you have printed "What do these ships carry?"

Another, but smaller, bulletin board is covered with a chart showing signal flags. Across the bottom of the chart hang four or five flags you have made from scraps of cloth. On a small table below the flags are small heaps of scrap cloth.

You cover the library table with books. In each are two or three colored markers, each inserted at a colorful picture or an exciting passage.

You set a large fish tank on the sink counter and fill it with water. You toss in a small wooden ship. Next to it you leave two metal ships (one must be large enough so that its displacement of water can be observed). You add a sign, "Why do metal boats float?" You drop a ruler and grease pencil next to the sign.

In one corner of the room you pin up, just above floor level, 6 feet of paper that will take tempera paint. Cans of paint and brushes sit nearby. Above the paper is an accurate picture of a port. In front of the paper you drop enough scraps of lumber so breakwaters and docks can be built.

Above the science table goes a picture of a lighthouse. On the table goes a set of instructions on how to build a lighthouse. Next to the instructions are batteries, wire, wood, tacks, bulbs—everything needed to build a lighthouse.

You use masking tape to hang a display. It shows men and women at work on ships and around the port. The caption asks, "What are these workers doing?"

You drop some more scraps of wood in the construction corner. Next to them go three small, dull saws, three small hammers, and an assortment of nails. You also leave a small ship that you made.

You put a song of the sea on the record player, slip on your coat, and head for home. The trap has been baited. The quarry is the interest of your pupils.

PLAY, DISCUSSION, AND RESEARCH

On Monday morning your class can't miss the changes in the classroom. When school begins, tell the class they may spend a little time wandering around the room, looking at things, and playing with the objects.

Give them enough time to prowl, but not enough time to satisfy their curiosity. (The interrupted pleasure is sure to be returned to eagerly.) Then ask, "Well, what do you think this is all about?"

"Boats!"

"Sailing!"

"The ocean!"

"Etc.!"

You ask, "What did you see that you liked most?"

"The boats!"

"The lighthouse!"

"The tools!"

"Etc.!"

Pick out from one-third to one-half of the class (depending on the size of the class, the amount of free space you have, and the number of toy ships available). Say, "OK, each of you get a ship or boat, and you can play with it."

They play. You watch. The other pupils watch. You circulate among the watchers and ask quiet questions.

"What is Billy doing?"

"Why is Mary running her boat up the wall?"

"How would you do that?"

Then you shift the groups until everyone has had his chance to play with the toy ships. The class has finished its first session of *dramatic play*.

The next step is discussion of what went on during play. You will probably pursue several ideas that occurred to you as you observed the play, but I'll just use one example.

"Billy, why were you and Kathy hitting your ships together?"

"Because. I was sailing along, and she ran into me."

"Why'd you run into his ship, Kathy?"

"Because he was in my way. He should have let me by. He's a boy and I'm a girl, and boys are supposed to be polite to girls."

"What happens if two ships smash into each other out in the ocean?"

"They sink."

"The policeman comes out in a rowboat and gives them a ticket."

"What policeman?"

"Oh, you know. It was a joke."

"Do ships smash into each other on the ocean?"

"Sure, and some of them smash into ice cubes . . . uh, icebergers and sink."

"Do all the ships that are on the ocean smash into each other all the time?"

"No."

"Why not?"

"I dunno."

"How can you find out?"

"Look it up."

"Where?"

"In the books."

"How else?"

"Ask somebody."

"Who?"

"My dad."

"A sailor."

"A sixth grader."

"The principal. He thinks he knows everything."

"OK. Who wants to work with Billy and Kathy on this question?"

And so it goes. A small research group is formed. You move on to another mistake or question or problem.

"Now, about that policeman in a rowboat. Do you really believe . . .?"

And so on.

When children play, they reflect what they know. They do some things correctly, and they make some mistakes. The mistakes are used to stimulate discussion that leads to questions that can be researched.

You do *not* say, "Billy, you are doing that wrong. Someone show him the right way." What you want is for the pupil to *find* the right way by his own (or his research group's) efforts.

You keep at these questions until everyone has elected a research group. The next day, you begin the period by asking each group to get together. Then you review, with each group, what they are trying to find out. Don't tell them! Ask them.

"Everybody set? OK, how much time do you want?"

And off they go, some to the library table, some to the library. They will waste time this first time. Why not? They have to become acquainted with many new books. They have to find what will be useful. They skim and finger and look at pictures. You visit each group, praising and prodding. Research takes time. And you must be willing to let them take time.

Your responsibility is to be certain that they can find out. You have to be sure the answers are in materials available to them. Why else did you do your research and write that resource unit?

Of course, someone always comes up with a question you didn't, and couldn't, anticipate. Then you have to dig out the answer. If third graders can't read your source, then you rewrite the source as simply as you can. I don't think I ever taught a unit of any kind where I didn't have to do some rewriting for the class.

Then, after one day or three days—however long it takes to find answers or partial answers—each group makes its report. When all are armed with this new knowledge, you go back to a play session.

Let's review for a moment. You create an environment. The class explores that environment. You let the class play with the ships. You observe the mistakes in the play. The class discusses the mistakes. Research groups are formed. Research takes place. The results of research are reported. The class plays again.

Source: Reprinted with permission of the The Free Press, a Division of Macmillan, Inc. from TEACHING SOCIAL STUDIES IN THE ELEMENTARY SCHOOL by John R. Lee. Copyright © 1974 by John R. Lee.

Lee has illustrated how dramatic play can be used as an opportunity (or stimulus) for raising questions children can then research. Of course, at lower grade levels, children's reading and research skills may be such that you will need to provide some of the answers for them. In fact, in some instances it may be necessary for you to raise *and* answer some of the key questions associated with dramatic-play activities. Indeed, one of the most difficult aspects of conducting dramatic-play activities—or almost any group-based inquiry activity, for that matter—is getting students to the point at which *they* ask the questions.

With dramatic play, you need to be careful that whatever you are trying to represent in your classroom does not teach incorrect or distorted ideas. Historical reenactments, for example, are particularly susceptible to distortion. Recreating a 1849 westward journey in a covered wagon, for example, is hardly likely to sensitize children to the problems encountered by pioneers, especially since most classrooms are poor duplicates of the rugged terrain the pioneers had to cross. In this instance, instead of a dramatic-play activity, which could be of questionable value unless handled very carefully, why not consider a decision-making activity? For example, you could provide small groups with topographic maps of a small area for one of the trails West—the Oregon Trail, the Santa Fe trail, etc.—and then ask them to plot the best route to follow. Indeed, students may find that the most commonly agreed upon route follows an existing road, and in that discovery they gain some insight about how early roads were located.

The amount of preparation and detail that went into the episode that Lee described should indicate that dramatic play does not happen spontaneously. It takes extensive preplanning and, often, quite a lot of materials. In summary, well-planned dramatic play can have the following outcomes:

Stimulate questions that children can then research

Provide a means for children to use and understand concepts and symbols

Reveal the natural behavior of children

Reveal needs that can be addressed in subsequent instruction

Stimulate different kinds of expressive activities (paintings, models, etc.)

Reveal new information and understandings the children have gained

ROLE PLAYING

In dramatic play, one child might play a father or mother, another child might play a store owner, someone else might play a ship's captain or an airline pilot, and so forth. Because children may assume different roles in dramatic-play experiences (although they are not required to do so), the distinction between dramatic play and formal role playing may seem a little fuzzy.

The difference between dramatic play and role playing lies in three factors: (1) *intent,* (2) the amount of teacher *structuring*—which can range from loosely

Role playing does not involve a predetermined script; its primary purpose is to provide students with opportunities to experience, analyze, and resolve a problem situation. (© *Mimi Forsyth/Monkmeyer Press Photo Service*)

organized (unstructured) to more tightly controlled (structured), and (3) the extent of *student involvement*. In dramatic play, the intent is to recreate an experience so that as the children play their roles they get a vicarious feel for that experience, and hopefully raise questions that lead to further research and investigation. In role playing, on the other hand, the intent is to provide children with opportunities to experience *and analyze a problem situation*. There is not much of a problematic nature associated with ships in a harbor, for example, as opposed to, say, a situation in which a pioneer family is moving West and, because of space restrictions, must decide between taking the family Bible or a set of heirloom china. Of course, the Bible-china question *might* arise in the course of dramatic play (that involved pioneers moving westward), but as a rule, role-playing situations are more narrowly defined. To this extent, role playing is somewhat more structured and teacher-directed than dramatic play.

In role playing, a small group of students reenacts a human situation while the rest of the class acts as observers. This is the third difference between role playing and dramatic play; in dramatic play there is usually no audience—everyone is involved in the "play." How a role-playing group resolves a problem—whether it be a Bible-china kind of question, the policeman-and-the-boy problem we noted earlier, or the recreation of a dispute that actually took place between individuals in the class—becomes the focus for discussion and analysis after the enactment is completed. However, unlike plays in which the actors follow a script, role-playing situations are by definition open-ended. The role players themselves must determine how the situation will be resolved.

In *Role Playing in the Curriculum,* Shaftel and Shaftel (1982) recommend the following procedure for handling role-playing activities:

1. **"Warming up" the group (problem confrontation)**
2. **Selecting the participants (the role players)**
3. **Preparing the audience to participate as observers**
4. **Setting the stage**
5. **Role playing (an enactment)**
6. **Discussing the enactment**
7. **Further enactment (replaying revised roles, suggested next steps, exploring alternative possibilities)**
8. **Further discussion (which may be followed by more enactments)**
9. **Sharing experiences (relating the role playing to one's life experiences), which may result in generalizing (p. 557)**

To help teachers introduce role-playing activities in their classrooms, Fannie and George Shaftel have developed a program that uses large photographs of problem situations. Students use the photographs as a basis for their role playing and discussion. The program is organized by levels and is intended primarily for kindergarten through fourth grade, but could be used at higher grade levels as well. A sample photograph and a page from the accompanying teacher's guide are presented in the following Model Student Activity.

MODEL STUDENT ACTIVITY

"People in Action"—Role Playing

THE PHOTOGRAPH
A mother comes home from work to find her living room in shambles, with children playing.

IDEAS TO BE DEVELOPED
Children carry responsibilities in the family, especially when their mother must work. A child's responsibilities must be suited to his age and maturity.

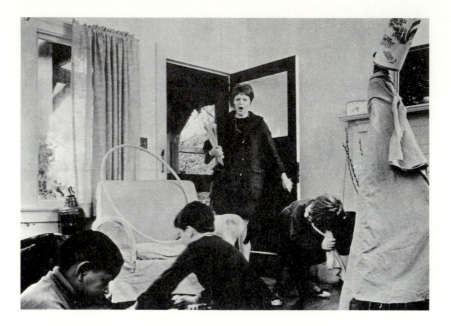

GUIDELINES FOR ROLE PLAYING AND DISCUSSION—
A PROBLEM-SOLVING LESSON: "OH, MY!"

Warm-Up

Teacher: Does your mother ever ask you to "take care of the house" while she's away? What does she mean? (Allow the children to discuss this, and then ask,) Do you ever ask friends to come and play with you at your house? What do you play?

What Is Happening Here?

Teacher (showing the photograph): What is happening in this photograph?

Children: The mother just came home from shopping—Maybe she's been at work—Those boys made a big mess—Maybe she just cleaned the house today!

Teacher: How do you think the mother feels?

Children: She's awful' mad—Somebody's going to get it good!

Invite the children to role-play what happens when the mother arrives home.

Enactment—   The mother angrily orders the visiting children home. She scolds her son furiously and sends him to his room, and she cleans the house in a rage.

Teacher: Well, how does everyone feel now?

Inviting Alternative Solutions

Teacher: Can you think of another way that the mother might handle matters?

Children: Maybe she makes them clean up?—She sends them to play in the yard.

Enactment The mother reminds the boys of their responsibilities and then "matter-of-factly" directs them to clean up, and sends them to play in the yard or other play area.

Source: Shaftel and Shaftel, TEACHER'S GUIDE: PEOPLE IN ACTION, LEVEL B, p. 24. Holt, Rinehart and Winston, 1970. Used by permission.

ROLE PLAYING AND DECISION MAKING

Role playing often plays a part in decision-making activities. Depending on the way you structure the activity, you have the option of emphasizing either the role-playing dimension or the decision-making dimension. The following student activity could be used in either a decision-making or role-playing framework.

MODEL STUDENT ACTIVITY

The Lunch Policy

Provide the following information to students:

A fast-food restaurant (e.g., McDonald's or Burger King) is to open next week across the street from Meridian Elementary School. Some students have requested permission from the principal to eat lunch there. Presently students may eat at home only if they bring a signed permission slip from their parents. The principal has called a meeting with the following people:

A parent

A student

A cafeteria director

A teacher

Tell students that they—as a group—must decide what to do.

PROCEDURE

Role-playing option   Identify individuals to play each of the roles and have them try to arrive at a decision agreeable to everyone. Then have the rest of the class evaluate and discuss both their decision and the procedures they used in arriving at it.

Decision-making option   Divide the class into small groups with each individual taking one of the roles. When all groups have made their decisions, these should be reported and evaluated by the class as a whole.

The format for role-playing and decision-making activities is the same as illustrated in "The Lunch Policy" and the examples presented in Chapter 10. Both methods involve (1) an open-ended problematic situation and (2) roles for the students to play.

In the case of "The Lunch Policy" and other activities like it, you could select either the role-playing or the decision-making option. Several factors might influence that decision. For example, if you think a group could handle this activity in five to ten minutes, you might select either (or both) option. If it might take longer than five to ten minutes or the role-playing enactments might drag, you could lose the observers' attention. In that event, you might select the decision-making option in which all students are involved (in small groups) in the same situation simultaneously.

UNSTRUCTURED ROLE PLAYING

In all types of role playing, students must deal with some kind of problematic situation. Teachers must also identify the role players and be certain that everyone understands the situation. In other words, there is a certain amount of teacher direction in all role-playing activities. There is also a certain amount of spontaneity.

Virtually all of the role-playing examples presented thus far are "unstructured." This means that the role players are allowed to define their roles without specific teacher direction. In "The Lunch Policy" illustration, for example, the teacher may have no idea how the situation will be resolved or whether the role players will become aware of all the various factors that might influence the decision. In other words, in unstructured role playing, the teacher really cannot be certain that a specific issue (such as safety in crossing the street) will emerge from the role-playing enactment. Of course, the teacher could decide to introduce a neglected issue (such as the safety element) in the follow-up discussion. However, teachers who wish to have certain issues considered in the role-playing enactment have the option of using a more structured role-playing format as described in the next section.

STRUCTURED ROLE PLAYING

The element that distinguishes structured from unstructured role playing is the addition of positions or points of view that one or more of the role players incorporate into their enactments. For example, if you were concerned that students might not know how a cafeteria director might feel about the lunch-policy question, you could structure the activity by adding position statements to the various roles, as illustrated below.

1. The parent wants her children eating well-balanced meals, not hamburgers every day.

2. The student feels the school should not dictate his eating habits.

3. The cafeteria director needs a full cafeteria to meet operating expenses, and must know a week in advance the number of students who will be eating in the cafeteria.

4. The teacher doesn't want to be bothered with permission slips and checking up on where kids eat, and feels it is up to the parents and children to decide where lunch will be eaten.

The procedures for managing this modified activity are the same as for the original. The format, however, is changed to reflect the new dimension. It involves

1. An open-ended problematic situation.

2. Roles for the individuals involved.

3. Position statements for each role player.

You are free, of course, to add other roles and/or positions. Or you might use a mixture of each, specifying positions for some roles while leaving others open so that players can operate according to their own convictions. No one way is better than another; it all depends on what you wish to accomplish. If you wish to heighten the sense of drama and add an element of mystery, you can distribute the role positions on separate slips of paper so that, initially, only the role players know who they are. These "secret" positions soon become apparent in the group interaction. This approach reduces spontaneity, but it also tends to heighten interest at the outset of role playing.

Handling Conflict

Should you choose to use activities with conflicting role positions, a note of caution is in order. By doing this you will have intentionally built *conflict* into the activity. Thus, you will need to be prepared to help the group cope with the conflict that is almost guaranteed to occur. In role-playing settings, conflict built into a group activity presents a beautiful opportunity to use process-observation skills. Indeed, a process observer's report could serve as the basis for at least part of the post-role-playing analysis.

Some students are such enthusiastic role players that they sometimes trap themselves in win-lose situations; they get so involved in a position that they take on a "this is my position, and I'll be darned if I'm going to change it or listen to anyone" attitude. To avoid this—at least to the extent that it can be avoided—you would be wise to establish a ground rule to the effect that individuals are free to change their minds (or positions) based on reasonable information. This will not eliminate win-lose situations, but it may reduce them to the extent that they don't interfere unduly.

GROUP INVESTIGATION

There are essentially three ways that group investigations can be conducted: (1) the entire class acts as a research group in which all individuals investigate the same problem simultaneously, (2) individual research groups investigate one aspect or dimension of a class wide problem and then pool their findings, and (3) individual research groups investigate separate problems. The "Detergent Survey" activity presented in Chapter 10 (pages 314–315) is an example of the first approach, and the "Prairie Dog" activity (pages 376–378) is an example of the third approach. The following activity, which is presented in a case-study format, illustrates the second approach to group investigation.

"THE WEARIN' OF THE GREEN"—A CASE STUDY
IN GROUP INVESTIGATION

It was March, a time when the winter months stretch out longer and longer, and when everyone must work at keeping a good mood. It was also the day before St. Patrick's Day.

Ms. Fleury, a fourth-grade teacher, commented to the class that a number of students were likely to wear green clothing the next day. She added that students in the intermediate grades were more likely to wear green than children in the primary grades. Her comment prompted a curious "why" from one student, Stephen. Everyone knew that St. Patrick's Day was coming up and that some students would wear green clothing; Stephen's concern was with why older children were more likely to wear such clothing than children in the lower grades.

The teacher responded by saying that intermediate students were older and more likely to wear green clothing because other students would be wearing green. Stephen suggested that primary children wear the clothes that their mothers lay out for them, and that the mothers would be sure to see that their children wore something green. In other words, there were two competing views; one based on peer pressure and the other based on parental influence.

Ms. Fleury recognized that the question could be resolved by gathering data, and asked the class as a whole to determine how they could find out which one was correct.

The students decided to observe each classroom in the building. Some students would be observers and others would stay in the classroom—the "control room"—to process the results. As the planning progressed, the principal came into the room. She asked how much green someone needed to wear to be counted, and whether it needed to be solid green. The students decided that someone had to have at least a sweater, shirt, blouse, skirt, slacks, scarf, or ribbon to be counted, and that the dominant color had to be green. When everything seemed in place, the observers went to the different classrooms to ask permission to visit that room the next morning. The students agreed in advance to tell the various teachers why they wanted to visit. However, they knew that if they told each class what they were doing, it could change their results.

The next morning, the students observed their assigned classrooms and then gave the data to the student-tabulators. The results were as Ms. Fluery had predicted: more intermediate students wore green than did primary-level students. Ms. Fleury was going to let it go at that, but one student said she thought that there were more intermediate students than primary students. Because of this, there were more intermediate students who *could* wear green, and naturally they would win.

This was something Ms. Fleury had not planned on. The issue involved percentages, which was something the students had not worked with yet. The talliers provided the total number of primary- and intermediate-level students and the numbers at each level who wore green, which Ms. Fleury then used to determine the percentage. The new results: 76 percent of the primary children wore green clothing, compared with 64 percent of the intermediate-level children. Ms. Fleury admitted that she had been wrong and that Stephen's hypothesis seemed to be true.

SIMULATION AND GAMING

Simulations are instructional activities in which elements from the real world are recreated (or simulated) in the classroom. For example, after an experience in which the classroom is turned into a miniature factory to mass-produce valentine cards, which we describe in detail in this section, the children have an opportunity to discuss what it is like to repeat the same task over and over again, as one would on a real assembly line. Likewise, in the computer simulation *Oregon Trail,* the child has an opportunity to experience the tribulations of traveling West in a covered wagon during the nineteenth century. If the children playing *Oregon Trail* fail to plan properly, they may die before reaching their destination—as was true of some real pioneers. Because simulations recreate only a portion of reality, the child's "death" leaves no lasting effects; he or she simply learns from "experience" and tries to do better next time.

Simulations, which often involve considerable role playing and decision making, are a comparatively recent innovation in education. Games, which rarely involve role playing, have been around much longer. We are not suggesting that either simulations or games are widely accepted as learning devices; both have "fun" aspects that make them suspect in some educational circles.

Despite the "fun" elements that are a part of educational games and simulations, students can also learn from playing them. In the simulation *Democracy*, for example, students play the role of legislators seeking reelection. By negotiating for the passage or defeat of legislation in keeping with their constituents' interests, the student legislators may be able to win reelection. But students who do not negotiate well enough to satisfy their constituents' desires may not be reelected.

Students playing *Democracy* simulate a legislature in session, and in doing so learn about factors that can influence the passage or defeat of legislation. In reality, however, the legislative process is so complex that were you to attempt to recreate it in a classroom, your students would undoubtedly have so many things to consider that they would be overwhelmed. About the only place you will find a totally realistic legislative process is in a real legislature, and that, unfortunately, cannot exist very practically in most classrooms. Thus, *Democracy* and all other simulations necessarily simplify whatever real-world equivalent they represent.

Because simulations simplify and focus the reality they deal with, it becomes possible to analyze the situation without a lot of other variables clouding the picture. And so students playing the first stage of *Democracy* have an opportunity to analyze the negotiation phase of the legislative process, without the confounding influence of political parties or other factors. In later stages of the simulation, the legislator's own convictions and the influence of political parties are added so that the simulation more nearly reflects the real legislative process. The players are then faced with the task of reanalyzing the process with the new dimensions added. (*Democracy* was originally developed by James S. Coleman for the 4-H Foundation, and is available from Western Publishing Company, 850 Third Ave., New York, NY 10022.)

To repeat: no simulation completely replicates reality or pretends to. Instead of being a liability, simplification is probably a prime educational asset of simulations; they simplify real situations to the extent that students are better able to see what is taking place.

The real world provides the model on which almost all simulations and many games are based. For example, if you were to drive down the streets of Atlantic City, New Jersey, you would encounter street names such as Baltic Ave., St. James Place, Park Place, and the Boardwalk. You might notice also that the socioeconomic levels of the various neighborhoods roughly parallel the property values on a Monopoly board—or at least they did when Monopoly was developed in the 1920s. That's because the model for Monopoly is based on real estate transactions in Atlantic City, New Jersey. However, to make a game of it, Monopoly developers had to take some liberties with reality. The major change they made involved adding more chance factors than are found in the real world. Consider, for example, that you cannot buy property unless you land on it, and that the property you land on is controlled by the dice. Other chance factors include "Community Chest" and "Chance" cards, "Go to Jail" (without having violated a law), "Luxury Tax," "Income Tax," and the total absence of insurance (except for "Get Out of Jail Free"). All of these make Monopoly fun to play because you never know what will happen next. But, because the chance factor so exceeds reality, you couldn't use Monopoly to teach the principles of real estate investment and development.

Many board games (though not all) are based on realistic models. Chess, for example, is based on the strategies of medieval warfare. Checkers, on the other hand, lacks a clearly identifiable model; it's simply a strategy game. Still other games, like craps and roulette, reflect no reality whatsoever; they are simply a matter of luck.

Most games are actually a kind of contest in which winning is determined by a combination of luck and skill. This includes those old classroom standbys, spelling bees and Twenty Questions, as well as the takeoffs on TV game shows like *Concentration* and *Password*. In games, opponents are pitted against one another, and, depending on luck and skill, someone will emerge victorious. Simulations usually lack the "contest" quality of games; even though simulations have outcomes, they usually lack the clear flavor of winning or losing that is more typical of games. In addition, the chance or luck factor in simulations tends to be lower than in most games. As a result, simulations tend to be more realistic than most games. These and the other characteristics of simulations and games are shown in Table 13.1.

From a child's perspective, most simulations and games offer enjoyable ways to learn something. In our judgment, whatever children learn by using a game or simulation should be the main focus, not the technical distinctions between the two formats (which students probably don't care about anyhow). From a teaching perspective, however, the distinctions are more important, especially if you try your hand at developing either simulations or games.

TABLE 13.1 Differences Between Simulations and Games

Characteristics	Simulations Tend To	Games Tend To
Size	Involve more students, often the entire class	Be limited to fewer players, typically four, seldom more than eight
Length	Be of longer duration (more than one period)	Be of shorter duration (one period or less)
Chance	More realistically reflect the real world	Contain a "chance" factor that exceeds reality
Result	Produce an outcome usually without winners or losers	Have defined winners and losers
Preparation and materials	Require considerable advance preparation and materials	Require minimal preparation and materials

COMPUTER-BASED SIMULATIONS

The real world outside of classrooms is amazingly complex. One asset of computer-based simulations, which are becoming increasingly available, is their ability to reflect more real-world complexities than would be possible through nontechnological means. For example, as pioneers journeyed westward in the last half of the nineteenth century, they encountered one set of conditions and problems as they crossed the plains and other kinds of problems as they crossed the deserts and the mountains. In the *Oregon Trail* simulation that we noted earlier, microcomputers make it possible to replicate some of the conditions that pioneers faced at various points on their journey. Bears do not live in the desert, for example, so the players need not concern themselves with being attacked by bears at that point in their travel. However, once the pioneers reach the mountains, they must beware. Computers are capable of taking information from a player's prior decisions and incorporating that data into the next decision the player must make, often with lightning speed.

Some computer-based simulations provide an excellent opportunity for children to employ map skills. In the simulation *Geography Search* (McGraw-Hill) for example, players must make navigation decisions as they sail to the New World. The computer then provides them with the precise location of their ship. In the simulation *Lemonade Stand* (Minnesota Educational Computer Consortium), players experience the interaction of basic enonomic factors as they attempt to make a profit from their lemonade stand.

Limitations

Lest we create the wrong impression here, be advised that despite some recent increases there are still relatively few computer-based social studies simulations suitable for elementary children, and almost none for primary-level children. The fact that children must be able to read the instructions on the computer screen (monitor) is a limitation, especially for younger students. In some instances, the program may require knowledge that students do not have. For example, we reviewed the simulation *Rails West,* about building the transcontinental railroad. Although we found it interesting, it also required prior knowledge about financial markets (stocks and bonds) that we, as adults, found taxing. Computer-based simulations are available from several sources, which we identify in Chapter 15, but we strongly recommend that you review and test such materials before you buy them.

Most noncomputer-based simulations are designed or can be adapted for an entire class. Computer-based simulations, on the other hand, are usually limited to one or two participants. The length of time it takes for an entire class to experience a particular simulation depends upon the number of computers available, of course, but restrictions on the number of players can sometimes constitute a limitation.

BUILDING SIMULATIONS

Commercially produced simulations and games are available from a variety of sources, such as The Social Studies School Service (10000 Culver City Blvd., Culver City, CA 90232). Some teachers, however, develop their own simulations.

The first step in designing a simulation is deciding what aspect of the real world you are going to simulate. For your first effort, the rule of thumb is to keep it simple. Attempting to simulate the judicial system, for example, will prove overwhelming. However, you could simulate one aspect of the judicial process, such as a jury's deliberation, as a starter. As a rule, processes of almost any kind offer fertile subject matter for simulations.

If you want to try your hand at some simulations, here are a few situations that can be used to generate simulation activities:

1. *Zoning questions.* Should a gas station, liquor store, or high-rise low-income housing be permitted in a residential neighborhood?

2. *Community priorities.* What should a community spend its money on—sewers, parks, playgrounds, more police and fire fighters?

3. *Deciding what is newsworthy.* Put together the front page of a newspaper, given an assortment of articles—news, sports, features, etc.—clipped from a local paper. Which stories should be given prominence? Why?

4. *School-policy questions.* Should recess be abandoned? (Or should children be permitted to go to fast-food restaurants for lunch?)

If some of these sound a bit like decision-making activities, that's because they could be used in that form too. Decision-making and role-playing activities are often integrated into a simulation format.

The following Model Student Activity presents a sample simulation that was developed by a teacher who was interested in teaching the elements of mass production under nineteenth-century factory conditions.

MODEL STUDENT ACTIVITY

The Holiday Card Factory—A Simulation

The entire class will be organized into production areas to produce holiday greeting cards (in this case, for Valentine's Day). To recreate some of the working conditions of the nineteenth century, the room should be darkened somewhat and students asked to stand at their workstations (desks) throughout. Talking unrelated to work is not permitted.

The greeting card consists of a white heart, pierced by a pink arrow, placed on a red circle, all of which is then mounted on a white paper doily. The completed product should resemble the one on the next page.

ORGANIZATION

In general, each phase of the card-making process is divided into drawing, cutting, and inspecting. For example, you will have a team of heart drawers, heart cutters, and a heart inspector. For a class of twenty-six students, you should have the following roles:

Heart department
4 heart drawers
3 heart cutters
1 heart inspector

Circle department
3 circle drawers
2 circle cutters
1 circle inspector

Slit department
(for making the hole where the arrow pierces the heart):
1 slit drawer
1 slit cutter
1 slit inspector

Arrow department
3 arrow drawers
2 arrow cutters
1 arrow inspector

Assembly department
3 assemblers
1 final inspector

(If you have fewer than twenty-six students, you can drop some of the inspectors; if more than twenty-six, add them to the drawers in any department.)

Cluster the desks into five areas. In advance make a sign identifying each area; e.g., heart department. Each student should then make a small sign identifying his or her particular task; e.g., circle cutter. The inspectors are responsible for maintaining quality control and taking the finished products to the assembly area. Provide the following materials and instructions to the appropriate department.

Heart department

Heart drawers

Materials: plain white paper (8½ × 11), pens, rulers

Instructions: "Draw the largest heart you can that will fit into an 8-inch square."

Heart cutters

Materials: scissors

Instructions: "Cut the heart as accurately as you can."

Heart inspectors

Materials: a sample heart (which you have made ahead of time)

Instructions: "Make certain that your hearts closely resemble the sample before taking them to the slit department. If anything is wrong with a heart, give it back to the heart drawers or cutters."

Slit department

Slit drawers

Materials: ruler and pencil

Instructions: "Your job is to locate the 1½-inch slit where the arrow will pierce the heart. Your inspector has a sample heart to show exactly where the slit should be located."

Slit cutters

Materials: scissors

Instructions: "Your job is to cut the 1½-inch slit where the arrow will pierce the heart. Cut as accurately and neatly as you can."

Slit inspector

Materials: sample heart with slit

Instructions: "Make certain that your slitted hearts closely resemble the sample before taking them to the assembly area. If anything is wrong, return it to the slit drawers or the slit cutters."

Circle department

Circle drawers

Materials: red paper, pencils or pens, compasses

Instructions: "Your job is to draw an 8½-inch circle on the red paper. It must be exactly 8½ inches in diameter. The circle inspector has a sample you can see."

Circle cutters

Materials: scissors

Instructions: "Your job is to cut the 8½-inch circle from the red paper. Work as neatly and as accurately as you can."

Circle inspector

Materials: sample red circle

Instructions: "Make certain that your finished circles resemble the sample before taking them to the assembly area. If anything is wrong, return them to the circle drawers or the circle cutters."

Arrow department

Arrow drawers

Materials: pink paper (8½ × 11), rulers, and pencils

Instructions: "Your job is to draw a 7-inch-long pink arrow. Your inspector has a sample you can follow. You should get at least four arrows from each sheet of paper."

Arrow cutters

Materials: scissors

Instructions: "Your job is to cut out the 7-inch pink arrows. Work as neatly and as accurately as you can."

Arrow inspectors

Materials: sample arrow

Instructions: "Make certain that your finished arrows resemble the sample before taking them to the assembly area. If anything is wrong, return the arrows to the arrow drawers or the arrow cutters."

Assembly department

Assemblers

Materials: 9- or 10-inch white paper doilies; paste, fast-drying glue or rubber cement

Instructions: "Your job is to insert the arrow through the slits in the heart, and then glue the heart onto the red circle. The heart and the circle should then be glued onto the doily. Your inspector has a sample you can follow."

Final inspector

Materials: sample completed heart

Instructions: "Your job is to make certain that each finished card resembles the sample. If it does, place it in a pile labeled 'finished'; if not, place it in a pile labeled 'reject.' "

Wages

Remind the students that work is to be done quickly and accurately; time is money! Also, only the inspectors can leave their stations. One candy heart for every ten minutes of cooperation and work.

Do not stop the activity until students have become visibly bored with what they are doing (which, unfortunately, may take longer than you might anticipate).

In the debriefing, consider some of the following questions:

1. How did you like your job?

2. How would you describe what we have done?

3. How would you go about improving conditions in this factory? What would you change?

4. What are some different ways we could use to produce greeting cards like these?

5. If you were the foreman on an assembly line, what kinds of problems do you think you might have?

Variation A useful variation is to have one class (or half the class) use the approach described above, while another class (or the other half of the class) uses a cottage-industry approach. In the latter approach, each student constructs the card by completing all of the different tasks—there is no division of labor.

DEVELOPING BOARD GAMES

Many elements of social studies, especially processes that result in a product—such as the production of milk, bread, steel, etc.—readily lend themselves to a board-game format.

A sample board-game format is illustrated in Figure 13.1. We developed this sample, which we call "The Milk Game," after first identifying the various stages of milk production: the dairy farm, transporting the milk from farm to dairy, the dairy itself, etc. We then outlined segments of the game-board pathway so that it corresponded, in sequence, to the different stages of milk production. Note that our game board uses straight pathways only because they are easy to draw neatly; curved trails would work equally well.

The idea of this and similar board games is that as small groups of students move their tokens around the game board, they will become familiar with the stages in the process—in this case, the process of milk production. It is possible to build much more complex and thought-provoking board games, of course, but for illustrative purposes, we have restricted ourselves to a very simple example.

Once we had our basic game board outlined, we needed to find a way to make the game appealing and fun for students. We accomplished this by first determining how the winner would be decided (the first student to reach "home"). Second, we determined how the movement of tokens would be governed. We decided to use a spinner made from a piece of popsicle stick affixed to the top of a plastic margarine container—although a die or cards (with the number of spaces indicated on them) could work equally well. Third, we decided to add additional interest by using "chance cards" that players would draw when they landed on a square marked with a tiny carton of milk. Note that we could have handled the chance element by marking directly on the squares, but we opted instead for the additional variety that the chance cards provide. To make our game even more realistic, we keyed the chance cards to things that might actually occur in the process of producing milk: "Your farm is struck by a power failure and you must milk the cows by hand—miss one turn," "The milk truck encounters light traffic—move ahead two spaces," etc.

FIGURE 13.1　Sample Board Game

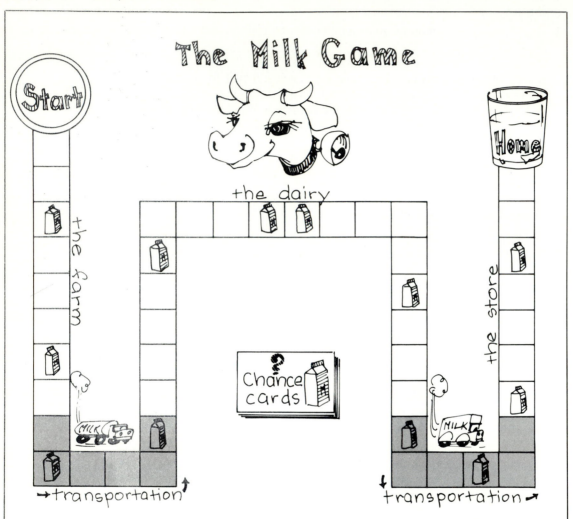

After writing a set of simple rules, we tried "The Milk Game" with students. We found that we had forgotten to indicate which player should go first, and corrected that by having each player spin to see who got the highest number; that player went first. In the course of playing the game, we also discovered that we had too many negative chance cards ("Miss a turn," "Go back to start," etc.), so that the players began grumbling about how this game was impossible to win. We corrected this by producing additional positive chance cards—"Move ahead, "Take an extra turn," and so on—to balance out the bad things that happened. On the second tryout, things went much better.

Either simple or complex, a good board game can offer students a thought-provoking and motivational means of learning about many of the elements of social studies. (© *Ed Malitsky/The Picture Cube*)

The principles we applied in developing "The Milk Game" would be equally appropriate for other kinds of board games, including those based on the history or geography of a region. Instead of drawing the pathway on a plain posterboard or oaktag, we would use a map of the region as the background. Actually, because most maps are too flimsy to withstand a lot of use, we would affix (glue or dry mount) them to pieces of posterboard. We would then be ready to draw the trail (or pathway) for "Sherman's March Game" on a road map of Georgia (or the southeastern United States), for example, while "The Oregon Trail" game could be done on a map of the western United States.

Card Games

Most paper-supply houses sell blank playing cards that can provide the basis for excellent card games. Consider, for example, an instance in which you want students to be able to match inventors with their inventions. By placing the inventors and their inventions on separate cards, students could attempt to match the appropriate cards using the rules for "Old Maid." In this instance, of course, you would need an extra card that doesn't match, possibly the "Old Inventor."

The "Rummy" game format might work equally as well, particularly for inventors who produced several inventions, like Thomas Edison.

In building card and board games, it is important to determine the extent to which they will be concealed tests. For the "Inventors Game" described above, we would place both the name of the inventor and the invention on the same card. Thus, an "Edison" card would have a picture of a light bulb on it, while a "Light Bulb" card would have Edison's name on it. The student would need both cards to have a match. If that information were not on both cards, the "game" would actually be a test of the student's knowledge of inventors. Students who do not know that Edison invented the light bulb, for example, could only guess which two cards went together, and the game could come to a screeching halt.

The intent of the card games described above is to help the student learn to match two or more elements that are associated (e.g., inventors with their inventions), not to test the students' knowledge. Likewise, "The Milk Game" was intended to familiarize students with the various stages of milk production, not to test their knowledge of it. Having students correctly answer a question such as "How much milk does a cow give each day?" before they can take their next turn, for example, could introduce elements that defeat the purpose of your game. If nothing else, you would need a referee or answer sheet (or both) to determine whether the question was answered correctly. The point here is that games can be structured so that they test a student's knowledge of whatever the game deals with. Although there is nothing necessarily wrong with doing so, we suggest that you avoid adding test-like elements wherever possible.

SUMMARY OF STEPS FOR DESIGNING A SIMULATION OR GAME

Designing a simulation or game begins with an idea. Thereafter, it requires a few materials, a little creativity, and often more time than you might imagine. The steps for designing a simulation or game are as follows:

1. Identify the process or system that you want to simulate.

2. Identify the specific characteristics of the system or process. These include the various stages in the process or system as well as the human components involved. Note that it may be necessary to narrow your focus; it may be possible to simulate only part of the nineteenth-century factory system, but not the entire system, for example.

3. Determine which characteristics of the system or process you wish to emphasize, and those you are willing to omit. Recall that simulations simplify reality. In the Holiday Card Factory, for example, the workers' long hours and a host of other working conditions were not present. Sweatshops or other conditions that might endanger the students' welfare are better left to history.

4. Determine which format—simulation or game—is best suited to the topic.

5. Decide what the players will be doing. Will they be making something, playing a role, moving tokens around a board, or what?

6. Decide on an outcome. When will the simulation or game end—after the players have reached a decision, been reelected, reached "home," made the most points, or at the end of a time limit?

7. Determine how you will introduce the chance element (to make the activity more interesting). Make certain that negative and positive chance factors are equally balanced.

8. (Simulations only) Determine how you will get information to the players. (Will each player get separate roles? Separate instructions?)

9. Determine if everything you have decided upon thus far "fits" together. If so, begin developing or collecting whatever materials you will need.

10. Prepare a preliminary set of written rules or directions.

11. Try out the simulation or game on a small group of "guinea pigs." (This is one of the most essential steps in the entire process—you will be amazed at what you forgot to take into account.)

12. Make necessary adjustments as indicated by the field test.

EXPRESSIVE AND ENACTIVE EXPERIENCES

Expressive and *enactive* experiences refer to what noneducators might call "projects." *Expressive experiences* refer to activities in which children have an opportunity to express themselves, either through drama—plays, skits, pageants, etc.—or through dramatic play, music, role playing, or other forms of sociodrama. *Enactive experiences* refer to activities in which students build or create something—models, murals, etc. Opportunities for children to express their creative or artistic talents are common to both kinds of experiences.

Because we have already dealt with several forms of expressive experience—dramatic play, role playing, and so forth—we will say little more about them, except to note that whatever is being dramatized should be portrayed accurately. Enactive experiences, too, must be carefully planned lest they degenerate into activities that produce only marginal learning outcomes. Thelen's example of the community-history TV project (see Chapter 12) is evidence of this.

Enactive experiences involving foods of various kinds seem to have become increasingly popular recently, and tend to crop up at many grade levels. If you wish to use food as a reflection of a culture, it is essential that children see the skill, the artistry, and the labor that goes into the preparation of a particular dish. To be effective, enactive experiences should be part of a broader study. In other words, before boiling the first grain of rice for an Oriental meal, for example, the children should have identified what kinds of things might be served at such a meal, what goes into the various dishes, how they are prepared, how they are served, and on what occasions they are eaten. The same is true for whatever food you are preparing. The actual preparation and eating—the enactive phase—may be only a small part of the larger study. The library's collection of cookbooks may very well become a major reference source. If the children are too young or otherwise unable to do library research, you may need to do it for them.

You may also find that worthwhile enactive experiences have a *problem-solving* dimension. In the previous example, the question guiding the students' search might be "What are the components of a typical Japanese meal?" Similarly, before building a Roman chariot, students should have researched the construction of an original; the question guiding their problem solving would be "How were Roman (or Greek) chariots built, and of what materials?" Before building a model dairy farm, primary students (or even intermediate ones) should have compared a series of pictures of dairy farms (or visited a dairy farm, if that is feasible) in order to identify their common characteristics.

A research component is a vital part of enactive experiences. In many instances, the children will be so anxious to begin an enactive experience that they think they cannot take the time to complete the necessary research. But the failure to do so can produce countless problems—for themselves and for you as the teacher—as we describe below.

ON BUILDING A MODEL IGLOO

Imagine yourself in the place of a teacher whose program calls for the study of Eskimos. There are a number of enactive experiences you might use with students, but you will undoubtedly reject some of those activities—such as building model harpoons—because of the safety hazard they could pose for exuberant children. Among some of those children, the temptation to throw their harpoons might be too great to resist.

Building a model igloo from sugar cubes (which are the color and texture of snow without painting) lacks most of the physical danger associated with activities such as harpoon building, but igloo building is not without its problems. First, you will need to decide if every student must build an igloo—including those students who dislike model-building activities of any kind. Perhaps it would be better to give such students the option of reading a collection of Eskimo folktales and then dramatizing one or two of them for the class.

Once those decisions have been made and the igloo building gets underway, you are apt to encounter "the glue problem." What kind of glue works best with sugar cubes? Most children may have small bottles of "Elmer's" glue available, but it doesn't set quickly enough for this kind of activity. You'll probably need to obtain some fast-setting household cement—the faster setting, the better.

Getting rectangular sugar cubes to slope inward to form the igloo's roof can also present a problem. You could have students glue the sugar cubes to pieces of styrofoam that's been cut to shape, but that isn't very realistic—igloos are hollow in the middle. To produce a realistic finished product, it's necessary to cut off one edge of each sugar cube so that it leans inward properly. Cutting sugar cubes without crumbling them can be accomplished with saw-toothed steak knives, but for safety's sake, this operation requires close supervision. (Actually, it's a good idea to use the styrofoam form to hold the sugar cubes in place while the glue sets, but the glue should be placed on the sugar cubes only; that way the form can be removed and the result is a realistic—though fragile—igloo.)

As they build their models, students will usually stack the sugar cubes as if they were building a cement block wall, as illustrated in Figure 13.2 (left). Real igloos, on the other hand, are constructed in a continuous upward spiral, also illustrated in Figure 13.2 (right). Eskimos are able to sculpt the spiral readily because the snow they work with is fairly soft—much softer than sugar cubes. In other words, the amount of cutting the students must do to create a realistic igloo can prove tedious—at least until they have gotten the first course of cubes in place. Thereafter it is much easier.

When the students' models are nearly completed, they should have the rounded shape of an igloo, but there are likely to be gaps and holes on the surface. The same thing happens with real igloos. The Eskimos cover the almost-finished igloo with loose snow that fills in the gaps and holes and creates the finished appearance. Students can approximate this by spraying their igloos with a *light* coat of water (from a spray bottle) and then sprinkling granulated sugar over their model—a process that may need to be repeated several times. The result should be a relatively respectable model igloo.

In this description of igloo building, we have provided considerable information on how the Eskimos build a real igloo and on the kinds of construction problems that children are likely to encounter. None of the problems are major, by any means, but the seemingly trivial problems occupied a large chunk of time when we first tried this activity with students. When we had twenty or so students complaining that "my roof keeps falling in," you can bet that we had some second thoughts about whether our "brilliant idea" (about building igloos) was worth it.

We would do things quite differently were we to try this activity with students again. First, we would be certain that they had scoured the library to find every bit of information about igloo building they could locate. We would also show the film *Autumn River Camp, Part II* (National Film Board of Canada)—which shows the Eskimo building an igloo—before we ever began construction. Most important of

FIGURE 13.2 Igloo Building

"WRONG"
Student-built igloo

"RIGHT"
Eskimo-built igloo

all, however, we would review our rationale for using this activity. At the time we first did it, we felt the children would learn about life in the Arctic—about what it was like to find shelter in a land of scarce resources. Whether our rationale was valid is debatable at best. In fact, what our students actually learned from the activity may have little or nothing to do with our stated purpose. Rather, the activity may simply have become a lesson in construction, in how to cut and glue sugar cubes.

Should your class study the Far East, you might have your students sit on the floor as they eat an Oriental meal (complete with chopsticks), even though the connection between that experience and your students' broader understanding of Oriental cultures may be doubtful. Placing a scoopful of canned chow mein on a plate, for example, is a far cry from the artistry that accompanies a formal meal in the Far East. Unless your class experiences that artistry—by deciding exactly how and where the food will be placed on their plate, for example—it is questionable whether they will either understand and/or appreciate an Oriental meal—or a Far Eastern culture.

By no means are we trying to put a damper on some of the fun activities you can have with social studies. Indeed, enactive experiences often have a dimension that cannot be measured in precise terms. The "hands-on" approach they reflect can often permit students to contribute to class activities in ways that would be denied them through more formal, reading-oriented activities. The appropriate use of expressive and enactive experiences probably lies somewhere between two extremes—between teachers who are *always* building something or getting ready for another play or pageant, and teachers who never use any of these experiences. In general, we feel that you should be encouraged to use expressive and enactive experiences when they (1) are integral to whatever you are studying, (2) involve an inquiry or research component, and (3) are done "right," that is, they are a genuine reflection of the culture, period, or phenomena.

SUMMARY

Group-based student activities range from those in which you establish a setting and then let the students' creativity come forth to those in which the children follow precise, step-by-step directions. The more you structure an activity, the more you begin to lose spontaneity and creativity. That loss, however, may be offset by the fact that you have a greater assurance that the children will consider the issues and questions that you have built into a more structured activity. And so, you are faced with another trade-off. Whichever kind of group-based strategy you use—structured or unstructured, expressive or enactive—will ultimately depend on your purposes for developing the activity in the first place.

Arguments as to whether an activity is or is not a dramatic play, or is or is not a simulation, are not very productive. The boundary line between such activities is usually sufficiently fuzzy that individuals often draw their own. In the final analysis, all group-based teaching activities are means toward an end. If the activity permits you to reach that end—whether it be to have children raise questions that they can then research, or to experience and analyze a situation they might encounter in the real world—it really doesn't make much difference what label you attach to the activity. Personally, we prefer the more structured forms of group-based activities because they are more likely to get us to where we want to go.

In the next chapter, we shift the focus from groups to individuals. No one is likely to suggest that managing group instruction is not a challenge, yet adapting instruction so that it meets the individual needs of your students will probably rank as one of the more challenging aspects of teaching.

SUGGESTED ACTIVITIES

1. Design a board game following the suggestions in this chapter. It may take time, but your students will love it.

2. Design a dramatic-play activity following Lee's format but involving a different content area.

3. Design an unstructured role-playing activity. Then identify the techniques you could use to add greater structure to the experience.

4. Suppose a teacher informs you that he or she plans to serve raw fish to a class so that the students will have better appreciation of Eskimo life. Identify the positive and negative learning outcomes that might result from this experience.

REFERENCES

Aronson, E. 1978. *The Jigsaw Classroom.* Beverly Hills, Calif.: Sage Publications.

Lee, John R. 1974. *Teaching Social Studies in the Elementary School.* New York: Macmillan.

Lippitt, Rosemary. 1958. "The Auxiliary Chair Technique." *Group Psychotherapy,* 11 (January), 8–23.

Shaftel, Fannie R., and George Shaftel. 1982. *Role Playing in the Curriculum.* Englewood Cliffs, N.J.: Prentice-Hall.

———. 1970. *Teacher's Guide: People in Action.* New York: Holt, Rinehart, and Winston.

SUGGESTED READINGS

Sharon Pray Muir. 1980. "Simulation Games for Elementary Social Studies." *Social Education,* 44 (January), 35–39. This article contains one of the most recent directories of available simulations and games.

Fannie R. and George Shaftel. 1982. *Role Playing in the Curriculum*. Englewood Cliffs, N.J.: Prentice-Hall. The name Shaftel has become almost synonymous with role playing and other group activities. This is the most complete and authoritative source by far.

David W. Zuckerman and Robert E. Horn. 1973. *Guide to Simulations/Games for Education and Training*. Lexington, Mass.: Information Resources. The directory portion of this volume is outdated, but the reference materials remain pertinent.

CHAPTER 14

Individualizing Instruction

On individual differences among children: "To paraphrase Churchill, never in the field of human behavior has so much been written by so many about a single idea—and perhaps utilized by so few."   Vincent Rogers

KEY QUESTIONS

☐ How do you individualize social studies programs?

☐ What is involved in diagnosing student learning?

☐ What is "learning style?"

☐ How does one establish social studies learning centers?

KEY IDEAS

☐ Individualized instruction is a reflection of efforts to make schools "fit" students and their individual needs more effectively.

☐ The basic elements of individualized instruction are diagnosing student's learning needs and providing prescriptive treatments.

☐ Exceptional children are usually defined as students at either end of the educational spectrum—those with special abilities and those with special needs.

☐ In individualized instruction, all students are considered "exceptional."

☐ Interest centers and learning stations are two devices for encouraging student-directed individualization.

INTRODUCTION: New Approaches to Perennial Problems

Were it safe to assume that children had learned everything they've been taught—which it isn't—and were it safe to assume that all children have similar abilities and learning styles—which they don't—there would be little need for individualized instruction. One could simply provide the same experiences for all students and leave it at that.

All of us know that children sometimes forget things that they've learned, and all of us know that children don't always learn something the first (or second) time around, *and* most of us also know that some children learn differently from others. Despite what we know, we have tended to overlook or ignore these realities in traditional educational practice. Such "ignoring" was hardly the result of an evil plot, but rather, we suspect, a reflection of the belief that it was the child's responsibility to "fit" the school—to learn and to act in ways the school deemed proper. Historically, the school has been seen as society's sorter and molder—as the institution that separates the fit from the unfit—and it has been the child's responsibility to conform to the school's expectations as best he or she could. Over time, however, that view has shifted somewhat, perhaps because of an increasingly large number of students who either haven't fit in very well or, in some instances, have rejected the school entirely. Instead of the one-way relationship that once prevailed—where the student either fit in or got out—the relationship today is two-way; the child's responsibility to fit the school is balanced by the school's responsibility to better fit the child.

Striking a balance between the children's responsibility to the school and vice versa is a continuing problem. Although many teachers agree with the need to maintain clearly identified standards for student performance, they also recognize that rigidly defined standards may not accommodate the wide range of individual differences they face in their classrooms every day. Variations within a class are often so great that at the beginning of the year some students can already demonstrate much of what will be expected of them at the end of the year and, theoretically at least, could skip that grade level entirely. For other students, however, the hope is that they will be able to meet the entry-level standards for their grade level before they leave it. (The latter is less likely to occur in states that have banned social promotion, but we are not talking about unique cases here; we're talking about the kinds of situations you are likely to find in a typical classroom.) Currently, the range of individual differences may be even wider than it was previously, as students who were once segregated into special classes have been "mainstreamed" into regular classrooms. When all of these factors are taken into consideration, it should be apparent that for many teachers the need to individualize instruction is not entirely a matter of principle; it has become a matter of necessity.

Operationally, the model for individualized instruction shares several characteristics with the medical model. Terminology such as *diagnosis* and *prescription,* for example, is much in evidence. The medical model, however, is based on the notion that something is wrong with the patient. Once the ailment is diagnosed, treatment to make the patient well again can begin. Unfortunately, when that model is transferred to classroom settings, the feeling of "wrongness" associated with illness sometimes comes with it. As a result, students who need remedial instruction may be perceived as "having something wrong with them." While being ill has always been acceptable in the medical model, only recently have schools begun to acknowledge the legitimacy of educational exceptionality. That acknowledgment is not universal by any means, but individualized instruction extends far beyond the simplistic notion that remedial instruction is something "bad," something only for poor students who can't handle regular instruction. All children can benefit from individualized instruction. In fact, some schools are moving toward providing individualized instruction for every student.

In this chapter we deal first with some of the traditional approaches for dealing with differences among students. We then consider some contemporary forms of individualizing, with special emphasis on diagnostic techniques that you might wish to use with your students. Finally, we examine strategies associated with what we call student-directed individualizing, that is, providing students with a range of choices in their social studies programs.

INDIVIDUALIZING INSTRUCTION

Two general approaches—one administrative and the other instructional—have traditionally been used to accommodate individual differences. *Administrative approaches* refer to policies and practices like homogeneous grouping, acceleration, retention, and special classes, which are employed on schoolwide or districtwide bases. *Instructional approaches* refer to techniques and practices that individual teachers employ to meet their students' needs, and include diagnosing performance, operating independent study centers, and the like. We examine each of these approaches in the following sections.

ADMINISTRATIVE APPROACHES

Acceleration and Retention

Ten or twenty years ago, the worst fate imaginable for many children was to fail and thus be required to repeat a grade level. The social stigma—for both parents and children—was often tremendous. For other children, however, there was the unrelenting hope that they would be among the privileged few who would be accelerated, who'd get to skip a grade.

From a student's point of view, administrative policies permitting *acceleration* and *retention* were undoubtedly seen as forms of reward (for superior performance) or punishment (for poor performance). From an instructional perspective, however, the effect of these policies (and sometimes their real intent) was to narrow the range of individual differences teachers would face in the classroom. In other words, by retaining less able students and accelerating more able students, the remaining students presented a narrower range of abilities for teachers to take into account. Then, too, students who were actually accelerated or retained would be in environments that more closely matched their instructional needs. At least that's how these policies were supposed to work in theory.

Although accelerated students were often younger and less mature than their classmates, the problems associated with the age differences were apt to be of a social rather than of an instructional nature. But retention, especially repeated retention, has sometimes created situations in which eleven- or twelve-year-olds were placed in classes where the majority of students were eight or nine years old. Should you ever encounter such a situation—as well you might—you can anticipate both social and instructional problems. Recognize that for children who measure their age in half-years, being eight and a half is considered "much older" than plain old eight. Even a two- or three-year age differential can produce very striking social consequences that, ultimately, may be reflected in students' academic performance. These factors (and others) have led many school systems to abandon retention as an administrative policy and move instead to *social promotion*.

Social Promotion

Promoting students even though they are unable to complete the work required at a lower grade level (social promotion) actually increases the range of individual differences a teacher must deal with. Unless teachers are able to provide some type of individualized instruction for students who have been socially promoted, the results are apt to be cumulative. In other words, such students may be increasingly unable to demonstrate the skills required at each higher grade level, and may thus fall further and further behind. (See "How Well I Remember Keith.") In addition, you may find that grades have lost much of their potency as motivators for socially promoted students; it's difficult to argue that grades are important when students know they will be passed on to the next grade level regardless of the grades they get.

Grouping

Another administrative approach is *homogeneous grouping* (or "tracking"). The effect of grouping students together on the basis of one or more criteria such as IQ, reading ability, achievement test scores, and/or teachers' ratings, is to narrow the range of student abilities a teacher must deal with.

Homogeneous grouping is a popular practice in many schools, and often results in classes described as "prekindergarten," "prefirst," "excelled fourth," or "advanced sixth." Even with tracking or homogeneous grouping, however, you are apt to find that students vary in their ability to deal with different subject areas.

Thus, you may also find that further subgrouping and/or one or more of the instructional approaches to individualizing are required.

HOW WELL I REMEMBER KEITH: A CASE STUDY IN RETENTION

Keith was a sixth grader when I (Welton) first met him; at least he was as old as the other sixth graders I taught that year. When Keith showed up at school, which wasn't very often, he just sat there, unmoving. He almost never talked to anyone and was one of the few students I've encountered who had absolutely no friends in the class. Later I discovered he hung around with a group of much older boys in his neighborhood, but within the class—nothing!

Keith was responsible for my first encounter with a truant officer; I didn't even think they existed in rural Ohio. I discovered that Keith had been that route before and was a well-known case. It turned out that Keith had never liked school very well to start with; but because of a legitimate illness, he had missed most of second grade. When he was promoted "socially" to third grade, Keith found he just couldn't handle the work—especially in reading. With both of his parents working, he found that he could avoid the entire hassle by staying home—which he did, regularly!

After a year (actually a nonyear) with Keith in my class, I knew he didn't have the skills to make it in seventh grade, and I decided to stop all this social-promotion nonsense and retain him. Some of the other teachers agreed, so, over the principal's objections, we "held Keith back."

It was in about the middle of my second nonyear with Keith in the sixth grade that I discovered that this was one of those occasions when the principal was right. He'd agreed that Keith wasn't ready for seventh grade but said another year in the sixth grade wouldn't make him any readier. I discovered what I believe I already knew—that Keith wasn't equipped to handle seventh grade, nor was he equipped to handle sixth grade. A second time through sixth grade wouldn't make him any better prepared. What he really needed were some second-, third-, and fourth-grade skills.

I erred in believing that if one dose of sixth grade didn't help Keith, a second dose would. My failure with Keith, which is perhaps why I remember him so well, lay in the fact that I didn't accurately diagnose his problem. Upon retaining him, I should have approached him as an individual and provided instruction in the skills he needed. I also realized, however, that it wasn't necessary to retain Keith to teach him those skills, for the same thing could be accomplished with individualized instruction in a seventh-grade class.

Indeed, how well I remember Keith!

Special Considerations for Exceptional Students

The need to provide appropriate instructional environments for exceptional students has necessitated still other administrative approaches for dealing with individual differences. There is no question, in our minds at least, that every child is unique and exceptional, but the term *exceptional students* refers to children whose learning disabilities, handicaps, or special abilities set them apart from the bulk of the students that teachers encounter. As Kirk and Gallagher noted (1986, p. 5):

> **The exceptional child is [one] who differs from the average or normal child in (1) mental characteristics, (2) sensory abilities, (3) communication abilities, (4) social behavior, or (5) physical characteristics. These differences must be to such an extent that the child requires a modification of school practices, or special education services, to develop to maximum capacity.**

This definition reflects two elements that warrant special mention. First, exceptionality is an extremely broad concept that encompasses a wide range of characteristics. Second, it includes both ends of the educational spectrum: students who may encounter difficulties in school because of their handicapping conditions or disabilities, as well as students who excel in academic, athletic, intellectual, or creative endeavors.

Table 14.1 illustrates the number of students with physical and educational handicaps who were enrolled in elementary and secondary schools in 1977 and 1984. Because gifted and talented students are *not* included in Table 14.1, the total number of exceptional children is much larger than that indicated. Nevertheless, it's clear that the number of handicapped students—especially students with

TABLE 14.1   Public Elementary and Secondary School Students in Programs for the Handicapped, by Type of Handicap, 1977 and 1984

Type of Handicap	Percent by Year 1977	1984	Change in percent
Learning disabled	21.5	42.0	+20.5
Speech impaired	35.3	26.2	−9.1
Mentally retarded	26.0	16.9	−9.1
Emotionally disturbed	7.6	8.4	+0.8
Hearing impaired/deaf	2.4	1.7	−0.7
Orthopedically handicapped	2.3	1.3	−1.0
Other health impaired	3.8	1.2	−2.6
Visually handicapped	1.0	0.7	−0.3
Multihandicapped	NA	1.5	—
Deaf/blind	NA	0.1	—
All conditions (in thousands)	3,692	4,298	+14.1

Source: U.S. Center for Education Statistics.

learning disabilities—has grown considerably since 1977. This may be the result of (1) changes in the nature of the handicapped population, (2) better diagnostic techniques, or (3) changes in the categories into which individuals are placed. Whatever the cause, this increase has significant implications for classroom teachers, which we consider later in this chapter.

Estimates on the total number of exceptional students vary. Gallagher (1974), for example, suggests that one out of every eight or ten students can be considered "exceptional." If you were to include students who exhibit milder forms of exceptionality yet who function within the normal population, the total may increase to 25 percent of the students in a typical classroom.

At one time, students with learning handicaps or other disabling conditions were placed in separate classes with special teachers. Such placements were sometimes regarded as "temporary"—as something to help the child overcome certain problems—but Dunn (1973, p. 22) found that fewer than 10 percent of the students placed in such classes ever returned to regular classrooms. Dunn also found that when mildly handicapped students remained in regular classrooms, their educational achievement exceeded that of students who had been segregated in separate classrooms (1968, p. 22). This type of evidence provided the basis for recommendations that segregated children be placed back into the "mainstream" of public education. Those recommendations ultimately became a part of federal legislation so far-reaching that it has affected virtually every teacher and exceptional student in the country.

Legislative Mandates   Two key pieces of federal legislation, Public Law 94–142, the Education for All Handicapped Children Act of 1975, and Public Law 93–380, the Education Amendments of 1974, have had far-reaching effects on the treatment of exceptional children. A major provision of P.L. 94–142 defined the concept of *least restrictive environment,* which is illustrated in Figure 14.1, and which spawned the practice of "mainstreaming." Basically, the law requires that whenever possible handicapped children should be educated in the most normal environment in which they can function successfully, usually a regular classroom. Further, it requires that students be placed in a *more* restrictive environment (special classrooms, special schools or institutions, etc.) only when it is impossible to work out satisfactory placements in less restrictive settings.

A second key provision of P.L. 94–142 requires that an individualized educational plan—an IEP—be prepared for each exceptional child. An IEP must identify both long- and short-term educational goals and the specific services to be provided to the student, and must be developed by a team that includes a representative of the local educational agency (usually the building principal), the teacher, the resource teacher, and the child's parents or guardians.

Public Law 94–142 has succeeded in removing mildly handicapped children from segregated classrooms, but it has not eliminated the conditions that led to students being separated from the "mainstream" to begin with. A learning disability or physical handicap, for example, does not disappear when a child is placed in a regular classroom. As a consequence, teachers almost always need to employ

FIGURE 14.1   The Least-Restrictive-Environment System of Placement

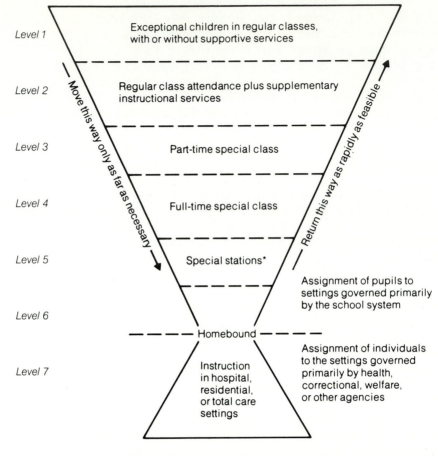

*Special schools in public school system

(Source: "Special Education as Developmental Capital" by E. Deno, 1970, Exceptional Children, 35, p. 236. © 1970 by the Council for Exceptional Children. Reprinted with permission.)

one of the instructional approaches to individualized instruction that we describe shortly.

To provide continuing assistance to students with special needs, many school systems have adopted the administrative policy of providing *resource teachers* and/or *resource classrooms*. Individuals or small groups of students are usually pulled out of their regular classes to work with specially trained resource teachers for short periods. Under the provisions of P.L. 93–980, many schools also provide enrichment classes and, in some instances, special teachers for gifted and talented students.

The Impact of Administrative Policies

Administrative policies, such as acceleration, retention, social promotion, mainstreaming, and resource classes, primarily affect the types of students you may have in your classroom. In some instances, such as in the case of homogeneous grouping, the policy may narrow the range of individual differences you must deal with, while in other instances, as in the case of "mainstreaming," the policy may have the opposite effect. In either event, and although administrative policies can influence *which* students will be in your classroom, they have almost no impact in determining what you *do* with those students once you get them. For that, it's necessary to turn to one or more of the instructional approaches we deal with in the next section.

INSTRUCTIONAL APPROACHES

There is a story about a monkey trying desperately to survive a flood. The monkey had clambered up a tree and was perched precariously on a limb overlooking the turbulent water. Below was a fish that seemed to be struggling against the rapidly moving current. With the best of intentions, the monkey reached down and scooped the fish from the water. Unfortunately, the monkey never fully understood why the fish was ungrateful, and why it died shortly after being "rescued."

Teachers, too, sometimes go out on a limb to help students having difficulties in school. Some of those students may be handicapped by physical, intellectual, and emotional disabilities that interfere with learning, while others may be children from different cultural backgrounds. Still other students may be "different" in other ways. Some academically gifted students, for example, may excel in every subject area, while other gifted students may excel in one or two specific areas, such as math, the visual arts, or poetry writing, and yet be quite average in most other respects. The logical conclusion is that the only way to accommodate the range and nature of exceptionality is to provide individualized instructional programs that recognize that in some situations all children are exceptional. Indeed, "exceptional children" may be a misnomer; exceptional instruction may actually be more appropriate.

Individualized Instruction

As a concept, individualized instruction is disarmingly simple; the intent is to provide instruction that is keyed to the student's needs, interests, and abilities, and that permits the student to maximize his or her potential. Implementing individualized instruction, however, is anything but simple. In fact, to *do* individualized instruction involves the following:

1. Differentiating among the different aspects of teaching: diagnosing, prescribing, evaluating, motivating, etc.

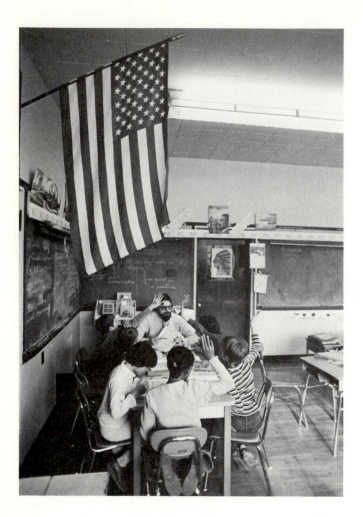

Even in a group, good instruction is individualized, for it is geared to each student's needs, interests, and abilities, and it permits the student to maximize his or her potential. (© *J. Holland/ Stock, Boston*)

2. Accommodating, managing, and being accountable for a wide range of student knowledge, skills, interests, and cultural backgrounds

3. Translating broad instructional goals into specific instructional objectives

4. Organizing learning activities so that they are sequential, developmental, and ensure student achievement

5. Managing the use of instructional time to maximize student achievement

6. Providing an environment in which each student realizes his or her potential

7. Providing ongoing feedback to students, parents, and others so as to assist children in mastering their learning goals

Doing all of this, much less doing all of it well, isn't easy. The difficulties are often compounded because teachers find themselves in school settings that (1) categorize and group children by age level, (2) fail to distinguish between different teacher roles, (3) often fail to operationalize educational goals, (4) often force teachers to "cover" a predetermined course of study rather than respond to students' needs, (5) typically assume a single cultural norm, and (6) usually organize the curriculum according to the logic of the subject matter and not to the logic of learning the content. All of these are obstacles that teachers must either combat or work around.

Despite this, the need to individualize instruction has become ever more crucial. How, then, does one go about doing it?

Little Beginnings

How do teachers provide an individualized program in each subject area for each of twenty-five, twenty-seven, or even thirty students? Where do they start? How do they keep track of all those different student programs? And how do they avoid what could become one of the most massive management nightmares of all time?

How? By beginning slowly—sometimes very slowly.

We're not trying to be funny here, nor are we in any way challenging the importance of providing instruction geared to individual needs. Rather, we're suggesting that attempting to individualize programs for each student in all subject areas from day one, especially for children who are not used to working in such programs, is likely to result in utter chaos—for you and your students. Thus, we recommend a small-scale approach at the outset, that is, beginning with only one subject area and perhaps with only two or three students. Once you feel comfortable, you can expand your program to include more students and more subject areas.

One of the myths of individualizing—that thirty students must be doing thirty different things at all times—is important in this context. This is an unrealistic expectation in terms of a teacher's psychological and physical survival. Individualized instruction may actually involve all students doing the same thing at the same time, or four groups of students doing the same thing, or selected individuals doing independent work, or any number of planned alternatives. It need *not* involve everybody doing their own thing at all times.

COMMENTARY: The Myths of Individualized Instruction

For some teachers, prospective and experienced alike, the thought of providing individualized instruction for students gives rise to fears and misgivings about their ability to individualize successfully. In environments where one is not encouraged to admit such reservations openly, individualizing has at times been attacked in such a way as to create and perpetuate a series of myths about the nature of individualized instruction. Some of these myths are presented below.

continued

Myth 1: In order to individualize, the teacher's philosophical disposition must either be "progressive" or "liberal."

Fact: *Both process-oriented and content-oriented teachers can find effective individualized approaches to use as means to reach their respective goals.*

Myth 2: Individualized instruction is a sudden, revolutionary, and radical departure from what is now being done, one that calls for a complete change in teaching functions.

Fact: *Individualizing need not involve an abrupt and radical departure from what is being done, but rather can involve a relatively slow and managed process of transition.*

Myth 3: Individualizing instruction causes insecurity among students and thus contributes to a breakdown of discipline.

Fact: *If individualizing is more than random activity, and if it is conducted in a planned way—one that gradually shifts responsibility from the teacher to the students—then it may provide an even better tool for classroom management.*

Myth 4: Individualizing demands that the teacher have access to a multitude of teaching materials before beginning, and that all the complementing and supporting aspects be determined first.

Fact: *If individualizing instruction is viewed as an evolving process rather than as a preset, packaged curriculum, it can be initiated even when the materials are based on a single text.*

Myth 5: Individualizing instruction is unrealistic because it requires far more planning and feedback time than teachers have available within the existing structure.

Fact: *Individualizing does call for different teacher roles and, thus, for different time demands. However, teachers can individualize only one part of their total teaching responsibility—it need not be all or nothing.*

Myth 6: Individualizing instruction is little more than a mechanistic system that emphasizes low-level behavioral objectives.

Fact: *If one takes into account such things as motivation, individual maturity, cognitive-skill levels, and learning styles, and if one recognizes that such factors can be modified, then individualizing instruction is far from mechanistic.*

TEACHER-DIRECTED INDIVIDUALIZING

The key elements in individualized instruction are finding out where an individual learner is, and then providing appropriate instruction for that individual. These are, in simplest form, the essence of *diagnosis* and *prescription*.

Students themselves will sometimes provide an initial clue that they're having a problem when they approach you and say, "I can't do this." This will only occur, however, in a climate where it's okay to have a problem and, more importantly, where one is free *to admit* that a problem exists. So why might a student approach you? For one of three reasons, we suspect, and you'll have to decide which. Either he or she (1) has a legitimate problem and wants help, (2) wants some personal attention and has discovered that this is one way to get it, or (3) a little of both.

To a plea of "I can't do this," the human response tends to be "Well, why not? What's the problem?" Realistically, if students could answer those questions, they wouldn't have "the problem" to begin with, and they probably wouldn't need a teacher's assistance. The situation is roughly equivalent to the patient who enters a doctor's office and says, "I think I'm sick!" The patient may not know *why* he is sick, just that he is. The doctor's immediate task is diagnosing the patient's problem and then prescribing accordingly. Likewise, in educational diagnosis the teacher's immediate task is to identify the *specific* problem, the precise cause or causes underlying the student's difficulty. In many instances, students indicate a general problem, as when they say "I just don't understand this stuff" or "I'm having trouble with maps," but these are usually symptoms of a more specific, underlying problem. In the case of "having trouble with maps," for example, there may be several underlying causes—the inability to interpret the map's key, the inability to identify the various symbols on a map, etc. Just as doctors interpret their patient's symptoms, the teacher must interpret the student's symptoms in order to determine why Johnny is having reading problems or Sarah can't read a map. Thus, determining *why* the student is having difficulty is the key element in educational diagnosis and, ultimately, in prescribing treatment.

THE WHAT, WHY, AND HOW OF DIAGNOSIS AND PRESCRIPTION

How does one diagnose—educationally speaking? Again, the diagnostic steps are similar to a doctor's: systematically gathering data, observing student performance (with a clear idea of what one is observing *for*), and asking questions. In a very real sense, the teacher's role in diagnosis is that of a quasi-researcher: the teacher builds a theory, generates hypotheses (about where students are having problems and why), develops treatments to test the hypotheses, gathers and analyzes what is learned, and then, sometimes, goes back to the drawing board. In other words, educational diagnosis is a process, not an end state, which involves the student, the task the student is expected to do, and the materials the student will use to do it. A key ingredient in that process is the teacher's awareness of the elements that make up a learning task. If the teacher is unaware of the components that go into map reading, for example, it will be exceedingly difficult for that teacher to diagnose the specific problems of children having difficulties with map reading. Indeed, without that information, the prescription is apt to be of the hit-or-miss, "go back and try it again" sort that has almost nothing to do with the student's real problem. (On the other hand, if the student's problem is carelessness, "go back and try it again" could be an appropriate prescription.)

The two types of diagnosis most closely associated with teaching social studies are reflected in the following questions: "Does the student have the necessary knowledge in his or her possession?" and "Is the student able to apply the necessary knowledge in a given situation?" The first question deals with the *knowledge dimension* of learning, while the second question—the application and manipulation of information—is related to the *skills dimension* of learning. The two dimensions are obviously related, but from a diagnostic perspective we examine them separately in the following sections.

Knowledge-level Diagnosis

One of the most straightforward ways to determine if children have certain knowledge in their possession is to ask them, for example, "What does interdependence mean?" If they can't answer adequately, then they probably need more experience (prescription) with situations involving interdependence in action.

Low-level Knowledge Diagnosis   At the lower levels of the knowledge category (of Bloom's *Taxonomy*), especially with factual information (UN concepts), determining why a child doesn't know something can prove more challenging than it might seem. Just ask yourself, for example, why a child might not know that the Declaration of Independence was signed in 1776.

Why? Several reasons are possible. Perhaps the child (1) never studied it in the first place, (2) has difficulty memorizing facts, (3) has difficulty making associations, (4) has forgotten it, even though it was studied at one time, (5) has repressed it, or (6) saw no reason to bother remembering it.

In this and other low-level cognitive diagnoses, most implications are for prescribing, not diagnosing. That is, of the possible explanations above, there is only one we could do something about. Indeed, we could provide children with more association-making experience (categorizing or conceptualizing), but that's not necessarily an adequate explanation for *why* they don't know something. Also, upon reteaching the fact, we could try to provide reasons for a child to remember it. That might help a second time around but it, too, may not explain why a child failed to learn something in the first place.

Inasmuch as knowledge-level diagnosis at the factual level may defy a search for causes, or may realistically take more time than it's worth, the teaching implications are fairly apparent. You either assess (pretest) students to see if they have the prerequisite knowledge, or you provide them with some experiences to refresh their memories before moving on to more complex issues.

Higher-level Cognitive Diagnosis   When you attempt to diagnose a student's knowledge at higher cognitive levels—when you attempt to ascertain a student's knowledge of generalizations or theories, for example—your problems become considerably more complex. Let's assume for the moment that you intend to teach the notion of interdependence to a second- or third-grade class. You have several options open to you.

One is to assume that your students know nothing about interdependence, and set out to expose them to the idea. Another is to see if they have an experiential understanding of interdependence—that is, if they recognize and have a feeling for the fact that people depend on others for certain goods and services—and then associate a label, the term *interdependence,* with their existing feelings. In some instances, we get into the problems of "label learning" or definition learning noted in Chapter 3. It may well be, for example, that a child has an implicit understanding of interdependence but is unaware of the correct cue-concept label to attach to it. Thus, one of the first steps in diagnosing at higher cognitive levels is to determine if you are dealing with a "labeling" problem or one that is more basic.

It's at about this point that higher-level cognitive diagnosis begins to get fuzzy. To pursue our previous example, suppose a student does not recognize the term "interdependence." The question becomes whether or not the child has a set of ideas or relationships that, when clustered, would constitute interdependence. In this case, the prescription would be to show the child how those ideas are related and then give them the label "interdependence." An alternative prescription would be to state that "Interdependence means . . .," and pray that the child makes the necessary relationships. A more fundamental problem occurs when the child does not comprehend the basic ideas that make up a cue concept such as interdependence. For example, if the child does not understand the notion of dependence, you can bet that he or she is unlikely to understand interdependence. And if dependence is the problem, you can begin the cycle once again. Is it a labeling problem? Does the child recognize the ideas that make up dependence? and so forth.

We suspect that one of the problems with higher-level cognitive diagnosis is that the *diagnoser* sometimes does not understand the concept or generalization well enough to know what questions to ask. What, for example, are the prerequisite ideas necessary for understanding capitalism, socialism, or culture? These are difficult questions indeed. To further complicate matters, if your education was anything like ours, we spent considerable time memorizing the definitions for capitalism, socialism, culture, and interdependence, and *not* clustering related ideas to build a definition. Had we learned our social studies the latter way, perhaps we'd have fewer problems with higher-level cognitive diagnosis.

Skills Diagnosis

Diagnosing skills, like higher-level knowledge diagnosis, poses a two-dimensional problem. First, the child may lack the knowledge (skill rule) component of a skill or, second, he or she may be unable to apply the skill rules in a particular situation. If the child is able to differentiate between facts and opinions, for example, this distinction is moot; if the child can apply the skill rules successfully, there is nothing to diagnose. But when the child cannot differentiate between facts and opinions, the diagnostic questions become: (1) does the child know the underlying skill rules—in this instance, the characteristics of facts and opinions and, (2) is he or she able to apply the skill rules in actual situations. If the children are unable to recognize a fact or opinion when they see one, the problem almost assuredly lies at the skill-rule (knowledge) level. However, if children can identify facts and opinions in one situation but not in another, the problem probably lies in how they apply their knowledge (assuming they are not making wild guesses, of course). The succeeding problem then becomes one of identifying the differences between the two situations to pinpoint what might be preventing the children from making the transfer.

The nature of skills diagnosis can be illustrated by examining the ways in which children place events and objects in categories or classifications. Unless students are able to classify and categorize the different kinds of data they encounter, they face the prospect of dealing with a random collection of tidbits of information. The relevant questions here include (1) How do children classify? (2) What is similarity and how is it recognized? (3) What criteria does a child use to make systems out of discrete objects and events?

Elementary children classify and make associations well before they ever knock on the kindergarten door. They may group certain toys according to shape, size, color, or function, just as they may group, collect, and store all sorts of objects around the house. Some educational toys actually force children to make associations by requiring them to place squares, triangles, or other shaped blocks through openings having the same shape. Even children's puzzles have a theme— the barnyard, etc.—and require that children relate shapes and sizes as well as color. All of these activities ask the child to create *order* out of bits of chaos. Yet even at the physical grouping level, individual children differ in their ability to achieve the desired ordering.

How does one diagnose the way children classify? The following can serve as a guide.

Behaviors to Observe While a Child Is Involved in Activities

A. The child uses descriptive criteria for classifying
   color
   size
   shape
   physical features (shiny, dull)

B. The child classifies by functions:
   purpose
   what objects *do*

C. The child uses personalized relationships as a basis for classifying
   mine
   yours

ours
valued (like/dislike)
aesthetic (beautiful/ugly)

D. The child classifies by using criteria:
hammer/nail
engine/power
seed/flower

E. The child uses inference to place objects into categories:
dog/animal
orange/fruit
girl/human

F. The child classifies by *one* attribute only.

G. The child categorizes by using several attributes.

H. The child verbalizes the criteria used in classifying.

I. The child combines two or more attributes when classifying.

Fundamental Diagnostic Questions Related to a Learner's Categorizing Style

1. How does this particular child categorize?

2. What kinds of criteria are apparently used when the child classifies?

3. In what kinds of situations was the child motivated to do classification?
Kinds of materials?
Kinds of play activities?
Kinds of selected or given tasks?
Kinds of social situations?

4. To what extent does the individual child verbalize why he did what he was observed to be doing?

5. Does the individual child maintain his or her criteria throughout the activity or does he or she apply different criteria in a random way?

6. Is the child's categorizing style consistent when observed over a period of time and when working on several tasks?

A word of caution: do not be too hasty to infer that a child follows a particular behavior pattern based on just one or two observations. Because children *do not* classify in a particular way doesn't necessarily mean they *cannot* do so. Nor do we know whether what is observed on one or two occasions is necessarily an optimal performance by a particular child. In fact, diagnosing the way children conceptualize and classify will probably require several periods of rather careful observation.

To see how well *you* are able to classify, study the three illustrations below and then answer the questions that follow.

MATCH THE PAIRS

In how many different ways (different criteria) could the items above be paired? (For example, could there be aesthetic considerations/criteria?) Which pairing would be considered correct?

What specific knowledge do you think the illustration above is trying to identify? What inferences about a pupil might you make if a student meets the knowledge criteria? What background experiences influence how a pupil might respond? How is the situational aspect of the matching controlled? How else might the matching ability be tested (other than by drawings)? How might having too much information get in the way?

What response considerations might be taken into account in trying to determine the number sequence in the illustration on page 445? Just what ability is being tested with the dominoes? (The first and third (odd) dominoes are decreasing while the second and fourth (even) are increasing. Thus, the sequence that begins 8, 5, 7, 6 would continue as follows: 6, 7, 5, 8, 4, 9, and so forth.)

Several other elements of skills diagnosis are illustrated by the following assignment: "Analyze Jefferson's first and second inaugural addresses and identify how they are similar and how they are different." Such a task would challenge many adults, to say nothing of elementary and middle-school children, because it

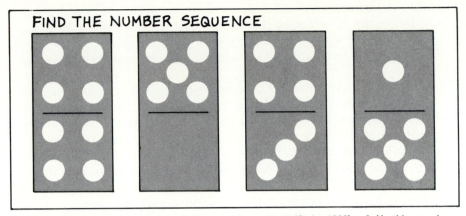

FIND THE NUMBER SEQUENCE

(Source: Illustrations on pp. 444–445 from Carnegie Quarterly, 14 *[Spring 1966] p. 6. Used by permission of the Carnegie Corporation of New York.)*

requires the application of several skills simultaneously. One must be able to analyze, translate, comprehend, compare—and the list goes on.

When attempting to diagnose children's skills, the key questions that teachers need to answer for themselves are (1) How many skills am I asking the student to apply in this situation? and (2) Has this student been successful in applying multiple skills before? If the answer to the second question is no, you may be dooming the child to failure if you persist in presenting the assignment. You can also be fairly certain that this is not a situation where the child will learn from his or her mistakes. Indeed, the child may be so ill-equipped to handle the task that he or she is unable to make mistakes.

Our final point on skills diagnosis is a fairly obvious one, we think, but one that also has some interesting implications. That is, in most instances it is the teacher who presents students with tasks that require that they apply their skills. Almost never will you encounter a student who asks "Can I do some more story problems?" or says "Gee, I can't wait to analyze this paragraph." Most children just don't respond that way. In presenting tasks to children, there needs to be a challenge, yes, but the teacher must also be sensitive to the relationship between the challenge that a task poses and the children's skill level necessary to meet it.

LEARNING STYLE

Are you primarily an auditory or a visual learner? In other words, when faced with learning something would you prefer to have it explained in a good lecture, or would you rather go off and read about it by yourself?

When given an assignment, how much structuring do you prefer? Would you prefer that the teacher specify everything you should do beforehand, or would you rather work it out as you see fit? Or doesn't it matter?

Your preferred instructional mode (auditory, tactile, or visual) and the amount of teacher structuring you desire are two examples of several generic factors that can influence learning, which, when clustered, are referred to as "learning style." These factors are generic since they are not restricted to social studies alone; they may influence student performance in all subject areas.

Six factors that contribute to one's learning style are described below.

1. *Instructional modes*   Students often prefer certain ways of gaining access to the content they are expected to learn. For example, some learners work better when their access to new information is through listening to verbal presentations. Others learn better through reading, through observation, or through hands-on activities. Admittedly, students' preferences for a particular instructional mode may vary depending on the kind of information they are dealing with. Some students, for example, may prefer to read social studies materials but would rather listen to a mathematics explanation.

   At least two studies (Dunn and Price, 1980; and Griggs and Price, 1982) indicate that gifted students have an aversion to a listening-based (auditory) learning mode. Those students also tend to prefer learning alone, and they require less teacher motivation and structuring (see following categories) than nongifted students. These studies do not pretend to describe every gifted student, of course, but they suggest some interesting directions for working with the gifted.

2. *Structure*   Students vary in the amount of organizing they can do on their own and the amount that must be done by someone else. Some students—including some of the brightest—require that teachers do most of the structuring in learning situations. For them, an assignment like "Read about Topic X" virtually drives them up the wall. What they want are page numbers—"Read from page 34 to page 37"—and once given that, they'll breathe a sigh of relief. Others, however, are quite capable of determining the limits of a task or assignment on their own. The basic structuring question, then, concerns how much organizing students can do for themselves and how much they depend on teachers to set the limits for assignments and activities.

3. *Social context of learning*   Students often function differently in different social/learning environments—something that should surprise almost no one. Two of the key factors that can influence this aspect of learning style are (1) how the student views authority, particularly the teacher's authority, and (2) how the student feels about working in group situations.

   Some students demand that teachers exercise their authority in a particular way. Some want the teacher to be an authoritarian taskmaster at all times, while other students want teachers to act as relaxed and casual counselors or guides (and never adopt a sterner stance). Sometimes those conflicting expectations come from students in the same class. Primary-age children are especially likely to regard teachers as surrogate parents. For them, the teacher's word is gospel, and things are "so" because "Teacher says they are so." Quite the opposite view may be held by older students, some of whom seemingly want to turn everything teachers say into debatable propositions.

If your intent is to use lots of small-group activities in your classroom, be prepared to deal with those students who have little use for group activities and would much prefer to go off somewhere and read an assignment (or otherwise avoid the social interaction necessitated in a small-group setting). Other students may tolerate group activities, but they certainly don't look forward to them. At the other end of the spectrum are students who feel that they learn best when they can talk over an assignment or task with a group.

4. *Physical context of learning* Some students demand absolute silence when they study, while others can tolerate noise no matter how loud it is. Others tend to be "morning people" and do their best work then, while some (though fewer) don't function well until after lunch.

5. *Reward/praise* Individuals vary in their need for and their response to reward and praise. In fact, some of your students will do everything they can to avoid public praise; it's almost a kind of punishment for them. Other students need and want constant attention and feedback. To an extent, students can be grouped in terms of whether they prefer external praise—either from teachers or other authority figures—or whether they rely primarily on internal praise and/or self-satisfaction.

6. *Goal preference* Some learners work more effectively and efficiently when goals are short-range and within their immediate grasp. For example, children who feel that the most important objective is "finishing homework" or otherwise completing a short-range assignment may never see how all of the smaller assignments fit together into a larger pattern. Other students may be willing to forego short-range goals in favor of working toward a longer-range objective. For some children, of course, "long-range" may be something one or two weeks away.

Although our list of factors involved in learning style in not exhaustive, its implications are significant for both individualized and whole-group instruction. For example, to provide verbal praise to students who don't like attention from an authority figure, or to provide almost no structuring for students who demand considerable teacher structuring, whether in individualized or group settings, could create problems for you *and* the students. The same could be true if you present only long-range goals to students whose concern is with meeting immediate, short-range objectives.

How does one go about diagnosing a student's learning style? Once again (as is true for all aspects of diagnosis), it's essential that you have identified what you are looking for. Once you've determined your focus—be it goal preference, response to praise, or something else—your actual technique may consist of one or more of the following: (1) systematically observing students as they participate in learning activities; (2) questioning—"Does the noise level bother you?" etc.; or (3) a written learning-style inventory/questionnaire, such as the one illustrated in Appendix C.

PRESCRIBING

After an extensive review of the research on teaching and learning, Barak Rosenshine (1977) concluded that one cannot assume that children know what they have not been taught. Now, if this finding reeks of common sense, you would probably be amazed at how often teachers assume the reverse, that is, that children know what they have not been taught. Seldom does this misguided assumption become more apparent than when teachers prescribe learning activities. Consider, for example, that you have discovered several children in your class who have difficulty identifying similarities and differences among objects, and this inability prevents them from placing objects into classes or categories. Would you give them a classification activity based on the illustrations—the different hats and the other objects—that we presented earlier in this chapter? (page 444)

Before responding, consider that most instructional materials do not teach per se. They can be used to teach, to be sure, but without appropriate instruction they are more likely to *test* the student's existing ability. In other words, giving students an activity based on the classification illustrations on page 444 in the absence of teaching would likely confirm what you already know; that they can't classify. The implication for teaching is the same as when you find that students cannot read a map or apply any one of a thousand other skills: the teacher should show (teach) the students a step-by-step procedure through which they will be able to demonstrate the desired behavior.

It isn't necessary to employ fancy questioning strategies either. Recall that every question presupposes certain knowledge and skills on the students' part. If students lack the knowledge or skills needed to complete a task, there is no reason to assume that they have the knowledge necessary to answer questions about the task—unless, of course, you're still not certain that you have accurately diagnosed the problem. In that instance, further questioning may be entirely appropriate. Otherwise, we suggest that you consider using some old-fashioned direct instruction; either show or tell the student how to complete the task, whichever is most appropriate.

DIAGNOSIS AND PRESCRIPTION: EXCEPTIONAL CHILDREN

Different types of exceptionality pose different challenges for the teacher. For example, when dealing with a mentally retarded child, it may be necessary to modify the goals and objectives the child is expected to achieve. On the other hand, when dealing with a sight-impaired student, the challenge is in locating instructional materials and techniques appropriate to that child's handicap. In other words, some types of exceptionality may make it necessary to revise the *ends* toward which instruction is directed (the goals and objectives), whereas other handicapping conditions make it necessary to revise the *means* of instruction—the materials and techniques used to reach one's goals.

For some forms of exceptionality, such as "health impaired" for example, the child's condition may influence the kinds of physical activities that he or she may engage in, but have very few or no instructional implications. This means that although the child manifests a form of exceptionality, the condition does not require a teacher to make any special educational provisions.

Learning-disabled children can pose special challenges to teachers. "Learning disabled" refers to the condition associated with a child's inability to perform school tasks at a level expected of him or her. The National Advisory Committee on Handicapped Children described a "learning disability" as a disorder in one or more of the basic psychological processes involved in understanding and using spoken and written language, including disorders in listening, talking, reading, writing, spelling, and some thinking processes. This category is so broad that it has almost become a catch-all classification that includes anything not related to visual, hearing, or motor handicaps, mental retardation, emotional disturbance, and environmental factors (Coles, 1978). Indeed, some authorities (Smith et al., 1977) have suggested that educators use the term "learning disabled" because it is less demeaning than "mentally retarded." The point here is that labels such as "mentally retarded," "health impaired," and especially "learning disabled" may provide an extremely limited basis upon which to identify and prescribe alternative learning activities.

COMMENTARY: Labeling Children

All cultures devise ways for designating individuals who vary from the perceived "normal" range, and ours is no exception. This means that all of us learn and respond to various social designations, categories, and labels. Once someone is labeled a "weirdo" or a "retard," for example, we may alter our actions and feelings about such individuals accordingly.

For handicapped children, both their handicapping condition and the labeling process can have social consequences. For example, Richardson (1973) found the following:

Nonhandicapped students usually select other nonhandicapped students for social interaction.

There is a perceived "stigma of association" that makes extended interaction between handicapped and nonhandicapped individuals either avoidable or easily terminated.

Nonhandicapped students often feel their handicapped peers need special consideration.

Handicapped students are less likely to receive accurate and spontaneous feedback on their social skills than their nonhandicapped peers.

Individuals or groups who are labeled often assume characteristics associated with the role identity that is projected upon them. In other words, once someone is labeled a "weirdo," that individual's actions may become increasingly weird. This phenomenon, which tends to perpetuate the

continued

stigmatizing, is especially evident in Robert Scott's (1969) *The Making of Blind Men.* Scott contends that once an individual is diagnosed, that person is encouraged to accept the role of a blind person as defined in our society.

In light of the effects that labeling can have, consider that educational diagnosis can be a two-edged sword. Although the intent may be to identify the problems that a child is experiencing in order to provide appropriate educational treatments, one result of that process may be the creation of a new label, a new category into which the child is placed. To say that a child is "learning disabled," for example, may seem simple enough, but it is equally likely that at some time in the future one could expect a teacher to say "Oh, he's learning disabled. We can't expect much out of him." Before long, the well-intended diagnosis can become a self-fulfilling prophecy in which the child believes that he or she cannot do things that "normal" people do—because he or she is learning disabled (or subject to some other handicapping condition).

Because of the problems associated with labeling children and the stigma of deviance sometimes placed on exceptional children, the field of special education is moving away from the medical model that we referred to earlier, and moving toward an ecological model (Kirk and Gallagher, 1986). Rather than try to "cure" the child, which may not be possible in many cases, the idea is to work with the various agencies and institutions—notably the family and school—with which the child comes into frequent contact. This shift in orientation is relatively recent and has not yet become widely known outside of special education. The point here is that regardless of one's motives, educational diagnosis has significant social implications for both the individual being labeled and for those who do the labeling.

ENRICHMENT

Enrichment refers to the process of providing instructional activities that supplement a basic program—activities that enhance and add fullness and richness to it. Although all social studies programs should be rich and varied to start with, enrichment is usually associated with programs for gifted and talented students.

Three types of enrichment are associated with social studies programs. Among the least common of these is *acceleration,* in which students with specific academic aptitudes move to higher grade-level classes for a particular subject and then return to their regular classes for other academic work. In analytic subject areas such as mathematics, for example, acceleration is a fairly common practice. A third-grade student with sixth-grade math skills, for example, may benefit from being placed in a sixth-grade math class. In synthetic areas such as social studies, however, you seldom find the well-developed, grade-to-grade-level skills sequence that is more common in the analytic subject areas. Thus, a third-grade student with sixth-grade map skills, for example, might be almost totally lost in a sixth-grade social studies class where map skills are only a minor part of the program. In other words, neither the content nor the skill-development sequence of most traditional social studies programs, especially those based on the expanding-environments approach, permits the type of acceleration that is possible in the analytic subject areas.

A second approach to enrichment involves giving gifted students (or others who finish their regular work early) the "privilege" of doing more work than everyone else. This means that instead of doing a ten-page report, for example, gifted students might be required to prepare a fifteen- or twenty-page report. Or instead of doing just the odd-numbered problems on a page (like everyone else), gifted and talented students may be required to do every problem on a page. This type of enrichment provides students with practice—often practice they don't need— but most students quickly realize that what teachers may intend as enrichment is really a kind of punishment. That's why we refer to this approach as *penalty-type enrichment*. Note that there's probably nothing at all punitive about the teacher's intent, it's just that students may look upon the additional work as a penalty. Also note that it usually isn't long before most students discover that they can avoid the penalty of extra work by slowing down and finishing their assignments with everyone else.

A third approach, *breadth/depth enrichment,* is probably the most desirable. Instead of asking students to do more work, as is usually true of penalty-type enrichment, in this approach students are provided with assignments that are qualitatively different. In some instances, students may select from several alternative activities suggested by the teacher, while in other instances they may initiate and undertake activities on their own. Whichever way it's done, the intent is to provide students with ways to explore topics or problems in greater breadth or depth than they otherwise might.

Literature is a frequently used vehicle for breadth/depth enrichment. One of the most obvious techniques is to permit students to read stories, either fiction or nonfiction, relating to topics or problems the class is studying. A less obvious technique is to use literature comparatively. On an occasion when a second-grade class was studying George Washington, for instance, one student read two biographies of his life. To her amazement, she discovered that the two accounts differed in several respects. As she put it, "One of these books is lying." She then proceeded to read almost everything the library had on George Washington, the *Encyclopaedia Britannica* included, in her quest to determine what actually happened.

Another means for providing breadth/depth enrichment is through special reports or projects, including model making and other enactive experiences. Before using any of these techniques, two key elements should be considered. First, make certain that whatever students do is really something special, not simply a longer or more detailed version of what everyone else is doing. In fact, unless students volunteer to do longer reports, the activities could become a form of penalty-type enrichment. Second, keep in mind that a steady diet of written reports can become tedious very quickly, regardless of a student's ability. To cope with this, many teachers try to balance written assignments with nonwritten presentations including various forms of sociodrama (skits, plays, pageants, etc.) or other visually oriented presentations (linear charts, pictures, slide-and-tape presentations, etc.).

DEALING WITH DIFFERENTIATED INSTRUCTION

Providing differential treatment to select groups of students, whether gifted or less able, can sometimes introduce an unintended and often undesirable dynamic to your classroom. After providing several enrichment experiences for gifted and talented students, for example, you may hear one of your average students say "Why do *they* always get to do all of the neat stuff, when all *we* ever get to do is the same old boring thing?" Or, after providing less able students with an assignment geared to their ability level, you may hear other students say "How come we don't get to do the easy stuff like they do?" When you hear either complaint, you'll know there may be problems ahead (if they are not upon you already).

There are essentially two ways to avoid the resentment that may accompany differentiated instruction. One way is to teach social studies on a whole-class basis and provide the same experiences and assignments for everyone. Although this can help avoid problems associated with feelings of unfairness, you can also be fairly certain that your academically talented students will go unchallenged, your less able students will experience their share of failure, while your average students will continue plodding along. Our point here is that by apparently solving one problem—feelings of resentment and unfairness—you may find yourself a victim of other, potentially more serious problems.

A second and far more preferable way to deal with preferential treatment that may seem to accompany differentiated instruction is to individualize instruction even more, so that it is an everyday occurrence that students come to expect. In classrooms where individualized instruction is the main method of operation, students are less apt to find anything unusual or unfair about it. Of course, things may be a bit rocky at first as students become accustomed to differentiated instruction (see case, pages 455–456), but once individualized instruction is the norm—when it's what students expect—feelings of resentment or unfairness should diminish considerably. The fact that individualized instruction provides a means for meeting students' varied skill and ability levels only adds to its appeal. In fact, it even permits you to provide enrichment activities for less able students, activities that can provide welcome relief from the day-to-day drudgery that often accompanies remedial work.

STUDENT-DIRECTED INDIVIDUALIZING

Johnny: I've finished this assignment. What should I do now?

Analysis: Johnny may need considerable teacher structuring.

Teacher: Everyone else is still working. How did you manage to finish so quickly?

Analysis: Probably represents a ploy (on the teacher's part) to gain time to think of something for Johnny to do.

Johnny: It was easy!

Analysis: Confirms Johnny's ability.

Teacher: Well, why don't you go on and do the next assignment?

Analysis: An assignment is phrased as if it were a question.

Johnny: Gee, do I have to? Can't I go to the library?

Analysis: Unhappy with the prospect of more work, Johnny turns the assignment into a debatable question, and then offers a more palatable option.

To accommodate students who finish early or who have nothing to do, some teachers establish interest centers or learning stations around the room. Students are generally free to go to the area and work on activities of their choice. Thus, the "reward" for students who finish early is the freedom to select activities that interest them and, hopefully, that they want to do.

What may have begun as a way to deal with students who finish early is certainly not limited to that, however, for some teachers have opted to use interest centers and learning stations as the basis for their entire program. In some respects, their efforts reflect the height of individualized instruction. We hasten to add that when teachers use a centers approach, you can be fairly certain that they require students to complete certain activities; it's not a matter of completely free choice. Otherwise students might avoid some subjects entirely.

Permitting students to participate in the selection and development of instructional activities is what student-directed individualizing is all about. It is an approach in which the teacher shares *some* (not all) of the instructional decision making with students.

Permitting students to exercise a greater role in instructional decision making sometimes necessitates physical changes in the classroom—changes intended to facilitate student choice making. In order to provide space in your classroom for interest centers or learning stations, you'll probably need to rearrange the room. Thus, instead of a conventional classroom with perfectly aligned rows of seats (Setting A of Figure 14.2), you'll typically find a much more flexible arrangement, as illustrated in Setting B of Figure 14.2. The intent of the centers approach, which is also called "centering," is to create a physical space where students can go as they pursue activities related to a particular subject area or to their own interests.

Several years ago we conducted an informal poll of over 1,200 teachers from across the country. We asked them which of two classroom settings—Setting A or B as shown in Figure 14.2—required more teacher effort. Almost to a person they indicated that it was easier to manage a teacher-directed classroom like the one shown in Setting A. We also asked the teachers what they thought would be the biggest problem in moving toward a more open classroom like the one shown in Setting B of Figure 14.2. Again, their response was almost universal: helping students accept the greater sense of responsibility that open classrooms require.

FIGURE 14.2 Two Classroom Arrangements

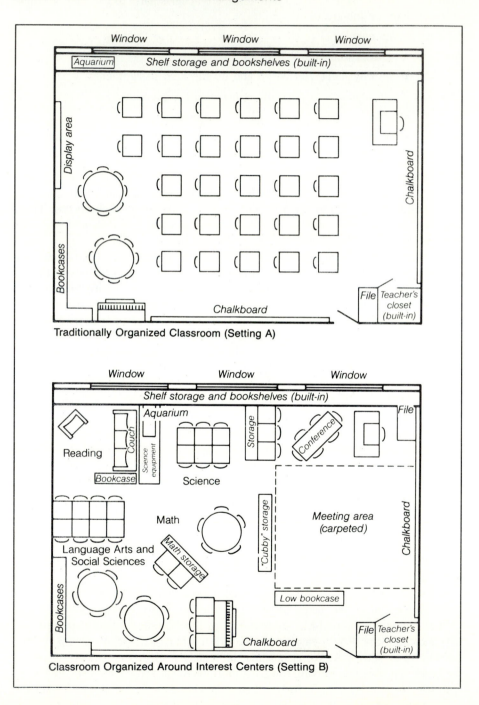

Traditionally Organized Classroom (Setting A)

Classroom Organized Around Interest Centers (Setting B)

For students who have spent most of their school life in traditional, teacher-directed classrooms, shifting to a more open setting could be a chaotic experience. However, if your goal is to share instructional decision making with students and to help them accept greater responsibility for their learning, you may find Gary Van der Haven's experience helpful.

GARY VAN DER HAVEN'S CLASSROOM: A CASE STUDY

Gary Van der Haven's fifth-grade classroom is a large room with a huge aquarium in the center. The floor is covered with a multicolored collection of carpet remnants and old rugs. A couch and some overstuffed chairs stand in one corner, and tables, chairs, and other working spaces are set up in clusters around the room. It's a classroom that reflects warmth, informality, and a lot of time spent collecting things.

Aside from its overall layout, two things are especially striking about Gary's classroom. First are the book reports written on large sheets of paper and mounted on the ceiling. Students lie on the floor to read them. The second thing is a sign over the chalkboard that reads: *You will have as much freedom as you have responsibility.* As Gary indicates, "The only way that this classroom can function is if everyone accepts responsibility for it. If someone goofs off, everyone gets hurt. Although you often hear that statement in traditional classrooms, in our setup it becomes even more important. Sometimes, like before vacations, I have to be the bad guy and sit on everybody."

"How do other teachers react to the way you operate your class?" we asked.

"It varies," Gary replied. "Some teachers think it's great, but then some of the old guard think I'm crazy."

"Have you always taught this way—in this kind of classroom?"

"No," he answered, "it's taken me eleven years to reach this point. I started out in a fairly traditional classroom—clusters of chairs and tables, that sort of thing—and have gradually changed to what you see now."

"In other words, you didn't consciously plan to teach in this kind of setup?"

"Not really," Gary said. "I had a general idea, but nothing specific that I could point to. Sometimes it depends on the kids. I learned the hard way that I couldn't take kids from a traditional fourth-grade classroom and turn them loose in this kind of environment—they went wild. So in September this room looks much more like a traditional classroom than it does now. I have assigned seats, everything. Then I gradually add things; the stuff in the quiet corner first, then the rugs and the other materials as the kids show that they have the responsibility to accept it.

"Two years ago," he continued, "I had a group that just couldn't handle the responsibility. I tried bringing in the rugs and the other stuff but

I had to take them out again. That group just couldn't deal with the freedom."

"Don't a lot of teachers use that as an excuse for not doing things—that their students can't handle it?" we asked.

"Yeah, that's true," Gary replied, "but many teachers say that without having tried it. They think their students can't handle something but they really don't know for sure. When I failed with that group, it wasn't because I hadn't tried."

There are several morals here, if we can call them that. One, before plunging into a major reorganization, "test the water" on a small scale. Move into it gradually. Second, don't assume that your students cannot do something until you (and they) have given it your best effort. Third, when you attempt something and it fails, the cause may not lie entirely with your ability. Remember that children who can function in unstructured situations can also function in highly structured situations. The reverse is not necessarily true, however; children who require a great deal of teacher structuring may flounder hopelessly in unstructured environments.

SOCIAL STUDIES CENTERS

We have used two terms, *interest centers* and *learning stations,* as if they were synonymous when, in practice, they are not. Although interest centers and learning stations may be quite similar in appearance, they differ in how they are used. An interest center is, by definition, a place students *may* go if they are interested in whatever that center contains. A learning station, on the other hand, is an area of the classroom that students *must* visit, either to complete tasks assigned by the teacher or to select from a range of alternative activities. In essence, there's more teacher direction associated with learning stations than with interest centers.

How does one create a social studies center? And, what do you put into it besides a couple of maps, a globe, and a set of encyclopedias?

The first thing you'll need to do is carve out some space for your center. Exactly how you do that depends on what kind of space you have available, so we can't be of much help in this area. Again, Setting B of Figure 14.2 shows one possible model. If need be, you could combine a social studies center with a science or language arts center. However you decide to proceed, you should mention your plans to one of the most important persons in any school—the custodian. If he or she must clean your room at night and prefers desks in neat, straight rows, you probably ought to inform him or her in advance of what you are trying to do. In addition, you'll probably want to mention your plans to the principal, particularly if most classrooms in your building have a more traditional format.

A social studies center should be comfortable—carpeted or cushioned—and should involve motivational materials such as posters, artifacts, magazines, records and tapes. (© *Paul Conklin/ Monkmeyer Press Photo Service*)

Once you get the preliminaries out of the way, you're ready to begin collecting materials. The following was abridged and adapted from a listing compiled by Evelyn Berger and Bonnie A. Winters (1973, pp. 14–15).

1. Several copies of selected social studies texts, especially those with lower reading levels, if available.

2. Trade books, cookbooks, songbooks, even fiction related to whatever you plan to study.

3. Maps of all shapes and sizes, especially topographical maps of your area.

4. Magazines and newspapers, depending on your grade level. Even at the primary level, you can never have too many magazines.

5. Filmstrips, records, tapes, transparencies, etc.

6. Artifacts—coins, stamps, etc.—from areas of the world you may be studying during the year.

7. Study prints, pictures, or travel posters.

8. A large "treasure chest" of materials for costumes to use in role playing or sociodrama.

9. Cushions, carpet pieces, perhaps even a rocking chair.

10. Large appliance cartons—for puppet stages and any variety of "buildings."

11. Some means to store everything on this list. These may be file cabinets, storage cases, mobile carts, bookcases, etc. The essential thing here is that the students have access to most materials when they need them (and thus not be forced to bother you every time they need something).

If you were to ask the typical open-classroom teacher what his or her biggest problem is, we suspect you'd find it's not teaching, not management, not discipline, but *storage!*

TASK AND ACTIVITY CARDS

Once you've collected enough materials, you'll still need a way to manage your centers. One successful strategy for doing that involves the use of task and activity cards. These are just what the name implies, cards—usually 5 by 8 inches or 7 by 11 inches—describing a task or an activity. Students can select task or activity cards that interest them, or they can be assigned by the teacher, depending on how you want to use your center.

The range of tasks or activities you make available on task or activity cards can be almost endless. Some of them may require that students go elsewhere—the library, outside, etc.—to complete the activity, while others will be self-contained, that is, everything the student will need will be located in the center or station. The difference between going elsewhere and being self-contained is the basis for our distinction between activity and task cards.

As a rule, activity cards reflect the following characteristics:

1. *They are open-ended;* they present activities for which there are no previously established answers. "Write a short story about what you see happening in this picture" and "Go out and find a million of something and then prove it" are examples of open-ended activities students might wish to pursue.

2. *They are not self-contained;* they do not include whatever information the student will need to complete the activity. "Conduct a survey to determine whether most students prefer frozen or canned corn" and "Go to the library and prepare a five-page report on . . ." are examples of activities that students must go elsewhere to complete.

On the other hand, task cards (illustrated in Figure 14.3 and Figure 14.4) reflect the following characteristics:

1. *They are self-contained;* they include the information students will need to complete the task.
2. *They have a readily identifiable skill focus.* Note that in the teacher-made task card (Figure 14.3) the second sentence, "Then, go back over your story and underline what you observed with a black pen and what you inferred with a red pen," shifts what would otherwise be an open-ended activity card to a task card with an identifiable skills focus—observing and inferring.

FIGURE 14.3   Teacher-Made Task Card

Write a short story about what you see in the picture.

Then, go back and underline what you observed with a black pen and what you inferred with a red pen.

Share your story with us when you are finished.

(Source: Cultural Resources Council, 411 Montgomery Street, Syracuse, N. Y. 13202.)

FIGURE 14.4   Commercially Made Task Card

Normal Temperatures for Ten U. S. Cities

City and state	January		July	
	High	Low	High	Low
Boston, Massachusetts	37	22	80	64
Denver, Colorado	43	20	86	62
Detroit, Michigan	33	19	84	63
Helena, Montana	27	8	84	52
Houston, Texas	62	46	92	75
Juneau, Alaska	31	21	62	47
Miami, Florida	74	63	87	76
Nashville, Tennessee	49	31	91	69
Portland, Maine	31	11	79	57
Portland, Oregon	44	35	79	58

Number your paper from 1 to 20. Read the questions below. After each question are several answers. Look at the table to see which answer is correct. Then write its letter on your paper after the number of the question. Be sure to read *all* the answers before you decide which one is correct.

1. The main purpose of this table is to show **A.** the ten largest cities in the United States **B.** temperatures each month during the year **C.** the normal temperatures for ten U.S. cities during January and July **D.** the highest and lowest temperatures ten U.S. cities have ever had in January and July

2. The table lists the normal temperatures for **A.** two months **B.** four months **C.** ten months **D.** each half year

3. The city that has the lowest temperature in January is **A.** Portland, Maine **B.** Helena **C.** Juneau **D.** Detroit

4. The warmest city in July is **A.** Nashville **B.** Miami **C.** Denver **D.** Houston

5. The coldest city in July is **A.** Portland, Maine **B.** Helena **C.** Juneau **D.** Portland, Oregon

6. The July temperatures in Portland, Maine, are most nearly like the July temperatures in **A.** Portland, Oregon **B.** Boston **C.** Juneau **D.** Helena

7. The city with January temperatures most nearly like those in July is **A.** Houston **B.** Miami **C.** Portland, Oregon **D.** Nashville

8. The city that has the greatest difference between the lowest and highest temperatures in July is **A.** Juneau **B.** Portland, Maine **C.** Houston **D.** Helena

9. The city in which the July high temperature is most nearly the same as the July high temperature in Houston is **A.** Denver **B.** Miami **C.** Nashville **D.** Detroit

10. Which city has about the same high and low temperatures in July as Houston has in January? **A.** Nashville **B.** Miami **C.** Detroit **D.** Juneau

(Source: Rath et al. [1969]. Reprinted by permission of Benefic Press.)

Just about any activity that appeals to you or your students can end up on a task or activity card. For convenience, you may wish to use a color-coding system, such as putting observing and inferring tasks on blue cards, research activities on red cards, and just plain "fun" activities (puzzles, riddles, etc.) on green cards. You'll also want to keep a supply of task and activity cards tucked away so you can change cards when your current crop begins to get a little stale. Actually, you might place a fresh set of task or activity cards in your center each time you begin a new area of study.

MODULES: LAPS, ILPS, AND OTHER FORMS OF ALPHABET SOUP

Modules are self-contained instructional packages that can be included in a center, and are intended to teach students about a particular topic. Since most modules contain (or indicate) almost everything students will need—a statement of objectives, a pretest, possible readings and activities, and a posttest—they can greatly simplify individualized instruction.

Modules go by a variety of names. An LAP, for example, indicates a Learning Activity Package, while an ILP is an Independent Learning Package. Regardless of what they are called, most modules contain the following components.

1. *Objectives*   Most modules clearly indicate to students what will be expected of them when they have completed the packet. Most modules will be stated behaviorally, and often in the form of "Upon completing this module, you will be expected to. . . ."

2. *Pretest*   If you know in advance that a student knows nothing about a module's topic, a pretest may be unnecessary. However, the inclusion of a pretest provides students with a way to determine if they are already proficient in the knowledge or skills a module deals with. If students complete the pretest successfully, they usually need go no further in the module.

   Note that the pretest, or at least the key to the pretest, is not usually packaged with the rest of the module materials.

3. *Activities*   The instructional activities in a module are usually keyed to certain objectives. If the pretest indicates that students are already able to meet the objectives, they are usually permitted to skip activities pertaining to those objectives.

4. *Posttest*   Posttests are not typically included with the rest of the module's materials even though they are a component of the program. Generally, students must get the posttest from the teacher (to avoid cheating, however unintentional it might be). When the module's objectives are clearly stated, students should have a good idea of what to anticipate on the posttest.

Some teachers use modules as the basis for their entire social studies program, and others—probably the majority—use them as a supplement. Some teachers require that students complete each module, and others allow students to select among those that interest them. Because there are no established guidelines in this area, teachers can use modular-based instruction as they see fit.

From everything we've said thus far, it should be apparent that individualizing instruction tremendously enlarges the scope of what it means to teach. It asks that you develop and use diagnostic skills that you may not have seen used before, or that weren't used on you (or at least you didn't know were being used on you); it also demands that you prescribe appropriate learning activities accordingly. What sounds so easy in theory will undoubtedly prove to be another difficult challenge. The essential question should not be whether or not to individualize instruction, but rather *how* you'll go about it.

We've tried to suggest some ways to begin—and we realize that they are only a beginning. However you go about it, we repeat our earlier advice: begin slowly.

SUMMARY

To believe that all students will learn the same things at the same time, at the same rate, and with the same degree of retention is sheer fantasy. In almost any classroom at any grade level, the range of students' abilities, interests, talents, knowledge, previous experiences, personalities, learning styles, dispositions, and needs is so great that it's staggering. In many instances, individualizing instruction so that these characteristics are taken into account is not simply a matter of principle, it's a matter of necessity.

We have suggested that individualized instruction has resulted from efforts to make schools more responsive to individual students and their instructional needs. We identified several administrative policies—homogeneous grouping, acceleration, retention, and special classes—that are aimed at narrowing the range of needs and characteristics with which teachers must deal. Although administrative policies help to determine *which* students will be in a particular class, the policies have relatively little impact on *how* students will be taught. For that, teachers must turn to instructional approaches to individualization.

Instructional approaches to individualization take two basic forms: teacher-directed and student-directed. In teacher-directed individualizing, the focus is on diagnosing the student's learning problem and then prescribing appropriate instruction. Diagnosing is a procedure (borrowed from the world of medicine) in which the teacher attempts to identify the factors that are influencing a learning situation. Prescribing, which is also borrowed from medicine, reflects the teacher's attempts to alter or modify instructional activities so that there is a close match between the tasks and the student's ability to deal with them. In some instances, the teacher may alter the task so that it more closely corresponds to the student's learning style. Learning style refers to generic factors such as preferred instructional mode, the need for structure, the social and physical contexts of learning, responses to reward/praise, and goal preferences that can influence how a student learns in any subject area.

Student-directed individualizing reflects efforts to provide options and opportunities for students to participate in instructional decision making, particularly in selecting the kinds of learning activities they will encounter. Permitting students to play a more significant role in instructional decision making necessitates a more open learning environment, as well as a greater sense of responsibility on the student's part.

The legislation relating to exceptional children has resulted in a sharpened focus on individualized instruction. We noted that exceptional children are students at either end of the educational spectrum—those children with handicaps and special needs as well as the gifted and talented. In view of the increased attention and funding being directed toward exceptional students, it is becoming apparent that we cannot overlook the needs of any child. In certain situations and in certain ways, every student is exceptional. Indeed, "exceptional children" may be a misnomer; exceptional (individualized) instruction for *all* children may actually be more appropriate.

SUGGESTED ACTIVITIES

1. There is a widespread, though usually unstated, feeling among many Americans that schooling should be the same everywhere, and that providing special programs for exceptional students is somehow undemocratic. Associated with this is the impression that Americans have accepted special education out of a sense of sympathy and sorrow for "those poor kids," a spirit similar to the one that causes us to help the needy at Christmastime and then ignore them the rest of the year.

   Most Americans accept the principle that every child has the right to an education. But do they also accept the principle that every child has the right to an education appropriate to his or her needs and abilities?

2. "If a child doesn't measure up, well, that's her problem." Identify your personal position with regard to this frequently heard comment.

3. As a group, design and actually build some of the instructional materials you would include in a social studies learning center.

REFERENCES

Berger, Evelyn, and Bonnie Winters. 1973. *Social Studies in the Open Classroom: A Practical Guide.* New York: Teachers College Press.

Coles, Gerald S. 1978. "The Learning Disabilities Test Battery: Empirical and Social Issues." *Harvard Educational Review,* 48 (August) 3, 313–40.

Deno, E. 1970. "Special Education as Developmental Capital." *Exceptional Children,* 37, 236.

Dunn, Lloyd M. 1968. "Special Education for the Mildly Retarded—Is Much of It Justified?" *Exceptional Children,* 35 (September), 5–22.

————. 1973. *Exceptional Children in the Schools.* 2nd ed. New York: Holt, Rinehart and Winston.

Dunn, R. S., and G. E. Price. 1980. "The Learning Style Characteristics of Gifted Students." *Gifted Child Quarterly,* 24, 33–36.

Gallagher, James J. 1974. "Phenomenal Growth and New Problems Characterize Special Education." *Phi Delta Kappan,* LV (April), 516–20.

Griggs, S. A., and G. E. Price. 1982. "A Comparison Between the Learning Styles of Gifted Versus Average Suburban Junior High School Students." *Gifted Child and Adult Quarterly,* 7, 39–42.

Haring, Norris G., ed. 1978. *The Behavior of Exceptional Children.* Columbus, Ohio: Charles Merrill.

Hobbs, Nicholas. 1975. *The Futures of Children*. San Francisco: Josey-Bass.

Kirk, Samuel A., and James J. Gallagher. 1986. *Educating Exceptional Children*. 5th ed. Boston: Houghton Mifflin.

Raths, Louis E., et al. 1969. *The Thinking Box*. Chicago, Ill.: Benefic Press.

Richardson, Stephen A. 1973. "The Effect of Physical Disability on the Socialization of a Child." In *The Handbook of Socialization Theory and Research,* ed. David A. Goslin. Chicago: Rand-McNally. pp. 1047–64.

Rosenshine, Barak V. 1978. "Academic Engaged Time, Content Covered, and Direct Instruction." Paper presented at the Annual Meeting of the American Educational Research Association.

Rowan, Helen. 1966. "Meritocracy: Ability Testing and the American Spirit." *Carnegie Quarterly,* 14 (Spring), 5–7.

Scott, Robert. 1969. *The Making of Blind Men*. New York: Russell Sage Foundation.

Smith, Monte D., Michael J. Coleman, Paul R. Dodecki, and Erle E. Davis. 1977. "Intellectual Characteristics of School-Labeled Learning Disabled Children." *Exceptional Children,* 44 (March), 185–95.

Ysseldyke, James E., and Bob Aglozzine. 1984. *Introduction to Special Education*. Boston: Houghton Mifflin.

SUGGESTED READINGS

Evelyn Berger and Bonnie A. Winters. 1973. *Social Studies in the Open Classroom: A Practical Guide*. New York: Teachers College Press. The subtitle on this one should read "A Very Practical Guide." In fewer than a hundred pages, the authors show you both what to do and how to do it.

John Herlihy and Myra Herlihy, eds. 1980. *Mainstreaming in the Social Studies,* Bulletin No. 62. Washington, D.C.: National Council for the Social Studies. This volume is made up of short articles dealing with the different aspects of mainstreaming in the social studies. Very helpful.

Kim Marshall. 1975. *Opening Your Class with Learning Stations*. Palo Alto, Calif.: Learning Handbooks. This is a brief, lively, to-the-point guide for establishing learning stations and for avoiding the chaos that sometimes accompanies them.

CHAPTER 15

Managing Instructional Resources

First Grader: Why does Daddy bring all those papers home in his briefcase?
Mother: Because he can't finish them at the office, so he has to work nights.
First Grader: Then why don't they put him in a slower group?

KEY QUESTIONS

□ What resources are available for teaching social studies?

□ What considerations are involved in using those resources?

□ What do teachers do when a school district lacks the resources they want?

KEY IDEAS

□ Instructional resources used improperly may be worse than having no resources at all.

□ Using resources effectively depends heavily on preplanning.

□ Identifying community resources is often less difficult than using those resources effectively.

□ Textbooks sometimes become the basis for a social studies program, not a resource to be used with it.

□ Instructional resources may lurk in unlikely places.

INTRODUCTION: "The Year They Taught the Telephone Directory"

Imagine a situation in which the teachers at one grade level were to pioneer a new program based on one thing only—the telephone directory. According to Merrill Harmin and Sidney Simon's (1965) satirical description of that situation, there was some grumbling from the teachers. This was not too unusual because complaints and grumbling often accompany a major curriculum change. Their complaints notwithstanding, come September the teachers set out to teach their assigned material.

Homework assignments typically required that students memorize small sections of the phone book. During September, for example, this included the names, addresses, and phone numbers of individuals in the As and Bs. Some students found this challenging at first, but they became increasingly bored and disgruntled as the semester progressed. Other students didn't like the activities to begin with. The teachers discovered that developing worthwhile and interesting in-class activities was an almost impossible challenge, especially since there weren't many ways to vary questions like "What is the phone number of AAA Auto Service?" and "Who lives at 126 North Hathaway?"

As the year progressed, the grumbling and complaints continued to increase. In fact, come January, the teachers found that even the midterm exam, which covered the letters A–M, failed to motivate even the most grade-conscious students. But the superintendent of that district, who had instituted the change to begin with, was facing a revolt—or so it was reported.

Harmin and Simon don't tell us how the mythical situation ended; rather, the superintendent defends the program by suggesting that studying the telephone directory develops discipline, concentration, and good study habits. Those time-worn arguments are not very convincing, especially because they apply to something that seems patently absurd to begin with. However, the irony of a satire such as this one is that there's usually a kernel or two of truth hidden somewhere within it. In this instance, a telephone directory could serve as a legitimate resource for teaching social studies. Unfortunately, in Harmin and Simon's account the telephone book was not used as a *resource*, it was the entire curriculum.

A resource is something teachers use to teach with; it's something they use to reach certain goals and objectives. In Chapter 3, for example, we used two cans of corn to develop a unit on resource utilization, and in Chapter 10 we used information from the telephone book as the basis for an activity on the residential pattern of doctors. In both instances, we did not attempt to teach about the resource itself; rather, we used the information for other purposes.

Our point here is that resources for teaching social studies are almost everywhere. The key question you need to ask yourself is "How could I use *that* (whatever the resource is) to teach?" The question you need *not* ask yourself is "What can I teach about that?" Individuals asking the latter question could find themselves teaching the names of people listed in the telephone directory.

Consider, for a moment, how a teacher might use the information in the Yellow Pages as the basis for legitimate instructional activities. Here are a few suggestions:

Identify the different government services available in your local community.

Identify different ways in which the Yellow Pages could be organized. Then consider what those organizational patterns would mean for (1) users, (2) advertisers, and (3) the telephone company.

Determine what it costs, if anything, to be listed in the Yellow Pages. If charges do apply, speculate on how they are determined as well as on why businesses might pay to be listed. When schools are listed in the Yellow Pages, do you suppose they pay? Or are some things listed free?

Using a Yellow Pages from the 1960s or 1970s and a current directory, determine the location of selected businesses—florists, hardware stores, video rental outlets (which did not exist in the 1960s), movie theaters, etc. Plot the location of each industry on a city map, and determine how the number and locations of the businesses have changed over time?

Whether you are fortunate enough to obtain a teaching position where you have a wealth of instructional resources available or whether you have relatively few materials, we suspect that the quality of your social studies lessons will depend not on the amount of materials you have, but on how you use them. Of course, it's nice to have lots of instructional materials to teach with, but the key ingredient is not the materials themselves, but you—the teacher—and how you *use* those materials with your students.

There is such a wealth of resources to use in teaching social studies that organizing the balance of this chapter in a way that made sense proved more difficult than we had anticipated. As a consequence, we have turned to an arbitrary and somewhat eclectic scheme that ranges from printed materials through computers, nonprint, and visual resources, and finally to community resources.

PRINT MATERIALS

TEXTBOOKS

One resource above all others—the textbook—dominates the print materials category. Almost every school has textbooks; in fact, some classes have access to several different texts. This doesn't mean that children use them—willingly or otherwise—just that they have access to them. We used the expression "almost every school" because we have found prospective teachers who, upon returning from school visits, were amazed to find that some schools—even those with ample financial resources—did not use social studies textbooks.

The absence of social studies texts can usually be explained by one of two factors: default or design. *Default* comes about when teachers feel so pressured to teach other subjects that there is little time left for social studies. Where social studies is treated only incidentally, if at all, there is little need for a textbook.

In some school systems, the availability of social studies texts may be limited by *design*. In Texas, for example, there is a prescribed social studies curriculum, but the state does not provide primary-level (K–3) social studies textbooks. This means that unless local schools are willing to purchase textbooks from their own funds, primary teachers are forced to rely on their own resources to teach the state curriculum.

In other schools, the number of texts available may be limited to a specified figure—often to no more than ten copies of a particular book. Because those classrooms may have as many as forty or fifty texts, it is technically incorrect to say that they don't have any social studies texts. What they don't have are enough copies of a single text for every child to have a copy of the same book. In such instances, teachers use a *multitext* approach in which they select elements from different books as needed. This reduces the pressure that teachers sometimes feel to cover every chapter in a book, and it also tends to prohibit teachers from turning social studies into an oral reading activity.

Generalizing about social studies textbooks can be a risky business, but we will barge ahead to suggest that

Elementary social studies textbooks today are much more similar than they are different.

You can get usable teaching ideas from every existing social studies textbook or accompanying teacher's guide—no matter how old and decrepit.

Textbooks have a way of becoming the basis for a social studies program, not a resource to be used with it.

Using Textbooks

When we first began working with prospective teachers, we identified several general procedures that applied to using textbooks. We identified things like reading the selection before assigning it and helping children with the new vocabulary, the table of contents, and the index. Upon reflection, however, most of our suggestions were things that almost anyone should find fairly obvious. The first time we presented those suggestions to a class, some students were insulted. That was the last time we tried to generalize about using social studies textbooks.

It is easy enough to say that textbooks are tools—resources to be used for particular purposes—but for many of us, the textbook *was* the social studies program. Everyone would read a certain number of pages each week and answer the end-of-chapter questions, and, if there was time (there usually wasn't), the entire text was covered in one school year. There was little or no selection of material. In fact, about the only difference between social studies and a typical reading lesson was the kind of content one read about.

As much as we disapprove of totally textbook-based social studies programs, we also recognize that an identifiable basis is necessary, and that using a social studies textbook for that purpose may be the lesser evil—for one's first year of teaching at least. In addition, every textbook series has an accompanying teacher's guide, some of which are more helpful than you might imagine.

For teachers who wish to depart from a textbook-dominated program, the first step in that process is to shift your perception of the textbook. When you come to regard a text as a resource, as something to use if it suits your purposes—then you will have made the transition.

What are some different ways you might use textbooks? Consider the following possibilities:

As a source of background information that may be read either (1) prior to studying a topic or concept or (2) *after* the need for the information has been established

As something students read on their own whenever they feel the need for additional information on a topic

As a source of in-class activities (or test questions)

As a contrasting point of view or as data for further analysis

As a means to confirm certain hypotheses *after* group discussion; "India is a 'poor' nation," etc.

As a vehicle to identify the main idea of several related paragraphs

As a source for establishing the meaning of various terms (so that they need not be dealt with in class)

As a way of placating those people who think that a course isn't worthwhile unless it has a textbook associated with it

Each of the above may be an appropriate use for an elementary social studies textbook, depending on your purpose.

SUPPLEMENTARY PRINT MATERIALS

The kinds of supplementary materials available to elementary social studies teachers are astounding. They range from periodicals and current events newspapers (*My Weekly Reader, Scholastic News,* etc.) through an almost unbelievable assortment of trade books (children's books), to prepackaged, skill-building kits on almost any topic you can name. We will examine supplementary materials in terms of these categories.

Current Events Publications

If your elementary school was like our elementary school, some of your teachers used one of the weekly or monthly current affairs periodicals: *My Weekly Reader,* from American Education Publications (245 Long Hill Rd., P.O. Box 360, Middletown, CT 06457), *Let's Find Out* (Kindergarten) or *Scholastic News* (Grades 1–6) from Scholastic, Inc. (730 Broadway, New York, NY 10003-9538), or *Junior Review* (Grades 6–9) from the Civic Education Service (1733 K St., Washington, DC 20006). These publications are still available and all are quite well written.

Instead of current events periodicals, your teachers may have relied more heavily on daily newspapers. From time to time, you may have been asked to bring in a current events article to share with the rest of the class. Unless certain limitations were put on the kind of clipping one could bring in, a typical assortment was likely to deal with topics such as a serious auto accident, last Saturday's Little League game, or a bank robbery in northeastern Nevada. Seldom would a child-selected article focus on Central America or the Middle East, changing views of morality, or the problems of international diplomacy—unless, that is, the teacher insisted on it. Even then, most children are likely to be at a loss to either understand or interpret the significance of such events. Such an assignment reflects the current events dilemma: as much as we might like children to be interested in and aware of the events and issues that may influence their lives, many of those events and issues may go beyond their level of comprehension and concern. The fact that some teachers have difficulty explaining something such as inflation or the Palestine Liberation Organization illustrates another dimension of the problem.

Current Events or Current Affairs   Amid these realities, you have at least two options for keeping students abreast of happenings around them: one is to maintain a current *events* program, where an event is defined as anything that has happened or is happening, either trivial or potentially significant; the other is to establish a current *affairs* program, one that focuses on continuing, ongoing issues or concerns. Unless you are able to establish realistic limitations on a current *events* approach, you may find that it can quickly degenerate into a warmed-over version of the nightly news, the purposes for which might be better served if the class actually watched the six o'clock news on TV.

Because current *affairs* programs focus on fewer, in-depth studies of ongoing issues, they're less likely to reflect the piecemeal approach that can occur in a current events program. In a current affairs program, for example, your focus might be on different dimensions of the farm crisis. Or you might use changes in the price (or weight) of bubble gum or candy bars as an entree to the continuing study of rises in the cost of living. The farm crisis, for example, is characteristic of a continuing problem whose full significance may initially exceed the comprehension of elementary children. The idea of a current affairs program is to tie together the separate events of a continuing problem to help build the child's understanding of the significance of a problem that could remain beyond their comprehension if dealt with on an isolated "events" basis.

Weekly news periodicals often furnish the background so essential for providing children with a context within which they can begin to interpret a particular current event. At the same time, however, these periodicals typically feature different topics each week, and this tends to support a piecemeal "events" approach. But what they lack in depth of coverage may be compensated for by their broad coverage of events and happenings. Thus, the basic decision you face in developing a current affairs or current events program (and in deciding whether or not to use one of the current events periodicals) depends on how much in-depth understanding you are willing to sacrifice to gain broader topical coverage. In addition, since some current affairs may be extremely esoteric for elementary children, even if reduced to their simplest dimensions, you may be better off opting for the broader coverage you gain with an "events" approach, especially at the primary level. But if you plan to teach at the intermediate levels, the possibility of pursuing an "affairs" approach becomes much more realistic.

Newspapers

Daily newspapers provide what the current events periodicals don't, including coverage of local news. But teachers who look to newspapers solely as a source of local news are not looking far enough. In fact, in some schools teachers base almost their entire program—including social studies, math, language arts, and reading—on the daily newspaper. Their students do comparison shopping using the grocery ads, compute batting averages (math) using the sports page, invest (mythically) in the stock market, examine weather patterns (using the weather map and forecast), realphabetize the newspaper's directory, put scrambled headlines back together again, compare the amount of space devoted to various categories of articles (international news, national news, etc.), use small sections of the paper to compare the amount of factual data (reporting) with the amount of opinion (editorials), or compare the amount of space devoted to ads with the space devoted to news.

You might also give student groups identical collections of stories clipped from several newspapers and ask them to compose a front page, noting their reasons for including the articles they did. You could also remove the headlines from various articles and have children create their own based on the content of the story. They could then compare their headlines with the originals. Or they could take several days' accumulation of TV schedules and try to identify patterns in TV programming.

There are still other things you could do with a daily newspaper, but these examples should serve to illustrate the idea. Note also that, for many of these activities, it isn't always necessary for the child to be able to read the articles in order to use the newspaper as a learning tool. As with most instructional resources, the essential idea is that you begin to consider the newspaper as something you can teach *with,* not simply teach *about.*

Many local newspapers maintain a "Newspaper in Education" department to provide teaching tips and other aids for integrating newspapers into the curriculum. If your local paper does not offer such a service, contact the American Newspaper Publishers Association Foundation (The Newspaper Center, Box 17407, Dulles International Airport, Washington, DC 20041) for information.

Trade Books

A book designed for use in classroom settings is considered a textbook. But a book—fiction or nonfiction—intended for sale to the general public is considered a trade book. *Mike Mulligan and His Steam Shovel* (Burton, 1939), which we referred to earlier, is a juvenile trade book, as is Kenneth Grahame's (1954) classic, *Wind in the Willows,* and thousands and thousands of others. There are so many trade books available that the National Council for the Social Studies reviews only those books considered "most notable" during a given year. Thus, unless the book (1) is written primarily for children (K–8), (2) emphasizes human relations, (3) presents an original theme or a fresh slant on a traditional topic, (4) is highly readable, and (5) includes maps and illustrations where appropriate, it will not be included in that bibliography.

Most teacher's guides and curriculum guides suggest trade books to accompany almost any social studies topic you can name. Likewise, children's literature textbooks, such as *Through the Eyes of a Child* by Donna Norton (1987), *Children and Books* by Zena Sutherland and May Hill Arbuthnot (1986), and *Children's Literature in the Elementary School* by Charlotte Huck (1979), are excellent resources. All of these provide brief reviews of some of the outstanding trade books in an area.

Historical fiction, nonfiction, biography, you name it—somewhere there's a trade book that applies to whatever your class is studying. To determine quality works of children's fiction that you might wish to use with your class, McGowan (1987) recommends the following criteria:

1. Determine if the book is *developmentally appropriate.* (Can the prose be understood by its intended audience, and are the setting, plot, and themes relatively familiar to young readers?)

2. Determine if the book has *literary value.* (Is it meaningful, enjoyable to read, and has the author written with attention to character development, dialogue, plot, imagery, and message?)

3. Determine if the book presents *valid information.* (Is the story told with reasonable accuracy and in a "true-to-life" fashion?)

4. Determine if the book's *message is of value.* (Does the author examine an issue worthy of the reader's attention or does the story involve values that the reader must eventually assimilate?)

One area of children's fiction particularly appropriate to social studies involves ethnic literature. For example, *The Big Push* by Betty Baker (1972) is based on a historical incident that occurred when white men forced Hopi Indian children to go to school, and is almost guaranteed to generate an active discussion. Children will also enjoy *The Hundred Penny Box* by Sharon Bell Mathis (1975), a poignant story about a young boy who convinces his mother not to throw out all of the old things that belong to his great-great-great-aunt, who lives with them.

Another subcategory of trade books that offers real potential for social studies classes are those having no text. *The Chicken and the Egg* by Iela and Enzo Mari (1970), for example, is a sequence of beautiful illustrations following the development of a chicken. Since there are no words, the children must supply them, and this adds immeasurable excitement to the book.

Trade books are like other instructional resources—you cannot use them unless you have them. But once you have the book in hand, you then have the option of using it in any one of several ways:

As supplementary reading for children

As background reading for yourself

As reference material for children to use

As the basis for units or lessons

As the basis for an individualized reading program that parallels whatever you are dealing with in social studies

COMMENTARY: Reading to Children

When we first began teaching in an elementary school, we did so with the conviction that children were older and more grown up than kids used to be, and that they wouldn't tolerate childish things—things like being read to by an adult. Such things might be okay for primary youngsters, but older children wouldn't sit still for such practices—or at least so we thought. Yet in teaching an average group of sixth graders, it became our practice to read vignettes from various children's books about whatever we happened to be studying. They loved it.

Were our classes unique? We wondered about that until one day when we had the opportunity to visit a fifth-grade class. As it happened, the teacher was reading them a story—at their request. The story? *Peter Rabbit.* We could hardly believe it—a group of fifth graders, sitting in rapt attention while their teacher read them *Peter Rabbit.*

The moral? Perhaps it's that we shouldn't underestimate the power of a good story. But then perhaps children may not be quite as old as they act, or as we (and they) may think they are.

Teaching Kits

Teaching kits are self-contained packages of instructional materials. Some kits, such as the MATCH (Materials and Activities for Teachers and Children) units (Delta Education, Box M, Nashua, NH 03061) offer one- to two-week units on a variety of topics such as "The City" (K–4), "The Japanese Family" (4–6), "Medieval People" (4–8), and "A House of Ancient Greece" (5–10). The MATCH kits include a teacher's guide, an assortment of student materials, reference materials for students and teachers, and sometimes even filmstrips or films.

A growing number of museums and state departments of education offer specialized teaching kits on a loan or rental basis. The Institute for Texan Cultures in San Antonio, for example, offers rental kits on "The Indians of Texas." If that topic is not something your students might study, consider the "Mysteries in History" toolbox available from the Indianapolis Children's Museum. Or contact the Education Coordinator at the nearest historical museum or reconstructed settlement (e.g., Old Sturbridge Village in Massachusetts, Connor Prairie Settlement in Indiana, etc.) or your state department of education to determine if they have instructional materials available for loan or rent. Considering that self-contained teaching kits can cost upward of $750, the relatively lower cost of loan or rental kits (approximately $25 plus shipping) often makes them more attractive to cost-conscious administrators.

Other commercially available kits focus on access and process skills rather than topics, which means that students can use them throughout the year. "The Thinking Box" (Benefic Press, 1900 N. Narragansett St., Chicago, IL 60639), for example, consists of a series of activity cards based on thinking skills and keyed to different subject areas. Other kits tend to focus on specific skill areas. For example, SRA's Basic Skills series (Science Research Associates, 155 N. Wacker Dr., Chicago, IL 60606) includes some nicely packaged activities dealing with map and globe skills, and graph and picture analysis. In each case, the skills are broken down into their smallest components and then each subskill or series of subskills is presented to the student on sequentially organized task cards. After completing the task, students can check their results on the answer card provided. Note that skill kits are being replaced by computer programs in some subject areas, as we will describe shortly.

Programmed Instruction

Until computer-based instruction gained popularity, most programmed instruction materials followed a workbook format in which the children wrote their responses to various questions. Correct answers were made available after the responses were entered. Computers greatly simplify this process by (1) indicating if the child's answer is correct or incorrect, (2) maintaining a record of the child's performance, and (3) preventing children from peeking at the correct responses, as was sometimes possible with written materials.

By design, most programmed materials require one-word or short-phrase responses, and, as such, focus heavily on factual material. In addition, it is difficult to skip around in written programmed materials (and almost impossible in computer-based materials) because of their rigidly sequential nature. This apparent limitation, however, can become an asset for children who flourish on structured, factually based material.

Workbooks

Workbooks are available for many social studies textbook series, although you usually have to order them separately—they don't just come with the texts. Also, you may find that they are called *pupil study guides, activity guides,* or something similar, perhaps in an effort to avoid the unsavory reputation sometimes associated with *workbooks*.

Like programmed materials, workbooks tend to emphasize factual material. However, if you are teaching in a program that demands the kind of reinforcement workbooks offer, you may find them helpful.

COMPUTER-BASED RESOURCES

The first two editions of this book were written on a typewriter. This edition was written on a personal computer. We now make changes and correct errors without retyping the entire page. The *hardware,* which includes the computer, the printer, and the monitor; as well as the *software,* which includes the word-processing program, the spelling-checker program (which we use quite often), and the other programs, costs approximately $2500—or the equivalent of roughly two thousand bottles of correction fluid.

As teachers, we use our computers extensively. All of our course syllabi, most of our instructional materials (class handouts), and many of our examinations are now created and stored on the computer. Were we teaching in a school where we had to keep lots of student records, we would use one of the computer-based grade-book programs that are currently available. Those can provide an up-to-date analysis of a student's progress and can provide almost instant grades at the end of the semester.

A computer is an information-processing machine. It's fast, efficient, and accurate. When there are errors, they can invariably be traced back to the humans who are operating the machines. Some of our programs are so sophisticated that the computer will alert us to the possibility that we have made an error. Considering the amount of information and routine paperwork that teachers must deal with, our computers have proven to be a remarkably error-free resource for managing classroom-related tasks. Indeed, we sometimes wonder how we ever did without them. What we have yet to mention, however, are instructional uses for computers.

Computers offer a variety of possible applications within the social studies classroom—
ranging from tutorial programs that actually provide information to drill-and-practice
programs that reinforce learning. (© *Susan Lapides 1987*)

INSTRUCTIONAL APPLICATIONS

There are four basic modes of computer-assisted instruction (CAI): (1) tutorial,
(2) drill-and-practice, (3) data base problem-solving, and (4) simulation (Cacha,
1985). Each of these is described briefly below.

Tutorial Mode

Tutorial programs present information to students, typically in a step-by-step
manner. In other words, in a tutorial program the computer takes the place
of the teacher, the textbook, or some other source as the provider of information.

Tutorial programs are available for a variety of topics, including basic economics
and introductory American history, but most of these are geared toward the
secondary level. At the elementary level, tutorial programs tend to be more
general (less subject-specific). *Kids on Keys* (Spinnaker Software), for example, is
a tutorial program designed to help very young children become familiar with the
computer keyboard.

Drill-and-Practice Mode

Most programs in the drill-and-practice mode reinforce prior learning through repetitive practice. Should you wish your students to learn the states and capitals or to practice locating places using latitude or longitude, for example, there are a number of programs available that can help them. Most of the computer-based social studies programs currently on the market fall into the drill-and-practice mode.

Drill-and-practice programs have been likened to electronic workbooks. Unlike most traditional workbooks, however, the interactive quality of computer-based instruction provides immediate feedback. For example, when students enter an incorrect answer, the computer will typically respond with an encouraging "Try again." Unfortunately, most computer-based programs do not give credit for partially correct answers (as human graders might). To the question "What is the capital of Missouri?" for example, a student might respond with "Jeferson City" [sic]. This particular error could reflect either a student's inability to spell or inadequate keyboarding (typing) skills. Regardless of the source of the problem, the computer will invariably display its "Try again" response for what is essentially a correct answer. Further, when the teacher gets a printout of the child's performance, "Jeferson City" will be included in the percentage of "wrong" answers.

Some drill-and-practice programs avoid the spelling/typing problem by asking questions in a multiple-choice format. In those instances, the child need enter only the letter (A, B, C, or D) for the correct response. Less often will you find drill-and-practice programs that take variant spellings into account. Despite these limitations, the interactive nature of computer-based drill-and-practice programs can add life to what might otherwise be deadly dull material.

Problem-Solving Mode

"How do underdeveloped nations differ from developed nations?" This was the problem that Tama Traberman (1984), a middle-school teacher from New Jersey, posed to her students in a global studies course. After entering data from almanacs and other sources into their computers, the children were able to develop computer-generated profiles of various nations around the world. They found, among other things, that underdeveloped nations have significantly higher birth rates than developed nations.

Ms. Traberman's students spent considerable time entering data into their computers. Today, a growing number of information collections, known as *data bases,* are available. In other words, much of the information now found in a library's reference collection is being placed into a form that computers can access almost instantly. Instead of traditional floppy discs, some schools now have the capability of computer-to-computer communication over telephone lines. In the not-too-distant future, elementary children sitting before a computer monitor will be able to gain access to an information source the equivalent of the Library of Congress. Whether they will actually need such a resource remains to be seen.

Simulation Mode

Using simulation programs, children are able to place themselves into lifelike situations. As we described in Chapter 13, children can attempt to sail from Europe to the New World, travel from Missouri to Oregon in the 1840s, or attempt to succeed in business by opening a lemonade stand. A growing number of other simulation programs are also available.

The basic idea of computer-based simulations is the same as the simulations we described in Chapter 13; that is, to place children in realistic situations in which they must make decisions similar to those that had to be made in whatever real-life situation the simulation depicts. The player must decide, for example, how much food and water to take on the trip to Oregon, and how much can be obtained along the way. The point, however, is not to teach the amount of food that must be taken, but rather that food, water, and other materials were factors that pioneers had to consider, regardless of their destination.

Children sometimes approach computer-based simulations in much the same way they do video games; that is, their objective is to outwit the program to the extent that they "win." Such situations may require human intervention, such as a teacher-led discussion, that refocuses the children's attention on the content being simulated.

EVALUATING SOFTWARE

The quality of social studies software can vary tremendously. In some cases, the program's instructions may be unclear, while in other instances, the program may produce inaccurate stereotypes or require information the students do not have. Such flaws may make the programs unusable by children, or, as in the case of inaccurate stereotyping, inappropriate for use with children.

Recommended criteria for evaluating computer software are illustrated in Figure 15.1.

SOURCES OF INFORMATION

Resources for computer-based education change rather rapidly; new companies and new materials may appear while other companies go out of business, almost overnight. Some of your best sources of information include publications such as the following:

1. *The Computing Teacher,* International Council for Computers in Education, University of Oregon, 1878 Agate St., Eugene, OR 97403-1923.
2. *Classroom Computer Learning,* 5615 W. Cermak Rd., Cicero, IL 60650.
3. *Electronic Learning,* 1311 Executive Center Dr., Tallahassee, FL 32301.

The publications listed above regularly publish evaluations of educational software. Other sources of such evaluations include the following:

FIGURE 15.1   Computer Software Evaluation Form

Program (title) _____ Grade Level(s) _____

Producer_____ Cost_____

Hardware Required:_____
_____

I. Program Description (describe briefly):

II. Instructional Design
(Briefly summarize any of the following elements that apply; note any problems):

1. Is the content accurate, appropriate, and worthwhile?   Yes ____   No ____

2. Is the content appropriately sequenced and free from stereotyping or biases?   Yes ____   No ____

3. Does the reading level fit the recommended audience?   Yes ____   No ____

4. Does the program make unusual demands of the student, e.g., excessive background knowledge, reading lengthy narratives, etc.?   Yes ____   No ____

III. Technical Considerations:

1. Are the instructions/documentation well organized, clearly written, and complete?   Yes ____   No ____

2. Are all needed materials included?   Yes ____   No ____

3. Does the program operate as it is supposed to?   Yes ____   No ____

Overall Rating _____ *Evaluated by:* _____

---

1. *Microcomputer and Software Information for Teachers,* Northwest Regional Educational Laboratory, 300 W. Sixth Ave., Portland, OR 97204.

2. *Educational Products Information Exchange,* P.O. Box 620, Stony Brook, NY 117909.

NONPRINT MATERIALS

Reading and the written word—the print media—so dominate American schools that nonprint media—videotape, pictures, films, filmstrips, and the like—have a long way to go before they approach the educational impact of the printed word. Nevertheless, there have been substantial increases in both the amount of nonprint media available and in the different kinds of nonreading-based materials designed for educational purposes.

PICTURES, FILMS, AND VIDEOTAPES

The largest and most obvious category of alternatives to the printed word is pictures—those things that are "worth a thousand words." They come in many forms: collections of study prints, films and filmstrips, videotapes, and paintings and other works of art. Or they can be nothing more than illustrations and advertisements that you have clipped from a magazine, calendar, or some other source.

Study prints can be homemade, like the culture cards we described earlier, or purchased from commercial sources. The major difference is usually a matter of size; commercial study prints are typically large enough that they can be viewed by a group. Some school systems have the equipment and expertise that enable them to enlarge small pictures so they are large enough to be used in group settings, or you can project a small picture on an opaque projector (at considerably less expense). A sample commercial study print, in this case a cartoon, is illustrated in Figure 15.2.

One of our favorite student activities involving artwork was developed by a fourth-grade teacher who had obtained reproductions of three different paintings of the Battle of Concord. Each painting was from a different time period. The earliest showed a ragtag group of American colonists fighting a well-outfitted British Army. In the second painting, the patriots appeared much more organized and well dressed while the British looked slightly less robust and in somewhat greater disarray than in the earlier picture. In the most recent painting, the colonists were depicted as muscular, well fed, and well outfitted, while the British troops had taken on the slovenly appearance of the patriots in the first picture. The teacher's point? To show how the depiction of an event—or at least artists' interpretations of an event—can change over time.

Photographs can sometimes reflect a photographer's biases, just as a painting may reflect an artist's view of the world. It depends on the kind of photograph you are dealing with; one needn't be concerned about a photographer's biases in an aerial photograph, for example.

The real beauty of photographs lies in their ability to present selected yet uninterpreted data (as we described in the section on culture cards, page XXX). Unfortunately, educators often interpret the data for viewers almost immediately; explanatory captions are provided for photographs and illustrations, and a narration serves this purpose for films. The intent, traditionally, has been to use the

FIGURE 15.2 Commercial Study Print

"I STILL THINK NANOOK SOLD OUT TO THE OIL COMPANIES."

(Source: Don Wright. The Miami News.)

narration or picture caption to convey additional information. However, educators have discovered that eliminating the caption or narration increases the viewer's involvement with a picture because viewers are forced to add their own interpretation. A traditional educational film, for example, might show a jungle scene in which it is raining heavily. As the scene flashes on the screen, the narrator announces "It often rains heavily in the jungle." Educational filmmakers have discovered that it is not essential to tell viewers that it rains heavily in the jungle, but that the same thing can be accomplished by showing several scenes in which it is raining—heavily.

Narrated films are available for almost any topic you can name, but there is also a growing body of educational films that have no narration, only the natural sound of whatever the film depicts. For example, over six hours of nonnarrated film that beautifully and simply portrays the life of the Netselik Eskimos (*Fishing at the Stone Weir, Caribou Hunting at the Crossing Place, Autumn River Camp, Parts I and II,* and *Winter Sea Ice Camp, Parts I and II*) are available from several film libraries across the country. A similar series of films traces the daily lives of the Bozo people, an African tribe living on the Niger River.

Eliminating the narration automatically eliminates any vocabulary problems the narration might present. Consequently, the same nonnarrated film can sometimes be used by primary students, twelfth graders, and even adults, usually with a different emphasis at each level.

Videotape cassettes and, to a lesser extent, video discs, have begun to replace traditional 16 mm films in many areas. This has come about not because videotape is a superior medium—in fact, sometimes the same material is available on either videotape or film—but because of lower costs and, more importantly, convenience. The purchase price of an hour-long film can range from $600 upward; the same material on videotape may cost less than $100. If the teacher records a TV network production—such as the Civil War saga *The Blue and the Gray*—the cost is reduced significantly. (Caution: Making copies of commercially produced videotapes—even for school use—is a violation of federal law.)

Because films are so expensive, most schools rent or borrow them from film libraries, educational service centers, and the like. It is not unusual to schedule films up to a year in advance—and then hope that the film arrives when your class needs it. Because the school (or teacher) owns the videotape, the scheduling hassle is eliminated—as much as possible. Whereas teachers once faced problems scheduling the film projector for their room, they now discover that many schools don't have enough videocassette recorders to meet the demand.

FILMSTRIPS, SLIDES, TAPES, AND RECORDS

Filmstrips offer a valuable pictorial resource and, like films, are available on almost any topic. Also, since most schools buy their own filmstrips but are forced to rent or borrow films on a predetermined schedule, you will typically have greater flexibility in scheduling filmstrips for your use. In addition, you can vary the amount of time you spend on each frame, something you cannot do very readily with a film. This can be an important feature, especially if you wish to use several frames from a filmstrip as the basis for an inquiry activity or supplement the narrative with additional information.

In an attempt to make filmstrips more involving—that is, involve more senses than just sight—some filmstrips are accompanied by records or tape cassettes that provide a narration. Aside from the fact that the quality of the narration (or even the filmstrips themselves) varies tremendously, you also lose a degree of control over the time you can spend on each frame when you use the narration. Of course you could always stop the narration, but if you've never tried to find the correct spot on a record in a darkened room—without cutting new grooves in the record—you may be in for an ear-shattering experience. Recording the narration on a tape cassette will save a lot of unnecessary frustration and gain considerably more flexibility. By all means, preview any film or filmstrip (and accompanying narration) before you use it.

If the sequence in which you show a series of pictures is important, you are probably better off with slides, not filmstrips. Of course, a filmstrip can be cut apart and the individual frames mounted as slides. But doing so might incur the wrath of your colleagues, especially those who desire the self-contained package a filmstrip offers.

Tapes and records are instructional resources that are both nonprint and nonvisual. But, because they appeal to only one sense—hearing—they tend to require a greater degree of concentration than do multisensory media. Thus, unless the tape or record is especially interesting or unless it accompanies something else—a written script, a worksheet, or a filmstrip, etc., as tapes and records often do—there is a possibility that the children will tune out after a relatively short time.

In many instances, tapes (and tape recorders) can be helpful tools, especially when used by students to collect data rather than by teachers to present data. When students interview people, for example, tape recordings can provide an accurate record of what was said; they also eliminate the need to write everything down. Tapes and portable TV minicams have also proved useful in helping children rehearse presentations of various kinds. In fact, sometimes student-recorded material may become an integral part of a group presentation. However, should you wish to use taped or recorded materials as a means of conveying information to students, the general rule is to keep it short. If you don't, your students may very well "tune out" more quickly than you would anticipate.

REALIA

Remember when a fellow student brought in his "genuine" Indian arrowhead collection to share with the class? Or when someone's relatives had been to the Orient and brought back an authentic Japanese fan? These things—the arrowheads, the Japanese fan, and other real objects that might be associated with social studies teaching—are all encompassed by the term *realia*.

Most realia tend to be an adjunct to rather than an integral part of social studies teaching, primarily because the objects are precious to their owners, often part of a collection, and as such they would rather not have them handled and possibly broken. Thus they often become things to be displayed—looked at but not used—in the course of a teaching activity, and perhaps rightfully so. In fact, some realia are probably best handled via display and in a passing fashion, such as when a student brings in a World War II bayonet during your study of colonial America. Using realia unrelated to whatever your class is studying is difficult to justify on almost any grounds. But assume, for a moment, that somewhere in your travels you acquired a colonial candle mold (and your class will be studying colonial America). What are your options? You have several.

First, you could display the device and say, "This is a colonial candle mold." You could then proceed to describe how it was used. That's one option.

You might also place the mold in a prominent location but say nothing about it. Questions are going to be asked about it, you can be sure. But to the question "What is it?" you could respond "What do you think it is?" You might then mount a large sheet of paper near the mold and ask the children to list what they think it is. At a convenient time, you might display an illustration of someone using a candle mold, again saying nothing about it. Someone will soon notice it, and you may not even need to say anything else at all. Or, you might pose the question "How are candles made today?" which will initiate another adventure.

You could also make the candle mold the focus of study for an activity by asking students to identify the different functions it might serve and what they know about the people who made it. In other words, it can be the basis for a structure-function lesson.

If the function of the realia is obvious, you might wish to take a different tack. Take the Japanese fan mentioned earlier, for instance. You might want to ask who uses fans in Japan and why. Are they necessarily to keep Japanese women cool? And does this mean that Japan has a warm climate? Should you pursue this line of questioning, identify—in advance—some sources the students can go to to validate their possible answers. Indeed, they may find that fans are an integral part of a Japanese dancer's equipment, much as jewels play a role in the activities of some belly dancers.

COMMUNITY RESOURCES

Every community, regardless of size, has someone who has been somewhere or who knows something that can be useful in your social studies program. And almost every community has something or some place you can visit that would also be an asset to your social studies program. In fact, most teachers have little problem identifying community resources. Their problem lies in *selecting* among those resources that most closely match their social studies program (and their school system's budget).

RESOURCE PERSONS

Identifying individuals in the community who have specialized knowledge or experience is not especially difficult. The list can go from authors to zookeepers. The more challenging task is using those resource people effectively.

Part of the problem occurs because resource people are, by definition, specialists in an area. As such, they are familiar with the intricacies, the nuances, and the jargon of their specialization. Your students, however, may be at a level where their primary concern is with the most fundamental aspects of a specialized area. Of course, most resource people recognize that they are dealing with children and adjust their presentations accordingly, but sometimes they unwittingly slip anyhow.

All things considered, the local history buff who, for example, gets enmeshed in the minutiae of who married whom in the early 1840s can't count on maintaining student interest for very long. Once their interest is lost, your students may begin to get a bit restless—and understandably so—but your guest speaker may take it as a personal affront and, rightly or wrongly, present a public relations problem for you by suggesting that "They can't maintain discipline in that school anymore" (or

Students who have prepared for a field trip to a farm will have established a focus for their visit and may have identified questions ahead of time, such as "How is the care of pigs different from that of cows?" (© *Gloria Karlson*)

something to that effect). It may seem an imposition, but you'll be doing yourself and your resource person a favor if you clarify in advance exactly what you want that person to cover. The intent is to ensure a successful experience for both the resource person *and* your class.

A related problem arises because some resource people are ill-equipped to do more than talk to students. Unless they deal with children on a regular basis, they are unlikely to have audiovisual aids or other media to enliven their presentation. Even if they have such media, however, the more basic issue depends upon you and your class. That is—and this cannot be stressed too heavily—you will need to have worked with your class to establish a need or desire for whatever information the resource person can provide. One of the most helpful things you can do is provide resource people with a list of questions or topics your class has developed in advance of the presentation. This helps ensure that (1) the class has at least a passing acquaintance with whatever the resource persons will deal with (otherwise they wouldn't be able to frame intelligent questions) and (2) the resource persons will have an idea of the level of the class's concerns and can prepare themselves accordingly.

The key to using resource people successfully probably lies as much in the advance preparation as it does in the visit itself. Our intent here is not to suggest that using resource people is an insurmountable problem, by any means. But you do need to be aware that there are some dimensions to a seemingly simple task (getting someone to talk about something) that can yield unhappy consequences for all concerned if left unattended.

A final suggestion about using resource people: be wary of those individuals who insist upon talking to your class. Among the thousands of people who volunteer their services, there are always those few who would use the schools as a platform for their special causes. Even if you are sympathetic to the cause—whatever it may be—you may risk your professional future by honoring their offer. Before issuing an invitation, be certain to check school policies and inform the appropriate administrative personnel (principal, etc.) of your intentions.

FIELD TRIPS AND TOURS

What teachers sometimes call "field trips" are actually tours. By taking students on tours of museums, bakeries, fire stations, and the like, teachers provide enriching, hands-on experiences that would be impossible in a classroom. Other teachers, however, take their students on field trips to museums, bakeries, fire stations, and so forth. The distinction between *tours* and *field trips* is based on (1) what has taken place in the classroom before leaving on the trip and (2) the students' perceptions as to why they are going. When scientists "go out into the field," for example, they have usually identified their purpose for going in advance. Thus, when archaeologists decide to "dig" at a particular site, that decision is usually based on (1) prior research, (2) a clear sense of purpose (for digging), and (3) previously identified questions or problems that they hope to have answered. Likewise, when students go on a field trip to a bakery, for example, they arrive armed with *previously identified* questions that they want answers for; "Do bakeries grind their own flour?" "Do bakeries use the same kind of flour available in supermarkets?" etc. In other words, as a result of the students' previous classroom experience, they arrive at the bakery with a clearer sense of *why* they are there. The fact that they may probably enjoy the experience and learn things they don't have questions about is simply extra frosting on the cake. On the other hand, students taking a tour of a bakery may have a general interest in what bakeries do, but because they may lack previous classroom experience, their sense of purpose is apt to be more vague than for students on a field trip.

Logistics

Tours and field trips add a dimension of virtually immeasurable value to education. However, most experienced teachers can tell you horror stories about things that went wrong on a field trip or tour—the time someone got lost, the time four children spent all of their lunch money at the souvenir stand, or the time they neglected to have the children visit the lavatory before leaving on the return trip. These kinds of logistical problems can have you tearing your hair out in short order. Then, too, students sometimes assume that rules for classroom conduct don't apply to activities outside of school, as on a field trip or tour, giving rise to discipline-related problems. Our hunch is that the clearer sense of purpose associated with field trips may result in fewer discipline problems, but there is certainly no guarantee in that. Indeed, most students realize that a teacher's disciplinary options on a field trip or tour are limited, which may be why teachers often bring several allies (parents) along with them.

Preplanning can eliminate some of the logistical and discipline-related problems associated with field trips and tours. The following suggestions are based on Rathbun, 1977, and Midgett, 1979:

Obtain administrative approval *before* announcing the trip to students. (On the application form, always use "field trip," even if you're planning a tour to the zoo—it sounds better and may be easier for the administrator to justify.)

In picking a date, avoid Mondays. Over the weekend, kids often forget to bring their lunches, spending money, etc.

Recruit, screen, *and instruct* parent chaperones so that they will be able to contribute significantly to the trip. Don't wait until just before leaving to tell parents what you expect of them. Send a note home beforehand that outlines (1) what you expect parents to do, (2) rules you have discussed with students, and (3) any other pertinent information.

Divide students into task groups well before the trip is to take place. Each task group should have a specific responsibility; e.g., recorders (keep records and journals), collectors (obtain necessary items for or from the trip), photographers, public relations (thank-you note writers), and maintenance (clean up).

If taking a tour, select an impressive place. If you were bored on your last trip to the sewage-treatment plant, for example, your students will probably be bored too.

Take everyone, including your troublemakers. Leaving them behind for disciplinary reasons could lead to deep-seated resentment that you may never overcome.

Send parental permission slips home even if the school uses a blanket permission form covering all field trips for the year.

Even with signed permission slips, you may be legally liable if you agree to supervise students in too large an area. We're not talking about the Astrodome here, since trying to supervise students in two large halls of a museum could make you liable if something happened to someone. Err on the safe side and take one adult for each group of five children.

Use name tags (including the school name). This is often essential for young students; for older students it enables chaperones to call them by name.

Avoid going in private cars whenever possible; the legal hazards (insurance coverage, etc.) are considerable.

Be sure to take a first-aid kit and a list of the children's home and emergency phone numbers.

Prepare a worksheet or guidesheet for students to complete while at the museum or other resource.

Be certain to debrief the activity. What happens after a field trip is as important as what takes place during or before it.

Don't overlook walking field trips to nearby locations. Supermarkets, banks, bakeries, as well as those old standbys—the post office and fire station—often welcome visits from school children. Whether you walk or take a bus, the crucial element is that your students understand why they are going on the field trip. Otherwise, field trips and tours may be seen as a "lark" or just another day off from school.

USING COMMUNITY RESOURCES

We have suggested that using community resources—either in the form of resource persons or field trips—involves both a logistical and substantive dimension. The logistical side involves such things as contacting individuals, arranging for buses (and rest stops, and parental approval and assistance, etc.), while the substantive dimension includes things related to the content that you and your class (and perhaps a resource person) will be dealing with.

Many school districts have specific guidelines concerning resource persons and field trips that specify the logistical (and legal) considerations you need to be aware of. Sometimes they also deal with substantive questions. Could you, for example, invite an avowed communist to speak to your class, or take your students on a field trip to a slaughterhouse or a funeral home? Consider how you would respond if you were an elementary principal and a teacher came to you with such a request. If the teacher could demonstrate a clear relationship between the slaughterhouse (or the funeral home, or the communist) and whatever the class had been studying, would it make any difference in your decision? The issues here are far from simple.

Once you have gotten the necessary permissions, the ultimate success of the experience will probably depend on the preliminary work you do before a resource person enters your classroom or before your class leaves on the field trip. The basic questions you need to ask yourself include the following:

Is a community resource appropriate for the purposes of my group?

Have I planned preliminary activities that provide a context within which my class can interpret whatever they hear or see?

Have I identified appropriate follow-up activities?

Does my class have an identifiable need for the information the resource can provide?

Do my students understand what is expected of them—both in terms of their conduct and what they are to learn?

If you can answer these questions in the positive, you'll be on the way to making effective use of the resources your community can provide. If not, keep your aspirin handy.

ACQUIRING INSTRUCTIONAL RESOURCES

Where do teachers get the things they teach with? The school system usually furnishes paper, chalk, paper clips, and that sort of thing, and it may (but not always) provide teachers with a budget from which they can purchase additional teaching materials. Where such budgets exist, they have one universal characteristic—small! It's the rare school that can supply teachers with everything they might like to use for teaching purposes.

In acquiring instructional resources, your first step is to identify what is available from commercial publishers or other sources. There are several large publishers of educational materials and a host of smaller ones, and you will usually find their catalogs in the school library, the resource center, or sometimes even in the teachers' lounge. Or you can obtain copies of the major teacher's magazines—*Learning88* (the year varies with the current year; 1111 Bethlehem Pike, Springhouse, PA 19477) or *Instructor* (7 Bank Street, Dansville, NY 14437). Buy yourself a bunch of stamps, and begin answering the ads for materials that appeal to you. The two major social studies journals, *Social Education* (Journal of the National Council for the Social Studies, 3501 Newark St. N.W., Washington, DC 20016) and *The Social Studies* (4000 Albemarle St. N.W., Suite 500, Washington, DC 20016), are also good sources for identifying current materials. Some of these periodicals also have special introductory rates for student teachers.

Some school systems accept teachers' requests for materials in the spring and purchase the materials during the following summer. This often means that you don't have the opportunity to purchase materials during your first year of teaching. In that event, you will be forced to do what hundreds of other teachers do—buy materials yourself. But before doing that, you have a couple of other options. First, find out if there isn't something you could use that is free (or inexpensive), and/or, second, consider making your own materials. There are so many free or inexpensive materials available that schools often subscribe to one or more of the guides to free materials. These include:

Educator's Guide to Free Social Studies Materials, edited by Patricia H. Suttles and William H. Hartley. Educators Progress Service, Inc., Randolph, WI 53956. Note: guides to other free and inexpensive material are also available.

Free and Inexpensive Materials on World Affairs, by Leonard S. Kenworthy. Teachers College Press, 1234 Amsterdam Ave., New York, NY 10027.

Free and Inexpensive Teaching Aids, by Bruce Miller. Box 369, Riverside, CA 92502.

Free and Inexpensive Learning Materials (updated annually). George Peabody College of Vanderbilt University, Nashville, TN 37203.

Selected Free Materials for Classroom Teachers, 5th ed., by Ruth H. Aubrey. Fearon Publishers, 6 Davis Dr., Belmont, CA 94002.

Guides to other sources of materials include:

Social Studies School Service Catalog (free). 10,000 Culver Blvd., P.O. Box 802, Culver City, CA 90230.

Where to Find It Guide, published annually in a fall issue of *Scholastic Teacher.* Scholastic Magazines, Inc., 50 W. 44th St., New York, NY 10036.

The quality of free and inexpensive materials can vary tremendously, so you'll need to be selective. One of the first questions you might want to consider is why various concerns would be willing to sell materials inexpensively or give them away. Indeed, before using some free or inexpensive material with students, you ought to "look your gift horse in the mouth."

Some of the best teaching resources we have encountered are those teachers have developed themselves. Most of the student activities in this book, for example, were built by teachers. Most of the activities went through some refining—that is, they were tried out with students and then revised—but once developed, they become a resource to be used in future years.

The process of developing your own teaching materials is not as difficult as you might suspect (a large dose of common sense is about as helpful as anything). Typically, you would

1. Identify (a) the major concept(s) you want to teach and/or (b) the major question(s), issue(s), or skill(s) you want the children to deal with. Note: This is sometimes the most difficult step of all.
2. Decide what kind of format you want to use—a fact sheet, a mini case study, role playing, limited-choice decision making, etc.
3. Build the activity (and duplicate as needed).
4. Use it with your students.
5. Revise as needed, based on what you found in Step 4.

Sometimes it's wise to add a Step 3(a). That is, before you duplicate an activity for students, share it with someone you can rely on for honest feedback—a colleague, a fellow student teacher, etc. You are almost certain to find that what you thought was perfectly obvious isn't, and thus gain a chance to make appropriate adjustments before trying it out with your students.

Finally, we recommend the same caution as we did for individualizing instruction. That is, to start small and then build your collection of materials slowly and steadily.

SUMMARY

Common sense would suggest that the more senses a particular medium can appeal to, the better the learning experience that should result. However, there are some recent data that suggest this isn't necessarily the case; these findings indicate that films, for example, do not necessarily produce better learning experiences than, say, tape recordings or filmstrips.

In radio's heyday, families gathered to listen to their favorite adventure stories—"The Shadow," "The Green Hornet," "The Lone Ranger," etc. Because everyone was dependent on only one sense, hearing, they were forced to build mental pictures of what was happening in the story. They had to use their imaginations to fill in the "blanks." With television, however, came both picture and sound. Viewers no longer had to imagine what was going on because everything was presented for them. Thus, TV (and movies) may tend to require less imagination and, hence, somewhat less mental participation on the viewer's part. So contrary to what common sense might suggest, media that appeal to only one sense may produce better learning experiences than some multisensory media.

The implicit expectation for all instructional media and materials is that they reflect accurate, quality "stuff." The prime requirement for almost any media form is that it be able to capture the children's attention. Unless it does, it may not make a lot of difference how many senses it appeals to. Our main point, however, is that your choice of media or materials should depend on your instructional purpose.

SUGGESTED ACTIVITIES

1. Congratulations! Your budget request has been approved and the Board of Education has authorized $150 per teacher for social studies teaching materials. You can really use some new materials since your textbook, for example, carries a 1980 copyright. Your other materials consist of a wall map of the world and one of the United States, a sixteen-inch globe, and an almanac dated 1985. How will you (or your team) spend those funds?

2. In small groups, plan a field trip for an elementary class. Then, as a group, go on the field trip you have planned, making certain someone brings a camera. Share your findings with the rest of the class; include your preliminary research, slides of the trip itself, and the way in which you would follow it up.

REFERENCES

Baker, Betty. 1972. *The Big Push*. New York: Coward, McCann & Geoghegan.

Burton, Virgina Lee. 1939. *Mike Mulligan and His Steam Shovel*. Boston: Houghton Mifflin.

Cacha, Frances B. 1985. "Microcomputer Capabilities in the Elementary Social Studies Program." *The Social Studies,* (March/April), 62–64.

Finkelstein, Judy, Steve Stearns, and Barbara Hatcher. 1985. "Museums Are Not Just for Observing Anymore." *Social Education,* 49 (February), 150–54.

Grahame, Kenneth. 1954. *The Wind in the Willows*. New York: Charles Scribner's Sons.

Harmin, Merrill, and Sidney Simon. 1965. "The Year the Schools Began Teaching the Telephone Directory." *Harvard Educational Review,* 34 (Summer), 326–31.

Huck, Charlotte S. 1979. *Children's Literature in the Elementary School*. 3rd ed., updated. New York: Holt, Rinehart and Winston.

Mari, Iela, and Enzo Mari. 1970. *The Chicken and the Egg*. New York: Pantheon Books.

Mathis, Sharon Bell. 1975. *The Hundred Penny Box*. New York: Viking Press.

McGowan, Thomas M. 1987. "Children's Fiction as a Source for Social Studies Skill-Building." *ERIC Digest* (No. 37). Bloomington, Ind.: Clearinghouse for Social Studies/Social Science Education.

Midgett, Barry. 1979. "Tight Ship Trips." *Teacher,* 97 (September), 90–94.

Norton, Donna E. 1987. *Through the Eyes of a Child*. 2nd ed. Columbus, Ohio: Charles Merrill.

Rathbun, Dorothy. 1977. "Foolproof Field Trips." *Learning,* 5 (April), 70–75.

Robinson, Sherryl B. 1984. "Textbook Evaluation." *Social Education,* 48 (May), 35–36.

Rooze, Gene E., and Terry Northup. 1986. *Using Computers to Teach Social Studies*. Littleton, Colo.: Libraries Unlimited.

Sutherland, Zena, and May Hill Arbuthnot. 1986. *Children and Books*. 7th ed. Glenview, Ill.: Scott Foresman.

Traberman, Tama. 1984. "Using Microcomputers to Teach Global Studies." *Social Education,* 48 (February), 130–37.

SUGGESTED READINGS

Thomas M. and Meredith McGowan. 1986. *Children, Literature, and Social Studies: Activities for the Intermediate Grades*. Omaha, Neb.: Special Literature Press. This excellent publication provides a wealth of information on basing social studies activities on children's fiction.

Joan E. Schriber. 1984. *Using Children's Books in Social Studies: Early Childhood Through Primary Grades*. Washington, D.C.: National Council for the Social Studies. This is the early-childhood equivalent of the McGowan book noted above.

John Searles and Richard A. Diem. 1985. *Computers and the Social Studies: Promises and Practices.* New York: Holt, Rinehart and Winston. Although aimed more at the secondary level, this volume provides a good overview.

Mark Schug and R. Berry, eds. 1984. *Community Study: Applications and Opportunities.* N.C.S.S. Bulletin No. 73. Washington, D.C.: National Council for the Social Studies. This small volume describes many ways in which the community can be used as an object of study; strong emphasis on oral history.

CHAPTER 16

Evaluation Strategies

"If you are teaching things that cannot be evaluated, you are in the awkward position of being unable to demonstrate that you are teaching anything at all." Robert Mager

KEY QUESTIONS

☐ How does one gather and use good evaluative data?

☐ How do norm-referenced and criterion-referenced evaluation differ?

☐ Are evaluation and grading compatible?

☐ How does one evaluate higher-level cognitive skills?

KEY IDEAS

☐ Evaluation is closely tied to objectives.

☐ The quality and accuracy of evaluative judgments are a function of the quality and accuracy of evaluative data.

☐ Subjectivity is inherent in evaluation; the goal is to limit and control its influence.

☐ Materials and strategies for evaluating higher-level cognitive skills may closely resemble the materials and strategies used to teach those skills initially.

INTRODUCTION: Evaluation and Grading

In the cartoon on page 495, Sally Brown has raised some of those thorny questions that students and teachers have wrestled with for years. Indeed, should teachers grade their students by applying the same standards for everyone or should they take the students' efforts into account? Or should both factors be taken into consideration?

Discussions involving grading, testing, and evaluation often generate more heat than light, simply because many people use these terms as if they were synonymous—which they are not. Some people, for example, erroneously assume

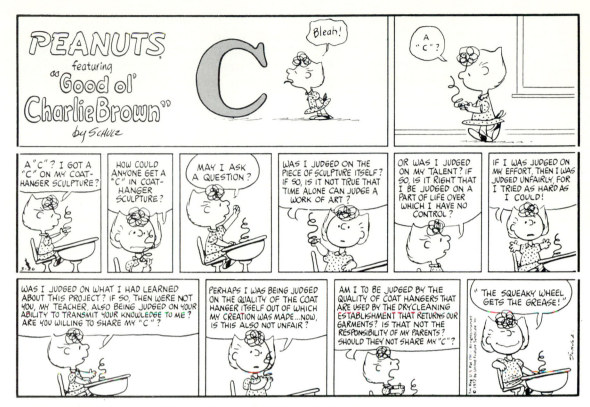

(Source: Charles M. Schulz, © 1956 United Features Syndicate. All Rights Reserved.)

that evaluation takes place only at the end of an instructional episode, usually in the form of a test. They don't realize that a significant amount of evaluation takes place during instruction, as teachers determine how well students are progressing. Other people erroneously assume that once you've taken a test, you necessarily get a grade. It's true that testing and grading often go hand in hand, but the two are actually quite separate processes—as we explain in this chapter.

Evaluation has always been an essential component of instruction, and student performance—as in Lucy's case above—has been its traditional focus. Students are still the major focus of evaluation, but the emphasis on accountability associated with the "back to the basics" movement has significantly expanded the scope and nature of educational evaluation. In many areas, course grades are no longer sufficient to assure that students will pass to the next grade level; those students must also pass state- or district-mandated tests to prove that they are indeed competent. In some of those areas, judgments about your ability to teach may also be based, in part, on how your students perform on certain tests. Of course, schools, too, use evaluation to demonstrate that they are accountable, that they are producing students who can perform competently. Our point here is that evaluation is no longer simply an element of the instructional process by which teachers judge their students' progress; rather, it has become a major force in American education—one that can have significant political ramifications.

Distinguishing among the various forms of evaluation as well as testing and grading is one of three major purposes of this chapter. Our second purpose is to examine the various functions that evaluation serves. Finally, we examine some recommended test-construction techniques as well as several alternative (non-test) evaluation strategies you might wish to employ.

THE EVALUATION PROCESS

The purpose of educational evaluation is to provide data that enables us to make qualitative judgments about students' (and teachers' and schools') performances. In other words, evaluation is a process that permits us to determine how well students (and in some instances, teachers or schools) are doing.

Evaluation is a three-part process that consists of: (1) identifying criteria or standards (determining what students will be expected to do), (2) gathering data on the student's performance with respect to those standards (often in the form of a test), and then (3) making judgments about the individual's performance (based on the information you have gathered). These elements are present in all forms of evaluation, but their relative emphasis sometimes changes depending on (1) the type of information desired and (2) the phase of the instructional cycle in which the evaluation is being done.

The evaluation process should enable teachers to answer two basic questions: (1) "Is student X able to demonstrate a desired behavior (knowledge or skill)?" and (2) "How is student X doing in comparison to the rest of the students in the class?" As these questions suggest, a teacher's evaluation focus is usually in terms of how *individual students* (a) are able to perform a particular task or (b) are performing in relation to other students in the class. When school systems enter the evaluation arena, the focus invariably shifts from individual students to larger groups (of students) or even entire schools. In other words, the evaluation questions that most school systems focus on are variations of Question 2 above: "How are the students in this class doing in relation to other students at the same grade level?" or "How are the students in this school doing in comparison to students from other schools in the system?" or "How are our schools doing in comparison with other schools across the nation?"

APPROACHES TO EVALUATION

The questions above reflect two different approaches to evaluation, each of which provides different information. The type of information that a teacher or school system desires determines the type of evaluation to be used. In Question 1, for example, the teacher was interested in determining whether students could demonstrate specific knowledges or skills. If the teacher expects the child to identify the location of the United States on a world map, for example, this expectation becomes the criterion, the desired behavior. Determining whether a

Students' performance can be evaluated in several different ways, including norm-referenced (for comparisons among students or classes) and criterion-referenced (for comparison with a specific knowledge or skill). (© *Dennis Mansell*)

student can or cannot demonstrate desired behaviors (and thereby meet the criterion) is called *criterion-referenced* evaluation.

In Question 2 above, and for most of the evaluation questions a school system might ask, the focus shifts from a child's ability to demonstrate certain behaviors to the child's (or group's) performance relative to an identifiable norm or standard. The basis for comparison (the norm) could be the performance of other students in the class, other students in the school, other students at the same grade level across the state or nation, or whatever other group that students might be compared with. In *norm-referenced* evaluation, an individual's or a group's performance is related (or referenced) to an identifiable norm or standard. We examine these two basic types of evaluation in the next sections.

Criterion-referenced Evaluation

The focus of criterion-referenced evaluation is on how individual students perform relative to a specific knowledge or skill. In other words, this type of evaluation is "referenced" or keyed to certain knowledges or skills, each of which serves as a criterion the child is expected to demonstrate. If the child can demonstrate what is expected, such as identifying the location of the United States on a world map, he or she is then ready to move on to something else. However, if he or she can't demonstrate the desired behavior, then further instruction is probably in order. Because criterion-referenced evaluation can be used to determine whether or not children need additional instruction, it is sometimes referred to as *diagnostic evaluation*.

Criterion-referenced evaluation can be used at any point in an instructional experience. It can be used as a pretest prior to instruction, it can be used to determine how things are going during instruction, and it can be used to determine if students have mastered the expected behaviors after instruction. Based on the students' performance on the criterion-referenced pretest, for example, neither you nor your students would need to waste valuable class time going over what they have proved they already know. You could then devote your attention to those areas where students need additional instruction.

Criterion-referenced evaluation is an integral component of *mastery learning*. Determining whether a student has mastered a particular behavior or skill is common to both. The key idea in mastery learning is that students should not move on to something else until they have mastered previous learning tasks.

Criterion-referenced evaluation and mastery learning are also reflected in many—though not all—of the *competency tests* that some states and school systems require before students can pass to the next grade level. In essence, the student must demonstrate that he or she has mastered—is competent in—the learning tasks specified for that grade level.

During instruction, teachers typically focus their efforts on helping students master single behaviors (competencies)—such as identifying the location of the United States on a world map or distinguishing between a fact and an opinion. The questions on most competency tests are keyed to competencies (behaviors) that students have supposedly dealt with separately throughout the year. If the concept of mastery learning were adhered to in its purest form, students would be expected to answer every question on the competency test correctly; doing so would mean that the child has mastered the desired behaviors. However, when specific behaviors or competencies are clustered together on a test, the standard or criterion for performance or nonperformance is usually established in terms of a percentage of questions that must be answered correctly. The criterion for competence may or may not be determined arbitrarily, which could mean, for example, that to demonstrate mastery the student would be expected to complete at least 80 percent (or some other percentage) of the test items correctly. If all students can demonstrate 80 percent mastery, all would be promoted to the next grade level (because all have met or exceeded the criterion).

Norm-referenced Evaluation

Instead of determining whether students can or cannot perform certain tasks, which is the focus in criterion-referenced evaluation, the focus in norm-referenced evaluation shifts to comparing a student's performance with other students' (or groups') performances on the same or similar tasks. If you were teaching third grade, for example, you might wish to compare your students' performance with that of third graders elsewhere, as one would when using a nationally standardized test. Or you might want to compare individuals in your class with your class's overall performance. In either case, whatever you use as the basis for comparison serves as the norm.

Norm-referenced evaluation would permit you to say, for instance, that "Johnny did better than 31 percent of the third graders who took this test on map skills." Actually, the quality of Johnny's performance may not be very good; in fact, it may be awful. But unless you shifted to criterion-referenced evaluation and analyzed Johnny's performance on each test item, it's doubtful that you would be able to determine the specific problems Johnny encountered and why he scored as he did. In other words, norm-referenced evaluation permits you to compare an individual's overall performance with that of a group; it doesn't provide information to indicate, for example, that Johnny's problem may lie in his inability to deal with cardinal directions.

The results of norm-referenced evaluation are always stated comparatively, that is, in relation to whatever norm is being used. Thus, to say that Maria got a 95 on her test, for example, might seem rather impressive at first, especially if you assume that it was a 100-item test. Your interpretation is likely to change, however, when you find that it was a 200-item test and the average performance for students the same age as Maria was 161. It might change even more so when you find that Maria is a perfectly average eight-year-old, whose native language is Spanish, who has been in this country just over a year, and whose score of 95 was on a test of English vocabulary (or American history). Our point here is to indicate that, unless the group Maria is being compared with (the norm) shares Maria's characteristics (including age, linguistic background, etc.), the results of normative evaluation could be very misleading.

Because norm-referenced and criterion-referenced evaluation serve different purposes, it's pointless to say that one is better than the other. However, from a purely instructional point of view, criterion-referenced evaluation provides the type of information that teachers must have in order to target instruction toward the needs of individual students. In the next section, we examine the relationship between instruction and criterion-referenced evaluation in greater detail.

INSTRUCTION AND EVALUATION

We noted earlier that evaluation was a three-part process that consists of (1) identifying criteria or objectives to be met by instruction, (2) gathering data on students' performance, and then (3) making judgments about how well the students have performed. We also suggested that the relative emphasis of these components can change depending on *when* in the instructional cycle the evaluation is being conducted. For example, although you should determine your instructional objectives and criteria during planning, you would obviously need to wait until after instruction to determine how well your students have performed. Then, too, you might want to check up on your students' performance during instruction—instead of waiting until the end of a lesson, unit, or grading period. The point here is that elements of evaluation are appropriate to and can apply at various points in the instructional cycle, as we describe below.

PLANNING AND EVALUATION

To the extent that instructional planning is a process for determining where you (and your students) are going, evaluation is a process for determining whether you (and your students) have arrived at your intended destination(s). Our reason for noting this here is to indicate that the first component or phase of evaluation—identifying objectives and criteria—actually takes place during planning. Once you have identified the objectives for a teaching activity, you will have identified the criteria for what your students will be expected to do. In other words, objectives identify the behaviors that students are expected to demonstrate.

When objectives are stated precisely in the planning phase, the evaluation criteria are clear-cut. For example, if your objectives indicate that students should be able to identify four of the five Great Lakes, or distinguish statements of facts from statements of opinion with at least 80 percent accuracy, your evaluation criteria are already established. You need merely to pose the evaluation task to students in some appropriate form. However, if a teacher were to ask students to correctly identify all five Great Lakes (Superior, Michigan, Huron, Erie, and Ontario) to receive credit on a test, there would be a clear mismatch between the objective and the evaluation item. Teachers are free to change the criteria in their objectives, to be sure, but upon doing so, they should advise students accordingly.

Students who know what will be expected of them tend not to ask that time-worn question "What's going to be on the test?" Students recognize, perhaps implicitly, that every test question is an indicator of the teacher's (or whomever's) real objectives. In your own case, you may not have discovered what those expectations were until you took the test. In some instances, that situation probably existed because your teachers waited until the night before the test to make out the questions, and it was then that their real expectations (criteria) became known. We are not suggesting that teachers should provide answers to test questions in advance, nor are we suggesting that tests are the preferred way to evaluate one's objectives. Our point is that identifying precise objectives in the planning phase can reduce much of the mystery (and fear) with which students approach evaluation.

CHECKING PROGRESS: FORMATIVE EVALUATION

When students seem to be encountering unanticipated problems, or even if they are not, it is simply common sense to stop periodically to evaluate how things are going. Evaluating students' progress during instruction—instead of waiting until the end—is known as *formative evaluation.* In other words, formative evaluation is a phase of criterion-referenced evaluation that occurs during instruction. What distinguishes formative evaluation from the common sense or intuitive pauses that occur spontaneously is its planned nature. In using formative evaluation, you (1) consciously plan to pause periodically during instruction to assess how things are going and (2) you use explicit (previously identified) criteria to assess the situation. This distinction does not mean that you should ignore what your intuition or your senses tell you, of course, because such information can be extremely useful.

The purpose of formative evaluation is to monitor learning progress *during* instruction and to provide continuous feedback to students and teachers. To obtain that information, teachers may use commercially prepared tests, their own criterion-referenced evaluation, observation, or some combination of these techniques. That information can then provide a basis for modifying instructional activities and for prescribing group or individual remedial work (Gronlund, 1985).

Formative evaluation, like all criterion-referenced evaluation, begins in the planning phase—when you identify what students are expected to do. Objectives identify the potential criteria (the desired behaviors) that you can use in either final or formative evaluation. However, for formative evaluation, you also need to determine *when*—at what point within an instructional activity—students should be able to demonstrate what you are expecting of them. The following example should illustrate what we mean.

Let's assume that you are two weeks into a four-week unit on communities in which one of the major concepts is "interdependence." You have already had several activities in which interdependence played a prominent role, and at this point most of your third graders are able to pronounce and define the term properly. Let's also assume that in your original planning, you indicated that after two weeks of instruction, you expected that at least 90 percent of your students would be able to provide examples of how communities are interdependent. (Note that if this is your first year of teaching, you might not have a very solid basis for determining if your expectation was realistic.) With the criterion (behavior) identified, you look for a way to assess student performance.

You might consider some of the options we deal with later in this chapter (interviewing, etc.), but for the sake of this illustration, let's assume that you settle on a simple question presented orally: "What are some ways that communities depend on each other?" That is really a double-barreled question because, initially at least, you are not concerned with how students answer it. Rather, for formative evaluation purposes, your initial concern lies in determining how many children indicate a willingness to answer the question. If almost every hand goes up, your focus can then shift to the quality of the students' answers. However, if only four hands go up, and if the majority of non-handraisers are trying to look disinterested or have expressions that say "Please don't call on me," you have a preliminary indication that the majority of your students cannot (or choose not to) demonstrate the desired behavior.

You might then call on the students whose hands are raised, hoping that their responses will provide accurate examples of what you are seeking. You might also reword your question—e.g., "Can anyone else give an example of ways that communities are interdependent?" and then reassess your students' willingness to respond. If the same situation prevails, you might then (1) reassess your original expectation, (2) consider developing additional activities that provide concrete examples of interdependence, or (3) do nothing in the hope that everything will work itself out with additional time and experience. Keep in mind that formative evaluation need not be a long, drawn-out process. In fact, once you have identified your criteria, you can probably do formative evaluation in far less time than it has taken you to read this rather elaborate example.

GRADING PROGRESS: SUMMATIVE EVALUATION

Formative evaluation takes place during instruction—as learning is "forming up"—whereas summative evaluation always occurs at the end of an instructional period. Summative evaluation is intended to "summarize" the changes that have occurred as a result of instruction. Students who are unable to distinguish between facts and opinions at the beginning of an instructional period, for example, should be able to do so by the end of that period. However, in addition to this particular skill, the student will be expected to demonstrate other knowledges, skills, and attitudes. Rather than report on each of these elements separately, schools have traditionally assessed the quality of a learner's performance on a number of measures, including test scores, individual effort, achievement relative to the rest of the class, deportment, etc., the results of which are "summed" into judgmental statements or, more commonly, a grade.

There are no precise guidelines for the procedures for summative evaluation, the criteria to be employed, or the elements that should be included. Because of this, summative evaluation can vary considerably from teacher to teacher and situation to situation. Despite such variations, the basic question one asks is "All things considered, how would you judge the quality of a particular student's performance (or product)?"

Grading

Grading is clearly the most common form of summative evaluation—for all practical purposes, the two terms are almost synonymous. Grading, as almost everyone knows, refers to the process of judging whether or not someone (or something) belongs in a particular category. The key element of grading (and summative evaluation) lies (1) in determining the characteristics of the categories to be used for reporting purposes and then (2) determining whether an object or person reflects those characteristics. Thus a meat inspector, for example, examines a carcass to determine the amount of marbleized fat it contains, and then assigns that carcass to a category—"prime," "choice," "good," etc.—usually by stamping it with the appropriate purple label. Once the inspector has identified the characteristics of a particular category, the label isn't essential; it just makes communicating about that carcass much simpler. As long as you know the characteristics of the categories, the labels "prime" or "choice" will have significance.

In most schools, grading labels are defined by school policy. Typically they are letters (A, B, C, D, F), numbers, descriptive expressions ("Satisfactory," "Excellent," etc.), or some combination of these. The labels we've got! What we don't have are consistent descriptions of the categories to which they apply, and therein lies the basis of the grading problem in schools. The result? There isn't a student alive who doesn't know that one teacher's A can be another teacher's B, C, or sometimes even worse.

Some teachers use norm-referenced evaluation for grading purposes; that is, the student's grade is based on an individual's performance relative to the class's performance as a whole. That procedure, which is commonly called "grading on the curve," should be well known to most college students. Other teachers attempt to identify grading categories using a criterion-referenced format. In those instances, the standards—such as "A grade of 90 or over is an A"—are usually established in advance. Things usually work out fine *if* the preestablished standards are appropriate and *if* there are a relatively limited number of elements that grades are based on. But when teachers indicate that "In determining your grade, I'm going to 'count' your test scores, class participation, and group work," the standards can become very fuzzy. Exactly how that "counting" will take place sometimes remains unknown. Other teachers, however, establish mathematical formulae (e.g., "Class participation counts one-fifth") in an apparent effort to make a subjective process more objective. Be advised that elaborate formulae and mathematical manipulation of scores do not necessarily make grading more objective or scientific. Rather, teachers who use such devices may be doing little more than objectively manipulating subjectively selected data.

Even though teachers sometimes deny it, most students are well aware of the fact that judgment and subjectivity are integral parts of the evaluation process. When one human being, the teacher, is put in the position of judging the performance of other human beings, the students, it is all but impossible to eliminate the human element in evaluation. It can be controlled, of course, which helps to explain our emphasis on behaviorally stated objectives and on establishing clear expectations (criteria) for students (and teachers). Actually, despite the presence of the human element, there is nothing intrinsically unfair about evaluation and grading; the only thing intrinsic about the process is that it is subjective.

In light of the inherent subjectivity of grading, our recourse is to gather as much *good* evaluation data as possible before making a judgment. The more data one has, the less likely one is to be misled in evaluating a student's performance. The sheer quantity of data is not the only issue, however, since a set of thirty test scores, for example, is not necessarily a better basis for making a decision than a set of ten test scores. Indeed, the quality of the data is just as important as the quantity. Thus, information gathered through systematic interviews with students will provide a better base for evaluative decision making than, say, several random impressions. Likewise, descriptive, anecdotal notes jotted on a student's profile sheet usually prove superior to mental notes made as you evaluate a student's class participation. Furthermore, should your evaluation and grading practices ever be questioned by anyone, the quantity *and* quality of your evaluation data will assume paramount importance.

A summary of the different types and phases of evaluation is shown in Table 16.1.

TABLE 16.1 Types and Phases of Evaluation as Reflected by Teachers' Questions

Teachers' Questions	Types of Evaluation	Comments
"Is the student able to perform a designated task? Or demonstrate a desired behavior?"	Criterion-referenced	Used to determine a student's skill proficiency. Sole focus is on individual performance.
"How does this student's performance compare with the class's performance as a whole?" or "How does the performance of my students compare with that of similar students across the country?"	Norm-referenced	Used to compare an individual's performance to that of a group, or one group's performance with another group; characteristic of standardized testing.
"How well am I doing? As a teacher? As a student?	Self-Evaluation	Criteria and results are usually private.
"What do my students already know? In what skills are students already competent? What do my students need to learn?"	Planning and setting objectives	Purpose is to determine and diagnose needs prior to instruction; invariably criterion-referenced.
"How well are students moving toward our objectives?" ("How are we doing?")	Formative	Purpose is to determine progress during instruction; invariably criterion-referenced.
"All things considered, how does the student's overall performance rate?"	Summative	Is used after instruction; may be norm-referenced, criterion-referenced, or a combination of both.

COMMENTARY: On Self-Evaluation and Grading

We have not discussed self-evaluation in this chapter, even though it's a form of evaluation that all of us use, sometimes to excess. The reason for this is that self-evaluation is among the most private forms of evaluation; the criteria are usually private, as are the results—unless, of course, you choose to make them public.

Self-evaluation demands a considerable degree of self-awareness and self-direction. In an attempt to help our students develop these qualities, we

continued

agreed on one occasion to permit them to give themselves their citizenship grades. They would identify the grade they deserved and we agreed to mark it on their report card. To make certain that everyone used somewhat similar criteria, we spent quite some time talking about what constituted "good citizenship." However, when the children turned in their grades, we were amazed and slightly shocked. Almost without exception, their grades were one to two grades lower than we would have given. Upon investigation, it turned out that what we had considered trivial incidents, such as the failure to complete a homework paper on time, were often blown out of proportion, and that the students had downgraded themselves accordingly. We ended up spending considerable time helping children examine their conduct in a broader perspective and trying to convince them that they were being too harsh on themselves.

On another occasion we permitted a college class to use self-evaluation as a basis for determining their course grade. And again, we attempted to identify mutually agreeable criteria. This time, however, the results were quite different; all thirty-four students gave themselves an A.

It became apparent that, although our elementary students had taken self-evaluation more seriously than we had anticipated, by the college level any connection between grading and self-evaluation had become tenuous at best. For many of those college students, grading had apparently become a kind of game where one "got" whatever one could. From some students at both levels, however, we also received vociferous objections to any attempt to base grading on self-evaluation. They claimed that grading was a teacher's responsibility while self-evaluation was a private matter, one that should remain private. Where do you stand?

PROCEDURES FOR GATHERING EVALUATIVE INFORMATION

To gather evaluation information, teachers sometimes use fairly unobtrusive techniques, such as observing their students perform a task. Or they may employ much more obtrusive procedures, such as giving a test. The unobtrusive procedures, such as observing and interviewing, are seldom threatening to most students, but the more obtrusive procedures—particularly paper-and-pencil testing—can sometimes evoke fear in the heart of the most able student. Despite the fear it sometimes generates, testing is an information-gathering process, nothing more. It is one of several techniques for gathering data about student performance, and if it is not viewed that way, it should be.

Testing, like most other measurement procedures, provides a way of gathering information that can then be used (1) to determine areas where students need instruction (in other words, a test used diagnostically), (2) to prescribe additional learning experiences or make other adjustments in instruction (as determined by formative evaluation), (3) to compare a student's performance with others (as in norm-referenced evaluation), or (4) to provide a basis for grading. Perhaps it's teachers' penchant for using tests almost solely for grading purposes that makes them such awesome things in the eyes of students.

The key to gathering useful evaluative information depends, first, on identifying the kind of information you want and, second, on using an appropriate means to get that information. The kind of information we need to evaluate social studies usually relates to (1) what children know and are able to do (cognitive domain) and (2) what they believe and how they respond to what they believe and feel (affective domain). We examine evaluation in the cognitive and affective domains in the following sections.

EVALUATING COGNITIVE KNOWLEDGE AND SKILLS

If there is any area in which education has developed a reasonable degree of expertise, it is in measuring what students know at the knowledge level. More recently, we have also made strides in evaluating skill development beyond the knowledge level.

Undoubtedly the most common technique for evaluating cognitive knowledge and skills involves a teacher's questions presented verbally. Either individually or in group settings, the child is presented with a task and then requested to answer appropriately. The second-most-common technique involves some type of testing, in which the questions are usually posed in written form.

There are three major categories of evaluation instruments (*instruments* being the technical name for an evaluation technique or scale). They are (1) nationally standardized tests and scales, (2) achievement tests developed by local, regional, or state agencies, which may or may not be normed, and (3) tests developed by teachers themselves.

Standardized Tests

Standardized tests are often ordained as part of statewide or schoolwide testing programs. School systems often want the norm-referenced data such tests provide so they can compare the performance of their students with performances of children across the state or nation. Unfortunately, some teachers, who know that *their* effectiveness may also be judged in terms of how well their students perform, may find themselves "teaching for the test." In other words, the nature of the test—especially in states with mandated competency test requirements—can play a significant role in determining the kind of social studies program that is established.

Most nationally standardized tests have sections dealing with basic social studies knowledges and skills. Often the skill section will emphasize reference or study skills, such as using an index or reading a chart, rather than information-processing skills such as interpretation or analysis. To determine a test's skill focus, it's usually necessary to examine and judge each test item separately.

Several sample standardized test items are illustrated in Figure 16.1. For test items that involve cognitive skills, the necessary information (to which the child applies the skill rules) must be provided. If it is *not* provided, the child is necessarily forced to recall both the skill rule and the information from memory. In the case of the sample items shown in Figure 16.1, for example, it would be reasonable to expect the child to remember the skill rule that "The directions on a map are indicated by the compass rose." The sample map supplies the information that would permit the child to apply that skill rule. However, some standardized test items can be deceiving in this respect; although they appear to present information the child could use, they actually ask questions that test the knowledge level—and not the child's ability to apply a skill rule. For example, the first set of questions on a popular standardized test are based on an illustration of different products on a grocery-store shelf. According to the picture caption, the store is located in Ohio. A sample question asks students to "Identify which of the following products was grown closest to the store: (a) bananas, (b) pineapples, (c) coffee, or (d) apples." Because all of the items on the shelf have labels—the pineapples have a sign that says "Pineapples" nearby—the children can refer to pictures of items for words they might not otherwise know. In this instance, and although the illustration is helpful for vocabulary purposes, it does not provide the information needed to answer questions such as the sample listed above. Despite appearances to the contrary, the question is actually testing the child at the knowledge level. Other questions, however, do present information that children must use to arrive at an answer.

Sources of standardized tests for elementary social studies include the following:

California Achievement Tests (CTB/McGraw-Hill, Del Monte Research Park, Monterey, CA 93940)

Iowa Tests of Basic Skills (Riverside Publishing Company, 1919 South Highland Ave., Lombard, IL 60148)

Metropolitan Achievement Test: Social Studies (The Psychological Corporation, 757 Third Ave., New York, NY 10017)

Primary Social Studies Test (Houghton Mifflin, One Beacon Street, Boston, MA 02108)

Sequential Tests of Educational Progress: Social Studies (Addison-Wesley Publishing Company, 2725 Sand Hill Road, Menlo Park, CA 94025)

SRA Achievement Series (Science Research Associates, Inc., 155 N. Wacker Drive, Chicago, IL 60606)

Stanford Achievement Test (The Psychological Corporation, 757 Third Avenue, New York, NY 10017)

FIGURE 16.1 Sample Standardized Test Items

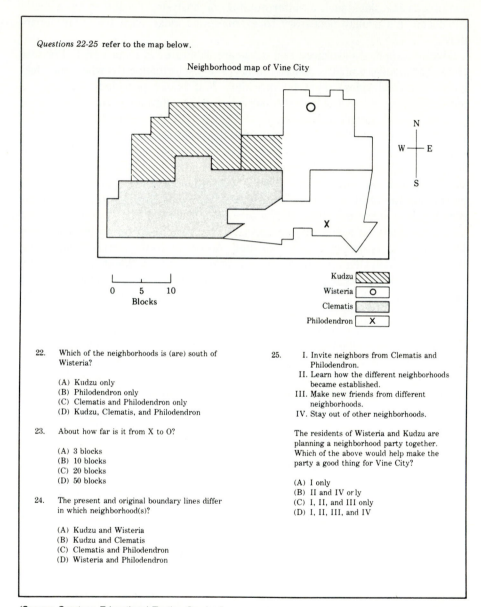

Questions 22-25 refer to the map below.

Neighborhood map of Vine City

Kudzu
Wisteria O
Clematis
Philodendron X

0   5   10
Blocks

22. Which of the neighborhoods is (are) south of Wisteria?

(A) Kudzu only
(B) Philodendron only
(C) Clematis and Philodendron only
(D) Kudzu, Clematis, and Philodendron

23. About how far is it from X to O?

(A) 3 blocks
(B) 10 blocks
(C) 20 blocks
(D) 50 blocks

24. The present and original boundary lines differ in which neighborhood(s)?

(A) Kudzu and Wisteria
(B) Kudzu and Clematis
(C) Clematis and Philodendron
(D) Wisteria and Philodendron

25. I. Invite neighbors from Clematis and Philodendron.
II. Learn how the different neighborhoods became established.
III. Make new friends from different neighborhoods.
IV. Stay out of other neighborhoods.

The residents of Wisteria and Kudzu are planning a neighborhood party together. Which of the above would help make the party a good thing for Vine City?

(A) I only
(B) II and IV orly
(C) I, II, and III only
(D) I, II, III, and IV

(Source: Courtesy Educational Testing Service.)

Although creating a fair, reliable, and valid test can be a challenging task, a teacher-made test can be an invaluable, tailor-made evaluation tool for a particular class's needs. (© *David S. Strickler/ The Picture Cube*)

Teacher-made Tests

The teacher's edition of most textbook series contains sample test items that you could use with your students. The key element in deciding which, if any, of those items to use would be how closely the objectives that the sample test items seek to measure match your objectives for whatever you are teaching. Unless that match is fairly close, your students might find themselves being tested on knowledge and skills that they had little idea would be expected of them. When that match does not exist, you will undoubtedly need to develop your own test questions (or identify some other way to determine that students have attained the objectives).

Developing Teacher-made Tests   Developing valid, unambiguous test questions may seem easy enough, but this is yet another instance where appearances can be deceptive. To be sure, there is nothing very difficult about writing a test item such as "Abraham Lincoln was born in _____ ," for example, but such an apparently straightforward question can place an unfair burden on students who must determine which of a multitude of possible answers (place? month? year?) the teacher has in mind. In other words, the students' problem with questions such as this one may lie not in their ability to demonstrate what they know about Lincoln's birth but in trying to determine the teacher's intent.

Validity   When students are unsure about what a test item expects of them—whether they are to supply a date (August 1809), a place (Kentucky), or something else—the likelihood is high that the item will not measure what it was intended to measure. This characteristic of test items (or entire tests)—namely, that they actually measure what they are intended to measure—is called *validity*. Lest there be any doubt about it, our Lincoln question is clearly invalid. All is not lost, however, for the validity of a test item can usually be improved by adding information that clarifies the teacher's intent. To do this, you must first eliminate any fuzziness from your original objectives so as to identify precisely what you expect of the student. Thus, an objective such as "From memory, the student will identify something about Abraham Lincoln" won't do; the term "something" is too vague to convey your real expectation. So, depending on what you really want students to know, the objective could be, "From memory, the student will identify the place (state) in which Lincoln was born." In this instance, the test item could then be stated as follows: "Abraham Lincoln was born in the state of _____ ."

Providing additional information often improves the clarity and, hence, the validity of a test question. In some instances, this can also be accomplished by changing the form of the question. Instead of using short-answer (completion) format, for example, our sample Lincoln item could be presented as a multiple-choice or true-false question. In multiple-choice form, the question could be stated as follows:

_____ **Abraham Lincoln was born in**
    a. Illinois
    b. Kentucky *
    c. Indiana
    d. None of the above

As a true-false item, the question could be phrased as

_____ **Abraham Lincoln was born in Indiana (F).**

In both examples, the intent of each question is clear. At the same time, we've compromised their validity somewhat by introducing a larger "chance" or guessing factor than was true for the short-answer (completion) format. For the true-false question especially, students have a fifty-fifty chance of guessing the correct answer. This may help to explain why some students prefer true-false test items simply because luck is on their side. This does not mean that you should forego using true-false or multiple-choice test questions, but it does mean that you cannot be as confident that such questions validly measure what they are intended to measure.

Appropriateness Regardless of the form in which our Lincoln test item is asked, a crucial question still remains: should students be expected to recall such information? On one hand, expecting children to know the date or place of Lincoln's birth could help to reinforce the notion that social studies is a collection of irrelevant facts. On the other hand, some individuals argue that such information is part of our historical heritage, and as such represents the kind of thing every citizen should know. Whichever position you lean toward will influence your judgment as to both the appropriateness of the question and the objectives on which it is based. And although this is a tough issue to deal with, our point in raising it is to indicate that determining the validity and appropriateness of test questions are separate issues and should be treated accordingly. Thus, a perfectly valid test question, such as "List the states in order of their admission to the Union," must still be judged in terms of its appropriateness. In fact, if test items (and the objectives they are based on) are unreasonable or inappropriate to begin with, validity doesn't even enter the picture. In other words, trying to develop valid test items for questionable objectives is an exercise in futility.

If you can't write good test items, you are unlikely to get a true indication of a child's abilities. In the sample test that follows, we have intentionally violated almost every existing practice of test construction. We have, in effect, produced a nontest. However, after each sample question we suggest ways in which it might be improved. In some instances, of course, it's impossible to improve a poor test question. Yet even when the form of a test question conforms to recommended practices, the items must still be judged in terms of its appropriateness.

A NONTEST—COLONIAL AMERICA

Completion

Fill in the blanks with the correct answer.

1. *Poor:* **The _____ _____ _____ were among the first white men to trade with the Indians.**

   Better: **The first white men to trade with the Indians in the Northwest Territory were the _____ fur traders; *or,* The first white men to trade with the Indians in the Northwest Territory were the French _____ _____ .**

   Analysis: **Ordinarily only one key word or phrase should be omitted, not three key words, and ordinarily the omitted word or phrase should be at or near the end of the sentence, so the student need not continually reread it in order to determine the subject. In addition, the lines where students write their responses should be of approximately equal length, so as not to provide clues to the desired answer. In this instance, however, there are so many blanks in the "poor" question** that the short response line was needed to provide a necessary clue as to what the question was asking.

Responding to a direct question is sometimes easier than completing a sentence, particularly if the test item (and its objective) contains multiple elements. Thus, an alternative short-answer format for this test item would be:

What was the occupation of the first white men who traded with the Indians in the Northwest Territory? _____

2. *Poor:* Manhattan Island was purchased from the Indians on July _____ , _____. (July 14, 1649)
   Better: None

   Analysis: Desired responses should deal with important information, not trivia. In addition, this item strongly resembles the kind of statement one would find in a social studies textbook. Using lines from a textbook as the basis for short-answer test items (and other test questions) encourages memorization, not understanding.

3. *Poor:* At the first _____ , the _____ brought _____ and the _____ brought _____ and other wild animals.
   Better (if used at all): At the first Thanksgiving, the Pilgrims brought several kinds of food including _____ and _____ .

   Analysis: Whether students should know who brought what to the first Thanksgiving is questionable to start with, but the question as originally stated contained so many blanks that its intent was not clear. Even in restated form, there are a number of correct answers, all of which should receive credit.

4. The colonists who attended the first Thanksgiving were called _____ .

   Analysis: There's nothing wrong with the form of this question, it's just that the answer is provided by the previous question.

True-False (Alternative Response)

Use a + for true and a 0 for false unless directed otherwise. (Capital T's and capital F's can look very much alike—sometimes intentionally so.)

5. *Poor:* The Puritan religion was best suited for the colonies.
   Better: None.

   Analysis: The question asks the student to make a value judgment in the absence of clearly defined criteria.

6. *Poor:* The Indians never helped the Puritans.
   Better: None.

   Analysis: Specific determiners and absolute terms such as *none, never,* and *always,* tend to be associated with false statements;

associated with true statements. Generally, specific determiners and absolutes should be avoided unless you are dealing with situations where they are appropriate; e.g., "Evaluation always requires the identification of criteria."

7. *Poor:* The first Thanksgiving was held over the winter of 1720–1721, and was attended by the Pilgrims, the Indians, the English, and the Dutch.
   Better: The first Thanksgiving was held during the winter of 1720–1721.

   Analysis: As originally stated, the question is misleading, especially since a false element, the date, is subordinate to the main thrust of the question. In addition, it is not clear whether the accuracy or the completeness of the list of attendees is the concern. As a general rule, avoid statements that could be misinterpreted or those that are partly true and partly false.

   An alternative technique for handling true-false questions that involve multiple elements is illustrated below.

   French explorers who visited North America included

   (+) 1. La Salle

   (0) 2. De Soto

   (+) 3. Champlain

   (0) 4. Hudson

   (+) 5. Cartier

   Another variation sometimes used with alternative-response questions requires students to supply the correct version of a false item. This technique is illustrated below.

   Native Americans sailed the lakes and rivers of the eastern woodlands in hickory canoes.

   (correct statement) _____

Multiple Choice

Select the best answer and write the letter in the space provided.

8. *Poor:* A red-orange root plant grown by the Indians was (a) corn, (b) yam, (c) pumpkin, (d) asparagus.
   Better: As multiple choice, none; if used at all, the question could be asked in a completion or true-false format.

   Analysis: Distractors for multiple-choice items should be plausible. In this instance, only one root plant is listed.

9. *Poor:* The Puritans
   a. were not the group that founded the Massachusetts Bay colony.
   b. went to southern Georgia.
   c. didn't believe in taking a bath.

d. left England, went to Holland, and then fled to the North American colonies of Great Britain, where they could avoid religious persecution.

Better: The Puritans settled in Massachusetts in order to

a. establish a fur-trading company.

b. avoid the high taxes they had been forced to pay in England.

c. practice their religion without interference.

d. prevent Spain and France from claiming the area.

Analysis: Where possible, the major portion of the statement should be presented in the introduction, or stem, of the question. In addition, all incorrect answers should be plausible, of the same general style, and of approximately the same length as the correct answer.

10. *Poor:* The name of the minister who headed the colonial government in Rhode Island was (a) John Smith, (b) Bunker Hill.

   Better: The name of the minister who headed the colonial government in Rhode Island was

   a. John Smith.

   b. John Adams.

   c. Roger Williams.

   d. Cotton Mather.

   e. None of the above.

   Analysis: Multiple-choice questions should have a minimum of three and preferably four or five alternative answers. The fewer the alternatives, the higher the probability that students may guess the right answer. More importantly, the correct (or best) alternative response must be provided (which it is *not* in the "poor" form of this question). Further, alternative answers should be of the same general type, such as the names of people, places, statements, etc. Mixing different types of alternative responses or providing obviously false distractors should be avoided. Also to be avoided are multiple-choice questions in which the correct answer is revealed by clues in the item itself, such as "Many colonial families used a (a) ax, (b) apple peeler, (c) candle mold, (d) ox." Only *c* is grammatically correct. Such questions should be reserved for grammar tests.

   You might have noticed that for the bulk of our sample multiple-choice questions the correct answer was *c*. Test-wise students often look for such a pattern, so you are safer to distribute the position of correct responses randomly throughout the test.

Matching

Write the letter from Column II in the space provided in front of the correct term in Column I.

11. *Poor:*

Column I	Column II
1. _____ Patroon	a. The Indian word for corn
2. _____ Maize	b. a Dutch system for landholding along the Hudson River
3. _____ Mayflower	c. one of the middle colonies
4. _____ Delaware	d. a ship

Better: Instructions: Write the letter for the occupation described in Column II in the space provided in front of the term associated with that occupation (Column I).

Column I	Column II
1. _____ blacksmith	a. barrelmaker
2. _____ chandler	b. hatmaker
3. _____ cooper	c. wheelmaker
4. _____ deacon	d. iron worker
5. _____ teamster	e. ship's supplier
6. _____ wheelwright	f. jewelry maker
	g. wagon driver
	h. church official

Analysis: The items in our "poor" example are so few and so dissimilar that almost anyone could complete the exercise, even if they knew nothing about "patroons." In addition, guessing is facilitated because the items in each column match exactly. Even though students may object loudly, guessing is minimized if one column contains more items than are used, or contains responses that are used more than once.

Among the most difficult aspects of developing quality matching questions is the problem of identifying enough similar items to place in the respective columns without resorting to trivia. Some of the following examples, which are adapted from Gronlund (1985), could be used for matching purposes. Note that all entries for one column of a matching test item would be examples of *one* entry shown in Column I below; the second column of the item would be examples from the parallel entry shown in Column II.

Column I	Column II
People	Achievements
Inventors	Inventions
Dates	Historical events
Objects	Names of objects
Terms	Definitions
Places	Geographical locations
Rules	Examples
Principles	Illustrations
Machines	Uses

Whenever your tests begin to look like our "poor" examples, you've got problems. Not only will the form of your test items be questionable, but you may also be guilty of emphasizing the kind of trivia that has given social studies an unsavory reputation, one that in this case is justly deserved. In addition, our "poor" test items also lend credence to the notion that evaluation is a kind of "game" intended to trick students, not an honest attempt to assess what they actually know.

Evaluating Skills

So much emphasis in traditional social studies has been placed on evaluating children's knowledge that efforts to evaluate children's skills has sometimes been inconsistent or neglected. Actually, it's not more difficult to evaluate a student's ability to deal with skills, it's just different. One difference is that evaluating skills, especially process skills, usually requires fewer evaluation questions or tasks. Instead of a fifty-item test, for example, three, four, or five questions will often suffice.

Essay-test items are a form of evaluation that permits teachers to "get inside" students and to gain insight into how they think and process information. In fact, essay tests are a form of testing for which it is almost impossible to "fake it." However, before essay testing is a possibility, students must be mature enough to express themselves in writing. Because of this, and because essay tests are often more difficult to grade, they are not widely used in elementary schools.

Some problems associated with essay-test items are shown below.

SAMPLE NONTEST—COLONIAL AMERICA, PART II
Write a good essay on one of the following questions.
1. *Poor:* **What crops did the early Pilgrims grow?**
   Better: **None.**

   Essay-test questions should ask students to do more than simply reproduce information. Indeed, if a list of the Pilgrims' crops is desired, a short-answer (completion) question would be more appropriate; e.g., "List five crops grown by the Pilgrims."

2. *Poor:* **Discuss Indians.**
   Better: **Describe with examples at least three different ways in which the early colonists' contact with the Indians benefited both groups.**

   Analysis: **"Discuss Indians" is so broad that it is difficult to know (1) where to begin and (2) what the intent of the question actually is. The improved question clearly conveys what the student is to do.**

3. *Poor:* **Tell all you know about why people should always be brave and thankful.**
   Better: **None.**

Analysis: Although the task in the "poor" question is clear enough, establishing valid criteria for evaluating students' responses would be difficult, if not impossible. This is a particularly common problem in attempting to evaluate attitudes, which is what this question seems geared toward. Of course, teachers could gain insight into their students' attitudes by asking them to respond to questions such as "Why do you think some people are thankful?" but using those responses for grading purposes would be inappropriate. Some of the observational techniques suggested later in this chapter may prove to be more valid indicators of children's attitudes than direct or written questions like the ones illustrated here.

A second difference that marks skill-test items from their knowledge-level cousins is their presentation of information to be interpreted, analyzed, evaluated, and so forth. In other words, what you are really looking for is the student's ability to *transfer* their skill of processing information from whatever kind of information they have worked with previously to the data presented on a test. The thing to be transferred is the skill and not necessarily the information itself. What you find when evaluating students' information-processing skills is that the *way* in which you present information in a testing situation may be very similar to the way you presented it in the original situation. Indeed, the manner of presentation may remain exactly the same; only the information will be changed to protect the student from thinking it has to be memorized.

The following are some examples of what we've been talking about. Note that in the case of the information from the *Works of James I* (Example 1), it was necessary to rewrite the material at a lower reading level.

EXAMPLE 1

Skills: Analysis and interpretation of data.

Instructions: Read the following quotes. Do they show the same position about the responsibility of an individual? Or about the way in which individuals control themselves? Explain.

Kings are like God. If you think of what God can do, you can think of what a king can do. For example, a king can do anything with his people. He can make them a success or make them a failure. He can judge whether or not what people do is right. But no person shall judge the king. A king's people are like chess pieces and the king is like a chess player. He decides the moves. He decides what the pieces will do. The people should serve the king. No person is to change the government. The government is the king's responsibility.

Adapted from the
Works of James I (1603)

Having taken this trip for the glory of God and to help the Christian faith, we agree to work together for the Glory and the Faith.

From *The Mayflower Compact* (1620)

EXAMPLE 2

Question 1: Skill area: Interpreting data.

Instructions: Use the data below to answer the following questions. (True-False: use + for true, 0 for false)

Population growth of two cities between 1875 and 1975:

Date	City A	City B
1875	111	72
1900	190	220
1925	1,621	400
1950	11,006	1,890
1975	24,000	2,773

_____ 1. City A has always been larger than City B. (0)

_____ 2. City A has grown faster than City B. (+)

_____ 3. City A was larger than City B in 1975. (+)

_____ 4. City A is likely to have more city employees than City B. (+)

_____ 5. City B is likely to have more schools than City A. (–)

Question 2: Skill area: Logic.

Instructions: Circle the correct answer.

1. Suppose three men need food for their families. Suppose also that the same three men realize that if they hunt together, it will be easier to shoot a buck. Each takes his position and the deer is shot. Which of the following would be most likely to take place?
   a. Each family would get more food.
   b. Each family would get the same amount of food.
   c. Each family would get the same quantity of food.
   *d. The three men would have to work out some way of dividing up the food.

2. If in your studies you find that (1) all humans have certain needs, (2) all humans strive to satisfy these needs, and (3) different people have different ways of satisfying their needs, you would be able to say that
   a. there is only one right way for people to satisfy their needs.
   b. people who do not satisfy their needs the same way we do are ignorant.
   *c. the different ways in which people satisfy their needs are learned and thus can undergo change.
   d. the ways people satisfy their needs cannot be changed.

3. If you depend on a classmate to help you with your homework, and the classmate in turn depends upon his brother to help him with his chores so he can find time to help you, you

    a. **are more concerned with your classmate than you are with his brother.**

  *b. **you are just as concerned with your classmate's brother as with your classmate.**

    c. **depend on one and not the other.**

    d. **don't take the brother into account.**

Interviewing and Observing

With any kind of written test, there always exists the problem of those students whose inability to read prevents them from demonstrating either what they know or are able to do. If students can't read the questions, the answers are immaterial, and they will be forced into a kind of guessing game. Interviewing and observation/rating scales are nonreading-dependent, data-gathering techniques that can prove useful, even when reading skills are not a potential problem.

Finding out what students know or are able to do just by talking with them or watching them is hardly a new idea. Even Socrates did more than just ask questions. But traditionally, talking with students or observing them has tended to be a casual affair. When a student was obviously having difficulty, for example, teachers would just as obviously walk over and talk with the student. Or, for one reason or another, a teacher's attention might be drawn to a particular student or a group of students. What distinguishes interviewing and observing from their more casual cousins is their systematic quality. The interview is not another casual conversation. It is systematic (though not rigidly so), and it is conducted for a particular purpose: to find out what children know about something and/or how they feel about it. The interview is not a teaching device in the narrowly defined sense of the term. That is, it is not primarily an opportunity to correct children's misconceptions or teach them something. Rather, it is an opportunity for teachers *to learn* something from and about their students.

A major deterrent to interviewing is the amount of time it can take. Even ten-minute interviews with a class of twenty-four students represents a considerable time commitment. The clear and sometimes preferable alternative to individual interviews is group sessions. Group sessions permit other students to share the focus of the teacher's attention, which is particularly valuable when an individual student might feel uncomfortable alone.

Suggested interview procedures include:

Identifying sets of similar questions on whatever it is you want to find out so that you don't ask the same questions all the time.

Keeping your facial expression as "interested" but as unevaluative as possible.

Making it clear that everyone will have an opportunity to talk (and shift to someone else if one student begins to monopolize things).

Not being put off by an immediate response of "I don't know." Often it's just the way children gain time while they think something through. Give them time to think, and then probe.

Observation/Rating Scales   An observation/rating scale is probably best described as a "scoresheet," something on which either teachers or students record their observations or, more accurately, judgments based on their observations. The basic observation/rating scale lists the students' names and the criteria against which they will be observed. Of course, if you have a lot of criteria, you may need a separate sheet for each student—in effect, a student profile. Then, periodically, you review each student's performance in terms of the criteria. It is often to your advantage to make the scale quite explicit, as shown in Figure 16.2.

EVALUATING ATTITUDES AND VALUES

In many schools, so much time is devoted to evaluating cognitive skills that the time devoted to evaluating students' attitudes and values seems almost minuscule by comparison. No matter how much teachers stress the importance of attitudes and values, the disproportionate amount of time spent evaluating cognitive skills may lead students to believe that all the talk about attitudes and values is just that—talk! Yet despite the apparent difference in time spent on each activity, evaluating attitudes and values is an area in which appearances can be deceiving.

Consider that to evaluate cognitive skills, it is necessary that students do something to demonstrate their ability. This could involve taking a test, participating in an interview, or somehow demonstrating what they can do, usually during a time period specifically reserved for such activities. (When evaluation is ongoing,

FIGURE 16.2   Sample Rating Scale for Student Responses

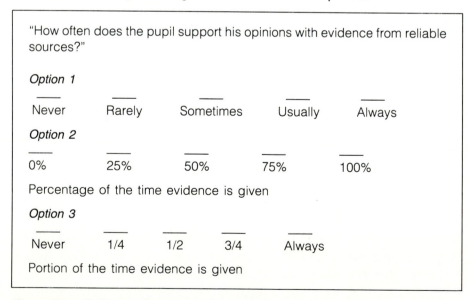

"How often does the pupil support his opinions with evidence from reliable sources?"

Option 1

____   ____   ____   ____   ____
Never   Rarely   Sometimes   Usually   Always

Option 2

____   ____   ____   ____   ____
0%   25%   50%   75%   100%

Percentage of the time evidence is given

Option 3

____   ____   ____   ____   ____
Never   1/4   1/2   3/4   Always

Portion of the time evidence is given

(*Source: Murray R. Thomas. "Education: The Case for Rating Scales," in* Teaching Elementary Social Studies: Readings. *1972. Belmont, Calif.: Wadsworth Publishing Company. Used by permission of the author and the publisher.*)

this is much less the case.) Students' attitudes and values, on the other hand, are more likely to be expressed in the natural course of their day-to-day activities. Their attitudes and values are expressed in everything they do. And so, simply by observing students' activities over a period of time, it becomes possible to infer what their attitudes and values are. In other words, a special time set aside for attitudinal evaluation usually isn't required. Evaluators need to know what behaviors they are looking for, of course. But attitudinal evaluation doesn't require any special behavior on the student's part. In fact, students' behaviors may more accurately reflect their underlying beliefs and values if they do *not* know they are being observed; that way they're less likely to behave in ways they think are expected of them. We are also suggesting here that observation is one of the most accurate techniques for gathering information on students' (or anyone's) attitudes and values.

COMMENTARY: Halos—Negative and Positive

In the process of selecting a name for our first child, I suggested Michael. My wife, a former teacher, responded with an immediate "No." Inexperienced as I was in name-choosing, I soon discovered that it is not an entirely rational process.

"What's wrong with Michael?" I asked.

"Well [emphatically], when I was teaching fourth grade I had a student whose name was Michael. He picked his nose, smelled of garlic, and always needed a bath. There is no way that we're going to name *our* son Michael."

We now have three sons, none of whom is named Michael. Although we have several friends and relatives named Michael with whom my wife gets along well, it's apparent that the thought of giving that name to one of our children elicited certain strong feelings about a certain Michael from my wife's past. The incident also illustrates the *halo effect,* an extremely common phenomenon that can influence a teacher's observation of students. Just as my wife's feeling about the name Michael had been biased by that former student, it is not unusual for teachers to generalize from certain specific behaviors to *all* of a child's actions. In other words, based on just a few behaviors, the teacher may form a uniformly negative or positive (but not both) opinion of a student that extends to almost everything the student does. That's why children with positive halos can sometimes get away with almost anything, whereas a child with a negative halo may be always suspect, even when wholly innocent.

Observation and rating scales will not eliminate the halo effect, for that is something all of us must deal with; however, they can provide a systematic process for gathering valid information that might otherwise consist only of random impressions.

One factor that makes evaluating attitudes and values more difficult than evaluating cognitive skills is the difficulty associated with identifying precise behavioral indicators for an attitude or value. No matter how desirable a particular attitude or value may be—"tolerance" or "appreciation," for example—it is difficult to identify behavioral characteristics (or indicators) for such values that do not tread on an individual's personal liberties. As long as an individual's behavior doesn't interfere with someone else's rights, the individual has the right to like or dislike whatever (or whomever) he or she chooses.

The difficulties involved in identifying precise behavioral indicators of an attitude or value, combined with an unwillingness to infringe on personal liberties, help to explain why attitudes and values are often expressed as general goals rather than as specific, measurable objectives. This lack of precision also helps to account for the absence of formal instruments to measure the development of attitudes and values. Although some attitude scales and inventories are available, these invariably are point-in-time measures; they attempt to identify an individual's attitudes or beliefs at a particular time, but they seldom make any pretense of explaining how attitudes or values develop. Despite this limitation, when such attitudinal measures are used in conjunction with other techniques, they may provide information and a point of departure that would otherwise be denied the teacher. In the following sections we examine several techniques for assessing attitudes and values.

Attitude Scales

Attitude scales differ from conventional tests in that tests usually have correct answers; attitude scales don't. An attitude scale consists of a set of questions or statements such as "Students should willingly share ideas and materials with others" or "I think cats are smarter than dogs." The individual is asked to respond to such questions or statements in terms of beliefs or personal preferences (which is why there are no previously established "right" answers).

Most attitude scales have several items that deal with a particular attitude or belief, to which the individual responds using a familiar Likert-type scale, such as "Strongly Agree," "Agree," "Undecided," "Disagree," and "Strongly Disagree." By analyzing the pattern of responses, it then becomes possible to infer the individual's attitude or belief toward the topic in question.

Questionnaires and Inventories

Most people have responded to questionnaires and interest inventories at one time or another. Questionnaires, of course, can deal with a wide range of topics, while interest inventories are usually restricted to what an individual likes or dislikes. Questions like "What do you like to do in your spare time?" and the familiar "What subjects do you like best (or least) in school?" are typical.

Questionnaires and inventories are relatively easy to develop. You simply identify open-ended questions to which the student supplies a written response.

In interview settings, the students' responses would be verbal. Regardless of how you administer the questionnaire or interest inventory, a potential problem may arise in determining what to do with the information once you've obtained it. Determining what your students do in their spare time, for example, is probably most useful in providing additional insight into your students and the activities they pursue.

Checklists and Rating Scales

A checklist consists of a series of descriptive statements such as "Works willingly with others" or "Participates in class discussions," next to which the evaluator makes a check mark when an item is observed. In the case of checklists used for self-evaluation, individuals mark the items that apply to them. There is no restriction on who should use a checklist; it could be the teacher, other students, or, as in self-evaluation, individual students themselves.

The format of checklists and rating scales is often similar. The difference between the two usually lies in the kind of marking system employed. On a checklist, the evaluator marks a preidentified category, as illustrated on the sample rating scale/checklist shown in Figure 16.3. On rating scales, evaluators usually use a qualitative rating to judge or rate the individual's characteristics or performance.

A retired elementary teacher of our acquaintance always used a rating scale to gather information on her students' class participation. She simply listed her students' names and then evaluated each student's class participation at the end of the day. The unique thing about her scale was her use of music symbols—sharps, naturals, flats—to indicate each child's performance. The scale on our former colleague's rating sheet was implied, that is, from good (sharp) to bad (flat).

Remember that what observers see may be colored by their perceptions. Remember also that a student's responses may be geared to what he or she thinks you want to hear, not the way he or she really feels about a topic or issue. And finally, remember that your evaluation of a shy child's lack of participation in class discussion, as might be identified by an evaluation using the instrument shown in Figure 16.3, may be based on elements that are far removed from the evaluation itself. In other words, although your evaluation may indicate that certain children do not participate regularly in class discussions, faulting those children for their failure to participate could aggravate the problem. The point here is that although an initial evaluation may indicate the presence of a certain problem, that evaluation may not necessarily indicate the reason or basis for the problem. Discovering why a shy child is reluctant to participate in class discussions will undoubtedly necessitate additional observation. Our second point here is that assessing students' attitudes and values, or even their class paticipation, can be more involved than it appears, and may demand that you gather information from as many different and varied sources as you can.

FIGURE 16.3 Sample Rating Scale/Checklist for Class Participation

	Rating		Checklist Criteria		
			Always	Usually	Seldom
Participates willingly/regularly					
Provides relevant ideas					
Respects rights/opinions of others					
Identifies or clarifies problems or questions					
For rating scale, use Outstanding = 4, Above Average = 3, Satisfactory = 2, and Needs Improvement = 1.					

SUMMARY

For years teachers have been using evaluation as more than just a basis for grading. The problem they face, however, stems from the fact that grading is such a powerful phenomenon that it tends to overshadow everything else. And so, although most teachers know that evaluation and testing are *not* synonymous with grading, they don't necessarily feel (or act) that way. Sometimes, quite unintentionally, they may find themselves stressing "a *very* important test on Friday," thereby perpetuating the evaluation-grading mystique.

Evaluation, like planning, is an ongoing process. Just as teachers' goals and objectives help to identify *what* they are attempting to do, evaluation helps them identify *how well* they (and their students) are actually doing it.

Evaluation always consists of identifying or accepting evaluative criteria (the standards against which evaluative judgments are made); measuring performance, behavior, or products in relation to those standards; and making judgments about the individual's performance. The form that evaluation takes is largely determined by the teacher's purpose. If you are interested in determining whether or not a student can demonstrate a certain skill or knowledge, you will undoubtedly turn to *criterion-referenced* evaluation. However, if you wish to compare your students' performance with that of another group, you will turn to a form of *norm-referenced* evaluation. In instances when you are interested in determining how things are going during an instructional episode, you may turn to *formative* evaluation. If you are interested in determining the overall quality of a student's performance or product at the end of an instructional period, you will turn to *summative* evaluation. Finally, if your purpose is to determine how well you are doing as a teacher, you will undoubtedly turn to *self-evaluation*.

Despite its close relationship to traditional grading, we defined *testing* as an information-gathering device. Testing, like observing, interviewing, checklists, attitude scales, interest inventories, and rating scales, are ways of gathering different kinds of information. Some of these techniques, however, are more likely to measure what they are intended to measure than others, and thus have higher validity.

Actually, we have barely scratched the surface of evaluation in this chapter. Although we have shown you some things to avoid, we also recommend that you consult one of the books on evaluation and test construction listed in the Suggested Readings section at the end of this chapter.

SUGGESTED ACTIVITIES

1. During one of our first years of working with prospective teachers, we decided to use self-evaluation as the basis for grading. At the end of the term we asked everyone to submit a self-evaluation and to recommend a grade for themselves. Despite wide discrepancies in individual performances, 95 percent of the self-evaluations indicated that our students felt they had learned a lot, had worked hard, and, in their minds, had earned the grade of A. Where did we go wrong? Or did we?

2. Obtain any one of the standardized tests that deals with elementary social studies (your psychology department should have copies if your education department doesn't). First, take the test so that your attention is not distracted by the content of the questions. Then analyze the items in terms of the skills they are really testing.

3. Assume that the students in your fifth-grade class need help in developing the following skills: (1) classification, (2) inductive reasoning, (3) question posing, and (4) hypothesis development. Using social studies content, develop at least two activities designed to promote skill development in each of the above areas.

   Using the same activity format but substituting data different from that used in the learning activities, develop a way to evaluate student performance in these skill areas.

4. It has been argued that creativity, evaluation, and grading are totally incompatible; that you can't have one as long as you have the other. What do you think? Is there any way to reconcile creativity, evaluation, and grading?

REFERENCES

Gronlund, Norman E. 1985. *Measurement and Evaluation in Teaching*. 5th ed. New York: Macmillan.

Krathwohl, David R., Benjamin Bloom, and Bertram Masia. 1956. *Taxonomy of Educational Objectives, Handbook II: Affective Domain*. New York: Longman.

Muir, Sharon Pray, and Candace Wells. 1983. "Informal Evaluation." *The Social Studies,* 74 (May/June), 95–97.

Saunders, Norris M. 1966. *Classroom Questions: What Kinds?* New York: Harper & Row.

Thomas, R. Murry. 1972. "Education: The Case for Rating Scales." In *Teaching Elementary Social Studies: Readings,* eds. R. Murry Thomas and Dale L. Brubaker. Belmont, Calif.: Wadsworth Publishing.

SUGGESTED READINGS

Note: As we began writing the annotations for the books in this listing, we found that all of them said essentially the same thing: excellent. So if you are interested in pursuing topics related to evaluation or test construction, any of the books selected from the list below should serve that purpose.

Harry D. Berg, ed. 1965. *Evaluation in Social Studies.* 35th Yearbook of the National Council for the Social Studies. Washington, D.C.: The Council.

Norman E. Gronlund. 1985. *Measurement and Evaluation in Teaching.* 5th ed. New York: Macmillan.

Making the Classroom Test: A Guide for Teachers. 1969. Princeton, N.J.: Educational Testing Service.

John U. Michaelis. 1985. *Social Studies for Children: A Guide to Basic Instruction.* 8th ed. Englewood Cliffs, N.J.: Prentice-Hall. An excellent chapter on evaluation.

Horace T. Morse and George H. McCune. 1971. (Revised by Lester E. Brown and Ellen Cook.) *Selected Items for the Testing of Study Skills and Critical Thinking.* 5th ed. Bulletin No. 15. Washington, D.C.: The National Council for the Social Studies.

P. L. Williams and J. P. Moore, eds. 1980. *Criterion-Referenced Testing for the Social Studies.* NCSS Bulletin 64. Washington, D.C.: National Council for the Social Studies.

EPILOGUE

Remember when you

□ couldn't understand why Australia was a continent but Greenland wasn't?

□ thought Paris, Boston, and Chicago were states?

□ had current events every Friday?

□ memorized the preamble to the Constitution, the Gettysburg Address, or the presidents of the United States, in order?

□ were taught that "mail carriers deliver the mail" when you already knew it?. . . .

INTRODUCTION: Reflecting on Things Past

We began this book many chapters ago by asking if you remembered some of the things we listed above. We end this book with the hope that you have a better context for explaining and interpreting some of those things you may have remembered. We hope that you understand, for example, that the perspective from which some maps are drawn makes Australia appear smaller than Greenland (when it is actually about three times larger), or that children often have difficulty distinguishing between cities, states, and even countries (such as Paris, Boston, and Chicago) until they gain more experience with their world. We also hope you understand that social studies is a subject that many teachers approach quite differently. Some of those teachers (and many parents) believe that having children memorize the preamble to the Constitution or the Gettysburg Address teaches patriotism; others believe that such activities help train the mind (mental discipline). Still others, ourselves included, believe that children could spend their time more profitably by engaging in other kinds of activities.

We have seen a lot of changes take place in social studies education over the years, ranging from efforts to teach "history as history" and "geography as geography," through attempts to teach children to become miniature historians, miniature political scientists, etc., to teaching children to use the social and behavioral sciences as they deal with the worlds in which they live. To whatever extent we have an opportunity to influence the direction that social studies education in the future may take, we wish to suggest the following as possible emphases for the 1990s.

Because it has to do with our world and how people interact within that world,
social studies instruction can offer a teacher almost unlimited challenges and rewards.
(© *Rick Kopstein 1986/Monkmeyer Press Photo Service*)

Instructional Premises for the 1990s

Observation and listening should receive increased emphasis as access skills.

There should be an increased emphasis on helping students to become more skillful in and cognizant of the thinking processes they use.

There should be increased awareness of the extent to which mathematics can be a tool and a form for communicating social information.

There should be increased recognition of the power of electronic media to place a world of data at students' fingertips.

From the primary grades onward, students should be increasingly involved in designing and conducting their own investigations (their own "social studies" if you will—which does not involve copying information from an encyclopedia).

Social studies curricula and teaching should emphasize systems of relationships among social phenomena rather than learning particular bits of information.

In social studies teaching, increased emphasis should be on helping students to become skillful in making and testing social ideas.

Skills-based teaching should become more systematic and more structured.

As long as the "back to the basics" movement continues to hold much of the country in its grasp, it is questionable whether the major focus in social studies can shift from the current emphasis on knowledge toward greater emphasis on skills-based teaching. But even in a "back to the basics" context, the essential question continues to be: Basic what? Basic facts? Basic skills? Basic knowledge?

Clearly there are certain fundamentals, certain basics, that all children should know. How you identify *which* fundamentals depends upon your view of the world for which you are educating children. In some cases this may mean a return to "Columbus discovered America" and "New Delhi is the capital of India," assuming, of course, that social studies programs have ceased emphasizing such information. But if this is what "the basics" means, then we need to ask ourselves how such information will help children to function in the increasingly information-rich world in which they will be living—a world where such information is readily available to everyone via computers and other electronic media. In other cases, the "basics" might refer to skills—the basic information-processing skills that we identified earlier. We would rather not cast this as an either-or question, but given the option, we place our emphasis on the skills dimension, for those skills are children's keys to their world.

As a kind of benediction, we'd like to share with you a proverb that we used in the first edition of this book, and that has served us well (and grown increasingly popular) over the years. It goes:

> Give a man a fish
>
> and you feed him for one day.
>
> Teach him how to fish, and
>
> he feeds himself for a lifetime.

Social studies as teaching children "to fish"? Consider it.

Best of luck!

APPENDIX A
DATA CARDS FOR PRESIDENCY
ACTIVITY

CARD 1

Data about Franklin D. Roosevelt, as of 1945   The American people elected Roosevelt president four times. Because of his New Deal programs designed to combat the severe financial depression of the 1930s and his leadership during World War II, many historians have classified him as one of the most effective chief executives ever to hold the office. Some of Roosevelt's critics, however, felt that he misused the power of the presidency by exerting extensive political pressure on Congress in order to secure passage of the New Deal legislation. He served as president from 1933 until his death in 1945. An attack of polio in the early 1920s left Roosevelt's legs partially paralyzed for the remainder of his life.

CARD 2

Data about Benedict Arnold, as of 1801   Before he joined the British in their attempt to defeat the rebels during the American Revolution, Arnold had served George Washington with distinction during military campaigns from 1776 to 1779. Distressed with financial worries and with a feeling of not receiving adequate recognition from the Continental Congress for his services, he abandoned the American cause and became one of the most well-known traitors in American history.

CARD 3

Data about Martin Luther King, Jr., as of 1968   Before he was assassinated in 1968, the Reverend Martin Luther King, Jr., had become one of the most active champions of the nonviolent civil rights movement. Beginning with his successful boycott of segregated city buses in Birmingham, Alabama, King rose to become leader of the Southern Christian Leadership Conference—one of the most effective organizations to lobby for federal civil rights legislation during the 1960s.

CARD 4

Data about Andrew Jackson, as of 1829   According to most historians of American life, Jackson was one of our most forceful chief executives. As president, Jackson asserted the supremacy of the federal government when South Carolina attempted to nullify federal tariff laws. His opposition to any form of monopoly was evident in his veto of legislation to recharter the powerful and half-public Bank of the United States.

CARD 5

Data about Alexander Hamilton, as of 1804   Until his death in a duel with Aaron Burr, he had served his country as an advisor to George Washington. His arguments for adoption of the federal Constitution were instrumental in its final approval. His financial genius helped to establish the young United States on a firm financial footing during its early years.

CARD 6

Data about Eleanor Roosevelt, as of 1949   Eleanor Roosevelt, wife of Franklin D. Roosevelt, became one of our country's most active champions of the poor, minority groups, women's labor unions, and civil rights. As Franklin Roosevelt's wife, she constantly served as an unofficial advisor for many of his New Deal domestic policies. After her husband's death in 1945, Mrs. Roosevelt was appointed a United States delegate to the United Nations.

CARD 7

Data about George C. Wallace, as of 1974   Until an attempt on his life crippled him in 1972, George Wallace had been an active and outspoken proponent of the cause of states' rights. This was especially evident when he began his first term as governor of Alabama, ran as a presidential candidate for the American Party in 1968, and campaigned as a Democratic candidate for the presidency in 1972. Since the attempt on his life, Wallace has been paralyzed from the waist down.

CARD 8

Data about Abraham Lincoln, as of 1865   With the exception of George Washington and Franklin D. Roosevelt, probably no other president ever entered office facing such immense problems as did Abraham Lincoln. Historians of Lincoln's life generally agree that he did as much as any chief executive could have to lead the Union to victory in the Civil War, and attempt to heal the wounds of that conflict for both the North and the South. On numerous occasions before and during his presidency, Lincoln suffered periods of severe mental depression. His untimely assassination occurred in 1865.

APPENDIX B
SPACE RENDEZVOUS ANSWERS

Items	Reasoning	Ranking	Your Ranks	Error Points*	Group Ranks	Error Points*
Box of matches	no oxygen on moon to sustain flame, virtually worthless	15	___	___	___	___
Food concentrate	efficient means of supplying energy requirements	4	___	___	___	___
50 feet of nylon rope	useful in scaling cliffs, tying injured together	6	___	___	___	___
Parachute silk	protection from sun's rays	8	___	___	___	___
Solar-powered portable heating unit	not needed unless on dark side	13	___	___	___	___
Two .45 caliber pistols	possible means of self-propulsion	11	___	___	___	___
One case of de-hydrated Pet milk	bulkier duplication of food concentrate	12	___	___	___	___
Two 100-lb. tanks of oxygen	most pressing survival need	1	___	___	___	___
Stellar map (of the moon's constellation)	primary means of navigation	3	___	___	___	___
Self-inflating life raft	CO_2 bottle in military raft may be used for propulsion	9	___	___	___	___
Magnetic compass	magnetic field on moon is not polarized, worthless for navigation	14	___	___	___	___
Five gallons of water	replacement for tremendous liquid loss on lighted side	2	___	___	___	___

*Error points are the absolute difference between your ranks and these (disregard plus or minus signs).

Items	Reasoning	Ranking	Your Ranks	Error Points*	Group Ranks	Error Points*
Signal flares	distress signal when mother ship is sighted	10	_____	_____	_____	_____
First aid kit containing injection needles	needles for vitamins, medicines, etc., will fit in space suits	7	_____	_____	_____	_____
Solar-powered FM receiver transmitter	for communication with mother ship, but FM requires line-of-sight transmission and short ranges	5	_____	_____	_____	_____
			Total _____		Total _____	

Scoring for individuals:

0–25 = excellent	33–45 = average	56–70 = poor
26–32 = good	46–55 = fair	71–112 = very poor, suggests possible faking or use of earthbound logic

*Error points are the absolute difference between your ranks and these (disregard plus or minus signs).

APPENDIX C
SAMPLE LEARNING STYLE
INVENTORY

_____ 1. When you really want to study something and learn it well, would you rather (a) work alone, (b) study with others having similar interests, (c) work by yourself but in a setting where there are other people around?

_____ 2. Assuming that each of the following modes is effective and that you have a choice, would you most prefer to learn something by (a) reading, (b) listening, (c) observing?

_____ 3. Learning situations that cause you the most concern are those that appear to be (a) ambiguous, (b) rather closely defined as to the desired outcome, (c) without guidelines, where you are completely on your own.

_____ 4. Do you have most trouble learning things that (a) use abstract symbols, (b) use diagrams and charts, (c) use mathematical numbers and figures?

_____ 5. When not really interested in something you are studying, do you find yourself (a) able to discipline yourself to study, (b) easily distracted by other things, (c) going through the motions to look as though you are studying?

_____ 6. When memorizing something, do you find yourself (a) developing a theme within which to relate the parts, (b) creating a pattern that cues the parts, (c) trying to picture the thing in your mind?

_____ 7. Would you prefer to study something that (a) involves some creative effort of your own, (b) calls for you to apply analytical and critical skills, (c) lays out all the points in front of you so you have a chance to understand it?

_____ 8. When do you find that you do your best learning—(a) in the early morning, (b) around midday, (c) in the afternoon, (d) during an "all nighter"?

_____ 9. When studying, do you find that you (a) create relationships without being told, (b) understand the material but have some difficulty putting it together, (c) must be given the "whole" before the "parts" make sense?

_____ 10. In most classes, would you rather be taught by someone who (a) knows the material and can tell it to you clearly and precisely, (b) knows the material and teases/leads you to conclusions, (c) knows the material but primarily raises questions?

_____ 11. Do you feel most comfortable when asked (a) to analyze the material studied, (b) to report on the material studied, (c) to summarize the material studied?

_____ 12. When studying something completely new, do you (a) need someone around to encourage your efforts, (b) prefer to figure it out for yourself, (c) tend to give up easily even if encouraged?

_____ 13. Do you classify yourself as a student who (a) grasps new ideas quickly, (b) goes at a slightly slower pace, yet masters ideas well, (c) deals with new material so thoroughly that you are able to identify new ideas and/or relationships that extend beyond those explicit in the original materials?

_____ 14. When studying with a particular instructor, are you (a) very conscious of the teacher's reaction to how you are doing, (b) indifferent to what the teacher thinks about your progress, (c) interested in the teacher's response but only after you have completed the task on your own?

_____ 15. If taking a class in which there were no grades or other rewards, would you probably (a) work just as hard as you would if there were grades, (b) end up doing something else you really wanted to do, (c) exert minimal effort?

_____ 16. Do you like taking courses where (a) both the objectives and procedures are clearly spelled out, (b) the procedures are fairly clear but the objectives are vague, (c) both the objectives and procedures are vague but there is a lot of excitement and drive on the part of the instructor?

_____ 17. When studying something new, would you say your attention span is (a) continuous, (b) irregular, (c) short but concentrated, (d) without particular pattern?

_____ 18. Do you sense the most satisfaction when (a) you've been able to figure out and repair something using your hands and your mind, (b) you've been able to conceptualize or see some meanings in academic work, (c) other people say they think you've done a good piece of work— regardless of what that work is?

_____ 19. When you find yourself in a situation determined by the clock, do you usually (a) start making all sorts of mistakes under pressure, (b) slow down and do what you can, (c) speed up and surprise yourself at how much you can do when the heat is on?

_____ 20. If you asked those people who know you best, they would probably say that (a) you are usually level-headed and have a lot of common sense, (b) it takes you a long time to get an idea but when you do you hang on to it, (c) always coming up with far-out crazy ideas—that sometimes work?

_____ 21. When bored in a class, do you usually (a) daydream, but of things related to what you are studying, (b) daydream of things seldom related to what you are studying, (c) pay attention even though it doesn't mean very much?

_____ 22. Do you find that when something new comes up you (a) adapt rather easily, (b) fight it for awhile but are willing, usually, to give it a try, (c) make darn well sure it makes sense and/or is right before making any effort to accept it?

_____ 23. When in a classroom with other students and observing a teacher teaching, do you (a) think of other ways to present the material and to teach, (b) listen to what the teacher is saying rather than watch how he or she is teaching, (c) wonder what the teacher wants and how you can deliver?

_____ 24. If you don't like the instructor, for whatever reason, do you (a) have a tendency to not do well, (b) find every reason possible for not studying/learning, (c) not let it affect how hard you try?

_____ 25. Do you get upset when studying something that (a) has no immediate and practical application, (b) appears to have some application but you're not sure just what, (c) is too darn practical and immediate?

_____ 26. When a particular teacher fails to "come across," do you have a tendency to blame (a) the teacher who, after all, is responsible for the class, (b) the subject matter—especially if the teacher tries, (c) both the teacher and yourself for not making it worthwhile.

_____ 27. If you took a course in social studies, would you want it to (a) focus primarily upon the facts, (b) pose some insight into contemporary problems of society, (c) have some payoff in your daily life?

_____ 28. The problem with a great number of teachers is that they (a) overkill, that is, teach too much of the same thing, (b) try to cover too much, (c) do not allow the student to really wrestle with the content.

_____ 29. Do you believe that most students gain confidence through (a) having rather well-established objectives and procedures, (b) being allowed to try different things, (c) psyching out the reward system and playing the game?

_____ 30. When studying, do you prefer (a) absolute silence, (b) low background noise, including music, (c) relative quiet, (d) loud conversation or music, etc., (e) sometimes one way, sometimes another?

_____ 31. Where do you prefer to study—(a) in your own room, (b) in a learning center, (c) at the library, (d) at a media center?

_____ 32. What type of assignments do you most prefer—(a) teacher-directed projects, (b) contracts, (c) self-directed projects, (d) a combination of these?

_____ 33. How do you most prefer to be evaluated on something—(a) by formal tests, (b) through teacher conferences, (c) on research papers or other written projects, (d) on the amount of your class discussion?

_____ 34. Which of the following is most likely to bring forth your best performance—(a) self-satisfaction, (b) clearly defined teacher expectations and deadlines, (c) public recognition of your achievement, (d) working in a subject area with which you are quite comfortable and familiar?

SUMMARY

Instructional Modes   Determine preferred instructional mode from responses to questions 2, 4, 7, 8, 11, 17, and 19.

_____

_____

Structure   Determine the degree of structuring from responses to questions 3, 6, 9, 12, 13, 16, 20, 22, 23, and 32.

High   Medium   Low

Social Context of Learning   Determine the general expectations for the way in which teachers handle their authority from questions 1, 10, 19, and 24.

_____

_____

Group-Related Activities   Determine preference for group-related activities from responses to questions 1, 12, 30, 31, and 34.

_____

_____

Physical Context of Learning   Determine preferences regarding the physical environment from the responses to questions 8, 17, 30, and 31.

_____

_____

Reward/Praise   Determine preferences for reward/praise from responses to questions 14, 15, 26, 29, 33, and 34.

_____

_____

Goal Preferences   Determine general goal preferences from the responses to questions 5, 18, 25, and 27.

Longer range   Shorter range

NAME INDEX

SUBJECT INDEX

AN INVITATION TO RESPOND

We would like to find out a little about your background and about your reactions to the Third Edition of *Children and Their World*. Your evaluation of the book will help us to meet the interests and needs of students in future editions. We invite you to share your reactions by completing the questionnaire below and returning it to: *College Marketing; Houghton Mifflin Company; One Beacon Street; Boston, MA 02108.*

1. Please tell us your overall impressions of the text.

	Excellent	*Good*	*Adequate*	*Poor*
a. Was it written in a clear and understandable style?	____	____	____	____
b. Were difficult concepts well explained?	____	____	____	____
c. How would you rate the Model Student Activities?	____	____	____	____
d. How comprehensive was the coverage of major issues and topics?	____	____	____	____
e. How does this book compare to other texts you have used?	____	____	____	____
f. How would you rate the *Commentary* feature?	____	____	____	____
g. How would you rate the study aids at the beginning and end of each chapter?	____	____	____	____
h. How would you rate the exercises and direct questions that were addressed to *you* the reader?	____	____	____	____

2. Can you comment on or illustrate your above ratings?_____

_____

_____

_____

3. What chapters or features did you particularly like?_____

_____

_____

_____

4. What chapters or features did you dislike or think should be changed?____

_____

_____

5. What material would you suggest adding or deleting?_____

_____

_____

_____

6. What was the title of the course in which you used this book? _____

_____

_____

7. Are you an undergraduate student?_____If so, what year?

_____

8. Are you a graduate student?_____If so, have you taught before?_____

9. Have you taken any other courses in education? If so, which courses?

_____

_____

10. Do you intend to keep this book for use during your teaching career?____
    Why or why not?_____

_____

11. Did you like the physical appearance of this book?_____ Did you
    find that the design of the text made using and finding material simple or
    difficult?_____ Why or why not? _____

12. We would appreciate any other comments or reactions you are willing to
    share._____

_____

_____